"A Country Nourished on Self-Doubt"

"A Country Nourished on Self-Doubt"
Documents in Post-Confederation Canadian History

Second Edition

Edited by

Thomas Thorner
with Thor Frohn-Nielsen

broadview press

National Library of Canada Cataloguing in Publication
"A country nourished on self-doubt" : documents in Post-Confederation Canadian history / edited by Thomas Thorner with Thor Frohn-Nielsen. — 2nd ed.
Previous ed. had title: "A country nourished on self-doubt" : documents in Canadian history, 1867-1980.
Includes bibliographical references and index.
ISBN 1-55111-548-4
1. Canada—History—1867- —Sources. I. Thorner, Thomas II. Frohn-Nielsen, Thor, 1955-
FC18.C68 2003   971.05   C2003-904248-0

Broadview Press Ltd. is an independent, international publishing house, incorporated in 1985. Broadview believes in shared ownership, both with its employees and with the general public; since the year 2000 Broadview shares have traded publicly on the Toronto Venture Exchange under the symbol BDP.

We welcome comments and suggestions regarding any aspect of our publications—please feel free to contact us at the addresses below or at broadview@broadviewpress.com.

North America
Canada: PO Box 1243, Peterborough, Ontario, Canada K9J 7H5
United States: 3576 California Road, Orchard Park, NY, USA 14127
Tel: (705) 743-8990; Fax: (705) 743-8353
e-mail: customerservice@broadviewpress.com

UK, Ireland, and Continental Europe
Plymbridge Distributors
Estover Road
Plymouth, UK PL6 7PZ
Tel: 44(0) 1752 202301; Fax: 44(0) 1752 202333
e-mail: orders@plymbridge.com

Australia and New Zealand
UNIREPS, University of New South Wales
Sydney, NSW, Australia 2052
Tel: 61 2 9664 0999; Fax: 61 2 9664 5420
e-mail: info.press@unsw.edu.au

www.broadviewpress.com

Broadview Press Ltd. gratefully acknowledges the financial support of the Government of Canada through the Book Publishing Industry Development Program for our publishing activities.

Printed in Canada

Contents

NOT ANOTHER EDITION

Many publishers annually incorporate relatively minor changes to produce yet another edition of their textbooks. This usually prevents students from selling their old editions and from purchasing cheaper, used books for courses. In this case well over half of the material is entirely new. The idea of a revised edition originated with a number of specific problems. First, one of the most compelling documents in the original collection turned out to have been fabricated. Without any hint of its fictional nature, Gerald Keegan's diary can still be found in one of the best anthologies concerning the Irish in Canada. Yet its authenticity sparked a major controversy in Ireland during the early 1990s. The "diary" turns out to have been written as a short story by a Scottish immigrant 50 years after the events it describes, and was not the account of a genuine Irish famine victim. The Keegan material also leaves the impression that the main motives for migration centred upon dispossession, nationalism, and Anglo-phobia, a version sharply contradicted by the De Vere account which now forms part of this new edition. Second, students wanted to hear more from the perspective of native peoples. Therefore a new opening chapter comparing cultural perspectives as well as an entire chapter devoted to native dissent was added to Volume One. Third, some critics thought that a single chapter on the early Maritime colonies was grossly inadequate. In its place are four new chapters. With the volume covering the period after 1867, many readers sought more material on classic Canadian issues and coverage beyond 1982 (which still remains the termination date for our post-Confederation history at Kwantlen University College). Another common suggestion was to include study questions, which previously had been available only in the study guides provided to instructors.

The first edition also failed to provide sufficient acknowledgement to the library staff at Kwantlen—in particular Margaret Giacomello and Jean McKendry—as well as Karen Archer, Jacinta Sterling, Kathie Holloway, Ann McBurnie, Judy Issac, and Nancy Smith—who always managed to keep the interlibrary loan material, upon which so much of this book was based, flowing.

Finally, this project would never have been possible without the steady support of Michael Harrison, Vice-President and Editor of Broadview Press.

Introduction

a country nourished on self-doubt
where from the reverse image of detractors
an opposite nation is talked into existence
that doesn't resemble any other one
a cross-breed plant that survives the winter

Al Purdy, "A Walk on Wellington Street," 1968

Ours is a history of self-doubt. From the moment of Confederation Canada has often been threatened by disintegration. Part of this problem stems from the fact that neither cultural symbols, a shared heritage, nor even a common language united Canadians when the nation emerged in 1867. Because much of the nation's growth in the years that followed could be attributed to immigrants who often retained their hyphenated ethnic status and never felt totally at home here, ambiguity about the significance of Canada or what it meant to be a Canadian was hardly surprising. The sheer problem of communication over vast distances and distinct regional economies also promoted disunity. By the 1880s Canada had already lost much of its lustre. Political tensions and economic depression caused many to doubt whether the nation could or should continue to exist. In Quebec separatist emotions had grown more pronounced, and the Nova Scotia legislature had endorsed a resolution favouring secession. Young Canadians by the thousands expressed their discontent with their feet when they left for better opportunities south of the border. After Macdonald's "national policy" had failed to generate prosperity or unite the country, the country's leading intellectual, Goldwin Smith, asked: What justifies Canada's existence? He concluded that Canada could not be considered a nation because it had failed to mould competing cultures and regions into a single community. In his mind Canada was nothing but an artificial entity totally at odds with the natural geographical and economic factors operating in North America.

The twentieth century, however, saw some Canadians beginning to celebrate the cultural diversity that Smith found so abhorrent. Particularly in contrast to the American "melting pot," they put forth the idea of the cultural mosaic as the very foundation of Canada's strength and identity. But as articulated by

W.D. Scott in Chapter 5, most Canadians remained doubtful whether building a nation with the discontented and dispossessed of the world was sound practice. Canada's immigration policies of the period between the two world wars could hardly be characterized as promoting cultural diversity and tolerance. Instead, many immigrants found the pressure to conform just as pronounced as it was in the United States.

But the gravest doubts about Canada in the mid-twentieth century focused upon foreign relations, not domestic affairs. While it had taken several decades of the new century for Canada to finally cut most of the vestiges of British control, the Second World War saw a nervous Canada give up much of its military independence in return for American protection. The school texts of the period proudly proclaimed our growth from colony to nation, but based upon American economic and cultural domination, critics increasingly characterized Canada's status as having shifted from a British colony to an American satellite. In 1965 the philosopher George Grant went so far as to announce Canada's death as a sovereign nation.

More recently the challenges to Canadian sovereignty came from within as demonstrated by the F.L.Q. crisis and the rise of the Parti Québécois. When the separatists came to power as the government of Quebec in 1976 and remained a viable political entity throughout the 1980s and '90s many wondered if Canada would indeed survive.

Yet Purdy's poem alludes to positive aspects: a "nourishing" self-doubt, a nation that "doesn't resemble any others," and a "cross-breed plant" that survives the winter. While Canadians have remained profoundly uncertain of who they are and their place in the world, other nations have regarded this modesty as comfortably non-threatening, especially in comparison to the crass boosterism of the Americans, and as such viewed Canada as an ideal candidate for international peacekeeping assignments. It is also a rather strange quirk of history that Canada's inhibited national consciousness is now taken by many outsiders as a sign of our maturity in an increasingly post-national world.

Many collections of Canadian readings on the market today reprint articles from academic journals as models of scholarship. Although such articles may certainly be of great value, they naturally tend to be written with a scholarly audience in mind. Coupled with standard survey texts, the near-total reliance upon secondary sources has had wide-ranging consequences. A student registering for a course on the Victorian novel would, no doubt, expect to read Victorian novels, not simply digest what secondary sources had to say about them. Even if the raw materials were as dense, drab and dull as the popular perception of

Canadian history makes them out to be, bypassing them would be disturbing. But primary sources are far from dull. What historians usually find most enjoyable about the craft is research—the labyrinthine quest in primary sources for answers about the past. What follows is a volume that attempts to bring together compelling excerpts of divergent eyewitness accounts of specific topics in post-Confederation Canadian history. The fascination of primary sources lies in their personal perspective and the immediacy of experience they convey. However lacking in objective insight they may be, they were written by people at or close to the source of the events they describe. In the same way, readers of this book are encouraged to analyze the arguments and information in the sources for themselves.

This is still very much a book aimed at those largely unfamiliar with the subject. In order to make available the greatest possible amount of original material that is interesting and important, some less pertinent passages have been deleted. Exercising even a minimal shaping hand will sacrifice some dimensions of the past, but even if the occasional reader feels uncomfortable that the integrity of some documents has been violated, one hopes that in the interest of engaging a wider readership and lifting the veil of boredom from Canadian history, the end will have justified the means.

Editors of document collections such as this must also be sensitive to the criticism that reproducing historical documents such as these perpetuates negative images, particularly about ethnic groups, and as such constitutes hate literature. Without a doubt many documents written by ethnocentric Anglo Canadians form part of a literature written to justify assimilation and domination. But it hardly follows that reprinting these inaccuracies constitutes disseminating hate literature. Instead these documents may provide a means of exposing those falsehoods, of demonstrating the basis of intolerance, and of understanding that prejudice is commonplace. In some respects these documents may be used to confront the current complacency or smugness of Canadians who assume that especially compared to the United States, ours has been a kinder, gentler history and therefore lacks a foundation for bigotry and racism.

Chapter One

"OUR RIGHTFUL PLACE": CONTINENTALISM, IMPERIALISM, OR NATIONALISM

1. William Norris, "Canadian Nationality: A Present-day Plea," *The Canadian Monthly and National Review,* February 1880.
2. Hon. Mr. Longley, Speech, *Debates and Proceedings of the House of Assembly of the Province of Nova Scotia,* Nova Scotia, May 8, 1886.
3. George M. Grant, *On Imperial Federation,* 1889.
4. Goldwin Smith, *Canada and the Canadian Question,* 1891.
5. Jules-Paul Tardivel, "Changing Perspectives," *La Vérité,* March 18, 1893
6. Henri Bourassa, "The French Canadian in the British Empire," *The Monthly Review,* October 1902.

Introduction

Many British North Americans felt deeply suspicious about federation and the creation of the Dominion of Canada when it occurred in 1867, a scepticism descending into outright hostility in some quarters by the 1880s. This was a time of profound and anxious soul-searching as the fledgling nation stumbled toward the twentieth century. John A. MacDonald's "National Policy" had, after all, not lived up to its billing and generated neither national unity nor sustained prosperity. But if not federation in its present guise, then what? There were also ideological questions. What should motivate Canada's decision on its own future? Should an emotional sense of nationalism form the foundation, or was this a quaint anachronism in an age of dynamic, transnational capitalism. And if money does indeed make the world go 'round, then surely captains of industry, not sentimental politicians, should determine Canada's future according to market forces. Finally, naive as it seemed, perhaps commerce and nationalism could coexist—but then in what form?

As the debate intensified, separatism among Quebecois simmered with new-found vigour, threatening to boil over in response to imperialist calls for

closer ties to Britain. In Nova Scotia, the bubbling anti-Confederationist sentiment, cooking since 1867, brewed into a legislative resolution favouring secession.
Some wistfully sought inclusion under the Stars and Stripes. Federally, the Liberals touted free trade with America as the nation's most viable route. Meanwhile,
aghast Loyalist descendants, ultra-Protestant Orange Order members and An-
glophiles clung fiercely to the Union Jack through the Imperial Federation League
and championed Canada's membership in the British Empire as a vital bulwark
against what they perceived as catastrophic Yankee annexationism.

Anguish over Canada's future reached far beyond the domain of traditional political hacks, journalistic pundits, the socio-political elite, malcontents,
and special interest groups. It became, in fact, a popular topic among ordinary
Canadians in everyday parlours, shops, and offices. Even writers like Sara Duncan
joined the fray with her popular and perceptive novel, *The Imperialist* (1904).
Canadians sensed that the nation's future was at stake.

Two wildly different events, occurring in quick succession and interpreted
in conjunction with one another, brought the issue into sharp relief: the Boer
War; and the Alaska boundary dispute. The former erupted in 1899 in South
Africa. There, Britain sought to reestablish sovereignty against the Boers, descendants of Dutch settlers, who created two independent republics in the heart
of what Britain claimed as part of its Empire. The initial result was a humiliating
military debacle when, the wily Boers decisively defeated Britain. In panic, Britain called for Empire support. Wilfred Laurier, Canada's Prime Minster, considered
contribution an absurd and dangerous precedent that could rend the fragile
fabric of the Canadian cultural duality since many French Canadians shared the
Boers resentment of British colonialism. However, an affronted English Canada
vehemently disagreed. Laurier had to think twice. The resultant Canadian compromise was a purely volunteer force of 7000 men—for which Britain bore the
cost. As far as most Canadians were concerned, Britain sought our assistance
and the Dominion responded.

Few cared about the exact boundary demarcation between Alaska and British
Columbia as long as the land remained valueless. That changed with the Klondike
gold rush of 1897. Suddenly the rugged coast, and sovereignty over it, became
very important indeed, because whoever controlled coastal ports such as Skagway
realistically controlled all traffic in and out of the Yukon gold fields, and therefore the rush itself. Not surprisingly, the American interpretation of the border
saw Skagway as US territory. Canadians insisted otherwise. The United States
and Britain, which negotiated all international treaties on Canada's behalf, agreed
in 1903 to convene a six-man panel to resolve the issue. Theodore Roosevelt, the

American president, appointed three members, Britain the rest, among whom two were Canadian. A pugnacious Roosevelt, however, had no intention of losing Skagway, and put considerable pressure on Britain's acquiescence—by threatening war. Roosevelt's adage of "walking softly while carrying a big stick" did the trick and Britain caved in. This, from a Canadian perspective, was a gross betrayal—to the point where the two Canadian judges resigned from the panel. For Canadians the incident was particularly galling when taken in conjunction with the Boer war: Canadians helped Britain when it needed them, but when Canada needed British assistance nothing seemed to be forthcoming. What was the Empire for, if not mutual support? Who were Canada's allies? What policy was best for the nation?

Discussion Points

1. Imperialism, continentalism and nationalism offered three options to Canadians. Identify the advantages and disadvantages of each movement.
2. Which author makes the best argument?
3. Were French Canadians, as Bourassa contended, the most nationalistic of all Canadians?
4. Goldwin Smith raised a critical question: what values does Canada embody that justifies its existence?
5. These authors were all white males. Is cultural and/or gender bias evident in their accounts? Would non-white males or females have expressed different points of view?

Documents

1. William Norris, "Canadian Nationality: A Present-day Plea," *The Canadian Monthly and National Review,* February 1880.

We are on the eve of startling events. Public opinion in Canada has come to the conclusion that something must be done, or some change made, to meet the crisis that is approaching. Half a continent cannot be settled and peopled by a colony; a nation may plant colonies, a colony never can. The Canadian people have assumed the responsibility of populating the North-West, and they must rise equal to the emergency ...

  It is said there are two ways out of the difficulty—Canada must either assume nationality, or join the United States. The first is the legitimate and only solution. Generally speaking, England would never permit annexation, unless forced on her by a long and disastrous war, which would almost destroy Canada, for her soil would be the battle ground of the contending nations. Independence could be obtained without embittering the relations which now exist. But annexation would be no remedy for the evils from which we suffer. Politically, it would only be a change of masters; and, as a means of settling and developing our country, it would be more than doubtful. Indeed, it would be the sure means of killing all our projects. No one can believe that the Americans would build our Pacific Railway to the detriment of their own Northern Pacific and the one already in operation. Neither is it likely that our sea-board would be developed to the injury of Portland, Boston and New York. Hence, annexation would be of no use to further the projects upon which, for good or evil, the Canadian people have set their hearts.

Politically, annexation would surely render Canada tributary to the States. There are those who think, and say, that suitable enactments could be made to secure the liberties of Canada; but no enactments could make a dwarf equal to a giant; and we do not see that enactments, even among Americans themselves, have much force to protect their own people when the supposed interests of one of the parties require that any particular section should be oppressed ... The only valid ground which the advocates of annexation have to stand on, is that the measure would give us access to the markets of the United States—a very dear privilege if it would entail the loss of our liberties—and if this result could be obtained by a means which would not also bring with it the evils of annexation, then their only argument is gone ...

It would seem plain, then, that the present colonial position of Canada prevents her from obtaining a proper reciprocity treaty with the United States, and shuts up the markets of the world to her goods, while giving no possibility of securing any better position for her goods in British markets than that possessed by other countries. It would also seem that independence would enable us to make such a treaty with the United States, and treaties with other countries, as would enable us to gain access to their markets without lessening our present privileges in those of Britain. There is no question that access to these markets, especially to those of our own continent, would be to the great and lasting benefit of Canada: every one is agreed on that.

There is also no doubt that independence would elevate the character and status of our people. It would give Canada a national credit in the money markets of the world, and better enable it to raise money by borrowing, or, by the creation of a national currency, similar to that of the United States, for the purpose of building the Canadian Pacific Railway.

There is one more argument in favour of independence greater than all the others put together. Without population, a great North-West is useless to Canada. So is a Pacific Railway. If there be no one to use the railroad, the money required to build it may as well be thrown into the sea ... Leave Canada in her present condition, and the chief use of a Canadian Pacific Railway will be to carry food to starving Indians, or to serve the Americans. Who will use it? There is not much use of expecting the people of foreign countries to come hither and occupy our lands. Our emigration agents were arrested in Germany a few years ago as frauds and cheats, in trying to get the people to emigrate to a place where they would have no country, as Canada cannot make a British subject, and she has no citizenship of her own. Then look at the statistics of British emigration for the year 1878. One-half of all the people who left the United Kingdom went to the United States, and one-tenth only came to Canada. What else is to be expected? ... We never can expect to retain even our own Canadian population until we can give them the same advantages they can get in the United States—that is, a country with all that a nationality implies and manhood suffrage. As to obtaining the people of the old countries, we must remain content, as long as we are a colony, with the poorer classes of immigrants which charity and paid passages send to our shores.

Apart, however, from the advantages and disadvantages of independence, we must make up our minds to look the inevitable in the face. We have resolved not to cast in our own lot with the Americans, and their continual precarious political condition confirms our resolution. Coming events will surely force us shortly to take up the destiny which every one admits must necessarily ultimately be borne ...

It, therefore, behooves all true Canadians to be prepared for whatever may occur. There is but little to be done. A Governor elected every seven years by both our Houses of Parliament, the appointment of a small diplomatic body, and the adoption of a flag are all that is needful. Surely, a people who have an independent and final Supreme Court is equal to this. The flag may cause some difficulty, but not necessarily. We have the colours already—it is only necessary to place them. The red first, representing Englishmen and Scotchmen; the white, representing the French who first colonized Quebec and the French Canadian people who now inhabit it; and the green, though questioned by some, is acknowledged by all to represent the Irish. These colours, placed vertically, with the Union in the upper corner as now, would make a good Canadian flag and attract the regard of a majority of the people who inhabit the Dominion. The green, especially, would be worth 100,000 men to the Dominion in case of any difficulty with our neighbours, and would effectually Canadianize the Irish.

The near prospect here held out may frighten the timid, but timidity is one of the things nationality is intended to remove. "You are big enough and strong enough for independence," said the *Times*, "and if not, the education of self-reliance will soon make you so." But there is nothing to fear but weakness and cowardice. We shall have 5,000,000 of brave, hardy, industrious people, unused to luxuries and all enervating influences. We have a commercial marine second only to that of America to carry a fully developed national trade. We have 800,000 men between the ages of 16 and 45, should they be required to defend our liberties. We have resources in natural wealth—lumber, coal, iron, and gold—almost measureless, while our agricultural lands in the North-West give double the average of the yield of the North-Western States. We are already Confederated and bound together in one Dominion, having executive, legislative, and judicial bodies, the last of which is independent, and the other two nearly so. And, lastly, we shall have the good will of England and possibly her guarantee for our independence.

We can then look forward to the future with hope and confidence. In twenty years of Canadian independence, twelve or fourteen states will occupy what is now an unbroken solitude, whose trade, and that of the whole North-West of the continent, will flow in one stream through our territory, either through Lake Winnipeg and Nelson's River into Hudson Bay, or down the Great Lakes and the St. Lawrence to the Atlantic, fertilizing and enriching the country through which it passes. Political power follows in the steps of material wealth. Modern nations on this continent grow with prodigious strides. In one hundred years the United States have passed through all the phases of national life that took a thousand to mould Europe, and they are fast hastening to a premature old age. Our country has come into existence at a grand period of the world's history. Humanity, on this continent, has advanced beyond the evils of the old civilization. Feudalism, slavery, and extreme ignorance and poverty, have never been known to any extent among us, and we shall never be handicapped by them. Our great competitor and rival will never recover from the evils of one of them—slavery. Already she shows signs of dissolution. The evils of the old civilization amid which she was begotten, and the corruption engendered by the civil war, are doing their work. A hot-bed progress among alien and half-assimilated people will surely accelerate the end. They are in a dilemma either horn of which is fatal. They must either submit to the mob and the commune, and see their cities blaze as they did three years ago, or to a standing army and a general who will destroy their institutions and make himself dictator. In either event, disintegration is sure to follow. As power steps from the disorganized grasp of the United States, it will fall to Canada as her natural right, making her the first nation on this continent, as she is now the second. United closely, as we shall be from the Atlantic to the Pacific by a common nationality, our country will go on, increasing from age to age in wealth, in power and in glory; and it may not be too much of a stretch of the imagination to think, that as it is the latest developed portion of a new world—as it was the first, by millions of years, to nurse and cradle in her bosom the first spark of animal life in the eozoon,—it may be the country where a last great, and fully developed humanity may find its fitting habitation and abode.

2. Hon. Mr. Longley, Speech, *Debates and Proceedings of the House of Assembly of the Province of Nova Scotia*, Nova Scotia, May 8, 1886.

I now state the real ground for my position on this question. I say that that man should be branded as a traitor that would attempt to break up a consolidated nationality if the elements of strength existed there, but if there is an abortive attempt to bind together that which has no national connection, and which hinders and obstructs our trade and progress, then sir it becomes our duty to say that the abortive attempt should be at an end. And, sir, I say that no germs of nationality exist to properly unite these scattered and disjointed provinces. That is impossible. I say that whether we pass this resolution to-day or not the people of Nova Scotia will endorse and sanction the policy inaugurated to-day, and that throughout all sections of the Dominion of Canada the dissatisfaction existing will break out and will eventually destroy the union ...

I say I am justified—anxious in my heart to promote the best interests of the country—in declaring this confederation a failure, a total failure, and in stating that it can never be successful, that God and nature have decreed that there can never be a nationality built up on such a system, and that all attempts will be abortive to the last degree—that every part at least will crumble to pieces or seek its natural prosperity and growth by a commercial identification with the great and prosperous people with which we hope to share the glory of this great English-speaking continent of North America. That is my justification for the present vote. I may say that the record of the development of Nova Scotia has been one of most bitter disappointment to all its sons truly bound up in its interests. Sir, it has been charged by hon. gentlemen opposite and their organs that the party with which I am identified is a dismal-doleful party. I deny the charge. I myself believe in a spirit of true patriotism. I believe in love of country. I believe in rallying round that body politic with which you are identified. I have no respect for the man that does not love his country and does not desire its success and prosperity. But how can we, as true loyal Nova Scotians, stand by and see it robbed of its legitimate progress and see it hampered by trade laws, shut out from valuable markets and put in a position in which prosperity is impossible, and yet not raise our voices against the system which is the real obstacle to our success. I have always been accustomed to believe that Nova Scotia is the gem of the continent of North America. I say that between the Gulf of Mexico and the North Pole there is only Pennsylvania, in which iron and coal be side by side as in Nova Scotia, and as great states grow up the coal and iron will be wanted, and if we have commercial identification with the United States we shall see the development of our coal fields, and vast manufacturing interests springing up, because people will not be afraid to risk their money when they are going to have,—not the markets of five millions of people with whom they cannot trade, but when we can have free access to all these markets which are natural to us and to which every steamer and every vessel that leaves our shore naturally goes. Then we shall see prosperity, happiness and true development in this province of Nova Scotia, then we shall see something to be proud of, and I believe, sir, that we are now entering upon a crusade which will give life and hope to every Nova Scotian interested in the prosperity of his country. Sir, it has been stated that he is the greatest man who can make two blades of grass grow where one blade grew before. I desire to propound a policy whereby the people may realize two dollars where one dollar was realized before—a policy that will remove the hampering barriers now affecting our trade, and will substitute in place of these the natural and geographical identification with the people of the United States, with whom God and nature intended us to trade.

3. George M. Grant, *On Imperial Federation*, 1889.

Imperial Federation, from a Canadian point of view, means simply the next act in a process of political and historical development that began in 1763, when Canada—with the consent of all parties concerned—was declared to be British. From that day, the development of Canada from the position of a British colony into that of a British nationality has gone on steadily. The colonial condition is one of incomplete political development, and Canada has passed through various stages, each of which marks a greater measure of self-government than the previous stage. The various Acts in the drama are indicated by successive civil conflicts always ending in constitutional changes that widened our liberties or by struggles against external enemies and influences that sought to interfere with our legitimate development. The making of Canada into a nation has been a long process, and the process is not yet ended. But to those who complain of the length of time, I would ask them to give an example of a nation or a tree that has been made in a day. Mushrooms grow in a night, but not cedars of Lebanon. It took Germany and Italy centuries to grow into their present stately strength and unity. The making of France and Britain into nations was in each case a long process. The United States of America—with all their immense advantages and with the aid of nineteenth century methods and speed—did not attain to that condition of stable political equilibrium which ensures permanence and prosperity till 1865, or almost a hundred years after their secession from Britain. With us the process of making Canada into a nation must end in one or other of two ways:—either clothing Canadians in a legitimate share in the supreme rights, privileges and responsibilities of the Empire to which they belong, that is in full citizenship, or in a Revolution which means the gradual disintegration or violent breaking up of the British Empire. Canada cannot continue long a mere dependency. Clearly, that is impossible. No living organism can continue long in a condition of arrested development. It must grow to its full stature or petrify. Even dwarfing means death. Besides, who wants to belong to a nation of dwarfs?

This brief sketch prepares us for a definition. Imperial Federation, then, may be defined as a union between the Mother Country and Canada that would give to Canada not only the present full management of its own affairs, but a fair share in the management and responsibilities of common affairs. As British citizens, ought we to ask for more? As Canadians and full-grown men, ought we to be satisfied with less?

In the meanwhile the object of the Imperial Federation League is to form branches all over Canada to discuss the question from every point of view, with the confident expectation that in due time our Parliament will feel itself warranted by public opinion to instruct the Government of the day to enter into negotiations with the British Government on the subject. Then will be the time to draw up a scheme.

Before forming a branch of the league, all that is necessary is that a number of people in the locality should have two principles rooted and grounded in them: 1. that Britain and Canada must continue to have one flag, in other words that the present union must be maintained; 2. that Canadians are prepared for full citizenship, in other words that they are determined to be the peers and not the dependents of their fellow-citizens in the British Islands. As to the particular form in which the movement may take shape, eventually, we are quite indifferent. We welcome the production of plans and of criticism on them, but we are committed to no scheme …

… "What are the objections to Imperial Federation?"

It will not be necessary to dwell on the important objections that have been mentioned in some influential organs of public opinion— … the objection that some vigorous writers have called Imperial Federation a fad. I may, however, note other arguments:

(a) It is said that "Imperial Federation would involve us in foreign relations." We are so involved already, from the fact every nation has neighbours, and that we in particular are a trading people; only, at present, we are without a voice as regards these relations. "We might be involved in European politics." We are so involved already, from the fact of our being united to Britain, only we cannot use any constitutional influence to detach the Empire from what is of less importance to what is of greater importance, from the affairs of Europe to the interests of an ever expanding Colonial Empire.

(b) "We might be involved in war." We may at any day now without our permission being asked. Ought we not to be in a position to give our voice for peace? Remember that democracy now rules in England, that its great interest is peace, and that we ought to reinforce it against any influence that might make for war. Ought we not to contribute our share towards securing the peace of the empire and even the peace of the world, instead of being selfishly satisfied that we ourselves are out of reach of war?

(c) "There would be expense." I have pointed out that Imperial Federation is simply the full development of self-government. Now, it is quite true that every development of self-government has brought with it additional expenses but would we on that account have been better off under tutelage or bondage? A Crown colony has usually little debt. In the old days of an irresponsible executive the debt of Canada was nominal. Now, our debt has attained to figures that are quite respectable. But, would we therefore go back to the old family compact regime? The sensible question to put is this: Are there corresponding advantages to the increase of expense? As regards the debt of Canada, no doubt mistakes have been made. Governments are not always wise and Government works are perhaps built and managed less economically than works under private management. But on the whole, we believe that we have got our money's worth and that no greater mistakes have been made in Canada than in other countries.

(d) "Our interests are different." Against whom, I ask. Not against enemies, for two are stronger than one. Canada and Britain must be stronger than either by itself. Not as against each other, for in almost every respect we are complementary ...

(e) "We would have little influence in the Federation." Well, in the first place, we would have more than we have now. We have none at all now, except that which is indirect and conceded by the generosity of Britain. We deserve to have none, for we have not shown that we value it, except by newspaper clamour when the inconvenience of our position is felt. It is humiliating to read articles in our papers calling on Britain to send *her* ships, for instance to Behring's Sea. I do not undertake to say whether ships of war should be sent there from Esquimault or not; but until we are able to change the pronoun and use the phrase *our* ships, we should have the grace to keep silent. Oh, but you say, think of the expense if we undertook to bear a share of the cost of the Imperial navy. Certainly, but if we go in for Independence, we shall have to build our own ships. Which will be the heavier burden, to build them at our own cost or in conjunction with the wealthiest Empire in the world? Again, if we go in for Annexation, we shall have to pay not only our share of the United States fleet, but our share of the pension fund. That of itself would be seven or eight millions a year, as the total is ninety millions—a good deal more, that one item, than our share in the British-Canadian fleet! Two or three years ago a Montreal newspaper made out that our connection with the Mother Country was only nominal, but when neighbours began to bully us for protecting our fisheries and to threaten war, the same paper pointed out that we were an integral part of the Empire, and that at the first movement in the direction of war the British fleet would destroy all the coastal cities of the United States. When the President threatened non-intercourse, the same paper pointed out clearly that he could not discriminate between one part of the Empire and another, and that non-intercourse with us meant commercial war with Great Britain too. In other words, the present union is nominal when it suits us, and real when it suits us. We run with the hare and hunt with the hounds. There is not much dignity in such a position. It has hardly the merit of impudence. It is simply childish. Is it too much to ask the gentlemen of the press who discuss this question to calmly consider these two questions: Ought we to ask for the service of a fleet for which we do not pay a cent? and is it not our right to ask for a share in the direction of the fleet which protects our coasts and our commerce? ...

The Empire to which we belong is admittedly the greatest the world has ever seen. In it, the rights of all men are sacred and the rights of the great men are also sacred. It is world-wide and therefore offers most opportunities for all kinds of noblest service to humanity, through the serving of fellow-citizens in every quarter of the globe. Let Canada ask for some emblem—let it be maple leaf or beaver—to represent it on the flag that represents so marvellous a past and present. Is it to be thought that we would separate from such a flag without cause, still less place our country in a position of antagonism to it? Think what it has always represented—personal and national freedom; civil and commercial, intellectual and religious freedom; righteousness in private and public affairs and the proclamation of eternal life to every son of Adam ...

What do I mean by our rightful place in the history of the world? This, to be the link that shall bind into a world-wide brotherhood, into a moral—it may even be a political—unity the mother of nations and all her children, the great daughter in the south of us as well as the youngest born of the family. Mark it well, an independent Canada is out of the question. The days of small nations are over forever. Of the few great nations of the future the English-speaking people is destined if we are only true to ourselves, to be the greatest, simply because it represents most fully the highest political and spiritual life that humanity has yet realized. Break up the British Empire, and what prospect is there of a worthy place in history for any—even the greatest—of the parts? Bind the Empire into unity and we shall have solved the problem that Spain and her Colonies could not solve, though two centuries ago the future of the world seemed bound up with them. We have to choose between our rightful place in history or absorption, or a position somewhat like that of a South American Republic. Take your choice.

4. Goldwin Smith, *Canada and the Canadian Question*, 1891.

Whether the four blocks of territory constituting the Dominion can for ever be kept by political agencies united among themselves and separate from their Continent, of which geographically, economically, and with the exception of Quebec ethnologically, they are parts, is the Canadian question ...

Let those who prophesy to us smooth things take stock of the facts. When one community differs from another in race, language, religion, character, spirit, social structure, aspirations, occupying also a territory apart, it is a separate nation, and is morally certain to pursue a different course, let it designate itself as it can. French Canada may be ultimately absorbed in the English-speaking population of a vast Continent; amalgamate with British Canada so as to form a united nation it apparently never can ...

From British as well as from French Canada there is a constant flow of emigration to the richer country, and the great centres of employment. Dakota and the other new States of the American West are full of Canadian farmers; the great American cities are full of Canadian clerks and men of business, who usually make for themselves a good name. It is said that in Chicago there are 25,000. Hundreds of thousands of Canadians have relatives in the United States. Canadians in great numbers—it is believed as many as 40,000—enlisted in the American army during the civil war … A young Canadian thinks no more of going to push his fortune in New York or Chicago than a young Scotchman thinks of going to Manchester or London. The same is the case in the higher callings as in the lower: clergymen, those of the Church of England as well as those of other churches, freely accept calls to the other side of the Line. So do professors, teachers, and journalists. The Canadian churches are in full communion with their American sisters, and send delegates to each other's Assemblies. Cadets educated at a Military College to command the Canadian army against the Americans, have gone to practise as Civil Engineers in the United States. The Benevolent and National Societies have branches on both sides of the Line, and hold conventions in common. Even the Orange Order has now its lodges in the United States, where the name of President is substituted in the oath for that of the Queen. American labour organizations … extend to Canada. The American Science Association met the other day at Toronto. All the reforming and philanthropic movements, such as the Temperance movement, the Women's Rights' movement, and the Labour movements, with their conventions, are continental. Intermarriages between Canadians and Americans are numerous, so numerous as scarcely to be remarked. Americans are the chief owners of Canadian mines, and large owners of Canadian timber limits. The railway system of the continent is one. The winter ports of Canada are those of the United States. Canadian banks trade largely in the American market, and some have branches there. There is almost a currency union, American bank-bills commonly passing at par in Ontario, while those of remote Canadian Provinces pass at par only by special arrangement. American gold passes at par, while silver coin is taken at a small discount: in Winnipeg even the American nickel is part of the common currency. The Dominion bank-bills, though payable in gold, are but half convertible, because what the Canadian banks want is not British but American gold. Canadians go to the American watering-places, while Americans pass the summer on Canadian lakes. Canadians take American periodicals, to which Canadian writers often contribute. They resort for special purchases to New York stores, or even those of the Border cities. Sports are international; so are the Base Ball organisations; and the Toronto "Nine" is recruited in the States. All the

New-World phrases and habits are the same on both sides of the Line. The two sections of the English-speaking race on the American continent, in short, are in a state of economic, intellectual, and social fusion, daily becoming more complete. Saving the special connection of a limited circle with the Old Country, Ontario is an American State of the Northern type, cut off from its sisters by a customs line, under a separate government and flag ...

The isolation of the different Canadian markets from each other, and the incompatibility of their interests, add in their case to the evils and absurdities of the protective system. What is meat to one Province is, even on the protectionist hypothesis, poison to another. Ontario was to be forced to manufacture; she has no coal; yet to reconcile Nova Scotia to the tariff a coal duty was imposed; in vain, for Ontario after all continued to import her coal from Pennsylvania. Manitoba and the North-West produced no fruit; yet they were compelled to pay a duty in order to protect the fruit-grower of Ontario 1500 miles away. Hardest of all was the lot of the North-West farmer. His natural market, wherein to buy farm implements, was in the neighbouring cities of the United States, where, moreover, implements were made most suitable to the prairie. But to force him to buy in Eastern Canada 25 per cent was laid on farm implements. As he still bought in the States, the 25 per cent was made 35 per cent ...

Without commercial intercourse or fusion of population, the unity produced by a mere political arrangement can hardly be strong or deep ...

The thread of political connection is wearing thin. This England sees, and the consequence is a recoil which has produced a movement in favour of Imperial Federation. It is proposed not only to arrest the process of gradual emancipation, but to reverse it and to reabsorb the colonies into the unity of the Empire. No definite plan has been propounded, indeed, any demand for a plan is deprecated, and we are adjured to embrace the principle of the scheme and leave the details for future revelation — to which we must answer that the principle of a scheme is its object, and that it is impossible to determine whether the object is practically attainable without a working plan. There is no one in whose eyes the bond between the colonies and the mother country is more precious than it is in mine. Yet I do not hesitate to say that, so far as Canada is concerned, Imperial Federation is a dream. The Canadian people will never part with their self-government. Their tendency is entirely the other way. They have recently ... asserted their fiscal independence, and by instituting a Supreme Court of their own, they have evinced a disposition to withdraw as much as they can of their affairs from the jurisdiction of the Privy Council. Every association, to make it reasonable and lasting, must have some practical object. The practical objects of

Imperial Federation would be the maintenance of common armaments and the establishment of a common tariff. But to neither of these, I am persuaded, would Canada ever consent; she would neither contribute to Imperial armaments nor conform to an Imperial tariff. Though her people are brave and hardy, they are not, any more than the people of the United States, military, nor could they be brought to spend their earnings in Asiatic or African wars ... Remember that Canada is only in part British. The commercial and fiscal circumstances of the colony again are as different as possible from those of the mother country ...

Annexation is an ugly word; it seems to convey the idea of force or pressure applied to the smaller State, not of free, equal, and honourable union, like that between England and Scotland. Yet there is no reason why the union of the two sections of the English-speaking people on this Continent should not be as free, as equal, and as honourable as the union of England and Scotland. We should rather say their reunion than their union, for before their unhappy schism they were one people. Nothing but the historical accident of a civil war ending in secession, instead of amnesty, has made them two ...

That a union of Canada with the American Commonwealth, like that into which Scotland entered with England, would in itself be attended with great advantages cannot be questioned, whatever may be the considerations on the other side or the reasons for delay. It would give to the inhabitants of the whole Continent as complete a security for peace and immunity from war taxation as is likely to be attained by any community or group of communities on this side of the Millennium. Canadians almost with one voice say that it would greatly raise the value of property in Canada; in other words, that it would bring with it great increase of prosperity ...

Again, Canadians who heartily accept democracy wish that there should be two experiments in it on this Continent rather than one, and the wish is shared by thoughtful Americans not a few. But we have seen that in reality the two experiments are not being made. Universal suffrage and party government are the same, and their effects are the same in both Republics. Differences there are, such as that between the Presidential and the Cabinet system, of a subordinate kind, yet not unimportant, and such as might make it worthwhile to forego for a time at least the advantages of union, supposing that the dangers and economical evils of separation were not too great, and if the territorial division were not extravagantly at variance with the fiat of Nature. The experiments of political science must be tried with some reference to terrestrial convenience. Besides, those who scan the future without prejudice must see that the political fortunes of the Continent are embarked in the great Republic, and that Canada will best promote her own ultimate interests by contributing without unnecessary delay all that she has in the way of political character and force towards the saving of the main chance and the fulfilment of the common hope. The native American element in which the tradition of self-government resides is hard pressed by the foreign element untrained to self-government, and stands in need of the rein-forcement which the entrance of Canada into the Union would bring it ...

In the present case there are, on one side, geography, commerce, identity of race, language, and institutions, which with the mingling of population and constant intercourse of every kind, acting in ever-increasing intensity, have brought about a general fusion, leaving no barriers standing but the political and fiscal lines. On the other side, there is British and Imperial sentiment, which, how-ever, is confined to the British, excluding the French and Irish and other nationalities, and even among the British is livelier as a rule among the culti-vated and those whose minds are steeped in history than among those who are working for their bread; while to set against it there is the idea, which can hardly fail to make way, of a great continent with an almost unlimited range of produc-tion forming the home of a united people, shutting out war and presenting the field as it would seem for a new and happier development of humanity ...

5. Jules-Paul Tardivel, "Changing Perspectives," *La Vérité*, March 18, 1893.

Since our newspaper began we have often stated our hope of seeing a French Canada, a New France, emerge on the shores of the St. Lawrence River. Confed-eration never appeared to us as the final state of our national destinies. It is too vast and contains too many jarring and even hostile elements to become a true fatherland. It is large enough to permit the formation and peaceful co-existence of several independent nations. Our ambitions, as French Canadians, must be to establish solidly in this St. Lawrence Valley, cradle of our race, a new father-land, French, and let us not fear to add, Catholic.

How and when will the French-Canadian people assume the place to which they are so evidently called among the autonomous nations of the earth? That is God's secret. But sooner or later that hour will certainly strike if we remain true to the Providential mission which He has assigned to us. This mission consists of carrying on in North America the work of Christianization and civilization which Catholic France accomplished through so many centuries and which she might still accomplish today if only she returned to what in the past were her sources of strength and glory.

This providential hour will strike, be certain of it, for it is inconceivable that God could not have willed to make a true nation of the French-Canadian people whose birth and youth he has so visibly protected. It is folly to believe that the destiny of this prolific and vigorous race, which has acquired such strong roots in the St. Lawrence Valley, is to merge with its surrounding elements or to remain eternally in this violently unnatural state of a race distinct but not independent.

For despite all one might say or do, the French Canadians do form a people apart in Confederation and unless they are renegades to their mission they will never allow themselves to be assimilated. Once this principle is admitted, political union with people with whom they have nothing in common will always appear as an abomination ...

Some will perhaps say that the withdrawal of Quebec from Confederation is today impossible. We do admit that it is difficult, but difficult or even very difficult is not the same as impossible.

What appears to be manifestly impossible is the continuation of the present political régime for any length of time, unless the French-Canadian race accepts collective suicide and disappearance as a distinct entity. Change appears inevitable. Some speak of annexation, others of independence ...

Annexation to the United States would mean a struggle for national existence against 65,000,000 people. And we already find this struggle difficult against three or four million.

As for the independence of Canada, it would in no way ensure the independence of French Canada. We would still be riveted to a people who hate us and who yearn for our disappearance.

Confederation was perhaps necessary twenty-five years ago to avoid a civil war. But it was a transitory form of government and it has now run its course. It has become a threat both to French Canada and to public peace and order. What was supposed to avoid a racial war is today the cause of worsening clashes and must necessarily end in catastrophe.

6. Henri Bourassa, "The French Canadian in the British Empire," *The Monthly Review*, October 1902.

The present feeling of the French-Canadian is one of contentment. He is satisfied with his lot. He is anxious to preserve his liberty and his peace ... Upon any proposed modification of the constitutional system of Canada he is disposed to look with distrust, or at least with anxiety. He cannot forget that all changes in the past were directed against him, except those that were enacted under such peculiar circumstances as made it imperative for the British Government to conciliate him. He asks for no change—for a long time to come, at least. And should any change be contemplated, he is prepared to view it, to appreciate its prospective advantages and inconveniences, neither from a British point of view nor from his own racial standpoint, but to approach the problem as it may affect the exclusive interests of Canada. He has loyally accepted the present constitution; he has done his ample share of duty by the country; and he feels that he is entitled to be consulted before any change is effected.

How thoroughly and exclusively Canadian the French-Canadian is should never be forgotten by those who contemplate any change in the constitutional or national status of Canada. This is so patent a fact, so logical a consequence of historical developments, that nothing short of absolute ignorance or wilful blindness can justify the language of those who talk of drawing him either by persuasion or by force to a closer allegiance to the Empire. As a matter of fact, he constitutes the only exclusively Canadian racial group in the Dominion. A constant immigration from the British Isles has kept the English-speaking Canadians in close contact with their motherland; so that even now they still speak of the "Old Country" as their "home," thus keeping in their hearts a double allegiance. On the soil of Canada, his only home and country, all the national aspirations of the French-Canadian are concentrated. "Canadian" is the only national designation he ever claims; and when he calls himself "French-Canadian," he simply wants to differentiate his racial origin from that of his English, Scotch, or Irish fellow citizen, who, in his mind, are but partially *Canadianised*.

When he is told that Canada is a British country, and that he must abide by the will of the British majority, he replies that Canada has remained British through his own loyalty; that when his race constituted the overwhelming majority of the Canadian people, Canada was twice saved to the British Crown, thanks to him and to him only; that he has remained faithful to Great Britain because he was assured of certain rights and privileges; that his English-speaking fellow citizens have accepted the compact and should not now take advantage of their greater numerical strength to break the agreement; that when settling in Canada, newcomers from the British kingdom should understand that they become citizens of Canada, of a Confederacy where he has vested rights, and should not undertake to make the country and its people more British than Canadian ...

Independence is to his mind the most natural outcome of the ultimate destinies of Canada. But so long as the present ties are not strengthened he is in no hurry to sever British connection. He realises that time cannot but work in favour of Canada by bringing to her population and wealth, and that the later she starts on her own course the safer the journey ...

Now, apart from his instinctive reluctance to contemplate any political evolution, what are the feelings of the French-Canadian with regard to Imperial Federation or any form of British Imperialism?

First, as may be naturally expected, sentimental arguments in favour of British Imperialism cannot have any hold upon him. To his reason only must appeals on this ground be made. That the new Imperial policy will bring him, and Canada at large, advantages that will not be paid by any infringement on his long-struggled-for liberty, he must be clearly shown.

Towards Great Britain he knows that he has a duty of allegiance to perform. But he understands that duty to be what it has been so far, and nothing more. He has easily and generously forgotten the persecutions of the earlier and larger part of his national life under the British Crown. He is willing to acknowledge the good treatment which he has received later on, though he cannot forget that his own tenacity and the neighbourhood of the United States have had much to do with the improvement of his situation.

In short, his affection for Great Britain is one of reason, mixed with a certain amount of esteem and suspicion, the proportions of which vary according to time and circumstances, and also with his education, his temperament, and his social surroundings.

Towards the Empire he has no feelings whatever; and naturally so. The blood connection and the pride in Imperial power and glory having no claims upon him, what sentiment can he be expected to entertain for New Zealand or Australia, South Africa or India, for countries and populations entirely foreign to him, with which he has no relations, intellectual or political, and much less commercial intercourse than he has with the United States, France, Germany, or Belgium?

By the motherland he feels that he has done his full duty; by the Empire he does not feel that he has any duty to perform. He makes full allowance for the blood feelings of his English-speaking partner; but having himself, in the past, sacrificed much of his racial tendencies for the sake of Canadian unity, he thinks that the Anglo-Canadian should be prepared to study the problems of Imperialism from a purely Canadian standpoint. Moreover, this absence of racial feelings from his heart allows him to judge more impartially the question of the relations between Canada and the Empire.

He fully realises the benefits that Canada derives from her connection with a wealthy and mighty nation. He is satisfied with having the use of the British market. But this advantage he knows that Canada enjoys on the very same terms as any other country in the world, even the most inimical to Britain. From a mixed sense of justice and egotism he is less clamorous than the British

Canadian in demanding any favour, commercial or other, from the motherland, because he has a notion that any favour received would have to be compensated by at least an equal favour given.

His ambition does not sway him to huge financial operations. Rather given to liberal professions, to agricultural life, or to local mercantile and industrial pursuits, he is more easily satisfied than the English-speaking Canadian with a moderate return for his work and efforts. He has been kept out of the frantic display of financial energy, of the feverish concentration of capital, of the international competition of industry, which have drawn his English-speaking fellow citizen to huge combinations of wealth or trade; and therefore, he is not anxious to participate in the organisation of the Empire on the basis of a gigantic co-operative association for trade. He would rather see Canada keep the full control of her commercial policy and enter into the best possible trade arrangements with any nation, British or foreign.

He is told that Canada has the free use of British diplomacy, and that such an advantage calls for sacrifices on her part when Britain is in distress. But considered in the light of past events, British diplomacy has, on the contrary, cost a good deal to Canada. So far the foreign relations of Canada, through British mediation, have been almost exclusively confined to America. That the influence and prestige of Great Britain were of great benefit to Canada in her relations with the United States is hardly conspicuous in the various Anglo-American treaties and conventions in which Canadian interests are concerned.

Not only did the American Republic secure the settlement of nearly all her claims according to her pretentions, but Canadian rights have been sacrificed by British plenipotentiaries in compensation for misdeeds or blunders of the British Government ...

It may be argued that all those concessions, made by Great Britain at the expense of Canada, were imposed by circumstances. It may be said also that by those same concessions Canada at large was affected, and that the French-Canadians had no greater cause of complaint than their English-speaking fellow citizens. But that exclusive Canadian sentiment which I have described makes the French-Canadian feel more deeply any encroachment upon the integrity of Canada. Unlike the Anglo-Canadian, he does not find in the glory of Empire a compensation and a solace for the losses suffered by Canada. That he entertains any rancour against Britain on that account would, however, be a false conclusion. For the international intricacies in which Great Britain has been and is still entangled he makes full allowance. With his strong sense of self-government, he does not expect the motherland to endanger her own position on behalf of Canada.

But if Great Britain is either unable or unwilling to take risks for the sake of Canadian interests, he does not see why Canada should assume new obligations towards Great Britain and run risks on her behalf.

As far as war and defence are concerned, he is still less disposed to consent to any Imperial combination. First there is that aversion to militarism that I have mentioned. Then he has a notion that all the sacrifices he may make on this ground will be so much that Canada will give without any probable return.

When he turns towards the past, what does he find? He finds that for the hundred and forty years that he has been a British subject, no more than his English-speaking fellow citizen has he ever been the cause, near or distant, of any trouble to Great Britain. Never did Canada involve the Empire in any war or threat of war. But the policy, right or wrong, of the British Government did cause his country to be the battlefield of two Anglo-American struggles. Upon those two occasions Canada was saved to the British Crown, thanks to the loyalty of his own race. During the Secession war, the peace of Canada came very near being disturbed once more, and her territory was threatened with invasion because of the attitude of Great Britain. And if he has been spared this and other bloody contests, it was only by the granting to the United States of such concessions as are referred to above.

So much for the past. When he considers the present and the future, the French-Canadian does not see any reason why he should enter into a scheme of Imperial defence.

The argument that if Canada stands by the Empire, the Empire will stand by Canada, cannot have much weight with him; and his objections on that ground are founded both on past events and on prospective developments. In the South African War he has witnessed an application of the new doctrine. Of the expenditure of that war he has been called upon to pay his share — a small one if compared with that of the British Kingdom, but a large one when it is remembered that he had no interest whatever in the contest, and no control over the policy which preceded the conflict, or over its settlement. Should the principle of military Imperialism predominate, he foresees that he may find himself involved in wars occasioned by friction between Australia and Japan, between New Zealand and Germany, between Great Britain and France in Europe, or between Great Britain and Russia in Asia. He does not see any eventuality in which the Empire may be called upon to help Canada.

He is ready now, as he was in the past, to support a sufficient military force to maintain internal peace and to resist aggression on the territory of Canada. But these eventualities are most unlikely to occur in the near future.

The enormous area as well as the vast resources of the country offer such opportunities to the care and activity of its population, that social struggles are almost impossible in Canada for many years to come. Foreign invasion, from the United States excepted, is most improbable. The Canadian territory is easy to defend against attacks on her sea borders, which would offer great difficulties and little benefit to any enemy of the Empire. Moreover, from a purely Canadian standpoint such occurrences are most unlikely to happen. Left to herself Canada has no possible cause of conflict with any other nation but the United States. On the other hand, by entering into a compact for Imperial defence, she may be involved in war with several of the strongest Powers. Therefore, as far as concerns any country outside America, the French-Canadian feels that the scheme of Imperial defence brings upon him new causes of conflict not to be compensated by any probable defensive requirement …

From all those considerations the French-Canadian concludes that Canada has never been, and never will be, the cause of any display of Imperial strength, with the single exception of a possible encounter with a nation that he is not desirous of attacking, and against which, in his mind, the Empire would be either unwilling or incapable of defending him. He does not therefore feel bound to assume military obligations towards any other part of the Empire.

The stronger Canada grows in population and wealth, the slighter will be the dangers that may threaten her security, and the greater her contribution to the welfare and glory of the Empire. The French-Canadian thinks therefore that the best way in which he can play his part in the building up Empire is not by diverting the healthiest and strongest portion of its population from the pursuits of a peaceful and industrious life and sending them to fight in all parts of the world. He does not believe in fostering in Canada the spirit of militarism. He is only anxious to make his country attractive and prosperous by keeping aloof from all military adventures.

Indifferent as he is to commercial Imperialism, hostile as he is to military Imperialism, the French-Canadian cannot be expected to wish for any organic change in the constitution of Canada and to look favourably upon any scheme of Imperial Federation.

For years he fought to obtain full control of his laws, of his social system, of his public exchequer. With the principles of self-government, of self-taxation, of direct control over the legislative body, no other citizen of the British Empire is more thoroughly imbued than he is. His local organisation, in Church, educational or municipal matters, is still more decentralised and democratic than that of the English provinces of Canada. He likes to exercise his elective franchise and to keep as close as possible to the man, the law and the regulation that he votes for. He cannot view with favour a scheme by which any power that has heretofore been exercised by his own representative bodies may pass under the control of some Council sitting in London.

There remains to be considered the question of annexation to the United States.

As I have stated, left to himself, the French-Canadian is not eager for a change. He requires nothing but quietness and stability in order to grow and develop. He is satisfied with and proud of his Canadian citizenship. But should a change be forced upon him by those who aspire to a greater nationality, he would rather incline towards Pan-Americanism.

For a long time annexation to the United States was most abhorrent to the French-Canadian. In fact, when an agitation in that direction was started by several leading English-speaking Canadians, his resistance proved to be the best safeguard of the British connection. But should his past fidelity be now disregarded, and Canadian autonomy encroached upon in any way, should he be hurried into any Imperial scheme and forced to assume fresh obligations, he would prefer throwing in his lot with his powerful neighbour to the South. His present constitution he prizes far above the American system of Government; but if called upon to sacrifice anything of his Federal autonomy for the working of the Imperial machinery, he would rather do it in favour of the United States system, under which, at all events, he would preserve the self-government of his province. Should Imperial re-organisation be based on trade and financial grounds, he would see a greater future in joining the most powerful industrial nation of the world than in going into partnership with the British communities; and this sentiment is gaining greater force from the present influx of American capital into Canada. The fact that the union of Canada and the United States would bring again under the same flag the two groups, now separated, of his nationality has no doubt greatly contributed towards smoothing his aversion to annexation.

I have so far analysed the sentiments of the higher classes among the French-Canadian people, of those who control their feelings by historical knowledge or by a study of outside circumstances, political, military or financial. If I refer to the masses, mostly composed of farmers, I may say that they entertain similar feelings, but instinctively rather than from reflection. The French-Canadians of the popular class look upon Canada as their own country. They are ready to do their duty by Canada; but considering they owe nothing to Great Britain or any other country, they ask nothing from them. Imbued with a strong sense of liberty, they have no objection to their English-speaking fellow countrymen going to war anywhere they please; but they cannot conceive that Canada as a whole may be forced out of its present situation. They let people talk of any wise and wild proposal of Imperialism; but if any change were attempted to be imposed on them, they would resist the pressure, quietly but constantly.

To sum up, the French-Canadian is decidedly and exclusively Canadian by nationality and American by his ethnical temperament. People with world-wide aspirations may charge him with provincialism. But after all, this sentiment of exclusive attachment to one's land and one's nationality is to be found as one of the essential characteristics of all strong and growing peoples. On the other hand, the lust of abnormal expansion and Imperial pride have ever been the marked features of all nations on the verge of decadence.

Readings

Berger, C. *A Sense of Power: Studies in the Ideas of Canadian Imperialists 1867 to 1914*. Toronto: University of Toronto Press, 1970.

Berger, C., ed. *Imperialism and Nationalism, 1884–1914: A Conflict in Canadian Thought*. Toronto: University of Toronto Press, 1970.

Carr, G. "Imperialism and Nationalism in Revisionist Historiography: A Critique of Some Recent Trends," *Journal of Canadian Studies* 17, 2 (1982).

Christian, W. "Canada's Fate: Principal Grant, Sir George Parkin and George Grant," *Journal of Canadian Studies* 24, 4 (Winter 1999-2000).

Coates, C. ed. *Imperial Canada 1867–1917*. Edinburgh: University of Edinburgh, 1997.

Cole, D. "Canada's 'Nationalistic' Imperialists," *Journal of Canadian Studies* 5, 3 (1970).

Cook, R. "Nationalism in Canada or Portnoy's Complaint Revisited," *South Atlantic Quarterly* 69, 1 (1970).

Cook, R. *The Maple Leaf Forever: Essays on Nationalism and Politics in Canada*. Second edition. Toronto: Macmillan, 1971.

Cook, T. "George R. Parkin and the Concept of Britannic Idealism," *Journal of Canadian Studies* 10, 3 (1975).

Grant, I. "Erasmus Wiman: A Continentalist Replies to Canadian Imperialism," *Canadian Historical Review* 53, 1 (1972).

Levitt, J. *Henri Bourassa and the Golden Calf: The Social Program of the Nationalists, 1900–1914*. Second edition. Ottawa: University of Ottawa Press, 1972.

Levitt, J. *Henri Bourassa on Imperialism and Biculturalism, 1900–1918*. Toronto: Copp Clark, 1970.

Moniere, D. *Ideologies in Quebec: The Historical Development*. Toronto: University of Toronto Press, 1981.

Murrow, C. *Henri Bourassa and French Canadian Nationalism*. Montreal: Harvest House, 1968.

Penlington, N. *Canada and Imperialism, 1896–1899*. Toronto: University of Toronto Press, 1965.

Russell, P. *Nationalism in Canada*. Toronto: McGraw-Hill Ryerson, 1966.

Shortt, S. *The Search for an Ideal: Six Canadian Intellectuals and Their Convictions in an Age of Transition, 1890–1930*. Toronto: University of Toronto Press, 1976.

Smith, A. *Canada- An American Nation?: Essays on Continentalism, Identity and The Canadian Frame of Mind*. Kingston and Montreal: McGill-Queen's, 1994.

Underhill, F. "Goldwin Smith," in his *In Search of Canadian Liberalism*. Toronto: Macmillan, 1960.

Wallace, E. *Goldwin Smith: Victorian Liberal*. Toronto: University of Toronto Press, 1957.

Warner, D. *The Idea of Continental Union: Agitation for the Annexation of Canada to the United States, 1849–93*. Lexington: University of Kentucky Press, 1960.

Chapter Two

"THE INSANE EXUBERANCE OF GENEROSITY": ANTI-POTLATCH LEGISLATION

1. Cornelius Bryant, "Sir," January 29, 1884.
2. "The Evil Potlatch," Toronto *Empire*, 1893.
3. Wise-As-You, Simh-Sam, and Naas-Quah-So, "Petition of Rights," February 26, 1896.
4. Kwakiutle Chief, 1896.
5. Maquinna Chief of Nootka, "To the editor," *Victoria Daily Colonist*, April 1, 1896.
6. Dr. Franz Boas, "To the editor," Victoria *Province*, 1897.
7. Rev. J.B. McCullagh, "The Indian Potlatch," *The Caledonian Interchange*, September 1900.

Introduction

The federal government in 1884 enacted legislation outlawing the West Coast Potlatch ceremony and maintained the ban until 1951. During that period, authorities charged Natives with breeching the law and seized ceremonial Potlatching goods. Today westcoast Canadian Natives perceive the Potlatch, and efforts to quell it, as symbolic of the struggle against the tyranny of White rule which they alleged had changed traditional Native culture beyond recognition, leaving the people semi-assimilated and culturally devastated. Potlatching experienced a renaissance in the 1970s, and much of the ceremonial material, at least that which is not in private collections, has been returned to its original owners.

Was this simply a case of paternalistic and bigoted White laws doing irreparable and indefensible damage to an innocent culture and people? What superficially appears as a clear case of racism, or as some would have it, cultural genocide, on closer inspection may be far "more complex." Arriving at a fair and balanced interpretation of such a highly charged issue logically requires establishing the essence of the ceremony itself and establishing the historical events that unfolded around its illegalization.

What was a Potlatch? The Potlatch was different things to different people and therefore defies definitive description. At its core, however, it was an ancient ceremony held by individual west coast Native families to celebrate the major events in their lives: primarily births, deaths, female puberty, and marriages. A family calling a potlatch invited friends and relatives from other coastal communities, often far distant ones, to join them in celebration. Thus, if it were a large Potlatch, hundreds of people descended upon their hosts from across the entire Pacific Northwest and Alaska, and often stayed for months. Hosting a potlatch was very costly and typically required the family to save for years in advance. Not only did one have to feed the guests, one also hosted the singing and dancing rituals, and ended the Potlatch by distributing large quantities of material goods such as blankets, boats, clothing, utensils, flour, and even articles like pool tables. The single most valuable item was the "copper," a piece of metal presumed to have originated from the bottom of eighteenth century British ships and then beaten into various shapes. These coppers came to represent enormous value to the Native owner.

The host family demonstrated its stature within the wider community by the generosity of its gifts, and could be left quite destitute as the last guest bade farewell and headed home. The expectation, however, was that guests would subsequently invite the family to their own Potlatches, at which they would receive back more than they originally gave. As such, early anthropologists like Franz Boas likened the ceremony to an economic system, similar to capitalism, which kept goods in circulation and allowed families to "invest" for their long-term futures. Native people agree, but argue that it is much more than that: that the Potlatch formed the preservative hub of their culture by affirming a family's social standing and perpetuating Native history through ritual songs, stories, dances, and the regular reunion of a geographically scattered people.

Under pressure, primarily from missionaries administering to West Coast Native communities, the federal government decided, on April 19, 1884, to amend the Indian Act, thereby illegalizing the Potlatch. The amendment read:

"Every Indian or other person who engages in or assists in celebrating the Indian festival known as the "Potlatch" is guilty of a misdemeanour, and liable to imprisonment for a term of not more than six nor less than two months in any gaol or other place of confinement; and every Indian or persons who encourages, either directly or indirectly, such a festival or dance, shall be liable to the same punishment."

A law, however, is only as effective as it is either acceptable or enforceable, and it was neither, at least not to Native people who openly defied it and continued Potlatching, either in its traditional form or in a modified version that cleverly circumvented legal limitations. This should, of course, have invoked punishment, but rarely did. Local Indian agents advised against prosecution for a number of reasons: fears of rebellion; the Potlatch was good business for those who sold Natives the materials distributed during the ceremonies; and many agents simply did not see the ceremony as wrong. There were other reasons for ignoring the lawbreakers. Though the Indian Act was federal, provinces were obliged to enforce it, which the British Columbia government in this case refused to do, largely because of the staggering costs and unlikely subsequent convictions. The overall effect was for government officials, in the form of Agents and police, to turn a blind eye to the Potlatch and instead rely upon missionaries to acculturate their flock away from such "heathen" practices.

An exception to this unwritten policy occurred during 1921 and 1922 when Duncan Scott, Deputy Superintendent of Indian Affairs, decided to enforce the law. The Kwakiutl of Alert Bay, in particular, felt his heavy hand. Dozens of Kwakiutl ended up languishing in Okalla prison in Vancouver after Dan Cranmer's Potlatch at Christmas, 1921. Of the fifty-eight charged, nine cases were dismissed and forty-nine convicted. Of those, twenty-three saw their sentences suspended in exchange for surrendering their Potlatching goods. Police collected 450 such pieces, which they sent to the Victoria Museum (now the Museum of Civilization) and Toronto's Royal Ontario Museum. Though Scott theoretically succeeded in his mission, seizing the ceremonial Potlatching gear had the opposite effect by contributing to West Coast Native political consciousness. Scott admitted defeat and day-to-day practice reverted to ignoring the ceremony—much to the chagrin of local missionaries who continued to rail against it. The police did make periodic and symbolic arrests, but judges invariably acquitted the accused, not so much from sympathy as from the Natives' shrewd understanding of the law and its loopholes. This, of course, made the law a joke, and Natives supposedly guffawed whenever officials or missionaries threatened them with it.

The federal government finally repealed the moribund Potlatch law in 1951, long after it ceased being anything more than a symbolic irritant. The final chapters of the saga began in 1963 when two Alert Bay Kwakiutl went to Ottawa, demanding return of their confiscated ceremonial gear. It took considerable time, but they succeeded and the Museum of Civilization sent the final piece to Alert Bay in 1987. Retrieving the Potlatch paraphernalia became a manifestation of Native independence and strength, and of the Potlatch revival.

Was it justified for one group of a given society to force its will upon other members? Although the anti-Potlatch law appeared very ethnocentric, a considerable number of Natives supported its passage.

The ceremony frequently took place to celebrate a forced marriage in which the women were in their early teens. Potlatching ceremonies also often involved self-mutilation,and led to considerable privation for members of the community—particularly its women, children and elderly. By the beginning of the twentieth century, most coastal people were devout Christians and as such believed that Potlatching must be abandoned on religious grounds—but could not effect that change because of coercion from traditionalists. The argument could therefore be made that the Potlatch law was justified because it sought to assist Native victims from being forced into participation. The law, in this light, upheld humanistic principles of individual liberty. This justification, in fact, gained strength with the passage of time. Increasing numbers of young Natives, in particular, rejected the Potlatch and described it as a form of tyranny that kept them socially dependent, and often in abject poverty. Many Natives argued that the Potlatch tradition simply perpetuated an outmoded paternalistic gerontocracy in a modern democracy, but that refusing to participate led to ostracization, public humiliation, and subsequent hardship. This position became particularly strong after the Second World War when a new generation of young Natives, particularly in the far Northwest of B.C., wished to join mainstream society but found themselves impeded by limitations imposed upon them by their Potlatching elders.

Some describe the Potlatch law as a tool for cultural genocide because it eradicated the foundation of west coast Indian life. Does this stand up to scrutiny? Perhaps not. Anthropologists state that Potlatching was already waning by the time of its banning. This is supported by an examination of the American situation where it had largely disappeared, despite being perfectly legal. The Makah of Cape Flattery, for example, retained far less Potlatching than their Nootka brethren on Vancouver Island—where it was illegal. The fact that the law was *not* applied, and that Canadian Natives Potlatched at will throughout the illegalization period, further suggests that the law's impact could not be genocidal. But then, if the Potlatch was on the wane in 1902, why is it still practised today?

Legislators' motivation and intent must also come under scrutiny if historians are to determine the law's justifiability. There is no doubt that most, if not all, missionaries and not a few politicians, sought the Potlatch's eradication on purely euro-centric grounds. Evangelical missionaries hated what they perceived as idol-worship and, to them, the notion of accumulating material only to give it away was a logical absurdity—despite Natives pointing out that Christian Christmas festivities involve rather similar features. There was also the serious issue of the perceived waste of time: time spent away from work. This did not sit well with industrious Protestants for whom laziness was sinfully unproductive. Finally, it is likely that the very exotic "foreignness" of the ceremony lay at the heart of White concern.

Discussion Points

1. If Canada professes to be a nation built on religious freedom, how could the anti-potlatch laws have been passed?
2. Although the law was not effectively implemented, could it still have had a profound impact on westcoast native life?
3. What made the Potlatch distinct from the exuberance of gift-giving during non-native weddings or Christmas celebrations?

Documents

1. Cornelius Bryant, "Sir," January 29, 1884.

In reply to your favor of 24th inst. in which you do me the honour of asking for any suggestions I may be able to offer respecting the custom of "Potchlatching" among the Indians on this coast, allow me to say that it is with pleasure that I accede to your request, inasmuch as it affords me an opportunity of conveying to the Government through an official channel the strong and decided opinion which I hold, after a personal knowledge of upwards of 26 years with our Indian tribes (chiefly on this E. coast and partly on Fraser river), of what you aptly designate as 'the demoralizing custom of "Potchlatching",' which, as you say, seems to be on the increase among the Indians of this coast.

My uniform experience, but especially my experience as a Christian missionary in this Province for the past 13½ years, sustains your view that these "potchlatching" customs are demoralizing, without any redeeming feature.

1. As to the *Individual*, who, in accordance with the well-known habit of giving away absolutely all they happen to possess in many cases, thereby reduce themselves to beggary and distress, but beyond mere impoverishment, and what is very much worse, physical misery and evils resulting from exposure to the elements in travelling to and from these 'Potchlatches,' which they do in their

canoes in all kinds of weather, and the debauchery produced by intoxication in which they often indulge upon such occasions,—leaves no doubt as to the personal demoralization which follows these native feasts.

Indeed, it is well-known that, at such times, knives and fire-arms are freely used in their drunken feuds, and too commonly with deadly effect. So that what is true of the individual, is also true

2. of the *Family* and the *Tribe*. The impoverishment and dissipation already referred to, have a most deplorable effect upon hapless children and aged people, who in their dependent condition ought to enjoy the comforts of convenient homes and wholesome food, which are denied them, owing to the reckless and spendthrift customs which are maintained at these Potchlatches. Improvident habits are of course too common among Indians, but they are fostered sadly too much by the Potchlatching system. Indeed not only the *Family* but the whole *Tribe suffers*.

For instance how many times have I appealed in vain to those who have been hoarding up their wealth in order to give it away at the next "Potchlatch," to assist in some sanitary improvement, such as the repair or renovation of their own dwelling house, or the grading or laying out of some street or road, or the fencing of, or supply of conveniences for their local cemetery? What is true in this respect is no less so in any attempts to elevate the natives intellectually and religiously, for,

3. The *Church* and the *School* cannot flourish where the "potchlatching" holds sway. In this my experience accords I doubt not with others who have had similar facilities for observation. Thus all the objects or advantages to be secured by good government are frustrated by this very demoralizing custom; and as the wards of the Government, the native tribes should be prevented by judicious counsel and governmental interference,—that is, by some kind of paternal restraint,—from indulging in their "Potchlatching" feasts. Of course, my knowledge of the Indian character, suggests the danger of attempting any *co-ercive* measures. Added to this, the situation of the Government in seeking to suppress the "Potchlatch" is rendered the more critical by the ill-advice and malignant designs of the dissipated class of whites who commonly hover around Indian camps, and from whom the natives are only too ready to take counsel. But I have also discovered that the Indians have been advised to rebel against the idea of discontinuing the "Potlatching" too, by respectable traders whose business interests have been temporarily benefitted by the "Potchlatches" being held in their neighbourhood. I could hardly have thought it possible that the good intentions of the Government, in seeking to suppress so pernicious a practice would have been discouraged and opposed, simply for the selfish purpose of selling a few

hundred dollars' worth of goods, had not the names of white-traders (one or two) been mentioned to me by the Indians themselves. It is hardly necessary to say that such an adverse opinion to "Potchlatches," was quoted by my Indian informant with approval, as sustaining his view of the unnecessary and unjust interference of the Gov't, as he termed it, with their long-standing custom. In the presence therefore of such embarrassing difficulties it is very perplexing indeed to say just what would be the most advisable course for the Gov't to pursue in trying to put down the "Potchlatching" system ...

2. "The Evil Potlatch," Toronto *Empire*, 1893.

The Season When the Red Man Gives Away His Blankets

A party of missionaries a few weeks ago paid a visit to the Indian reserve at Cape Mudge, B.C., where they found the red man engaged in a great 'potlatch.' The word means 'to give.' The visitors went from Comox by the mission boat Glad Tidings. On landing at the village they found some 1,200 Indians congregated from a radius of 100 miles or more. Their tents were made some of white cotton, some of cedar bark and some of cedar slabs. Into these places the hordes were huddled until there was scarcely room to step. Strewn about in all directions were pieces of refuse, food and other filth, in which the young children were rolling, some of them entirely nude, others with a mere rag of clothing on them. To make the mixture complete, were scores of Indian dogs lying about with the children, others in their beds, or nosing about their foods ... until

The Scene Was Disgusting

in the extreme. This is a meagre sketch of the scene by daylight, when a great many of the family were out. Under the cover of darkness this seething mass of corruption puts on another aspect. Morality among the Indians themselves, under these circumstances, is at a very low ebb; but when a score of white men come in with a few gallons of 'fire water,' and spend the night with the Indians, the scenes become indescribable ... the picture is more like hell upon earth than anything ever heard of.

Now for a few side pictures, and they were by no means scarce. The visitors stepped into one tent to see a poor woman whose leg was actually rotting off. She was all alone, her husband having left here, and her son 'thrown her away,' or left her to herself. The poor creature was entirely without food or care. Hearing some woman crying in another tent, we went in, and found a baby dying. We asked where the father was, when the poor mother told us that he was up on the raised platform

Throwing Away His Blankets

in which he took a great deal more interest than in his dying child. A great drumming was going on in one of the large houses, upon entering which they found a number of Indians beating on boxes and boards, as an accompaniment to the death-song which they were chanting. They enquired why they were singing it and were told that a woman had died that morning, and, after hurrying her away to the graveyard before the corpse was cold, they were singing the death-song to drive away the spirit that it might not linger near them, as they have an awful dread of spirits of departed friends. Piled on the top of that house were hundreds of blankets, which the owner was throwing to the ground one by one, at the same time calling out the names of the persons to whom they were given. These blankets are carried away to other villages, when potlatches are called and the blankets returned to their owners; thus it goes on from month to month and from year to year ...

In places where the potlatch has ceased the missionaries claim that the morality of the people has risen to a higher standard and as a natural result the people, especially the children, are more numerous and more healthy; whereas, in some of the villages where this fearful vice remains, the few children that may be found are full of disease, and few of them live to grow up; and even if they do, their life is a burden to them.

A few years ago a law was passed prohibiting the potlatch. This was as good as winked at by some of the officials; and when a certain tribe asked permission to hold 'just one more potlatch,' and that permission was granted, the Indians said, 'If one tribe can break the law by permission, we will try breaking it without permission,' and they have done so ever since. The law remains on the Dominion statutes, but is practically a dead letter; and the Indians, instead of being an upright and industrious people, are a filthy, indolent, degraded set, a disgrace and a curse to our country.

3. Wise-As-You, Simh-Sam, and Naas-Quah-So, "Petition of Rights," February 26, 1896.

To G. E. Corbould, Representative at Ottawa:

The undersigned, a delegation of Indian chiefs, in view of the hereditary right of our ancestry would respectfully represent: That we were at the Indian department in the city of Victoria this day at 11 o'clock. In an interview with Mr. Vowell, Indian commissioner, we were informed by an explanation of how that any person giving a potlach would be imprisoned for six months. It is the desire of the Indian department to civilize us, which meets with our approbation;

but we were born Indians, educated according to the laws of our ancestry, and, as nature dictates to us we enjoy their vested rights as an inheritance. We came to Victoria to obtain our natural rights.

We see in this a contradictory state of affairs adorning your civilization. Churches are numerous; theatres are located in the various sections of the town; and saloons multiply in numbers; all of which are in conformity with your laws, consequently we wish to know whether the ministers of the gospel have annihilated the rights of white men in these pleasures leading to heaven and hell exactly in different directions. They have kindly forced us out, as we are "not in it."

In the difference of your wisdom have we committed any offence against the Almighty God or civilized humanity by bestowing on our poor Indian brethren the pleasure of our hearts by donation of charity in token of friendship. If it is a sin against nature, or a damage to government, society or otherwise, we will yield with the kindliest feeling to your imperial mandate.

You have your Christmas, First of July and 24th of May, all of which you celebrate without interference—sine que non. Money is spent in squandrous profusion with no benefit to the poor of your race.

We go to the entertainments of your theatres and you charge us money for the privilege. We give our dances at which our guests are welcomed by the testimonial of donations, according to our custom—the inheritance of our fathers.

If we wish to perform an act moral in its nature, with no injury or damage, and pay for it, no law in equity can divest us of such right.

We see the Salvation Army parade the streets of your city with music and drum, enchanting the town; leading wanderers, and helping the poor—by making him pay for all he gets.

We are puzzled to know whether in the estimation of civilization we are human or fish on the tributaries of the Nass river, that the felicities of our ancestors should be denied us.

Our lands and our fishing grounds are converted to other hands; licenses are imposed for fishing the waters of the White Crest mountains, which we pay with pleasure, for such is your law, and we only ask in connection that our potlatches may meet with your approbation.

We see in your graveyards the white marble and granite monuments which cost you money in testimony of your grief for the dead. When our people die we erect a large pole, call our people together, distribute our personal property with them in payment for their sympathy and condolence; comfort to us in the sad hours of our affliction. This is what is called a potlach—the privilege denied us ...

4. Kwakiutle Chief, 1896.

We want to know whether you have come to stop our dances and feasts, as the missionaries and agents who live among our neighbors try to do. We do not want to have anybody here who will interfere with our customs. We were told that a man-of-war would come if we should continue to do as our grandfathers and great grandfathers have done. But we do not mind such words. Is this the white man's land? We are told it is the Queen's land; but no! it is mine! Where was the Queen when our God came down from heaven? Where was the Queen when our God gave the land to my grandfather and told him, "This will be thine?" My father owned the land and was a mighty chief; now it is mine. And when your man-of-war comes let him destroy our houses. Do you see yon woods? Do you see yon trees? We shall cut them down and build new houses and live as our fathers did. We will dance when our laws command us to dance, we will feast when our hearts desire to feast. Do we ask the white man, "Do as the Indian does?" No, we do not. Why then do you ask us, "Do as the white man does?" It is a strict law that bids us dance. It is a strict law that bids us distribute our property among our friends and neighbors. It is a good law. Let the white man observe his law, we shall observe ours. And now, if you are come to forbid us to dance, begone, if not, you will be welcome to us.

5. Maquinna Chief of Nootka, "To the editor," *Victoria Daily Colonist*, April 1, 1896.

My name is Maquinna! I am the chief of the Nootkas and other tribes. My great-grandfather was also called Maquinna. He was the first chief in the country who saw white men. That is more than one hundred years ago. He was kind to the white men and gave them land to build and live on. By-and-by more white men came and ill treated our people and kidnapped them and carried them away on their vessels, and then the Nootkas became bad and retaliated and killed some white people. But that is a long time ago. I have always been kind to the white men. Dr. Powell knows it and Mr. Vowell and all the white men who come to my country. And now I hear that the white chiefs want to persecute us and put us in jail and we do not know why.

They say it is because we give feasts which the Chinook people call "Potlatch." That is not bad! That which we give away is our own! Dr. Powell, the Indian agent, one day also made a potlatch to all the Indian chiefs, and gave them a coat, and tobacco, and other things, and thereby we all knew that he was a chief; and so when I give a potlatch, they all learn that I am a chief. To put in prison people who steal and sell whiskey and cards to our young men; that is right. But do not put us in jail as long as we have not stolen the things which we give away to our Indian friends. Once I was in Victoria, and I saw a very large house; they told me it was a bank and that the white men place their money there to take care of, and that by-and-by they get it back, with interest. We are Indians, and we have no such bank; but when we have plenty of money or blankets, we give them away to other chiefs and people, and by-and-by they return them, with interest, and our heart feels good. Our potlatch is our bank.

I have given many times a potlatch, and I have more than $2,000 in the hands of Indian friends. They all will return it some time, and I will thus have the means to live when I cannot work any more. My uncle is blind and cannot work, and that is the way he now lives, and he buys food for his family when the Indians make a potlatch. I feel alarmed! I must give up the potlatch or else be put in jail. Is the Indian agent going to take care of me when I can no longer work? No, I know he will not. He does not support the old and poor now. He gets plenty of money to support his own family, but, although it is all our money, he gives nothing to our old people, and so it will be with me when I get old and infirm. They say it is the will of the Queen. That is not true. The Queen knows nothing about our potlatch feasts. She must have been put up to make a law by people who know us. Why do they not kill me? I would rather be killed now than starve to death when I am an old man. Very well, Indian agents, collect the $2,000 I am out and I will save them till I am old and give no more potlatch!

They say that sometimes we cover our hair with feathers and wear masks when we dance. Yes, but a white man told me one day that the white people have also sometimes masquerade balls and white women have feathers on their bonnets and the white chiefs give prizes for those who imitate best, birds or animals. And this is all good when white men do it but very bad when Indians do the same thing. The white chiefs should leave us alone as long as we leave the white men alone, they have their games and we have ours.

I am sorry to hear the news about the potlatch, and that my friends of the North were put in jail. I sympathise with them; and I asked a white man to write this in order to ask all white men not to interfere with our customs as long as there is no sin or crime in them. The potlatch is not a pagan rite; the first Christians used to have their goods in common and as a consequence must have given "potlatches" and now I am astonished that Christians persecute us and put us in jail for doing as the first Christians.

6. Dr. Franz Boas, "To the editor," Victoria *Province*, 1897.

... The economic system of the Indians of British Columbia and Alaska is largely based on credit, just as much as that of civilized communities. In all his undertakings the Indian relies on the help of friends. He promises to pay them for this help at a later date. If the help furnished consisted in valuables—which are measured by the Indians by blankets as we measure them by money—he promises to repay the amount so loaned with interest. The Indian has no system of writing and, therefore, in order to give security to the transaction it is performed publicly. The contracting of debts on the one hand and the paying of debts on the other is the potlatch. This economic system has developed to such an extent that the capital possessed by all the individuals of the tribe combined exceeds many times the actual amount of cash that exists. That is to say the conditions are quite analogous to those prevailing in our community: If we want to call in all our outstanding debts, it is found that there is not, by any means, money enough in existence to pay them, and the result of an attempt of all the creditors to call in their loans results in disastrous panic from which it takes the community a long time to recover.

It must be clearly understood that an Indian who invites all his friends and neighbors to a great potlatch, and apparently squanders all the accumulated results of long years of labor, has two things in his mind which we cannot but acknowledge as wise and worthy of praise. His first object is to pay his debts. This is done publicly and with much ceremony, as a matter of record. His second object is to invest the fruits of his labor so that the greatest benefit will accrue from them for his own benefit as well as for his children. The recipients of gifts at this festival receive these as loans, which they utilize in their present undertakings. But after the lapse of several years they must repay them with interest to the giver or to his heir. Thus the potlatch comes to be considered by the Indians as a means of insuring the well-being of their children if they should be left orphans while still young; it is, we might say, his life insurance.

The sudden abolition of this system, which in all its intricacies is very difficult to understand, but the main points of which are set forth in the preceding remarks, destroys all the accumulated capital of the Indians. It undoes the carefully planned life-work of the present generations, exposes them to need in their old age, and leaves the orphans unprovided for. What wonder, that it is resisted with vigor by the best class of Indians, and that only the lazy ones support it because it relieves them of the duty to pay their debts.

But it will be said, that the cruel ceremonies connected with some of the festivals make their discontinuance necessary. From an intimate knowledge of the Indian character and of these very ceremonies I consider any interference with them unadvisable. They are so intimately connected with all that is sacred to the Indian that their forced discontinuance will tend to destroy what moral steadiness is left to him. It was during these ceremonies that I heard the old men of the tribe exhort the young men to mend their ways, that they held up to shame the young women who had gone to Victoria to lead a life of shame and that they earnestly discussed the question of requesting the Indian agents to help them in their endeavor to bring the young back to the good moral life of old.

And the cruelty of the ceremonial exists alone in the fancy of those who know of it only by the exaggerated descriptions of travelers. In olden times it was a war ceremony and captives were killed and even devoured. But with the encroachment of civilization the horrors of the old ceremony have died out. I heard an old chief addressing his people thus: "How lovely is our time. No longer do we go in fear of each other. Peace is everywhere. No longer is there the strife of battle; we only try to outdo each other in the potlatch," meaning that each tries to invest his property in the most profitable manner, and particularly that they vie with each other in honorably repaying their debts.

The ceremony of the present day is no more and no less than a time of general amusement which is expected with much pleasure by young and old. But enough of its old sacredness remains to give the Indian, during the time of its celebration, an aspect of dignity which he lacks at other times. The lingering survivals of the old ceremonials will die out quickly, and the remainder is a harmless amusement that we should be slow to take away from the native who is struggling against the over-powerful influence of civilization.

7. Rev. J.B. McCullagh, "The Indian Potlatch," *The Caledonian Interchange*, September 1900.

The Indian Potlatch presents a most difficult problem, not only to solve for the betterment of the race, but even to understand. Indeed no one who has not been born and reared as an Indian among Indians practising it can rightly comprehend what it all means. Though I cannot lay claim to this privilege (!), yet I have had the Potlatch under close observation for sixteen years, and have studied it on the spot both in theory and practice as far as one may do so without actually making one ...

Although not an idol itself, the Potlatch puts all the idols of heathendom in the shade, for not only does it swallow up the sustenance of an entire community but the community itself ... It consumes five clear months out of every twelve in simply gorging, sleeping and dancing; the most that any of its followers can earn is all too little for it; the money that ought to be spent upon the necessaries of life is squandered on this idol, which is feted and glutted to its heart's content, while the poor, the aged, the feeble and the sick lie in poverty, filth, and rags—dying for want of a little nourishment.

It is a pitiable sight to behold sick folk, invalids, delicate children and babies travelling to and fro over fifty miles of waste ice and snow, the themometer perhaps below zero at the time, for the sole purpose of paying and receiving homage before this idol. I have seen dying persons and children suffering from measles hauled about the country in mid-winter on sleds, camping out in the snow at night, in order to be present, or that those on whose tender mercies they were dependent might be present at Potlatch; and I have seen them taken back from Potlatch in their coffins ...

Among those who practise it, its influence is baneful in the last degree; it puffs up while exhausting, and its victims while being destroyed think they are being established; ... it is fatal to all idea of thrift and comfort in family life—to be thrifty is to be bad, to be economical is criminal; it is destructive of individual liberty and, consequently, of the development of the race; it is inimical to all social progress and education; although not a religious system it is intensely repugnant to religion, and the civilization of the Indian is an abomination to it; it produces such a strange condition of society that if we can get in five years' work among the people in twenty years we may claim to do well; it places our best actions in a false light—while we think we are showing kindness and charity to the poor and needy we are in reality paying homage to exalted personages; our greetings, salutations and smiles very often appear in the same light; our efforts for the salvation of souls are nothing less than a hunt for men of title with which to adorn our missions, while everything containing the element of a free gift—and much of our work is of that nature—is liable to appear in the light of a "bid" for favour ...

I must now say a few words about the effect of the potlatch system upon those Indians who have come out on the side of religion and civilization.

If after an Indian leaves the Confederacy to join a mission the potlatch would let him alone all would be well. But it does no such thing. If the man be a chief the potlatch immediately usurps his chieftainship, promotes another chief in his place, takes away his name and title, and ignores him. This is very hard for some men to bear, not so much because of the humiliation as because of the injustice.

If when a Christian Indian dies the potlatch would leave the matter alone much heart-burning would be avoided. But it does no such thing. If the deceased has been a person of any social position some heathen clansman is sure to make a potlatch for the corpse in order to take that position, thus raising trouble among the Christian relatives.

If the potlatch would leave their young men alone the Christian Indians would not be very much opposed to it. But it will not leave them alone; it inveigles them back into heathenism ... and ties them up to debts from which they may not be able to get free for years ...

It is the duty of everyone who has the welfare of the Indian at heart to protest against the present unsatisfactory state of affairs. If the existing law is to be retained, enforce it; if not, take it off the statute book. But if it may not be repealed, let it be amended; and if it be amended, let it be so amended that it shall touch the core of the evil and ensure relief where relief is wanted, and restraint where restraint is required.

Readings

Adams, J. *Gitksan Potlatch: Population Flux, Resource Ownership and Reciprocity*. Toronto: Holt, Rinehart and Winston, 1973.

Codere, H. *Fighting with Property, A Study of Kwakiutl Potlatching and Warfare 1792–1930*. Seattle: University of Washington Press, 1966.

Cole, D. and I. Chaikin, *An Iron Hand Upon the People: The Law Against the Potlatch on the Northwest Coast*. Vancouver: Douglas and McIntyre, 1990.

Fisher, R. *Contact and Conflict: Indian-European Relations in British Columbia 1774–1890*. Vancouver: University of British Columbia Press, 1977.

Jonitas, A. ed. *Chiefly Feasts: The Enduring Kwakiutl Potlatch*. Vancouver: Douglas and McIntyre, 1991.

Kan, S. *Symbolic Immortality: The Tlingit Potlatch in the Nineteenth Century*. Washington: Smithsonian Institution Press, 1989.

Loo, T. "Dan Cranmer's Potlatch: Law as Coercion, Symbol, and Rhetoric in British Columbia, 1884-1951," *The Canadian Historical Review* 73, 2 (June 1992).

Pettipas, K. *Severing the Ties that Bind: Government Repression of Indigenous Religious Ceremonies on the Prairies*. Winnipeg: University of Manitoba Press, 1994.

Rosman, A. and P. Rubel, *Feasting with Mine Enemy: Rank and Exchange among Northwest Coast Societies*. New York: Columbia University Press, 1971.

Sewid-Smith, D. *Prosecution and Persecution*. Cape Mudge: Nu-Yum-Baleess Society, 1979.

Simeone, W. *Rifles, Blankets and Beads: Identity, History and the Northern Athapaskan Potlatch*. Norman: University of Oklahoma Press, 1995.

Tennant, P. *Aboriginal Peoples and Politics: The Indian Land Question in British Columbia. 1849–1989* Vancouver: University of British Columbia Press, 1990.

Titley, E. *A Narrow Vision: Duncan Campbell Scott and the Administration of Indian Affairs in Canada.* Vancouver: University of British Columbia Press, 1986.

Chapter Three

"Two Distinct Personalities": The Question of Riel's Sanity

Introduction

The enigmatic Louis Riel still stirs controversy well over one hundred years after his execution in the Regina police barracks. The man, his legacy, and his place in the national pantheon continues to foment debate, historical papers, and letters to editors. Riel has, since his death, metamorphosed in the public mind from traitor to a brave hero of Canadian minority rights and one of the Fathers of Confederation. He still serves as a lightning rod for issues of social justice, civil and minority versus government rights.

The question of Riel's sanity before, during, and after the Northwest Rebellion of 1885 generated considerable debate. What would it say about the Metis, for example, if they willingly followed a bone fide lunatic? Could that not imply that they, as a people, were either equally misguided, hopelessly gullible, or both? The federal government, meanwhile, could perhaps be justified for its action, or inaction, before and during the rebellion if Riel were insane—but then he should not have hanged. Conversely, finding him sane, even in retrospect, justifies his execution and simultaneously elevates his followers in the public's eye. The Catholic church, too, discussed the issue of Riel's sanity. Was he indeed a mad heretic to be dismissed or excommunicated? Perhaps, but there are Catholics who believed, and still believe, that Riel, like Joan of Arc, will eventually and deservedly win ecclesiastical recognition and honour as a saint, not a lunatic.

Tackling the issue from an entirely different perspective, some interested parties debate whether Riel's sanity is really an issue at all, or simply a red herring conjured to deflect people's attention from the truly significant issues around the North-West Rebellion. And if not a red herring, could historical and contemporary efforts to brand Riel a madman arise from those issues, both then and now, to discredit a Native who dared oppose colonization?

Establishing Riel's guilt as a traitor posed few problems in the narrow eyes of English Common Law, then or now. The evidence overwhelmingly proved that he indeed broke the Elizabethan Statute of Treasons by "most wickedly and traitorously [making] war against our said lady the Queen." Where the issue became ambiguous was whether he knew he broke the law and whether, if he did, he knew it was wrong to do so. An affirmative answer to either indicated sanity: that he knew what he was doing. This made him guilty of intent, for which the state had every right to punish him. If, on the other hand, he did not know what he was doing, or did not recognize his actions as wrong, then he could not be held responsible by virtue of insanity, and a jury had to acquit him. The conundrum, of course, lay in interpreting the word "wrong" because legal and moral "wrongs" were, and are not necessarily the same thing. Riel, for example, did not believe it morally "wrong" to defend his people against federal incursion, despite it being legally "wrong" to do so.

British Common Law recognized insanity through a series of precedent setting cases, and accepted the notion that an insane criminal must be pitied, not punished, because "they knew not what they did." "Pity" could ironically mean indefinite incarceration in an insane asylum which, considering conditions in 19th century asylums, was harsh punishment indeed— but it wasn't dangling from the end of a noose. The difficulty lay in developing criteria for testing and definition because "sanity" was subjective and interpretive: one man's visionary is, after all, another's lunatic. To address this, British judges in the 1840s created a set of cognitive tests, known as the McNaughten Rules, to establish an accused's sanity. The individual answered a series of questions that purportedly ascertained their ability to distinguish right from wrong. Though controversial and rejected by many in the fledgling psychiatric community, the

Rules remained in force throughout the empire and for the rest of the century. Using these Rules very few succeeded in pleading insanity.

Interested parties at the time of the Riel trial interpreted known facts in an effort to plead their side of the case and establish Riel's mental status. Riel had indeed spend time in insane asylums, twice, during the 1870s, but he was deemed in each case "cured" and released. Riel readily admitted to hearing God-sent voices directing him to lead the Metis people under new religious tenants. Though erratic and holding rather unorthodox religious views, Riel did enjoy support from Metis and white settlers. Several hundred men willingly followed him into battle in 1885. Throughout his trial Riel insisted on his sanity, a claim which in an awkward twist of logic, his defence team used as proof of his insanity.

The case became particularly awkward for the federal government when the jury returned a guilty verdict, implying sanity, but recommended clemency, which federal cabinet had legal rights to grant. This knot put the case back into MacDonald's hands, where he did not want it, since it put him in the unenviable political position of juggling Ontario's wish for "Riel's head in a sack" against the court's and Quebec's call for mercy. Clemency also implied federal culpability in the rebellion, which MacDonald found unacceptable. The Prime Minister opted for a set of manoeuvres which, though legal, pushed the envelope of justice and interpretations of "wrong." It called for a series of carefully orchestrated medical examinations which found that Riel was indeed a sane criminal ready for hanging. Louis Riel walked to the scaffold at dawn on November 16, 1885.

Discussion Points

1. Based upon the documents in this chapter, should the jury have found Riel sane or insane?
2. Some argue that prayer is still a common means of communicating with God, should Riel's divine communications be taken as evidence of instability? Would this behaviour have been more acceptable in the nineteenth century than today?
3. Is there any evidence to suggest that the whole issue of insanity was designed to take the focus away from the central issue of the federal government's administation in the West?

Documents

1. Judge Richardson, Charge to the Jury, 1885.

... If you are conclusively convinced that the prisoner was implicated, then has anything been shown here to relieve him from responsibility? His counsel urged that at the time he committed the acts charged he was of unsound mind, that he did not know what he was doing, and for that reason he should be acquitted. This question of unsoundness of mind has given rise in former years to a very great deal of consideration. I heard a case referred to yesterday which resulted in a great scandal in Great Britain. That was not the only case, it was followed some years afterwards by a case involving still greater scandal. The law has been put in such a shape now that when the question was set up, judges may be able to tell the jury fixedly in words what their duties are in regard to responsibility for crime when insanity is set up as a defence. As to insanity, as you saw yesterday, doctors differ as do lawyers. Month by month I may say, week by week, additions are made to classes of mania, new terms are used, branches which were under the simple category of mania come out with new names. I heard a name given in evidence yesterday that I never heard before, megalomania, but it seems to be accepted as a symptom or as a fixed branch of insanity, but it is not every man who is pronounced insane by the doctors and who from charity or kindness should be placed under restraint and be put in one of the asylums; it is not I say, every one of them that is to be held free from being called upon to answer for offences he may commit against the criminal law ...

Witness after witness gave evidence as to what occurred in March, at the time of the commencement of this rebellion. Some of them speak of the prisoner being very irritable when the subject of religion was brought up. It appears, however, that his irritability had passed away when he was coming down with Captain Young, as we do not hear anything of it then. Does this show reasoning power?

Then at what date can you fix this insanity as having commenced? The theory of the defence fixes the insanity as having commenced only in March, but threats of what he intended to do began in December. Admitting that the insanity only commenced about the time of the breaking out of the rebellion, what does seem strange to me is that these people who were about him, if they had an insane man in their midst, that some of them had not the charity to go before a magistrate and lay an information setting forth that there was an insane man amongst them, and that a breach of the peace was liable to occur at any moment, and that he should be taken care of. I only suggest that to you, not that you are to take it as law, I merely suggest it to you as turning upon the evidence. Having made the remarks I have, I am simply called upon to tell you what is legal insanity, insanity in the eye of the law, so far as crime is concerned. The Crown must in all cases, particularly such as this, bring home conclusively the crime charged to the prisoner. If the Crown has done that, on the prisoner rests the responsibility of relieving himself from the consequences of his acts. The law directs me to tell you that every man is presumable to be sane and to possess a sufficient degree of reason to be responsible for his crimes until the contrary be proved to your satisfaction. And that to establish a defence on the ground of insanity, it must be clearly proved that at the time he committed the act, the party accused was laboring under such defective reasoning from a diseased mind as not to know the nature and quality of the act he was committing, or that if he did know it, that he did not know that he was doing wrong. That I propound to you as the law.

If the evidence conclusively satisfied you that the prisoner was implicated in these acts or in any of them I may say, has it been clearly proved to you that at the time he committed those acts he was laboring under such defective reasoning caused by disease of the mind as not to know the nature and quality of the act he was committing, or if he did know it, that he did not know that he was doing wrong? If the evidences convinces you and convinces you conclusively that such was the case, then your duty is to acquit the prisoner on that ground, and you are required to declare that he is acquitted by you on account of such insanity ...

2. Francois Roy, Testimony.

Q. What is your position in Quebec? A. For a great number of years I have been medical superintendent and one of the proprietors of the lunatic asylum at Beauport.

Q. How long have you been connected with the asylum as superintendent? A. More than fifteen or sixteen years.

Q. You are also a member of the society of America—of the Society of the Superintendents of the Insane Asylums of America? A. Yes.

Q. During these fifteen or sixteen years your duties caused you to make a special study of diseases of the brain? Is it not true that it has been necessary for you to make a special study of diseases of the brain? A. Yes; it was my duty to go to the principal asylums in the United States and see how the patients were treated there.

Q. Had you any connection with the asylum of Beauport in 1875 and 1876? A. Yes.

Q. You were at that time superintendent of the asylum? A. Yes.

Q. In those years, or about that time, did you have occasion to see the prisoner? A. Certainly; many times.

Q. Where did you see him? A. In the asylum.

Q. Can you tell the date? A. Yes, the date was taken from the register when I left Quebec.

Q. What date is that? A. I took the entry from the register in the hospital in the beginning of this month.

Q. Was he admitted with all the formalities required by law? A. Yes.

Q. Will you tell me what time he left the asylum? A. He was discharged about the 21st of January, after a residence in the house of about nineteen months.

Q. Had you occasion to study at that time the mental disease by which the prisoner was affected at that time? A. Yes.

Q. Did you have relations with him during that time, and did you watch him carefully during that time? A. Not every day, but very often.

Q. Can you say now what mental disease the prisoner was then suffering from? A. He was suffering from what is known by authors as megalomania.

Q. Will you give the symptoms of this disease? A. Many of the symptoms of that disease are found in the ordinary maniac. The particular characteristic of this malady is, that in all cases they show great judgment in all cases not immediately connected with the particular disease with which they suffer.

Q. Will you speak from memory or by referring to the authors, what are the other symptoms of this disease? A. They sometimes give you reasons which would be reasonable if they were not starting from a false idea. They are very clever on those discussions, and they have a tendency to irritability when you question or doubt their mental condition, because they are under a strong impression that they are right and they consider it to be an insult when you try to bring them to reason again. On ordinary questions they may be reasonable and sometimes may be very clever, in fact without careful watching they would lead one to think that they were well.

Q. Was he there some weeks or months before you ascertained his mental condition? A. Yes. I waited till then to classify him as to his mental condition. We wait a few weeks before classifying the patient.

Q. Does a feeling of pride occupy a prominent position in that mental disease? A. Yes, in different forms, religion, and there are a great many with pride; we have kings with us.

Q. Is the question of selfishness or egotism prominent in those cases? A. Yes.

Q. Are they liable to change in their affections rapidly? A. Yes, because they are susceptible to the least kind of attraction.

Q. In that particular malady are the patients generally inclined to be sanguine as to the success of their projects? A. The difficulty is to make them believe that they will not have success; you cannot bring them to change that, it is a characteristic of the disease.

Q. Are people who suffer from this particular form of disease liable to be permanently cured or are they liable to fall back into the old malady? A. Generally remain in that condition; they may have sensible moments and then intermission would interfere.

Q. In a case of this kind could a casual observer without any medical experience form an estimate as to the state of the man's mind? A. Not usually, unless he makes a special study of the case; there is more or less difference in each case.

Q. What is the position of the mind of a man suffering from this disease in reference to other subjects which do not come within the radius of his mania? A. They will answer questions as any other man with the sense of reason; it is only when they touch the spot of their monomania that they become delirious.

Q. You stated that the prisoner left the asylum in 1878? A. In January 1878.

Q. Have you ever seen him from that time till yesterday? A. No, never.

Q. Do you recognize him perfectly as the same person who was in your asylum in 1876 and 1878? A. Yes.

Q. Were you present at the examination of the witnesses that took place to-day and yesterday? A. Partly.

Q. Did you hear the witnesses describing the actions of the prisoner as to his peculiar views on religion in reference to his power, to his hoping to succeed the Pope, and as to his prophecies, yesterday and to-day? A. Yes.

Q. From what you heard from these witnesses and from the symptoms they prove to have been exhibited by the prisoner, are you now in a position to say whether or not at that time he was a man of sound mind? A. I am perfectly certain that when the prisoner was under our care he was not of sound mind, but he became cured before he left, more or less. But from what I heard here to-day I am ready to say that I believe on these occasions his mind was unsound ...

Q. Do you believe that under the state of mind as described by the witnesses and to which you referred that he was capable or incapable of knowing the nature of the acts which he did? A. No, I do not believe that he was in a condition to be the master of his acts, and I positively swear it and I have people of the same character under my supervision.

Q. Will you swear from the knowledge you have heard? A. From the witnesses.

Q. That the man did not know what he was doing or whether it was contrary to law in reference to the particular delusion? A. No, and for another reason the same character of the disease is shown in the last period, the same as when he was with us, there is no difference, if there was any difference in the symptoms I would have doubts, but if it was of the same character so well described by Dagoust, who is taken as an authority and has been adopted in France as well as in America and England.

Q. The opinion you have formed as to the soundness of his mind is based upon the fact that the symptoms disclosed by the witnesses here yesterday and to-day are to a large extent identical with the symptoms of his malady as disclosed while he was at your asylum? A. Yes.

3. Sir Charles Fitzpatrick, Address of Defense Counsel.

... We have stated that this man was suffering from that form of disease known as megalomania. It is not necessary for me to tell you more than that the characteristic symptom of this disease is an insane, an extraordinary love of power and extraordinary development of ambition, a man that is acting under the insane delusion that he is either a great poet or a god or a king or that he is in direct communication with the Holy Ghost; and it may be well for me here to remind you that I do not speak here of my own authority. I tell you here that from books, the most reputed authorities on this subject, one of the distinguishing characteristics of this disease is that the man might reason perfectly and give perfect reasons for all that he does and justify it in every respect, subject always to the insane delusion. They are naturally irritable excitable, and will not suffer that they can be contradicted in any respect ...

But, gentlemen, if his conduct is entirely inconsistent with the possession of a sound mind, is it not consistent with the possession of an unsound mind? And here I may as well tell you that you are entire masters of the fact in this case, that all the evidence given here is given for the purpose of enabling you to arrive at a conclusion, that you are not to take your verdict from me, from the Crown nor from the court; that the oath which you have taken, as you understand thoroughly, obliged you, when you came into the box, to stand indifferent as you stood unsworn, and the true deliverance made between our Sovereign Lady the Queen and the prisoner at the bar, according to your conscience and to your judgment.

Therefore, gentlemen, you have these facts in evidence, that this man, laboring under the insane delusion that he at some future day would have the whole of the North-West Territories under his control, and being thoroughly convinced that he was called and vested by God, for the purpose of chastising Canada and of creating a new country and a new kingdom here, acting under that insane delusion, what do we find him doing? We find him then taking such steps as would enable him to carry out the object which he then had in view. We find this man believing himself to be inspired by God and believing himself to be in direct communication with the Holy Ghost, believing himself to be an instrument in the hands of the Lord of Hosts. We find him with forty or fifty men going out to do battle with against the force of Canada. If the man was sane, how is it possible for you to justify such conduct as that? If the man was insane you know it is one of the distinguishing characteristics of his insanity that he could see no opposition of his objects, that he believed himself to be under the guidance of the Lord of Hosts, and natural reason, he could reason naturally, subject to his insane delusion, he reasoned naturally that the All Powerful will necessarily give him the victory no matter what may be the material that may be placed in his hands, no matter how inadequate that material may appear to a sane man, I, knowing that I am inspired by the Almighty, knowing that I am the instrument in the hands of God, I know that I will necessarily gain the victory; and he goes forth and gives battle with these men. Therefore, gentlemen of the jury, you have one illustration of the insanity, of the unsoundness of this man's mind in those very facts.

... Now, gentlemen, I say that the conduct of Louis Riel throughout the whole if this affair is entirely inconsistent with any idea of sanity, but is entirely consistent with his insanity. As I said to you a moment ago in speaking at the opening of this case, the fact of his delivering himself up is one of the characteristics of a man suffering from the insanity from which he is suffering, because he cannot appreciate the danger in which he is placed. It is impossible for him to appreciate the danger in which he places himself, and he never sees that there is any possibility that any harm can happen to him. If that man was perfectly sane, gentlemen, if that man was perfectly sane in doing as he did do, then you have to say whether or not, as I said before, there are not some redeeming features about this man's character, in the heroic act which he did in delivering himself up to Middleton. On the other hand if he is insane, as I contend he is, you see then the proof, for any man of ordinary prudence knows that this man could have escaped and could have evaded the officers of the law and the soldiers. Notwithstanding all that, he comes and gives himself over to General Middleton and is prepared to take the consequences, no matter what they are. I say that that is one of the characteristics of his malady, that that is one of the proofs of his insanity and that is one of the characteristics which are laid down in all the books, as being characteristic of the disease of those men who believe themselves to be in constant intercourse with God, because they think God is always around them, that He is constantly taking care of them and that no harm of any kind can befall them ...

4. Mr. Robinson, Address of Crown Counsel.

My learned friends must make their choice between their defences. They cannot claim for their client what is called a niche in the temple of fame and at the same time assert that he is entitled to a place in a lunatic asylum. I understand perfectly well the defence of insanity; I understand perfectly the defence of patriotism, but I am utterly unable to understand how you can be told in one breath a man is a noble patriot and to be told in the next breath that every guiding motive of his actions, every controlling influence which he is bound by his very nature to give heed to, is that of overweening vanity, a selfish sense of his own importance and an utter disregard to everything but his own insane power. There must be either one defence or the other in this case.

Unfortunately it becomes my duty to show to you, that the case which the Crown believes it has made out is, that this prisoner at the bar is neither a patriot nor a lunatic.

But before I proceed further as to that, I would ask you in all seriousness, as sensible men: do you believe that a defence of insanity could have any conceivable or possible applicability to a case of this description? ...

Now, gentlemen, just remember what you are told and what you are asked to believe: The half-breeds of this district number, I understand, some 600 or 700. I am speaking entirely of the French half-breeds. I believe the English half-breeds are more numerous than that.

In July 1884, the French half-breeds, believing that the prisoner at the bar was a person in whose judgment, whose advice, whose discretion they could trust and rely upon, sought him out in the place where he was then living with a view of getting him to manage for them their affairs, and to represent their grievances, and to endeavor to obtain for them those rights and that justice which they believed to be theirs.

They sent men, I suppose, in whom they had confidence to ask the prisoner to come for that purpose. They, in their intercourse with him, discovered nothing wrong in his mind, no unsoundness in his reason. The prisoner came here. He remained here from July 1884, till March 1885, and during all that time he was before the public; he addressed, I think we have been told, seven meetings, and there were, I suppose, many more in which he also participated. There was in the district a population of at least 2,000 altogether, for there were six or seven hundred French half-breeds and the English half-breeds outnumbered them. There can be no question, I say, that the prisoner at the bar addressed on public affairs at least two thousand people.

During that time was there ever a whisper of his insanity heard? Have you had one single soul who heard him during that time, one single person of the community among which he lived, and which believed in him; have you heard, I say, one single suspicion from any of them that the prisoner was insane?

The next thing we find in regard to these men is that under the guidance of the prisoner they embark in an enterprise full of danger and gravity. They place their lives and property under his control and direction, and trusting in his judgment they risk both in obedience to his advice, and we have not heard from any one of them that during all that time there was the smallest suspicion he was affected with any unsoundness of mind whatever.

Now, gentlemen, am I speaking reason or am I not speaking reason? Unless all reason and common sense has been banished from the land is it possible that a defence of insanity can be set up in the case of a person of that description? If so, I should like to know what protection there is for society, I should like to know how crimes are to be put down. I should like to know more; I should like to know if the prisoner at the bar is not in law to be held responsible for this crime, who is responsible? He was followed by some six or seven hundred misled and misguided men. Are we to be told that the prisoner at the bar was insane but that his followers were sane? Is there any escape from the one inevitable conclusion either that the prisoner at the bar was perfectly sane and sound in mind or that all the half-breed population of the Saskatchewan were insane. You must have it either one way or the other.

What in reality is the defence set up here; what in reality is the defence which you, as sensible men, are asked to find by your verdict? You are asked to find that six or seven hundred men may get up an armed rebellion with its consequent loss of life, its loss of property, that murder and arson and pillage may be commited by that band of armed men, and we are to be told they are all irresponsible lunatics ...

There are, I say, other features connected with the prisoner's conduct which

I think ought to be submitted to you to show that his mind was strong and clear, that he was not merely a man of strong mind but unusually long-headed, that he was a man who calculated his schemes and drew his plans with shrewdness, and was controlled by no insane impulse.

In the first place do you think his treatment with regard to the rising of the Indians is a piece of insanity? Do you think that the manner in which he addressed them to rise? Do you think the communications which he sent them were suited to their purpose, were adapted to answer the object he had in view? Or do you think you can discover in any one of these communications the insane ravings of an unsound mind? I shall come to this on another branch of the case in a few minutes ...

The only peculiarity in this case is that some eight or nine years ago the prisoner was in a lunatic asylum, and I cannot help saying that the evidence we have had here on that subject was to my mind unsatisfactory. I should like to have known how, and under what circumstances, the prisoner was placed in that asylum, under an assumed name. I should like to know who were responsible for his being placed there. I should like to have seen the register and records which are kept in every asylum from week to week, and I should like to have seen not only why he was received into that asylum, but how he came to be discharged ...

I have nothing more to say in that respect except this: It has been said by learned judges over and over again that insanity is not a question which is only decided by experts. Any man of intelligence and sense, and ordinary capacity is said to be a perfectly good witness, and in many respects as capable to decide on cases of insanity as medical experts can be ...

The medical experts have none of them had any opportunity of observing the prisoner at the bar and his state of mind at the only time when his state of mind is in question, at the time when his crimes were planned and carried out. Our witnesses are men who saw him at that very time and who observed his demeanor, who had much better opportunities of observing him ...

Gentlemen, as to latent insanity, all I can say is this: There are cases of latent insanity; human nature is always fallible, but if it be possible in any civilized community for a man to go through the career which the prisoner at the bar has had, for a man to exercise all that influence over his fellow-creatures which he has exercised, and if sensible men are then to be told that during that time he was practically irresponsible, then all I can say is that there is no safety for society—can be no safety for society at all. If we are to be told that these six or seven hundred men who entrusted themselves to his guidance were all a band of lunatics, following a lunatic leader, and that they are not responsible for murder, pillage, arson, spread throughout this country, then all we can say is that it is not a country for human beings to live in.

5. Louis Riel, Statement.

Your Honors, gentlemen of the jury: It would be easy for me to-day to play insanity, because the circumstances are such as to excite any man, and under the natural excitement of what is taking place to-day (I cannot speak English very well, but am trying to do so, because most of those here speak English), under the excitement which my trial causes me would justify me not to appear as usual, but with my mind out of its ordinary condition. I hope with the help of God I will maintain calmness and decorum as suits this honorable court, this honorable jury ...

It is true, gentlemen, I believed for years I had a mission, and when I speak of a mission you will understand me not as trying to play the roll of insane before the grand jury so as to have a verdict of acquittal upon that ground. I believe that I have a mission, I believe I had a mission at this very time. What encourages me to speak to you with more confidence in all the imperfections of my English way of speaking, it is that I have yet and still that mission, and with the help of God, who is in this box with me, and He is on the side of my lawyers, even with the honorable court, the Crown and the jury, to help me, and to prove by the extraordinary help that there is a Providence to-day in my trial, as there was a Providence in the battles of the Saskatchewan ...

To-day when I saw the glorious General Middleton bearing testimony that he thought I was not insane, and when Captain Young proved that I am not insane, I felt that God was blessing me, and blotting away from my name the blot resting upon my reputation on account of having been in the lunatic asylum of my good friend Dr Roy. I have been in an asylum, but I thank the lawyers for the Crown who destroyed the testimony of my good friend Dr Roy, because I have always believed that I was put in the asylum without reason. To-day my pretension is guaranteed, and that is a blessing too in that way. I have also been in the lunatic asylum at Longue Pointe, and I wonder that my friend Dr Lachapelle, who took care of me charitably, and Dr Howard are not here.

Even if I was going to be sentenced by you, gentlemen of the jury, I have this satisfaction if I die—that if I die I will not be reputed by all men as insane, as a lunatic. A good deal has been said by the two reverend fathers, André and Fourmand. I cannot call them my friends, but they made no false testimony. I know that a long time ago they believed me more or less insane. Father Fourmand said that I would pass from great passion to great calmness. That shows great control under contradiction, and according to my opinion and with the help of God I have that control.

As to religion, what is my belief? What is my insanity about that? My insanity, your Honors, gentlemen of the jury, is that I wish to leave Rome aside, inasmuch as it is the cause of division between Catholics and Protestants. I did not wish to force my views, because in Batoche to the half-breeds that followed me I used the word, *carte blanche*. If I have any influence in the new world it is to help in that way and even if it takes 200 years to become practical, then after my death that will bring out practical results, and then my children's children will shake hands with the Protestants of the new world in a friendly manner. I do not wish these evils which exist in Europe to be continued, as much as I can influence it, among the half-breeds. I do not wish that to be repeated in America. That work is not the work of some days or some years, it is the work of hundreds of years.

My condition is helpless, so helpless that my good lawyers, and they have done it by conviction (Mr Fitzpatrick in his beautiful speech has proved he believed I was insane) my condition seems to be so helpless that they have re-course to try and prove insanity to try and save me in that way. If I am insane, of course I don't know it, it is a property of insanity to be unable to know it. But what is the kind of mission that I have? Practical results. It is said that I had myself acknowledged as a prophet by the half-breeds. The half-breeds have some intelligence. Captain Young who has been so polite and gentle during the time I was under his care, said that what was done at Batoche, from a military point of view was nice, that the line of defence was nice, that showed some intelligence.

It is not to be supposed that the half-breeds acknowledged me as a prophet if they had not seen that I could see something into the future. If I am blessed without measure I can see something into the future, we all see into the future more or less. As what kind of a prophet would I come, would it be a prophet who would all the time have a stick in his hand, and threatening, a prophet of evil? If the half-breeds had acknowledged me as a prophet, if on the other side priests come and say that I am polite, if there are general officers, good men, come into this box and prove that I am polite, prove that I am decent in my manner, in combining all together you have a decent prophet. An insane man cannot withhold his insanity, if I am insane my heart will tell what is in me ...

If it is any satisfaction to the doctors to know what kind of insanity I have, if they are going to call my pretensions insanity, I say humbly, through the grace of God, I believe I am the prophet of the new world.

I wish you to believe that I am not trying to play insanity, there is in the manner, in the standing of a man, the proof that he is sincere, not playing. You will say, what have you got to say? I have to attend to practical results. Is it practical that you be acknowledged as a prophet? It is practical to say it. I think that if the half-breeds have acknowledged me, as a community, to be a prophet, I have reason to believe that it is beginning to become practical. I do not wish, for my satisfaction, the name of prophet, generally that title is accompanied with such a burden, that if there is satisfaction for your vanity, there is a check to it ...

If you take the plea of the defence that I am not responsible for my acts, acquit me completely since I have been quarrelling with an insane and irresponsible Government. If you pronounce in favor of the Crown, which contends that I am responsible, acquit me all the same. You are perfectly justified in declaring that having my reason and sound mind, I have acted reasonably and in self-defence, while the Government, my accuser, being irresponsible, and consequently insane, cannot but have acted wrong, and if high treason there is it must be on its side and not on my part.

... Up to this moment I have been considered by a certain party as insane, by another party as a criminal, by another party as a man with whom it was doubtful whether to have any intercourse. So there was hostility, and there was contempt, and there was avoidance. To-day, by the verdict of the court, one of those three situations has disappeared.

I supposed that after having been condemned, I will cease to be called a fool, and for me, it is a great advantage. I consider it as a great advantage. If I have a mission—I say 'if,' for the sake of those who doubt, but for my part it means 'since,' since I have a mission, I cannot fulfil my mission as long as I am looked upon as an insane being—human being, as the moment I begin to ascent that scale I begin to succeed.

You have asked me, your Honors, if I have anything to say why my sentence should not be passed. Yes, it is on that point particularly my attention is directed.

Before saying anything about it, I wish to take notice that if there has ever been any contradiction in my life, it is at this moment, and do I appear excited? Am I very irritable? Can I control myself? And it is just on religion and on politics, and I am contradicted at this moment on politics, and the smile that comes to my face is not an act of my will so much as it comes naturally from the satisfaction that I proved that I experienced seeing one of my difficulties disappearing. Should I be executed—at least if I were going to be executed—I would not be executed as an insane man. It would be a great consolation for my mother, for my wife, for my children, for my brothers, for my relatives, even for my protectors, for my countrymen. I thank the gentlemen who were composing the jury for having recommended me to the clemency of the court ...

Besides clearing me of the stain of insanity, clearing my career of the stain of insanity, I think the verdict that has been given against me is a proof that I am more than ordinary myself, but that the circumstances and the help which is given to me is more than ordinary, are more than ordinary, and although I consider myself only as others, yet by the will of God, by his Providence, by the circumstances which have surrounded me for fifteen years, I think that I have been called on to do something which, at least in the North-West, nobody has done yet. And in some way I think, that, to a certain number of people, the verdict against me to-day is a proof that maybe I am a prophet, maybe Riel is a prophet, he suffered enough for it.

6. Dr. Francois-Xavier Valade, "Report on the Sanity of Louis Riel."

On the thirty first of October last I was appointed to a medical commission named to investigate the then mental condition of Louis Riel, lying under sentence of death for the crime of High Treason.

... After having heard the above statement, Dr. Lavell went alone to interview the prisoner. On the same afternoon I had occasion to spend about one hour and a half with the prisoner. During this visit after much conversation and having questioned him at length in regard to the Northwest troubles and many other matters entirely foreign to that question, I established that Riel was suffering from religious and political hallucinations. Although he was very clear I may even say very rational upon certain questions foreign to what was engrossing his mind, still I assert positively that it was impossible for him to keep up any serious conversation with sustained attention, or to speak upon any moral or philosophical matter without travelling off into vagaries to say the least of it. His phophetic themes, his divine mission, his revelations in regard to the regeneration of the whole world, of the different governments and the northwest in particular, the voices that were speaking to him, and in one word his wild fantasies completely absorbed him ...

He came to us with his book of prophecies wherein he had noted down all his revelations, and with several other documents, two of which I shall quote since they establish to my mind a well defined proof of the politico-religious monomania under which he was really and unfeignedly labouring. Dr. Lavell and I questioned him in turn, upon the northwest troubles and other matters, as we had done on the preceding day. Then as usual, according to the evidence mentioned above, he was at times lucid, rational, and even logical on certain points, but this lucidity and logic lasted for a moment only, his mind would wander at once to his favorite topics and it was then impossible to bring him back to the points. Thus upon Dr. Lavell asking why he had proposed giving up the rebellion if the government would pay him the sum of thirty five thousand dollars, he answered: "Do I inquire of you how you employ your money? Have I not children to educate and provide for?" And on my asking if it were not his intention to return to the states and establish there a great newspaper, "Oh yes," he exclaimed. "This is my divine mission. I must establish a paper for the spread of my views and plans, and with it I must raise an army of twenty or thirty thousand men to carry out my vocation as a Prophet and to reconquer the northwest which I have been chosen to govern." ...

Let us now examine genuine insanity:

1st—From the best informations I could collect there have been cases of folly in Louis Riel's family. His mother even is subject to hallucinations.

2nd & 3rd—Riel was confined for four years in two lunatic asylums, which clearly indicates some premonitory symptoms in his case.

4th—These are well defined characteristics of politico-religious monomania.

5th—Riel has on every occasion maintained that he was of thoroughly sound mind, and would become indignant on this point being questioned.

6th—He never attempted to escape, he did the very reverse, and he was constantly proclaiming that he had been unable to prevent the committal of the crime for which he was condemned, since it was in fulfilment of his divine mission.

7th—He constantly argued on the same political and religious questions in presence of doctors and other visitors. Dr. Jukes testifies that he never spoke to him on outside matters.

8th—He was generally indifferent to disastrous consequences of his doings as Dr. Jukes has stated on his testimony, viz: there is one point which struck me: he has given up all interest in anything.

9th—In my opinion there was a marked expression of insanity in his look and manner. In fact, these various signs of insanity were strongly marked in Louis Riel's case.

The lengthy interviews we had together, the perusal of some of his papers besides those cited above, the prisoner's evident and unfeigned conviction in the truth of his revelations, his faith in his prophecies, his excitement, the wildness of expression about his eyes, his excessive action, his dissertations and speeches on the two favorite topics, religion and politics, which were ever uppermost in his thoughts, all this together was sufficient to convince me that Riel was suffering from uncontrollable politico-religious hallucinations ...

We have observed and discovered in the conversation and conduct of the prisoner Riel the evidence of fixed delusions, the expressions of which could by no logical sequence be linked on to ideas previously expressed. It is of no consequence that he manifested lucid intervals, and that he could even talk like a philosopher; nor is it of any importance that taking his fixed delusion as a starting point, he could reason logically in that direction; this would only go to prove that the reasoning faculty was not entirely destroyed. A railway train running off the track keeps going for some time.

Besides do not maniacs sometimes give utterance to sensible and even deep sayings in the midst of their ravings: even idiots have now and then lucid intervals. While conversing with monomaniacs they suddenly become incoherent and wild, when a moment before they were rational. It is because they have entered upon the ground of their delusions in spite of every effort to keep them from it. This was precisely Louis Riel's case. It was useful to attempt by interruptions or questions asked in the midst of his disposition on politics and religions, and entirely foreign to these matters, to turn away his thoughts, he was invariably and fatally recalled to his fixed delusion which was ever pursuing and worrying him. Reason and Justice and science agree as to the responsibility of an insane man, calling himself a monomaniac when he acts outside of the range of his delusion but they also agree to free him from all responsibility when he has committed a crime deriving from the very delusion itself.

In conclusion we may state that for the advocates of partial responsibility there exists in the monomaniac two distinct personalities, the one sane, the other insane: now the latter alone is not answerable for his acts, since he has been pushed to commit them by a hallucination, a delirious conception or a delusion.

I have stated that Louis Riel was suffering from political-religious hallucinations but on all other matters, he was responsible for his acts, and could distinguish right from wrong. All this means and meant very clearly that in the sphere of the fixed delusions which were constantly occupying his mind and which were the one theme of his writings, speeches, and conversations, he was not fit to perceive the crime of High Treason of which he had been guilty; and that when I examined him he could not in my humble opinion, distinguish between right and wrong on politico-religious questions.

7. Dr. Michael Lavell, "Report."

Louis Riel was physically well developed, and in his prime, when I saw him early in November, 1885, manly expression of countenance, sharp eyes, intelligent and pleasing address. His conversational powers were remarkable, voice capable of any amount of modulations, with a rare charm about it. At times in conversation he maintained all the characteristics of his race, excitable and enthusiastic, while at other times, when speaking of circumstances having reference to his present position and prospects, his voice was soft, mellow and sweet, interesting to a degree, drawing out the sympathies of the listener.

I knew I had a wily, clever and ambitious man to deal with, and therefore took every precaution against possible imposition. ... The presumption of insanity was based upon delusions and hallucinations of a religious and political character. He posed as an inspired Leader and Prophet, and as such had not much difficulty in impressing a simple and superstitious people. He was a man having force of character, education, and a thorough knowledge of the people and country, shrewd, cunning, selfish, ambitious and vain. Attractive in person, manner and speech, he could easily sway his followers to deeds of daring—they believed and trusted him, and he well knew it.

He replied that his people being superstitious, he would be more able to lead them to follow him if he impressed them with a belief that he had a divine gift. In other words, that he could sway them more easily and this is shown in an incident of the Duck Lake fight, which I alluded to. I asked him to explain why he had acted so wildly then, running about displaying a Crucifix before his followers. His reply was that he had a superstitious people to do with and could by such means retain his influence and control over them and in this manner excite enthusiasm.

He frequently talked of his children, and when speaking of his execution as a criminal, and the disgrace of it to his family, he was overcome with emotion. When informed that a respite of six days was given him, his manifestation of gratitude was touching in the extreme, thanking God for having more time for giving him preparation. He asked to have a shorthand writer to whom he could dictate what he might have to state in vindication of his course, so that his children when they grew up, would not feel ashamed of their father. ...

I departed from him with depressed feelings. The consciousness of the convictions I held as to his accountability gave me pain. I became during my interviews with him very much interested. He impressed me as a notable character, with other characteristics I have mentioned. He was enthusiastic and impulsive and if those characteristics had been diverted in proper channels he would have made his mark for good in the Great North West.

8. Alexander Campbell, Minister of Justice, "Memorandum Respecting the Case of the Queen v. Riel," November 25, 1885.

... With regard to the sanity of the prisoner and his responsibility in law for his acts, there has been much public discussion.

Here again it should be sufficient to point out that this defense was expressly raised before the jury, the proper tribunal for its discussion; that the propriety of their unanimous verdict was challenged before the full court in Manitoba, when the evidence was discussed at length and the verdict unanimously affirmed ...

The learned Chief Justice of Manitoba says in his judgment: "I have carefully read the evidence and it appears to me that the jury could not reasonably have come to any other conclusion than the verdict of guilty. There is not only evidence to support the verdict, but it vastly preponderates."

And again: "I think the evidence upon the question of insanity shows that the prisoner did know that he was acting illegally, and that he was responsible for his acts."

Mr. Justice Taylor's conclusion is: "After a critical examination of the evidence, I find it impossible to come to any other conclusion than that at which the jury arrived. The appellant is, beyond all doubt, a man of inordinate vanity, excitable, irritable, and impatient of contradiction. He seems to have at times acted in an extraordinary manner; to have said many strange things, and to have entertained, or at least professed to entertain, absurd views on religious and political subjects. But it all stops short of establishing such unsoundness of mind as would render him irresponsible, not accountable for his actions. His course of conduct indeed shows, in many ways, that the whole of his apparently extraordinary conduct, his claims to Divine inspiration and the prophetic character, was only part of a cunningly devised scheme to gain, and hold, influence and power over the simple-minded people around him, and to secure personal immunity in the event of his ever being called to account for his actions. He seems to have had in view, while professing to champion the interests of the Métis, the securing of pecuniary advantage for himself" ...

Mr. Justice Killam says: "I have read very carefully the report of the charge of the Magistrate, and it appears to have been so clearly put that the jury could have no doubt of their duty in case they thought the prisoner insane when he committed the acts in question. They could not have listened to that charge without understanding fully that to bring in a verdict of guilty was to declare emphatically their disbelief in the insanity of the prisoner."

And again: "In my opinion, the evidence was such that the jury would not have been justified in any other verdict than that which they gave ... I hesitate to add anything to the remarks of my brother Taylor upon the evidence on the question of insanity. I have read over very carefully all the evidence that was laid before the jury, and I could say nothing that would more fully express the opinions I have formed from its perusal than what is expressed by him. I agree with him also in saying that the prisoner has been ably and zealously defended, and that nothing that could assist his case appears to have been left untouched."

The organization and direction of such a movement is in itself irreconcilable with this defense; and the admitted facts appear wholly to displace it. The prisoner, eight months before this rebellion broke out, was living in the United States, where he had become naturalized under their laws, and was occupied as a school teacher. He was solicited to come, it is said, by a deputation of prominent men among the French half-breeds who went to him from the North-West Territories, and, after a conference, requested him to return with them, and assist in obtaining certain rights which they claimed from the Dominion Government, and the redress of certain alleged grievances. He arrived in the Territories in July, 1884, and for a period of eight months was actively engaged in discussing, both publicly and privately, the matters for which he had come, addressing many public meetings upon them in a settlement composed of about six hundred French and a larger number of English half-breeds, together with others. The English half-breeds and other settlers observed his course, and saw reason to fear the outbreak which followed; but the suggestion of insanity never occurred, either to those who dreaded his influence in public matters over his race, and would have been glad to counteract it, or to the many hundreds who unhappily listened to him and were guided by his evil counsels to their ruin.

If, up to the eve of the resort to arms, his sanity was open to question, it is unaccountable that no one, either among his followers or his opponents, should have called public attention to it. If the Government had then attempted to place him under restraint as a lunatic, it is believed that no one would have been found to justify their action, and that those who now assert him to have been irresponsible would have been loud and well warranted in their protest. It may be well also to call attention to the obvious inconsistency of those persons—not a few — who have urged the alleged maladministration of the affairs of the North-West Territory by the Government as a ground for interfering with the sentence, without ceasing to insist upon the plea of insanity. The prisoner cannot have been entitled to consideration both as the patriotic representative of his race and an irresponsible lunatic. It may be asked, too, if the leader was insane, upon what fair ground those who were persuaded by and followed him could be held responsible; and, if not, who could have been punished for crimes which so unquestionably called for it?

It has been urged, however, that his nature was excitable, and his mental balance uncertain; that as the agitation increased his natural disposition overcame him, and that the resort to violence was the result of over-wrought feelings, ending in insanity for which he cannot fairly be held accountable—that, in short, he was overcome by events not foreseen or intended by him ...

A simple statement of the facts will show that this view is wholly without foundation; that throughout he controlled and created the events, and was the leader, not the follower; and that the resort to armed violence was designed and carried out by him deliberately, and with a premeditation which leaves no room whatever for this plea ...

It may be asserted with confidence that there never has been a rebellion more completely dependent upon one man; that had he at any moment so desired, it would have come to an end; and that had he been removed a day before the outbreak, it would, in all probability, never have occurred. A dispassionate perusal of the whole evidence will leave no room for doubt upon this point ...

Finally, under this head, as regards the mental state of the prisoner, after his trial and before execution, careful enquiry was made into this question by medical experts employed confidentially by the Government for that purpose, and nothing was elicited showing any change in his mental powers or casting any doubt upon his perfect knowledge or his crime, or justifying the idea that he had not such mental capacity as to know the nature and quality of the act for which he was convicted, as to know that the act was wrong, and as to be able to control his own conduct.

9. Dr. Daniel Clark, Medical Superintendent of the Asylum for Insane, Toronto, "A Psycho-Medical History of Louis Riel," *Journal of Insanity,* July 1887.

On July 28, 1885, the writer made a first visit to Riel in the prison at Regina, Northwest Territory. He was found to be a stoutly built man and of splendid physique. He was in good health, about forty-two years of age. He had a swarthy complexion and black eyes of great brilliancy, restless and searching. His movements were nervous, energetic and expressive as are so characteristic of the French. This was evidently a normal condition and not from apprehension as to his fate. He was very talkative, and his egotism made itself manifest, not only in his movements, but also in his expressed pleasure in being the central figure of a State trial, which was likely to become historic. The writer stated to him that his lawyers were trying to save his life by proving that he had been insane. At this statement he got very much excited, and paced up and down his cell like a chained animal until his irons rattled, saying with great vehemence and gesticulation, "My lawyers do wrong to try to prove I am insane. I scorn to put in that plea. I, the leader of my people, the centre of a national movement, a priest and prophet, to be proved to be an idiot. As a prophet, I know beforehand, the jury will acquit me. They will not ignore my rights. I was put in Longue Pointe and Beauport Asylums by my persecutors, and was arrested without cause when discharging my duty. The Lord delivered me out of their hands."

I questioned him very closely as to his plans in the past, but he did not seem to be communicative on these points. He said he would insist on examining the witnesses himself. He did not feel disposed to allow his lawyers to do it for him, if they were determined to try to prove he was insane. During the trial he made several attempts to take the case into his own hands, as in the questioning of witnesses, his importance seemed to be ignored by his counsel. I asked him if he thought he could elicit more on his own behalf than men expert in law could. He proudly said: "I will show you as the case develops." During a long conversation with him, I found him quite rational on subjects outside of those connected with his "mission" and personal greatness. He walks about a good deal as he talked, at the same time putting on his hat and taking it off in a nervous way. His fidgety way, his swagger, his egotistic attitudes, his evident delight at such a trying hour—in being so conspicuous a personage—impressed me very strongly as being so like the insane with delusions of greatness, whether paretics or not. A hundred and one little things in appearance, movement and conversation, which can not be described in writing, are matters of every day observation by asylum medical officers. I may say they are almost intuitions in this respect. Such knowledge as this, which we acquire by every day acquaintance of the insane, would be laughed out of court by the legal profession, who can not discern any valid evidence that does not tally with a metaphysical and obsolete definition.

It was evident to me that Riel was concealing to some extent the inner workings of his mind, and that he had an object in view in hiding his thoughts. I endeavored to make him angry by speaking contemptuously of his pretensions.

He only shrugged his shoulders and gave me a smile of pity at my ignorance. I touched upon his selfishness in asking $35,000 from the government, and on receipt of it, to cease agitation. He smiled at my charge, and said that the money had been promised to him and was due to him. Had he received it he would have established a newspaper to advocate the rights of his kindred. It would have been a glorious work for him to be able to control a newspaper, and to promulgate in print his mission to the world.

Dr. Roy and myself had a second examination of Riel at the Police Barracks, on the evening of the 28th of July. He was closely catechised by Dr. Roy in French, and by me in English. He evaded giving direct answers to our questions, although he knew we were to give evidence for the defense, if his insanity were a fact. He thanked us for our kindly interest in him, but repudiated our plea with scorn. We took that ground to possibly put him off his guard, but in this he was consistent with himself and his record. We elicited little from him except that great developments, of a national character, were near at hand, according to his prophecy, and he was to be the central moving power. The insanity plea was abhorrent to him, and he scorned to take that ground, even to save his life. Friends and foes were convinced of his honesty and candor in his repudiation of this defense. He would rather die as a deliverer than live as a lunatic.

I had a third visit alone with Riel, in his cell, on the 29th of July. He was very much excited, and paced his narrow enclosure like an enraged tiger would, yet in this mood he said nothing. I accused him of hiding his motives to his own hurt, and told him that his friends from Quebec could do nothing for him because of his obstinacy. Suddenly he calmed down and with great self-possession said: "His legal friends had mistaken his mission. At present he was an important State prisoner, and he was suffering, not only for himself, but also for others." He also told me that he wrote a book which was still in existence. In it he clearly proved that he was a great prophet, and as a prophet he *knew* beforehand that a verdict would be given in his favor. I closely questioned him as to why he thought so, but his only reply was in putting his hand over his heart and saying pathetically, "It is revealed to *me*." I informed him that there was a bitter feeling hostile to him outside, and that so far the evidence was strongly against him and that he would probably be hanged as a felon. He smiled cynically at my ignorance, but the alternative did not seem to affect him. I told him the feeling had not subsided for the murder of Scott, in 1879. In reply he said the Northwest Council sentenced Scott to death for treason. He was only one of thirteen. He suddenly broke away from this subject and began to pour out a torrent of vigorous language on the head of Dr. Steultze, of Winnipeg, whom he associated in some way with Scott and the rebellion of 1870. Before I left he came back to the fulcrum idea that he was yet to be a great political and religious leader, who would revolutionize the world.

These were the notes I took at the time. To me they were significant, but as legal evidence they would be considered of little value.

I wish again to repeat the statement which is a truism to alienists. He had a look and movement so characteristic of insane people, which it is impossible to put in words, but known so well to us. He had that peculiar appearance, which is hard to be described, of a man who is honest and sincere in his insane convictions and statements. There could be no doubt he was stating what he himself believed to be true. In acting as he did he was not a pretender, and did not assume those feelings to his own hurt for the occasion. The most cunning deceiver could not simulate the appearance and actions which he presented. A malingerer would never utter so much wisdom, mixed with so much that showed insanity. Riel's great aim, even at the trial, was to falsify the charge of insanity, and to show by his words his mental capacity to be a leader of men. Anyone who has read his letters and addresses to the jury will see that a great deal of shrewdness, and irony, and sarcasm, of rather an intelligent kind, were mingled with his delusions of greatness. This is perfectly consistent with his form of insanity. Every asylum could produce men and women just as clever, cunning, and able to write as good letters as Riel did, and even hide their delusions when it suits their purpose so to do. His frowns, facial disgust and deprecatory shakes of the head when evidence was given to prove his insanity, and his egotistic walking up and down the dock, with swinging arms and erect head when his sanity was witnessed to, were no actor's part. His actions and speeches carried conviction of their genuineness even to the minds of many who were bitterly hostile to him. Much evidence was given by the Crown after mine was rendered. His two speeches made to the jury and much of his excited conduct in the dock towards the end of his trial impressed me very strongly as to the prisoner's mental unsoundness. His whole aim was to show that he was responsible in all his conduct, and not demented. He was a saviour and leader of his people, and this glorious position was to be taken from him by his friends trying to prove his insanity. He repudiated the plea with scorn ...

... it is recorded in law books, and was asserted by a learned Queen's Counsel at the trial, that any ordinary common sense man could detect an insane man as easily as could an expert. Had this sweeping assertion been made of cases of acute mania, there might have been some force in it; but any one who has even a limited experience of the insane knows that there are many phases of insanity in all our asylums which in their subtility and masked form, would baffle the common sense but inexperienced man, and even the legal theorist, with his ethical and antiquated absurdities of definition. I have seen judges, lawyers, and members of grand juries trying their mental acumen at selecting the sane from the insane in our wards, with most ludicrous results. Only a few days before his execution he wrote to his clerical friend in Winnipeg a farewell epistle. It is closely written in French, and contains fourteen pages of foolscap. He knew that his day of doom had come, yet it is full of the old delusions of prophecy and other rubbish concerning his power and greatness. One sentence will suffice as a specimen. He says: "The pope of Rome is in bondage and is surrounded by wicked counsellors. He is, however, not infallible, and the centre of the hierarchy should be located on this continent. I have elected Montreal as its headquarters. In a year of weeks after this change the Papal See will be centred in St. Boniface, Manitoba. The new order of things will date from December 8, 1875, and will last four hundred and seventy-five years."

Then again: "Archbishop Bourget told me of my supernatural power on the 18th of December, 1874. I felt it on that day, while I was standing alone on a high hill, near Washington, D.C. A spirit appeared to me and revealed it out of flames and clouds. I was speechless with fear. It said to me, 'Rise, Louis *David* Riel. You have a mission to accomplish for the benefit of humanity.' I received my divine mission with bowed head and uplifted hands. A few nights before this the same spirit told me that the apostolic spirit which was in the late Archbishop Bourget, and who was the pope of the new world, had taken possession of Archbishop Taché. It is to remain with the latter until his death, and then will re-enter the archbishop of Montreal. It will remain in him and his successors for one hundred and fifty-seven years. At the end of that time it will return to the ecclesiastical head of St. Boniface and his successors for 1,876 years."

Such delusional and egotistic nonsense could be quoted to any extent. Enough has been transcribed, not only to show the groove in which his mind ran when these frenzies took hold of him, but also to indicate how consistent throughout his whole career of over a quarter of a century, his mental activity was in respect to the uniformity of these vagaries.

Archbishop Taché, in speaking of Riel and his condition, said: "For many years I have been convinced beyond the possibility of a doubt, that, while endowed with brilliant qualities of mind and heart, the unfortunate leader of the Metis was a prey to what may be termed 'megalomania' and 'theomania,' which alone can explain his way of acting up to the last moments of his life."

The prosecution brought forward a number of witnesses to show that such had known Riel and had conversations with him, but saw no signs of insanity. It need scarcely be said that such *negative* evidence is worthless. A person may be insane and yet *rational*. Such having delusions can mask them with a great deal of shrewdness in ordinary conversation. All asylums have this experience, until some pertinent remark or favorable condition evokes and brings into prominence and activity the abnormal and diseased mental bias. A thousand persons may see no insanity in a patient, but one reliable witness who has seen indubitable evidence of mental alienation, will cancel the whole negation. Leaving out the evidence for the defense altogether, the witnesses for the crown gave facts enough to establish the prisoner's mental unsoundness, at least in the estimation of the writer.

There is no doubt that Riel was responsible for some years, up to the time of the Duck Lake fight. The excitement of that fight caused another attack of insanity, and from that time there is no evidence that he was accountable for what he did. While he was suffering from these attacks he was not responsible for anything he did. I spoke to some of the half-breeds who were in all the engagements with Riel, and they uniformly said he was not the same man after the first fight. He seemed to have changed entirely, and became frenzied. He organized no opposition after this time, did no fighting, but was looked upon as inspired by his deluded followers, and ran about from rifle pit to rifle pit, holding aloft a crucifix, and calling upon the Trinity for aid. The military organizers, leaders and fighters were Dumont and Dumais. These sane, shrewd and brave rebels have been amnestied by our government, but the mental weakling was hanged ...

The writer challenged the government to hold a *post mortem* on Riel's brain, and submit it to the examination of any competent pathologist. He was prepared to abide by the opinion and verdict of such an expert. This challenge was made through the press, and especially through the government organ. The writer was sure that organic changes would be found in Riel's brain, even of a gross nature, after such mental storms of a life-time. The footprints of disease were there, and within that skull was evidence of the prisoner's aberrations. Two medical men were present at his execution, but they also were government officers, under instructions. No *post mortem* of the brain was made. He was buried beside the scaffold where he bravely died. His body was kept under military supervision for about four weeks, and at the expiration of that time it was delivered up to friends. Decomposition had set in, and so the brain records were forever destroyed ...

Readings

Barron, F., and J. Waldram. *1885 and After: Native Society in Transition.* Regina: University of Regina, 1986.

Beal, B., and R. Macleod. *Prairie Fire: The 1885 North-West Rebellion.* Edmonton: Hurtig, 1984.

Bingaman, S. "The Trials of the 'White Rebels' 1885," *Saskatchewan History* 25 (1972).

Bowsfield, H., ed. *Louis Riel: Rebel of the Western Frontier or Victim of Politics and Prejudice?* Toronto: Copp Clark, 1969.

Bowsfield, H., ed. *Louis Riel: Selected Readings.* Toronto: Copp Clark Pitman, 1988.

Brown, D. "The Meaning of Treason in 1885," *Saskatchewan History* 28 (1975).

Flanagan, T. *Riel and the Rebellion: 1885 Reconsidered.* Saskatoon: Western Producer, 1983.

Flanagan, T. *Louis 'David' Riel: Prophet of the New World.* Toronto: University of Toronto Press, 1979.

Flanagan, T. "Louis Riel: Insanity and Prophecy," in H. Palmer ed. *The Settlement of the West.* Calgary: Comprint, 1977.

Flanagan, T. "Louis Riel: A Case Study in Involuntary Psychiatric Confinement," *Canadian Psychiatric Association Journal* 23 (1978).

Flanagan, T., and N. Watson. "The Riel Trial Revisited," *Saskatchewan History* 34 (1981).

Lee, D. "The Militant Rebels of 1885," *Canadian Ethnic Studies* 21, 3 (1989).

McLean, D. *1885: Metis Rebellion or Government Conspiracy?* Winnipeg: Pemmican, 1985.

Morton, D., ed. *The Queen v. Louis Riel.* Toronto: University of Toronto Press, 1974.

Sprague, D. *Canada and the Metis, 1869–1885.* Waterloo: University of Waterloo Press, 1988.

Stanley, G. *Louis Riel.* Toronto: McGraw Hill Ryerson, 1963.

Stanley, G. *The Birth of Western Canada: A History of the Riel Rebellions.* Third edition. Toronto: University of Toronto Press, 1970.

Thomas, L. "A Judicial Murder—The Trial of Louis Riel," in H. Palmer ed. *The Settlement of the West.* Calgary: Comprint, 1977.

Verdun-Jones S. "'Not Guilty by Reason of Insanity,' The Historical Roots of the Canadian Insanity Defence, 1843–1920," in L. Knafla ed. *Crime and Criminal Justice in Europe and Canada.* Waterloo: Wilfrid Laurier Press, 1981.

Chapter Four

"UNCEASING CONFLICT AND UNRELENTING DETERMINATION": UNIONS AND INDUSTRIALIZATION

1. Goldwin Smith, "The Labour Movement," *Canadian Monthly,* December, 1872.
2. *Royal Commission on the Relations of Labor and Capital in Canada,* 1889.
3. Jean Scott, *The Conditions of Female Labour in Ontario,* 1889.
4. "There is a Reason for it," *Industrial Banner,* February 1897.
5. *La Presse,* December 6, 1902.
6. A. Siegfried, *The Race Question in Canada,* 1906.
7. "The Glace Bay Strike," *Canadian Mining Journal,* August 1, 1909.
8. E. Bradwin, *The Bunkhouse Man: A Study of Work and Play in the Camps of Canada 1903–1914.*
9. "The Winnipeg Strike," *The Gazette,* May 22, 1919.
10. *Western Labour News,* May 28, 1919.

Introduction

Labour unions have, since their emergence during the nineteenth century in Canada, generated considerable controversy. Why? Pare away the hyperbole, peel back the layers of rhetoric, and the answer that emerges is the fundamental clash of ideas: the rights of the collective versus those of the individual.

The industrial revolution produced profound changes in society when it gathered momentum in Europe toward the end of the eighteenth century. Mechanization and the birth of the assembly line encouraged production with fewer hands; hands that could belong to cheaper semi-skilled workers, women, children, or immigrants. Longer working hours with abbreviated breaks meant increased production, as did strict division of labour and lowering wages. At its simplest, harnessing steam power to manufacturing made the individual self-employed and skilled craftsman working at his bench at home a quaint anachronism. Instead, he now shuffled off to the factory gates to await the morning whistle. Often workers saw their independence, their skills, pride, and sense of place disappear in the face of industrial capitalism as it rolled across much of northern Europe and eventually North America during the nineteenth century. A positive consequence was dramatic and sustained price reductions for manufactured goods, resulting in far more products available to a far wider spectrum of the population.

Life in the factories, what Charles Dickens called the "dark satanic mills," was anything but pleasant. Job security disappeared, the workday increased to a typical ten to twelve hours per shift, often six days per week, and wages dropped to the point where Canadian workers struggled to make ends meet. Discipline became harsh and authoritarian, with fines, corporal punishment and firings for infractions such as talking on the job, accidentally damaging machinery, absenteeism, or perceptions of laziness. Workplace safety concerns did not exist, and many workers lost fingers, limbs, or lives to one of the hundreds of whizzing belts propelling the machinery in front of which they toiled. The seasonal nature of industrial work exacerbated working class hardship in Canada because factories typically shut down for periods during the winter, without any systemic social safety nets to catch the unemployed.

Did factory owners and politicians lack all moral and social conscience by allowing such desperate conditions? Was the entrepreneur really a fat, cigar-puffing sociopath with the politician in one pocket and wads of dollars in the other? The nineteenth century was the age of unbridled individualism where the philosophy of the era assumed that humans were each responsible for their own success or failure. It was the time of capitalism as codified by Adam Smith, augmented by scientists and social theorists such as Charles Darwin and Thomas Malthus who added ideas of survival of the fittest in the commerce, not just the animal kingdom. According to this philosophy that supposedly explained human existence: those who rose to the top did so naturally, at their own accord, and with God's blessing. Putting in place rules and regulations that might interfere with the individuals responsibility to sink or swim on his own was therefore not only illogical but ungodly. Thus it made perfect sense for factory owners to squeeze what they could from workers, unencumbered by legal or moral limitations. Employers could go home at the end of the day feeling genuinely self-righteous, honourable, and Christian—in fact more Christian than their workers whose lowly position on the social ladder indicated some fundamental failing. Subscribers to this view of human existence logically considered the notion of workers banding together into a union and speaking as a collective, rather than as individuals, as unnatural, outrageous and unacceptable.

And what of the politicians? Perceived as a landmark by some, the Trade Unions Act passed by John A. Macdonald's government gave unions the right to exist, but related legislation still criminalized various acts related to organizing workers. Until the mid-twentieth century employers retained the right to obstruct unions with strikebreakers or blacklists and sue unions for damages caused by strikes or breaches of contract. Macdonald's 1889 Royal Commission on Labour and Capital travelled from the coal pits of Cape Breton, through the cotton mills of New Brunswick, to Toronto and Montreal factories, interviewing over 1800 workers and witnesses on subjects as disparate as child and female labour, sanitation and safety provision. Although the Commissioners reflected Conservative party views, many of its members came from within the working class and included a printer, a carpenter, a journalist and several builders. This commission enjoyed a unique opportunity to examine and evaluate the new industrial economy, but apart from the implementation of the Labour Day holiday, most of its recommendations came to naught and it had little impact. Later the Mathers Royal Commission would cover much of the same ground, while the Winnipeg general strike generated its own study—the Robson Royal Commission. Accelerating confrontations also prompted the creation of the Department of Labour in 1900 and its various attempts, such as the Industrial Disputes Investigation Act, to serve as an "impartial umpire" between unions and management. But labour legislation remained primarily a provincial responsibility. As such many provinces passed the original legislation concerning workingmen's compensation, child labour, hours of work, and minimum wages. Provincial factory inspectors submitted detailed annual reports which provided a far more detailed and regular assessment of working conditions than the episodic federal royal commissions.

Workers tended to agree with the prevailing ethos that government should stay out of their lives. Thus rather than depend upon legislation for protection, and rather than the single worker bargaining for his job contract, banding together among themselves seemed logical. Canadian craft unions—composed of skilled workers who could not be easily replaced—date back to the 1830s but came into their own by the 1860s and '70s in a more broadly based, less exclusive form, as the most powerful weapon in the workers' limited arsenal. Their relative success generally followed overall national business cycles. Unions expanded in good times and workers often gained significant concessions, but economic downturns led to contractions and setbacks. The original idea behind unions was simple: if everyone from a particular craft, carpenters for example, banded together and made demands as a tight group, management faced one of two choices: concede, either partially or totally, or face a strike. Strikes meant no production and therefore a loss of profits for employers. Striking, of course, involved perils for workers too: no income, and the threat of being fired and replaced with "scab" labour—often recent immigrants desperate for jobs. The shift toward semi-skilled workers indeed led to the creation of more comprehensive and inclusive unions. If all wage earners regardless of craft or skill, for example, banded into a single large organization, it would be sufficiently strong to wrest generous contracts from recalcitrant factory owners while simultaneously defending against management counterattacks. Taken to its logical conclusion, if all workers banded together everywhere into one big union, their weapon became the formidable General Strike, which could shut an entire community down—as it did in Winnipeg in 1919 when a dispute involving a comparatively small number of sheet metal workers brought the city to a standstill as some 30,000 other union members walked out in sympathy. The new all-inclusive union generally sat well with those promoting socialist and communist visions, and with those at the bottom of the labour ladder, but craft based unions, feeling their power and prestige at stake, often felt reluctant to join together with the more egalitarian industrial based unions. Concerns about the ultimate outcomes of union activity also took on new dimensions for both unionists and their opponents once the Bolsheviks had secured power in Russia and claimed to have created the first workers' state.

Unions were nowhere as ubiquitous, monolithic, or powerful as many anti-unionist scaremongers insisted. Whole segments of the working class, such as the navvy "bunkhouse men," remained unaffected. These men, often recent immigrants, toiled by the thousands in isolation at backbreaking jobs like railroad construction, logging, mining, and canal digging far from union influence but ironically in desperate need of their help. This was also true of the "sweated trades" in which countless urban workers, primarily women and children, sweated away in their homes at jobs like hand-sewing buttonholes for pennies per dozen. Nor were unions particularly united. Clashing egos among leaders, regionalization, ideological differences, and Canada's vast distances, often made unions more suspicious of one another than of their common foe. There was also the significant issue of American unions making inroads into the Canadian labour scene. American organizers arrived from positions of strength, holding out promises of significant labour victories if Canadian workers abandoned their locals in favour of affiliation with giants like the American Federation of Labor. Many did and their fellow workers often accused them of selling out to Yankee imperialism. Women's place in the labour movement also generated considerable debate in union circles. Many men perceived women workers as unfair competition since they worked for lower wages and were not primary bread winners. Usually women only worked in the factories for relatively short periods of time prior to marriage. This short-term tenure made many union organizers wary of making any substantial efforts to organize them. Some argued that regardless of gender, women should receive equal union protection and consideration. Finally, there was the position of the church, particularly in Quebec. The Catholic church generally railed against unionism, feeling threatened by workers taking control of their own destinies rather than leaving it in the hands of the church and traditional authority figures. The debate made unionization in Quebec particularly contentious especially when Catholic bishops threatened excommunication. Quebec's Catholic church eventually temporized by creating sanctioned Catholic unions that offered neither strength nor independence—but which Quebec workers joined by the thousands.

Discussion Points

1. Should workers have joined unions in this period?
2. What limited the effectiveness of unions?
3. Employers argued that union demands for a "standard living wage" would violate the basic tenets of supply and demand, raise the costs of production, fail to recognize that not all workers had the same ability or motivation, and violate individual freedom. Were employers justified in opposing unions?
4. To what degree did class consciousness begin to emerge? What evidence indicates that it took precedence over ethnic, religious, regional, or gender affiliations?
5. Did the Winnipeg General Strike exceed the boundaries of workers' legitimate rights to protest? Where does unionism end and socialism begin?
6. What role, if any, should the state play in the relationship between workers and management?

Documents

1. Goldwin Smith, "The Labour Movement," *Canadian Monthly,* December, 1872.

We are in the midst of an industrial war which is extending over Europe and the United States, and has not left Canada untouched.

Flushed with confidence at the sight of their serried phalanxes and extending lines, the unionists do like most people invested with unwonted power; they aim at more than is possible or just. They fancy that they can put the screw on the community, almost without limit. But they will soon find out their mistake. They will learn it from those very things which are filling the world with alarm— the extension of unionism, and rest of the community, including the baker: then the baker strikes against the builder, and the collier strikes against them both. At first the associated trades seem to have it all their own way. But the other trades learn the secret of association. Everybody strikes against everybody else: the price of all articles rises as much as anybody's wages; and thus, when the wheel has come full circle, nobody is much the gainer. In fact, long before the wheel has come full circle, the futility of a universal strike will be manifest to all. The world sees before it a terrible future of unionism, ever increasing in power and tyranny; but it is more likely that in a few years unionism, as an instrument for forcing up wages, will have ceased to exist. In the meantime the working classes will have impressed upon themselves, by a practical experiment upon the grandest scale and of the most decisive kind, the fact that they are consumers as well as producers, payers of wages as well as receivers of wages, members of a community as well as workingmen.

The unionists will learn also, after a few trials, that the community cannot easily be cornered; at least, that it cannot easily be cornered more than once by unions, any more than by gold rings at New York, or pork rings at Chicago. It may apparently succumb once, being unable to do without its bread or its newspapers, or to stop buildings already contracted for and commenced; but it instinctively prepares to defend itself against a repetition of the operation. It limits consumption or invents new modes of production; improves machinery, encourages non-union men, calls in foreigners, women, Chinese. In the end the corner results in loss. Cornering on the part of workingmen is not a bit worse than cornering on the part of great financiers; in both cases alike it is as odious as anything can be, which is not actually criminal; but, depend upon it, a bad time is coming for corners of all kinds.

I speak of the community as the power with which the strikers really have to deal. The master hires or organizes the workmen, but the community purchases their work; and though the master, when hard pressed, may, in his desperation, give more for the work than it is worth rather than at once take his capital out of the trade, the community will let the trade go to ruin without compunction rather than give more for the article than it can afford ...

A great fact has dawned upon their minds. Note too that democratic communities have more power of resistance to unionist extortion than others, because they are more united, have a keener sense of mutual interest, and are free from political fear. The way in which Boston, some years ago, turned to and beat a printers' strike, was a remarkable proof of this fact.

Combination may enable, and, as I believe, has enabled the men in particular cases to make a fairer bargain with the masters, and to get the full market value of their labour; but neither combination nor any other mode of negotiating can raise the value of labour or of any other article to the consumer; and that which cannot raise the value cannot permanently raise the price.

All now admit that strikes peaceably conducted are lawful. Nevertheless, they may sometimes be anti-social and immoral. Does any one doubt it? Suppose by an accident to machinery, or the falling in of a mine, a number of workmen have their limbs broken. One of their mates runs for the surgeon, and the surgeon puts his head out of the window and says—"the surgeons are on strike." Does this case much differ from that of the man who, in his greed, stops the wheel of industry which he is turning, thereby paralysing the whole machine, and spreading not only confusion, but suffering, and perhaps starvation, among multitudes of his fellows?

... There are some who say, in connection with this question, that you are at liberty to extort anything you can from your fellow men, provided you do not use a pistol; that you are at liberty to fleece the sailor who implores you to save him from a wreck; or the emigrant who is in danger of missing his ship. I say that this is a moral robbery, and that the man would say so himself if the same thing were done to him.

A strike is a war; so is a lock-out, which is a strike on the other side. They are warrantable, like other wars, when justice cannot be obtained, or injustice prevented by peaceful means, and in such cases only. Mediation ought always to be tried first, and it will often be effectual; for the wars of carpenters and builders, as well as the wars of emperors, often arise from passion more than from interest, and passion may be calmed by mediation. Hence the magnitude of the unions, formidable as it seems, has really a pacific effect: passion is commonly personal or local, and does not affect the central government of a union extending over a whole nation. The governments of great unions have seldom recommended strikes. A strike or lock-out, I repeat, is an industrial war; and when the war is over there ought to be peace. Constant bad relations between the masters and the men, a constant attitude of mutual hostility and mistrust, constant threats of striking upon one side, and of locking out upon the other, are ruinous to the trade, especially if it depends at all upon foreign orders, as well as destructive of social comfort. If the state of feeling, and the bearing of the men towards the masters, remain what they now are in some English trades, kind-hearted employers, who would do their best to improve the condition of the workman, and to make him a partaker in their prosperity, will be driven from the trade, and their places will be taken by men with hearts of flint, who will fight the workman by force and fraud, and very likely win. We have seen the full power of associated labour; the full power of associated capital has yet to be seen. We shall see it when, instead of combinations of the employers in a single trade, which seldom hold together, employers in all trades learn to combine.

We must not forget that industrial wars, like other wars, however just and necessary, give birth to men whose trade is war, and who, for the purpose of their trade, are always inflaming the passions which lead to war. Such men I have seen on both sides of the Atlantic, and most hateful pests of industry and society they are. Nor must we forget that Trade Unions, like other communities, whatever their legal constitutions may be, are apt practically to fall into the hands of a small minority of active spirits, or even into those of a single astute and ambitious man.

Murder, maiming, and vitriol throwing are offences punishable by law. So are, or ought to be, rattening and intimidation. But there are ways less openly criminal of interfering with the liberty of non-union men. The liberty of non-union men, however, must be protected. Freedom of contract is the only security which the community has against systematic extortion; and extortion, practised on the community by a Trade Union, is just as bad as extortion practised by a feudal baron in his robber hold. If the unions are not voluntary they are tyrannies, and all tyrannies in the end will be overthrown.

The same doom awaits all monopolies and attempts to interfere with the free exercise of any lawful trade or calling, for the advantage of a ring of any kind, whether it be a great East India Company, shutting the gates of Eastern commerce on mankind, or a little Bricklayers' Union, limiting the number of bricks to be carried in a hod. All attempts to restrain or cripple production in the interest of a privileged set of producers; all trade rules preventing work from being done in the best, cheapest and most expeditious way; all interference with a man's free use of his strength and skill on pretence that he is beating his mates, or on any other pretence; all exclusions of people from lawful callings for which they are qualified; all apprenticeships not honestly intended for the instruction of the apprentice, are unjust and contrary to the manifest interests of the community, including the misguided monopolists themselves. All alike will, in the end, be resisted and put down ...

I sympathize heartily with the general object of the nine hours' movement, of the early closing movement, and all movements of that kind. Leisure, well spent, is a condition of civilization; and now we want all to be civilized, not only a few. But I do not believe it possible to regulate the hours of work by law with any approach to reason or justice. One kind of work is more exhausting than another; one is carried on in a hot room, another in a cool room; one amidst noise wearing to the nerves, another in stillness. Time is not a common measure of them all. The difficulty is increased if you attempt to make one rule for all nations, disregarding differences of race and climate. Besides, how, in the name of justice, can we say that the man with a wife and children to support, shall not work more if he pleases than the unmarried man, who chooses to be content with less pay, and to have more time for enjoyment? Medical science pronounces, we are told, that it is not good for a man to work more than eight hours. But supposing this to be true, and true of all kinds of work, this, as has been said before, is an imperfect world, and it is to be feared that we cannot guarantee any man against having more to do than his doctor would recommend. The small tradesman, whose case receives no consideration because he forms no union, often, perhaps generally, has more than is good for him of anxiety, struggling and care, as well as longer business hours, than medical science would prescribe. Pressure on the weary brain is, at least, as painful as pressure on the weary muscle; many a suicide proves it; yet brains must be pressed or the wheels of industry and society would stand still. Let us all, I repeat, get as much leisure as we fairly and honestly can; but with all due respect for those who hold the opposite opinion, I believe that the leisure must be obtained by free arrangement in each case, as it has already in the case of early closing, not by general law.

I cannot help regarding industrial war in this new world, rather as an importation than as a native growth. The spirit of it is brought over by British workmen, who have been fighting the master class in their former home. In old England, the land of class distinctions, the masters are a class, economically as well as socially, and they are closely allied with a political class, which till lately engrossed power and made laws in the interest of the employer. Seldom does a man in England rise from the ranks, and when he does, his position in an aristocratic society is equivocal, and he never feels perfectly at home ...

... But on the whole class distinctions are very faint. Half, perhaps two-thirds, of the rich men you meet here have risen from the ranks, and they are socially quite on a level with the rest. Everything is really open to industry. Every man can at once invest his savings in a freehold. Everything is arranged for the convenience of the masses. Political power is completely in the hands of the people. There are no fiscal legacies of an oligarchic past. If I were one of our emigration agents, I should not dwell so much on wages, which in fact are being rapidly equalized, as on what wages will buy in Canada—the general improvement of condition, the brighter hopes, the better social position, the enlarged share of all the benefits which the community affords. I should show that we have made a step here at all events towards being a community indeed. In such a land I can see that there may still be need of occasional combinations among the working men, to make better bargains with their employers, but I can see no need for the perpetual arraying of class against class, or for a standing apparatus of industrial war ...

2. *Royal Commission on the Relations of Labor and Capital in Canada, 1889*

LABOR ORGANIZATIONS

Labor organizations are necessary to enable workingmen to deal on equal terms with their employers. They encourage their members to study and discuss matters affecting their interests and to devise means for the betterment of their class. It is gratifying to be assured by many competent witnesses that labor bodies discourage strikes and other disturbances of industry, favor conciliation and arbitration for the settlement of disputes, and adopt conservative and legitimate methods for promoting the welfare of the producing members of society. It is in evidence that most labor bodies strive effectively to promote temperance throughout the country, and especially among their members.

LABOR UNIONS

Workingmen's organizations have spread very rapidly of late years and with much apparent good to their members and trade. They have made it possible, in cities where they are strong, for workingmen to maintain their wages at a living rate. Much testimony was given of their influence for good in the discouragement of strikes and in advocating mediation and arbitration for the settlement of disputes between capital and labor. By stimulating their members to aim at a higher standard of proficiency in their callings they have done much to improve the skill of our artizans. To them is largely due the improved sanitary conditions in factories and workshops, the shortening of the hours for child and female labor and the separation of the conveniences for the sexes. In nearly all of these societies benevolence forms a prominent part of their work—the caring for the sick and injured, and the providing for the families of deceased members by their insurance departments. They inculcate a spirit of self-control, of independence, and of self-reliance in matters that affect their material welfare, and are the earnest promoters of temperance principles among the working classes. Your Commissioners recommend that in view of the good already accomplished the increase of such societies be encouraged by all legitimate means, and that one day in the year, to be known as Labor Day, be set apart as a holiday by the Government.

INFLUENCE OF LABOR ORGANIZATIONS

Among other matters brought out by this Commission is the interesting and important bearing on the labor question of the influence of workingmen's organizations. Nothing could be more striking than the contrast furnished between organized districts and others where as yet the principles of a trade organization are little known and still less acted upon. And if the progress that has been made towards uniting capital and labor in cities that are comparatively well represented in the ranks of labor bodies is to be taken as a criterion of the usefulness of such societies, we may well believe that they are destined to be a very important factor in the solution of the labor problem. And as the work of consolidating the ranks of labor makes progress, so will its influence extend and its usefulness become more apparent. Slowly but surely are capital and labor becoming drawn more closely together, as the aims and principles of united labor are better understood ... That great progress has been made in the last few years is evidenced by the fact that a large percentage of the disputes that have arisen between employers and their employés have been amicably adjusted, either by conciliation or arbitration brought about by the efforts of the various trade societies involved ...

One of the good results ... of labor organization in other countries has been to place capital and labor in such a position that it is reasonable to expect that in the near future the strike will be a thing of the past and boards of arbitration will have taken its place. That this is also the goal of Canadian workingmen is fully borne out by the testimony of hundreds of witnesses who were examined by the Commission, many of whom were especially appointed by the societies to which they belonged to give evidence bearing on this matter; and it is gratifying to state that in many instances, where labor organizations existed, very many of the largest employers of labor have endorsed what the men have stated in reference to their desires in this respect.

That the wage question is the most prolific source of trouble there can be no doubt, and it is for the removing of this cause of friction in a friendly way that labor bodies have most strenuously persevered. The claim that workingmen do not receive full value for their labor, that they are too frequently unable to make ends meet and that capital often takes advantage of their necessities to regulate the price of labor, appears to be well founded, when judged by the evidence given before the Commission. This state of affairs is, however, more apparent in the places that are not organized, and where wages are invariably lowered in the winter season. But in cities and towns where labor is organized, higher wages not only rule, but usually remain the same throughout the year. This is to be attributed to the fact that these societies claim an equal right with the employer in determining the amount to be paid for the labor given, the principle laid down being that the minimum rate shall be a living rate of wages for all ... Workingmen ask why should not capital and labor meet together and fix the rate of wages to be paid for the production of the goods. An industrial partnership of this kind would at once settle the wage question, and in like manner dispose of the question as to the length of the day's labor. Labor says: Remove or settle these two questions, and the unity of capital and labor will be an accomplished fact.

The principal objects of labor societies, until recently, were the protection of the worker in his wages and the prevention of undue competition among them by shortening the hours of labor. But these organizations have extended their field of usefulness, and their educational value cannot be overestimated. They have been very beneficial in promoting a spirit of self-control, in instilling a knowledge of parliamentary proceedings and in conducting meetings. A spirit of independence and self-reliance has grown with their progress, looking rather to their own efforts to accomplish their objects than appealing to the Government for assistance. Though much can be done by legislation, they themselves have, and can do, a great deal to better their condition by united action. In a mob men trample on each other, but in a disciplined army they brace one another up. So labor unions prevent disorder to trade. Nor should the character of those who compose these societies be overlooked. In nearly all of them proficiency in their calling, as well as a good character, is made a condition of membership ...

To the persistent efforts of labor organizations may also be traced, very largely, the advanced state of public opinion in relation to the sanitary condition of factories, workshops, and dwellings of the working classes. It is now impossible in organized labor centres to neglect these matters. Employers find it difficult to carry on business where no attention is given to the health and comfort of their employés. In many places where these societies exist there is now an entire separation of the conveniences for the sexes, and care is taken that no corrupt influence shall gain any foothold where males and females are employed in the same building. The shortening of the hours of labor for women and children has for years been kept before the public by labor organizations, though as yet with indifferent success. Much progress has also been made in preventing the sending to this country, by interested people and charitable societies in other lands, an undesirable class of immigrants, and it is due to the reiterated persistency in protesting against this wrong, by organized labor, that the practice of sending the helpless and pauper classes to become burdens on our people and charities has been very much lessened and will, it is hoped, be prevented altogether.

Thus in many ways the influence of labor organizations have had a beneficial effect to those who have taken advantage of the opportunity they afford of discussing the whole labor problem in its economic, social and political aspects.

Some of the especial benefits are better wages, shorter hours of labor, better protection from accident, a more friendly relation to capital, prevention of child labor, higher education, a better knowledge of their trades through the discussion of their wants, voluntary and compulsory insurance, payment of sick and death benefits, and the extension of relief to the needy.

There have been many mistakes in the past; the enemies of labor can point to follies, and even crimes, that have been committed, for which in some cases the organizations were responsible, but the same may be said of all bodies of men, public or otherwise. Even Parliaments are not free from such errors ... It would be unfair, therefore, to expect that associations composed of working-men, often half educated, or not educated at all, would be free from mistaken motives and acts at times. Tracing such societies from their earliest history to the present time and noting the immense amount of good they have conferred on their members, all must admit that the benefits conferred far outweigh the loss....

To this may be added the fact that where organization has made much progress the moral standing of the people is also high. No one can become a member who is not sober, and, as a consequence, union men and women are temperate and industrious in their habits. The universal testimony of wage-earners is that the money paid by them to support their societies is as good an investment as they have ever made. In some of the States of the American Union

a day has been set apart as a general holiday, known as Labor Day. This movement has spread in our Dominion and of late years several of the towns and
cities of Canada have proclaimed one day in the year as a municipal holiday in
honor of labor. It would be well to make this system a general one—to choose a
suitable day, about the 1st of September in each year, and to proclaim it labor
holiday, in the same way as Thanksgiving Day is now proclaimed, and made a
holiday throughout the Dominion.

3. Jean Scott, *The Conditions of Female Labour in Ontario*, 1889.

1. *Trades Unions.*

Trades unions of women in Ontario have not been numerous nor remarkably successful; but still they have been formed at various times. In a number of
cases, also, women have joined the men's unions. In Hamilton, Kingston and
Toronto, Assemblies of the Knights of Labour have at various times been formed
of women alone; but at present none seem to be active.

In Toronto as far back as 1883 a union was formed among telegraphers;
and women were asked to join as well as men. A strike organized by them having
failed, the union was for the time dissolved.

About 1885 an Assembly of the Knights of Labour was organized of women
in various occupations. It was called "Hope Assembly," and lasted for some
time, but finally succumbed.

About 1888–9 the "Silver Fleece" Assembly was formed, composed of
women in the tailoring business. It is not now active.

In 1889 the corset-makers organized an Assembly to carry on a strike to
resist a reduction of wages. A compromise is said to have been effected; and the
assembly has ceased to exist. Women belong at present to the cigar-makers and
typographical unions, but their numbers are so few that practically women are
not a factor in trades unions or Knights of Labour assemblies at present in Toronto
at all.

The non-success of trades unions among women is partly attributable to
the same causes as the but limited success of such movements among men in
Canada and America generally. Both men and women in various trades in Canada
are always looking forward to bettering their condition in some way, and do not
expect their connection with a trade to be permanent. This is particularly the
case among those who are apt to be the leading spirits in the movements. Women,
moreover, have in the past lacked the training necessary to carry on such unions,
and were often altogether ignorant of the nature of labour combinations. And
again, since women on the whole do not remain long in employment, benefit

and superannuation schemes in connection with the unions were not much appreciated. Moreover there does not exist that "class spirit" among women in employments that is necessary to organized progress; and men with reason complain that it is difficult to operate plans of any sort which require unselfish action among large bodies of women.

There is no doubt that in unions among men and women employed at the same trade, where equal wages are demanded, the women gradually become fewer and finally drop out, if they are physically unfit for as severe labour as the men; and they know in such cases that it is not to their individual advantage to belong to the unions. Where equal pay is demanded for equal labour, the "survival of the fittest" is alone possible.

4. "There is a Reason for it," *Industrial Banner*, February 1897.

A sermon was recently delivered by a clergyman in this city in which he contrasted the condition of affairs to-day with what existed at the commencement of the century, and among other things he stated that the artizan did not labor as many hours as he used to do. While this is true, it is as well to understand how it has come about. It has been accomplished not because humanity and civilization has advanced so much as because labor was organized. The reduction of the hours of toil has been gained as the price of unceasing conflict and unrelenting determination on the part of the Trades Unions.

They have been resisted and opposed at every turn by capital and the capitalistic class. Every concession gained has been wrung from unwilling hands; and at the present moment the same conflict is being waged for an eight-hour day, and it is being just as resolutely opposed, and by the same class of people as have stood in opposition all along. Therefore, if the mechanic and laborer is working a less number of hours per day now than he was fifty years ago, he can thank the organizations of labor that such is the case. Without organization the capitalist would not hesitate to make him work his twelve or fourteen hours straight. It is a fact, however, that workingmen are working too many hours as it is.

With the multiplication of labor-saving machinery the science of production has advanced with such tremendous strides that one man can now turn out as much material as demanded the skill of twenty men a few short years ago, and hence as a result thousands of unemployed abound in the land.

The only possible chance to place this class at profitable employment is to reduce the hours of toil to keep pace with the increased power of production, and this is what the employing class is resisting, tooth and nail.

It is no virtue for the pulpit to inform the producing classes that they work less hours now than they used to do. Rather let them boldly proclaim the truth, and acknowledge that the conditions under which workingmen and workingwomen now earn a livelihood are more onerous than when they worked twelve hours a day.

The struggle for a bare existence is more bitter at this moment than it ever was before. More workers are out of employment, and their ranks are constantly swelling. Work in the past was at best reasonably sure; not so in the present.

And, pray, who is fighting the battle for shorter hours now—the pulpit, the press, the universities, the employers, or the men of business? Most certainly not. It is the workingman himself, and he is met with opposition on every hand. In the future, we doubt not, when progressive trade unionism has succeeded in still more materially reducing the hours of toil, some preacher will arise and tell the producers how much better off they are than we to-day. If the organizations of labor had never existed, it is safe to say no preacher could take such unction to his soul as to think humanity was advancing, and point to these decreasing hours of toil as a proof.

If workingmen are better off in this respect to-day than formerly, they know whom they have to thank. They are intelligent enough to understand that the working classes must work out their own salvation; that if they have gained concessions in the past it was because they were in a position to demand them and able to enforce the demand. They are not so ignorant as to believe that the leopard will change his spots, or the lion become a lamb. They recognize that the class who have antagonized their legitimate claims for justice in the past will likewise oppose them in the future; that any concession they may gain will be conceded only when the opposing class is powerless to withhold it. In a word, the laborer is becoming aware that only as he becomes organized and intelligent has he any show whatever of securing the least recognition in the community, or any consideration of his rights.

Because the hours of labor have been reduced in the past it would be unsafe to say that humanity was getting better. First recognize how and why they have been reduced, and then ask yourself the question: "Why should men even work eight hours a day when the advanced mechanical skill and productive power of the world is sufficient to feed, clothe, house and provide every luxury requisite to happiness with less than four hours of toil a day?" Is it not a fact easily proved that even at eight hours a day, the worker is just toiling four hours too long?

It is well to recognize that the reason why so many men are in poverty, with no work to do is because they who do the work have to toil so long.

5. *La Presse*, December 6, 1902.

As has been seen, unionized typographers were dissatisfied, in 1887 and 1888, with the conduct of the Knights. We will see that several other organizations were hardly happier with them.

In 1882, the General Assembly of the Amalgamated Association of Iron and Steel Workers felt obliged to deliver a stern rebuke with respect to the conduct of the Knights, who had attempted to sow discord within the ranks of that association.

Nor had the Brotherhood of Carpenters been spared. It had solicited the support of the Knights in vain when preparing the launch of its initial campaign for the 8 hour day; in vain, did it ask the general secretary of the Order to authorize the assemblies of carpenters to exchange work permits with the Brotherhood's Unions so as to force out of unionized workplaces those who would not or could not procure one.

The cigar makers were also displeased. In 1884, the Knights of Labor took in scabs expelled by the International Union of Cigar Makers, and in 1883, they helped New York manufacturers inflict defeat on the union.

The Union local [...] of that city materially and morally helped Mr Samuel Gompers, who had been its first president, to publish the "Picket" in order to defend New York's unions against the Knights.

The latter succeeded in setting up within the Order a national assembly of cigar makers who caused a yellow label to be affixed to the boxes of cigars rolled by its members.

From what happened in Montreal, it is easy to understand the difficulties that arose from this organizational dualism among the cigar makers each time they had to discuss working conditions with their employers.

Consequently, they rushed to respond to the appeal launched in early 1886 by the general secretary of the "United Brotherhoods of Carpenters and Woodworkers of North America" to, together with the principal Unions involved, look into the situation in which they found themselves.

The Knights were at that time registering members by the thousands daily, and their local assemblies were multiplying by the hundreds. Strikes were spreading like a contagion from one end of the United States to the other, and the Executive Council of the Order was obliged, in certain localities, to suspend the initiation of new members. The Knights had just shown their true colours: they declared that there was no further reason for ordinary Trade Unions to exist.

Twenty-two national and international unions were represented at the conference held in Philadelphia by P. J. McGuire, W. H. Foster, typographic worker and secretary of the Federation of Organized Trades and Labor Unions, Strasser, chairman of the International Union of Cigar Makers and two other leaders representing stone masons and foundry workers. Twelve other national and international unions sent members.

This conference of Trade Unions proposed to the Knights of Labor the following convention:

1st In any trade in which there is a union, the Knights shall not initiate any person, nor shall they set up any assembly without the consent of the most immediate national union involved;

2d They shall admit no individual who agrees to work at a rate inferior to the wage scale set by the Union of his trade, or having committed any offence whatsoever against the union of his trade;

3d All Charters granted by the Knights to assemblies recruited exclusively within a trade where there exists a national or international union shall be revoked, and their members required to join a mixed assembly or to found a union local under the jurisdiction of the relevant national or international Union;

4th Any organizer of the Knights who has tried to bring about the dissolution of trade unions or undermine their development or privilege shall be removed;

5th No assembly of the Knights shall interfere in a strike or lockout involving any trade union whatsoever before a settlement is reached that is to the satisfaction of the latter;

6th The Knights shall issue no label that might compete with that of a national or international union.

The Knights of Labor rejected these proposals and addressed to the trade unions a circular written by a special committee of which Frank Foster was the chairman and which counted among its members Robert Shilling, former chairman of the Industrial Congress held at Rochester, in 1874, and George MacNeil. Here are several extracts:

"We make no distinction with regard to trade, sex, faith, colour, or nationality. Our desire is to raise wages, reduce working hours, prevent through laws the unfair accumulation of wealth, and the merging of large corporations; our desire is to prepare for the 'substitution of wage earners' by means of cooperation and through the suppression of castes and classes.

"We acknowledge the services rendered to humanity and the working cause by trade unions, but we believe that the time has come or that the time is near for all workers to be enrolled under the same banner.

"We undertake to cooperate with organizations that wish to preserve their present structure, to achieve the outcomes that they and we pursue, and our special committee will confer with the committee that all the national and international Unions see fit to appoint with a view to resolving any difficulties that might arise between us.

"The basis on which an agreement can be reached necessarily involves some system for protecting all workers' associations from men who have been expelled, suspended, or fined and from all those who have taken the place of Unionists or Knights involved in a strike or lockout.

"As far as possible, we should adopt uniform wage scales and hours of work and a system allowing an exchange of work permits.

"Finally, we believe that whenever a request is made for a wage increase or a reduction in working hours, a conference should be held between the various organizations represented in the establishments in question and that the same should be done for resolving any difficulties that might arise between employers and employees, with a view to achieving an outcome satisfactory to both organizations."...

I needed to present these facts in order to make it clearly understood what I intend to show: that the principles, methods, and sympathies of the Knights of Labor are incompatible with the principles, methods, and sympathies of Trade Unionists.

A Trade Unionist.

6. A. Siegfried, *The Race Question in Canada*, 1906.

By reason of this dispersion of a relatively small number of artisans over an enormous expanse of territory, by reason still more of their striking differences of origin, language, and character, there really does not exist, properly speaking, any working class in Canada. Moreover, there is not so wide a gulf between the industrial artisan and the agricultural labourer as exists with us—the distance between them is easily bridged. Thus no one ventures to talk to the "Canadian workman," for this expression does not convey any precise meaning, covering as it does many different types of men with nothing in common but the name.

In the Maritime provinces the industrial workman is generally a native of the country, though the Sydney steel manufactories have imported a good deal of American skilled labour. In this part of the colony, which stands somewhat to one side, the working population is mostly British, stolid, and somewhat slow-going. The more active elements are tempted, as everywhere in America, to go West.

If we pass to the French province, the contrast is remarkable. The French-

Canadian artisan is usually a peasant attracted to the factory by the bait of regular wages. He provides an inferior kind of manual labour not exacting high wages, just as is the case in the great factories in New England. The psychology of the Quebec countryman turned artisan undergoes little change. He remains entirely under the control of the clergy, and his new role effaces in no way his national character. Many strikes have been stopped through the influence of the priests, and in many cases the workmen have accepted terms which otherwise they would have rejected, simply because the priests counselled submission. The Church does all it can to keep the French workmen apart from the English—this separation being essential, she feels, to the preservation of their race. Montreal, it should be mentioned, presents an exceptional state of things: the time is perhaps not far distant when the working class of this great city will become emancipated.

In Ontario we find workmen of a more purely Canadian kind. The Toronto artisan, akin to the artisan of the United States, but educated and trained in a very British atmosphere, is pre-eminently Canadian. If one could speak at all of the "Canadian workman," it is certainly in the great English province that it would be necessary to seek the type.

In the West—Manitoba, Alberta, Saskatchewan—American influence is very strong, the number of American immigrants being so considerable. The still greater number of European immigrants of all kinds when assimilated to their surroundings produce a type of workmen very different from those of Eastern Canada.

The province which has become most Americanized is British Columbia. With the exception of Victoria, which is a very English city, the whole of this region resembles most strikingly the neighbouring states of Washington, Idaho, Montana, and Oregon—themselves neighbouring states to California. Indeed, in spite of the Canadian Pacific Railway, British Columbia has more intimate connection with the American Northwest than with Eastern Canada. To the north as to the south of the frontier, you find mushroom cities springing up suddenly in the midst of a wonderful country, with a composite population of British, Americans, Europeans of all kinds, Chinese and Japanese; small wooden shanties, as many bars as dwelling-houses, on one side the trim residences of respectable folk, on the other whole streets given over to prostitution, swarming hives of Chinamen, such is the character of these Western cities, which have nothing in common, not merely with the cities of the East, but even with Winnipeg, Regina, or Calgary. You feel that the everlasting "boom" of California is not far distant.

... Employers have not a very well-defined attitude toward their employees. Some are ready to recognize the unions, others take their stand openly for resistance. It would seem that the Canadian working class are not yet sufficiently self-conscious to awaken the fears of the rich. The rich are at the stage where they declare themselves to have at heart the welfare of the workers, while preferring that these should not go too thoroughly into the question for themselves. In this respect the Liberal employers do not seem to differ appreciably from the Conservative.

The workers have begun the work of organizing themselves according to American methods, but have been retarded greatly by all their differences of race, language, moral and material conditions. In imitation of what has been done in the United States, they have established in most of the towns special trade unions for each trade; the different trade unions in each locality take part frequently in Trades and Labour Councils. There is a general federation of these for the whole of Canada, known as the Trades and Labour Congress, which holds a general convention every year. The majority of the unions belonging to this Congress are affiliated to the American Federation of Labour. The word "general" which I have used is not quite accurate, however, for Nova Scotia, Prince Edward Island, and British Columbia have remained the centres of separate organizations.

These unions have until now devoted themselves principally to professional ends—the securing of higher wages, the reduction of the hours of labour, the improving of the conditions of employment either through their own action or by means of amicable negotiations with employers or through the mediation of the state. However, they have lately shown a tendency to take a larger part in politics, if not actually by asserting themselves at elections, at least in a general sense. The tendency of the Trades and Labour Congress is undoubtedly to exercise influence over the social legislation of the country. Some of the unions, chiefly in British Columbia, are of a distinctly socialistic character, but these are the exception. The others in their manifestoes are content to employ vague formulas by which they do not commit themselves ...

Coming now to the political side of the matter, we find that the Canadian workers, in spite of some isolated victories at the polls, have not yet succeeded in constituting themselves a third party. The organization of such a group involves, in truth, numerous difficulties. The agricultural predominance, the scattered condition of manufacturing industries, the absence of marked differences between the social classes, have all combined to prevent the growth of any real class feeling. If such a feeling exists in British Columbia and shows signs of coming into existence in Montreal, it cannot be said to be evident elsewhere. In a new country, prospering and developing rapidly, the general interests of all classes are too interlaced and interdependent for it to be easy to organize a class policy; the policy of national prosperity comes before all else.

7. "The Glace Bay Strike," *Canadian Mining Journal*, August 1, 1909.

... It is scarcely a correct use of words to refer to the present labour troubles at Glace Bay as a "strike." The cessation of work by the adherents of the United Mine Workers, and the intimidation of hundreds of other men who wish to work, has not arisen out of the struggle of legitimate trade unionism against oppressive capitalism. It is not one incident out of the many that daily occur in the never-ending struggle of the proletariat against plutocratism that is as old as time and will still be waging when our civilization and our race is but a memory. Many of the deluded men who have gone on strike believe otherwise, and are honest in their belief, not realizing that they are the miserable victims of men whose mouths are filled with lies ...

Probably there never was a strike in Canada that had less justification. The Dominion Coal Company are now dealing with the first strike in their history, and, in fact, there has only been one strike of any consequence in the coal mines of Cape Breton since 1868. The Canadian press, with the exception of one ephemeral and intermittent broadsheet that has made its appearance on perhaps a dozen occasions, has with one voice condemned the action of the United Mine Workers. Some provincial newspapers that have assiduously fanned the agitation for months past are now trying to lay the fire they have caused, much to the bewilderment of those simple people who believe what they read in the newspapers. All shades of public opinion, religious, political, and commercial, unite in deploring this strike as a national calamity. Nevertheless, a very large amount of misapprehension exists as to the true magnitude of the trouble. The vastness of the Dominion Coal Company's enterprise has so impressed itself on the public that it is assumed that any labour trouble that seriously affects its operations must have behind it the support of a large and determined body of men. This, however, is not the case. The United Mine Workers are in a decided minority of the Coal Company's employees, and their determination is a mixture of desperation and American money. At the end of the second week of the strike two-thirds of the Coal Company's employees are working, and many of them have risked and are risking their lives, voluntarily, to protect what they conceive to be their company's interests and their own. Before the strike the U.M.W.A. publicly announced in the newspapers that they were about to call out 95 per cent of the Coal Company's employees. On the first day of the strike the output of the company's mines was just about half a normal output, and the number of men that absented themselves was well under two thousand. Taking into consideration the number of men who were waiting to see how things would develop, it is safe to assume that the actual number of strikers did not exceed 1,700, which is generally supposed to be approximately the number of U.M.W.A. men in the Coal Company's employ. The day following was marked by disgraceful and riotous scenes. Men were beaten, stripped naked, assailed by the most opprobrious epithets imaginable, and things were said and done that deserve the most emphatic and sternest condemnation. As a result men were intimidated from coming to work, and we in Glace Bay witnessed the terrorizing of a community of ten or twelve thousand people by a body of persons who did not represent ten per cent of the population ...

The United Mine Workers have evidently a keen desire to control the mines of the Dominion Coal Company. At the Glace Bay Hotel, which during the past fortnight has provided rest and refreshments for the leaders of the opposing forces, and a horde of newspaper reporters, the U.M.W.A. have five of their officers from the United States, assisted by a clerical force of two female clerks and a male clerk. The business of these gentlemen in Cape Breton is to lead and supervise the campaign of an American labour union in its attack on one of the most important industries of Canada, in the attempt of a foreign union to usurp and destroy a Canadian union, which was in existence and was doing a good work many years before the U.M.W.A. had emerged from the womb of time. A gentleman prominent in American governmental circles, who has made a special study of industrial conditions on this continent, recently stated that the U.M.W.A. were very anxious to control the eastern mines of Canada in order to be able to neutralize them whenever a strike was considered necessary in the bituminous coal fields of the United States. This, and this only, is the reason for the presence of these U.M.W.A. gentlemen in Glace Bay. Their efforts will fail; must fail, in fact, because American domination in any shape is something that Canada will not tolerate. Annexation was once a live issue in the Dominion. It is now dead as Moses. Labour legislation and labour organization always lags a decade or two behind the general progress of our race, but when the time comes—and it is not far distant—when Canada chooses between international trade unionism, or, in other words, domination of Canadian unionism by that of the United States, and national trade unionism—when that time comes, the national spirit will assert itself ...

8. E. Bradwin, *The Bunkhouse Man: A Study of Work and Play in the Camps of Canada 1903–1914*

TO ORGANIZED LABOUR

... What have organized labour and its leaders been doing for the navvy and those men employed on seasonal works? And further: Why were the recognized leaders of union labour in Canada so long indifferent to the wage conditions of the navvy on the National Transcontinental? Only in the closing years of the period, so far, at least, as the writer has been able to discover, was any official action taken by them in an effort to protect the interests of the workers in the camps.

It may be recalled, too, that organized labour in Canada, during those same years, was by no means inactive in other fields. Men among them were vocable enough in the cities and larger industrial centres. They interested them-selves in education and other measures for the betterment of the workers: evening classes were multiplied, technical schools were inaugurated that have since in-creased in mighty strides, compensation laws were enacted in the different provinces, and other practical results achieved, which in themselves were a direct recognition of the demands of organized labour, and most of these have since proven their worth.

But, meanwhile, organized labour has never convinced the man in the bunkhouse that it is so valiant in its fight for the consideration of the labourer on frontier works. The bushman has had some gesture of sympathy but the navvy is overlooked entirely. Is Labour not concerned about camps, wherein men engage in tasks that require of each strong personal assets? Is this apparent neglect a penalty for broadbacked men, who, in their toil strive largely as indi-vidualists? This oversight is serious. It lets down the bars for more radical movements which secure a foothold among the unorganized workers in the iso-lated work-groups of the frontier.

While in cities organized labour can man its walls with plenty of sentinels, in camps and frontier works the opposite prevails. There, the rights of workers may frequently be infringed. On all stretches of new railway construction, the building of culverts and the draining of muskegs are closely scrutinized; the piles that enter into the building of trestles are carefully inspected by officials on the job, but on the human side the conditions of work and wage may be overlooked.

Solitude fosters the independence of a man's nature, but to be continu-ally ignored and deprived of healthy leadership is but to add dignity to the more virulent. The migratory workers of the camps and the frontier, shifting, homeless and womanless, come in contact with the ugliest features of human hire and pay. It is not desired simply that all such men be assured fair pay, but that they have more wisdom to govern the use of their wages. In this they claim the guidance and intelligent sympathy of the leaders of the better organized and more successful labour. Given this, and with fair conditions of employment, they would become a bulwark rather than an enemy of ordered government ...

These very qualities, however, of shifting and unrest so inherent in seasonal workers, need not prove a permanent barrier to recognition by labour in some form. The right of the navvy and other frontier workers to organize is fundamental. It is even necessary. To be able to negotiate with the employer in an effective manner is just as essential to the campman at some isolated work as it is to the machine man in the mill of a factory town. If conditions of work and pay in camps do preclude effective organization, all the greater is the need for a tangible recognition from organized labour in some other form.

This is a challenge to leaders whose concern is for the protection of workers. Has organized labour in respect to men in camps lived up to its opportunities? Or is its chiefest concern bounded largely by the horizon of the local unions? To the occupant of the bunkhouse, it lends the impression that its efforts are confined wholly to the sacred groves in urban places where it rears its many temples.

Leaders of organized labour could be better informed of work conditions in isolated places. To many of them the frontier camp, employing often a large force of men, is a closed book. Representatives of labour, duly accredited, should require freer access to all isolated works, for at times a whole plant may be forbidden one whom the company mistrusts. This is a detriment to the campman. He is unvoiced. Strange things happen to labour under such conditions. More is not heard of them, because the man of the bunkhouse is not naturally querulous. He will grin and bear, but inwardly resolve at the same time that there will be two moons in the sky when he is caught in such meshes again. But, with the coming out and the relaxation, his modest stake is spent before he leaves the frontier town, so he drifts back again to the camps. That class of worker looms large on all seasonal works. They are fit material for the supervision and counsel of a reliable representative of organized labour ...

All frontier works give rise to exceptional placements in labour. Such camps frequently are situated beyond the effective jurisdiction of regularly appointed law-officials. Disputes regarding phases of work and pay often arise in far-out places, which require immediate decisions. Any delay with perhaps a subsequent tramp back over the trail, or down the lake by canoe to the nearest magistrate, is always at the expense of the worker himself. This simply means that disputes of any kind are a disadvantage to the campman. Neither, on the other hand, does the bunkhouse man consider the battle fairly drawn when he must remain on the work and confront lone-handed the decision of the company or its agents.

9. "The Winnipeg Strike," *The Gazette*, May 22, 1919.

The dimensions of the labor strike in Winnipeg have been a rude shock to the people of Canada. It was unthinkable that in this democratic country the social life of any large community could be interrupted, its business blocked, its industries prostrated, municipal services dislocated and civic government paralysed, at the mandate of Trades Union leaders; yet that is what has happened. Labor has boasted of its power, and labor has given an example of its power of which the most dangerous feature is that it may become infectious. The strike of the metal workers was not in itself a matter of great moment, and sooner or later would have been adjusted. The disturbing thing is the sympathetic strike, the cessation from work of all the members of all the unions not because of grievances of their own but to coerce the metal trade employers into granting the demands of their employees, and inferentially to give warning that the Labor Unions are conducted on the principle of all for one and one for all. It is futile to exclaim that the whole proceeding is wrong in ethics and economics, and that none suffer in greater relative degree than the laborers who voluntarily deprive themselves of work and pay. Labor neither philosophizes nor inclines to logic. It presents demands on a bludgeon, and if the demands are not acceded to the work shop is closed and so picketed that none can enter, because a basic rule of unionism is the destruction of individualism, suppression of the will of the individual.

In the last five years what is colloquially termed labor has made an immense stride forward. The cataclysm of war gave an impetus, high wages added an influence, and revolutionary propaganda coming from Russian and German sources sowed seeds of unrest and perverted conceptions, the consequences of which are seen in Winnipeg. Labor has rights, labor has privileges, and the rights and privileges of labor were never so much regarded as now. President Wilson spoke by the book when he declared that the question which stands before all others in every country is the question of labor, the creation of a community of interest between capital and labor, shortening hours of work, paying wages that will enable the worker to live in tolerable comfort, better fed, better housed, better clothed, better schooled than he has been. Governments everywhere are seeking to attain this end. The eight-hour day is in force quite generally in Great Britain, and on this continent. Public money is being devoted to prevent unemployment, and schemes for old age pensions, insurance against sickness, the prevention of child labor, better sanitary surroundings in factories are engaging the earnest study of legislators. It is under these circumstances when labor may look hopefully for the dawn of a better day that the attempt is made to set up in Winnipeg Soviet government after the Russian pattern. We do not believe for a moment that the people of Canada will tolerate the autocratic rule of the unions, whose combined membership is not a very large proportion of the population. Labor leaders, however, Rev. Mr. Evens for instance, retort "What are you going to do about it?" And if the strikers refrain from overt acts of criminality, the answer is not obvious. Unionism of labor is lawful, and there is no compulsion upon unwilling men to work. But there are silent forces operating always to restore order and normality; the moral influence of the people at large, the conscience of many strikers, and the pangs of hunger. If capital cannot coerce labor, neither can labor coerce capital. There is a limit set to the wage scale, namely, the ability to market the product of labor at profitable price. Some revolutionists talk of limiting hours of work to six, or even four hours, of fixing wages at a high minimum, and of restricting production to actual necessities of the people, as if a Chinese wall could be built about Canada and a new Heaven and a new earth made therein. Madmen who preach these doctrines will not long hold their congregation, and it will be a proper act for the Government to invite them to return to the countries whence they came. But the Canadian workingman has at bottom sufficient saving grace of sense not to embrace the pernicious teaching of Bolshevism, and to realize that the high cost of living which has given him unrest and dissatisfaction is not to be reduced by increasing the cost of production.

It is sometimes asked: "Why does not the Government intervene and settle the Winnipeg trouble?" Those who put the question ignore the fact that the Government is but another name for the people, that it derives all its functions and powers from the people. Law and order must be maintained if Canada is not to relapse into a state of anarchy; and with the first outbreak of violence in Winnipeg—which may Heaven avert—the duty of prompt action will be laid upon the Government. Swift should be the action to punish and repress, confident in the sanity and support of the overwhelming mass of the Canadian people.

It may be that press despatches give too lurid a color to the situation, but even allowing for exaggeration, it is shockingly bad. Orderly government has ceased to exist. The strike committee suppresses the Press and determines the conditions upon which food, water, gasoline and oil shall be distributed to the citizens, and there is no authority to say it nay, so weak is the spinal column of the constituted authorities. Is there no one to show courage and do the right? Can the crisis produce no man of nerve and fortitude and sense to restore sanity to a people swept from their moorings by Bolsheviks? The Dominion Government is set at defiance by its own officers, sworn guardians of the peace look with kindly eye on the prostration of municipal authority; and a pious prayer that the strikers will not run into excess, and that time will bring a remedy seems the only recourse of those clothed with responsibility. It will all pass away and be forgotten, of course; the sympathetic strikers will weary of their holiday and yearn for the pay envelope, sanity will once more have sway. If these thing are not to be, then governments, municipal, provincial and federal, may as well abdicate their functions and confess their incapacity; since Canada will cease to be a democratic country in which law and order are maintained, the rights of property upheld and personal liberty protected.

10. *Western Labour News*, May 28, 1919.

The workers have never liked to down tools. It means hard times for them. Many never have enough to live on. The strike takes away all their living. For this reason they strike only when they are driven to desperation.

Why then, it will be asked, do unions that have no direct disagreements of their own walk out with others who have a disagreement. Why do they join in a general strike.

Others add the question, why should they put the whole community to a disadvantage because they take up the quarrel of others.

To answer adequately this question would take a volume. But we can indicate the answer.

First, labor will not call a general strike on a question of wages alone. It wants a decent wage, but so far as we know, no general strike was ever called for this reason alone. It is when principles that cannot be arbitrated are involved and would be defeated unless there were a general stand made by labor that a general strike is possible. It is never possible otherwise.

That was the issue in this city a year ago. The right of the firemen and police to organize was challenged, and labor by a very gradual process brought out one union after the other until the unions concerned were recognized.

This year the issue arose over the Metal Trades. The employers here were arrogant and defiant. They threatened to practically close up and the men might starve. Such was the essence of the matter.

In the case of the Building Trades workers it was the matter of wages. But not a mere matter of wages either. Their demands were acknowledged to be fair and reasonable. But the banking interests were behind the scenes, and the employers were not free to pay the reasonable wage. Thus, labor was face to face with a wage crisis that had never before appeared. It was a straight demand on the part of our financial barons that the workers should work for less than a living wage, while they piled up more millions. That was why the men involved struck work. That is—they just stopped working on those terms. A couple of weeks sufficed to demonstrate that the employers had determined that they would not run the foundries or erect buildings, and the workers were faced with the alternatives of going on under impossible conditions or calling the whole force of labor to their assistance.

They did the latter. Will those who oppose the general strike say that there was a better way? Will they say that labor had any alternative?

But others suffer besides the original parties, they say. That is true. But, is labor responsible for that? Is it not the financial autocrats and barons who are responsible? The answer is clear. Labor has no choice. Moreover, for thousands of workers to stop work and lose their wages in the interests of others is the highest form of brotherhood. It cannot be condemned. Still further, it is wholly a negative method. It does not consist in destruction or violence, but merely is a cessation of work. It has no other phases. It is wholly a cessation of work.

If the general public is so considerably inconvenienced when labor ceases to work, is it not convincingly clear that it is the business of all the people to see that labor gets such a wage and such working conditions as tend to contentment and efficiency? Yet, when was the public interest in labor?

Readings

Acton, J., ed. *Women at Work: Ontario, 1850–1930.* Toronto: Women's Press, 1974.

Babcock, R. *Gompers in Canada: A Study of American Continentalism Before the First World War.* Toronto: University of Toronto Press, 1975.

Bercuson, D. *Confrontation at Winnipeg: Labour, Industrial Relations and the General Strike.* Montreal and Kingston: McGill-Queen's University Press, 1974.

Bercuson, D. *Fools and Wise Men: The Rise and Fall of the One Big Union.* Toronto: McGraw-Hill Ryerson, 1978.

Bliss, M. *A Living Profit: Studies in the Social History of Canadian Business, 1883–1911.* Toronto: McClelland and Stewart, 1974.

Bradbury, B. *Working Families: Age, Gender, and Daily Survival in Industrializing Montreal.* Toronto: McClelland and Stewart, 1993.

Bullen, J. "Hidden Workers: Child labour and the Household Economy in Early Industrial Ontario," *Labour* 18 (Fall 1986).

Copp, T. *The Anatomy of Poverty: The Condition of the Working Class in Montreal, 1897–1929.* Toronto: McClelland and Stewart, 1974.

Craven, P., ed. *Labouring Lives: Work and Workers in Nineteenth-Century Ontario.* Toronto: University of Toronto Press, 1995.

Craven, P. *"Impartial Umpire": Industrial Relations and the Canadian State, 1900–1911.* Toronto: University of Toronto Press, 1980.

Harvey, F., ed. *Aspects Historiques du Mouvement Ouvier au Quebec.* Montreal: Boreal-Express, 1973.

Heron, C. *The Canadian Labour Movement: A Short History.* Toronto: James Lorimer, 1989.

Hurl, L. "Restricting Child Factory Labour in Late Nineteenth-Century Ontario," *Labour* 21 (Spring 1988).

Jamieson, S. *Times of Trouble: Labour Unrest and Industrial Conflict in Canada 1900–1966.* Ottawa: Queen's Printer, 1972.

Kealey, G. *Toronto Workers Respond to Industrial Capitalism 1867–1902.* Toronto: University of Toronto Press, 1980.

Kealey, G., and B. Palmer. *Dreaming of What Might Be: The Knights of Labour in Ontario.* New York: Cambridge University Press, 1982.

Kealey, L. *Enlisting Women for the Cause: Women, Labour and the Left in Canada, 1890–1920.* Toronto: University of Toronto Press, 1998.

Leir, M. *Where the Fraser River Flows: The Industrial Workers of the World in British Columbia.* Vancouver: New Star, 1990.

MacIntosh, R. "The Boys in Nova Scotia's Coal Mines, 1873–1923," *Acadiensis* 16, 2 (Spring 1987).

McCormack, A. *Reformers, Rebels and Revolutionaries: The Western Canadian Radical Movement 1899–1919.* Toronto: University of Toronto Press, 1977.

McNaught, K., and D. Bercuson. *The Winnipeg Strike: 1919.* Toronto: Longman, 1974.

Morton, D., and T. Copp. *Working People.* Ottawa: Deneau and Greenberg, 1980.

Naylor, J. *The New Democracy: Challenging the Social Order in Industrial Ontario 1914–1925.* Toronto: University of Toronto Press, 1991.

Palmer, B. *A Culture in Conflict: Skilled Workers and Industrial Capitalism in Hamilton, Ontario, 1860–1914.* Montreal: McGill-Queen's University Press, 1979.

Palmer, B. *Working Class Experience: The Rise and Reconstitution of Canadian Labour, 1800–1980.* Second edition. Toronto: McClelland and Stewart, 1992.

Roberts, W. *Honest Womanhood: Feminism, Femininity and Class Consciousness among Toronto Working Women, 1896–1914.* Toronto: New Hogtown Press, 1977.

Robin, M. *Radical Politics and Canadian Labour, 1880–1930.* Kingston: Queen's University Press, 1968.

Chapter Five

"THE UNFRIENDLY RECEPTION": IMMIGRATION

1. W.A. Cum Yow, Testimony before the *Royal Commission on Chinese and Japanese Immigration*, 1903.
2. "Chinamen," *Saturday Night,* September 1906.
3. "Western Blacks," *Saturday Night,* April 1911.
4. Dr. Sundar Singh in Empire Club of Canada, *Addresses Delivered to the Members during the Session of 1911–12.*
5. W. Scott, "The Immigration by Races," 1914.
6. Maria Adamowska, "Beginnings in Canada."

Introduction

"Come to Canada," they said, "and satisfy all your needs!" In 1900 the federal Immigration Branch published and distributed over one million pamphlets, in many languages, extolling the Canadian West to Europeans anxious for a fresh start on a young continent far from the stultifying social inertia, poverty, and perpetual turmoil of their homelands. Though earlier Canadian immigration policy favoured British Isles residents to the virtual exclusion of others, Prime Minister Wilfred Laurier and his Minister of the Interior, Clifford Sifton, changed that by boldly inviting immigrants from east and central Europe too—which caused considerable consternation among those wishing to perpetuate the Anglo-Saxon temper of Canada.

Sifton understood that ignoring majority sentiment, especially over issues as sensitive as immigration, could be politically suicidal. He therefore did not accept just anyone as an immigrant. Mainstream Canadians, he knew, judged immigrants' desirability like the concentric rings formed by a pebble tossed in a pond: London represented the epicentre, and the closer the ring to the point of impact, the more welcome the immigrant. Thus Scandinavians and North Germans were fine, as were the Dutch. Travelling further outward, however, raised eyebrows. Distant rings, representing Mediterranean nations, were really too remote to be desirable. Italians and other "Latins," after all, suffered from excess passion, and East European rings were simply too Slavic for mainstream accept-ability. Sifton, however, successfully argued that a "stalwart peasant in a sheepskin coat with a stout wife" from Eastern Europe could develop the Canadian North-west as well, if not better, than newcomers from Great Britain. To assuage fears, he assured Canadians that a Ukrainian immigrant would soon assimilate and become as indistinguishably Britannic as the majority. And what of the far-flung rings representing prospective immigrants of colour: Africans, Indians, and Asians?

Many, perhaps most, Canadians viewed newcomers with non-white faces with concern if not downright suspicion and hostility. This was particularly true in British Columbia where a disproportionate number of prospective immi-grants arrived from non-European countries like Japan, China, and India. Those newcomers bore the brunt of stereotyping, and usually found their presence unwelcome—except when it served employers' needs. Racism and xenophobia came in various guises, but B.C. residents worried that the outsiders, if not barred, would arrive en masse and take over.

Federal and provincial governments responded to local anxieties and soon erected barriers against those immigrants deemed "undesirable." And if the bar-rier proved too low? Raise it. Do whatever was necessary to keep them out. Thus Chinese immigrants paid head taxes upon arrival, taxes that rose from an initial fifty dollars, to one hundred, and finally to five hundred dollars. The federal government created a "gentleman's agreement" with Japan whereby the Japanese government forbade all but a few of its citizens from travelling to Canada. India and Indian emigrants, however, posed a special conundrum. Members of the British Empire had a legal right to travel and live anywhere within the Empire. Thus Indians could legally immigrate to Canada if they so wished—and, much to the dismay of many in British Columbia, a growing number did. In response, the Federal Government enacted the Continuous Passage Act that neatly cir-cumvented legal niceties by requiring prospective Indian immigrants to travel by continuous passage from India to Canada—which was impossible. Efforts to evade the act came to a head in the summer of 1914 when the *Komagata Maru* and its nearly 400 passengers sailed directly from Calcutta to Vancouver. Stuck on board for nearly two months waiting for the right to land, the ship was finally forced out of Canadian waters at gunpoint.

Sifton's settlement of the prairies proceeded at a rapid pace and with less anti-immigrant hostility than on the West Coast. The Canadian west's popula-tion of 300,000 before 1896 grew to 1.5 million by the eve of the First World War in 1914. The prairies ceased being primarily Native and Métis homelands, and instead developed a multicultural milieu unlike any other in the country.

But it was not easy. Certainly, the prairies offered better opportunities and more potential than their original homelands, but life proved much harsher than immigrants expected. Canadian government propaganda, after all, only described success stories, never failures. Pamphlets failed to mention the expectation of assimilation, the racism, bigotry, and discrimination. Immigration agents in Europe never commented upon homesickness, loneliness, or any of the other traumas so common to new immigrants. The Canadian Pacific Railroad, which played a major part in recruiting and transporting immigrants, even failed to mention winter or snow in its promotional advertisements on the Canadian prairies.

Discussion Points

1. Would you agree with Scott's description of the federal government's immigration policies as "just and humane"? If not, how would you define them?
2. On what basis did Canada rank immigrants?
3. Compare the experiences of visible minorities such as the Chinese and Sikhs with those of Adamowska.
4. Did the federal government take advantage of newly arrived immigrants? Did it have an obligation to provide more support to these people?
5. Three decades passed between Adamowska's initial immigration experience and its publication. Would her description have been different if it had been recorded earlier? What distinguishes "history" from "memory"?
6. Scott's account contains many racial stereotypes and demeaning images of ethnic groups. Should we reprint and study these types of documents? Do they qualify as hate literature?

Documents

1. W.A. Cum Yow, Testimony before the *Royal Commission on Chinese and Japanese Immigration*, 1903

I was born at Port Douglas in this province in the year 1861. My parents are both Chinese. They have lived in the province for nearly 45 years. I was educated in the province. I am corresponding foreign secretary of the Chinese Empire Reform Association of Canada. I have been in close touch with the Chinese all my life, and I am familiar with their modes of living and of doing business. There has been no systematic importation of Chinese into this province since the construction of the Canadian Pacific Railway. At that time a large number were engaged and brought over. This was done by the Chinese contractors who were working under Mr. Onderdonk. Some of these men went back, but others had no means to pay their way back, and many who remained were in great straits for a long time. These men were all voluntarily hired, and were in no sense serfs. Serfdom is not practiced among the Chinese. All who come here come free men and as a rule pay their own boat fare and entry tax. These are paid in Hong Kong to the steamboat agents before they start. I am certain none of the Chinese labour contractors here have sent money to pay for a number of Chinamen to come here. Occasionally, Chinamen have sent money to bring out relatives or personal friends, but that is the extent to which this is done. There is never any bond given for repayment of such advances, but where there is an understanding that repayment will be made it is always faithfully done. Chinese merchants have sometimes taken action to limit the number of those coming when they find there are too many here. They do this by communicating with the merchants in China, who have great influence with the labouring classes. They took this course two years ago when the labour market was over-supplied owing to the number of Japs who had come in. There are not so many Chinamen or Japs here at present as there were a year ago. Many of those who were here have gone over to the States where liberal wages are being paid them, and they can do much better than here. Others have gone to the West Indies and settled there. Many of the Chinamen who previously went to the West Indies have made lots of money, and some of them have intermarried with the native races. There have been cases of importation of Chinese girls for immoral purposes, but not many. This has been the work of unscrupulous men, who, by gross misrepresentations, and free use of money have led poor people to entrust them with the care of their daughters. Proportionately, I believe, there is nothing like the same number of such cases among the Chinese as among white people, but there are wicked and unscrupulous men among the Chinese as among other races. I do not think any Chinese parents would willingly give up their daughters for such purposes. The Chinese who are here usually congregate in one part of the city. The chief reason for this is for companionship. Besides the Chinese know that the white people have had no friendly feeling towards them for a number of years. This has been most apparent since the Canadian Pacific Railway construction days, and it has been accentuated by those who since then have come into the province from all parts of the world, many of whom were not in touch with the Chinese before. This unfriendliness and want of respect has caused a feeling of want of confidence among the Chinese, and it certainly has not tended to induce them to abandon their own ways and modes of life. It was very different before the date referred to, when a feeling of mutual confidence and respect prevailed, and all were able to work in harmony. This system of doing business also tends to keep them together, as it enables them the better to have their own social functions and meetings. They have their own Board of Trade and other meetings as to their trade interests. We have not here the faction element which prevails to some extent in San Francisco. There are now in this province strong branches of the Chinese Empire Reform Association of Canada. This association has been incorporated. Its objects are duly set forth in the accompanying copy of the constitution and by-laws. The Reform Association has branches all over the world where there are Chinamen. They wish to elevate the Chinese and to promote the prosperity of the old land. The work is carried on here largely by public meetings and addresses. Some of the members are most eloquent speakers. This work cannot be carried on yet in China itself, but we hope for great good to China from the movement, and also to be able to do something for the good of the Chinese who are here. The association has also arranged for the translation of some of the best books in the English language into Chinese for distribution among Chinamen in China and other parts of the world. They are also sending students to different seats of learning to be educated. The Chinese have always a very high regard to their home land, and a strong filial affection. They sacrifice a great deal for themselves to be able to send money home to sustain their parents or their families, and if by any piece of good fortune or by success in gambling they make a large sum at any time, the larger part of that money will usually be sent to China for the use of their families. They do not spend it on themselves. There is proportionately a large amount of gambling among the Chinese. Some do gamble for large amounts, but more commonly the play is for amusement only, and for small sums to pass the time, as this is done in the common room of the boarding house, where all assembled, though differently occupied. If a police raid is made and any are caught playing, all are arrested for gambling or looking on. ... Chinese use intoxicating liquors, but not often, and usually in moderation. They use all kinds of liquor. They sometimes use a Chinese wine, which serves as a tonic for the system. They very seldom get drunk or drink to excess. They regard all who are excessive drinkers as barbarians and beneath contempt. So strong is the feeling among them, that if any one should indulge too freely, they are heartily ashamed of it, and they at once go to bed. A certain number indulge in opium smoking, but only a small percentage of the whole. The habit is induced by companionship with those who use it. I have seen white men in the Chinese quarter using opium, but not many of them here. The opium smokers realize the evil of the habit, but they are unable to break it off. The Chinese have a hospital for the treatment of sick men who are without means. It is a charitable institution, and is supported by voluntary subscriptions, contributed chiefly by the merchants. They have a Chinese doctor of their own, and he does the work for charity. The patients are cared for by the janitor of the hospital, and by their own friends. I have known of some cases of recovery there, but they generally go there as a last resort, hence the large percentage of deaths. In the boarding houses the attention is given to the sick. Of course those who have money secure better treatment than those who have none. It is not the case that any of the sick are neglected. They are cared for up to the ability of their friends, and after death they are given a proper burial by the undertakers at the friends' expense. I have never known a case of concealment of infectious disease among them.

The Chinese have a very high regard for the marriage relationship. They usually marry at from sixteen to twenty years of age. Many of those who are here are married and have wives and children in China. A large proportion of them would bring their families here, were it not for the unfriendly reception they got here during recent years, which creates an unsettled feeling. Both spouses are, as a rule, faithful to each other, and the wife stays with the husband's relations, the money sent home by the husband is of use to them all. Often the family property has to be mortgaged to help the son to come here, and the first thing he does is to try to lift the mortgage. Divorce is unknown in China, and it is a very uncommon thing for spouses to separate their relations on any ground. As a nation, the Chinese are very anxious that their children be well educated. There has been no serious attempt in China to teach other than the Chinese language until recently. Now English is largely taken up, as they are coming more and more into contact with the English speaking people. The desire to learn is not confined to any one class. The laboring or farming class are as anxious for education as the others, and they stand the same show to get it. The Chinese here are all anxious to have their children taught the same as other children are taught here. Regarding prospects of assimilation, I do not think this will be easily or soon brought about. I do not favor the idea of intermarriage, as the modes of life of the races are different in several respects, and it would not conduce to happiness. There are exceptional cases, such as where the parties have been brought up together or under similar conditions, but this seldom happens. Assimilation can only come through those who are born here, or at least are brought here in infancy, and are separated from the ideas of the old land and the mode of life there. For work, the Chinese are not so physically strong as the white people. This is due to the diet they take, but they are very patient and persevering workers, and they are quick in action. It therefore follows, that for light work they excel the white people, but for heavy work white men have the advantage. Their wages vary considerably. In the canneries they get from $45 to $50 a month, but the month must consist of 26 days of 10 hours each of actual work. As day labourers they get about $1 per day. Chinese farmers and laundrymen usually get from $10 to $20 per month and their board and lodging. In the cannery boarding-house the bosses supply the food and each is charged in proportion to the cost of it. This will amount to from $9 to $10 per month for each. The rule in regard to laundries applies to some other lines of light work. The boots and shoes and a large proportion of the clothing used by Chinamen are made in Canada or the United States. The silk goods and silk shoes come from China. They get some of their food stuffs from China, such as rice, which cannot be grown here. Rice is one of the essential parts of their dietary. The Chinese are especially suited for such light work as in the laundries, cooks in hotels or camps and in domestic service. They have been engaged in such work as long as I can remember, and always received with favour by the employers. They are quick in action, and ready to do what they are told, and able to do a greater variety of work than a girl can do in domestic service. In all my experience I have not heard of a Chinaman being indecent in his relation to the household where he works. As a rule they can be relied on and are very attentive to duty. The Chinese have been engaged largely in market gardening in this province for over thirty-five years, and they have during all those years been the chief source of supply of vegetables for our markets. They work late and early on their ground, and have it in a high state of cultivation, hence they can make a good living off ten acres of land. They have been engaged in the fish-canning work since the beginning of the industry over twenty-five years ago. They are thoroughly trained in all the different inside departments. I cannot see how they can be dispensed with, as so many hands are required, and all need a special training for the work. As a fact it would take years to train a sufficient number of white men or children. These could better do the work now done by Indians, but of course the Indians would resent this inroad on them. A great feature of their character is their frugality. In fact this is one of the chief complaints against them. They are trained to be frugal, and it seems to me a virtue rather than a cause of offence. True it enables them to save money and to send some of it to China to help their families there, but that is also a virtue. They are willing also to undertake work at a small wage rather than be idle, and they are very careful to live within their income, whether it be large or small, that they may have some provision for idleness or illness. In this respect it seems to me, that they are superior to many white men who will not work unless they get a high pay, and are extravagant and even reckless in their expenditure of the money they earn, who never think of providing for the future, and have very little consideration, even for their own wives and families. To some extent this may be due to the privileges the white men have of friendly and charitable societies to rely upon which are not available for the Chinaman. My opinion is, that if the Chinese were accorded the same respect as others here, they would prove themselves to be good citizens, and they would settle in the land with their wives and families. Being thrifty they would save money, and that money would be judiciously used in the country. Certainly, if their families were here, they would have no occasion to send their money away. It is not pleasure for them to be separated from their families (in a good many cases for 15, 20 and 25 years). They come here to improve their circumstances, and they would only be too glad to have their families to enjoy with them any improvements that are available. Many of the chief opponents of the Chinese are comparatively new arrivals in the province, who have very little idea of the facts of the case. Some of these men are unwilling to work themselves, and they misspend the earnings they do make, yet they are eager to run down the Chinese who are willing to work and who do work hard, and are very careful of their hard-earned money. Men are coming here from all parts of the world and of all nationalities. As regards industry and thrift, the Chinese will compare favourably with any of them. In many respects they are greatly superior to many of the men who come here during the canning season and claim the privilege of being British subjects. Some of these are wild, lawless drinking men who are a discredit to any community. During the canning season, though a large number of Chinese congregate at Steveston and other points, they are all very orderly and obedient to the laws. Referring to cannery work, it is well known that the Chinese contractors each year enter upon very onerous contracts with the canners for labour, and that under these contracts large advances are made by the canners to the contractors before the work of the season begins. I do not know of one single instance where a Chinese contractor failed to carry out his contract in full. I know of many instances where they have done it at a heavy loss to themselves, but they did it honourably. As regards further immigration, I think the matter will always fully regulate itself. The Chinese merchants will always take care that too many do not come. It is a serious burden on them if they come and do not get plenty of work. The head tax also presents a substantial barrier against them coming in present circumstances. I do not favour the existence of this tax. I think the same end could have been reached by diplomacy, as was done by the United States. I quite approve of certain conditions being attached to the granting of the franchise, such as are provided in the Natal Act, and that it be applicable to Japanese, Galicians, Italians and others all alike. I do think however, that if the Chinese pay admission to this country, and if they have educational qualifications they should not only be allowed the privilege of the franchise, but be treated otherwise as men and as British citizens. Already the Chinese have done good work in placer mining, as they are content to work up claims deserted by the white miners, if they yield even $1.25 to $2 per day. There are great areas of such properties, and the reclamation of this gold is a valuable provincial asset, which would otherwise remain worthless. Besides mining this province has a vast territory, and many other undeveloped resources. It has, therefore, opening for a very large industrial population, and as the Chinese are, as already stated, industrious, thrifty and persevering, and always amenable to the laws of the land, as far as they understand them, they should make valuable citizens and greatly aid in the development of this great country. This is particularly true of the opening up of the agricultural land, as the Chinese are born agriculturists and are accustomed to make the very best of the soil. Their experience should therefore in agriculture be most valuable to enable this province to provide for its own want as well as to become an exporting country. In view of the agitation being carried on by politicians and professional agitators against the Chinese here, it is a mystery to me as it must be to other observers that so many people in all ranks of life are so ready to employ Chinamen to do their work. Many of them are thus employed, and some at fairly high salaries, and this seems to nullify the allegations that they are either offensive or detrimental to the development of the country. It is as a fact a valuable testimonial of merit and proves that they are needed in the country.

In conclusion, my firm conviction is that the agitation which has arisen in connection with the orientals is more directed against the capitalists than against the Chinese themselves. They seem to think that the capitalists are benefiting from the labour of the orientals in a special manner; whereas it seems to me that the orientals are enabling the capitalists to carry on business which directly benefit all classes in the community. It is true there are also those who seem to dislike the appearance of the Chinamen and their oriental ways of living and dressing, and there is a large unthinking class who condemn them because it has become a custom to do so. I have always urged the Chinamen to adopt the British mode of dress and living; and, judging from the experience of the Japanese, I am satisfied the Chinese would greatly benefit if they did so.

2. "Chinamen," *Saturday Night,* September 1906

CHINAMEN

The word comes from British Columbia that there is a movement on foot to induce the Dominion Government to permit the importation of 5,000 Chinamen ... to construct the mountain section of the Grand Trunk Pacific, these men to be sent back to China on the completion of that work ... We don't want Chinamen in Canada ... This is a white man's country, and white men will keep it so. The slant-eyed Asiatic, with his yellow skin, his unmanly humility, his cheap wants, would destroy the whole equilibrium of industry. He would slave like a Nubian, scheme like a Yankee, hoard like the proverbial Jew. Turn these people loose in a country like ours and they would make progress like a pestilence. Race prejudice! This is race prejudice, of course. But so strong, so prevalent, is it that no Government could do any one thing that would bring it to more swift and sure disaster than to open the gates of this country to the yellow invaders. Let them swarm in once and the yellow stain on the country will be one that cannot be rubbed out. We cannot assimilate them. They are an honest, industrious, but hopelessly inferior race.

3. "Western Blacks," *Saturday Night,* April 1911

WESTERN BLACKS

If the Negro is a successful colonizer in the Canadian West he will have accomplished something that up to the present has been foreign to his nature. The Negro under favourable conditions is a fairly successful labourer, but when thrown upon his own resources he has failed to meet the demands made upon him. The servitude of centuries cannot be cast off in a day. The initiative is lacking. He is indolent, prodigal, and shiftless. In other words, he is by nature unfit for carving out for himself a home in the wilderness. Then, again, the rigorous climate of our Northwest is unsuitable for those of a dark skin. The Negro is far more susceptible to cold than is the Anglo-Saxon and the other hardier Northern races, and this is proven by the fact that north of the Mason-Dixon line the Negro does not thrive as he does in the sunny South ... There is every reason to believe that the Negro problem of our Northwest, if there is a problem, will adjust itself.

4. Dr. Sundar Singh in Empire Club of Canada, *Addresses Delivered to the Members during the Session of 1911–12*

Some few years ago a few troops of the Sikhs passed through Canada on their way to the jubilee of the late Queen Victoria, and the gentlemen who were in charge of them spoke very highly of them. These Sikhs went back home and they spoke of the vast prairies where they saw wheat growing the same as we grow wheat. The consequence was that a score of them came out in 1905—about forty of them came in that year and the next, and this went on till in 1909 there was quite a strong body of them, about 4,000 in all, engaged in agriculture; they were farmers in India, and of course they naturally took to farming when they came to this country.

They are British subjects: they have fought for the Empire; many of these men have war medals; but, in spite of this fact, they are not allowed to have their families with them when they come to this country; in spite of their being British subjects, they are not allowed to have their wives here. People talk about these Oriental races, and the phrase is understood to include not only the Chinese and the Japanese, but the Sikhs as well, which is absurd. Letters giving inaccurate statements are appearing in the press all the time. I do not know why all this objection should be directed against the Sikhs—against that people, more than against any other Oriental people.

These people are here legally; they have satisfied every process of law; they have been here over five years; they have been good to their employers—Colonel Davidson employs 350 of them in his mills in New Westminster—their work is equal to that of other labourers; their quarters are better, and they are making more wages now; they have fitted into the situation here; they have made good.

In spite of this, there are these letters going through the papers, and there are attacks upon these men; yet, although they are British subjects, nobody stands up for them. We appeal to you of the Empire Club, for we are only 4,000 in number, to help us in this matter, and to see that justice is done to these subjects of our King.

We are subjects of the same Empire; we have fought, we have sacrificed. We have fought for the Empire and we bear her medals; we have an interest in this country: we have bought about $2,000,000 of property in British Columbia; we have our church and pay our pastor, and we mean to stay in this country. I understand that there is a society called the Home Reformation Society and that it says that it is better for a man to have a wife and family. To others you advance money to come here, and yet to us, British subjects, you refuse to let down the bars. All we are asking of you is justice and fair play, because the Sikhs have believed in fair play, and have believed all the time that they will get justice; that ultimately they will get justice from the British people.

Many people have been telling me that it is useless my trying to bring this question before the Canadian people, but I am firmly persuaded that, if the question, is properly brought before right-minded Canadians, that they will say that the same rights should be given to the Sikh people as are given to any other British subjects.

Some people have spread the false statement that the Sikhs are polygamous; they are monogamous in India, and are not more polygamous than you are. They are strictly monogamous by their religion, and it is useless to spread these false stories. There are officers in India—perhaps some have come from Canada—and they can take their families to India to our people; are the laws made so invidious that it cannot work both ways! That law was meant to shut out the Japanese, yet, in the year 1908, 5,000 came from Honolulu, and they let them in. We do know that we are British subjects and we ask for our rights; if you can allow the alien to come over here, surely a British subject ought to have the same rights as an alien.

The position cannot hold good; it is inevitable that it cannot hold good. These Sikhs are the pick of their villages, they are not out here like the Japanese and Chinese. The Japanese has to show only 50 cents when he arrives, but the Sikh has to show $200, and, if he cannot, he is sent away. Of course you can understand what the reflex action of this treatment might be in the present state of India. These people who are here, are here legally; if they were new people coming in, it would be a different matter; but as such they have rights, and I think those rights ought to be respected. (Applause.)

It is only a matter of justice. If this Empire is to be and continue to be a great Empire, as it is sure to be, then it must be founded on righteousness and justice; your laws cannot be one thing for one set and a different thing for the rest of us.

These Sikhs are quite alone; they do the roughest labour; they do not come into competition with other labour, and yet this is the treatment they receive. They are plainly told: "We do not want you to bring your wives in." You cannot expect people to be moral, if you debar them from bringing in their wives and children. They can travel in Japan, they can travel in Europe; they can travel anywhere under the British flag, except here.

Just at present there are two Sikh women confined on board a boat at Vancouver; they came on the 22nd. One is the wife of a merchant, the other is the wife of a missionary. These men have been settled in this country for five years, and are well spoken of. They went back some time ago to bring out their wives and children. They asked the steamship company to sell them tickets, and the company told them that they would be refused admission. They came to Hong Kong, and the steamship company refused to sell them tickets; they waited ever since last March and last month the C.P.R. sold them tickets. On the 22nd, they arrived here, and the men were allowed to land, but the ladies are still confined as if they were criminals.

Now, if these men were allowed to land, why not their wives; why should they not be allowed to land, too? That is what they do not understand, and, although they are well versed in the occult sciences and mystical philosophy, why this should be so, they cannot see. (Applause.)

We have the promise of Queen Victoria that all British subjects, no matter what race or creed they belong to, shall be treated alike. These promises have been confirmed by King Edward, and by His Majesty King George the Fifth. When he was in India, he granted their full rights to the Hindoo people. The Indian people are loyal British subjects. They are as loyal as anybody else. Why should there be such a difference in the treatment of these loyal people?

We appeal to you, gentlemen, to say that in any country, under any conditions, the treatment that the Sikhs are receiving is not fair. We appeal to your good sense and to your humanity to see that justice is done, that this thing is not continued, for it has been going on for quite a long time. You may well imagine the feeling of these two men, who are suffering as I have described, for no fault at all, except that they are Sikhs.

5. W. Scott, "The Immigration by Races," 1914.

… Compared with other European settlers the British start with the advantage of having the same mother tongue as Canadians; with this exception they are on an equal footing with all others and must be prepared to compete on these terms. Much is said of the preference which Canada should give to persons from the mother country, but there is little sentiment in business, and if an Italian immigrant can do more work than an Englishman, the Italian "gets the job." Fortunately for Canada and for the immigrants there is usually work for both.

Considering the immense number of British immigrants arriving—some 674,000 in the first decade of the century—it speaks well for them and well for the country that so few have failed. Those who do not succeed are the exception. Although the success is of varying degree, it is as a rule according to the energy and tenacity of purpose displayed. There are few British immigrants in Canada who are not in a position much superior to that which they would now be occupying had they remained at home.

For the last twelve fiscal years, 1901–12, the immigration from Great Britain and Ireland amounted to 823,188 in the following proportion: English and Welsh, 601,963; Scottish, 171,897; Irish, 49,328. The largest number in any one year was for the twelve months ending March 31, 1912, when the total reached the immense figure of 138,121, made up of 96,806 English and Welsh, 32,988 Scottish and 8327 Irish.

United States Immigration
The people from the United States most readily adapt themselves to Canadian conditions. The greater portion come from the Northern and Western States, where climatic and agricultural conditions closely resemble those of the Dominion. As they are largely of the agricultural class and come to Canada to take up farming, they know the proper course to adopt immediately upon arrival. United States immigrants may be considered the most desirable for a number of reasons. They understand Canadian conditions so well that their success in the so called dry belt of Alberta has been greater than that of the Canadian born; immediately on arrival they put large tracts under cultivation, and induce the railway companies to provide transportation facilities in the districts where they settle; they use the most recent machinery and labour-saving devices, and are thus an object-lesson, more especially to foreign settlers, who, without this clear proof of the value of improved machinery, would be slow in commencing its use; and, lastly and most important of all, they employ upon their farms large numbers of the immigrants of all races, who yearly arrive without sufficient capital to commence operations at once on their own account, and who must seek employment with others until they have saved enough to begin work on their free homesteads.

Much is spoken and written of the danger that Western Canada may become Americanized. The force of such arguments depends upon what is meant by "Americanized." If it is to be taken to mean the growing up of a sentiment in favour of annexation with the United States, the charge is groundless; if it means that the progressiveness of the American will be copied by the Canadian, the more rapid the Americanization the better. The Western Canadian is never averse to learning, no matter who may be his teacher. Sometimes the American settler finds in turn that in many things he may safely follow the lead of his Canadian neighbour.

When speaking of the possibility of annexation to the United States it is well to remember that probably not more than 50 percent of the immigrants from the United States were born there, and that, in addition to the 10 percent of the immigrants who are Canadians returning to the Dominion, which they left when the conditions were adverse, there are numbers who, while born in the States, are children of Canadian parents, and look upon themselves as really Canadians. Nor must it be forgotten that a considerable portion were born in the British Islands, and, coming again under the same flag, immediately upon arrival look upon themselves as Canadians.

The immigrants from the United States become naturalized at the earliest opportunity, while those who may be repatriated upon a three months' residence are quick to avail themselves of the opportunity. Generally speaking, the Americans are staunch supporters of the Canadian system of government, and are ever ready to point out wherein it is superior to that which they have left. More especially is this true with regard to the Canadian system of judiciary. No warmer advocate of the appointive system of judges exists than the American, who has had experience of the elective system …

Austro-Hungarians

One of the largest contributors of immigrants to Canada of late years has been Austria-Hungary. The term Austro-Hungarian, however, has no very definite meaning. Such words as English, French, German, Norwegian convey to the mind a class of persons of certain language, type, appearance and peculiarities. Not so with the term Austro-Hungarian. Austria-Hungary is not a country wherein dwells a particular class of people, but is a certain area under two constituted governments, ruled over by one sovereign. The population is made up of a number of races with different languages, religions and social ideals. Divided into a large number of provinces, the country as a whole has an area of 240,942 square miles and a population of about fifty millions. Of these 45 percent are Slavs, 25 percent Germans, 16 percent Magyars; the remainder consist of Roumanians, Croatians, Ruthenians, Ser[b]ians, Poles, Bohemians, Jews and numerous other races. Of the different races the Germans are the most desirable in every respect, their educational standard being much higher, their industry more noticeable, and their ideals more closely approaching those of Canadians than is the case with the other races. The provinces which have contributed most largely to the movement of immigrants to Canada are Galicia and Bukowina. The North Atlantic Trading Company, which will be mentioned later, brought Canada to the attention of the people in these two provinces especially, and the movement once commenced continued through the indirect immigration work carried on by those who were successful in their new homes. The census of 1901 showed 28,407 persons in Canada who had been born in Austria-Hungary, and 18,178 of these were classified as Austro-Hungarians, the balance presumably being of German origin. Since that date the immigration movement has been large, nearly 140,000 arriving in the years 1901–12.

Coming from a country where agriculture is the principal industry, the Galicians and others from Austria-Hungary are fitted in some ways to make suitable settlers in Canada. They have been, however, embarrassed for want of capital. They have, moreover, preferred to settle on lands well covered with timber, and the cost of clearing the land and bringing it under cultivation has been higher than that of cultivating prairie land. In the majority of cases when the $10 entry fee for a homestead was paid and a not very habitable house erected, the head of the family, together with any other members able to act as wage-earners, found it necessary to seek work in order to secure funds to purchase stock and machinery. Employment could generally be secured with farmers in the harvesting season, with threshing outfits during the autumn, and in the bush during the winter. In this way the men have secured some knowledge of the English language, as have also some of the women who have become domestic servants.

The Galicians and other Austro-Hungarians are settled largely in the eastern portion of Manitoba and the northern sections of Saskatchewan and Alberta. They have improved their positions by coming to Canada, but whether or not they are a valuable acquisition to the Dominion is an open question. They are slow to assimilate and adopt Canadian customs, and, after all is said, this should be the final test as to the desirability of any class of immigrants. If they will not aid in forming a people united in customs and ideals, their room should be more acceptable than their company. Time will, no doubt, work wonders in their case, as it has in the case of other nationalities, and eventually it is hoped that they will make good Canadians. The process, however, will be slow.

What has already been said refers to those who have gone upon farms in

Canada. Those who have settled in the cities form an entirely different problem. Living as they do in crowded, insanitary and usually filthy quarters, existing upon food and under conditions which a self-respecting Canadian would refuse to tolerate, they enter into unfair competition with the wage-earners of Canada and constitute a source of danger to the national life. Crime is all too common among them, and it is without doubt the city element of this people which has brought about the prejudice which exists against Galicians in the minds of Canadians. Since 1906 no effort has been made by the Canadian government to secure further immigration of this class. But, although all the restrictive regulations mentioned later on are enforced against them, large numbers still arrive, and are likely to arrive for years to come. A flow of any particular class of immigrants is usually difficult to start, but when once commenced it is often just as difficult to check.

The Italians
According to the 1901 census there were then in Canada 6,854 persons born in Italy and 10,834 persons of Italian origin. Between the fiscal years 1901–2 and 1911–12 nearly 62,000 immigrants arrived from Italy. The large majority of the Italians cannot, however, in the true sense be classed as immigrants, for they do not come with the intention of making permanent homes. They are "hewers of wood and drawers of water" who, by living at the lowest possible expense and by working diligently, hope to accumulate sufficient wealth to enable them to live comfortably in "Sunny Italy." They arrive with little that cannot be carried tied up in a handkerchief, and leave with a travelling outfit of about the same dimensions. Stored about their persons, or transmitted already to their native land, is the money they have earned during their sojourn here.

If we except the hand-organ man and the fruit-dealer, practically all are engaged at work as navvies. In every city you see them digging drains; on railway construction from the Atlantic to the Pacific their services are eagerly sought. The Italian is a good navvy. He obeys the orders of the "boss." He is anxious [not] to go on strike, as he counts that any increase in wages would in the short period he intends to remain in the country no more than reimburse him for the wages lost while the strike was on. At construction work he boards himself, or, if eating at the contractor's boardinghouse, is likely to be satisfied with whatever fare is furnished. He has no desire to insist upon exceptionally clean sleeping quarters, and, in a word, is exactly the class of help which contractors desire for the rough work of railway construction. When times are slack the Italians flock to the cities, and in their little colonies in Montreal, Toronto, Winnipeg and

Vancouver huddle into their cheap boarding houses and live under appalling conditions, at a rate so low as almost to shatter belief in the much talked of "increased cost of living." When work is again available they are shipped off by employment agents to points at which their services are needed.

They have arrived from their native land with the idea that it is for them to right their own wrongs in person. Thus, while crimes committed by them against other than Italians are uncommon, stabbing and shooting affrays are all too common where men of their own race are the victims. Edward A. Steiner, in his book *On the Trail of the Immigrant*, writes thus of the Italian attitude towards crime:

> The worst thing about the Italians is that they have no sense of shame or remorse. I have not yet found one of them who was sorry for anything except that he had been caught; and in his own eyes and in the eyes of his friends he is "unfortunate" when he is in prison and "lucky" when he comes out. "He no bad," his neighbour says. "He good, he just caught." And when he comes out he is received as a hero.

Of the Black Hand societies, of which we hear so much in the large cities of the United States, little as yet has been heard in Canada. That they exist is admitted by those most familiar with the Italian in the Dominion, but as their threats are invariably addressed to members of their own race, information is unlikely to be furnished to the courts, or even to creep into the press of the country.

That labour is necessary to carry on the large public works throughout the Dominion is admitted; that, if not on hand, it must be brought to the country is conceded. We may, however, hold that the help should be secured from such immigrants as are considered desirable, so that the country may have as its labourers those who intend to become permanent residents. The Italians are not of this class. They merely save money with which to return to their native land.

The enforcement of the regulation requiring Italians upon arrival to present their penal certificates has resulted in the rejection of many. A penal certificate is a civil document showing the number of convictions registered against the person to whom it is issued. As each Italian is supposed by the laws of his own country to possess one, the fact that he is without one is taken as evidence that he does not wish it seen, or, in other words, that it shows him to have been convicted of crime. As many have been rejected, either on account of information furnished on the penal certificate or through not possessing a penal certificate, it is evident that many of the Italians attempting to come to Canada (and the same is true of the United States) belong to the criminal class. The government has never encouraged immigration from Italy, except, for a very brief period, in the case of some northern Italians. The large number of arrivals from Italy is accounted for simply by the fact that those emigrating desire work, and that the work awaits them in Canada.

The French

With the population of France at a standstill and the people prosperous, it is not to be expected that any great movement of settlers should take place from that country; nevertheless, since the beginning of the twentieth century there has been a steady flow of emigration to Canada. The number for the years 1901-12 was 17,970. As in 1901 there were only 7,944 persons in Canada who had been born in France, this class of population has more than doubled in the last decade.

The French coming to Canada have settled largely in Quebec, Ontario and the western provinces. There are several very progressive colonies in Saskatchewan. The French are an industrious and thrifty people, and will make a success of agricultural work in the Dominion.

More important than the movement from France is that of "Returned Canadians" from the Eastern States. These people left Quebec when Canada was far from being as prosperous as it now is, and are returning to Canada to take up free homesteads in the prairie provinces, or to secure crown lands in Quebec or Ontario.

The Belgians

The people from Belgium also make excellent settlers. Of these there were 2,280 in 1901, and since that date the arrivals have been 10,184.

The Dutch

The Dutch are as yet slightly represented in the Dominion, there being in 1901 only 385 in Canada who were born in Holland. In the first decade of the present century 4,895 arrived, and a heavier immigration is expected in the future. They make good settlers, and those who have already come have made very rapid material progress.

The Swiss

The Swiss are lightly represented in the immigration returns, only 1,717 having arrived between 1901 and 1912. They also make good settlers.

The Germans

In Canada in 1901 there were only 27,300 persons who had been born in Germany; there were, however, 310,501 of German origin, or almost 6 percent of the total population of the Dominion. In the early days ... Canada received considerable German immigration both directly from the Fatherland and indirectly from the German settlements in the United States. The descendants of these settlers form the greater part of the present population of German origin. The immigration from Germany during the years 1901–12 was about 25,000. In addition to the above a considerable portion of the immigration from Austria-Hungary and Russia is of German origin. For the fiscal years 1909–10 and 1910–11 the unnaturalized Germans from the United States numbered 2,378 and 1,123 respectively.

Sturdy, intelligent, honest and industrious, the German makes an ideal farmer, and he is in other walks of life a good citizen. Although he clings to his language he also acquires English, and the younger people especially adopt Canadian customs. They are amongst Canada's best settlers, and it is to be regretted that the laws of Germany prohibit the active immigration propaganda which would enable the Dominion to secure a much larger number than are now arriving.

The Scandinavians

... As of [Icelanders], so of the other Scandinavian races—Swedes, Norwegians, and Danes—nothing but good can be said. The larger part of the immigrants of these races go on the land; but whether they engage in agriculture or take up employment in the cities they prove hard-working, honest, thrifty and intelligent settlers of whom any country might be proud. In addition to those coming direct from the homeland many have been moving for years past from the Western States into Saskatchewan and Alberta, and are there looked upon as amongst the most progressive settlers. They readily acquire the English language, become naturalized at the earliest possible moment, take an interest in the political questions affecting their new homes, and, in a word, "become Canadians." In 1901 there were in Canada 2,075 Danes and 10,256 Norwegians and Swedes. Between 1901–1902 and 1911–12 over 4,700 Danes and over 36,500 Norwegians and Swedes arrived in the Dominion. With the Scandinavian race there is really no question of assimilation. They are sprung largely from the same stock as are the English, and, when they have acquired the language and become acquainted with Canadian customs, they will be as other Canadians. True, the first generation will be distinguished by their accent, but even this disappears in the second generation.

Turks, Armenians and Syrians

Turkey, Armenia and Syria supply some of Canada's most undesirable immigrants. With them assimilation is out of the question and, except rarely, they are not producers. The Italians have their faults; Canadians may not approve of the manner in which the Poles and many other Eastern European races live. But these people are at least workers. If they take money out of the country when they go back to their homes, they leave behind them tasks performed, for which as a rule they have received no more than they have earned. But with the Turks, Syrians and Armenians it is different. They live under conditions which are a menace to the country, and their time is spent in trade and barter. Like the Gypsies, they are quick to avail themselves of naturalization, not that they admire Canada's form of government or take any interest in political events, but merely because of the extra protection which naturalization affords or which they imagine it affords. They are of a wandering nature, and many of them have lived on both sides of the international boundary. It is not uncommon to meet people of these classes who carry with them when travelling naturalization papers from both Canada and the United States. They find them of value in passing from one country to the other. There were 1,571 Turks and Syrians in Canada in 1901, and of these 481 were naturalized. Since that date there have arrived 2,456 Turks, 5,229 Syrians and 1,473 Armenians. Pedlars are no great acquisition to any country, and there are few people in the Dominion who would care to see the day arrive when people of these races might be pointed out as fair samples of Canadian citizens.

Greeks, Macedonians and Bulgarians

The Greeks, Macedonians and Bulgarians are all dwellers in cities when that is possible. If city work is not available they take railway construction work, and, as they can live on very little, they are able to save a large part of their earnings. The Greek is rapidly branching out into two new callings, shoe-polishing and confectionery. Amongst the Macedonians and Bulgarians the highest ambition seems to be to keep small stores where they sell the necessaries of life, even if in a small way, as it gives them a better opportunity to prey upon their countrymen.

The modern Greek, Macedonian and Bulgarian have far from a high sense of truthfulness. The writer has seen squads of forty or fifty examined at the ocean port. Each one gave an address to which he was proceeding, and gravely informed the inspector that the person he was going to join was his brother. Each one gave the same address. When asked if he had any relatives accompanying him, each stated that he had none. When confronted with the statements of others of the party these dissemblers would then change their story and claim to be cousins, brothers-in-law, or to have any other convenient relationship to the one already in the country. A recent case occurred in which a Macedonian naturalized in Canada sent his naturalization papers to a friend in the United States who desired to come to the Dominion. This person, when stopped by an immigration official, demanded entry as a Canadian citizen. The fraud was discovered, the would-be immigrant was fined and deported, and the Macedonian Canadian citizen was fined $250 for aiding and abetting the entry of an undesirable.

Practically all these three classes in the Dominion have arrived since the beginning of the present century, the Greek and Macedonian immigration numbering 3,997 in the first decade and the Bulgarian 4,484 in the same time. Since the 1910 Immigration Act came into force the rejections amongst these classes have been very heavy. None are now admitted if they can be legally kept out.

The Chinese

Chinese immigration has undergone many changes. It was openly encouraged in the early eighties when Chinese labourers were needed in the construction of the Canadian Pacific Railway. In 1886 an agitation carried on by trade unions resulted in the imposing of a head tax of $50 on this class of immigrants. In 1901 this was increased to $100 and in 1904 to $500. In 1901 there were 17,043 persons in Canada who had been born in China. The number of those of Chinese origin was probably somewhat larger. Between 1901 and 1912 upwards of 30,000 entered Canada. Very few of the Chinese arriving in Canada come on their own initiative. Their fares and head tax are paid by "tyees" or contractors, who hold them practically in bondage until they repay the expense entailed in bringing them to Canada, together with an exorbitant profit. They are industrious workers, very thrifty, live well according to their standards, and insist upon receiving the highest rate of remuneration which their services can secure.

The Chinese in Canada may be divided into four classes: merchants, dealing largely in teas, silks, opium and other oriental products; gardeners who devote their attention almost entirely to garden products, and who in British Columbia appear able to make large profits after paying a yearly rental of $25 an acre for their land; restaurant keepers and laundrymen; and, lastly, domestic servants. In the last-mentioned occupation they give excellent satisfaction to their employers, but as their wages have doubled since the imposition of the $500 head tax, it is their proud boast that it is the Canadians and not themselves who are mulcted. For this boast they apparently have good grounds.

Generally speaking the Chinamen are quiet, inoffensive, law-abiding people, if we leave out of account their tendency to gamble and to indulge in opium.

Many missions exist for their conversion to Christianity. It is true, however, that while large numbers profess conversion some will admit to their intimate friends that they have done so because, as they say, it is "good for blizness." When gambling they are not averse to deception, but in business transactions they are credited with having a strict sense of honour; many who know them best say that a Chinaman's word is as good as his bond.

The large increase in numbers arriving during 1910–11 is reported to have been caused by the circulation of a report in China that the Canadian government intend raising the head tax to $1,000. Although not popular, the Chinaman may be said to be now the least hated Oriental on the western coast. As the desire of the Chinese is to accumulate wealth to take back to their native land, and as assimilation is out of the question, they cannot be classed as desirable, but, unless the numbers arriving increase very largely, they cannot be said to constitute any great menace to Canada.

The Japanese

The Japanese are, from a Canadian standpoint, the most undesirable of the Orientals. Belonging to an emigrating race, filled with patriotism for their own country, and living within such easy reach of Canada's western coast, they might, if allowed to come, flood the Province of British Columbia and dominate not only the labour market, but, through the investment of capital, the principal industries as well. That they are industrious and capable is admitted by all acquainted with them. They would, however, never become Canadians, and their arrival in large numbers is, therefore, a contingency which should be carefully guarded against. Unlike the other Orientals, they are not content to remain "hewers of wood and drawers of water." Possibly this desire to figure in all walks of life is not unconnected with the dislike which the white races bear towards them. There were about 4,700 Japanese in Canada in 1901. Between 1901 and 1912 about 15,000 entered the Dominion, the heaviest immigration being in 1907–8, when 7,601 arrived. There was a great falling off in the numbers (495) arriving in 1908–9 as compared with 1907–8; this was the result of an arrangement between Canada and Japan, whereby the Japanese coolies arriving in any one year were to be restricted to a certain number. Japan has kept well within the number arranged for. So long as this arrangement remains in force Japanese immigration need cause no anxiety to Canada.

The Hindus

Of the different immigration problems which from time to time have faced the

Dominion, that of the influx of Hindus appeared for a time to be possibly the most serious. This movement commenced in 1905. The arrivals up to the close of the fiscal year 1911–12 were 5,203. British Columbia, the nearest province to the Orient and the one possessing the climate most closely resembling that of their native land, was the ultimate destination of these unwelcome comers, and British Columbia was not slow in expressing her disapproval of them. "A White Canada" was her cry. That these immigrants were British subjects; that many had fought for the Empire; that many expressed their willingness to do so again should occasion arise—all this in no way lessened the antipathy of the white race towards them.

True, there were some imperialists who, recognizing in the Hindus subjects of the same sovereign, argued that they were entitled to enter the Dominion as a matter of right, and that any action towards restricting their movements from one part of the British domains to another would endanger the existence of the Empire. But the counsels of the advocates of "A White Canada" finally prevailed, and an order-in-council was passed providing that persons of Asiatic origin, other than Chinese and Japanese, must have in their possession $200 at the time of landing in Canada. This came into force in 1908, and the numbers arriving immediately dropped from 2,623 in that year to almost nothing.

The Hindus who came to Canada were largely from the Punjab and, physically, were a fine set of men. The term Hindu as here applied is a misnomer, denoting as it does a religious sect rather than a race of people. In religion they were divided, some being Hindus, others Buddhists and others Mohammedans. It is doubtful whether with their constitutions, suitable for the country and climate from which they came, they will ever become thoroughly acclimatized in Canada. Pneumonia and pulmonary troubles have already resulted in the death of no small number. Their bodies were disposed of by cremation, the burial method of their own country; possibly this is the only one of their customs which might with advantage be adopted.

Saw-mills and railway construction work afforded employment to the Hindus. While they were able at most times to secure employment, it was at a lower rate than that paid to white men or even to Japanese or Chinese. They were unaccustomed to Canadian methods, and though able to speak a little English were slow to learn more. Their greatest disadvantage, however, is their caste system, which prevents them from eating and sometimes even from working with white men, or even with others of their own race who belong to a different social scale—for this is practically the meaning of caste. Now that the influx is checked the Hindu problem is ended ...

The Jews
Scattered over the face of the earth, a people but not a nation, the Jews seek the land where they may hope to reap a harvest from their labours. Canada, in common with the United States, has proved a loadstone to draw these wanderers from the ends of the earth ...

Efforts at colonization on the land have been made. Two of the most important were at Wapella and Hirsch. Neither has proved a conspicuous success. More recently the Jews have attempted the cultivation of the finer grades of tobacco in the Province of Quebec, and although their efforts are apparently meeting with success it is as yet too soon to predict the final result. They cannot be classed as agriculturalists, and the number who have engaged in this occupation is small compared with those engaged in trade and barter or who take up manufacturing.

The Jews are pre-eminently dwellers in cities. The clothing trade in its various branches provides employment for many; other occupations that attract them are cigar and cigarette making, shoe-repairing, fruit-dealing and vegetable-dealing, and rag and other varieties of peddling.

The increase in the Hebrew population has been very rapid in Canada, rising from 667 in 1881 to 16,131 in 1901; since then the immigration of this race has amounted to over 50,000. According to the census of 1901, of the 16,131 Jews then resident in Canada 13,470 lived in twelve cities. In Montreal, Toronto and Winnipeg the conditions under which some, especially the Russian Jews, live are far from satisfactory, either as respects air-space, ventilation or cleanliness. Sweat-shops have not yet reached in Canada the deplorable condition found in the United States, but the tendency is in that direction, and the Jews are one of the strongest factors in bringing this about. No effort is or ever has been made by the government of Canada to induce Jewish immigrants to come to the Dominion, and the influx has been entirely unsolicited. In their movements to America they are aided largely by their philanthropic societies. These also do useful work amongst their own people by looking after those unable to support themselves ...

THE IMMIGRATION POLICY OF CANADA
The immigration policy of the government of Canada at the present time is, and for many years past has been, to encourage the immigration of farmers, farm labourers and domestic servants from countries which are classed as desirable. The list of countries had undergone change from time to time, and at the present includes the United States, the British Isles, France, Belgium, Holland, Switzerland, Germany, Denmark, Norway, Sweden and Iceland.

On the other hand, it is the policy of the government to do all in its power to keep out of the country undesirables, who may be divided into three classes:

1. Those physically, mentally or morally unfit whose exclusion is provided for by the immigration act already quoted.

2. Those belonging to nationalities unlikely to assimilate and who, consequently, prevent the building up of a united nation of people of similar customs and ideals.

3. Those who from their mode of life and occupations are likely to crowd into urban centres and bring about a state of congestion which might result in unemployment and a lowering of the standard of Canadian national life.

While neither the Immigration Act nor the orders-in-council passed thereunder prohibit the landing in Canada of persons belonging to the second and third classes above mentioned, still their entry has been made difficult. Their coming is discouraged in a number of ways. Chinese are subject to a head tax of $500. The number of Japanese coolies has been limited by arrangements between the two countries. Orders-in-council have been passed requiring (1) Asiatic arrivals to have $200 in cash at the time of landing; (2) the production of passports and penal certificates by persons coming from the countries which issue these; (3) the continuous journey of all immigrants from the country of their birth or citizenship on tickets purchased in that country or purchased or prepaid in Canada. All these regulations put obstacles in the way of immigrants from Asia and Southern and Eastern Europe, and, consequently, the numbers coming or likely to come from those countries are correspondingly diminished.

Briefly, this is the immigration policy of the government. In so far as the administration of the restrictive part of the policy is concerned the Immigration department has at all times endeavoured to be both just and humane, bearing in mind, however, that its duty is to Canada and to Canada only, and that while every applicant for admission who is likely to be an acquisition to the country shall be admitted if the law will permit it, on the other hand, every person who is likely to be a detriment to the country must be rejected if the law will allow it.

It may be here stated that until 1903 immigrants, upon arrival in Canada, underwent no medical examination which might result in their rejection through physical or mental unfitness. In 1903, however, a medical examination was commenced, and from that year rejections at the ocean ports have been frequent, both upon medical and civil grounds. The rejections at border points between Canada and the United States commenced in 1908-9. During the fiscal years 1902-12 8,500 rejections were recorded at ocean ports and 51,015 at border stations on the United States boundary. Even with the care exercised in the rejection of undesirables when they apply for admission, a certain percentage enter Canada who prove failures and who are deported. During the years 1902-12 5,626 such deportations were made ...

THE PROBLEM OF FUTURE IMMIGRATION

At the present time there is no large number of persons in Canada whose presence is a menace to the country from a political, moral or economic point of view. The reason for the absence of such a problem is that representatives of undesirable nationalities have as yet come in small number only. Who would care to see Alberta a second Mississippi or Georgia, as far as population is concerned? Who would wish to see the day arrive when British Columbia could be termed the "Second Flowery Kingdom," as might easily happen if the doors were thrown open to the Japanese? Who would not regret to see the ghettos and slums of New York, with her hived population and her reeking sweat-shops, duplicated in Montreal, Toronto and Winnipeg? These are the questions which today confront Canadians, and this is the problem of the future. More important than the drilling of armies, more important than the construction of navies, more important even than the fiscal policy of the country is the question of who shall come to Canada and become part and parcel of the Canadian people.

Fifty years ago the United States was receiving practically the class which is to-day coming to Canada. With the disappearance of free lands the character of the immigration to the United States has changed, and now Southern and Eastern Europe are furnishing most of her new settlers, and a large percentage of her immigrants remain in the cities. The people of the republic are now awake to the danger which this involves, and anti-immigration leagues and similar organizations are being formed to bring the question prominently before the public. Canada, with this object-lesson before her, has no excuse if she allows the same evils to grow. Much has already been done to prevent this. One suggestion for further checks is the introduction of educational tests. It is, for instance, suggested that no one over ten years of age shall be admitted who is unable to speak, read and write either English, Welsh, Gaelic, French, German, Dutch, Danish, Norwegian, Swedish or Icelandic. This would practically confine immigration to the countries where immigration work is now carried on ...

In checking undesirable immigration it must be decided what constitutes an undesirable, and the following definition is put forward for consideration: undesirable immigrants are those who will not assimilate with the Canadian people, or whose presence will tend to bring about a deterioration from a political, moral, social or economic point of view.

6. Maria Adamowska, "Beginnings in Canada."

... Finally, we sailed into port Halifax. On the shore, a crowd of people stared at us, some out of curiosity, some out of contempt. Our men, particularly those from Galicia, were dressed like gentlemen for the voyage, but the women and children traveled in their everyday peasant costumes. The older men from Bukovina attracted attention to themselves by their waist-length hair—greased with reeking lard—and by their smelly sheepskin coats. Perhaps that was the reason why the English people stopped their noses and glued their eyes upon us —a strange spectacle, indeed.

In Halifax, we boarded a train and continued on our journey. As we sped across Ontario with its rocks, hills, and tunnels, we were afraid we were coming to the end of the world. The heart of many a man sank to his heels, and the women and children raised such lamentation as defies description.

At last we arrived in Winnipeg. At that time, Winnipeg was very much like any other small farmers' town. From the train we were taken to the immigration home ...

One must remember that times were different then. Nowadays when an immigrant arrives in Canada, he feels more or less at home. Here he can find his own people everywhere and hear his own language. But in those days you had to wander far and wide before you could meet one of your countrymen. No matter what direction you turned, all you could see was the prairie like a vast sea on which wild animals howled and red-skinned Indians roamed. It was not until after our arrival that the mass immigration of Ukrainians to Canada began ...

From Winnipeg, we went to Yorkton, Saskatchewan. There we hired a rig which took us more than thirty miles farther north. At long last, after a miserable trip—we were nearly devoured alive by mosquitoes—we managed to reach our destination, the home of our acquaintances.

Our host, who had emigrated to Canada a year or two before, had written us to boast of the prosperity he had attained in such a short time. He said that he had a home like a mansion, a large cultivated field, and that his wife was dressed like a lady. In short, he depicted Canada as a country of incredible abundance whose borders were braided with sausage like some fantastic land in a fairy tale.

How great was our disenchantment when we approached that mansion of his and an entirely different scene met our eyes! It was actually just a small log cabin, only partly plastered and roofed with sod. Beside the cabin was a garden plot which had been dug with a spade. The man's face was smeared with dirt from ear to ear, and he looked weird, like some unearthly creature. He was grubbing up stumps near the house, and his wife was poking away in the garden. She reminded us of Robinson Crusoe on an uninhabited island. She was suntanned like a gypsy and was dressed in old, torn overalls. A wide-brimmed hat covered her head.

When mother saw this scarecrow, she started crying again. Later on, father reprimanded the man for writing us such nonsense. But his only answer was, "Let someone else have a taste of our good life here." ...

Our troubles and worries were only just beginning. The house was small, and there were eighteen of us jammed within its four walls. What was one to do?

My father had brought some money with him, and with it he bought a cow and, later, a horse. Needless to say, I was the cow-herd ...

Winter was setting in. Dreading the idea of having to spend the season in such cramped quarters, my father dug a cave in a riverbank, covered it with turf, and there was our apartment, all ready to move into. Oh, how fortunate we felt! We would not have traded that root cellar for a royal palace. To this spot, we carried hay in bed sheets on our backs and stacked it. We also dragged firewood on our backs and made other preparations.

Day by day, our provisions ran lower and lower. The older folk were able to put up with hunger, but the famished children howled pitifully, like wolves.

One day I sneaked into our hostess' garden and pulled a turnip. Then I slipped out of the patch and ran as fast as I could into a gorge where I planned to hide myself in the tall grass and enjoy a real treat. Unfortunately, our hostess spied me, grabbed a club, and chased after me with the speed of a demon. To escape, I hid in some tall grass, but this heartless woman searched until she found me. There she stood over me and, as she raised her club, hissed, "You detestable intruder! One blow with this, and you'll be dead like a dog."

Fear of death made me forget about the turnip. It did not matter now how hungry I was: life was still sweet. And the woman was so ferocious that one blow of that club would certainly have meant the end of my life.

With tears in my eyes I began to plead, "Auntie darling, forgive me. I'll never again set my foot in your garden as long as I live."

Spitting at me with disgust the woman said, "Remember! Write that down on your forehead."

And so, for a piddling turnip, I almost paid with my life.

Came winter. Our cow stopped giving milk. Aside from bread, there was nothing to eat at home. Was one to gnaw the walls? One time I happened to notice tears rolling down mother's cheeks as she sipped something from a small pot. We children began to weep with her. "Mother, why are you crying? Won't you let us taste what you're eating?"

Mother divided the gruel among us. She tried to say something, but all she could manage was "My chil—"; further words died on her lips. Only a moan of anguish escaped from her breast. We learned afterwards that, late in the fall, mother had visited the garden of our former host and painstakingly raked the ground for potatoes that had been too small to be worth picking at potato-digging time. She had found a few tiny ones, no larger than hazel nuts. From these potatoes, she had made a gruel that tasted like potato soup, and it was this gruel which we children shared, tears flooding our eyes. Who knows how we would have managed if father had not brought his gun from the old country. With it he went hunting, and we had game all winter.

Before spring arrived, father went to look for a farm. He found one some fifteen miles to the west of us, and we began to build a house. We dug a round pit in the ground about five yards in diameter, just deep enough to scrape the black earth off the top and reach clay underneath. We mixed hay and water with the clay and kneaded it with our bare feet. With this clay, we plastered our house. In the spring, we moved into it. By that time, all our provisions had run out.

And so it was that father left home one day, on foot, prepared to tramp hundreds of miles to find a job. He left us without a piece of bread, to the mercy of fate.

While father was away, mother dug a plot of ground and planted the wheat she had brought from the old country, tied up in a small bundle. Every day, she watered it with her tears.

That done, there was no time to waste; every moment was precious. Mother and I began to clear our land. But since I was hardly strong enough for the job, I helped by grabbing hold of the top of each bush and pulling on it while mother cut the roots with the ax. Next we dug the ground with spades. How well did I do? At best, I had barely enough strength to thrust half the depth of the blade into the ground, no deeper. But that did not excuse me from digging. Where the ground was hard, mother had to correct my work, and thus the two of us cleared and dug close to four acres of land.

We lived on milk. One meal would consist of sweet milk followed by sour milk; the next meal would consist of sour milk followed by sweet milk. We looked like living corpses.

In the beginning of our life in Canada, old and young alike had to work grievously hard, often in the cold and in hunger. The effects of this hard work can now be painfully felt in even the tiniest bones of our bodies …

Our Rumanian neighbor, who lived a mile from our place, had made himself a small handmill for grinding wheat into flour. In the fall, when our wheat was ripe, mother reaped it very thoroughly, every last head of it, rubbed the kernels out, winnowed the grain, and poured it into a sack. Then she sent me with this grain—about eight pounds of it—to have it ground at our neighbor's mill.

It was the first time I had ever been to his place. As soon as I entered the vestibule of the house, I could see the hand mill in the corner. Now a new problem faced me: I had not the faintest idea how to operate the mill, and there was no one around to show me. I sat down and began to cry. After a while, the neighbor's wife showed up and spoke to me, but I could not understand her so I just kept on crying. I had the feeling that she was scolding me for sneaking into her house. I pointed to the bag of wheat. She understood what I wanted, pointed to the hand mill, and went inside the house, leaving the door open. She sat down at the table, picked up a piece of bread which was as dark as the ground we walked on, dipped it in salt, and munched away at it.

As I watched her, I almost choked with grief. Oh, how strong was my urge to throw myself at her feet and plead for at least one bite of that bread. But, as she obviously was not thinking of me, I got ahold of myself. That piece of bread might well have been the last she had in the house. That experience gave me the most profound shock of my entire life. No one can fully appreciate what I went through unless he has lived through something similar himself.

Continually swallowing my saliva, I kept grinding the wheat until I had finished. Then I ran home with that little bit of flour, joyfully looking forward to the moment when we, too, would have bread.

But my joy quickly evaporated. Mother pondered a moment and said, "This will make two or three loaves of bread, and the flour will be all gone. Not enough to eat and not enough to feast our eyes upon. I'm going to cook cornmeal for you; it will last longer." And so we teased ourselves with cornmeal for some time.

On his way home from the other side of Brandon, where he'd been working, father stopped at Yorkton and bought a fifty-pound sack of flour. He carried it home on his back every inch of the twenty-eight miles. When we saw him coming home, we bounced with excitement and greeted him with joyous laughter mixed with tears. And all this excitement over the prospect of a piece of bread! Father had not earned much money, for he had lost a lot of time job-hunting. Then, at work, he had fallen from a stack onto the tines of a pitchfork and been laid up for a long time. But he had managed to earn something like twenty dollars, enough for flour to last us for a time.

The coming of winter presented new problems. We had nothing to wear on our feet. Something had to be done about that. Mother had brought a couple of woolen sheets from the old country. From these she sewed us footwear that kept our feet warm all winter.

That winter our horse died. We were now left with only one horse and he was just a year-old colt, though he looked like a two-year old. Father made a harness from some ropes, and a sled, and began to break him in.

… Even in winter we had no rest. We had settled in a low-lying area. In the summertime, water lay everywhere, and the croaking of frogs filled the air. And it never rained but poured in those days. Often the downpour continued for two or three weeks without a letup. In the winter, the water in the lakes froze up, the wells—always few in number—dried up, and there was nothing one could do about it. We were concerned not so much about ourselves as about our few head of livestock, which would have no water. We could not let them die; a way had to be found to obtain water for them.

Father found a piece of tin somewhere, shaped it into a trough, built an enclosure out of stones, placed the trough over it, built a fire in the enclosure under the trough, kept the trough filled with snow, and, as the snow melted, collected the water in a tub at the bottom end of the trough. But this was not the best way to water cattle. A cow could drink up a couple of tubs of water at a time and then look around and moo for more.

As a result, we messed around with snow all winter long, until at times the marrow in our bones was chilled. And talk about snow in those days! Mountains of it! Your cattle might be lowing pitifully in the stable, and you could not get to them because heaps of snow blocked your way. It might take a hard morning's work before a tunnel could be dug to the stable, and the cattle fed …

Ours was a life of hard work, misery, and destitution. Things got a little better only after we acquired a yoke of oxen to work with. But when we first got them, we experienced some unhappy and frustrating moments …

With each day of labor, our poor settlers could see some progress. They now lived in hastily built houses, as everyone was sick and tired of living in damp, smelly root cellars. Although these houses lacked in comfort, there was at least fresh air in them. By now, each settler had dug up a piece of land and owned a few head of cattle and other livestock …

In the spring, father was able to get some seed wheat. When he finished seeding our tiny, little field, he left home to look for a job again. At home, the family buckled down to clearing, digging, and haying. Mother mowed the hay with a scythe, and we children raked it, carried it home on our backs, and stacked it. We also brought a supply of wood for the winter.

In the meantime, the people from the old country had arrived. This added a touch of brightness to our social life. The newcomers, Mrs. D.F. Stratychuk and Mrs. P. Denys, even helped us to harvest our crop …

That autumn father's earnings were a little more substantial. He was able to buy another cow and another steer. And he bought me a pair of shoes and material for a skirt. Those shoes meant more to me than any ordinary ones …

As for their durability, suffice it to say that when one of us girls got married, she handed the shoes down to the younger sister, and the process was repeated until four of us had worn them, each for a few years. And who knows how many more generations those shoes would have survived if it had not been for mother. She got so disgusted with them that she threw them into the stove one day and burned them.

As for my skirt, it was made of the finest quality "silk," the kind used for making overalls. So one can imagine how I looked in that gorgeous costume. But, poor me, I was quite happy with it.

In the wintertime, father used to ask some of his neighbors to give him a hand in threshing his wheat with flails. Once the threshing was done, he had other work to do, such as making a yoke for the oxen and repairing the harrow and the plow, so that everything would be ready for spring work …

In our neighborhood, there were settlers of other nationalities, mainly Rumanian. One of them put on a wedding for his daughter and invited us to attend. We accepted first because there had not been such an event in the few years that we had been in Canada, and second, out of simple curiosity to see a Rumanian ceremony …

The town of Canora was founded five miles from our place. Our people were quite happy about that, and they were happy when its first store was opened by a Jewish merchant. For one thing, we were fed up with traveling all that distance to Yorkton to do our shopping. Secondly, with a Jew we could always speak in our own language, for at that time how many of us immigrants could speak English? When we did try, it was only by means of sign language …

Year by year the cultivated area of our farm grew in size. And when the field got too large to be harvested with sickles, father had to buy a binder. For the first couple of years we used it, we hitched our oxen to it. That was a miserable experience. Cutting grain of medium height posed no problem, but if it was heavy or lying flat and you had to give the binder a little more speed, you could not make the oxen move faster even by lighting a fire under them. They kept to the same slow pace no matter what. The only way to cope with this problem was to buy another horse. A team of horses made harvesting so much easier.

During the long winter evenings, I taught younger children to read in Ukrainian. Among my students were a girl [of] non-Ukrainian descent and an elderly gentleman. There were no schools anywhere around in those days. Children grew up like barbarians …

We had quite a few books at home. Father had brought a lot of them from the old country, all on serious subjects. Later on, when Ukrainian newspapers began to be published, none of them escaped father's attention. Even if he had to go without food and live on water for a whole week, he found the money for newspaper subscriptions. Since there were several literate people in our community, they used to get together at our home on the long winter evenings, to read the papers and discuss their contents. Many a sunrise found these men, though weary from the previous day's hard toil, going without a wink of sleep to forge a happier lot for themselves and their children.

Those sleepless nights were not spent in vain. In 1904-05, thanks to the efforts of our pioneer fathers, a small but beautiful school was built. Its first teacher was the scholarly and patriotic Ukrainian, the late Joseph Bychynsky …

As for churches or Ukrainian priests, you could not have found one if you'd searched the country with a fine-tooth comb. Occasionally a priest would stray our way, but he was what we called an "Indian priest," and we could not understand him, nor he us. Our poor settlers consulted among themselves and decided to meet every Sunday and sing at least those parts of the liturgy that were meant to be sung by the cantor. Since our house was large enough, that was where the meetings were held. On Sunday morning, everyone hurried to our house the way one would to church …

In due course, the Bukovinians built themselves a church in which services were at first conducted by a visiting Russian priest. Often we were invited to attend but we could not understand their service, which was in Rumanian …

That year Easter came very early. It was the Saturday before Easter, but only here and there was the snow beginning to melt. The day before, a severe blizzard had piled up banks of snow and drifted over all the roads. But there was no power on earth which could have stopped us from carrying out our plans …

Whatever the course of later events, it must be recognized that, in the beginning, the pioneer priests contributed a great deal to the cultural development of our people here, in what was then a foreign land to them. And for their efforts and troubles, they sought no favors from anyone. They suffered the same woes and miseries as did everyone else. In short, they proved themselves to be true sons of the Ukrainian people …

In those days, no one dreamed of such luxuries as paint or lime. For whitewashing jobs, people used a kind of ash-gray clay found under the surface of the ground cover in swampy areas. They dug this clay, pressed it into flat cakes, and dried it. Dissolved in water, it was used for whitewashing.

Bitter and unenviable were our beginnings, but by hard work and with God's help, we gradually got established. Not very far from our place a few neighbors pooled their resources and bought a steam threshing outfit in partnership. Father decided it was time, we, too, had our threshing done by a threshing machine …

In 1908, father traded farms with an Englishman, and our family moved thirty miles farther north, to the Hyas district …

By moving to Hyas, we had to start all over again and suffer the same hardships as in the beginning. But hope of better times lifted our spirits and gave us courage and strength to face future labors.

Such were the tremendous hardships our people had to endure in the early days of immigration. Since there were as yet no railways, they were compelled to travel hundreds of miles on foot. Toiling in cold and hunger, they cleared the forests, [cleaned] the land of rocks, and converted the inaccessible areas into fertile fields. Many of the pioneers who came here in the prime of their lives are no longer with us. Those who are still with us are stooped with age; tomorrow it will be their turn to leave us for their eternal rest …

Readings

Anderson, K. *Vancouver's Chinatown: Racial Discourses in Canada, 1875–1980.* Montreal-Kingston: Queen's University Press, 1991.

Avery, D. *Dangerous Foreigners: European Immigrant Workers and Labour Radicalism in Canada.* Toronto: McClelland and Stewart, 1979.

Avery, D. *Reluctant Hosts: Canada's Response to Immigrant Workers, 1896–1994.* Toronto: McClelland and Stewart, 1995.

Burnet, J., ed. *Looking into My Sisters' Eyes: An Exploration in Women's History.* Toronto: Multicultural History Society of Ontario, 1986.

Dunae, P. *Gentlemen Immigrants: From British Public Schools to the Canadian Frontier.* Vancouver: Douglas and McIntyre, 1981.

Hall, D. *Clifford Sifton.* Vancouver: University of British Columbia Press, 1985.

Jackel, S., ed. *A Flannel Shirt and Liberty: British Emigrant Gentlewomen in the Canadian West, 1880–1914.* Vancouver: University of British Columbia Press, 1982.

Johnston, H. *The Voyage of the Komagata Maru: The Sikh Challenge to Canada's Colour Bar.* Delhi: Oxford University Press, 1979.

Lehr, J. "Kinship and Society in the Ukrainian Pioneer Settlement of the Canadian West," *The Canadian Geographer* 29, 3 (1985).

Lindstrom-Best, V. *Defiant Sisters: A Social History of Finnish Immigrant Women in Canada.* Toronto: University of Toronto Press, 1988.

Luciuk L., and S. Hryniuk, eds. *Canada's Ukrainians: Negotiating an Identity.* Toronto: University of Toronto Press, 1991.

Lupul, M., ed. *A Heritage in Transition: Essays in the History of Ukrainians in Canada.* Toronto: McClelland and Stewart, 1982.

Martynowych, O. *Ukrainian Canadian: The Formative Years 1891–1924.* Edmonton: Canadian Institute of Ukrainian Studies, 1991.

Palmer, H. *Patterns of Prejudice: A History of Nativism in Alberta.* Toronto: McClelland and Stewart, 1982.

Palmer, H., ed. *Immigration and the Rise of Multiculturalism.* Toronto: Copp Clark, 1975.

Parr, J. *Labouring Children: British Immigrant Apprentices to Canada, 1869–1924.* Second edition. Toronto: University of Toronto Press, 1994.

Petryshyn, J. *Peasants in the Promised Land: Canada and the Ukrainians, 1891–1914.* Toronto: James Lorimer, 1985.

Potrobenko, H. *No Streets of Gold: A Social History of Ukrainians in Alberta.* Vancouver: New Star, 1977.

Ramirez, B. *On the Move: French-Canadian and Italian Migrants in the North Atlantic Economy, 1860–1914.* Toronto: MacClelland and Stewart, 1991.

Roberts, B. *Whence they Came: Deportation from Canada 1900–1935.* Ottawa: University of Ottawa Press, 1988.

Roberts, B. "'A Work of Empire': Canadian Reformers and British Female Immigration," in L. Kealey, ed. *A Not Unreasonable Claim: Women and Reform in Canada, 1880s–1920s.* Toronto: Women's Press, 1979.

Roy, P. *A White Man's Province: British Columbia Politicians and Chinese and Japanese Immigration, 1858–1914.* Vancouver: University of British Columbia Press, 1989.

Swyripa, F. *Wedded to the Cause: Ukrainian-Canadian Women and Ethnic Identity 1891–1991.* Toronto: University of Toronto Press, 1993.

Ward, P. *White Canada Forever: Popular Attitudes and Public Policy Towards Orientals in British Columbia.* Montreal-Kingston: Queen's University Press, 1978.

Chapter Six

"THE SMELL OF THE GOOD GREEN EARTH": RURAL VS. URBAN LIFE

1. E.B. Mitchell, *In Western Canada Before the War*, 1915.
2. Nellie McClung, *In Times Like These*, 1915.
3. Rupert Brooke, *Letters from America,* 1916.
4. Mary Joplin Clarke, "Report of the Standing Committee on Neighbourhood Work," *Canadian Conference of Charities and Correction,* September 23–5, 1917.
5. William Irvine, *Farmers in Politics*, 1920.
6. Maude Newcombe, "The Farm Woman's Lot," *Grain Growers' Guide*, April 15, 1925.
7. Mrs. R.C. Phillips, "A Farm Woman's Reply," *Grain Growers' Guide*, May 27, 1925.

Introduction

Aesop's fable "The Town Mouse and the Country Mouse" is a cautionary tale of the city's allure. So is Beatrix Potter's *The Tale of Johnny Townmouse*. In both, upstanding and wholesome country mice visit the city, a place they long dreamed of. They are made to feel like country bumpkins by their urbane rodent-cousins, and stay just long enough to realize that city living is not all it was supposed to be: that it was crass, superficial, degenerative, and very dangerous. The mice escape back to the hills and live happily ever after amid self-righteous bucolic splendour.

The early decades of the twentieth century was a time of significant soul searching among those in industrialized nations for whom urban life was both vital and the seductive fountainhead of all things evil. Canadians, too, grappled with the increasing tension between country and city, and failed to stem the tide. Already by the early 1920s more Canadians lived in urban centres than rural and many feared the complete demise of a better way of life. Agriculture also formed the recognized bedrock of a nation, without which it could not feed itself let alone continue its profitable international grain trade.

Why did country folk leave their "wholesome" farming life for the city?

There is no single explanation. Under MacDonald's "National Policy" farm equipment became more expensive because Canadian manufacturers no longer had to compete against their American counterparts who traditionally sold cheap implements into rural Canada. Coupled with the development of automated farm machinery that required far fewer workers, the end result was a consolidation of many small and marginal farms into fewer but more heavily capitalized and larger ones— with a commensurate drop in farm jobs. Pundits also offered more metaphysical reasons for the depopulation of the Canadian countryside. The root of the problem, so some said, lay in the softening of the steely Anglo-Saxon farmer's spine. He had lost his sense of morality, sense of co-operation, spirituality and Christian values to the siren call of the godless city. In its place, farmers supposedly accepted the urbanite's insatiable greed, competitiveness, and lack of social conscience. Was this all hyperbole?

And what of the city itself? Was life in its bosom as sweet as country people sometimes dreamed? The city, in reality, had plenty of problems among its ample attributes. Rapid industrialization and subsequent urbanization created all manner of social and physical ills: everything from dangerously high levels of pollution, to crime, squalor, homelessness, and what would today be called urban alienation. The middle and upper class could indeed enjoy the considerable amenities on offer with fewer of its drawbacks. Moneyed citizens had everything from music, theatre, art, shopping, restaurants, leisure, space, to a myriad of other services at their fingertips. This group, however, constituted a very small minority. For the urban masses, city life generally proved tough. Owning your own home was all but impossible and rents for dingy apartments were high. Jobs, contrary to popular belief, were neither plentiful nor well paid, and the hours were extraordinarily long and tedious. Public amenities such as safe drinking water, sewers, cheap mass transit, health care, policing, and leisure remained stunted if available at all, and city politicians had a justified reputation for corruption.

The situation gave rise to a new breed of social activists who set out to save urban Canada by attempting to dovetail rural life with the metropolitan environment. Their effort clearly demonstrated the nature of the urban-rural debate around the turn of the century. Urban activists began from two premises: that rural life was morally superior to urban living; and that abandoning the city was out of the question because cities represented progress and progress was good. The problem, of course, was how to overcome this apparent contradiction. What if some urban dwellers had regular access to nature? Would that solve the city's ills by fusing the contradiction? Activists, taking their cues from Europe and the

United States, emulated the City Beautiful movement, which created urban parks where weary and angry factory workers could refresh their exhausted souls amid the wholesome influence of greenery, and fresh air. Whether they made much impact on the workers of the day, however, remains debatable. The Garden City movement took a slightly different tack, arguing that workers should spend their days in the urban industrial core, as usual, but should then head for new outskirts in the evening, to spend their leisure hours in their own homes, each with its own green space. This approach to urban malaise led, of course, to the creation of suburbia, urban mass transportation and its own set of problems.

Discussion Points

1. Which provided the best environment in early twentieth century Canada, the city or the country?
2. Why was there a tendency for country folk to feel defensive toward their city brethren, and why was the reverse not true?
3. Were farmers actually more conservative, religious, community minded and family oriented than urban residents?
4. How reasonable were the solutions to the various social problems put forward in the documents?

Documents

1. E.B. Mitchell, *In Western Canada Before the War*, 1915.

Farming was not, as a fact, generally popular, and many who had tried it spoke of it with a certain horror. People who came West deliberately intending to farm, some of them good hardy country-men, had given up their land or left it. Various causes were stated, besides the mere attractiveness of town life, principally the loneliness of the prairie and the impossibility of making farming pay.

The loneliness of many parts is extreme. The farms are large, a quarter square mile at the least. In three districts I knew, blocks of empty "Company land" were constantly intervening, breaking up the settled country and harbouring gophers. These are lands granted tax-free to the Canadian Pacific Railway Company, as part of the bargain under which the line was built, and they have been held, for surrounding settlement to make them more valuable. The C.P.R. created Western Canada a generation ago, but now these empty lands are a perpetual irritant. Much of the rest of the land, for one reason or another, is not taken up, and in some districts much that is taken up is in the hands of foreigners. Roman Catholic settlers are influenced by their priests to settle together, but the true Anglo-Saxon of other communions shows his independence by wandering where he will. Thus an English-speaking family may be surrounded by Scandinavians or Galicians or Indian half-breeds, and there may be no neighbours at all, or no woman neighbours. I stayed with an Englishwoman on the borders of an Indian reserve in a most picturesque desolation, and I think she said the nearest Englishwoman was seven miles off; certainly the seven miles' trail by which we left their farm was bare of habitations. Far worse cases could be found; in this case there was a large family to keep things going. But I had an old-timer friend, a sort of mother to all her district, and at dishwashing time in the kitchen she told me stories of the prairie. It seemed as if her acquaintance might be divided into three sets—the "lovely" people, the "nice young fellows that don't know the first thing about farming," and the men and women who went mad. The prairie madness is perfectly recognized and very common still; the "bachelors" suffer most, and the women. For even if neighbours are not so impossibly far off, yet the homesteader has to work hard all day, and is in no great mood for exerting himself in the evening to walk to a neighbour's; if he is poor and has only oxen, their slowness is unendurable for a pleasure trip—they make about two miles an hour, ... A woman alone in the house all day may find the silence deadly; in the wheat-farming stage there may not even be a beast about the place. Her husband may be tired at night, and unwilling to "hitch up" and drive her out "for a whimsy"; or the husband may be willing and sympathetic, but she may grow shy and diffident, and not care to make the effort to tidy herself up and go to see a neighbour—any neighbour, just to break the monotony. Then fancies come, and suspicions, and queer ways, and at last the young Mounted Policeman comes to the door, and carries her away to the terrible vast "Sanatorium" that hangs above the Saskatchewan. There is still that kind of loneliness on the prairie. Also, with the country only half filled up, no neighbourhood is populous. Twenty houses, perhaps, or thirty, within reach for social purposes, make a good neighbourhood. Not all can bear such lack of variety; and cut-worms and your neighbours' ways lose their freshness at times as subjects of conversation.

Mixed farming is not so lonely or monotonous, because the pig falls mysteriously ill and has to be nursed, or a calf is born in a great frost, and has to be coaxed into life beside the kitchen stove, or a horse strays from the pasture over hill and dale, or the poultry get up a vast excitement because they see a white pigeon and think it is a new kind of hawk; but on the other hand the grind is worse. Day in day out, in fair or foul weather, in health or sickness, the cows *must* be driven from pasture and milked, the team-horses watered and fed, the poultry fed and shut up, the eggs gathered. No holiday or change is possible. It is the singlehandedness of the average prairie farm and the distance from neighbours that makes it all so difficult.

2. Nellie McClung, *In Times Like These*, 1915.

There is no class of people who have suffered so much from wrong thinking as the farmer; vicarious wrong thinking, I mean; other people have done the wrong thinking, and the farmer has suffered. Like many another bromide, the thought has grown on people that farmers are slow, uncouth, guileless, easily imposed on, ready to sign a promissory note for any smooth-tongued stranger who comes in for dinner. The stage and the colored supplements have spread this impression of the farmer, and the farmer has not cared. He felt he could stand it! Perhaps the women on the farm feel it more than the men, for women are more sensitive about such things, 'Poor girl!' say the kind friends. 'She went West and married a farmer'—and forthwith a picture of the farmer's wife rises up before their eyes; the poor, faded woman, in a rusty black luster skirt sagging in the back and puckering in the seams; coat that belonged to a suit in other days; a black sailor hat, gray with years and dust, with a sad cluster of faded violets, and torn tulle trimming, sitting crooked on her head; hair the color of last year's grass, and teeth gone in front.

There is no reason for the belief that farmers' wives as a class look and dress like this, only that people love to generalize; to fit cases to their theory, they love to find ministers' sons wild; mothers-in-law disagreeable; women who believe in suffrage neglecting their children, and farmers' wives shabby, discouraged and sad.

I do not believe that farmers' wives are a down-trodden class of women. They have their troubles like other people. It rains in threshing time, and the threshers' visit is prolonged until long after their welcome has been worn to a frazzle! Father won't dress up even when company is coming. Father also has a mania for buying land instead of building a new house; and sometimes works the driving horse. Cows break out of pastures; hawks get the chickens; hens lay away; clothes-lines break.

They have their troubles, but there are compensations. Their houses may be small, but there is plenty of room outside; they may not have much spending money, but the rent is always paid; they are saved from the many disagreeable things that are incident to city life, and they have great opportunity for developing their resources.

When the city woman wants a shelf put up she 'phones to the City Relief, and gets a man to do it for her; the farmer's wife hunts up the hammer and a soap box and puts up her own shelf, and gains the independence of character which only comes from achievement. Similarly the children of the country neighborhoods have had to make their own fun, which they do with great enthusiasm, for, under any circumstances, children will play. The city children pay for their amusement. They pay their nickel, and sit back, apparently saying: 'Now, amuse me if you can! What are you paid for?' The blasé city child who comes sighing out of picture shows is a sad sight. They know everything, and their little souls are a-weary of this world. It is a cold day for any child who has nothing left to wonder at ...

Not long ago I made some investigations as to why boys and girls leave the farm, and I found in over half the cases the reason given was that life on the farm was too slow, too lonely, and no fun.' In country neighborhoods family life means more than it does in the city. The members of a family are at each other's mercy; and so, if the 'father' always has a grouch, and the 'mother' is worried, and tired, and cross, small wonder that the children try to get away. In the city there is always the 'movie' to go to, and congenial companionship down the street, and so we mourn the depopulation of our rural neighborhoods.

We all know that the country is the best place in which to bring up children; that the freckle-faced boy, with bare feet, who hunts up the cows after school, and has to keep the woodbox full, and has to remember to shut the henhouse door, is getting a far better education than the carefree city boy who has everything done for him.

It is a good thing that boys leave the farm and go to the city—I mean it is a good thing for the city—but it is hard on the farm. Of late years this question has become very serious and has caused alarm. Settlements which, ten or fifteen years ago, had many young people and a well-filled school and well-attended church, with the real owners living on the farms, have now become depopulated by farmers retiring to a nearby town and 'renters' taking the place ...

Why any rational human being wants to 'retire' to the city, goes beyond me! I can understand the city man, worn with the noise, choked by the dust, frazzled with cares, retiring to the country, where he can heal his tired soul, pottering around his own garden, and watching green things grow. That seems reasonable and logical! But for a man who has known the delight of planting and reaping to retire to a city or a small town, and 'hang around,' doing nothing, is surely a retrograde step ...

It is very desirable for the world that people should be born and brought up in the country with its honest, wholesome ways learned in the open; its habits of meditation, which have grown on the people as they have gone about their work in the quiet places. Thought currents in the country are strong and virile, and flow freely. There is an honesty of purpose in the man who strikes out the long furrow, and turns over every inch of the sod, painstakingly and without pretense; for he knows that he cannot cheat nature; he will get back what he puts in; he will reap what he sows—for Nature has no favorites, and no short-cuts, nor can she be deceived, fooled, cajoled or flattered.

We need the unaffected honesty and sterling qualities which the country teaches her children in the hard, but successful, school of experience, to offset the flashy supercilious lessons which the city teaches hers; for the city is a careless nurse and teacher, who thinks more of the cut of a coat than of the habit of mind; who feeds her children on colored candy and popcorn, despising the more wholesome porridge and milk; a slatternly nurse, who would rather buy perfume than soap; who allows her children to powder their necks instead of washing them; who decks them out in imitation lace collars, and cheap jewelry, with bows on their hair, but holes in their stockings; who dazzles their eyes with bright lights and commercial signs, and fills their ears with blatant music, until their eyes are too dull to see the pastel beauty of common things, and their ears are holden to the still small voices of God; who lures her children on with many glittering promises of ease and wealth, which she never intends to keep, and all the time whispers to them that this is life.

The good old country nurse is stern but kind, and gives her children hard lessons, which tax body and brain, but never fail to bring a great reward. She sends them on long journeys, facing the piercing winter winds, but rewards them when the journey is over with rosy cheeks and contented mind, and an appetite that is worth going miles to see; and although she makes her children work long hours, until their muscles ache, she gives them, for reward, sweet sleep and pleasant dreams; and sometimes there are the sweet surprises along life's highway; the sudden song of birds or burst of sunshine; the glory of the sunrise, and sunset, and the flash of bluebirds' wings across the road, and the smell of the good green earth ...

3. Rupert Brooke, *Letters from America*, 1916.

1 Quebec
... Is there any city in the world that stands so nobly as Quebec? The citadel crowns a headland, three hundred feet high, that juts boldly out into the St.

Lawrence. Up to it, up the side of the hill, clambers the city, houses and steeples and huts, piled one on the other. It has the individuality and the pride of a city where great things have happened, and over which many years have passed. Quebec is as refreshing and as definite after the other cities of this continent as an immortal among a crowd of stockbrokers. She has, indeed, the radiance and repose of an immortal; but she wears her immortality youthfully. When you get among the streets of Quebec, the mediaeval, precipitous, narrow, winding, and perplexed streets, you begin to realise her charm. She almost incurs the charge of quaintness (abhorrent quality!); but even quaintness becomes attractive in this country. You are in a foreign land, for the people have an alien tongue, short stature, the quick, decided, cinematographic quality of movement, and the inexplicable cheerfulness which mark a foreigner. You might almost be in Siena or some old German town, except that Quebec has her street-cars and grain-elevators to show that she is living.

2 Montreal

... The outcome of it all was a vague general impression that Montreal consists of banks and churches. The people of this city spend much of their time in laying up their riches in this world or the next. Indeed, the British part of Montreal is dominated by the Scotch (sic) race; there is a Scotch spirit sensible in the whole place. The rather narrow, rather gloomy streets, the solid, square, grey, aggressively prosperous buildings, the general greyness of the city, the air of dour prosperity. Even the Canadian habit of loading the streets with heavy telephone wires, supported by frequent black poles, seemed to increase the atmospheric resemblance to Glasgow.

But besides all this there is a kind of restraint in the air, due, perhaps, to a state of affairs which, more than any other, startles the ordinary ignorant English visitor. The average man in England has an idea of Canada as a young-eyed daughter State, composed of millions of wheat-growers and backwoodsmen of British race. It surprises him to learn that more than a quarter of the population is of French descent, that many of them cannot speak English, that they control a province, form the majority in the biggest city in Canada, and are a perpetual complication in the national politics. Even a stranger who knows this is startled at the complete separateness of the two races. Inter-marriage is very rare. They do not meet socially; only on business, and that not often. In the same city these two communities dwell side by side, with different traditions, different languages, different ideals, without sympathy or comprehension ...

Montreal and Eastern Canada suffer from that kind of ill-health which afflicts men who are cases of 'double personality'—debility and spiritual paralysis.

The 'progressive' British-Canadian man of commerce is comically desperate of peasants who *will not* understand that increase of imports and volume of trade and numbers of millionaires are the measures of a city's greatness; and to his eye the Roman Catholic Church, with her invaluable ally Ignorance, keeps up her incessant war against the general good of the community of which she is part. So things remain.

3 *Ottawa*

Ottawa came as a relief after Montreal. There is no such sense of strain and tightness in the atmosphere. The British, if not greatly in the majority, are in the ascendency; also, the city seems conscious of other than financial standards, and quietly, with dignity, aware of her own purpose. The Canadians, like the Americans, chose to have for their capital a city which did not lead in population or in wealth. This is particularly fortunate in Canada, an extremely individualistic country, whose inhabitants are only just beginning to be faintly conscious of their nationality. Here, at least, Canada is more than the Canadian. A man desiring to praise Ottawa would begin to do so without statistics of wealth and the growth of population; and this can be said of no other city in Canada except Quebec. Not that there are not immense lumber-mills and the rest in Ottawa. But the Government farm, and the Parliament buildings, are more important. Also, although the 'spoils' system obtains a good deal in this country, the nucleus of the Civil Service is much the same as in England; so there is an atmosphere of Civil Servants about Ottawa, an atmosphere of safeness and honour and massive buildings and well-shaded walks. After all, there is in the qualities of Civility and Service much beauty, of a kind which would adorn Canada ...

     The streets of Ottawa are very quiet, and shaded with trees. The houses are mostly of that cool, homely, wooden kind, with verandahs, on which, or on the steps, the whole family may sit in the evening and observe the passers-by. This is possible for both the rich and the poor, who live nearer each other in Ottawa than in most cities. In general there is an air of civilization, which extends even over the country round ...

     ... What Ottawa leaves in the mind is a certain graciousness—dim, for it expresses a barely materialised national spirit—and the sight of kindly English-looking faces, and the rather lovely sound of the soft Canadian accent in the streets.

4 *Toronto*

Toronto (pronounce *T'ranto*, please) is difficult to describe. It has an individuality, but an elusive one; yet not through any queerness or difficult shade of eccentricity; a subtly normal, an indefinably obvious personality. It is a healthy, cheerful city (by modern standards); a clean-shaven, pink-faced, respectably dressed, fairly energetic, unintellectual, passably sociable, well-to-do, public-school-and-'varsity sort of city. One knows in one's own life certain bright and pleasant figures; people who occupy the nearer middle distance, unobstrusive but not negligible; wardens of the marches between acquaintanceship and friend-ship. It is always nice to meet them, and in parting one looks back at them once. They are, healthily and simply, the most fitting product of a not perfect environ-ment; good-sorts; normal, but not too normal; distinctly themselves, but not distinguished. They support civilisation. You can trust them in anything, if your demand be for nothing extremely intelligent or absurdly altruistic. One of these could be exhibited in any gallery in the universe, 'Perfect Specimen; Upper Middle Classes; Twentieth Century'—and we should not be ashamed. They are not vexed by impossible dreams, nor outrageously materialists, nor perplexed by overmuch prosperity, nor spoilt by reverse. Souls for whom the wind is always nor'-nor'-west, and they sail nearer success than failure, and nearer wisdom than lunacy. Neither leaders nor slaves ...

Such is Toronto. A brisk city of getting on for half a million inhabitants, the largest British city in Canada (in spite of the cheery Italian faces that pop up at you out of excavations in the street), liberally endowed with millionaires, not lacking its due share of destitution, misery, and slums. It is no mushroom city of the West, it has its history; but at the same time it has grown immensely of recent years. It is situated on the shores of a lovely lake; but you never see that, because the railways have occupied the entire lake front. So if, at evening, you try to find your way to the edge of the water, you are checked by a region of smoke, sheds, trucks, wharves, store-houses, 'depôts,' railway-lines, signals, and locomotives and trains that wander on the tracks up and down and across streets, pushing their way through the pedestrians, and tolling, as they go, in the Ameri-can fashion, an immense melancholy bell, intent, apparently, on some private and incommunicable grief. Higher up are the business quarters, a few sky-scrap-ers in the American style without the modern American beauty, but one of which advertises itself as the highest in the British Empire; streets that seem less narrow than Montreal, but not unrespectably wide; "the buildings are generally substantial and often handsome." Beyond that the residential part, with quiet streets, gardens open to the road, shady verandahs, and homes, generally of wood, that are a deal more pleasant to see than the homes in a modern English town.

Toronto is the centre and heart of the Province of Ontario; and Ontario, with a third of the whole population of Canada, directs the country for the present, conditioned by the French on one hand and the West on the other. And in this land, that is as yet hardly at all conscious of itself as a nation, Toronto and Ontario do their best in leading and realizing national sentiment. A Toronto man, like most Canadians, dislikes an Englishman; but, unlike some Canadians, he detests an American. And he has some inkling of the conditions and responsibilities of the British Empire. The tradition is in him. His father fought to keep Canada British ...

Toronto, soul of Canada, is wealthy, busy, commercial, Scotch, absorbent of whisky; but she is duly aware of other things. She has a most modern and efficient interest in education; and here are gathered what faint, faint beginnings or premonitions of such things as Art Canada can boast ... Most of those few who have begun to paint the landscape of Canada centre there, and a handful of people who know about books. In these things, as in all, this city is properly and cheerfully to the front. It can scarcely be doubted that the first Repertory Theatre in Canada will be founded in Toronto, some thirty years hence, and will very daringly perform *Candida* and *The Silver Box*. Canada is a live country, live, but not, like the States, kicking. In these trifles of Art and 'culture,' indeed, she is much handicapped by the proximity of the States. For her poets and writers are apt to be drawn thither, for the better companionship there and the higher rates of pay.

But Toronto—Toronto is the subject. One must say something—*what* must one say about Toronto? What can one? What has anybody ever said? It is impossible to give it anything but commendation. It is not squalid like Birmingham, or cramped like Canton, or scattered like Edmonton, or sham like Berlin, or hellish like New York, or tiresome like Nice. It is all right. The only depressing thing is that it will always be what it is, only larger, and that no Canadian city can ever be anything better or different. If they are good they may become Toronto.

5 Winnipeg

Winnipeg is the West. It is important and obvious that in Canada there are two or three (some say five) distinct Canadas. Even if you lump the French and English together as one community in the East, there remains the gulf of the Great Lakes. The difference between East and West is possibly no greater than that between North and South England, or Bavaria and Prussia; but in this country, yet unconscious of itself, there is so much less to hold them together. The character of the land and the people differs; their interests, as it appears to them, are not the same. Winnipeg is a new city. In the archives at Ottawa is a picture of Winnipeg in 1870—Mainstreet, with a few shacks, and the prairie either end. Now her population is a hundred thousand, and she has the biggest this, that, and the other west of Toronto. A new city; a little more American than the other Canadian cities, but not unpleasantly so. The streets are wider, and full of a bustle which keeps clear of hustle. The people have something of the free swing of Americans, without the bumptiousness; a tempered democracy, a mitigated independence of bearing. The manners of Winnipeg, of the West, impress the stranger as better than those of the East, more friendly, more hearty, more certain to achieve graciousness, if not grace. There is, even, in the architecture of Winnipeg, a sort of *gauche* pride visible. It is hideous, of course, even more hideous than Toronto or Montreal; but cheerily and windily so. There is no scheme in the city, and no beauty, but it is at least preferable to Birmingham, less dingy, less directly depressing. It has no real slums, even though there is poverty and destitution.

But there seems to be a trifle more public spirit in the West than the East. Perhaps it is that in the greater eagerness and confidence of this newer country men have a superfluity of energy and interest, even after attending to their own affairs, to give to the community. Perhaps it is that the West is so young that one has a suspicion money-making has still some element of a child's game in it—its only excuse. At any rate, whether because the state of affairs is yet unsettled, or because of the invisible subtle spirit of optimism that blows through the heavily clustering telephone-wires and past the neat little modern villas and down the solidly pretentious streets, one can't help finding a tiny hope that Winnipeg, the city of buildings and the city of human beings, may yet come to something. It is a slender hope, not to be compared to that of the true Winnipeg man, who, gazing on his city, is fired with the proud and secret ambition that it will soon be twice as big, and after that four times, and then ten times ...

> *"Wider still and wider*
> *Shall thy bounds be set,"*

says that hymn which is the noblest expression of modern ambition. That hope is sure to be fulfilled. But the other timid prayer, that something different, something more worth having, may come out of Winnipeg, exists, and not quite unreasonably. That cannot be said of Toronto.

6 Prairie Cities

These cities grow in population with unimaginable velocity. From thirty to thirty thousand in fifteen years is the usual rate. Pavements are laid down, stores and bigger stores and still bigger stores spring up. Trams buzz along the streets towards the unregarded horizon that lies across the end of most roads in these flat, geometrically planned, prairie-towns. Probably a Chinese quarter appears, and the beginnings of slums. Expensive and pleasant small dwelling-houses fringe the outskirts; and rents being so high, great edifices of residential flats rival the great stores. In other streets, or even sandwiched between the finer buildings, are dingy and decaying saloons, and innumerable little booths and hovels where adventurers deal dishonestly in Real Estate, and Employment Bureaux. And there are the vast erections of the great corporations, Hudson's Bay Company, and the banks and the railways, and, sometimes almost equally impressive, the public buildings. There are the beginnings of very costly universities; and Regina has built a superb great House of Parliament, with a wide sheet of water in front of it, a noble building.

The inhabitants of these cities are proud of them, and envious of each other with a bitter rivalry. They do not love their cities as a Manchester man loves Manchester or a Münchener Munich, for they have probably lately arrived in them, and will surely pass on soon. But while they are there they love them, and with no silent love. They boost. To boost is to commend outrageously. And each cries up his own city, both from pride, it would appear, and for profit. For the fortunes of Newville are very really the fortunes of its inhabitants. From the successful speculator, owner of whole blocks, to the waiter bringing you a Martini, who has paid up a fraction of the cost of a quarter-share in a town-lot—all are the richer, as well as the prouder, if Newville grows. It is imperative to praise Edmonton in Edmonton. But it is sudden death to praise it in Calgary. The partisans of each city proclaim its superiority to all the others in swiftness of growth, future population, size of buildings, price of land—by all recognized standards of excellence. I travelled from Edmonton to Calgary in the company of a citizen of Edmonton and a citizen of Calgary. Hour after hour they disputed. Land in Calgary had risen from five dollars to three hundred; but in Edmonton from three to five hundred. Edmonton had grown from thirty persons to forty thousand in twenty years; but Calgary from twenty to thirty thousand in twelve ...

4. Mary Joplin Clarke, "Report of the Standing Committee on Neighbourhood Work," *Canadian Conference of Charities and Correction*, September 23-5, 1917.

1 Bad housing conditions

Bad housing conditions are so prevalent as to be almost inseparable from the conception of a neglected district. They may be summarized under the following heads: (a) Acreage overcrowding, found principally in the older cities of the Dominion, and in its most aggravated form in the cities of Halifax and St John. (b) The unsanitary tenement, and the old-fashioned family dwelling house converted into a tenement, also the problem to a large extent of the older cities, where a one-time fashionable residential district has degenerated into a slum. (c) Shacks and rough cottages, without proper water supply or sanitary conveniences, found in the outlying neglected districts and also in conjunction with (b) in older cities. This is also the most characteristic condition in the neglected urban communities of the west. It is not within the power of the neighbourhood worker to remedy these conditions completely, that can only be done when public opinion refuses to tolerate the startling contrast presented by the slum and the fashionable residential section in our cities under our present system of taxation and distribution of wealth.

The problem, however, is very properly part of our subject, as it contributes so largely to all the undesirable conditions against which the neighbourhood worker must fight.

2 Inadequate food and clothing

This, like the housing problem, is a condition familiar to all social workers and, in its most aggravated form, is part of the problem of the Committee on Public and Private Relief, but it may be mentioned here as a possible stimulus to community action through some sort of co-operative purchasing enterprise.

3 Labour conditions

In addition to other handicaps, the members of neglected communities are usually employed at hard physical labour for so many hours a day that they have little inclination to use what scanty leisure they have in occupations that call for any sort of effort. Hence the saloon or its equivalent has acquired its popularity. The uncertainty of the labour market, too, is a real obstacle to constructive neighbourhood work among labouring men, who may be forced at any time to move in order to be within reach of a new place of employment. These facts again, are merely noted as they affect the conditions we are studying. We must look to the Committee on Social Legislation to provide a solution of the problem.

4 Lack of proper recreational facilities

A neglected district is usually characterized by (a) Absence of facilities for healthy recreation. (b) Presence of commercialized recreation of a cheap and often sordid variety. It is of course self-evident that in congested communities the home provides little or no opportunity for recreation, either to its adult or juvenile members. Nor is it possible for those who live there to escape from them to any great extent and take recreation in the outlying parks or surrounding country. They must, therefore, look to their own community to provide them with recreation. This is done in two ways, by public and commercial enterprise.

PUBLIC RECREATION: The movement to establish supervised playgrounds, more especially in the congested districts, is in various stages of progress in the different cities of the Dominion. Playgrounds are operated during the summer months in almost all the cities from which reports have been received. In Montreal there are six playgrounds, maintained by the city, in addition to five operated by the Parks and Playgrounds Associations, though not all are in charge of trained workers. In Halifax there are six playgrounds in the schoolyards, under a board composed of members of the school commissioners, the local Council of Women, and representative citizens, and in addition one large recreation centre is being developed this summer under the supervision of an expert. Winnipeg also has playgrounds in connection with the public schools, and Ottawa, Fort William, and Calgary are well supplied with supervised playgrounds. There is no mention of winter work being done in any of these cities, except in Winnipeg and Calgary, where there are open air rinks. St John has a Playgrounds Association which conducts six supervised playgrounds in the summer months, and a Boys' and Girls' club in the winter. In Toronto the Parks Department of the city conducts supervised playgrounds from May till October and three recreational centres during the winter months, as well as open air rinks in a number of the parks. The Board of Education also conducts supervised playgrounds during the summer vacations. Neighbourhood festivals and inter-playground athletic leagues constitute a part of the work done on the city playgrounds and have had considerable influence in developing community spirit among the young folk.

In addition to the supervised playgrounds, Halifax, Toronto, and Calgary possess parks which are easily accessible to those who live in crowded districts, and Toronto, Halifax and Ottawa maintain public bathing beaches.

Victoria has excellent natural facilities for outdoor recreation, but no organized playgrounds.

COMMERCIALIZED RECREATION: Competing with the very limited attraction of these public recreation facilities, the majority of which seldom appeal to persons much over eighteen years of age, we have in the slums of most cities, a number of commercial enterprises catering to the recreation needs of both young and old, with no higher purpose than that of achieving their own financial success. Consequently they appeal to the lowest appetites of humanity and thus exercise a pernicious instead of a healthful influence upon the community. Motion picture shows, vaudeville and burlesque shows of the cheapest and most lurid variety, pool rooms, dance halls, and where prohibition is not in force, saloons, located in neglected districts, derive their income, for the most part, from the patronage of those who live in their vicinity. Nor can prohibition be said to have completely solved the problem of the saloon. The popular 'hang-out' has in many cases been transferred to some other convenient spot, such as the ice-cream parlour, which, while seemingly innocent enough, in Toronto at least to our knowledge, is frequently connected with immorality. Even when there is no question of a positive evil influence, the habit of congregating in places of this kind is injurious in that it is conducive to idleness, and a disposi-tion to 'loaf,' which in turn militates against the development of a healthy and purposeful form of neighbourhood organization.

The popularity of this form of diversion, however, shows that there is a very real desire among the members of a community to 'get together' and sug-gests the possibility of directing this natural tendency into channels where it could be a constructive instead of a destructive force.

The problem of recreation, therefore, is very vitally connected with our subject. It presents at once an obstacle which must be overcome, in the develop-ment of community spirit, and one of the most fruitful means to the cultivation of that spirit.

Conditions resulting from the character of the population

It is remarkable that, with the exception of the older cities of Halifax and St John, and the city of Ottawa, the population of the neglected districts is almost without exception composed of British or foreign immigrants. It is not the pur-pose of this committee to discuss this matter in detail, but merely to comment upon the fact as it affects the subject under discussion. The greatest difficulty encountered in the attempt to develop community spirit on this continent is occasioned by the fact that, in so many instances, the population of our commu-nities is cosmopolitan in character. Not only are neighbours unable to converse with each other, but they often cherish racial and religious prejudices among themselves. Especially is this the case where English and Jewish immigrants live side by side. In addition to prejudice within these districts, the city as a whole usually fails to understand and sympathize with 'the foreigner,' preferring to leave him in isolation rather than attempt to assimilate him. Especial emphasis is laid upon this difficulty in the Winnipeg reports.

On the other hand, the British immigrant often brings with him a concep-tion of community co-operation which is as yet foreign to our soil, and supplies excellent material for the task that we have in hand, while foreign immigrants of almost all nationalities possess a cohesion within their own groups which can be used as a basis for community cohesion, if we will but make the effort to break down the barriers of mutual misunderstanding and distrust.

Neighbourhood work at present being done in Canada

We are not considering under this head the work of charity organization societies, and other relief organizations, as that is the province of another committee, but are confining ourselves to the work of organizations, public and private, which endeavour to improve the conditions in neglected districts.

1 Housing problem

In the first place, what is being done to cope with the housing problem? There is evidence that in most places there is at least a realization that this problem exists. St John has organized a Social Service Council, with the investigating of the housing problem as one of its duties. Ottawa has made a housing survey, not published however, at the time of going to press, and even where no definite steps have been taken to handle the situation, there is a realization of its seriousness.

In Toronto there has been persistent effort on the part of the Department of Public Health for the past few years, to close up unsanitary houses, abolish privy pits, and improve the regulations as to future building. Tenements, cellar dwellings, and dark rooms are illegal, and the number of persons who can occupy a given number of rooms is limited. These regulations are enforced by a staff of 28 sanitary inspectors, of whom 3 are women. Its staff of visiting nurses also attempt to cope with the results of bad housing in their fight against infant mortality and disease.

In Calgary similar work is being done by the Health Department.

In Halifax building laws have recently been revised, and efforts are being made by the Board of Health to remove the abuses connected with the old buildings. A housing company has been formed, and has secured land and plans for the erection of dwellings at moderate rentals, as in this city the actual scarcity of houses affects almost all classes of the population, and makes it very difficult to close up old houses even when they can legally be condemned.

2 Recreation

The task of supplying healthy recreation is perhaps the most widely accepted duty of the settlement, church-club, and YM and YWCA. We must consider the efforts of these various agencies, not only as they may offer competition to the commercialized amusements of their neighbourhoods, but as they contribute towards the development of community cohesion. The church club, while it may aim to be a neighbourhood organization, is seldom able to draw members to any extent, from outside its own adherents, and hence, while it may help to

fill the need for healthy recreation, it cannot perform the function of a co-
ordinating neighbourhood agency in our cosmopolitan communities. Its greatest
success in this direction is likely to be in an English-speaking community where
there is little or no religious prejudice.

The non-denominational mission sometimes provides recreation activities, and when these are available to all comers, and have no definite connection
with the religious services conducted by the same institution, they may offer
opportunities for community recreation. As a general rule, however, the missions, like the churches, aim to provide for their own people only. Those missions
which conduct definite neighbourhood work as a separate branch of their activities are classed as settlements for the purposes of this report.

The YM and YWCA in many instances provide recreation for the young
people of neglected districts, although their work is not confined to any one
class. It is impossible for these institutions, however, by their very character, to
meet the recreational needs of the community as a whole.

The social settlement is perhaps better fitted than any other institution to
bring together different nationalities in their play-time, organized as it is to
provide a common meeting ground for all its neighbours, without reference to
their particular nationality or religion.

There are the following nine social settlements in Canada: Montreal—
Chalmers House, Iverley Settlement, University Settlement. Toronto—Evangelia
Settlement, University Settlement, St Christopher House, Central Neighbourhood
House. Ottawa—Settlement House. Fort William—Wayside House. In addition to these, the following institutions are doing settlement work, though with
definite church connections: Winnipeg—All People's Mission. Toronto—Memorial Institute, Fred Victor Mission.

The work being done by these organizations varies somewhat in character
and extent. It will be necessary to generalize in describing it for the purpose of
this report. It is a common policy of settlements to provide for the people of
their district some of the things of which they would otherwise be deprived.
Classes in dancing, sewing, carpentry, play schools for small children, dramatics,
gymnasium work, entertainments, mothers' clubs, and clubs for boys and girls
of all ages are among the usual recreational activities.

In so far as these are a means to bring together the different people inhab-
iting the settlement neighbourhoods, they are valuable aids in breaking down
some of those barriers which stand in the way of community co-operation. It is
in the self-governing club, however, that the most important work is done towards the positive development of that co-operation, especially when the club

includes members of more than one nationality. By its means the younger people learn the elements of co-operation and citizenship, and are taught to develop their own resources rather than to rely on the efforts of other people in providing entertainment and occupation for them. Some of this recreational work is at present being carried on in the school buildings. An important experiment in this connection is being made in Toronto by the Playgrounds Association. The playgrounds that this association was instrumental in organizing have been taken over by the city, and it is now financing the operation of social centres in three of the public schools. The centres are under the direction of the headworkers of three of the settlements, and are conducted consequently in close co-operation with the work of those settlements. The activities include play hours, dancing classes, gymnasium work, games, club work, dramatic work, and entertainments of all sorts. The possibilities of the wider use of schools will be dealt with more fully later, under a separate section.

An interesting enterprise, of a kindred nature is being carried on among foreign immigrants in the Rochesterville Social Centre, Ottawa. Here the centre is a one-time saloon, and the work is operated by a sub-committee of the Civic Improvement League. This centre seems to be almost unique in that it is evidently attractive to the men of the community, providing facilities for pool, cards, smoking, reading, and boxing in addition to the usual attractions for children in the form of playground, clubs, sewing, and cooking classes. It also boasts a concert hall, and a coffee canteen in the winter, and is planning to add a skating rink in the immediate future. This provides an excellent suggestion as to a possible use of saloons that have been closed under prohibition, especially in the effort that has been made to make it a real substitute for that recreation centre in meeting the needs of the men.

Almost all neighbourhood organizations attempt to supply their clientele with some sort of substitute for the summer holiday of those with greater financial resources. Day outings and summer camps are conducted by settlements, missions, and church organizations alike. These may be made a means to the formation of friendships between those taking charge of the expeditions, and those benefiting by them, and in this way can be a very valuable assistance to the neighbourhood worker in the effort to obtain a knowledge of the people. Girls' and boys' camps can be even more valuable than clubs in developing co-operation among those for whom they are conducted. On the other hand fresh air work may be a means of pauperizing those who are benefited, if the latter are not required to contribute in some way towards the undertaking. At best it can be but a slight mitigation of the sufferings of slum dwellers in summer, unless it is made to contribute, in some such way as has been indicated, towards the development of group cohesion which can become a part of a permanent neighbourhood spirit.

5. William Irvine, *Farmers in Politics*, 1920.

Poverty is not confined to the cities. Its dreadful shadow is everywhere on the great fertile Canadian plains. It is produced through the monopoly of natural resources, and by the exploitation of the agrarian toilers. A glance at a few of the facts will suffice to demonstrate the truth of the statement. In the three prairie provinces there are 153,000,000 acres of tillable land, of which 16,000,000 acres only are cultivated, while 100,000,000 acres are held by speculators. Thousands of people, many of whom are returned soldiers, desire to use this land and production would be enormously increased if it were available to these people for use. But the prices charged by the speculators are prohibitive, and, as a matter of unexaggerated fact, most purchasers of land under the present unfavorable agricultural conditions simply bind themselves to slave their lives away for mortgage companies.

One of the largest land holders in the prairie provinces is the Canada Northwest Land Co., Ltd., whose board of directors is practically that of the Canadian Pacific Railway Co. In addition to an interest in the Canadian Pacific Railway townsites, this company owns 373,165 acres. The Canadian Northern Prairie Lands Co., under Canadian Northern Railway direction, holds 67,319 acres; the Hudson's Bay Co. has 4,058,050 acres; and the Canadian Northern Railway Co. owns 6,511,394 acres. The Canadian Pacific Railway Co. has been selling its land for twenty years or more. By the sale of 21,000,000 acres the company realized over $100,000,000.

Much of the land now under cultivation has been purchased by farmers from these privileged companies. This, together with the tariff, the high freight rates, and the low price of wheat, accounts for the fact that a large percentage of the farmers are operating to-day under the gentle care of mortgage companies. In Saskatchewan it is estimated that eighty per cent of all farm lands is mortgaged, and a similar condition of things exists in the other Canadian provinces.

The homestead policy can scarcely be said to have been devised either in the interests of agriculture, or of the homesteaders themselves. It was devised in the interests of railroads and land companies. Settlers were necessary to the country if the land values were to be improved, and if the railroads were to be profitable, and hence the free homesteads offered as alluring inducement. But these homesteads were not of the best lands; the best had already been picked; neither were they close to the railway, for land adjacent to the railroads had been disposed of already; and so the homestead farmer suffered from land monopoly from the very first. Forced to go anywhere from five to forty miles from a railroad, the pioneer lost by the increased cost of the production of his marketable commodities. He spent more time on the road, used more horses, and wore out more wagons. But he had also to build roads from his lonely homestead, over, and through, miles of unused land, much of which was untaxable. Schools, too, had to be supported, and the price of land kept settlers away, so that the burden fell more heavily on the small community. As time went on these pioneer farmers had built roads and established schools; small towns sprang up, and the land values created by the social toil of these people were added to the price of the exploiter's land. Farmers who came after the homestead lands were taken up were forced to pay to railway companies and land companies the values created by the toil of their fellow farmers. This was a burden which handicapped the later settlers, even though, by buying the land of the speculators, they were nearer to the railroads than the pioneers. And so in both cases, in the case of the first settlers on account of the extra work entailed, and in the case of the later settlers on account of the high prices paid for land, the cost of production was increased to that point where there was practically nothing left for the farmer except a bare existence. Unlike the manufacturer, you see, the farmer could not add the increased cost of production to the selling price of wheat, or beef, or whatever it was he produced on his farm; the prices were set—both ways—and all he could do was to pay what was asked, and take what was given, and still "keep smiling."

It was the greed of the land and natural resources exploiters that led to the building of the transcontinental lines of railroad. Instead of concentrating our railway system in that part of the Dominion that was already settled, and instead of developing the natural resources by which they were surrounded, for the national benefit, these resources were grabbed up everywhere, from coast to coast, and a railway was run across thousands of miles of waste like an ostrich track in a desert. It is safe to say that the population of Canada could all be concentrated in one province like Ontario, without suffering from over-crowding, and the railways which were necessary to span the Dominion, had they been built on a plan governed by the requirements of the case, would have given greater service at infinitely less expense. As it was, although our railroads were built by the people, according to the exploiters' idea of development, they resulted in a most costly undertaking, giving a minimum of service. Freight rates had to be raised so as to cover the extravagance in construction, and this fell upon the shoulders of the farmers, more than upon any other class. The farmer lost the price of freight on the selling price of his wheat, and had to pay the freight on all machinery and other commodities necessary to his life on the farm.

In addition to the enormous gifts of land to railroads, they received from the Canadian people in actual cash $244,000,000, besides guaranteed bonds to the value of $245,000,000. All this notwithstanding, the people of Canada did not own the Canadian railways. This is proved by the fact that latterly some of them, after having become bankrupt, have been bought again by public money, presumably in order to save the investments made by the magnates in control. Consequently, while our railway schemes necessitated high freights, the greed of profit made the freights higher still, all of which increased the burdens of the farmer, and made them heavier than they were.

The tariff, which has long been recognized by a large section of the people as a social crime, constitutes another of the economic prods which served to drive the farmers into co-operation. This subject has been so much talked about, and its injustice is so obvious that I need but to mention it. The tariff crime, sometimes committed in the sacred name of patriotism, at other times excused as a producer of revenue, and invariably represented to the workers as the salvation of their jobs, stands as one of the most glaring examples of class legislation which the history of Canada affords. Industries claimed that they needed protection on the grounds that they could not compete with manufacturers of the United States and Great Britain. This protection was granted because the financial interests engaged in manufacture controlled the government.

The farmers had to raise wheat, and sell it on the world's market for the current price, and in doing so the Canadian farmer was, and is, handicapped. There are natural disadvantages such as drought, hail, frost, rust, smut, hot winds, and so on, and numerous artificial ones, the long hauls, for instance, and their consequent high freight rates. Many of these difficulties are not found in other wheat-raising countries, hence while it is not easy for the Canadian farmer to compete with other countries, yet he has done it, and is continuing to do it, without protection. If the farmer, in the face of so many difficulties, gets no protection, and asks none, why should manufacturers be protected at the expense of the farmer, thus making it next to impossible for that which is the basic industry of the country to exist? This thought came to the farmers, as soon or later it was bound to come, and the longer he thought the plainer it became that the injustices of land and tariff monopolies under which he suffered, together with the many other tyrannies, high freights, etc., were slowly encroaching on his very life, threatening his existence, and if he would continue to live it was necessary that he should do something in his own behalf, do it without delay, and do it himself.

There came a time when the pressure of these injustices became so severe that farmers had to give up their land and move to the cities in order to be able to live. Then people began to wonder and talk and speculate on the reason why the farmers had left their farms. Some said that farmers who gave up and went to the city were lazy, others said it was the gaiety of city life that lured them. The farmer alone knew that the exodus was due to economic necessity. Manufacturers, railroad magnates, real estate dealers, and governments began a "Back to the Land" campaign, without making the slightest attempt to solve the problem which accounted for the vacant farms, without even understanding for the most part that such a problem existed. Perhaps it is one of the tragedies of our society that those responsible for much of the trouble are entirely unconscious of it.

Meanwhile the farmers, now alive to the necessity for sane action on their part, began to watch their oppressors. They saw that while they were themselves standing as individuals, in political and economic helplessness, the industrial magnates were organized, and through organization were able to dominate. They saw that through organization the banks were able to say how much they would charge for money, the manufacturers how much was to be paid for their manufactured article, the railroads how much was to be charged for freight; the land owner fixed the price of his land, and even the laborers were getting together and demanding a price for their labor. So the farmers said: "We, too, will organize, and see if by that means we cannot decide ourselves what shall be paid for wheat, instead of leaving it to be decided by wheat dealers as we have done for so long."

... There are doubtless many contributing causes for this outstanding radical aggressiveness on the part of rural women's organizations. Perhaps chief among these is the fact that women on the farms have in the past suffered enormously from lack of just such things as healthy social intercourse, a community spirit, opportunities for their children along educational and recreational lines, and more than all else, for lack of proper medical attention, or even medical attention of any kind. The actual urgency arising out of the conditions of life in rural Canada has helped to awaken the mothers especially to accept the responsibility for the health, development, and happiness of their communities. Farm women have little time and less inclination for the frivolities which occupy the attention of many "society" women. The mothers on the farms are grappling with real life problems, and their struggle against gigantic odds, during many years of pioneering, has been noble and heroic in the extreme ...

The farm women approached modern problems from the viewpoint of obtaining a fuller life. The loneliness of the farm, lack of social and intellectual intercourse, the disadvantages of isolated homes, combined to bring the farm women together. Before that was done there was no means of developing a community spirit. Community life was hindered rather than helped by such organizations as existed up till that time. Even the churches tended to divide, instead of to unite it. The great need was to find a means of bringing all people together, regardless of religious belief, nationality, or political bias. Party political organization, together with denominationalism in the churches, stood in the way of undertaking community tasks. There were many things that might be improved by co-operative effort—phases and branches of life left entirely untouched by such organizations as were in existence. There were the young without healthy recreation or well directed amusement, and without education in vital matters. The youth of the farm was growing up, and growing more and more discontented. The lack of social life, and the difficulty in finding expression for youthful impulses, were even harder to bear than poverty in material things, and so the young people were drifting to the cities. To remedy this state of affairs was the work which the United Farm Women undertook first. They began to meet together in order to break the monotony and drudgery of the farm. Their organization was a revolt against the drab existence which was their lot. Their aim was to improve conditions as much as possible under the present political and economic systems, and was, therefore, from its inception, constructive and positive.

Education, health, and work among the young people, with a view to making life worth while on the farm, have been specific objectives. For improvement in rural education the United Farm Women have advocated, and in many instances helped to make practicable, such reforms as making the school a community center; obtaining facilities for a resident teacher; beautifying the school and school grounds; the cultivation of school gardens; the introduction of the hot noon lunch; organized and supervised play; school fairs and field days; and the changing of the curriculum so as to make it more suitable to the needs of rural children.

6. Maude Newcombe, "The Farm Woman's Lot," *Grain Growers' Guide*, April 15, 1925.

Drudgery, routine, monotony, loneliness—see a repetition of those words in the columns of a magazine and one can be fairly sure that the subject is the lot of the farm woman. Whether farmers' wives first inspired the articles or the articles first inspired the wives I do not know. But we have all been quite ready to believe that those words do describe our lives ...

The truth is that we have not been doing any real thinking. We have been listening to those who believe that we live lives of hardship and suffering, and taking it for granted that we do. I've been doing something. My conclusions are that the prairie farmers' wives are the freest and happiest women on earth. I had previously believed that some quality peculiar to me alone had prevented my hair from falling out in the dry prairie climate, and my skin from becoming shrivelled and yellow, as my neighbours sadly predicted when I arrived. But I've suddenly realized that I have never yet seen a bald-headed woman, nor one with yellow, shrivelled, parchment-like skin.

We get up early but are rewarded by getting our work done early, and we can rest later in the day. We talk of sweeping, and scrubbing, and dusting when we detail our work for effect, and in the next breath complain because our houses are so small. We list washing and ironing, and grumble because we never have any clothes. We are hardly consistent.

Milking cows does fall to the lot of some of us. Sometimes we like to do it, though we would never admit it. Even if we do not enjoy it, we do get away from the kitchen for an interval, and the change does us good. It would do us more good if we did not always go to the barn with an injured feeling because we had to milk cows.

As for feeding hens, I have never yet seen a woman feeding her flock without so much pride and interest in her work that she spent a lot more time doing it than was necessary.

Only the other day I read that prairie farmers' wives never have any time to read. We do have time to read, and to do practically anything that we want to do. Even with a family, and a few hired men to work for, we have more time and opportunity for caring for our hair and complexion, and for cultivating our literary tastes than the average single girl working in a city. Because we have not realized this there is a marked tendency to envy the city girl or woman. This is detrimental in that we spend our time planning for a future that always remains a future, instead of making proper use of the present. We are waiting until we can leave the prairie farm and go to the city to live, or back East, or home to the Old Country. With such an attitude, is it any wonder that our hair turns grey and our faces wrinkle? We need not blame it on the climate. We make no attempt to beautify our surroundings because we are "going back." We are dissatisfied.

The truth is that we did want to go back wherever "back" happens to be, when we first came. Nobody "fits" at first. We are lost in the vastness of the space on the prairie. We feel the power of it and are helpless. But that power is so real that once we get in the grip of the prairie we cannot get beyond it. It follows us to the ends of the earth and forces us back. This has been proven by so many who leave and return again, that we may as well settle down now and be contented. For we cannot go back. We don't really want to.

We say we are lonely. We only long for company at times just as city people occasionally long for solitude. But if we had to allow half-a-dozen of our neighbours to move into our front yard to live we would not be happy until we got them out again.

We get a lot of sympathy because of our loneliness. No neighbours nearer than half-a-mile. Yet our sympathizers, and we, too, thrill when we read books about the "great open spaces" where the hero or heroine does not see a white person for six months.

We think we envy city women because of our own lack of modern conveniences. We may envy wealth if we are envious. But we need not envy the city woman who lives in the same circumstances that would be ours were we to go to the city. She has a bathtub and electric lights that we have not, but little else that we want. Shows soon become her amusement simply because "there's no place else to go" that her purse will afford, while our community gatherings never lose their attraction for us.

Our 10 or 15 mile trip to town is one of our main grievances. It would be a glorious outing for a city woman, and is for us. And we don't have to carry our purchases out to our buggies even. Would we like carrying armloads of bundles on crowded street cars again?

Would we skimp ourselves with eggs and butter again because we couldn't afford to buy all we wanted? Would we use the top of a quart of milk for the family's supply of cream after using that much in one cup of coffee on the farm? Would we be contented with a skinny chicken once a year?

We may all leave the prairie farms and go back East, or to the Old Country, or to cities, but the railways will have one busy time getting us back to our prairie homes as quickly as we want to come.

We need to stop complaining and make of our lives what we wish to, for our opportunities are unlimited. Our own mental attitudes are all that stand in our way. Let's go.

7. Mrs. R.C. Phillips, "A Farm Woman's Reply," *Grain Growers' Guide,* May 27, 1925.

It was with much interest and, I fear, a little indignation that I read the article, entitled The Farm Woman's Lot, in THE GUIDE of April 15. I must say that I disagree most emphatically with the writer on several points. I have lived on a farm practically all my life, 14 years as the wife of a farmer, and feel that I know a little about the subject of which we speak.

True enough we may be the freest and happiest women on the earth in some respects, but we are certainly the busiest. However, hard work is no hindrance to happiness or freedom either. As for our having time to read or do anything else we like, I certainly have not found this to be the case, neither in my own experience nor in that of my friends and neighbours.

I have found that farmers' wives seldom complain about their hard lot, accepting the drudgery and discomforts of pioneering quite as a matter of course. And certainly no other class of women on earth are such close partners in their husband's business.

The majority of people on farms in the West have come from places where the price of land is beyond their means. They have homesteaded or bought land on easy terms here and located with the intention of making this their permanent home. Very few had much capital with which to start and hence buildings were built and machinery bought "on time," and met by crop payments, which means so much out of each year's returns when the crop is sold. Those who have acquired land in this way can testify that it is only by the practice of the most rigid economy that the payments can be made in the first few years—at least. Therefore, we find farm women getting up early in the morning, preparing breakfast for six, seven, or sometimes more people; washing dishes, the cream separator and all the milk utensils, packing school lunches and speeding the children on their way; feeding and caring for the chickens (and in the hatching season this is no small task), hurrying back to the house to make beds, sweep and dust; and on certain days, ironing, washing, baking, scrubbing, to say nothing of the family sewing, which often means making over garments for the smaller members of the family from the cast-off clothing of their elders. Most farm women sew their own bedding, and there is also the never-ending mending and the contriving in every way possible to manage the household as economically as possible. Somehow time must be found for planting and caring for the garden as well as the canning and preserving of the fruit and vegetables for winter use.

In spite of careful planning and the elimination of all elaborate dishes from the menu, three well-balanced meals a day prepared in quantities sufficient to satisfy hungry men who work out-of-doors for long hours, requires a considerable portion of a woman's time. All of which leaves very little time through the day for rest and recreation, however early we may rise in the morning.

Don't ask why we do not hire help during the busy seasons and install modern conveniences to lighten our labour, for I assure you that is the very goal to which the majority of us are working. A new plow may enable the farmer to cultivate enough more land in a single year to pay for it, leaving the other year's profits from that piece of land to pay for some other necessity or improvement, while a vacuum cleaner would only give the housewife the benefit of a heavy task lightened, and not the cash so sorely needed to meet payments, so the cleaner must wait for awhile.

Were it not for the dreams of the future when our homes shall be paid for and labour-saving devices and comforts within our means, I am afraid a good many of us would give up in despair.

Now do not imagine for one moment that I do not like farm life, and am living with the expectation of leaving it. I enjoy every phase of farm life and would live nowhere else if I were given the opportunity of making a choice. But no one can deny that there is a lot of hard work for the average farm wife in the West where our homes are as yet only in the making. Even now my greatest dream of happiness, since my health broke with the strain of work a year ago, is that I may be able to take it up again where I was forced to lay it down. ...

I might say that we have enjoyed a fair measure of success in the past 15 years, but it has only been accomplished by hard gruelling labour and sacrifice on both sides, and could never have been attained any other way under the circumstances. At last we are beginning to find the path smoother, as I hope every homemaker in the West will in the near future. I, too, feel that we may attain any goal we like, but that the price paid sometimes seems almost too great for the gain.

Readings

Artibise, A. *Winnipeg: A Social History of Urban Growth, 1874–1914*. Montreal and Kingston: McGill-Queen's University Press, 1975.

Artibise, A., ed. *Town and Country: Aspects of Western Canadian Urban Development*. Regina: University of Regina, 1981.

Baskerville, P. and E. Sager. *Unwilling Idlers: The Urban Unemployed and their Families in Late Victorian Canada*. Toronto: University of Toronto Press, 2000.

Burnet, J. *Next Year Country: A Study of Rural Social Organization in Alberta.* Toronto: University of Toronto Press, 1951.

Copp, T. *Anatomy of Poverty: The Condition of the Working Class in Montreal, 1897–1929.* Toronto: McClelland and Stewart, 1974.

Danysk, C. *Hired Hands: Labour and the Development of Prairie Agriculture.* Toronto: McClelland and Stewart, 1995.

Fowke, V. *The National Policy and the Wheat Economy.* Toronto: University of Toronto Press, 1957.

Goheen, P. *Victorian Toronto 1850–1900: Pattern and Process of Growth.* Chicago: University of Chicago, 1970.

Halpern, M. *And On That Farm He Had a Wife: Ontario Farm Women and Feminism, 1900–1970.* Montreal: McGill-Queen's University Press, 2001.

Hann, R. *Farmers Confront Industrialism: Some New perspectives on Ontario Agrarian Movements.* Toronto: New Hogtown Press, 1975.

Harris, R. "Residential Segregation and Class Formation in Canadian Cities: A Critical Review," *Canadian Geographer* 1984.

Jones, D. *Empire of Dust: Settling and Abandoning the Prairie Dry Belt.* Edmonton: University of Alberta Press, 1987.

Jones, D. and I. MacPherson, eds. *Building Beyond the Homestead: Rural History on the Prairies.* Calgary: University of Calgary Press, 1985.

Kinnear, M. *Do You Want Your Daughter to Marry a Farmer? Women's Work on the Farm, 1922,* in D. Akenson (ed.) *Canadian Papers in Rural History* Vol 6. Gananoque: Langdale Press, 1988.

McCormack, A. and I. Macpherson, eds. *Cities in the West: Papers of the Western Canadian Urban History Conference.* Ottawa: National Museum of Man, 1975.

McDonald, R. "'Holy Retreat' or 'Practical Breathing Spot'?: Class Perceptions of Vancouver's Stanley Park, 1910-1913," *Canadian Historical Review* 1984.

Piva, M. *The Condition of the Working Class in Toronto, 1900–1921.* Ottawa: University of Ottawa Press, 1979.

Rutherford, P. *Saving the Canadian City: The First Phase, 1880–1920.* Toronto: University of Toronto Press, 1974.

Sampson, D. ed., *Contested Countryside: Rural Workers and Modern Society in Atlantic Canada, 1800–1950.* Fredericton: Acadiensis Press, 1994.

Sandwell R., ed. *Beyond City Limits: Rural History in British Columbia.* Vancouver: University of British Columbia Press, 1999.

Smith, A. "Farms, Forests and Cities: The Image of the Land and the Rise of the Metropolis in Ontario, 1860-1914," in D. Keane and C. Read, eds. *Old Ontario: Essays in Honour of J.M.S. Careless.* Toronto: Dundurn, 1990.

Spelt, J. *Urban Development in South Central Ontario.* Assen: Van Gorcum, 1955.

Stelter, G., ed. *Cities and Urbanization: Canadian Historical Perspectives.* Toronto: Copp Clark Pitman, 1990.

Stelter, G. and A. Artibise, eds. *The Canadian City: Essays in Urban and Social History.* Ottawa: Carleton University Press, 1984.

Stelter, G. and A. Artibise, eds. *Shaping the Urban Landscape: Aspects of the Canadian City Building Process.* Ottawa: Carleton University Press, 1982.

Taylor, J. *Fashioning Farmers: Ideology, Agricultural Knowledge and the Manitoba Farm Movement 1890–1925.* Regina: Canadian Plains Research Center, 1994.

Van Nus, W. "The Fate of City Beautiful Thought in Canada, 1893-1930," *Canadian Historical Association Report,* 1975.

Chapter Seven

"PERFECT JUSTICE AND HARMONY": VOTES FOR WOMEN

1. Hon. John Dryden, Minister of Agriculture, "Womanhood Suffrage," Speech, Ontario Legislature, May 10, 1893.
2. James L. Hughes, *Equal Suffrage*, 1910.
3. H. Bate, "Are Women to Blame?," *Grain Growers' Guide*, March 1, 1911.
4. Henri Bourassa, "Women's Suffrage, Its Effectiveness, Its Legitimacy," *Le Devoir*, 24 April 1913.
5. Nellie McClung, *In Times Like These*, 1915.
6. Stephen Leacock, "The Woman Question," in *Essays and Literary Studies*, 1916.
7. H.D.P., "The Failure of the Suffrage Movement to Bring Freedom to Women," *Woman Worker*, December 1928.

Introduction

Statistical data definitively shows how Canadian women still struggle for political and social equality in our new century, and the evidence even suggests outright regression in some areas. Though they are hardly shoeless and pregnant in the kitchen, a glimpse at the House of Commons, any university engineering faculty or corporate boardroom, graphically illustrates that women are far from sharing power commensurate to their proportion of the population. On average women still earn, three-quarters as much as men—though this is a significant improvement over the early part of the twentieth century when they could expect half. Social issues that directly affect women, such as a national daycare policy, remain unaddressed. Unfortunate as the present situation may be, it bears remembering that less than one hundred years ago women could not even vote, let alone run for Parliament. Engineering faculties in 1900 forbade their admission, and they entered the boardrooms of the nation not as executives but as stenographers. Thus progress has been made but the questions remain: why was obtaining the vote so difficult; and to what degree, if any, did enfranchisement actually fulfil their hopes and promises?

The Canadian feminist movement emerged simultaneously with those in the United States and Great Britain, but unlike the latter never became violent. First Wave feminism sprang from the ideological and social dilemmas posed by industrialization, urbanization, and a perceived decline of family values. As such, it shared ties with general reformist ideas challenging the ruthless and exploitive excesses of modern capitalism. For much of its history the core of the movement remained in Toronto, which served as the headquarters for groups such as the Dominion Women's Emancipation Association, the Dominion Enfranchisement Association, and the Canadian Suffrage Association. While claiming to be national in outlook, these organizations had little impact outside Toronto, and most suffrage campaigns began as intensely provincial, not national, movements. Nor did they represent a cross-section of Canadian womanhood. The associations were thoroughly upper class and often snobbishly so, urban, English, and led by women with leisure time to study and organize— and there weren't many of those.

Most national organizations took the stand that women's voting and political participation would spread natural maternal qualities to the society at large. This "maternal" feminist strain worried little about equality, believing instead that inasmuch as women perform different roles in society than men, they must champion those nurturing qualities from which the whole nation would benefit. For this group, achieving the vote was a means to social reform, not an end in itself. Thus it is hardly surprising that maternal feminists formed the vanguard of the prohibition movement. The other branch of feminism, the "equal rights" feminists, disagreed with their "maternal" sisters and argued in favour of the vote on the political principle that women, as equals to men, deserved the same political power. This group, in fact, saw "maternal feminists" as misguided and, not surprisingly, adopted a far more aggressive, and in some cases extremist, approach to gaining the vote.

Both feminist groups believed that Canadian women voters would significantly improve the national social fabric by bringing power to bear on areas male parliamentarians apparently chose to ignore. Social policy issues such as child labour, daycare, education, welfare, prohibition, and protection for women must all be addressed in the twentieth century and that, they argued, would only occur if women gained a direct political voice. Enfranchised women, by constituting half the voting population, would force change by electing candidates, male or female, who promised to push appropriate legislation through the provincial and federal corridors of power. Thus a sense of "women-as-national-saviours" permeated both branches of the suffrage movement.

Many men and women, however, argued that getting the vote would affect nothing, either for women or the nation. Power and the ability to enact change, they said, did not lie in a political gender balance but elsewhere. This was naturally a popular and effective weapon in the anti-suffrage arsenal, and led to a certain smugness when female voters and legislators arguably achieved limited success in the post-enfranchisement period—particularly compared to their high hopes and expectations. Today the limited agenda of first wavers earn it dismissal or derision from those who argue that its motivation had little to do with emancipating Canadian women.

Why did it take so long for Canadian women to gain the vote in the first place? Actually it didn't, at least not in relative terms. Canada compares very well to the rest of the world, both then and now, when it comes to developing women's rights. Still, there is no denying the protracted struggle Canadian women experienced in their march to the ballot box. In the final analysis, the patriarchal nature of Canadian society ensured that men wielded legislative power, and it was they who had to change, and they who had to accept the idea of women's suffrage before it could occur. Sharing, especially sharing power, did not necessarily come naturally or easily, and most men initially resented or feared the suffrage movement. Male farming associations in the prairies first broke the patriarchal mold by endorsing women's political rights, perhaps because prairie women so often worked as equals to their husbands as they jointly struggled to hew new lives from the unyielding prairie. Manitoba granted women the franchise in 1916, the first province to do so, and the other prairie legislatures soon followed. On the other hand, in 1922 44,259 Quebec women petitioned against giving women the vote and they remained provincially disenfranchised until 1940, some twenty years after Canadian women earned the right to enter a federal polling booth—but then Swiss women did not get the vote until 1971.

Discussion Points

1. Based upon these documents, summarize the arguments made for and against women getting the vote.
2. Leacock and H.D.P. all cast doubt upon the significance of women gaining the right to vote. Were they right? Was the original feminist movement misdirected?
3. While western Canada became the chief centre of support for suffrage Quebec lagged far behind. Why?

Documents

1. Hon. John Dryden, Minister of Agriculture, "Womanhood Suffrage," Speech, Ontario Legislature, May 10, 1893.

... Mrs. Harriet Law, an advocate of women's suffrage openly repudiates the Bible on the ground that "its teachings oppose that liberty of speech and action which she as a representative woman demands." Another lady writer states that "if the Bible stands in the way of women's rights then the Bible and religion must go." These are strong statements, which will not be endorsed by many who support this Bill in this Legislature or outside of it.

... I am free to say to you that these convictions as to whether this measure is right or wrong, have been formed from a careful study of the teachings of the Bible which bear upon it. I accept these teachings as of divine origin, and they cannot, therefore, change from age to age ...

If we go back to the account of creation, we shall find that man being created, the various animal creations which had been brought into existence were brought before him in order that he might name them. But among them all there did not appear any that could be utilized as his associate—after they have all passed before him he is still left alone and has no companion. Then the statement is made that "It is not good for man to be alone; we will make an help-meet for him." And in after ages, when the apostles made reference to this statement they used these words: "Man was made and then the woman; the man was not made for the woman, but the woman for the man."

The point I want to emphasize in this regard is that woman was formed to be an associate, a companion, a helper of man, and not to usurp authority or control over him. They are two persons, yet they are spoken of as one—of the same flesh, one the complement of the other. The same rule applies in their formation as in the animal creation everywhere. Man's appearance indicates force, authority, decision, self-assertion, while that of a woman shows exactly the opposite, and indicates instead, trust dependence, grace and beauty. In other words, man was made in such a form when compared to woman as stamps him with the attributes of authority, government and control ...

In view of these statements, and others which might be quoted, I therefore conclude that woman's place in accordance with Bible teaching is to be in submission to man, and not to assume the place of authority. When my honorable friend seeks to give them the ballot he in effect says, "I propose to give woman control of public affairs; I wish to place in her hands governing power to compel man to accept her dictation." That proposition, according to my argument, is against the teaching of Scripture, and therefore is not and cannot be right ...

Women have exercised and will exercise more power without the ballot than with it in matters of this kind. What has changed the drinking customs of this country from the drunken revels of the past to the orderly, sober conduct of to-day? It is largely due to the influence of women. How has this influence been exercised? Not by force, not by control, nor by authority, but by the strongest of all forces, loving persuasion. Women to-day can do much more in this direction than they have ever done in the past if they will unite in creating a sentiment in favor of sobriety and right conduct. Woman has in this regard immense power over man if she is willing to exercise it ...

I notice that Mrs. Rockwell, the lady who seems to stand at the head of this movement in this country, writes in one of the public papers that man cannot legislate for woman, and that woman, therefore, needs the franchise for her own protection. In that statement you have an utter repudiation of woman's dependence upon man; it is an assertion of independence; it is a desire to live and work separately. She says, "Give us the franchise and we will protect ourselves and our sex." Now, I repudiate entirely this doctrine. Do what you will you cannot, and you ought not if you could, reverse nature's law. Woman always was and always will be dependent upon man, and whether some women who are manhaters like it or not it cannot be changed. This lady's statement means that man has no regard for wife, mother, sister or daughter—that he, their rightful protector, will see them injured and refuse to come to their aid ...

This same lady tells us that women do not receive equal pay with men for equally good work. How can the ballot correct this? Can you compel by law the payment of a higher scale of wages? So long as women are willing and anxious to work for less wages than men, so long will they be paid less. Would the use of the ballot compel the mistress on Bloor street to give her servants higher wages? Would it insure the dressmaker down town more wage for her work? All this is regulated by the law of supply and demand, and is in no way affected by the ballot.

TO REFINE POLITICS.

The advocates of Women's Suffrage tell us that the ballot is wanted in order to refine politics, in order to bring better candidates before the public. That depends on what you consider better candidates. Is it better looking men who are required. I can easily understand looking around this Assembly, if a few, especially in this corner, were excluded, including the Attorney-General and perhaps the leader of the Opposition, it is possible better candidates in this regard might be secured. But speaking for myself, I am not aware that there is any particular necessity for refining politics in this country. I believe that our political campaigns in these days are conducted in a very orderly manner already ...

By my strongest objection to the Bill of my hon. friend is the evil effects which in my judgment would result to society and to woman herself. These results would not be seen immediately; they would not be observed at the first few elections, they probably would take years to work out, but in the end the result would be evil, and evil alone. The right to cast the ballot carries with it the right to be elected by the ballot. If woman is part of the people, as is alleged, if she stands on an equality with man, having the same rights in the body politic, having equal intelligence, equal education, equal business training, by what process of reasoning can you show that the right to vote in her case does not carry with it the right to be voted for? ... The right to vote for a member of the Legislative Assembly would carry with it the right to be elected a member of this Assembly, the right to preside here, the right to take part here in all its deliberations. I think I hear the question coming to my ears. And why should they not take part? My answer is, not because woman is not intelligent, nor because she is not sufficiently educated, but because she is woman, because by putting her thus out of her sphere you unsex her, you are seeking to make her a man, to induce her to fill the place of a man; to seat her in Parliament making laws and governing the stronger sex—sitting as judge on the bench and as juror in the box.

A LOW TYPE OF WOMANHOOD.

I am well aware that this is the ambition of some women, masculine in character, disliking their own sex, having only selfish ambitions, deploring the fate that brought them into the world as women, and determined at all hazards to break the bonds of womanhood, and to take the part of a man. Such a woman says, "give me a chance and I will show you that I am not dependent; I refuse to take the place of humble submission which nature has assigned me; I am as able as any man; I can fill his place anywhere." Such a person I describe as a manly woman—the lowest type of true womanhood. An effeminate man or a manly woman is not the ideal type of humanity. They are nowhere in demand. The masculine, manly woman is not respected by her own sex—they generally despise and mock her—and I am certain that she is not strongly admired by many men either. It is not her misery that she cannot be a man, but rather that she cannot be a woman.

I appeal to true womanhood if its highest joy is not to know that in man they have a protector, one who loves them, provides for their needs, not by force, but willingly, because he delights to do it, and I appeal to true manhood if the strongest incentive to active exertion to do their best in every way is not the fact that there is dependent upon them a loving, dutiful wife, or a mother, daughter or sister.

INJURY TO HOME.

Can you not see that when you have brought women into the rightful sphere of man you will have revolutionized society, and so changed altogether the relationship of man and woman? Will such a course bring greater harmony? Will the happiness of the people be thereby increased? Will, as these people imagine, all sin thus be stamped out? How will such a course affect the home life? Suppose that men and women voted differently, the mother against the son, the husband against the wife, and so on. If they did not thus vote differently, according to the argument, all these supposed wrongs could never be righted, and no object would be gained by adding this enormous number to the list of voters. If they did vote differently, is it possible that this would add to the joy of the home? Will it permit in many cases harmony and love to continue?

Women are more strongly partizan than men; they admire more strongly, and when one has become the idol of their choice there is nothing they would not do to secure his election ... Imagine the female portion of a household the members of one partizan committee and the men arrayed on the other side. Imagine the men of the opposite party holding consultations with the women of one's own household in the heat of a party contest. It is impossible under such circumstances that bitterness should not come into that home. Its harmony would be gone; it would no longer be a place of joy and love and trust; these would certainly give place to jealousy, hatred and malice.

I am firmly convinced that one of the curses of this age is that there is not enough of home life. I think that home life is the strength of any nation ... The demand for woman suffrage is a blow at this power. If I had the privilege, and wished to bring the greatest blessing possible to our people, I should choose to increase and develop the influence of the home, to endeavour to change the tendency of the times, and to encourage young people together to build homes where mutual companionship, harmony and love might prevail: such homes as would prove a greater attraction than the street parade, the saloon or the theatre: homes where character would be built which would increase right conduct and prove a shield from temptation.

WOMEN WITHOUT HOMES.

One reason urged why woman suffrage should be granted is because so many women are without homes. I know that this is true, and that the tendency in that direction is increasing, but it is largely the result of the prevailing fashion among young people to desire neither to be mistress of a home nor to work in the home of another. They choose in preference the factory, the counter of a store, and the tailor shop: anywhere to be entirely independent and to live unto themselves. I have no quarrel with them if they wish to do this, but I want to say that it is certainly not conducive to increasing morality. Intemperance is spoken of as the greatest evil, but I ask those who have observed more closely the workings of society whether or not the tendency to forsake home and home life does not lead directly to that end? I ask whether the prevailing vices of our cities and towns are not the direct outcome of forsaken homes, and do not lead directly in the way of the saloon and the grog shop? To introduce women into the political arena is to add to this tendency, and those who advocate it are incurring a great responsibility. I certainly shall not be one of them. The home is woman's place of power; if she is a true woman she rules there, although she does not assume that authority. This is her queenly station in every Christian country. Here her nobility, grace and moral power can be felt, and will always wield a greater influence on the nation than she ever could by assuming to take control in the political world.

DEGRADING WOMAN.

I have already stated that woman is most respected in Christian and civilized countries. Introduce her into politics; make her an active agent, an active canvasser in political campaigns; bring her upon the platform and let her try her hand at sarcasm and ridicule; let her drop her winning ways and patient persuasion; let her shake her fist in man's face; let her undertake to fight her way thus to fancied freedom, and declare her power to compel him to submit to her dictation, and what inevitably must be the result? Shall I still be expected to lift my hat in respectful deference? Will man anywhere give place to her, in the car or on the street? In so doing she declares her equality, and constantly states that she is not dependent. She will in the end be taken by most men at her word and left in public to look after herself ...

Example is given us of women in history who have figured as rulers of nations. We are frequently pointed to queens who have taken a notable place in history, but it will be observed always that these women have occupied this position only because they appeared in the direct line of descent, and because there was no male to fill the place. Our own Queen is pointed to as an example of what a woman can do in ruling a great nation. She has won the respect and admiration, not only of her own people, but of the whole civilized world. But how has she done this? Is it because she has assumed the position that these persons desire women generally to take? Has she assumed the position of a dictator, that she might have her will and her way? I think not.

She has always shown her dependence upon men by choosing from among her people the wisest and best men upon whom to place the responsibility of the great work of governing her vast empire. She is admired to-day, not because she is a ruler, but because, in the midst of all her queenly duties she still maintains the womanly part; she is esteemed because of the admirable example she has placed before her people as a dutiful wife and an affectionate mother.

I do not wish to be misunderstood by anyone. I am conscientious in my statement of the case. I am not seeking to degrade woman, but am anxious, rather, that she should maintain her present high place, and be beloved still more, if possible. What I have said here I have said in her defence. I am here to defend my wife and my daughters; I am here to stand in defence of our home; to stand in defence of the influence and power of woman in the home, in the church and in society, and I call upon the hon. members of the Legislature not to treat this matter as a trifling question, to pass it by with a smile and vote for the Bill because they think they are thus paying a compliment to woman. It is not a compliment to them to vote in favor of my hon. friend's proposition. I call upon them to take the manly part; to join with me in defending woman from the degrading influences which are sure to follow if she takes part in political warfare.

2. James L. Hughes, *Equal Suffrage*, 1910.

... 3. "*Women would not vote if they had the opportunity.*" Women do vote when they get the opportunity to do so. In all countries where they have the parliamentary franchise they vote quite as well as men. In some countries even a larger percentage of women vote than of men.

There is no use in theorizing about the question. Men proved conclusively that locomotives could not run on smooth rails, but they ran, and that settled the discussion. Women do vote in Church matters, in school elections, in municipal elections and in parliamentary elections wherever they have the legal right to do so. If women would not vote, no harm could come from making the experiment of granting woman suffrage.

4. "*All women do not wish to vote.*" True. Neither do all men. It would, therefore, be as logical to refuse to let men vote because some men do not care to vote as to refuse to let women vote because some of them do not yet wish to vote. Less than half the men vote at ordinary municipal elections in many places. It

would be utterly unjust on this account to disfranchise those who wish to vote. If only one hundred women in Canada believed it to be their right and duty to vote, there is no spirit of justice, human or divine, that would prevent their voting merely because other women do not wish to vote. Not one woman in a hundred wishes to teach school. The same argument would prohibit all women from teaching because all women do not wish to teach. The logical outcome of this argument allows no woman to do anything unless all women desire to do it. Many women do vote in municipal matters, and desire the right to vote on other questions. The indifference of women not yet aroused cannot affect the rights of those who are awake. The ballot was given to the negroes not because all negroes wanted it, but because it was right that they should have it. Duty is the broad ground on which the question rests. Thousands of true, pure, home-loving women sincerely believe it to be their duty to vote in order to help to decide great social and national questions that affect the well-being of their country and their homes. They surely have as well-defined a right to desire to vote as other women have to oppose woman's enfranchisement. The women who wish to vote do not try to compel those women to vote who oppose woman suffrage. This is an age of individual liberty. Right and duty and conscience should guide us. Each woman should be at liberty to decide for herself ...

10. *"Woman's mental nature is different from man's."* However it may be expressed, this is precisely the strongest reason why they should vote. God made man and woman different in characteristics, but He made the one the complement of the other. Perfect unity is wrought out of different but harmonious elements. Legislation will be essentially one-sided until man's ideals are balanced by woman's. Woman's individuality does differ from man's, and her individuality is necessary to perfect justice and harmony in the senate as well as in the home.

Woman's different mental attitude makes her vote valuable. She is the complement of man in the divine conception of humanity. Her vote should therefore be the complement of man's vote. The unity of related diversity produces harmony. The male and female elements of intellect and character when balanced produce the grandest unities of human intelligence. The enfranchisement of a sex means more than the liberation of a class chiefly because it brings a distinct and hitherto unrepresented element into the voting power of the world. There would be only a partial hope in securing woman suffrage if it would simply increase the number of voters. It will do much more than this. It will not only enlarge the voting power; it will enrich it.

11. *"Politics will degrade women."* *"It is because women have kept out of*

politics and generally out of the contentious arena, that they have remained gentle, tender and delicate women." Politics should not be degrading. It is discreditable to men that the sacred duty of statecraft should be associated with any processes or experiences of a debasing character. But the presence of woman purifies politics. The women of Wyoming are as womanly and as gentle as those in the neighboring States where women do not vote. The women who lead in municipal reforms in England, or who champion the cause of woman's enfranchisement there, are as true and pure and sweet-voiced as those who are conventional models. Politics should mean high thinking on social and national questions, and the carrying out of calm decisions by voting for right measures. Thinking about her country's history and present condition and hopes and relationships to other countries, need not destroy a woman's gentleness. Strength of character does not rob woman of her witching charm. The condition of politics, as admitted by this objection, indicates the need of woman's elevating, purifying influence.

Wendell Phillips crystallized the reply to this argument when he said, "Women will make the polling booth as pure as the parlor," and there is every reason to believe with Mr. Phillips that instead of politics degrading women, women would elevate politics. Why should it degrade a woman to do her part in making the laws of her country harmonize with her purest feelings and her highest thought? It is impossible to believe that such a result could follow such action. Character is not ennobled by thinking good thoughts, but by executing them. History proves conclusively that men have always risen to a higher dignity of manhood after being entrusted with the ballot. The result would inevitably be the same in the case of woman. The sense of responsibility would define and strengthen her character.

If politics are really degrading in themselves, men should be prohibited from taking part in them as well as women, but they are not necessarily degrading either to men or women. It is not necessary to theorize about this question, however. The test has been made for nearly forty years in Wyoming, and there has been no degradation of the women there, no unsexing, no loss of the sweetness and tenderness of woman's character ...

14. "*Wives might vote against their husbands, and thus destroy the harmony of the home.*" It is a strange conception of family harmony that husband and wife must think alike in regard to all subjects. This would not be true harmony, it would be mere sameness; and it is only logically conceivable on the surrender of the individuality of one to that of the other. This can never be done without degradation to the one who has to submit. Woman has had too much of such degradation. Why should two reasonable beings cease to recognize each other's

right to independent judgment because they are married to each other? Woman suffrage will elevate the condition of both husband and wife. The wife will be emancipated from a subjection pronounced by God to be a curse, and the husband will be saved from the debasing selfishness of believing himself to be the only member of his household worthy of being entrusted with the dignity of voting.

It would be a great advantage if the drunkard's wife and the moderate drinker's wife could vote in opposition to their husbands. Such opposition would result in ultimate peace and not discord ...

21. *"The transfer of power from the military to the unmilitary sex involves a change in the character of a nation. It involves, in short, national emasculation."*

The "war" argument is a very old one often answered. Women suffer as much as men from war. Their hardships at home are often equal, and their anxieties greater than those of the soldiers on the field or in the camp. Those soldiers are husbands, sons, brothers or lovers of sorrowing women. Many women labor in hospitals and various other ways for the soldiers. Woman's work is not man's work, nor man's work woman's, in war or in peace; but her work is quite as needful to the world's advancement, both in peace and war, as man's is. The time cometh, too, when "war shall be no more," and however man may sneer at woman suffrage, woman's work will aid in the fulfilment of this prophecy.

Then, too, very few men ever really fight for their country. The "war argument" would, therefore, disqualify most of the very men who use it from voting, and, carried to its logical limit, it would confine suffrage to soldiers alone. If the function of the State be only to raise armies and build court-houses and jails, woman may safely be refused the ballot; but if the State should deal with education, with moral, social, and industrial evolution, with art, science, charity, justice, manufactures and commerce, woman is entitled to her share in guiding the affairs of State.

22. *"Man alone can uphold government and enforce the law. Let the edifice of law be as moral as you will, its foundation is the force of the community, and the force of the community is male. Laws passed by the woman's vote will be felt to have no force behind them. Would the stronger sex obey any laws manifestly carried by the female vote in the interests of woman against man? Man would be tempted to resist woman's government when it galled him."* Women have made no proposal to establish a government by women. They strongly object to government by one sex, either male or female. It is not possible to have all the men voting on one side, and all the women on the other. All women do not think alike, nor will they ever vote unanimously any more than do the men. It is purely imaginary to

speak of woman's government. Government will always be maintained by a majority composed of the united votes of men and women. Moreover votes are now cast in the ballot box, and it will not be possible to find out whether the majority consists chiefly of men or of women. Therefore it is clear that the question of force cannot be brought into the suffrage discussion. The force of a nation must remain on the side of the majority. But modern governments do not rely on force for their existence or for the execution of their laws. The edicts of despots had to be forced on unwilling people. Rebels to-day know that their rebellion is not against kings or governments, but against the will of the people. Men submit to laws because they have shared in making them ...

27. *"Woman is weaker than man physically."* Has she strength enough to go to the polls and vote? If she has, the question of strength has nothing more to do with deciding the question of suffrage.

Men are allowed to vote who are carried in bed to the polls, so that by man's own physical standard set for himself, woman is competent to vote. No physical test has been adopted for men; none must be fixed for women. The strength test, and the sex test cannot be the same.

28. *"Woman's brain is not so large as man's, therefore she should not vote."* Size of brain has never been made a test in deciding man's right to vote, so this objection is irrelevant. No one ever saw an official at a polling booth with a tape-line to measure men's heads to decide whether they should vote or not. It is therefore perfectly illogical to raise the question of the size of woman's head in discussing her right to vote. If a standard could be fixed for the size of a voter's head, and applied in the case of men as well as women, there would be justice in the rule, but little sense. Only small-headed men, with their largest development in the back of their heads near the top, could be illogical enough to propose such a test. Quality of brain is more important than size of brain. Thousands of men vote in every country who are not equal in intelligence to the average woman. The great body of men most uniformly opposed to equal suffrage are not only small-headed, but small-hearted ...

30. *"Women are more nervous than men, and the excitement of elections would undermine their constitutions and tend to unbalance them."* Thousands of men vote whose nervous systems are in a worse condition than the nervous system of the average woman. Men indulge in smoking, in the drink habit and in other habits exhaustive to the nervous system more than women do, so men should take care lest, by suggesting a nervous test, they may be establishing a principle that will disfranchise the male sex at no distant date. If humanity demands that woman should be prohibited from voting in order to prevent her

physical deterioration in consequence of her present weakness, surely the same principle would prohibit those men from voting who are weaker than women, in order to prevent the further deterioration of their already enfeebled bodies.

It is very satisfactory to note that men as well as women are becoming aroused in regard to the physical deterioration of women under false conditions, and that widespread efforts are being made to improve the conditions of training and living so that woman may have the opportunity to develop vigor and endurance as freely as man.

Woman has been restricted in her physical development by conventionalities and erroneous notions that proscribed outdoor games as improper for her. She has, by custom, been confined to the house. Men have made it popular with women to be somewhat delicate, because they have too often shown a decided tendency to admire the frail, timid, dependent, "clinging little creatures." Robustness was really a disadvantage to a woman, and was likely to gain for her a reputation for masculinity ...

Sensible men and women have ceased to regard weakness as an essential characteristic of true womanhood. Women are freeing themselves from the tyranny of social customs which injure their health, and they are rapidly regaining the individuality which enables them to discard modes of dress that prevent the full and natural growth of their vital organs. Popular opinion and popular sentiment are removing the ban from girls and young women which made it immodest for them to play at outdoor sports, and so the women of the future are likely to get a fair chance to have better bodies. They need boating, the ball games, the running games and all sports that make energetic physical effort an essential to success quite as much as boys do, they need them more, indeed, to help to overcome the false training of centuries ...

3. H. Bate, "Are Women to Blame?," *Grain Growers' Guide*, March 1, 1911.

It is with interest, amusement and disgust that I read the arguments in favor of women's suffrage as advanced by contributors to your department of THE GUIDE. In the first place, I doubt very much if a majority of women are in favor of suffrage. It is a matter that should be decided for women by women. If it can be proven that the majority of women really desire so-called equal rights with men, I say let them have them at once.

I have taken the trouble to inquire to the different classes, professional, domestic and leisured women of my acquaintance and I find that 75 per cent do not bother their heads about it, and half of the other 25 per cent are in disfavor of the suffrage movement. I think I am safe in saying that these women are as intellectual, cultured and as up-to-date as the average.

It amuses me to see the horrible pictures that these suffrage exponents draw of mere man as a monster of oppression, and it leads me to mention that as women had the bearing and rearing of man, as they had the first chance to mold and form his character, why did they not make a better job of it? To my mind their arguments are an attempt at face saving, and a way they have of covering up their botch-work. According to the reasoning of a great many of the leading suffragists on account of the injustice and oppression of man in the past, it was impossible that our grandmothers and mothers could have been women of intellect, culture, virtue and purity. They must have been mere child-bearing, dish-washing, cooking machines. The suffragist has yet, I think, to advance arguments that will convince the world that the noble women of the past would have been more noble than they were if they had the privilege of so-called equal rights. They have yet to show me how so-called equal rights will cause the women of today to be able to rear more noble sons than Christ, Luther, Knox, Lincoln, or the great many other honorable and just men who lived in the past—who live today. How can it cause the women of today to bear and rear more beautiful and better daughters than Mary, Mother of Christ, Martha, Florence Nightingale or Queen Victoria, or our mothers, who we all agree were as pure and noble, as much a power for good in the world, as if they had had these so-called equal rights. If it can with logic and reason be proven to me that suffrage will cause the world to be richer in more honorable, Christ-like men, or more pure and virtuous women than the above, I am prepared to became a champion of woman's rights for all time.

It is a fact admitted by all who have made a study of the matter that it takes the average person a lifetime to make a success of any one thing. The average person cannot do two things well. I believe the all-wise Creator intended men for the sphere outside the home; women for the sphere inside of the home. If not we would have been made more alike in temperament. If the average woman is going to be a successful homekeeper she will find her life well and satisfactorily filled as our mothers did. In winning a satisfactory living from the world, no matter in what line of labor or endeavor, the average man will find his life well and satisfactorily filled as our fathers did. Outside the home women have not attained the heights of worldly endeavor as a Cromwell, Washington, Karl Marx, Lloyd-George, etc., did. They were not created of the same stuff or with that end in view, of if they had been all the oppression of man that ever was could not have kept them down. It did not keep those fellows down. It is true if the vote was given to women it might down the liquor traffic the sooner, but if we do not become temperate in all things what is the use? When the windows need washing we do not scrub up one pane of glass and call the job done; we wash them all.

When we see as we often do these reformer women wearing hats decorated with the innocent little birds and preaching the cause of humanity, we can only come to the conclusion that after all women are subject to the same inconstancies and errors that men have been. Let the women of today learn less worldliness and more of that good old book, the Bible, that our mothers and grandmothers knew so well and the result will be that both sexes will become more free and a force for good in the world to any extent they desire.

4. Henri Bourassa, "Women's Suffrage, Its Effectiveness, Its Legitimacy," *Le Devoir*, 24 April 1913.

... But where we no longer agree with the advocates of suffrage is in the suffragettes' narrow and peculiar conception of the way in which women can and must practise this collaboration and demonstrate their influence.

The idea that, within Anglo-Saxon civilizations—where the woman, long deprived of her characteristic charms and natural powers of influence, could hold no sway over society, in which, moreover, individual political prerogatives have been made the main source of social initiatives—women are looking to exert their influence by the same means as men, to play a role identical to that of men, is understandable, even while one remains sceptical as to the outcome. In England there is a saying, blunt but true, that: "Parliament can do anything ... except make a woman a man."

But in countries of French and Catholic mould, where the woman's dominant influence has been exerted for centuries in every sphere of heart, mind, and deed, where the saying "In all things, *cherchez la femme*" could be rendered banal, this mistaken idea of a woman's social role cannot prevail over tradition, over the general way of thinking, over the instinct of nature. The vast majority of women would reject it, and they would be right to do so. Instinctively obeying this supreme law, that all strength increases in proportion to its conformity with the laws specific to its nature, they sense that on the day they exercised the same powers of influence as men, they would cease to benefit from those that are their own, or at least, that the effectiveness of those powers would markedly diminish ...

The concrete examples that can be given by suffragettes in support of their argument prove nothing counter to this general law.

That in Australia or elsewhere, women electors have succeeded in bringing about this or that reform in no way proves that without being electors, the same women could not, by other means, have obtained the same reforms and even others. And in particular, it proves still less that, in other countries, women would gain, as electors, influence they could not more effectively exert on a personal or social plane.

That in Montreal, infant mortality, alcoholism, tuberculosis, worldliness, and a host of other social scourges,—whether physical or moral—call out for the dedication and individual and collective actions of women, is certain. But that, in order to influence society, laws, and the authorities, this dedication and action should require the right to vote and to participate in electoral struggles, is far less certain. Given our French mentality, it is the opposite that would happen.

Let the most intelligent, most dedicated women coordinate their efforts and focus them on those areas in which their womanly influence can bring pressure, through feminine ways with arguments that only the heart and charm of a woman can devise, and they will achieve their goal far more surely than through conferences, meetings, and electoral committees. The significant and unobtrusive work accomplished by a great number of French-Canadian women, religious or lay,—who, besides, are totally without experience in the use of un-seemly publicity—shows that they are capable of any initiative, of any productive dedication. Broadening their field of action and giving them the tools they need would be all that is required to solve the new and growing problems that are crying out for attention.

If this dedication unfortunately dried up, political action and exercising of the right to vote would certainly not be compensation for it ...

I will mention only in passing the question of women's suffrage envisaged as a woman's absolute right.

With that faculty which is characteristic of women, and which renders them as capable of accomplishing specific tasks as they are incapable of contemplating the broader issues, suffragettes see in the right to vote a concrete right, absolute, a sort of alpha and omega of the law of the equality of the sexes.

They seem unaware that the right to vote is but the corollary of a set of duties and roles necessary to the governing and defence of society.

The right to vote entails, in terms of power at least, eligibility for every administrative and legislative role, and the obligation to see to every civil and military responsibility.

Until the suffragettes have shown proof of women's aptitude for filling these diverse roles and their own willingness to assume any and all of these responsibilities, they merit no attention when they speak of "rights," "equality," and "enfranchisement."

If they object that a woman's physical constitution and the demands of motherhood preclude her from most of these roles and responsibilities, they themselves provide the fundamental argument that destroys their whole theory – which is that the difference between the sexes means, not an inequality of conditions, but a sharing of roles and social responsibilities, and also a sharing of the rights that correspond to those responsibilities and roles. That which feminists and suffragettes denounce as a deprivation of rights, as a mark of servitude, is in reality nothing but emancipation from numerous obligations incompatible with the roles of wife and mother, which remain, in spite of feminism, the normal roles of the majority of women ...

As for those suffragettes who confine themselves to demanding the right to vote without aspiring to eligibility for State office, they are even less logical than the others and are no more clearer-headed, and no more broad-minded.

They are unaware of that other basic truth—that the right to vote is simply the power given to those who have made it their mission to protect society to delegate their authority to a certain number among them.

No doubt, this power is supposed to involve, for those who exercise it, the necessary willingness and intelligence to make judicious choices and themselves perform, should the need arise, the functions they entrust to their representatives. And feminists have had no difficulty showing that a goodly number of electors and elected are very little suited to the exercise of their respective functions and duties. Some excellent arguments can be drawn from this against universal suffrage and against representative government—in the way that every political regime's injustices have provided convincing arguments against each of them.

But the fact that men fail to properly perform the functions incumbent upon them, and even that many women would be better able to handle this duty than would a number of men, in no way means that these functions should be entrusted to women—no more so than that the sizeable number of unfaithful wives and incapable mothers, or depraved, cruel, or stupid women, those of easy virtue or of spendthrift ways, show that they should be replaced by male incubators, male wet-nurses, male nannies, male housewives.

There is a great deal still to be done in terms of moral reform and the reform of laws and society, in Canada as elsewhere;—but these reforms will be that much more fruitful and enduring if they remain in keeping with the laws of nature and the dictates of Providence.

5. Nellie McClung, *In Times Like These*, 1915

Any man who is actively engaged in politics, and declares that politics are too corrupt for women, admits one of two things, either that he is a party to this corruption, or that he is unable to prevent it—and in either case something should be done. Politics are not inherently vicious. The office of lawmaker should be the highest in the land, equaled in honor only by that of the minister of the gospel. In the old days, the two were combined with very good effect; but they seem to have drifted apart in more recent years.

If politics are too corrupt for women, they are too corrupt for men; for men and women are one—indissolubly joined together for good or ill. Many men have tried to put all their religion and virtue in their wife's name, but it does not work very well. When social conditions are corrupt women cannot escape by shutting their eyes, and taking no interest. It would be far better to give them a chance to clean them up.

What would you think of a man who would say to his wife: 'This house to which I am bringing you to live is very dirty and unsanitary, but I will not allow you—the dear wife whom I have sworn to protect—to touch it. It is too dirty for your precious little white hands! You must stay upstairs, dear. Of course the odor from below may come up to you, but use your smelling salts and think no evil. I do not hope to ever be able to clean it up, but certainly you must never think of trying.'

Do you think any woman would stand for that? She would say: 'John, you are all right in your way, but there are some places where your brain skids. Perhaps you had better stay downtown today for lunch. But on your way down please call at the grocer's, and send me a scrubbing brush and a package of Dutch Cleanser, and some chloride of lime, and now hurry.' Women have cleaned up things since time began; and if women ever get into politics there will be a cleaning-out of pigeon-holes and forgotten corners, on which the dust of years has fallen, and the sound of the political carpet-beater will be heard in the land.

There is another hardy perennial that constantly lifts its head above the earth, persistently refusing to be ploughed under, and that is that if women were ever given a chance to participate in outside affairs, that family quarrels would result; that men and their wives who have traveled the way of life together, side by side for years, and come safely through religious discussions, and discussions relating to 'his' people and 'her' people, would angrily rend each other over politics, and great damage to the furniture would be the result. Father and son have been known to live under the same roof and vote differently, and yet live!

Not only to live, but live peaceably! If a husband and wife are going to quarrel they will find a cause for dispute easily enough, and will not be compelled to wait for election day. And supposing that they have never, never had a single dispute, and not a ripple has ever marred the placid surface of their matrimonial sea, I believe that a small family jar—or at least a real lively argument—will do them good. It is in order to keep the white-winged angel of peace hovering over the home that married women are not allowed to vote in many places. Spinsters and widows are counted worthy of voice in the selection of school trustee, and alderman, and mayor, but not the woman who has taken to herself a husband and still has him.

What a strange commentary on marriage that it should disqualify a woman from voting. Why should marriage disqualify a woman? Men have been known to vote for years after they were dead!

Quite different from the 'family jar' theory, another reason is advanced against married women voting—it is said that they would all vote with their husbands, and that the married man's vote would thereby be doubled. We believe it is eminently right and proper that husband and wife should vote the same way, and in that case no one would be able to tell whether the wife was voting with the husband or the husband voting with the wife. Neither would it matter. If giving the franchise to women did nothing more than double the married man's vote it would do a splendid thing for the country, for the married man is the best voter we have; generally speaking, he is a man of family and property— surely if we can depend on anyone we can depend upon him, and if by giving his wife a vote we can double his—we have done something to offset the irresponsible transient vote of the man who has no interest in the community.

There is another sturdy prejudice that blooms everywhere in all climates, and that is that women would not vote if they had the privilege; and this is many times used as a crushing argument against woman suffrage. But why worry? If women do not use it, then surely there is no harm done; but those who use the argument seem to imply that a vote unused is a very dangerous thing to leave lying around, and will probably spoil and blow up. In support of this statement instances are cited of women letting their vote lie idle and unimproved in elections for school trustee and alderman. Of course, the percentage of men voting in these contests was quite small, too, but no person finds fault with that.

Women may have been careless about their franchise in elections where no great issue is at stake, but when moral matters are being decided women have not shown any lack of interest ...

'Why, Uncle Henry!' exclaimed one man to another on election day. 'I never saw you out to vote before. What struck you?'

'Hadn't voted for fifteen years,' declared Uncle Henry, 'but you bet I came out today to vote against givin' these fool women a vote; what's the good of givin' them a vote? they wouldn't use it!'

Then, of course, on the other hand there are those who claim that women would vote too much—that they would vote not wisely but too well; that they would take up voting as a life work to the exclusion of husband, home and children. There seems to be considerable misapprehension on the subject of voting. It is really a simple and perfectly innocent performance, quickly over, and with no bad after-effects.

It is usually done in a vacant room in a school or the vestry of a church, or a town hall. No drunken men stare at you. You are not jostled or pushed—you wait your turn in an orderly line, much as you have waited to buy a ticket at a railway station. Two tame and quiet-looking men sit at a table, and when your turn comes, they ask you your name, which is perhaps slightly embarrassing, but it is not as bad as it might be, for they do not ask your age, or of what disease did your grandmother die. You go behind the screen with your ballot paper in your hand, and there you find a seal-brown pencil tied with a chaste white string. Even the temptation of annexing the pencil is removed from your frail humanity. You mark your ballot, and drop it in the box, and come out into the sunlight again. If you had never heard that you had done an unladylike thing you would not know it. It all felt solemn, and serious, and very respectable to you, something like a Sunday-school convention. Then, too, you are surprised at what a short time you have been away from home. You put the potatoes on when you left home, and now you are back in time to strain them.

In spite of the testimony of many reputable women that they have been able to vote and get the dinner on one and the same day, there still exists a strong belief that the whole household machinery goes out of order when a woman goes to vote. No person denies a woman the right to go to church, and yet the church service takes a great deal more time than voting. People even concede to women the right to go shopping, or visiting a friend, or an occasional concert. But the wife and mother, with her God-given, sacred trust of molding the young life of our land, must never dream of going round the corner to vote. 'Who will mind the baby?' cried one of our public men, in great agony of spirit, 'when the mother goes to vote?'

... Father comes home, tired, weary, footsore, toe-nails ingrowing, caused by undarned stockings, and finds the fire out, house cold and empty, save for his half-dozen children, all crying.

'Where is your mother?' the poor man asks in broken tones. For a moment the sobs are hushed while little Ellie replies: 'Out voting!'

Father bursts into tears.

Of course, people tell us, it is not the mere act of voting which demoralizes women—if they would only vote and be done with it; but women are creatures of habit, and habits once formed are hard to break; and although the polls are only open every three or four years, if women once get into the way of going to them, they will hang around there all the rest of the time. It is in woman's impressionable nature that the real danger lies.

Another shoot of this hardy shrub of prejudice is that women are too good to mingle in everyday life—they are too sweet and too frail—that women are angels. If women are angels we should try to get them into public life as soon as possible, for there is a great shortage of angels there just at present, if all we hear is true.

Then there is the pedestal theory—that women are away up on a pedestal, and down below, looking up at them with deep adoration, are men, their willing slaves. Sitting up on a pedestal does not appeal very strongly to a healthy woman— and, besides, if a woman has been on a pedestal for any length of time, it must be very hard to have to come down and cut the wood.

These tender-hearted and chivalrous gentlemen who tell you of their adoration for women, cannot bear to think of women occupying public positions. Their tender hearts shrink from the idea of women lawyers or women policemen, or even women preachers; these positions would 'rub the bloom off the peach,' to use their own eloquent words. They cannot bear, they say, to see women leaving the sacred precincts of home—and yet their offices are scrubbed by women who do their work while other people sleep—poor women who leave the sacred precincts of home to earn enough to keep the breath of life in them, who carry their scrub-pails home, through the deserted streets, long after the cars have stopped running. They are exposed to cold, to hunger, to insult—poor souls—is there any pity felt for them? Not that we have heard of. The tender-hearted ones can bear this with equanimity. It is the thought of women getting into comfortable and well-paid positions which wrings their manly hearts.

Another aspect of the case is that women can do more with their indirect influence than by the ballot; though just why they cannot do better still with both does not appear to be very plain. The ballot is a straight-forward dignified way of making your desire or choice felt. There are some things which are not pleasant to talk about, but would be delightful to vote against. Instead of having to beg, and coax, and entreat, and beseech, and denounce as women have had to do all down the centuries, in regard to the evil things which threaten to destroy their homes and those whom they love, what a glorious thing it would be if women could go out and vote against these things. It seems like a straightforward and easy way of expressing one's opinion.

But, of course, popular opinion says it is not 'womanly.' The 'womanly way' is to nag and tease. Women have often been told that if they go about it right they can get anything. They are encouraged to plot and scheme, and deceive, and wheedle, and coax for things. This is womanly and sweet. Of course, if this fails, they still have tears—they can always cry and have hysterics, and raise hob generally, but they must do it in a womanly way. Will the time ever come when the word 'feminine' will have in it no trace of trickery?

Women are too sentimental to vote, say the politicians sometimes. Sentiment is nothing to be ashamed of, and perhaps an infusion of sentiment in politics is what we need. Honor and honesty, love and loyalty, are only sentiments, and yet they make the fabric out of which our finest traditions are woven ...

For too long people have regarded politics as a scheme whereby easy money might be obtained. Politics has meant favors, pulls, easy jobs for friends, new telephone lines, ditches. The question has not been: 'What can I do for my country?' but: 'What can I get? What is there in this for me?' The test of a member of Parliament as voiced by his constitutents has been: 'What has he got for us?' The good member who will be elected the next time is the one who did not forget his friends, who got us a Normal School, or a Court House, or an Institution for the Blind, something that we could see or touch, eat or drink. Surely a touch of sentiment in politics would do no harm ...

There are people who tell us that the reason women must never be allowed to vote is because they do not want to vote, the inference being that women are never given anything that they do not want ...

That fact that many women are indifferent on the subject does not alter the situation. People are indifferent about many things that they should be interested in. The indifference of people on the subject of ventilation and hygiene does not change the laws of health. The indifference of many parents on the subject of an education for their children does not alter the value of education. If one woman wants to vote, she should have that opportunity just as if one woman desires a college education, she should not be held back because of the indifferent careless ones who do not desire it. Why should the mentally inert, careless, uninterested woman, who cares nothing for humanity but is contented to patter along her own little narrow way, set the pace for the others of us? Voting will not be compulsory; the shrinking violets will not be torn from their shady fence-corner; the 'home bodies' will be able to still sit in rapt contemplation of their own fireside. We will not force the vote upon them, but why should they force their votelessness upon us?

6. Stephen Leacock, "The Woman Question," in *Essays and Literary Studies*, 1916.

... 'Things are all wrong,' she screamed, 'with the *status* of women.' Therein she was quite right. 'The remedy for it all,' she howled, 'is to make women "free," to give women the vote. When once women are free everything will be all right.' Therein the woman with the spectacles was, and is, utterly wrong.

The women's vote, when they get it, will leave women much as they were before ...

For when the vote is reached the woman question will not be solved but only begun. In and of itself, a vote is nothing. It neither warms the skin nor fills the stomach. Very often the privilege of a vote confers nothing but the right to express one's opinion as to which of two crooks is the crookeder.

But after the women have obtained the vote the question is, what are they going to do with it? The answer is, nothing, or at any rate nothing that men would not do without them. Their only visible use of it will be to elect men into office. Fortunately for us all they will not elect women. Here and there perhaps at the outset, it will be done as the result of a sort of spite, a kind of sex antagonism bred by the controversy itself. But, speaking broadly, the women's vote will not be used to elect women to office. Women do not think enough of one another to do that. If they want a lawyer they consult a man, and those who can afford it have their clothes made by men, and their cooking done by a chef. As for their money, no woman would entrust that to another woman's keeping. They are far too wise for that.

So the woman's vote will not result in the setting up of female prime ministers and of parliaments in which the occupants of the treasury bench cast languishing eyes across at the flushed faces of the opposition. From the utter ruin involved in such an attempt at mixed government, the women themselves will save us. They will elect men. They may even pick some good ones. It is a nice question and will stand thinking about.

But what else, or what further can they do, by means of their vote and their representatives to 'emancipate' and 'liberate' their sex?

Many feminists would tell us at once that if women had the vote they would, first and foremost, throw everything open to women on the same terms as men. Whole speeches are made on this point, and a fine fury thrown into it, often very beautiful to behold.

The entire idea is a delusion. Practically all of the world's work is open to women now, wide open. *The only trouble is that they can't do it*. There is nothing to prevent a woman from managing a bank, or organising a company, or running a department store, or floating a merger, or building a railway—except the simple fact that she can't. Here and there an odd woman does such things, but she is only the exception that proves the rule. Such women are merely—and here I am speaking in the most decorous biological sense—'sports.' The ordinary woman cannot do the ordinary man's work. She never has and never will. The reasons why she can't are so many, that is, she *can't* in so many different ways, that it is not worthwhile to try to name them.

Here and there it is true there are things closed to women, not by their own inability but by the law. This is a gross injustice. There is no defence for it. The province in which I live, for example, refuses to allow women to practise as lawyers. This is wrong. Women have just as good a right to fail at being lawyers as they have at anything else. But even if all these legal disabilities, where they exist, were removed (as they will be under a woman's vote) the difference to women at large will be infinitesimal. A few gifted 'sports' will earn a handsome livelihood but the woman question in the larger sense will not move one inch nearer to solution.

The feminists, in fact, are haunted by the idea that it is possible for the average woman to have a life patterned after that of the ordinary man. They imagine her as having a career, a profession, a vocation—something which will be her 'life work'—just as selling coal is the life work of the coal merchant.

If this were so, the whole question would be solved. Women and men would become equal and independent. It is thus indeed that the feminist sees them, through the roseate mist created by imagination. Husband and wife appear as a couple of honourable partners who share a house together. Each is off to business in the morning. The husband is, let us say, a stock broker: the wife manufactures iron and steel. The wife is a Liberal, the husband a Conservative. At their dinner they have animated discussions over the tariff till it is time for them to go to their clubs.

These two impossible creatures haunt the brain of the feminist and disport them in the pages of the up-to-date novel.

The whole thing is mere fiction. It is quite impossible for women—the average and ordinary women—to go in for having a career. Nature has forbidden it. The average woman must necessarily have—I can only give the figures roughly—about three and a quarter children. She must replace in the population herself and her husband with something over to allow for the people who never marry and for the children that do not reach maturity. If she fails to do this the population comes to an end. Any scheme of social life must allow for these three and a quarter children and for the years of care that must be devoted to them. The vacuum cleaner can take the place of the housewife. It cannot replace the mother. No man ever said his prayers at the knees of a vacuum cleaner, or drew his first lessons in manliness and worth from the sweet old-fashioned stories that a vacuum cleaner told. Feminists of the enraged kind may talk as they will of the paid attendant and the expert baby minder. Fiddlesticks! These things are a mere supplement, useful enough but as far away from the realities of motherhood as the vacuum cleaner itself. But the point is one that need not be laboured. Sensible people understand it as soon as said. With fools it is not worth while to argue.

But, it may be urged, there are, even as it is, a great many women who are working. The wages that they receive are extremely low. They are lower in most cases than the wages for the same, or similar work, done by men. Cannot the woman's vote at least remedy this?

Here is something that deserves thinking about and that is far more nearly within the realm of what is actual and possible than wild talk of equalising and revolutionising the sexes.

It is quite true that women's work is underpaid. But this is only a part of a larger social injustice.

The case stands somewhat as follows: Women get low wages because low wages are all that they are worth. Taken by itself this is a brutal and misleading statement. What is meant is this. The rewards and punishments in the unequal and ill-adjusted world in which we live are most unfair. The price of anything—sugar, potatoes, labour, or anything else—varies according to the supply and demand: if many people want it and few can supply it the price goes up: if the contrary it goes down. If enough cabbages are brought to market they will not bring a cent a piece, no matter what it cost to raise them.

On these terms each of us sells his labour. The lucky ones, with some rare gift, or trained capacity, or some ability that by mere circumstance happens to be in a great demand, can sell high. If there were only one night plumber in a great city, and the water pipes in a dozen homes of a dozen millionaires should burst all at once, he might charge a fee like that of a consulting lawyer …

So it stands with women's wages. It is the sheer numbers of the women themselves, crowding after the few jobs that they can do, that brings them down. It has nothing to do with the attitude of men collectively towards women in the lump. It cannot be remedied by any form of woman's freedom. Its remedy is bound up with the general removal of social injustice, the general abolition of poverty, which is to prove the great question of the century before us. The question of women's wages is a part of the wages' question.

To my thinking the whole idea of making women free and equal (politically) with men as a way of improving their *status*, starts from a wrong basis and proceeds in a wrong direction.

Women need not more freedom but less. Social policy should proceed from the fundamental truth that women are and must be dependent. If they cannot be looked after by an individual (a thing on which they took their chance in earlier days) they must be looked after by the State. To expect a woman, for example, if left by the death of her husband with young children without support, to maintain herself by her own efforts, is the most absurd mockery of freedom ever devised. Earlier generations of mankind, for all that they lived in the jungle and wore cocoanut leaves, knew nothing of it. To turn a girl loose in the world to work for herself, when there is no work to be had, or none at a price that will support life, is a social crime …

I leave [readers] with the thought that perhaps in the modern age it is not the increased freedom of woman that is needed but the increased recognition of their dependence. Let the reader remain agonised over that till I write something else.

7. H.D.P., "The Failure of the Suffrage Movement to Bring Freedom to Women," *Woman Worker*, December 1928.

The great activity shown when occasion demands by political parties in their efforts to get the woman vote, brings to mind many of the promises and prophesies which were made by friends and foes in those not distant days when it required a little courage to wear a "votes for women" button.

Of course the "Antis" sounded their usual alarm—the home would be destroyed—and one admits that many suffragists also showed their ignorance of the "world process" by their optimistic arguments along opposite lines: And after it was all over what happened?

In the first place, the anti-suffragists who were loudest in proclaiming that "woman's place is the home" were the very first to step out and seek political and other offices. And of all the others who fought so well for this right of self-expression, only one or two, here and there over the whole country, saw that this was not the end of the struggle, but only a very small beginning.

To be sure, it was not a working class movement. The majority in it were middle class and fairly satisfied with conditions—as one well known club woman said to me "It seems so absurd that my gardener can vote and I can't." It was just a matter of status with her.

They were the sort who used to get up in meetings and enquire anxiously—"but who will do the menial work," when one was trying to picture a better social order. Evidently, if it meant work and responsibility for all, they were not going to stand for it. But they were mostly nice, kind ladies, and they often meant well, as on the occasion when one of them undertook to investigate conditions in a certain workshop, she brought back an excellent report, and when asked from whom she got her information, she said, "Oh, I went right to the manager!" And how they wanted to supervise the spending of working class housewives at the beginning of the war. It seems that some of these wasteful creatures were discovered buying oranges and pickles—and later on it was gramophones and pianos!

But when election time came these same fine ladies were very busy calling on women in various working class districts, and acting so "perfectly lovely," that many a foolish woman voted against her own interests and against her family and her class, because she was so flattered she was easily deceived.

In the U.S.A. a group of influential ones, called "The Women's National Party," are now going before Congress—supported by members of the employer's association—and opposing legislation that would aid great numbers of women to an approach to economic equality with men. They call it, asking for "equal rights." If, for instance, men are working ten hours a day in certain places, women employed there must also have the "right" to work ten hours a day. If successful, they will nullify the work of years done by trade unions and labor groups for the betterment and relief of working women. It may be that they do not grasp the serious problems of the woman worker, but, anyway, they are proving again that the business of fair play for all who work for wages is the worker's own task.

Another reason why the vote has been of so little use to us is the fact that hundreds of thousands are always disfranchised.

The law requires certain conditions and the worker following his job or moving about in search of employment is thus automatically off the voters' list.

And the working class generally is suffering today in "mind, body, and estate" because we've been too confiding, too good natured, too patient. We have failed to see that whatever value there was in the vote was lost entirely unless used for ourselves. And if this be intelligent selfishness there's little to argue about.

Certainly the so-called "dignity of labor" is only an election phrase, but there are enough workers to give it real meaning. We could very well take a lesson from the conduct of those in authority over us. They realize what class loyalty means, even though they may not like or in any way approve of each other individually. Yet they are rarely so silly as to be caught voting or acting in any way against their class interests. They stick together.

And since we have in Canada such a high class paper as "The Woman Worker" it must be now much easier to get together in great numbers with one common denominator—working class freedom.

If we meet just as working women, with no handicaps because of race, creed or color, it will speed up the day when voting will not be the force it now is, when governments will not be something remote and threatening, when the ruling of peoples will give place to the administration of things "for the well-being of all."

Readings

Bacchi, C. *Liberation Deferred? The Ideas of the English Canadian Suffragists, 1877–1918.* Toronto: University of Toronto Press, 1983.

Cleverdon, C. *The Woman's Suffrage Movement in Canada: The Start of Liberation.* Second edition. Toronto: University of Toronto Press, 1974.

Cohen, Y. *Femmes de Parole: L'Histoire de Cerlces de Fermieres du Quebec, 1915–1990.* Montreal: Le Jour, 1990.

Cook, R., and W. Mitchinson, eds. *The Proper Sphere: Women's Place in Canadian Society.* Toronto: Oxford University Press, 1974.

Crowley, T. *Agnes Macphail and the Politics of Equality.* Toronto: James Lorimer, 1990.

Crowley, T. "Adelaide Hoodless and the Canadian Gibson Girl," *Canadian Historical Review,* 1986.

Cramner, M. "Public and Political: Documents of the Women's Suffrage Campaign in British Columbia, 1871-1917: The View from Victoria," in B. Latham and C. Kess, eds. *In Her Own Right: Selected Essay on Women's History in B.C.* Victoria: Camosun College, 1980.

Flemengo, J. "A Legacy of Ambivalence: Responses to Nellie McClung," *Journal of Canadian Studies* 34, 4 (Winter 1999–2000).

Forbes, E. "Battles in Another War: Edith Archibald and the Halifax Feminist Movement," in his *Challenging the Regional Stereotype: Essays on the 20th Century Maritimes.* Fredericton: Acadiensis Press, 1989.

Hallet, M., and M. Davis. *Firing the Heather: The Life and Times of Nellie McClung.* Calgary: Fifth House, 1993.

Kealey, L., ed. *A Not Unreasonable Claim: Women and Reform in Canada, 1880s–1920s.* Toronto: Women's Press 1979.

Kealey, L., and J. Sangster, eds. *Beyond the Vote: Canadian Women and Politics.* Toronto: University of Toronto Press, 1989.

Kinnear, M., ed. *First Days, Fighting Days: Women in Manitoba History.* Regina: Canadian Plains Research Centre, 1989.

Latham, B., and R. Pazdro, eds. *Not Just Pin Money: Selected Essays in the History of Women's Work in British Columbia*. Victoria: Camosun College, 1984.

Lavigne, M. and Y. Pinard, eds. *Travailleuses et Feministes: Aspects Historiques*. Montreal: Boreal Express, 1983.

Le Clio Collectif, *L'Historie des Femmes au Quebec depuis Quatre Siecles*. Montreal: Women's Press, 1991.

Light, B., and J. Parr, eds. *Canadian Women on the Move, 1867–1920*. Toronto: New Hogtown Press, 1984.

Newton, J. *The Feminist Challenge to the Canadian Left, 1900–1918*. Montreal: McGill-Queen's University Press, 1995.

Roberts, W. *Honest Womanhood: Feminism, Femininity, and Class Consciousness among Toronto Working Women, 1893–1914*. Toronto: New Hogtown Press, 1976.

Sangster, J. *Dreams of Equality: Women on the Canadian Left, 1920–1950*. Toronto: McClelland and Stewart, 1987.

Silverman, E. *The Last Best West: Women on the Alberta Frontier, 1880–1930*. Montreal: Eden Press, 1984.

Strong-Boag, V. *The Parliament of Women. The National Council of Women of Canada 1893–1929*. Ottawa: National Museums of Canada, 1976.

Strong-Boag, V. "'Ever a Crusader': Nellie McClung, First Wave Feminist," in V. Strong-Boag and A. Fellman, eds. *Rethinking Canada: The Promise of Womens's History*. Second edition. Toronto: Copp Clark Pitman, 1991.

Strong-Boag, V. "Independent Women, Problematic Men: First and Second Wave Anti-Feminism in Canada from Goldwin Smith to Betty Steele," *Social History* 57 (May 1996).

Strong-Boag, V. *The New Day Recalled: Lives of Girls and Women in English Canada, 1919–1939*. Toronto: Copp Clark Pitman, 1988.

Trofimenkoff, S. "Henri Bourassa and the 'Woman Question,'" *Journal of Canadian Studies* 10 (November 1975).

Warne, R. *Literature as Pulpit: The Christian Social Activism of Nellie L. McClung*. Waterloo: Wilfred Laurier Press, 1988.

Chapter Eight

"What is Our Duty?":
Military Service in World War I

1. G. Starr, 123rd Battalion Recruiting Leaflet.
2. Peter McArthur, "Country Recruits," *Globe*, January 30, 1915.
3. *Saturday Night,* August 1915.
4. Talbot M. Papineau, "An Open Letter from Capt Talbot Papineau to Mr. Henri Bourassa," March 21, 1916.
5. Henri Bourassa, "Mr. Bourassa's Reply to Capt. Talbot Papineau's Letter," August 2, 1916.
6. "No More Canadians For Overseas Service. This Young Dominion Has Sacrificed Enough," *Sault Express,* June 23, 1916.
7. Robert Borden, *Debates,* House of Commons, 1917.
8. Francis Marion Beynon, "Women's View of Conscription," *The Grain Growers' Guide* May 30, 1917.
9. Joseph Ainey, "Canadian Labour and Conscription," *Le Devoir,* July 5, 1917.
10. Rev. S.D. Chown, "An Open Letter on the Duty of the Hour," *Christian Guardian*, Dec 12, 1917.

Introduction

Canada did not have a strong military tradition and was unprepared, psychologically and materially, for the Great War when it broke out in the summer of 1914. Just the same, the nation responded with aplomb to the British declaration of war. This, of course, was not a matter of choice. Under the British North America Act, Britain still chose the Dominion's friends and enemies, and the British declaration of war automatically included Canada—which suited most Canadians in the summer of 1914. The war, however, turned out to be less gloriously romantic than its initial billing. Modern mechanized warfare dehumanized combat to the point where the enemy became a faceless foe unleashing a relentless barrage of lethal shells. There was mustard gas, barbed wire, and hopeless charges into no-man's land. Living conditions at the front degenerated into raw survival in rat-infested, water-filled trenches. Soldiers were cold, hungry, flea-ridden, bored, terrified, and often deeply disillusioned. In total, some 620,000 Canadian men and several thousand women actively served over the course of the conflict, of whom 60,661 died. Those enormous numbers, from a national population of a mere eight million in 1914, may tempt Canadians to believe that the nation gave a disproportionate number of its young to the war. Canada did indeed make enormous sacrifices but its efforts were, in fact, proportionally smaller than some other members of the Empire. Part of the explanation lies in the difficulty of maintaining and increasing the size of Canada's manpower contribution.

Recruiting initially proceeded very successfully, with young men across Canada flocking to the recruiting stations. The flood of volunteers, however, dried to a trickle by 1916 when descriptions of the Western Front reached home and patriotic enthusiasm evaporated. The Federal government responded with an intense and relatively crude propaganda campaign geared to encourage recalcitrant young men to sign up. Prime Minister Robert Borden, after all, wanted 500,000 men in uniform, which indeed called for more concerted recruitment. The essence of the campaign was simple: any young, able-bodied man not in uniform was presumably shirking his responsibility to Canada and the Empire, and must be "encouraged" to see the error of his ways. This could be done by humiliating him through "white-feathering," appealing to his sense of duty, warning him of social stigmas if he did not volunteer, and by any other means the government thought might work. Propaganda posters glamorized the soldier's life and boldly implied that the war was a grand and noble adventure, despite what anyone said to the contrary. French-Canadians came under an especially withering propaganda barrage. This is hardly surprising. French-Canadian voluntarism, at five percent of total volunteers, lagged far behind its Anglo-Canadian counterpart throughout the war. Why? Likely for as many reasons as there were young men who refused to sign up, but distinct trends emerge. Some assumed that just as English Canadians still venerated their mother country, French Canadians would support France with which the British were allied. But French Canadians had few remaining ties to France. Tensions with English Canadians still lingered over their role in the Boer War, French language rights and separate schools in Canada. The organization of the Canadian army also guaranteed that French-Canadians would not show much enthusiasm: few officers spoke French; chances of promotion remained very limited; an Anglican Minister headed official recruiting in Quebec; and there were no French-Canadian speaking regiments until 1917 when the Vandoos (Royal 22nd) came into existence. Finally, Quebecois argued that they had proportionately greater family obligations that impinged on their liberty to sign up.

Close scrutiny of the recruitment data indicates that the Quebecois were, in fact, not the only reluctant volunteers. Western Canadians and Maritimers also demonstrated a lack of commitment when compared to areas with large pockets of recent British immigrants, a good portion of whom were single men without family responsibilities. Many western Canadians were first generation immigrants who fled Europe precisely to avoid repressive governments that forced young men to fight the interminable wars plaguing that continent. They would hardly return, or send their sons, after just escaping to more congenial climes. They also argued that their place was on Canada's farms where they and their families could contribute as much, if not more, to the war effort than by donning uniforms.

Lack of recruits and an appalling casualty rate eventually led Prime Minister Robert Borden to introduce conscription, an act of Parliament as contentious and divisive as anything since Confederation. It so badly divided the country that for the first and only time in Canadian history, the two main federal political parties split along ethnic lines, French Canadian Members of Parliament rallying to Laurier's anti-conscription Liberals. Borden, meanwhile, created the new Union party made up of pro-conscriptionist English-Canadian Liberals and Conservatives. The ensuing 1917 election was very bitter, with violence, unscrupulous political manipulation, intimidation, and propaganda on both sides. Borden won, and his Military Service Act led to clashes between troops and French-Canadians in Quebec that killed five civilians. In response the Quebec National Assembly discussed a resolution to secede from Canada.

Why was conscription so contentious? The country had little military experience and many Canadians found the concept of conscription foreign. Canada traditionally relied upon voluntarism for its armed forces. Many thought that the First World War simply was not Canada's fight: that it had nothing to do with us. Some, on moral principles, could not accept the notion of the state forcing its citizens into arms. But what about duty, others wondered? Canada, after all, belonged to the British Empire, and like it or not, membership in the club entailed responsibilities as well as privileges. And if not to the Empire, surely citizenship demanded duties and obligations to the nation. Thus, they argued, if Canada ran low on volunteers, the government must make up the deficit by conscripting its citizens.

Discussion Points

1. Summarize the arguments for and against increased Canadian participation in the First World War.
2. Based on these accounts, how ideologically motivated were Canadians? Did they understand what was at stake in the war?
3. Should governments have the power to coerce its citizens into military service? Should it be considered a duty of citizenship?
4. Explain the "conscription of wealth." Should it have taken place before or alongside the conscription of men? Was it even realistic?

Documents

1. G. Starr, 123rd Battalion Recruiting Leaflet.

To the Women of Canada

In addressing these few remarks exclusively to the women of the country, it is to be understood that we have arrived at that period in the struggle where we realize the utter futility of recruiting meetings.

The men who have as yet failed to join the colors will not be influenced by any eloquence from any platform.

The reason? The man we are trying to reach is the man who will never listen and the man who never for a moment considers the remarks as applicable to himself.

And so now we appeal to the women—the women who are the mainspring of all masculine action.

In the First Division of the C.E.F. we swept up the young manhood of the country in the first enthusiasm—we secured the cream of the country in the men who flocked to the colors taking thought of neither yesterday or tomorrow.

At the second call men were stopping to calculate and hesitate. Since then the hesitation has developed into stagnation. Men who see a desperate winter ahead are joining the colors, and a few others; the remainder are deadwood.

The reason? Firstly, the man who prefers to allow others to fight for him so that he may pursue a comfortable occupation, preserve his youth, be safe from danger, and explain to his friends that he would gladly join the colors could he obtain a commission—and yet take no steps towards that end.

Second. The man who is influenced by the selfish maternal appeal either from mother or wife.

Third. The man who claims his business would go to pieces without him, but is satisfied to let others throw away life and youth to sustain that business.

Fourth. The others—call them what you may.

And now my Appeal to Women

You entertain these wretched apologies in your homes. You accept their donations, their theatre tickets, their flowers, their cars. You go with them to watch the troops parade.

You foully wrong their manhood by encouraging them to perform their parlor tricks while Europe is burning up.

While Canada is in imminent danger of suffering the same were it not for the millions who are cheerfully enduring the horrors and privations of bloody warfare for the millions who stay at home watching the war pictures and drinking tea.

Bar them out, you women. Refuse their invitations, scorn their attentions. For the love of Heaven, if they won't be men, then you be women. Tell them to come in uniform, no matter how soiled or misfitting—bar out the able-bodied man who has no obligations, show that you despise him. Tell him to join the colors while he can do so with honor. And the day is not far off when he will have to go. The old mother has issued the last call to her sons.

Make your son, your husband, your lover, your brother, join now while he yet retains the remnants of honor. Compulsory training is in the offing.

Get the apologist, the weakling, the mother's pet, into the service. Weed out all, and we will find out who are the cowards. Analyze your friends—you women—refuse their attentions, and tell them why. Make them wake up.

GOD BLESS HIM THE KING CALLS! JOIN ROYAL GRENADIERS OVERSEAS BATTALION, 123rd C.E.F.

2. Peter McArthur, "Country Recruits," *Globe*, January 30, 1915.

With all the papers lamenting the fact that the rural districts are not contributing a satisfactory number of recruits to the war, it is perhaps unsafe for me to point out a few facts about rural conditions, for the last time I did so I was accused in a section of the press of preparing a defence for people who lack patriotism. I have surely put myself on record often enough as believing that the war must be supported to the utmost, but I am not going to let that belief make me unjust. I have told you how scarce men of military age are in this district and that if they enlist there can be none of the increased production that is being urged as an expression of patriotism. The Department of Agriculture is proclaiming that the man who produces more foodstuffs is doing a man's work for the Empire, and the few young men who are on the farms are practically all producers. Each one who went to the front would leave a hundred acres untilled.

It is high time that the Department of Militia and the Department of Agriculture got together and decided on a definite policy. If a man is doing his duty by producing more, he should not be open to criticism if he does not enlist. To show you how shorthanded this district is it is only necessary to point out that during the past ten years the population of the county of Middlesex has been so greatly reduced that at the recent redistribution one riding was wiped out. I have not the figures by me, but I understand that the population has fallen off something over ten thousand. This decrease is largely due to the exodus of young men to the west and to the cities. If the country had been at war for the past ten years we could not have lost a greater proportion of our population. If every young man of military age enlisted, the county could hardly make a fair showing and it would fall behind in production. Will those who are condemning the rural districts for not sending more recruits kindly tell what should be done in the case of Middlesex county?

While the above paragraph was in course of preparation I received a letter from a correspondent in Castorville which reports a similar condition. The writer says

"While reading *The Globe* last evening I noticed a considerable complaint that the country districts are not responding very heartily to the call for volunteers to go to the war. In thinking the matter over I felt that there is a danger of not giving the country due consideration for this seeming shortcoming.

"I do not wish to excuse the country where it is lacking patriotism but I feel that the conditions of farmers are not fully comprehended which I will note briefly:

"(1) The smallness of families in farming districts these days is noticeable. There used to be five and six boys in a family on the farm. Today there are only one or two.

"(2) The spare boy that could be gotten along without has gone to the city or the west, and now not one farm in three has even one boy or man eligible to be a volunteer.

"(3) Help is scarce on the farms and in the farming districts. Most of the farmers are and have been running their farms with as little help as possible, and even when we feel we would like to have someone to help it is almost impossible to get it for there are no spare hands in the community.

"(4) If Canada is to provide bread, beef, horses, etc. for the war, the farmer must have sufficient help to do it.

"(5) The overflow of country population has gone to the cities or west. The congestion in the labour market at the present time is found in the cities, therefore it is not surprising that the majority of volunteers should come from that quarter."

This letter is of interest because it shows that conditions in other parts of the country are the same as I find them here in Middlesex. The farmers cannot both increase production and give volunteers to the army.

There is a thought that suggests itself in connection with this state of affairs. In the present national crisis we have a right to expect every man who is capable of rendering service to do so patriotically. The man who enlists to go to the front is making the supreme sacrifice that it is possible for a man to make. He is offering to give his life for his country. The man who is eligible to give similar service but feels that his call of duty is to stay at home and help his country with increased products should also be prepared to make many and great sacrifices. He is not offering his life, and therefore he should not stint in offering his means. If the young men who avoid military service do so because they think that during war times farming will yield them increased profits they must expect to take their profits with a share of public contempt. Never before has the call for unselfish service been so urgent and so great. Those who elect to serve their country as producers must be prepared to give to their full capacity. Even if they give all, they will not be giving so much as those who are offering their lives. As the war progresses public sentiment will probably be educated to a point where men in all walks of life who try to make profits from the unhappy condition of their country will be scorned for their selfishness. If we cannot serve at the front we must be prepared to serve unselfishly at home. As a matter of fact, I think it would be quite justifiable to ask the young married men of military age who are not enlisting what proportion of their products they will give for patriotic purposes over and beyond what they will have to pay in the form of taxes. When the survivors of those who volunteer for service at the front come back wounded and broken the young men who stay at home cannot feel much self-respect if they have spent the time in accumulating profits. This should show definitely whether their "patriotism of production" is real or only an excuse.

3. *Saturday Night* August, 1915

This protest by French-Canadians against French-Canadians fighting the battles of Britain is the result of insular, bigoted upbringing, combined with dense ignorance. The French-Canadian of the type who marches and riots as a protest against recruiting is perhaps more to be pitied than blamed. He is ignorant and he is narrow, and so he will remain just so long as his schools refuse him facilities for a liberal education. He knows nothing beyond his Province, and he cares less. All Jean Baptiste wants is to be left alone.

4. Talbot M. Papineau, "An Open Letter from Capt Talbot Papineau to Mr. Henri Bourassa," March 21, 1916

In the Field, France, March 21, 1916.
My dear Cousin Henri,—

... Too occupied by immediate events in this country to formulate a protest or to frame a reasoned argument, I have nevertheless followed with intense feeling and deep regret the course of action which you have pursued. Consolation of course I have had in the fact that far from sharing in your views, the vast majority of Canadians, and even many of those who had formerly agreed with you, were now strongly and bitterly opposed to you. With this fact in mind, I would not take the time from my duties here to write you this letter did I not fear that the influence to which your talent, energy, and sincerity of purpose formerly entitled you, might still be exercised upon a small minority of your fellow countrymen, and that your attitude might still be considered by some as representative of the race to which we belong.

Nor can I altogether abandon the hope—presumptuous no doubt but friendly and well-intentioned—that I may so express myself here as to give you a new outlook and a different purpose, and perhaps even win you to the support of a principle which has been proved to be dearer to many Canadians than life itself.

I shall not consider the grounds upon which you base your opposition to Canadian participation in this more than European—in this World War. Rather I wish to begin by pointing out some reasons why on the contrary your wholehearted support might have been expected.

And the first reason is this. By the declaration of war by Great Britain upon Germany, Canada became "ipso facto" a belligerent, subject to invasion and conquest, her property at sea subject to capture, her coasts subject to bombardment or attack, her citizens in enemy territory subject to imprisonment or detention. This is not a matter of opinion—it is a matter of fact—a question of international law. No arguments of yours at least could have persuaded the Kaiser to the contrary. Whatever your views or theories may be as to future constitutional development of Canada, and in those views I believe I coincide to a large extent, the fact remains that at the time of the outbreak of war Canada was a possession of the British Empire, and as such as much involved in the war as any country in England, and from the German point of view and the point of view of International Law equally subject to all its pains and penalties. Indeed proof may no doubt be made that one of the very purposes of Germany's aggression and German military preparedness was the ambition to secure a part if not the whole of the English possessions in North America.

That being so, surely it was idle and pernicious to continue an academic discussion as to whether the situation was a just one or not, as to whether Canada should or should not have had a voice in ante bellum English diplomacy or in the actual declaration of war. Such a discussion may very properly arise upon a successful conclusion of the war, but so long as national issues are being decided in Prussian fashion, that is, by an appeal to the Power of Might, the liberties of discussion which you enjoyed by virtue of British citizenship were necessarily curtailed and any resulting decisions utterly valueless. If ever there was a time for action and not for theories it was to be found in Canada upon the outbreak of war.

Let us presume for the sake of argument that your attitude had also been adopted by the Government and people of Canada and that we had declared our intention to abstain from active participation in the war until Canada herself was actually attacked. What would have resulted? One of two things. Either the Allies would have been defeated or they would not have been defeated. In the former case Canada would have been called upon either to surrender unconditionally to German domination or to have attempted a resistance against German arms.

You, I feel sure, would have preferred resistance, but as a proper corrective to such a preference I would prescribe a moderate dose of trench bombardment. I have known my own dogmas to be seriously disturbed in the midst of a German artillery concentration. I can assure you that the further you travel from Canada and the nearer you approach the great military power of Germany, the less do you value the unaided strength of Canada. By the time you are within fifteen yards of a German army and know yourself to be holding about one yard out of a line of five hundred miles or more, you are liable to be enquiring very anxiously about the presence and power of British and French forces. Your ideas about charging to Berlin or of ending the war would also have undergone some slight moderation.

No, my dear Cousin, I think you would shortly after the defeat of the Allies have been more worried over the mastery of the German consonants than you are even now over a conflict with the Ontario Anti-bi-linguists. Or I can imagine you an unhappy exile in Terra del Fuego eloquently comparing the wrongs of Quebec and Alsace.

But you will doubtless say we would have had the assistance of the Great American Republic! It is quite possible. I will admit that by the time the American fleet had been sunk and the principal buildings in New York destroyed the United States would have declared war upon Europe, but in the meantime Canada might very well have been paying tribute and learning to decline German verbs, probably the only thing German she *could* have declined …

Nor disappointed as I am at the present inactivity of the States will I ever waiver in my loyal belief that in time to come, perhaps less distant than we realise, her actions will correspond with the lofty expression of her national and international ideals.

I shall continue to anticipate the day when with a clear understanding and a mutual trust we shall by virtue of our united strength and our common purposes be prepared to defend the rights of humanity not only upon the American Continent but throughout the civilised world.

Nevertheless we are not dealing with what may occur in the future but with the actual facts of yesterday and to-day, and I would feign know if you still think that a power which without protest witnesses the ruthless spoliation of Belgium and Servia, and without effective action the murder of her own citizens, would have interfered to protect the property or the liberties of Canadians. Surely you must at least admit an element of doubt, and even if such interference had been attempted, have we not the admission of the Americans themselves that it could not have been successful against the great naval and military organisations of the Central Powers?

May I be permitted to conclude that had the Allies been defeated Canada must afterwards necessarily have suffered a similar fate.

But there was the other alternative, namely, that the Allies even without the assistance of Canada would *not* have been defeated. What then? Presumably French and English would still have been the official languages of Canada. You might still have edited untrammelled your version of Duty … In fact Canada might still have retained her liberties and might with the same freedom from external influences have continued her progress to material and political strength.

But would you have been satisfied—you who have arrogated to yourself the high term of Nationalist? What of the Soul of Canada? Can a nation's pride or patriotism be built upon the blood and suffering of others or upon the wealth garnered from the coffers of those who in anguish and with blood-sweat are fighting the battles of freedom? If we accept our liberties, our national life, from the hands of the English soldiers, if without sacrifices of our own we profit by the sacrifices of the English citizen, can we hope to ever become a nation ourselves? How could we ever acquire that Soul or create that Pride without which a nation is a dead thing and doomed to speedy decay and disappearance.

If you were truly a Nationalist—if you loved our great country and without smallness longed to see her become the home of a good and united people—surely you would have recognised this as her moment of travail and tribulation. You would have felt that in the agony of her losses in Belgium and France, Canada was suffering the birth pains of her national life. There even more than in Canada herself, her citizens are being knit together into a new existence because when men stand side by side and endure a soldier's life and face together a soldier's death, they are united in bonds almost as strong as the closest of blood-ties.

There was the great opportunity for the true Nationalist! There was the great issue, the great sacrifice, which should have appealed equally to all true citizens of Canada, and should have served to cement them with indissoluble strength — Canada was at war! Canada was attacked! What mattered then internal dissentions and questions of home importance? What mattered the why and wherefore of the war, whether we owed anything to England or not, whether we were Imperialists or not, or whether we were French or English? The one simple commending fact to govern our conduct was that Canada was at war, and Canada and Canadian liberties had to be protected.

To you as a "Nationalist" this fact should have appealed more than to any others. Englishmen, as was natural, returned to fight for England, just as Germans and Austrians and Belgians and Italians returned to fight for their native lands.

But we, Canadians, had we no call just as insistent, just as compelling to fight for Canada? Did not the *Leipzig* and the *Gneisnau* possibly menace Victoria and Vancouver, and did you not feel the patriotism to make sacrifices for the protection of British Columbia? How could you otherwise call yourself Canadian? It is true that Canada did not hear the roar of German guns nor were we visited at night by the murderous Zeppelins, but every shot that was fired in Belgium or France was aimed as much at the heart of Canada as at the bodies of our brave Allies. Could we then wait within the temporary safety of our distant shores until either the Central Powers flushed with victory should come to settle their account or until by the glorious death of millions of our fellowmen in Europe, Canada should remain in inglorious security and a shameful liberty?

I give thanks that that question has been answered not as you would have had it answered but as those Canadians who have already died or are about to die here in this gallant motherland of France have answered it.

It may have been difficult for you at first to have realised the full significance of the situation. You were steeped in your belief that Canada owed no debt to England, was merely a vassal state and entitled to protection without payment. You were deeply imbued with the principle that we should not partake in a war in the declaration of which we had had no say. You believed very sincerely that Canadian soldiers should not be called upon to fight beyond the frontier of Canada itself, and your vision was further obscured by your indignation at the apparent injustice to a French minority in Ontario.

It is conceivable that at first on account of this long held attitude of mind and because it seemed that Canadian aid was hardly necessary, for even we feared that the war would be over before the first Canadian regiment should land in France, you should have failed to adapt your mind to the new situation and should for a while have continued in your former views;—but now—now that Canada has pledged herself body and soul to the successful prosecution of this war—now that we know that only by the exerci[s]e of our full and united strength can we achieve a speedy and lasting victory—now that thousands of your fellow citizens have died, and alas! many more must yet be killed—how in the name of all that you hold most sacred can you still maintain your opposition? How can you refrain from using all your influence and your personal magnetism and eloquence to swell the great army of Canada and make it as representative of all classes of our citizens as possible?

Could you have been here yourself to witness in its horrible detail the cruelty of war—to have seen your comrades suddenly struck down in death and lie mangled at your side, even you could not have failed to wish to visit punishment upon those responsible. You too would now wish to see every ounce of our united strength instantly and relentlessly directed to that end. Afterwards, when that end has been accomplished, then and then only can there be honour or profit in the discussion of our domestic or imperial disputes.

And so my first reason for your support would be that you should assist in the defence of Canadian territory and Canadian liberties....

The third reason is this: You and I are so called French-Canadians. We belong to a race that began the conquest of this country long before the days of

Wolfe. That race was in its turn conquered, but their personal liberties were not restricted. They were in fact increased. Ultimately as a minority in a great English speaking community we have preserved our racial identity, and we have had freedom to speak or to worship as we wished. I may not be, like yourself, "un pur sang," for I am by birth even more English than French, but I am proud of my French ancestors, I love the French language, and I am as determined as you are that we shall have full liberty to remain French as long as we like. But if we are to preserve this liberty we must recognise that we do not belong entirely to ourselves, but to a mixed population, we must rather seek to find points of contact and of common interest than points of friction and separation. We must make concessions and certain sacrifices of our distinct individuality if we mean to live on amicable terms with our fellow citizens or if we are to expect them to make similar concessions to us. There, in this moment of crisis, was the greatest opportunity which could ever have presented itself for us to show unity of purpose and to prove to our English fellow citizens that, whatever our respective histories may have been, we were actuated by a common love for our country and a mutual wish that in the future we should unite our distinctive talents and energies to create a proud and happy nation.

That was an opportunity which you, my cousin, have failed to grasp, and unfortunately, despite the heroic and able manner in which French Canadian battalions have distinguished themselves here, and despite the whole-hearted support which so many leaders of French Canadian thought have given to the cause, yet the fact remains that the French in Canada have not responded in the same proportion as have other Canadian citizens, and the unhappy impression has been created that French Canadians are not bearing their full share in this great Canadian enterprise. For this fact and this impression you will be held largely responsible. Do you fully realise what such a responsibility will mean, not so much to you personally—for that I believe you would care little—but to the principles which you have advocated, and for many of which I have but the deepest regard. You will have brought them into a disrepute from which they may never recover. Already you have made the fine term of "Nationalist" to stink in the nostrils of our English fellow citizens. Have you caused them to respect your national views? Have you won their admiration or led them to consider with esteem, and toleration your ambitions for the French language? Have you shown yourself worthy of concessions or consideration?

After this war what influence will you enjoy—what good to your country will you be able to accomplish? Wherever you go you will stir up strife and enmity—you will bring disfavour and dishonour upon our race, so that whoever bears a French name in Canada will be an object of suspicion and possibly of hatred.

And so, in the third place, for the honour of French Canada and for the unity of our country, I would have had you favourable to our cause.

I have only two more reasons, and they but need to be mentioned, I think to be appreciated.

Here in this little French town I hear about me all the language I love so well and which recalls so vividly my happy childhood days in Montebello. I see types and faces that are like old friends. I see farm houses like those at home. I notice that our French Canadian soldiers have easy friendships wherever they go.

Can you make me believe that there must not always be a bond of blood relationship between the Old France and the New?

And France—more glorious than in all her history—is now in agony straining fearlessly and proudly in a struggle for life or death.

For Old France and French civilisation I would have had your support.

And in the last place, all other considerations aside and even supposing Canada had been a neutral country, I would have had you decide that she should enter the struggle for no other reason than that it is a fight for the freedom of the world—a fight in the result of which like every other country she is herself vitally interested. I will not further speak of the causes of this war, but I should like to think that even if Canada had been an independent and neutral nation she of her own accord would have chosen to follow the same path of glory that she is following to-day.

Perhaps, my cousin, I have been overlong and tedious with my reasons, but I shall be shorter with my warning—and in closing I wish to say this to you.

Those of us in this great army, who may be so fortunate as to return to our Canada, will have faced the grimmest and sincerest issues of life and death—we will have experienced the unhappy strength of brute force—we will have seen our loved comrades die in blood and suffering. Beware lest we return with revengeful feelings, for I say to you that for those who, while we fought and suffered here, remained in safety and comfort in Canada and failed to give us encouragement and support, as well as for those who grew fat with the wealth dishonourably gained by political graft and by dishonest business methods at our expense—we shall demand a heavy day of reckoning. We shall inflict upon them the punishment they deserve—not by physical violence—for we shall have had enough of that—nor by unconstitutional or illegal means—for we are fighting to protect not to destroy justice and freedom—but by the invincible power of our moral influence.

Can you ask us then for sympathy or concession? Will any listen when you speak of pride and patriotism? I think not.

Remember too that if Canada has become a nation respected and self-respecting she owes it to her citizens who have fought and died in this distant land and not to those self-styled Nationalists who have remained at home.

Can I hope that anything I have said here may influence you to consider the situation in a different light and that it is not yet too late for me to be made proud of our relationship?

At this moment, as I write, French and English-Canadians are fighting and dying side by side. Is their sacrifice to go for nothing or will it not cement a foundation for a true Canadian nation, a Canadian nation independent in thought, independent in action, independent even in its political organisation—but in spirit united for high international and humane purposes to the two Motherlands of England and France?

I think that is an ideal in which we shall all equally share. Can we not all play an equal part in its realisation?

I am, as long as may be possible,
Your affectionate Cousin,
TALBOT M. PAPINEAU.

5. Henri Bourassa, "Mr. Bourassa's Reply to Capt. Talbot Papineau's Letter," August 2, 1916.

... As early as the month of March 1900, I pointed out the possibility of a conflict between Great Britain and Germany and the danger of laying down in South Africa a precedent, the fatal consequence of which would be to draw Canada into all the wars undertaken by the United Kingdom. Sir Wilfrid Laurier and the liberal leaders laughed at my apprehensions; against my warnings they quoted the childish safeguard of the "no precedent clause" inserted in the Order in Council of the 14th of October 1899. For many years after, till 1912, and 1913, they kept singing the praises of the Kaiser and extolling the peaceful virtues of Germany. They now try to regain time by denouncing vociferously the "barbarity" of the "Huns." To-day, as in 1900, in 1911, and always, I believe that all the nations of Europe are the victims of their own mistakes, of the complacent servility with which they submitted to the dominance of all Imperialists and traders in human flesh, who, in England as in Germany, in France as in Russia, have brought the peoples to slaughter in order to increase their reapings of cursed gold. German Imperialism and British Imperialism, French Militarism and Russian Tsarism, I hate with equal detestation; and I believe as firmly today as in 1899 that Canada, a nation of America, has a nobler mission to fulfil than to bind herself to the fate of the nations of Europe or to any spoliating Empire —whether it be the spoliators of Belgium, Alsace, or Poland, or those of Ireland or the Transvaal, of Greece or the Balkans.

Politicians of both parties, your liberal friends as well as their conservative opponents, feign to be much scandalised at my "treasonable disloyalty." I could well afford to look upon them as a pack of knaves and hypocrites. In 1896, your liberal leaders and friends stumped the whole province of Quebec with the cry "WHY SHOULD WE FIGHT FOR ENGLAND?" From 1902 to 1911, Sir Wilfrid Laurier was acclaimed by them as the indomitable champion of Canada's autonomy against British Imperialism. His resisting attitude at the Imperial Conferences of 1902 and 1907 was praised to the skies. His famous phrase on the "vortex of European militarism," and his determination to keep Canada far from it, became the party's by-word—always in the Province of Quebec, of course. His Canadian Navy scheme was presented as a step towards the independence of Canada ...

By what right should those people hold me as a "traitor," because I remain consequent with the principles that I have never ceased to uphold and which both parties have exploited alternately, as long as it suited their purpose and kept them in power or brought them to office?

Let it not be pretended that those principles are out of place, pending the war. To prevent Canada from participating in the war, then foreseen and pre-dicted, was their very object and *raison d'être*. To throw them aside and deny them when the time of test came, would have required a lack of courage and sincerity, of which I feel totally incapable. If this is what they mean by "British loyalty" and "superior civilisation," they had better hang me at once. I will never obey such dictates and will ever hold in deepest contempt the acrobats who lend themselves to all currents of blind popular passion in order to serve their per-sonal or political ends...

I will not undertake to answer every point of the dithyrambic plea of my gallant cousin. When he says that I am too far away from the trenches to judge of the real meaning of this war, he may be right. On the other hand, his long and diffuse piece of eloquence proves that the excitement of warfare and the distance from home have obliterated in his mind the fundamental realities of his native country. I content myself with touching upon one point, on which he unhappily lends credit to the most mischievous of the many anti-national opin-ions circulated by the jingo press. He takes the French-Canadians to task and challenges their patriotism, because they enlist in lesser number than the other elements of the population of Canada. Much could be said upon that. It is sufficient to signalise one patent fact: the number of recruits for the European war, in the various Provinces of Canada and from each component element of the population, is in inverse ratio of the enrootment in the soil and the traditional patriotism arising therefrom. The newcomers from the British Isles have enlisted in much larger proportion than English-speaking Canadians born in this country, while these have enlisted more than the French-Canadians. The Western Provinces have given more recruits than Ontario, and Ontario more than Quebec. In each Province, the floating population of the cities, the students, the labourers and clerks, either unemployed or threatened with dismissal, have supplied more soldiers than the farmers. Does it mean that the city dwellers are more patriotic than the country people? or that the newcomers from England are better Canadians than their fellow citizens of British origin, born in Canada? No; it simply means that in Canada, as in every other country, at all times, the citizens of the oldest origin are the least disposed to be stampeded into distant ventures of no direct concern to their native land. It proves also that military service is more repugnant to the rural than the urban populations.

There is among the French-Canadians a larger proportion of farmers, fathers of large families, than among any other ethnical element in Canada. Above all, the French-Canadians are the only group exclusively Canadian, in its whole and by each of the individuals of which it is composed. They look upon the perturbations of Europe, even those of England or France, as foreign events. Their sympathies naturally go to France against Germany; but they do not think they have an obligation to fight for France, no more than the French of Europe would hold themselves bound to fight for Canada against the United States or Japan, or even against Germany, in case Germany should attack Canada without threatening France.

English Canada, not counting the *blokes*, contains a considerable proportion of people still in the first period of national incubation. Under the sway of imperialism, a fair number have not yet decided whether their allegiance is to Canada or to the Empire, whether the United Kingdom or the Canadian Confederacy is their country.

As to the newcomers from the United Kingdom, they are not Canadian in any sense. England or Scotland is their sole fatherland. They have enlisted for the European war as naturally as Canadians, either French or English, would take arms to defend Canada against an aggression on the American continent.

Thus it is rigourously correct to say that recruiting has gone in inverse ratio of the development of Canadian patriotism. If English-speaking Canadians have a right to blame the French Canadians for the small number of their recruits, the newcomers from the United Kingdom, who have supplied a much larger proportion of recruits than any other element of the population, would be equally justified in branding the Anglo-Canadians with disloyalty and treason. Enlistment for the European war is supposed to be absolutely free and voluntary. This has been stated right and left from beginning to end. If that statement is honest and sincere, all provocations from one part of the population against the other, and exclusive attacks against the French-Canadians, should cease. Instead of reviling unjustly one-third of the Canadian people—a population so remarkably characterised by its constant loyalty to national institutions and its respect for public order,—those men who claim a right to enlighten and lead public opinion should have enough good faith and intelligence to see facts as they are and to respect the motives of those who persist in their determination to remain more Canadian than English or French.

... The most that can be said is, that the backward and essentially Prussian policy of the rulers of Ontario and Manitoba gives us an additional argument against the intervention of Canada in the European conflict. To speak of fighting for the preservation of French civilisation in Europe while endeavouring to destroy it in America, appears to us as an absurd piece of inconsistency. To preach Holy War for the liberties of the peoples overseas, and to oppress the national minorities in Canada, is, in our opinion, nothing but odious hypocrisy.

Is it necessary to add that, in spite of his name, Capt. Papineau is utterly unqualified to judge of the feelings of the French-Canadians? For most part American, he has inherited, with a few drops of French blood, the most *denationalised* instincts of his French origin. From those he calls his compatriots he is separated by his religious belief and his maternal language. Of their traditions, he knows but what he has read in a few books. He was brought up far away from close contact with French-Canadians. His higher studies he pursued in England. His elements of French culture he acquired in France. The complexity of his origin and the diversity of his training would be sufficient to explain his mental hesitations and the contradictions which appear in his letter ...

6. "No More Canadians For Overseas Service. This Young Dominion Has Sacrificed Enough," *Sault Express,* June 23, 1916.

The Express in its limited sphere has been advocating peace among the warring nations of Europe, but save in the undercurrent of Canadian sentiment which we know exists in the heart of many of our people there appears to be no desire for a termination of hostilities until the Germanic power in Europe has been utterly destroyed and many of the old world wrongs have been made right. We fear that if Canada is to continue to shed her life blood until that day arrives there will not be many Canadians remaining to celebrate the conquest, and the high purposes for which our forefathers on this continent strove will all have been in vain. And more than that, we have grave fears that if this horrible conflict goes on for another two years we shall not have our United Empire to cheer for. These words are spoken in the fullest consciousness of their meaning. The destruction of the Teutonic race is quite as impossible as the destruction of the Anglo-Saxon race, and the destruction of either would be nothing short of a catastrophe handed down to posterity as an example of our present day higher civilization. What our empire needs right now and what Canada needs right now is PEACE. But we have drifted away from what we started out to say, which was that this Dominion should not send any more of her sons overseas to engage in this frightful cataclysm. The truth is that there has already been too much Canadian bloodletting and the cost of British connection has been away and beyond what our people counted on. We have less than eight millions of population as against three hundred millions in India. If, as we are told, the shedding of blood overseas is the silicon which binds the steel of Empire, then why does England not draw upon her three hundred millions in India as she has drawn upon her seven millions in Canada?

"The Canadian troops made a most gallant stand;" "the soldiers from Canada well upheld the traditions of the race;" "thousands of our brave Canadian soldiers fell with honour," "we can never forget the heroism of those grand Canadians." That kind of salve from London does not bind up the hearts of the thousands of Canadian mothers and sisters whose loved ones sleep in a foreign land after dying for a foreign cause.

It is about time for Canadians to wake up and realize that they are living in America and not Europe; that old world empires rise and fall; that we are the last great land to the west on this great planet and that the Lord has so ordained; that our neighbors and we are of the same faith, our language is the same and there is a comity of blood existing between us which makes us brothers in the truest human sense. A century of peace exemplifies the silicon in the steel.

Canada will contribute more to the future greatness of the Anglo-Saxon race by pursuing her own ideals and minding her own business on this side of the Atlantic then by spending "her last son and her last dollar" across the water in a futile effort to adjust the wrongs which most of our ancestors left the old world to escape …

7. Robert Borden, *Debates,* House of Commons, 1917.

I approached a subject of great gravity and seriousness, and, I hope, with a full sense of the responsibility that devolves upon myself and upon my colleagues, and not only upon us but upon the members of this Parliament and the people. We have four Canadian divisions at the front. For the immediate future there are sufficient reinforcements. But four divisions cannot be maintained without thorough provision for future requirements ... I think that no true Canadian, realizing all that is at stake in this war, can bring himself to consider with tolera-tion or seriousness any suggestion for the relaxation of our efforts ... Hitherto we have depended upon voluntary enlistment. I myself stated to Parliament that nothing but voluntary enlistment was proposed by the Government. But I re-turn to Canada impressed at once with the extreme gravity of the situation, and with a sense of responsibility for our further effort at the most critical period of the war. It is apparent to me that the voluntary system will not yield further substantial results. I hoped it would. The Government have made every effort within its power, so far as I can judge. If any effective effort to stimulate volun-tary recruiting remains to be made, I should like to know what it is ...

     All citizens are liable to military service for the defence of their country, and I conceive that the battle for Canadian liberty and autonomy is being fought to-day on the plains of France and of Belgium. There are other places besides the soil of a country where the battle for its liberties and its institutions can be fought; and if this war should end in defeat, Canada, in all the years to come, would be under the shadow of German military domination. That is the very lowest at which we can put it ...

     Now the question arises as to what is our duty ... A great responsibility rests upon those who are entrusted with the administration of public affairs. But they are not fit to be trusted with that transcendent duty if they shrink from any responsibility which the occasion calls for ... The time has come when the au-thority of the state should be invoked to provide reinforcements necessary to maintain the gallant men at the front ... I bring back to the people of Canada from these men a message that they need our help, that they need to be sus-tained, that reinforcements must be sent to them. Thousands of them have made the supreme sacrifice for our liberty and preservation. Common gratitude, apart from all other considerations, should bring the whole force of this nation behind them. I have promised ... that this help shall be given. I should feel myself unworthy of the responsibility devolving upon me if I did not fulfil that pledge. I bring a message also from them, yes, a message also from the men in the hospitals, who have come back from the very valley of the shadow of death, many of them maimed for life ... But is there not some other message? Is there not a call to us from those who have passed beyond the shadow into the light of perfect day, from those who have fallen in France and in Belgium, from those who have died that Canada may live — is there not a call to us that their sacrifice shall not be in vain?

I have had to take all these matters into consideration and I have given them my most earnest attention. The responsibility is a serious one, but I do not shrink from it. Therefore, it is my duty to announce to the House that early proposals will be made to provide by compulsory military enlistment on a selective basis, such reinforcements as may be necessary to maintain the Canadian army in the field ... The number of men required not be less than 50,000, and will probably be 100,000 ...

It has been said of this Bill that it will induce disunion, discord and strife and that it will paralyze the national effort. I trust that this prophecy may prove unfounded. Why should strife be induced by the application of a principle which was adopted at the very inception of Confederation? ...

It was my strong desire to bring about a union of all parties for the purpose of preventing any such disunion or strife as is apprehended. The effort was an absolutely sincere one, and I do not regret that it was made, although the delay which it occasioned may have given opportunity for increasing agitation and for excitement arising from misunderstanding. I went so far as to agree that this Bill should not become effective until after a general election, in the hope that by this means all apprehension would be allayed, and that there might be a united effort to fulfil the great national purpose of winning this war. What may be necessary or expedient in that regard, I am yet willing to consider, for ever since this war began I have had one constant aim and it was this: to throw the full power and effort of Canada into the scale of right, liberty and justice for the winning of this war, and to maintain the unity of the Canadian people in that effort ...

God speed the day when the gallant men who are protecting and defending us will return to the land they love so well. Only those who have seen them at the front can realize how much they do love this dear land of Canada. If we do not pass this measure, if we do not provide reinforcements, if we do not keep our plighted faith, with what countenance shall we meet them on their return? ... They went forth splendid in their youth and confidence. They will come back silent, grim, determined men who, not once or twice, but fifty times, have gone over the parapet to seek their rendezvous with death. If what are left of 400,000 such men come back to Canada with fierce resentment and even rage in their hearts, conscious that they have been deserted or betrayed, how shall we meet them when they ask the reason? I am not so much concerned for the day when this Bill becomes law, as for the day when these men return if it is rejected.

8. Francis Marion Beynon, "Women's View of Conscription," *The Grain Growers' Guide,* May 30, 1917.

There are four objections to the government's announced intention of forcing conscription upon the people of Canada, the first and greatest being that the people have not been consulted about it, the second that it should include married as well as single men; third, that it should be accompanied by conscription of all wealth and all moneys invested in the war loans, and fourth, that the government of Great Britain no longer ago than last week closed out a motion saying that they were not fighting for imperialistic conquest or aggrandisement.

Before men are arbitrarily taken from their homes and put through the military machine, they and their mothers and fathers have a right to say that they are willing it should be done. More particularly is this the case since the killing or physical maiming of them is among the lesser evils that have befallen many of the Canadian boys who have gone to serve in the army. It was admitted in the British House of Commons the other day that in one Canadian camp alone there were seven thousand men suffering from venereal disease, and medical reports in Great Britain show that ten per cent of the forces are affected.

Of these thousands of men who have been ruined there are numbers who would not in any case have led a blameless life, but there are also thousands of clean-minded innocent young boys who would otherwise have been decent upright citizens who will now be nothing but a scourge to their country when they return and whose lives have been completely ruined. Their chances of marrying and having a happy home and healthy children have been taken away from them. Before any mother sees her son forcibly exposed to these temptations she has a right to say whether or not she is willing to have it so. When Everywoman's World took a vote of its women readers on the question of conscription recently it was defeated six to one. If this is any indication of public opinion it is certainly a minority decision the government has arrived at. If you feel at all strongly on this question, bombard Premier Borden with letters demanding a referendum, and write at once.

Although the government doubtless intends to follow the example of Great Britain of taking first the single men and then extending the principle to apply to the married men, as the demand increases, it seems fair to make it apply to both from the outset. If the good of the individual is to be set aside at the demands of the country, then the rights of the individual ought to be completely disregarded, and those men, married or single, left at home who are mostly useful to the country. There is nothing to be gained by deceiving ourselves, it means conscription for married men also, sooner or later, if the war goes on, as it seems likely to do, indefinitely. The Canadian government has followed so far, exactly the system that was followed in England at the beginning of the war, and it is likely that they will continue to follow it in every particular.

Then as regards the conscription of wealth. It has been said over and over again that this war will be won by the silver bullet, but instead of the government getting this silver bullet through war loans at five per cent and forever exempt from income tax, let them conscript the city houses and the bank accounts and the railways and the munition plants and the farms, and let all the citizens pay rent to the government. Then with this income pay a generous separation allowance to the wives of married men, and a liberal pension to their widows, and above all an especially generous pension to returned soldiers who are partially or completely disabled, so that these men who have faced death for their country may not need to be the objects of charity from people who have gotten rich out of war profits. Moreover it is obviously unjust to conscript the life of the poor working man, which is all that stands between his family and destitution, while another man can go to the front knowing that in the event of his complete disablement, neither he nor his family will have to eke out a miserable existence for years and years to come.

Finally, before men are compelled to go against their will to serve in the army they have a right to know what they are fighting for, whether it is indeed the principle of democracy, which they were assured at the beginning of the war it was, or whether it is for territory, the acquisition of which will lead to the shedding of the blood of hundreds of thousands of other men at a later date, as territory snatching almost invariably does ...

Now as has been pointed out in this column over and over again there is no territory in the world that is worth the slaughter of human beings, and, moreover, this snatching of territory is a positively bad and wicked thing, sowing the seeds of other wars for other men to be slaughtered in. It is utterly opposed to the principle of democracy for which the British Empire is supposed to stand and for which men believe they are dying in this war. No group of people have a right to be transferred from one government to another without their own consent, in a fair referendum, and they ought not so to be transferred at any time, whether in war time or peace. Therefore before conscription comes into force in Canada the British government should be compelled to repudiate any desire for territorial aggrandisement. Men have no right to be forcibly killed and maimed to acquire a few acres of land.

9. Joseph Ainey, "Canadian Labour and Conscription," *Le Devoir,* July 5, 1917

The workingmen, throughout Canada, are opposed to the Compulsory Service Bill now under discussion before the House of Commons.

This opposition is not confined to one province, as it has been stated in some newspapers. It is true that opinions have been expressed more freely in the Province of Quebec, but I have had the opportunity of coming in contact with the population of other provinces, and I have found opposition everywhere.

Apart from the constitutional and economic aspects of the question, the average workingman considers that if there is to be conscription of men, it should be accompanied, if not preceded, by conscription of wealth.

The workingmen hate war more than anybody else. War produces individual wealth and prosperity, but in other sections of the community. Unmolested profiteering has rendered ineffective many good recruiting speeches.

In the working classes are also found thousands of good citizens who have made this country their land of adoption, principally because they wanted to free themselves from the consequences of militarism. These cannot be expected to be very enthusiastic over the introduction of compulsory service.

The workingman of Canada is also aware of the crisis which his country is facing.

Canada has enlisted up to this date an army of over 400,000 men for overseas's service. For the purpose of illustration let us consider for a moment that in proportion to population, this would be equivalent to an army of 6,000,000, if recruited in the United States.

We are told by the best authorities that the Allies must rely on America for food. Are we in position to meet the demand? We have the land, but we are already short of hands. Our farmers are able to cultivate only part of their farms. Farm help is obtained with great difficulty and only at the price of skilled labor. Overproduction has become an impossibility under present conditions. We cannot even produce sufficiently to keep the cost of living within reasonable figures.

I find from official statistics that in the month of May 1914, the weekly cost of food for a family of 5 was estimated at $7.42, whilst in the month of May

1917, the same could not be obtained for less than $11.82. The general budget of a family of 5 in the month of May 1914 was estimated at $14.19 per week; in May 1917, it had reached $18.50.

The situation is alarming and the working classes feel what is coming, and they know who is to suffer first and longest.

For all these reasons, the great majority of workingmen in Canada are opposed to conscription, and from all parts of the country their representative bodies have passed resolutions accordingly.

10. Rev. S.D. Chown, "An Open Letter on the Duty of the Hour," *Christian Guardian*, Dec 12, 1917.

At the present time the supreme issue of winning the war so dominates the whole of Canada's present and future life, and will so affect the relation of our country to the world at large, that the old modes of political thought should be entirely superseded by loftier conceptions of patriotism, and our action as voters should be determined not by parochial, but by world-wide issues. The old bottles of party tradition must be burst with the new wine of national duty ...

This is a redemptive war, and its success depends entirely upon the height of sacrifice to which our people can ascend. It is under this conviction that ministers of the gospel feel in duty bound to enter the political arena. We shall fail and fail lamentably as Christian people unless we catch the martyr spirit of true Christianity and do our sacrificial duty between now and on the 17th of December. But if we do fail, I, for one, will never be sorry that I tried to bear aloft the banner of the cross amidst the fight ...

This war has so related our Dominion to the greatest nations on earth that we must ask regarding each ballot what effect it will have in London, Paris, Rome and Washington, on the one hand, and upon Berlin, Vienna, Sofia and Constantinople on the other. We must enquire what effect each ballot will have upon Christian civilization as opposed to undiluted barbarism: upon heaven as in contrast with hell. Surely we shall not permit ourselves to give a fiendish joy to the Turks, who, in their butchery of Armenian Christians, considered bullets too expensive, and used axes instead ...

The Borden Government certainly deserves criticism. Perhaps it should have punishment. But we are not dealing with it now, and if we stop to do so we would be like a man punishing a boy for some misconduct while the house about them both is burning to the ground.

To me it is as clear as the day that if we defeat conscription we cannot possibly get the last available man and fulfil our promise to Great Britain. We would then be a fit ally for the nation which has become notorious for tearing up scraps of paper. The Hun might well strike a medal to commemorate our defeat because it would be no less deadly to the national honor of Canada than the sinking of the *Lusitania* was to human life.

For these and other reasons I have been led to accept the policy of conscription or the selective draft. ... I believe ... that under any conditions it is the fairest, most democratic, most expeditious and least expensive method of raising an army in this country: and under present conditions it is the only possible way of fulfilling our obligations to Christian civilization. I also believe that socially considered it is the most moral and profoundly religious method of doing our national duty ...

If the Government be not sustained, the heart will be taken out of our soldiers. How could we face these men upon their return if we forsake them now? But I fear they would scorn to return. I fear they might forswear their country and die fighting, if need be, under another flag.

In my judgment, the elector who votes for the anti-conscription policy and the repeal of the Military Service Act, with the consequent inevitable withdrawal of Canada from the war, forges three links in a fatal chain of personal humiliation, public contempt and national decay. He alienates Canada from the rest of the Empire and from association with the respectable portion of mankind. He degrades the term Canadian from a synonym of glory to a badge of dishonour and a by-word of reproach. "Lo this man began to build and was not able to finish." If I voted against a Union Government candidate I would feel that I was opposing the most patriotic movement ever known in the Dominion of Canada ...

Readings

Armstrong, E. *The Crisis in Quebec, 1914–1918.* Toronto: McClelland and Stewart, 1974.

Berger, C., ed. *Conscription, 1917.* Toronto: University of Toronto Press, 1969.

Bray, R. "Fighting as An Ally: The English-Canadian Patriotic Response to the Great War," *Canadian Historical Review* 61, 2 (June 1980).

Brown, R., and D. Loveridge. "Unrequited Faith: Recruiting the CEF, 1914–1918," *Revue Internationale d'Histoire Militaire* 54 (1982).

Cook, R. "Francis Beynon and the Crisis in Christian Reformism," in C. Berger and R. Cook, eds. *The West and the Nation: Essays in Honour of W.L. Morton.* Toronto: McClelland and Stewart, 1976.

Gorham D., "Vera Brittain, Flora MacDonald Denison and the Great War: The Failure of Non-Violence," in R. Pierson., ed. *Women and Peace: Theoretical, Historical and Practical Perspectives*. London: Croom Helm, 1987.

Granatstein, J., and J. Hitsman. *Broken Promises: A History of Conscription in Canada*. Toronto: Oxford University Press, 1977.

Hyatt, A. "Sir Arthur Currie and Conscription: A Soldier's View," *Canadian Historical Review* 50, 3 (September 1969).

Morton, D. "French Canada and War, 1868-1917: The Military Background to the Conscription Crisis of 1917," in J. Granatstein and T. Cuff, eds. *War and Society in North America*. Toronto: Nelson, 1970.

Roberts, B. "Women Against War, 1914-1918: Francis Beynon and Laura Hughes," in J. Williamson and D. Gorham, eds. *Up and Doing: Canadian Women and Peace*. Toronto: Women's Press, 1989.

Robin, M. "Registration, Conscription, and Independent Labour Politics, 1916–1917," *Canadian Historical Review* 47, 2 (June 1966).

Socknat, T. *Witness Against War: Pacifism in Canada, 1900–1945*. Toronto: University of Toronto Press, 1981.

Socknat, T. "Canada's Liberal Pacifists and the Great War," *Journal of Canadian Studies* 8, 4 (Winter 1983–84).

Walker, J. "Race and Recruitment in World War I: Enlistment of Visible Minorities in the Canadian Expeditionary Force," *Canadian Historical Review* 70, 1 (March 1989).

Warne, R. "Nellie McClung and Peace," in J. Williamson and D. Gorham, eds. *Up and Doing: Canadian Women and Peace*. Toronto: Women's Press, 1989.

Willms, A. "Conscription 1917: A Brief for the Defence," *Canadian Historical Review* 37, 4 (December 1956).

Young, W. "Conscription, Rural Depopulation and the Farmers of Ontario, 1917-1919," *Canadian Historical Review* 53 (September 1972).

Chapter Nine

"NATIONAL ART":
THE GROUP OF SEVEN

1. Percy Moore Turner, "Painting in Canada," *Canadian Forum*, December 1922.
2. "Canadian Art," *Saturday Night*, May 1924.
3. "Canada and her Paint Slingers," *Saturday Night,* November 8, 1924.
4. "Freak Pictures at Wembley," *Saturday Night*, December 13, 1924.
5. Hector Charlesworth, "The Group System in Art," *Saturday Night*, June 24, 1925.
6. "The Group of Seven," *Canadian Forum*, February 1927.
7. "The Group of Seven," *Canadian Forum*, June 1930.

Introduction

What is more Canadian than a Group of Seven painting of Georgian Bay? Along with other national icons like the maple leaf (and syrup), the beaver, and hockey, Group of Seven images of Canada tug at the heartstrings and, in the twenty-first century, help define what it is to be Canadian. Institutions like the National Gallery promote the Group as visionaries who sought and created a proudly distinct Canadian style, not only in subject, colour and technique, but in ideology as well. Their paintings are indeed masterful expressions of the Canadian landscape, but their reputation as revolutionary iconoclasts who democratized art while creating a Canadian style stands on far shakier ground.

The Group, originally composed of Franklin Carmichael, Lawren Harris, A.Y. Jackson, Frank Johnston (replaced in 1926 by A.J. Cason), Arthur Lismer, J.E.H. MacDonald, and Fredrick Varley, formed in 1920. All except Harris, who was independently wealthy, supported themselves as commercial artists and had known each other since about 1911. The Group's purpose was a mystical and romantic crusade to create a uniquely Canadian style that captured the essence of the new country, physically, metaphysically, metaphorically, and emotionally.

This first meant rejecting norms set by the stodgy Royal Canadian Academy of Arts, which functioned as the arbiter of good taste in Canadian painting, but which members of the Group found stultifying and ultimately foreign. In the pre-First World War era, the Academy, with a typical colonial inferiority complex, looked across the Atlantic to England, Holland, and France for artistic inspiration and found it in the formalized portraiture and landscape painting of the pre-impressionist era. This it appropriated and promoted as the correct artistic style for Canada. The themes, subject matter and techniques were consciously Euro-centric and spoke, so the Group said, of a different continent and a different time, not of Canada on the edge of the twentieth century.

Loss of faith in what nineteenth century European salon-culture labelled "good art" placed the Group of Seven solidly in the Modernist school: that group of Europeans thinkers, initiated by the painter Edouard Manet in the 1860s, rejected the "safely representational and beautiful" school of art in favour of bold new horizons. Modernist painters had to reach for stylistic autonomy, and their canvases had to be both intuitive and deeply subjective rather than mere photographic likenesses that complimented the couch. This meant, in a word, that "modern" artists had to paint from wells deep in their subconscious and do so without concern for artistic or technical convention. It allowed Lawren Harris, for example, to paint landscapes that were less and less representational until they finally became purely abstract—it also meant that the Group was part of an international movement, not exclusively Canadian.

Modernists also claimed an arrogant aesthetic and moral authority, a position to which the Group of Seven certainly subscribed. Artists, the Group believed, had a closer understanding of spirituality than ordinary people, which led Harris to proclaim that there is "a divine being within each of us to be disclosed over the ages by self-devised creative effort and experience," and that "Art is the high training ground of the soul, essential to the soul's growth, to its unfoldment." Yet modernist artists also sought to make art accessible and part of everyday life.

The Group of Seven effectively transmitted its message by consciously courting controversy. The more arrogant their statements, the more controversial their paintings, the more interest it generated—the better. The right to choose the paintings to represent Canada at the 1924 British Empire Exhibition at Wembley in England was perhaps the single most controversial event. Traditionally the Royal Canadian Academy of Art made the selections, but the newly created National Gallery of Canada usurped control and sent the Group's work—much to the Academy's dismay. It was a prophetic choice, however, because the highly influential British critics praised the show. This, rather ironically, suggests that the imperial heartland gave its stamp of approval to the Modernist Canadians who sought to reject British influence. The show vindicated the National Gallery and consolidated its implicit right to define "good" Canadian art from then on. Finally, and perhaps most ironically of all, the fact that the renegade Group was the darling of the National Gallery ensured its place in the Canadian art establishment.

But why would a group of urbane commercial artists forsake the comfort of urban studios for extended and arduous camping trips painting northern Ontario? Surely they could have created a uniquely Canadian style around the familiar urban landscape. Their forays into Canada's wilderness were, in fact, typical of an era where the middle class wanted to escape the hustle and unhealthy industrial society. They sought mythical Arcadia, a primitive, romantic, and pre-industrial age when humankind supposedly lived in unsullied harmony with nature. In the Canadian context, the back-to-nature movement led to the creation of "Cottage Country" in the Muskoka area, and to founding the national parks. It popularized naturalists like Grey Owl and Ernest Thompson Seton, and established children's camps and the scouting movement. It also developed city parks that brought greenery to the masses, and suburbs where every house sported a bit of verdant nature. Thus the Group of Seven's collective yearning to head for the wilderness was common to much of middle class urban Canada at the time. This trend was, however, decidedly anti-modernist.

The Group of Seven did indeed create a style unlike any previously seen in Canada, and their unabashed nationalism still reverberates through their canvases. Their subject matter, however, is hardly "national," being predominantly northern Ontario. Their lofty position in the pantheon of Canadian artists, secure by the 1930s, also excluded or denigrated art from other Canadian regions—unless it was very similar, such as the paintings of Emily Carr. The Group recognized this problem and tried to create a more truly pan-Canadian vision by inviting Edwin Holgate from Quebec and L.L. Fitzgerald from Winnipeg to join them, but the result remained the same.

In an era when Canadians were desperately trying to define and assert their own identity through literature, poetry, music, and drama, only the Group of Seven was considered to have succeeded. By the time the Group disbanded in 1933 it had achieved a mythical status completely out of proportion to its achievements.

Discussion Points

1. Considering art's highly subjective nature, were the attacks on the Group justified? Was the praise warranted?
2. To what degree, if any, do the Group of Seven's paintings represent the Canadian identity? What was "distinctly" Canadian about them?
3. If the Group so clearly captured the spirit of Canada, why do we still have trouble defining what it means to be Canadian?
4. What, if anything, can historians gain from studying artists and their work?

Documents

1. Percy Moore Turner, "Painting in Canada," *Canadian Forum*, December 1922.

... Upon both these questions I had a keen remembrance of the sense of disappointment my previous visits had left with me. An insipid level of academic art, most of it the reflex of European teaching and outlook and dominated by it, technically accomplished, but very little distinctive of Canada in thought or presentation, had come to my notice. Then as I wandered through the few available public galleries I had realized under what disadvantages the artistic youth of Canada was unconsciously labouring. The galleries, themselves, seemed to me quite adequate for their purpose as buildings; but their contents were generally of a secondary and perfunctory order, acquired with but little regard to system or policy.

The officials were not to blame. The apathy of the governing bodies— national, provincial, and municipal—was but too evident on every hand. The directors, therefore, seemed in the main, to be thrown back upon the good will of isolated collectors who had accumulated a few odds and ends, generally of a sadly minor order, sometimes, in the case of the old pictures, of doubtful attribution, which these collectors had been good-hearted enough to give or bequeath to the public collection. This dilettante attitude was indelibly stamped upon the galleries. On almost every hand there was a want of understanding of the real import of art in its relation to life, a lack of comprehension of what great art really is. But amateurish direction is by no means limited to Canada. Great Britain can, unfortunately, furnish not a few instances in its provincial galleries.

Thus both sides of the question—indissolubly bound up with one another—
had evoked a feeling of despair in me.

Now, for the results of my present visit. I was soon in contact with the
same old academic art. It was neither better nor worse. I found the art of painting still tolerated as a superior kind of amusement by a mighty nation engaged
in a life and death struggle with the untamed forces of Nature, a nation imbued
with grim determination to set its material house in order, but which, as yet, had
had neither the opportunity nor the desire to realize what really great and virile
art means to a nation, and indeed, to civilization. A feeling of hopelessness at
finding any art representative of Canada was commencing to creep over me,
when a friend asked me if I knew the 'Group of Seven'. I confessed I did not. 'Go
and see it', he said. With mixed feelings I set out. Once in front of the paintings
of these men I realized that I was face to face with the one movement in Canadian art; a little body of enthusiasts endeavouring whole-heartedly, under appalling
difficulties, to work out their own salvation in feeling, outlook and subject—St.
Johns, as yet, crying in the wilderness.

I will not attempt to be laudatory. Such an attitude would be an imperti-
nence on my part. I will be critical. It will shorten my task; and perhaps my
homily, which is meant to be most kindly and I hope will be forgiven, may
induce these earnest men to weigh my views. To me, the 'Group of Seven'—I
believe it is really now a group of six—are so intent upon their objective that
they are impatient of European control. Laudable yearning to achieve complete
independence has induced a tendency to overshoot the mark. This criticism
demands an explanation from me, and I must do my best to make my meaning
clear.

I contend that art is divided into two distinct but closely related categories,
the one national, the other international or rather universal. National art represents the virile forward movement of a country, expressing its national intensity,
aspirations, and characteristics, ever forward in its outlook, seeking to uplift the
spiritual side of the nation, and, as such, being an integral and vital factor in its
aesthetic advancement. To become an enduring factor, national art must be based
upon the great stream of international art as it comes through the centuries.
National art cannot, however, break suddenly away from this stream; it cannot
deflect or modify the stream. That stream fundamentally supplies its aesthetic
nourishment, and national art must accept the precepts of the men who compose that stream and apply these precepts to its own development.

International art enunciates eternal and traditional principles, common to
universal art-development. I will cite a few patent instances:—The Italian Re-

naissance, Poussin, Claude, Rembrandt, Vermeer, Ruisdael, Corot, Courbet, Daumier, many of the Impressionists, and Cézanne. These are examples of the forces which have helped to mould the world in an aesthetic sense and will continue to do so. No new country can hope, at one jump, either to uproot or even modify this all-dominating continuity. National art can only aspire to enter the universal category after it has proved its worth in a national sense and begins, at a further stage, to break new ground of universal aesthetic import. The 'Group of Seven' for me, therefore, is in a national stage. It represents Canada and its spiritual aspirations in a pictorial sense as nothing has represented it before. It is pathetic, indeed, that most of the members of this important group are not sufficiently supported to be able to devote whole time and energy to their art. If such were the case they might effect more intimate communion with the best forward European art and lay solidly the foundation of a great Canadian school ...

2. "Canadian Art," *Saturday Night*, May 1924.

What some of us feared has come to pass ... It was feared that the group of painters which elects to present in exaggerated terms the crudest and most sinister aspects of the Canadian wilds, and which has steadily campaigned against all painters of more suave and poetic impulse, would be accepted by British critics [at the British Empire Exhibition] as the exclusive authentic interpreters of Canadian landscape ... "Emphatic design and bold brushwork are characteristic of the Canadian section," says [one critic in the *London Times*], "and it is here in particular that the art of the Empire is taking a new turn ... There can be no question that Canada is developing a school of landscape painters who are strongly racy of the soil." Flub-dub, every word of it, but no doubt sincere flub-dub, based on the conviction that this is the pure quill "Canadian" stuff; and that other types of landscape painting which present the beautiful pastoral phases of this country are false and insincere ... This school of painting is not of the soil, but of the rocks. The sections of Canada which its votaries in their harsh, uncompromising style (which of itself is alien to the Canadian temperament) delight to depict, undoubtedly do exist. Unfortunately, one must ... add, for the areas of primeval rock and jack-pine constitute Canada's gravest problem in an economic sense and the most serious barrier to her social and political unity. We cannot deny them; but they are not all of Canada, as the laymen who boost this school, as the only true, sincere and original Canadian art, would have the world believe.

3. "Canada and her Paint Slingers," *Saturday Night,* November 8, 1924.

There has been a great deal of talk of late in England and elsewhere about "representative Canadian art", especially in connection with a group of Toronto painters who hold that Canada is only truly interpreted through a single narrow and rigid formula of ugliness. Many Canadians of taste and discrimination who went abroad to visit the British Empire Exhibition this past summer, have lately returned, and expressions of disgust are to be heard on all sides at the unrepresentative character of what the London critics have been led to believe is "representative" Canadian art. There are some good pictures in the Wembley collection; but the cult of ugliness is so glaringly and insistently exemplified on the walls of the Canadian gallery that canvases of this order overshadow and "kill" pictures of a truly thoughtful and interpretative character.

As has been frequently pointed out in these columns the group, which is trying to force its wares on international attention do no good to Canada, for they cannot apprehend or put on canvas the beauties even of the subjects they instinctively choose. Many will read with mingled feelings the following extract from a review of the work of the Toronto blood and thunder school, published in the *Brooklyn Museum Quarterly* of recent issue:

> "The flavor of Canada to most of us is a mixture of the great Northwest, Quebec and French Canadians, snow, skis, rapids, canoes and forests primeval. All these connote one's mental image of Canada. And, logically, we expect to find some expression of this in her art, forgetful of the fact that stylization, standardization and modernism have done much to eradicate racial qualities in art, and that only painters of the most intense and vital personality can stand up against this levelling process."

The words "stylization, standardization and modernism" are well chosen to describe the efforts of this school to reduce all Canadian landscape painting to one graceless and depressing formula; but the images they evoke are obviously not those which Canadians accept as true generalizations. The blood and thunder school not only reject the circumstance that Canada in many sections is one of the richest pastoral lands in the world, lovely in its contours as a beautiful woman, glowing with exquisite and subtle gradations of tone. Not only do they reject beauty themselves but they urge that all painters who feel its existence be cast aside and their pictures excluded so far as possible from public galleries as "insincere" and "unrepresentative" from the standpoint of nationality. And the worst of it is they seem to be succeeding to some extent in spreading the belief that Canada is a land of ugliness; and its art a reflection of a crude and tasteless native intelligence.

4. "Freak Pictures at Wembley," *Saturday Night*, December 13, 1924.

It is to be hoped that the British scientists who have recently completed a tour of Canada will on their return to the motherland be good enough to enlighten the British public as to the libel on Canadian landscape involved in the freak pictures now on view at Wembley. As a result of what seems to have been a fairly effective lobby a number of London art critics were induced to compliment certain Canadian painters on the creation of a new school of art. C. Lewis Hind, for instance, who was never in the wilder parts of Canada oracularly proclaimed that these caricatures had "the very look and feel of Canada;" and were a true expression of the country's national life. Perhaps the favorable words of several critics were due to the fact that these pictures conform to a preconceived conception of Canada and Colonials generally as crude and ugly, though "virile."

Britishers, above all people, object to having preconceived opinions upset, and there is nothing in these pictures to disturb the popular belief we have all encountered among uninformed Englishmen, that Canadians are crude and commonplace in taste and ideals. Thus when a tawdry play "The Man from Toronto" was produced in London five years ago and the hero was depicted as a person of grotesquely bad manners, the critics hastened to compliment the playwright on creating a character that had the very look and feel of Canada. Thus, when two years ago a Canadian female orator distressed her countrymen by her impudent gaucheries on the public platform in London, her English auditors said: "How refreshing; how typically Canadian; a real breath from the prairies!" But in the main we think a good deal of the praise was dictated by some friendly theory that by strained compliments the ties of Empire are being cemented.

Anyone who has seen the Georgian Bay country where some of our freak painters claim to derive their inspiration, during the last few weeks, and revelled in the subtle and manifold beauties of Nature in that region, must laugh, albeit a little bitterly, at the hoax that has been perpetrated on the British public in the assumption that insincere and splashy pictures painted to create a sensation rather than to record beauty and emotion, truly interpret this Canada of ours. These pictures do undoubtedly provide a sensation for jaded palates, but we are quite sure that no stranger to this country having looked on them would ever want to visit our shores. From the standpoint of business they are as bad an advertisement as this country ever received.

5. Hector Charlesworth, "The Group System in Art," *Saturday Night*, June 24, 1925.

The group system in politics has of late been tried in several parts of the English speaking world, and found wanting; but there still seem to be persons who have a childlike faith in the group system in art. There is an analogy between the two. The new political groups in Canada have been congeries of regimented opinion, pledged to fixed programmes, in which it is treason to look aside at anything unrelated to the main objective, to bring up a question of realities, or to recognize validity or sincerity in other men's ideas. Something very like the same attitude of mind governs the body of painters known as "The Group of Seven," which aspires to dominate pictorial expression in this country, despite the well established fact that all groups or schools which adhere to fixed methods and opinions are a handicap to artistic progress. ...

The French instinct for classification has become responsible for the introduction of the words "school" and "group" into the vocabulary of art criticism; without reference to the fallacies involved. Consequently when last summer English critics tried to cement the Empire with friendly allusions to "an original Canadian school of art" it awakened no answering chord of patriotic enthusiasm in the breasts of some of us; for there can be little "originality" in a school. Originality is wholly bound up with individual vision. All it could mean was that a number of our painters had chosen to adopt a syndicated technique of sufficient novelty to attract attention. Syndicated painting, according to a rigid formula, chiefly based on rejections, may increase the output of one kind of thing, but it can have no beneficial effect on quality.

These reflections are not intended as an apologia—only as proof that the objections frequently voiced in these columns to establishment of a Canadian "school" or "group" are not mere capricious fault finding. An exhibition of more than 50 paintings and as many more drawings by the "Group of Seven" is now in progress at the Toronto Art Gallery, and reveals everywhere that narrowness of outlook to which the group system naturally tends. Some of its members are undoubtedly very clever craftsmen. Lawren Harris and A. Y. Jackson are experts in brushwork and know precisely what they want to say without muddying up their color and fumbling their designs. J. E. H. Macdonald, F. Horsman Varley and Arthur Lismer are very able draughtsmen with a selective grasp of essentials, as their exhibits in the graphic art collection prove. The two younger members, Frank Carmichael and A. H. Robinson (Montreal) have promising intuitions in the treatment of landscape if they will permit their individualities to develop. Yet when one passes from the gallery of drawings to the collection of paintings, the result is depression. To sensitive eyes it is like a chamber of horrors; a vision of things hard, glaring; repellent. Yet those of us who have throughout our lives known Canada in all her moods are asked to accept the collection as exclusively representative of Canadian art ...

With so much basic talent in the group, the arbitrary nature of their proceedings with paint becomes the more exasperating. The key note is over-emphasis of a few essentials and rejection of all other elements. Articulate this or that motif; cast aside the rest. This is the method of the anatomist with a cadaver, and the result is often as gruesome. Yet it would be unfair to say that all the paintings are bad. The perversity of Lawren Harris, who on many occasions has revealed fine aesthetic feeling for tone, is inexplicable. In his large canvases at present on display he twists the contours of nature into hard and turgid outlines; and most of his comrades show a tendency to do likewise. Angles and spirals abound as in mechanical drawings; and the rigid outlines enclose untoned masses of crude color.

The singular thing about many of these pictures is the entire absence of natural light, despite the fact that they are painted in high tones. The lighting is often akin to the weird glare of an unscreened calcium lamp. It has none of the radiating qualities of sunlight. The shadows in these pictures have no luminosity; they are solid blobs, even less expressive than murky effects of the pre-Impressionist days of the 19th century. And since there is no natural light there is no feeling of atmosphere, and little sense of depth. At one fell stroke the phalanx of seven deal out death to the nuances of nature. And as for poetic feeling and gentle emotion, these are dismissed as sentimental heresies.

Occasionally however members of the group escape from the rigors of their creed and make excursions in the direction of individualistic perception and sincerity. This is particularly true of the two younger men, Mr. Carmichael and Mr. Robinson. Four of Mr. Carmichael's pictures, "Late Evening," "White Rocks," "Bluff Rock, on the Upper Ottawa," and "The Upper Ottawa, near Mattawa," are among the best in the gallery. They are not mature work, but they give a sense of air and of a feeling for the subtle and evanescent moods of nature—sincere rather than sensational. Mr. Robinson's "Quebec from Levis" also has qualities of atmosphere and feeling with an effect of solidity and values in the handling of the impressive main subject; though perhaps as a concession to the ideals of the group he makes the cakes of floating ice in the foreground, starkly rectangular. Mr. Varley shows the head of a dusky woman in which warmth of color is exaggerated, but sound drawing and a suggestion of characterization make it interesting. In at least one of his pictures, "Afternoon Sun, North Shore, Lake Superior," Lawren Harris gets away from the calcium effect and gives us real sunlight, though the withered saplings at the right are flat as brown paper. In the main Mr. Harris's method is kaleidoscopic not merely in garishness of color, but in rigidity of design. Mr. Jackson also occasionally frees himself from the trammels of theory, and his color sympathies are broader than those of his colleagues. His "Moose Country" might as well be called "Crater"; but "The Winter Road," "Winter Moonlight" and "Dawn, Pine Island" are not merely decorative but felicitous. Most of the paintings of Messrs. Macdonald and Lismer are in harsh, unemotional moods, though in "The Factory Town" and "A Northern Town" an abundance of vari-colored detail is translated by Mr. Lismer into vivid synthesis and the light is that of nature. Taking the collection as a whole, the effect is singularly monotonous, despite the fact that it is a veritable riot of primary colors. Though superficially daring, most of the pictures seem to be essentially timid, as though each member were afraid of violating his fraternal oath.

6. "The Group of Seven," *Canadian Forum*, February 1927.

... The artists who performed this drastic operation upon our artistic conventions are the artists to whom *A Canadian Art Movement* is devoted, the Toronto group known chiefly as 'the Seven'. It was they who, now some fifteen years ago, first began to express vigorously as artists what they quite simply liked as men. Instead of respecting the preferences of their old-country forerunners, they followed their own preferences. They liked the bright sun on snow and set out to paint it in defiance of the old law which said that snow was not a fit subject to paint; in common with every Canadian lad they delighted to cut themselves adrift from civilization among the lonely Northern lakes and in like spirit they began to paint those regions, basing their style, as far as they were able, upon what they saw and felt in the wild North rather than upon what an Englishman had seen and felt in an English garden. At every point they broke with the old habits; in choice of subject, in mood and texture, and in medium. They painted all that was brilliant and Northern and undomestic, and they set Canadian painting free from a tradition with which no healthy compromise was possible.

The revolution which they brought about had been looked forward to for years by a number of thoughtful painters, but little had been done to speed its arrival. It was left chiefly to Lawren Harris, A. Y. Jackson, J. E. H. Macdonald, and Tom Thomson to effect the change. To be sure, they did not always paint successfully; they frequently displeased others and must occasionally have displeased themselves. But, count their faults and failures as we may, their service to Canadian painting is hard to exaggerate. Within fifteen years of their first tentative beginnings Canadian landscape painting has won its place in the sun. It is already seen to be by far the most vigorous expression of spiritual life in the country, and it is beginning here and there, inside and outside our political frontiers, to give a new meaning to the word 'Canada' ...

7. "The Group of Seven," *Canadian Forum*, June 1930.

The "Group of Seven" exhibition which was held during the month of April at The Art Gallery of Toronto and at The Montreal Art Association, this last month, has established without any compromise where the 'Seven' stand on the burning question of Modernism. (Speaking of the "Seven," it may be said that they are now eight, with Edwin Holgate of Montreal as the breaker of the magic number.) The Seven are modern and yet have evaded the formulae of modernism. Of all the art groups who, on this side of the Atlantic are called modern, there is probably no other that has escaped so fully the "academism of modernism" and remained so pure in its inspiration and in the techniques which its various members individually favour. If this should be the only contribution of the "Group" to Canadian Art, it would be well worth a mention in the art history of this country. On the other hand, from the standpoint of what the "Group" looked like in that exhibition one must frankly admit that it had all the airs of a posthumous exhibition. The cohesion which one implicitly expects to find in the work of members of an art group did not exist between the paintings in that show. One could not see the parenthood between the various canvases. Only in the work of A. Y. Jackson and in that of Edwin Holgate one did find a kinship of mental attitude, something which was in the nature of a brotherhood of art. The cement which once kept all the stones of this Canadian tower together has dried out and has fallen off, the stones have been disassembled and have been scattered. For the sake of sentimentalism or conservatism, bring them together if you will, but it takes more than the desire to see them, one next to the other, to make of them a unit with a symbol, having a common significance.

Contributions by outsiders which had been selected by the "Group" were, in the majority decidedly weak, and showed a clannish attitude which is incompatible with the growth of a movement. The paintings by Emily Carr, H. Mabel May, Yvonne McKague, George Pepper, and Sarah M. Robertson were exceptions, and helped to hold up the standard of the exhibition. All in all, however, there were paintings in the collection which, if produced by Americans in the United States, would arouse so much enthusiasm that the public would be given more than a little stale publicity about them, or the impertinent remarks of a few ignorant fools seeking the means of having their names played up in the columns of the dailies. Canadians should awake to the fact that they have great artists interpreting their country and its soul, and they should also be told the truth about those self-styled critics who have only contempt for what is best and finest in the field of art in Canada.

Readings

Atwood, M. "Death by Landscape," *Harper's* August, 1990.

Bordo, J. "Jack Pine- Wilderness Sublime or the Erasure of Aboriginal Presence from the Landscape," *Journal of Canadian Studies* 27, 4 (winter 1992-93).

Cole, D. "Artists, Patrons and Public: An Inquiry into the Success of the Group of Seven," *Journal of Canadian Studies* 13 (summer, 1978).

Cook, R. "Landscape Painting and National Sentiment in Canada," *Historical Reflections* 1, 2 (1974).

Davis, A. "The Wembley Controversy in Canadian Art," *Canadian Historical Review* 54, 1 (March, 1973).

Davis, A. "A Study in Modernism: The Group of Seven as an Unexpectedly Typical Case," *Journal of Canadian Studies* 33, 1 (Spring 1998).

Davis, A. *The Logic of Ecstasy.* Toronto: University of Toronto Press, 1992.

Harris, C. "The Myth of the Land in Canadian Nationalism," in P. Russell ed. *Nationalism in Canada.* Toronto: McGraw-Hill, 1966.

Hill, C. *The Group of Seven: Art for a Nation.* Ottawa: National Gallery of Canada/ McClelland and Stewart, 1995.

Jessup, L. "Prospectors, Bushwackers, Painters: Antimodernism and the Group of Seven," *International Journal of Canadian Studies* 17 (Spring 1998).

Mellen, P. *The Group of Seven.* Toronto: McClelland and Stewart, 1970.

Murray, J. *The Best of the Group of Seven.* Edmonton: Hurtig, 1984.

Nasgaard, R. *The Mystic North.* Toronto: Art Gallery of Ontario, 1984.

Osborne, B. "The Iconography of Nationhood in Canadian Art," in D. Cosgrove and S. Daniels, eds., *The Iconography of Landscape.* Cambridge: Cambridge University Press, 1988.

Reid, D. *The Group of Seven.* Ottawa: National Gallery of Canada, 1970.

Reid, D. et al. *Canadian Jungle.* Toronto: Art Gallery of Ontario, 1983.

Tooby, M. ed. *The True North: Canadian Landscape Painting, 1896–1939.* London: Lund Humphries, 1992.

Chapter Ten

"THIS IS MY LAST CHANCE": DEPRESSION AND DESPAIR

---

1. Thomas M. Gibbs, Sarnia, Ontario, December 1, 1930.
2. A Nanaimoite, February 22.
3. R.D., Ottawa, March 4, 1932.
4. Mrs. Ernest Ferguson, Ferguson, N.B., March 21, 1933.
5. Brief Presented by the Unemployed of Edmonton to the Hon. R.B. Bennett, December 30, 1933.
6. To Canadian Government, December 1934.
7. P.R. Mulligan, Debden, Saskatchewan, March 3, 1934.
8. Miss Elizabeth McCrae, Hamilton, Ontario, April 6, 1934.
9. L.M. Himmer, Blaine Lake, Saskatchewan, September 9, 1935.
10. Dorothy Franklin, Brechin, Ontario, February 28, 1935.
11. Mrs. Otto Brelgen, Dempster, Saskatchewan, April 15, 1935.
12. Bruce Bass, Whiteway, N.B., October 7, 1935.
13. A Mother.
14. Experiences of a Depression Hobo.

Introduction

Unemployment and distress grew to unimaginable levels when the Great Depression hit at the end of the 1920s. Canada was among the nations worst affected, quickly skidding toward insolvency and social catastrophe. The economic situation was bad enough, with some 20% of the population on relief over the worst years between 1933 and 1936. Environmental calamities on the southern prairies, however, exacerbated the problem by creating a dust bowl that thousands barely survived, and many did not. Drought made conditions so unbearable that the International Red Cross declared parts of Saskatchewan disaster areas. Social assistance, inevitably inadequate, barely existed for those desperate people, and it came at a high psychological cost. Collecting relief, after all, collided with proud and independent souls who believed in self-reliance, not charity. It is therefore hardly surprising that Depression survivors subsequently developed "depression mentalities" that had them hoard pieces of foil, twist-ties and plastic bags for the rest of their lives.

The Great Depression also offered unprecedented increases in the standard of living for employed people who did not suffer pay cuts, or for people with independent means. This, of course, worsened the Depression's impact by deepening and widening the financial and social gulf between the top and bottom of Canadian society. The Depression was, after all, a deflationary period when dollars, if one had them, bought more and more each day. Federal civil servants, for example, experienced a 25% increase in their standard of living over this period. Services, goods, food, entertainment—almost all became cheaper for those with money.

The Depression was particularly hard on the aged, sick, marginalized, and young, those least able to fend for themselves. Though historians know the cold facts, statistics do not adequately tell the story. Statistics do not, for example, count those eking out existences perched just above the poverty line, and therefore not officially "poor." Nor do the numbers include the thousands whose pride prevented them from seeking charity. Statistics cannot describe the humiliation of a father publicly avowing his failure to provide for his family in order to receive relief. Cold numbers do not show inspectors subsequently searching his home for luxuries, such as telephones and drivers' licenses, which made the family ineligible. Numbers cannot interpret a paranoid government encouraging people to inform on "relief cheats." Hard data cannot express the anguish a mother felt as she exchanged her meagre food vouchers for goods under her neighbours' watchful gaze.

Suspicious and cash-strapped governments in this era assumed that relief recipients created their own misfortune. They therefore made obtaining relief humiliating, and preferred issuing vouchers in kind (redeemable for food, heat, clothing) to cash, which profligate poor people would presumably squander. Municipalities which administered public relief, also often had applicants work for their assistance, creating make-work schemes that contributed little but further humiliation.

And for those without homes? Young men over 18 were ineligible for family relief. That left thousands of men riding boxcars from town to town, city to city, drifting and increasingly marginalized. No wonder they began to organize, to join the Communist Party of Canada, and to turn their backs on a mainstream society that betrayed their dreams. The federal government, fearing this social sub-class, enacted plans to contain it, but only ended up further marginalizing the men by establishing work camps in remote areas where they toiled for 20 cents per day at useless jobs under the watchful gaze of the Department of National Defence. Camp inmates even lost their right to vote and had their mail censored.

Ironically, Canadians elected the nation's first millionaire as prime minister in 1930. R.B. Bennett's annual income dropped considerably but never dipped below $150,000 per year during the depression, a time when families comfortably survived on $25 per week. He promised to end unemployment through stiff tariffs that were to encourage Canadian industry, but his policies did more harm than good, especially in the agricultural sector. His administration, however, did provide extraordinary funds for destitute provincial coffers. Bennett hated the concept of relief, fearing that it promoted "idleness." Yet the economy had all but halted, and even he had to admit that jobs were scarce. Nor was he heartless. Bennett and his secretaries responded to virtually every letter he received, and he regularly dipped into his own funds to alleviate particularly heart-wrenching stories. News of his philanthropy spread quickly, and the volume of mail increased to the point where he established a special donations fund, usually five dollars at a time. The number of gifts peaked around election time in 1935.

The historians who originally published the following letters changed the senders' names and addresses in the interest of privacy. They also chose the most poignant correspondence for publication and attempted to balance the regional, ethnic, and occupational perspectives. They discovered that Bennett and his staff had a slight preference for sending cash to youth, westerners, and Anglophones.

Discussion Points

1. List the recurring themes of these letters. What do they say about the causes, conditions and impact of poverty during the depression?
2. Many claim that women have a unique culture and voice often overlooked by historians. Did men and women experience the Depression differently?
3. Were Canadian governments negligent in their treatment of the poor during the Great Depression?
4. Why did welfare seem dangerous or unadvisable to so many people?
5. The document "Experiences of a Depression Hobo" provides a rather different perspective from many of the Bennett letters. What would account for this?

Documents

1. Thomas M. Gibbs, Sarnia, Ontario, December 1, 1930.

Hon. Mr. Bennet Ottawa Ont.
Dear Sir:

I am taking this priviledge in my own hands of writing you which a person of my class should be ashamed to take such athoraty. But I am down and out and do not know what to do. We have six children and I don't beleive it right to see them suffer for the want of food I tried everywhere to get things for them to eat this is Saturday and I must say we have to go all day Sunday with but one small meal that is dry bread and apple sauce which we have day after day the apples will soon run out then we will be out of luck. I asked for asistance from the township they never came near me. I was in the second Canadian infantry Battalion as a private. I wrote to London see if I could get releif there. Enclosed you will find a coppy which they sent me. I will not take up too much of your time just now. But in my case I am a good worker but the work is not to be had. My name has been in the employment office since June but there is no jobs comming in so I have to do something might soon I hate to go out and steal but the family can't starve to death. I am a butcher by trade and know cattle and understand them thourghly. Also farmed for twelve years. Am all willing to go anywhere to work if there is anything at all you can possible do for me this will be greatly appreciated if there is any dought these statements call Sarnia 1154 that will be Mr. A.E.Palmer Employment Bureau. Kindly over look the privledge Im taking I think this is my last chance to get help. If this fails I do not know what we will do.

2. A Nanaimoite, February 22.

Mr Bennett
Dear Sir

before we are much older there is going to be trouble in Nanaimo & Cumberland owing to the foreigners having jobs while the men & boys who are borne British subjects & who rightfully belong to these jobs have to go without jobs therefore they have to go without sufficient food & clothing, in Cumberland you have Japanese & Chinese working in & about the mines also other foreign-ers from other countrys who can neither read write or speak english & this is breaking the Coal Mines Rules and Regulation Act & they are a danger to both human life & property yet they hold the jobs which rightfully belong to us British although it is against the rules for these people to have jobs in the mines.

The same applied to Nanaimo only the Chinese are working on the surface here & not below but there are a very large number of foreigners working in the mines at Nanaimo who can neither read write nor speak English & apart from that besides having our jobs & getting the wages which is ours by right the money is not only going out of Nanaimo but it is going out of the country & that is not good for this country. I wish you could come yourself to the mines at Nanaimo & watch the ammount of foreigners who are employed at these mines & then look at the number of British men & boys who go to these same mines every day begging for a job only to be turned away & they have no money to buy bread & clothing while the foreigner has both the foreigners are also starting allkinds of stores & boarding houses & trying to buy beer parlours while the Britisher goes broke as there are not enough British men & boys in employment & the foreigner buys all from his own kind. It looks to me as though the chief Superintendent of these mines here is trying to cause a lot of trouble on this Island by employing as many foreigners as possible at the expense of the people who belong to this country if this is so he is going to see all the trouble & more than he wants before long as human nature can't stand for it much longer there is a lot of talk here (& men say they are prepared to prove it) that Robert Fox who is superintendent of these mines is accepting bribes from these foreigners for jobs. I hope government will take a hand in this before it is too late as there is so much money going out of this town & out of the country & our men & boys are asked to go to goverment camps & give up their homes to these foreigners the foreigner can come here and make a home while the men and boys who have a right to a home & a job have to get out to make room for the foreigner can you wonder that the Britisher is getting riled & again very many of these foreigners fought against our men & boys in the big war now they are given our jobs our bread & our homes if government does not take a hand in this at once I fear an uprising of all English speaking people on this Island & it may end in harm to the foreigner & also to property

3. R.D., Ottawa, March 4, 1932.

Dear Sir,

I am just writing a few lines to you to see what can be done for us young men of Canada. We are the growing generation of Canada, but with no hopes of a future. Please tell me why is it a single man always gets a refusal when he looks

the streets, & starve, than work on a
farm. That is a true statement. Myself I work wherever I can get work, & get a
good name wherever I go. There are plenty of young men like myself, who are in
the same plight. I say again whats to be done for us single men? do we have to
starve? or do we have to go round with our faces full of shame, to beg at the
doors of the well to do citizen. I suppose you will say the married men come
first; I certainly agree with you there. But have you a word or two to cheer us
single men up a bit? The married man got word he was going to get relief. That
took the weight of worry off his mind quite a bit. Did the single man here
anything, how he was going to pull through? Did you ever feel the pangs of
hunger? My idea is we shall all starve. I suppose you will say I cant help it, or I
cant make things better. You have the power to make things better or worse.
When you entered as Premier you promised a lot of things, you was going to do
for the country I am waiting patiently to see the results. Will look for my answer
in the paper.

4. Mrs. Ernest Ferguson, Ferguson, N.B., March 21, 1933.

Hon. R.B. Bennett
Ottawa, Can.
Dear Sir,

The respectable people of this country are *fed up* on feeding the bums for
that is all they can be called now. This "free" relief (free to the bums) has done
more harm than we are altogether aware of. The cry of those who get it is "Bennett
says he wont let anyone starve" They don't consider that the *people* (many poorer
than themselves but with more spunk) have to foot the bill. The regulations
(which are only a poor guide after all) were too loose from the start and *could be*
and *were* easily side stepped many times.

Getting relief has become such a habit that the majority think only of how
to get it regularly instead of trying to do without once in a while. Nearly all of
them have dogs too which are fed by the country and are of no practical use.

One family near me has three and another has two and others one and I know it is the same everywhere. I also know that food enough to keep one dog will keep at least four hens and keep them laying. The family that has the three dogs ate at least 550 pounds of meat from the second week in November until the first part of March. There are the parents, twins 10 years old and four children from one year to eight. Who but the dogs got a good part of that? Also dogs everywhere are chasing and catching deer but if a man tries to get one for the family he is either fined or jailed if found out. Or if he tries to get a few fish (he is mighty lucky if he succeeds above Newcastle on the Miramichi now) the wardens are right after him and he finds himself minus a net at the least.

Now the taxes are going to be forcibly collected to pay for the good-for-nothings for whom the debt was made. Those people should be made work and there wouldn't need to be much forcing for taxes. The taxpayers don't consider that they should keep people as well and sometimes better off than they are and their wives agree with them. We see plainly now that those being kept will not help themselves so long as they are fed for nothing.

Notice should be given at once to enable them to get crops in and so on and relief stopped altogether. The cost of that would pay for a good deal of work. Also please remember there are other people in the country who need your thought as well as those on relief as it is now though they are struggling along somehow. I think it only fair to state that if it continues or is considered for the future there will be a goodly number of Conservatives vote the other way for as I stated in the beginning we are sick and tired of being forced to keep the majority that are following the relief path. It hasn't been fair all through as any thoughtful man must know. I am not stating this idly because I have talked with many others many times and that is the general feeling. I think I can safely say too that the Liberals getting relief don't thank the Conservatives enough to give them a vote either because they nearly all say the country owes them a living and think no thanks are due.

I could write more but will let this suffice for this time but Please consider this question of relief as a very important one because a deal of trouble may brew from it.

5. Brief Presented by the Unemployed of Edmonton to the Hon. R.B. Bennett, December 30, 1933.

Mr. R.B.Bennett
Prime Minister of Canada

For three long, weary years you, Mr Bennett and your Conservative Party have held undisputed and unmolested sway in Canada. You and your coleagues were elected primarily because you gave the people two great promises, (1) you would end unemployment, (2) you would blast your way to foreign markets. As to the first of these promises, you Mr. Bennett as the chief Economic Doctor, have failed, miserable failed, not only to cure the dangerous disease, but even to give it an unbiased diagnosis; and the only blasting that has been apparent has been the inhuman wrecking of millions of once happy homes. You have repeatedly reminded us of the sacredness of our British Institutions. Mr. Bennett, is not the home an institution? Then why do you callously stand by while it is being wantonly destroyed by the Molloch of Big business? We have this to say Mr. Bennett. Even a yellow dog will resist, to the death, the ruthless destruction of his most priceless possession.

Surely, in three years of full political power you could have found, if you had tried, a better method of dealing with unemployment than the Direct Relief System. In view of the fact that you have not we hereby give you the only solution which is applicable in society as at present constituted. Non-contributary Unemployment Insurance. It must be non-contributary, otherwise the million and a half already unemployed will receive no benefit. Pending the enactment of this Bill, Relief allowances must be raised. Seeing that we are not allowed to earn in wages sufficient to maintain us and our families, we demand adequate relief. The perpetual cry of Mayor Knott, and Premier Brownlee is "We can do nothing. We have no money". Without discussing the truthfulness of these statements, Mr. Bennett, we know that the contribution from the Federal Treasury must be doubled if it is designed to even remotely approach the need ... We have not words in our vocabulary sufficiently strong to properly condemn your method of dealing with unemployed single men. Those slave camps are a blot on the record of any civilized country. That young men, the very flower of the race, those who must make the next generation are forced, by economic necessity, to enter those isolated prisons, where there is neither proper physical food, nor mental stimulation, cries to Heaven for correction. What are you trying to do to our young men? Make a generation of physical wrecks and mental dolts? Or perhaps they will be used for cannon fodder? The militarization of those camps strongly points to this latter hypothesis as being the correct one … placing the single men in camps under the control of the Department of National Defence is too apparent to be overlooked. We shall resist to the bitter end the slaughtering of those boys and young men in an Imperialist war. We demand that they be taken out of those camps and be given an opportunity to earn a civilized living, at a civilized wage, and live a normal life by taking a wife and raising a family. We protest against the increased appropriations for the National Defence. These monies should never be spent for these purposes, but instead, used to supplement the contribution to relief. The battleships and bombing planes, and big guns will never be used if it is left to the people to declare war. In this connection why has Japan been allowed to buy tremendous quantities of junk iron from Canada? Is it possible we shall again see and feel this iron in the form of bullets? If such a thing should come to pass, who is the butcher, the man behind the gun or the man who supplied him with the ammunition. We want it clearly understood that we consider the workers of Japan, Germany, France, Russia or any other country as nothing more nor less than brother workers and we strongly protest against the despicable and abominable part Canada is playing in hastening us toward another great Imperialist conflagation, the horrors of which were only too well forcast by the last World War.

Mr. Bennett, there was never a more damnable insult heaped upon a working class of any country than when armoured tanks and other highly perfected instruments of slaughter were sent into Stratford, Ontario. Are these the trying circumstances which will test the very best of our National fibre, which you mentioned upon your return from England? Why is it, that if our government is a Democratic institution, representing the whole people the armed forces of the nation is used to coerce the working class, who make up 95% of the population, and force them to submit to wage cuts and a general worsening of their living conditions? On the face of it, it appears that Big business, whose interest it is to force the working class into pauperism, is being protected and not we; that the minority is dictatorial machine, which our Democratic government allows to use the military power of the nation against the majority. Not only in Stratford does this phenomena manifest itself, but throughout the country, whenever the workers use the only economic weapon they have, the strike, the R.C.M.P. are rushed to the spot and club the workers into submission. We submit Mr. Bennett that we are a peaceful people. If you will send work at a living wage to strikers instead of tanks and machine guns your economic troubles will be considerably lessened. We protest against this Fascist terrorism, and demand the rights of free speech and free assemble. We protest against the policy of deporting foreign born workers simply because they can find no buyer for their labor power. The solidarity of the British Commonwealth of Nations is widely publicized, yet, we find workers born in the British Isles are subject to deportation. When a young and great country like Canada with only Ten million population finds itself in the position where it must deport labor power there must be something wrong with its economic system. Those workers, came to Canada in good faith, after being led to believe that this country was the land of their dreams. They did not come in order to get on Canada's Unemployed list. After promising them a Heaven. and then give them Hell is not a safe policy. The slightly lesser evil of the relief lists is, we feel, the worst that these people should be subject.

To sum up, Mr. Bennett, we are absolutely fed up with being on relief. The terrible waste that is implied in a million and a half idle man power is a crime against the human race. There is so much work to do, and here there are, unemployed. We don't know how the natural resources come to be where they are, but we do know, that neither you nor Big business created them. The material is here, land, lumber, iron, steel, etc. and so are we. If you can't supply the tokens of exchange that will bring us together, you had better resign and hand the country over to the workers. We may be ignorant uncouth men, belong to the lowest strata of a low society, but, and we don't boast, we will have enough sense to eat when there is food to eat, and work when there is work to be done and tools to work with.

6. To Canadian Government, December 1934.

Canadian Govt. at Ottawa, Canada

Well Mr. R.B. Bennet, arnt you a *man* or are you? to be the cause of all this starvation and privation. You call us derelicts, then if we are derelicts *what else are you* but one too, only *a darn sight worse*. You said if you was elected, you would give us all work and wages, well you have been in the Prime Ministers shoes, now, for 4 years and we are *still looking for work and wages*. You took all our jobs away from us. We can't earn any money. You say a releif camp is good enough for us, then *its too good* for *you* Mr Bennet, you are on releif your own self. You put away your big govt salary, then ask the gov't. to pay for your big *feasts*, while *we* poor fellows starve. While *you* jazz around the hotel girls. You think people don't know any thing well, even if we are *"derelicts" "as you called us"* and which we consider you as the leader of the derelicts Band you have fooled us a lot, in the last four years. We have lived on your hot air, so you may know you had to expell a *lot*. But you can't fool *all* of us, *all* the time.

… Well now Mr. Bennet, I hope this sinks clear down to your toes, and gives you swelled feet, instead of a swelled head. You have had a swelled head ever since you had the "Eddy" Match Co. signed to you by Mrs. Eddy, don't think people don't know anything.

P.S. this will take my last 3 cents, but we hope it goes to the bottom of *you*, and that you will hand us out *both work* and *living wages*. You have caused *lots* of people to kill their families and themselves rather than to slowly starve to death, or freeze to death. Try it you prime minister, just try it.

Now you are trying to get war going to make yourself richer. Well R.B. Bennet, I hope you get your share of the bullets.

We are going to give you a chance, (which you don't deserve) either you will stop this war, now, and give us fellows work and living wages enough to stop such starving, and freezing, because we *can't* buy any clothes, the doukabours are jailed because they wont wear any clothing while *we* are jailed trying to get clothing to wear. You say we live too extravagance, then you shall be able to hand out $5.00 to anyone and everyone, then we wont live so extravagant. You have heaps of money laid away. Well, it wont do you a bit of good if we have another war.

We are giving you this chance. We say again you do not deserve it at all. If we dont get work or wages, and "living wages" to, we are going to tell the Canadian government they have a "murderer", in the house at Ottawa. You said a rich uncle left you your wealth, bah. We know better. We are not trying to scare you, but we are tired, of relief camps and going hungry and cold. no homes, or any thing else.

7. P.R. Mulligan, Debden, Saskatchewan, March 3, 1934.

Hon. Mr. R.B. Bennet
Ottawa, Canada
Dear Sir —

I am writing to see if you could not give me a little help. I hear you are going to destroy some thousands of tons of wheat to get rid of it; while my family & stock are starving to death. There is lots of wheat and other things here but I have no money to buy them with. I have been farming in Central Sask. since 1909 until a yr ago when I was forced off my farm. So last yr I could not get a place for to farm so could only get what I could by working out on farms. Which was not near enough to keep my family in food. In the fall I moved to the North hoping to be able to keep my stock alive and to be able to get a homestead. I had applied to have my stock sent to Spiritwood but by some mistake somewhere I was sent to Debden instead so then I had neither buildings or feed in reach and dead broke in bitter cold weather. So could not buy feed or take a homestead either. As the relief officer for this part was in town here at the time I asked him for relief & for feed. I could not get any feed whatever out of him until my four horses and seven head of cattle (my two best cows included) 16 pigs (some of them weighed over 100 lbs) and most of my poultry had actually starved to death. All that was necessary was an order to get some feed from the relief officer, but though I asked him several times & did not get any until that many were dead. Since then I have had orders amounting to 1500 (fifteen hundred) oat sheaves but nothing to feed a pig or chicken. If I had been given sufficient feed in the first place my stock would be alive and most of those hogs would now be ready for market. We would then have some meat for our table and the rest would have repaid the relief I needed and most likely would have left something to take me off the relief list for a time at least. Now we cannot farm the land I had rented because I haven't a horse left to farm with. We kept off relief as long as we had a cent to buy food or a rag of clothes that would hang together. To date we have had $45.35 for food to feed ten of us from Dec 1st on until now, and I did relief bridge work to about that amount and was quite willing to do as much more as I would get the chance to do. But when I asked for a greater food allowance I was told that many were doing with much less as well as one insult upon another added thereto by the local relief officer. Yet I know several families right around here getting more relief according to the size of family and do not need relief at all but still they get it. I have 8 children ranging from 4 ½ yrs to 14 ½ yrs yet all we have had in the house for over a week has been dry bread and black tea and believe me Mr. Bennet it isn't very nice to listen hour after hr to young children pleading for a little butter or why can't we have some potatoes or meat or eggs. But how can I get it on what I have been getting when it takes most of it for flour alone. Because we were not sent where we asked to be sent to we have to live ten of us in cold one roomed shack instead of having a comfortable house to live in. We haven't a mattress or even a tick just simply have to sleep on a bit of straw and nearly every night we have to almost freeze because we haven't bed clothes. I did not ask relief to supply these but I did ask for pants, overalls and footwear for the children about two months ago, but to date we have had $15.95 of clothing (some of this had to be returned as it did not fit) and some of the children are at this time running barefooted & not one of them has either a pr. of pants or overalls to cover their nakedness. Neither can they go to school because they have no clothes and also because the local school board demand a tuition fee of $30 because we are not taxpayers as yet in this school and that after paying school taxes in this province for nearly 25 years. One result now is that the whole family have some kind of rash and running sores & I cannot take them to a Dr. as I have not the price to pay the Dr. or to buy the things that he would order. Also my wife has become badly ruptured and I can not have anything done about it for the same reason. I was born with one leg shorter than the other and am physically not a strong man but I have always done all I've been able to do and a lot more than many more able than I am and I am not in the habit of wasting any time or money on drinking, gambling or anything of the sort yet we have to sit here and see not only our stock starve but see my wife & children starve as well, and do the same myself. So for God's sake give us an order to get a few bus. of wheat to help us live and to raise a few chickens and pigs to eat at least and if we ever make enough to do it with I'll return it with interest too.

Yours in need

8. Miss Elizabeth McCrae, Hamilton, Ontario, April 6, 1934.

To His Excellency The Rt Hon. R B Bennett, Parliament Buildings,
Ottawa Ontario.
Dear Sir:

I am writing you as a last resource to see if I cannot, through your aid, obtain a position and at last, after a period of more than two years, support myself and enjoy again a little independence.

The fact is: this day I am faced with starvation and I see no possible means of counteracting or even averting it temporarily!

If you require references of character or ability I would suggest that you write to T.M. Sanderson of Essex, Ontario. I worked as Stenographer and Bookkeeper with him for over three years in the office of the Sanderson-Marwick Co., Ltd., in Essex. I feel certain that you have made his acquaintance for he was President of the Conservative Association at the time of the Banquet held in your worshipful honour a few years ago.

I have received a high-school and Business-college education and I have had experience as a Librarian. My business career has been limited to Insurance, Hosiery, and Public Stenography, each time in the capacity of Bookkeeper and Stenographer — briefly, General Office work.

My father is a farmer at Pilot Mound, Manitoba and during the past years his income has been nil, so I cannot get any assistance from him. In fact, until I joined the list of unemployed I had been lending the folks at home my aid. To save my Mother from worry I have continually assured her that I am working and till the end I will save her from distress by sticking to this story.

When the Sanderson-Marwick Co., Ltd, went out of business I had saved a little money and there being no work there for me I came to Hamilton. Since then I have applied for every position that I heard about but there were always so many girls who applied that it was impossible to get work. So time went on and my clothing became very shabby. I was afraid to spend the little I had to replenish my wardrobe. Always the fear was before me that I would fail to get the position and then I would be without food and a roof over my head in a short time. Many prospective employers just glanced at my attire and shook their heads and more times than I care to mention I was turned away without a trial. I began to cut down on my food and I obtained a poor, but respectable, room at $1. per week.

First I ate three very light meals a day; then two and then one. During the past two weeks I have eaten only toast and drunk a cup of tea every other day. In the past fortnight I have lost 20 pounds and the result of this deprivation is that I am so very nervous that could never stand a test along with one, two and three hundred girls. Through this very nervousness I was ruled out of a class yesterday. Today I went to an office for an examination and the examiner looked me over and said; "I am afraid Miss, you are so awfully shabby I could never have you in my office."

I was so worried and disappointed and frightened that I replied somewhat angrily: "Do you think clothes can be picked up in the streets?"

"Well," he replied with aggravating insolence, "lots of girls find them there these days."

Mr. Bennett, that almost broke my heart. Above everything else I have been very particular about my friends and since moving here I have never gone out in the evening. I know no one here personally and the loneliness is hard to bear, but oh, sir, the thought of starvation is driving me mad! I have endeavoured to be good and to do what is right and I am confident I have succeeded in that score but I can name more than ten girls here in Hamilton who I am sure are not doing right and yet they have nice clothes and positions. That is what seems so unfair. They never think of God nor do they pray and yet they seem so happy and have so many things I would like, while I, who pray every night and morning have nothing!

Day after day I pass a delicatessen and the food in the window looks oh, so good! So tempting and I'm so hungry!

Yes I am very hungry and the stamp which carries this letter to you will represent the last three cents I have in the world, yet before I will stoop to dishonour my family, my character or my God I will drown myself in the Lake. However, I do not hint that I have the slightest intention of doing this for I am confident that you will either be able to help me find employment or God will come to my aid.

But in the meantime my clothing is getting shabbier and I am faced with the prospect of wearing the same heavy winter dress, that has covered me all winter, during the coming summer.

Oh please sir, can you do something for me? Can you get me a job anywhere in the Dominion of Canada. I have not had to go on relief during this depression but I cannot get relief even here. Moreover it is a job I want and as long as I get enough to live I shall be happy again.

I have tried to get work at anything and everything from housework up but I have been unsuccessful and now I am going to starve and in debt to my landlady. I wouldn't mind if I could just lay down and die but to starve, oh its terrible to think about.

Mr. Bennett, even if you can do nothing for me I want to thank you for your kindness in reading this letter and if I were jobless and semi-hungry for a lifetime I would still be a Conservative to the last, and fight for that Government.

Thanking you again for your very kind attention, I am,

Your humble servant,

9. L.M. Himmer, Blaine Lake, Saskatchewan, September 9, 1935.

Hon. R.B. Bennett
Ottawa, Ont.
Dear Sir:

For some time I have been thinking what this new country of ours was coming to. I had the pleasure of talking with Mr. F. R. MacMillan M.P. of Saskatoon and Senator Hornor of Blaine Lake. They both insisted that I write you a line.

I wish to give my opinion of relief. First it is a shame for a strong young man to ask for relief in this country. To my mind the relief has helped out the C.C.F. and Social Credit. When you give an inch they take a foot. There are men, who have been on relief, now sitting on the street asking $2.50 and 3.00 per day. Many of them would not be worth a $1.00 per day to stook 60 ct wheat.

To my mind the poet is right nine times out of ten. The best thing that can happen to a young man is toss him overboard and compel him to sink or swim, in all my acquaintance I have never known one to drown who was worth saving.

When I hear young men, with their head full of book knowledge, complaining about no money no work. They say they'll try for relief and they get it, then they spend two or three months around a lake shore rolling in the sand and splashing in the water. When winter comes they have no preparations of any kind. They say they'll try for relief and they get it.

I say again a man must have a purpose in life if he hasn't he will never amount to much. He will eat that which he has not earned, he will clog the wheels of industry and stand in the way of progress. Thoughts of this kind should be empressed on the pupils by the teachers, and ministers, instead of the C.C.F. doctrine, and athletic sports. The people have gone silly over nonsense and it is our leaders that are teaching the younger generations to be useless.

I asked a young man to help me thresh, he said he would not pitch sheaves for less than $5.00 per day, he can get relief, no doubt. I have four young men four harvest and threshing, they blow their wages every Saturday night, some of them will be on relief this winter, if not all.

It takes hardship to make real men and women so cut out relief ...

Relief is like a sixteen year old boy getting money from dad, when the old man gets wise and tightens up the boy gets mad and cuts a shine just as the relief strikers did.

There are some people in this country who are in hard circumstances, but I can safely say there is no one having the hardships that we pioneers had 28 and 30 years ago

Yours turely

10. Dorothy Franklin, Brechin, Ontario, February 28, 1935.

I hope you will pardon me for writing to you but I feel that, as the head of our country you should be made acquainted with some of the things we of the poorer class are up against. Oh, I know you have all kinds of this stuff thrown at you but today I just have to unload. You may recall that I wrote to you about three years ago and you very kindly interceded for a farm loan for us at Kent, but to no effect. We were refused the loan and the mortgage was foreclosed and we lost everything. We made a sale to pay the taxes and I reserved about thirty P. R. Hens that were laying and the only bit of money we had coming in. Well, the sale day was terribly stormy and along with other things on that day, there was a very poor turnout. The sale amounted to $220 for what we had paid $770. and the $220. was $24. less than the taxes. So my hens were sold at 80¢ each, which paid up the taxes and left us with nothing. When you wrote to me you said you hoped that year would be our best. Well, perhaps it was, It left us nothing but our experience and that has been dearly bought. We lost $3500. a mere nothing to some perhaps but our life's work. We moved to the front here hoping things might be better but since Dec. 10th, my man has been able to bring in $3.00. He is out every day looking for work and always the same results. Yesterday he came home and told me there is some road work starting next week but in order to get on, the men must sign up for relief. I wonder why men who are self-respecting have to be subjected to such humiliation and embarrassment when they are only too willing to work if possible. It isn't only the men who suffer but the families of these men. We have a pair of twin boys, sixteen years old. Both at school yet but those boys have gone all winter without underwear and no over-coats and do not even own a suit of clothes. They are wearing the same pants and sweaters week day and Sunday. I have to mend and wash their pullovers so they are presentable for Sunday School but they will not go to church because they are so shabby. We were taught to believe God put us women here for the noble cause of Motherhood. I wonder how many would have suffered what we have, had we known our children were not even going to have the necessities of life. This week we have bought just 1 lb of butter & 3 loaves of bread. I'm ashamed to ask the grocer for any more credit. We have been eating stew. First potatoes & carrots and then carrots and potatoes. I'm so discouraged. I wonder which re-quires the greater courage, to carry on knowing how much we are all needing and cannot have or to end it all as that poor woman did this week in Oakville by sticking her head in a pail of water and drowning. My last coat that I bought was eight years ago for the fabulous sum of $10.75 and my sunday dress is an old one of a cousin's made over. I wouldn't feel so badly if we only had our home but having no prospect of ever having anything is killing me. The people around this gritty hole are saying "Wait until the new government gets in". Its all bosh. No party alone can change things much. My idea is that all must work together to accomplish much good. In trouble such as the country is laboring under now, the partyism should be forgotten for the good of all mankind. Yes, I'm tory to my toes but just the same I have no hard feelings toward those who think differ-ently from me. Some day things will turn out all right and I am very thankful that through it all I can truthfully say I can still maintain my faith and trust in God above.

Forgive me if I have taken too much of your time.

Yours respectfully,

11. Mrs. Otto Brelgen, Dempster, Saskatchewan, April 15, 1935.

R.B. Bennett Esq

Ottawa, 0nt

Dear Friend,

I just can not stand for our treatment any longer without getting it off our chest. We came out here in Aug 1932 from Saskatoon on the Government Relief Plan. So you will understand that we have practically nothing as we had very little to start on, and we have worked very hard but have had terrible bad luck. We have lost 3 horses since coming out here so now are stranded with one horse which is on last legs. So how is it possible to go ahead and farm without help from somewhere. Last spring we had a neighbor break some for us. We have 15 acres now broke here, and my husband was working nearly all summer to pay the neighbor back so that certainly isn't going to put us somewhere we are going back fast. Still we are working like slaves, never have enough to eat and very little to wear. We have 5 children and our 2 selves. My baby was born up here without help of doctor or help in the house. Only what the neighbors felt like helping out. Now she is 16 month old and doesn't walk mostly lack of proper food. The other children all boys have been sick this winter, but how would it be possible to be healthy in such a condition. Last August our relief was cut down to $8.25 a month, but since Jan have recieved $11.65 so you see it is impossible to give the children proper foods. We had no garden at all everything froze to the ground as soon as it was started growing. We have about 20 chicken 1 cow. no meat or potatoes only what we buy many a meal around here is dry bread and milk when our cow is milking otherwise its water, butter is an extra luxury which we cannot afford. None of us have proper footwear now its not fit to be outside unless clothed properly. Its is a sin and a shame to be in such circumstance as that. It sure does grieve one when there nothing to eat or wear. We loan settler from the city's do not seem to be treated as well as those that moved in from the dried-out areas as they are fully equiped with live stock and also machinery, where we have nothing. I sure would like to know why that is. You maybe able to understand how it would be possible to feed our family on less 2 1/2 cents each person each meal it is quite impossible as I have tried every way of getting by. But cannot make it go. My family don't live anymore we only exist. I think if the situation was more clearly put to the right parties they could help us more some less, as there are people who have cattle, garden, and could get by without gov. help still they receive assitance which does only makes it worse for those who really need it. I am looking forward that you may be able to help us in some way. We most certainly would like to be on the upward road. Just think how many families in these north woods are starving, trying to make things go. Such hard work without food to supply body energy. So first the body fails then the mind. I know Im very near a nerbous wreck. If we were allowed supose the doctor would tell me I had a nervous breakdown as it is I have to keep trudging along trying to make the best, but don't think I can stand the strain much longer. We never get out amongst any kind of entertainment as relief people are not allowed any recreation of any kind. We would be so thankful to you if you could help us in some way. Today is only the 15th of the month and our flour is all gone already and the stores will not give any credit out. So we'll all be quite hungry until the first of the month. Please give this your personal consideration and send me an answer of what could be done we are practally at the end of our rope now. Thanking you again for your attention

Your Faithfull Servant

12. Bruce Bass, Whiteway, N.B., October 7, 1935.

Right Hon. R B Bennett,
Dear Sir: —

I am writing to ask you if you could or would help me. As I have a big family and all are going to school at present, but I will soon have to keep them home as they have no clothes and very little to eat. I have been working nearly all summer but my pay was so small that I barley got enough to eat for them. There are six children, ages from 15 to 7, four of which are boys, one boy 13, and in Grade Vlll. I would like for him to be in school till he get through. But with out help of some kind, I can't. I try every way to get work. There is no work and wages so small. All I can do is to get something to eat for my wife and children, and so many school books to buy, besides three of our children have one book between them. No way of getting any more The times have been so hard around here that everything one had is all worn out. This very night we havn't a baking of flour in our house. I have order some whether we will get it I can't tell. No work nor no money I think it is a terrible thing for a man that is able and willing to work he has to see his little children go to school hungry and half enough cloth on them to keep them warm. I always support the Conservative Government, and intend to do the same next Monday if nothing happen.

I don't mind my self so bad, the children I am thinking most of now. I don't know How I am going to get cloth for them if your help me I would be very thankful to you.

I remain Your Truly,

13. A Mother.

Hon. R.B. Bennett
Ottawa
Sir:

This is from a mother who's son is wandering somewhere in Ont. trying vainly to get work. What are you going to do for these thousands of young men? There is lots of work to be done if you would only start them at it. You have never had to sleep out in the snow and rain or go days without food. Just stop and think of these hungry boys when you are at your next banquet.

You have no children, so you cannot realize how parents feel with their sons wandering in this useless search for work.

You have only a short time now to try to help these men or it will be up to the other party to do it.

14. Experiences of a Depression Hobo.

I arrived in Toronto a week ago but have not got work yet. The trip down took 5 ½ days and I did not visit any jails. My total expenses were 50 cents but I ate a slept well.

On the Saturday night of April 15 my friend and I took the last street car out to Sutherland having previously found out that a freight train was leaving for Winnipeg during the early hours of Sunday morning. We slunk around the yards till we came upon a brakeman and asked when the freight for the East was pulling out. Before he could reply a torch light beamed in our faces and the "bull" asked "Where are you guys going?" "East"—"Winnipeg." "Well that freight won't pull out till seven to-morrow morning." We thanked the police-man for this information and retired to the shadow of a nearby Pool Elevator, lighted cigarettes and attempted keep warm. Even I, with 2 pairs undercloth-ing, 2 shirts, a sweater, my brown suit, overalls, overcoat, winter cap & 2 pairs sox was getting chilly. Presently we became restless & walked out onto the tracks to spy an ancient looking empty coach with a light in it. Prowling lower we observed a notice on the side telling us it was for the use of stockmen only. A brakeman informed us that the coach was to be put on the freight to Winnipeg for the use of some stockman travelling. We entered the coach, found a fire burning in the stove, wiped the dust off the seats, spread them out bed fashion & were soon asleep. We were suddenly awakened by the guard who informed us that the train was pulling out in 5 minutes and that a "bull" was going to travel with the train. Observing the "bull" walking down the side of the train we waited till he rounded the end before ourselves, hopping out, walked after him & inspected the box cars. All but one were sealed, this "one" being half full of coal. There were already about ten other travellers sprawling in various positions amongst the coal.

The first division stop was Wynyard and here my friend turned back. He had a warm bed in Saskatoon, a mother, a father and home—not work. He explained that he was a decent fellow, had never been in jail in his life &, didn't like freight riding. What would his mother say if he was arrested? Besides, supposing there was no work in Toronto what would we do? We'd be arrested, vagrants. He had never been in a big city before, our money would not last long, we might even starve to death! In other words, he'd had enough … just chicken hearted.

The sun was warm and I rode on top of a box car all day. Towards evening the train pulled in at the next division stop, Bredenbury. I was hungry & made for the town semi-satisfying my appetite in a "Chinks". Returning to the train I fell in with two of my fellow passengers of the coal car who had been "bumming" the houses. They were lads of 23 also heading for Toronto — happy but broke. Arriving at the tracks we walked boldly towards the freight & walked right into the "bull" who instantly showed his ignorance. "What the hell d'you fellows want here." We put him right as to our wants whilst he accompanied us to the entrance of the yards and the freight steamed out. He informed us that should he see us around again he would put us all in "clink". One of my new-found confederates thanked him very much and suggested that as we had lost the freight and had nowhere to sleep we should very much appreciate his hospitality. But the "bull" was not so hospitable & we slept in the C.P.R. round house beside a boiler. I slept well in spite of the sudden change from feather to concrete mattress. Following morning a pail & water from the boiler brightened our appearance & we made for town agreeing that the inhabitants should pay dearly for their ignorant railway cop. Meeting the oldest resident, I think he must have been, on "Main Street" we enquired as to the whereabouts of the local "town bull", the mayor, the residences of the station agent, the railway cop and the R.C.M.P. local. With this information we commenced our labours for breakfast.

Seeing a man working in a garden we wondered whether he would like our aid or company. He was not impressed by either but gave us $1 for "eats". Entering the local hotel we explained our circumstances and gorged for 25 cents per head. During the morning we lay down on some open prairie & slept till roused by a crowd of children who had come to inspect us. One yelled "Hobo, hobo we've got some candy for you", but as I got up hopefully they took to their heals [sic] and ran for town. Our stomaches [sic] informed us dinner time had arrived, one of the boys set out for the mayors house and brought back a fine "hand out" which we consumed. The other set out for another of our addresses, split some wood & received a "sit-down". Then it was my turn to go "bumming". I set out for a large house set back from the town which looked hopeful. I tapped at the door nervously and a large man poked his head cautiously out of the door letting out an equally large dog as he did so. My knees knocked and I stuttered something about work & eat. The man told me he did not feed tramps & would set his dog on me. I moved toward the dog which instantly fled with its tail between its legs and the man slammed the door. As I was walking down the path the man popped his head out of an upstairs window and threatened to inform the police if I did not "get clear" immediately.

Towards evening the Winnipeg freight pulled in and we boarded it as it pulled out of the yards. There were no "empties" but a stock coach on the back, so we sat on the steps of this. As dusk fell we stopped for water at some place & the guard sighted us. He came up & inspected us, then unlocked the coach & told us to get in there for the night, we might go to sleep on the steps & fall off. Next morning we awoke to find our freight standing in the Portage La Prairie yards. Two "bulls" walked up the train, inspected the seals, glanced at the stock coach where we had assumed an attitude of sleep once more, walked off. We left the freight at a street crossing outside Winnipeg, yelled at a passing truck driver and were whirled into the city. The two lads I was with got a free shave at the Barber College and we learnt that the city was handing out meals to transients. After much walking and enquiring we obtained meal tickets and set out for the soup kitchens, which used to be the C.N.R. Immigration Hall where I stopped when first in Canada. The meal was awful! We walked down a counter gradually accumulating our ration which consisted of a piece of bread & square of butter, a small dish containing about a spoonful of sugar, a tin bowl containing a green fluid sometimes called soup, a tin plate on which had been dumped, dirty potatoes, two [sic] large hunks of fat, some carrots and thick gravy, and a mug contain -hot water the same colour as weak tea. We sat on a bench containing males of all types, nationalities and descriptions and attempted to eat.

The gentleman on my right had developed a strange habit of wiping a running nose with the back of his hand between each mouthful which did not increase the flavour of my meal. A large bowl of rice was placed on the table for desert but as I had my plate already filled with leavings I did not try any.

We left the soup kitchens and made enquiries about the times of freight trains. There was one leaving from the C.N.R. Transcona yards at around midnight for Toronto. We commenced the 9 miles walk to Transcona.

On the way we passed over a bridge on the side of which some humorist had written with chalk "I'm fed up; for further information drag the river." Over the bridge is St. Boniface where there is a large catholic church, seminary, school, nuns home etc. etc. Whilst passing the seminary and admiring its size and beauty we espied the kitchen through a basement window. Thoughts concerning the higher arts vanished from our heads, we looked at each other, looked for the nearest door, and entered, coming upon a fat cook. I moved my hand over my chest and wore my most pious expression and one of the boys addressing the cook as "brother" explained that we were extremely undernourished and should be pleased with some bread. The cook prepared some sandwiches containing cold slabs of steak and we departed praising the Lord, the cook and ourselves.

Towards late afternoon we arrived at the yards, parked ourselves on the grass outside the fencing and built a fire of old ties—and commenced a 7 hour wait. We consumed our sandwiches which were delicious—I think I'll become a priest.

As time passed more "travellers" appeared and settled around our fire; soon we had about a dozen fellow "unionists" and grew to discussing "this world of ours" as men often do. In London there are cockney tales, in Scotland, Scotch tales and on the road, hobo tales. Hoboes also have quite a language of their own. The same as farmers but without the large variety of 'swear words' usually associated with the barnyard.

The depression, the railway companies and Bennett were our chief topics. We wisely listened to each others views on depression. Its due to tariffs, to immigration, the price of wheat, the U.S.A., Russia, war, their "big-bugs", religion, the "bohunks". Nothing but war will bring back prosperity; no cancellation of war debts; no socialism; no God; let's have the good old days; scrap machinery, to hell with motor cars, deport the Reds, deport the "bohunks", oust Bennett ...

Quite evidently there is no use for a penniless person in this land of opportunity; a person without work and money is considered an outcast, no town or city wants him but he can usually get two meals per day and exist because even Canadians do not usually let dogs starve. When a person has lost all his money and cannot get work he can either take to the road and become a bum or stop in his home town and get a free bed and two meals a day from the city relief for which he has to do as many hours work per week. I estimate that this scheme breaks the spirit of the average man within a year; hence I chose the road. My spirit is by no means broken I just feel angry and the harder Canada kicks me the more I'll retaliate. I do not consider myself an ordinary "bum". If there is any work to be done I'll do it providing I receive what I consider a decent living wage. I will certainly not work for my board and I will not work for the pittance many are receiving today.

Until such time as I get a decent job I intend to live well, dress respectably, eat all thats good for me, keep myself clean and have clean clothes. Canada generally will pay for this. I will obtain what I need by bumming and other comparatively honest methods. If such ways and means should fail I shall resort to thieving and other criminal ways of which l have some knowledge ...

Readings

Ballageon, D. "If you had No Money, You had no Trouble, Did you? Montreal Working Class Housewives during the Great Depression," in W. Michinsen *Canadian Women: A Reader*. Toronto: Harcourt and Brace, 1996.

Ballageon, D. *Making Do: Women, Family and Home in Montreal During the Great Depression*. Waterloo: Wilfrid Laurier University Press, 1999.

Brown, L. *When Freedom was Lost: The Unemployed, the Agitator and the State*. Montreal: Black Rose, 1987.

Cadigan, S. "Battle Harbour in Transition: Merchants, Fishermen and the State in the Struggle for Relief in a Labrador Community during the 1930s," *Labour* 26 (1990).

Christie, N. *Engendering the State: Family, Work and Welfare in Canada*. Toronto: University of Toronto Press, 2000.

Dumas, E. *The Bitter Thirties in Quebec*. Trans. A. Bennett. Montreal: Black Rose, 1975.

Finkel, A. *Business and Social Reform in the Thirties*. Toronto: James Lorimer, 1979.

Francis, R., and H. Ganzevoort, eds. *The Dirty Thirties in Prairie Canada*. Vancouver: Tantalus, 1980.

Glassford, L. *Reaction and Reform: The Politics of the Conservative Party Under R.B. Bennett*. Toronto: University of Toronto Press, 1992.

Gray, J. *The Winter Years: The Depression on the Prairies*. Toronto: Macmillan, 1966.

Gray, J. *Men Against the Desert*. Saskatoon: Western Producer, 1967.

Healey, T. "Engendering Resistance: Women Respond to Relief in Saskatoon, 1930-33," in A. Moffat and D. De Brou, eds. *Other Voices: Historical Essays on Saskatchewan Women*. Regina: Canadian Plains Research Centre, 1995.

Hobbs, M. "Equality and Difference: Feminism and Defence of Women Workers during the Great Depression," *Labour* 32 (Fall 1993).

Horn, M., ed. *The Dirty Thirties: Canadians in the Great Depression.* Toronto: Copp Clark, 1972.

Horn, M., ed. *The Depression in Canada: Responses to Economic Crisis.* Toronto: Copp Clark Pitman, 1988.

Howard, I. "The Mothers' Council of Vancouver," *B.C. Studies* (1986).

MacDowell, L. "Relief Camp Workers in Ontario during the Great Depression of the 1930s," *Canadian Historical Review* 76, 2 (1995).

Neatby, H. *The Politics of Chaos: Canada and the Thirties.* Toronto: Macmillan, 1972.

Pierson, R. "Gender and Unemployment Debates in Canada, 1934–1940," *Labour* 25 (Spring 1990).

Safarian, A. *The Canadian Economy in the Great Depression.* Toronto: University of Toronto Press, 1959.

Struthers, J. *No Fault of Their Own: Unemployment and the Canadian Welfare State, 1914-1941.* Toronto: University of Toronto Press, 1983.

Struthers, J. *The Limits of Affluence: Welfare in Ontario, 1920–1970.* Toronto: University of Toronto Press, 1994.

Thompson, J., and A. Seager. *Canada 1922–1939: Decades of Discord.* Toronto: McClelland and Stewart, 1985.

Wilbur, R., ed. *The Bennett New Deal: Fraud or Portent?* Toronto: Copp Clark, 1968.

Vigod, B. "The Quebec Government and Social Legislation during the 1930s: A Study in Political Self-Destruction," *Journal of Canadian Studies* 14, 1 (1979).

Chapter Eleven

"THE QUESTION OF LOYALTY":
JAPANESE CANADIANS AND WORLD WAR II

1. "The Situation in 1940," *Report and Recommendations of the Special Committee on Orientals in British Columbia,* December 1940.
2. A. Neill, House of Commons, *Debates,* February 19, 1942.
3. Muriel Kitagawa, *This is My Own: Letters to Wes and Other Writings on Japanese Canadians 1941-1948.*
    i. December 21, 1941.
    ii. January 21, 1942.
    iii. February 19, 1942.
    iv. March 2, 1942.
    v. April 20, 1942.
    vi. We'll Fight for Home, 1942.
    vii. On Loyalty, 1942.
    viii. Mr. and Mrs. Kitagawa to Custodian of Japanese Properties, Vancouver, B.C., July 1943.
    ix. F.G. Shears, Department of the Secretary of State, Office of the Custodian, Japanese Evacuation Section, Vancouver, B.C., to Mr. and Mrs. Kitagawa, July 2, 1943.
    x. T.M. Kitagawa to Mr. F.G. Shears, July 8, 1943.
4. W.L. Mackenzie King, House of Commons, *Debates,* August 4, 1944.

Introduction

Vilifying other nations' histories is so much easier than attacking one's own. National self-flagellation hurts and threatens the collective psyche; it challenges a people's xenophobic chauvinism and selfrighteousness. That is why nations' histories often exclude firmly closeted skeletons. Canada is no exception, and the story of the Japanese Canadians in British Columbia during the Second World War stands out.

Even before any official declaration of war against Japan, the federal cabinet formed the Special Committee on Orientals in British Columbia. This occurred immediately after Japan announced its alliance with the Axis powers and amidst protests against Asian Canadians serving in Canada's armed forces. All Japanese Canadians were asked to voluntarily register with the RCMP and have their fingerprints taken. When the war with Japan finally came, Order-in-Council P.C. #1486, issued by the federal government on February 24, 1942, evacuated all people of Japanese extraction living in a "protected zone" within one hundred miles of the West Coast. Ottawa officially rationalized that this law lessened the chance that *Nisei* (those born in Canada of Japanese ancestry), or *Issei* (naturalized Japanese immigrants) could act as the vanguard for a Japanese surprise attack; and it protected those of Japanese ancestry from abuse in the hysterical aftermath of the bombing of Pearl Harbour. Order-in-Council #1486 was not based on nationality since the majority of the 21,000 men, women, and children evacuated into British Columbia's interior, Alberta, and Ontario were, in fact, Canadian citizens. Racial origin alone decided the internee's fate because it apparently determined patriotism or lack thereof.

To what degree, if any, was the evacuation based on genuine and legitimate fear, or was it purely an act of polite racism masquerading as a national security issue? The argument in favour of internment for the sake of national security certainly held sway during and immediately after the war. The Japanese government, after all, did launch a heinous and devastating surprise attack against Pearl Harbour in Hawaii halfway across the Pacific to British Columbia. Though there was initially no confirmed Japanese naval activity on Canada's coast, unconfirmed sightings abounded, and all generated very genuine anxiety if not terror.

Other issues heightened suspicion toward the Japanese Canadian community. Some perceived the Japanese-Canadians as an unassimilable culture consciously and dangerously isolated from the rest of society by an impenetrable cloak of a radically different culture, language, religion, and appearance. Current historiography posits racism as the primary motivation behind the evacuation. The Canadian government recently acknowledged this by offering an apology and financial compensation to the Japanese-Canadian community. Canada did indeed have a long history of racism, nowhere more so than along the West Coast and against "Orientals." Only racism, so the argument goes, can explain why evacuees could not return to British Columbia until four years after the war ended and why children and the aged—hardly security threats—were also evacuated. Further evidence supporting this interpretation comes from the RCMP and military intelligence which both stated, prior to the evacuation, that Japanese-Canadians on the West Coast did not constitute a threat to national security.

Prime Minister MacKenzie King also recognized in 1948 that "no person of Japanese race born in Canada [was] charged with any act of sabotage or disloyalty during the years of the war."

Order-in-Council #1486 astonished people like Muriel Kitagawa who probably did not really believe it until she heard the knock at her door. She should have seen it coming. The Americans, after all, had already passed legislation prohibiting 120,000 Japanese-Americans from living within one hundred miles of the west coast, and simultaneously seized their property. The new Canadian law mimicked American actions by allowing the RCMP to enter homes without warrants and to confiscate property deemed a security risk. This included fishing boats, cameras, radios, and firearms. Vehicles also had to be surrendered, and the government imposed a dusk-to-dawn curfew. Japanese-Canadian newspapers and schools closed. After the evacuation, the Custodian of Enemy Alien Property seized all unmoveable goods, such as businesses, homes and property, and held them in trust until January 1943 when they auctioned them off without the owners' consent. Monies raised alleviated the relocation cost, thereby addressing the demand that Canadian taxpayers should not bear the financial burden of incarcerating the country's enemies. Selling their possessions, of course, also ensured that Japanese-Canadians could not easily return to their former homes once hostilities ended. Interestingly, the American government released Japanese-Americans from detention well before the end of the war, and returned their seized possessions.

Discussion Points

1. To what extent was Japanese relocation a product of the war or did the war simply provide a convenient means for expressing long standing racism?
2. Kitagawa implies that Canada's treatment of its Japanese citizens compares to Nazi Germany's anti-semitic policies and that Canada deluded itself into thinking it fought a war for democracy when, in fact, it was just as guilty of denying civil liberties to its citizens. Was she right?
3. The federal government acknowledged its responsibly for injustices suffered by Japanese-Canadians in the Second World War through a formal apology and compensation for survivors. Are modern Canadians accountable for mistakes in the past?

4. What, if any, lessons should Canadians learn from examining the treatment of Japanese-Canadians in World War II?

Documents

1. "The Situation in 1940," *Report and Recommendations of the Special Committee on Orientals in British Columbia*, December 1940

22. In the examining of witnesses the members of the Committee first directed their attention towards discovering whether, in fact, hostile feeling existed in any important degree. It became immediately apparent that there was in some quarters an active hostility towards the Japanese; and that, while many witnesses expressed a liking for them, or an admiration for their individual and national qualities, this was coupled with a greater or less degree of suspicion of the Japanese as a people and a feeling that their racial solidarity was likely in an emergency to override their loyalty to Canada and produce subversive or otherwise dangerous activities. No concrete evidence was adduced in support of this sentiment, and charges of disloyal conduct brought by witnesses against individual Japanese or groups of Japanese proved in every instance upon further examination to arise from unsubstantiated rumour and hearsay ...

... The police officers who appeared before the Committee, while in some cases they differed in their personal views on the questions at issue and in their attitude towards the Japanese as a people, all agreed that they formed one of the most law-abiding elements in the population of the Province and that they were in general industrious and inoffensive citizens.

24. Nevertheless, despite this favourable testimony, the Committee was obliged to recognize that, even granting the Japanese in British Columbia to be innocent of acts or speech conducive to suspicion and hostility, they are in fact mistrusted and disliked by many people, particularly in those districts where they are most thickly congregated. It was, therefore, necessary to discover the true causes of this ill-feeling, and this point was put specifically to every witness examined. The almost invariable reply was to the effect that the chief cause of animosity was economic. The Japanese are disliked by those whom they injure (or who consider themselves injured) in competition with white Canadians as labourers, as fishermen, as farmers, as retail storekeepers or in other occupations, where they accept lower wages or subsist on a less expensive standard. This sentiment may sometimes be justified by the facts, since it is natural for a white competitor to resent the existence of a class which appears deliberately to depress

standards of income, working hours, and living conditions. But even where it is not justified, it is easily rationalized by representing the Japanese as a community who, besides being economically undesirable, are politically dangerous.

25. It is doubtful whether these sentiments of dislike and mistrust would persist to any significant degree in times of normal economic activity and relatively full employment, unless they were kept alive and stimulated by other agencies. Unfortunately the Committee received ample evidence to show that hostility towards the Japanese has been deliberately inflamed by certain individuals for reasons which can only be ascribed to a desire for personal political advantage. While considering such practices to be objectionable at all times, and particularly dangerous in present circumstances, and, although not suggesting that to suppress those practices will remove the anti-Japanese sentiment which now exists, the members of the Committee are convinced that, as a first step towards diminishing the mutual antagonism between certain elements of the white population and the Japanese community, it is essential to prevent acts tending to create public suspicion and alarm. In this sense, the suppression of public statements arousing antagonism against the Japanese in British Columbia should be an integral part of plans for civil security and national defence ...

27. While there may be differences of opinion as to how far the charges levelled against the Japanese in respect of underselling and underliving their white competitors are justified, it is probable that many grievances could be removed by the proper enforcement of existing legislation, or the enactment of new laws or by-laws, which would prevent some forms of unfair competition, e.g., the custom of some Japanese food retailers of sleeping in their stores and thus reducing overhead costs for rent. In general, any policy designed to raise the standard of living and the standard of income of the Japanese would tend to narrow their competitive margin and thus to remove causes of ill-feeling against them. In this connection it was brought out clearly by the evidence of many witnesses that it is the exclusion of Japanese from one occupation after another in British Columbia which has driven them into occupations of a different grade, e.g., when driven out of the fisheries they turned to small storekeeping, tailoring, dry-cleaning, where their inexpensive standards permit them to drive out white competitors. There is no doubt that the Japanese themselves have a sense of persecution when after being excluded from one occupation they are blamed for resorting to another. The animosity of the white population thus has its counterpart in the resentment of the Japanese; and it is obvious that such conditions make for neither loyalty nor harmony. It is indeed in some respects astonishing that the native born Japanese are not more vocal and active in their resistance to the discrimination to which they are subjected. This can partly be

explained by the fact that, by and large, they are at least as well off, and in most cases are better off, materially than they would be in Japan. They are, moreover, a traditionally disciplined and obedient people, accustomed to thinking in terms of the interest of their community as a whole, so that any tendency toward imprudent action can be readily held in check by the leaders of their several groups.

28. While it is probable that, given patience and the lapse of time, the most serious economic causes of ill-feeling between white and Japanese could be modified, it was clear from the statements of many witnesses that most of the occidental population of British Columbia regard the Japanese as unassimilable because of their distinctive racial character. No doubt in the most favourable conditions racial animosity might, with the lapse of time, be expected to diminish, and it is possible that such conditions could be produced by legislation, good will and individual effort. But the chief problem before the Committee was the short-term problem. It was therefore obliged to recognize that, in addition to the economic factor, racial prejudice is an important element in producing dislike and mistrust of the Japanese. It does not matter whether this racial prejudice is reasonable or not. It exists and it has to be taken into account. Moreover, the present international situation, in which Japan has declared herself on the side of the enemies of the British Empire, has in itself intensified not only national feeling but also racial feeling.

29. It was very apparent, and in this the majority of the witnesses who appeared before the committee agreed, that this complex of economic, national and racial factors has produced a dangerous situation, but it was most significant that, with one exception, all the witnesses examined, even those most hostile to the Japanese, agreed that the greater danger was to be expected not from the Japanese themselves, but from the white population, who with only the slightest additional provocation, might suddenly resort to violence against Japanese individuals or groups. The Japanese themselves are alive to this hostility, and their fear and perplexity and their natural determination to protect themselves if attacked, are further elements of danger.

30. The committee recognized that the situation in British Columbia may be further complicated at any time by acts committed outside of Canada; acts which cannot be foreseen, but which may be intensely provocative. Any occurrence of that nature might not only provoke action against the Japanese in British Columbia, but, if there were Canadians of Japanese race serving at the time in the armed forces of Canada, they also might be in danger of attack by the less responsible element among their comrades.

31. In view of these considerations the members of the committee reached

the conclusion that one of their main duties must be to point out that the first and perhaps the greatest potential source of danger is not disloyalty on the part of the Japanese in Canada but the animosity of white Canadians against the Japanese in general. The Committee's recommendations therefore deal principally with the measures which can be taken to prevent acts of hostility against Japanese resident in British Columbia. Among such measures must be included not only military and police precautions, but also the removal, so far as may be possible, of conditions likely to produce mistrust and anxiety among both the white and the Japanese populations.

32. ... While the committee is convinced that the investigation made by the Board of Review in 1938 indicated that these beliefs are, and for some years have been, unfounded, it is nevertheless true that some sections of popular opinion in British Columbia still accept the charges as true. For this and other reasons the demand for a complete registration of the Japanese population is still foremost in the minds of a considerable element in the population.

33. ... the General Officer Commanding in Chief, Pacific Command, was consulted, and stated that he was in full agreement with the Committee's view of the situation; that he had already taken, and would continue to take, all possible military precautions against civil disturbance. With regard to police precautions it is believed, on the evidence of the witnesses examined, that all police authorities in the province are fully aware of the dangers to be guarded against and have laid plans accordingly.

34. An important aspect of the problem of protecting loyal Japanese against violence is the choice of methods to be used for the purpose of distinguishing potentially hostile elements from the loyal Japanese who are legally domiciled in Canada. For this purpose, it is, in the Committee's opinion, desirable to impress upon the responsible leaders of the various Japanese communities that the wrongful act of a single Japanese would, even in present circumstances, and *a fortiori* if the international situation were to deteriorate further, imperil the lives and property of *all* Japanese, whether loyal or otherwise; and that consequently it is their duty and in their interest to co-operate fully with the authorities by keeping a close watch on their own communities and reporting without delay any suspicious circumstances ...

37. Although the members of the Committee sympathize with this attitude, they are bound to consider the question in relation to other facts, and those facts are that opinion in British Columbia is on the whole against allowing persons of Japanese race to take military training or to serve in the armed forces. This opposition is based in part upon racial prejudice, as is shown by the

statements of several witnesses who were offended by the prospect of white and Japanese youths being together in camp or in barracks. But what seems to the Committee to be a more valid objection was raised by those who urged that, particularly in the event of increased tension between Japan and the democratic states, the situation of Japanese Canadian youths in training or serving in military units with large numbers of white Canadians would be one of great danger should racial or national passion be aroused by some untoward incident at home or abroad. A quarrel in a canteen might lead to the gravest results to the Japanese directly concerned, and it might further set in motion currents of race hatred in other parts of the world, with the usual sequels of reprisals and counter-reprisals. Therefore, it has been decided to recommend, though most reluctantly and not unanimously, that at least for the present, Canadians of Japanese race should not be given military training (except of course the Basic Training provided for all students in public schools and universities) and should not be enlisted generally in the armed forces of Canada. Such exclusion will certainly give offence to a number of Japanese Canadians, and it would therefore be prudent to explain the Government's decision to them in a sympathetic way, dwelling upon the fact … that it is largely based upon a desire to protect and to ease the position of the Japanese themselves, and not upon any mistrust of their patriotism.

2. A.W. Neill, House of Commons, *Debates*, February 19, 1942.

Mr. Speaker, I have listened to that appeasement talk for twenty years from the government benches, and I think the time has come to take a different stand. I believe we can best serve the interests of our country, and promote peace, by having plain talk, straightforward discussions and, I hope, definite action, with respect to the issues before us …

In September, 1940, Japan signed the deal, agreement or whatever you call it with Italy and Germany. In plain English, they bound themselves to enter into war against us and the United States whenever it suited Germany or Hitler. Pressure was put upon the government by British Columbia, and I suppose some realization of the situation also led the government to take action. They appointed a hand-picked committee to investigate the subject, which… came back with a number of recommendations, I believe ten in all. There were only two of any importance, Nos. 5 and 7, and I shall deal with them. No. 5 recommended against allowing Japanese to enlist in our volunteer army then being raised. That was a very good idea, otherwise we would have had perhaps 1,500

Japanese training in our army, possibly in key positions, petty officers and the like. They would have been familiar with every detail of our army operations. Protests were made by the mayor of Nanaimo, and I think by other cities and by myself, and the recommendation of the committee carried. That was all right.

Recommendation No. 7 was that there should be a re-registration of the Japanese in Canada. It had been claimed by many people that the registration that had been taken was just a fake as regards the Japanese. Only those who felt like it registered, and there was a demand for a new registration. The recommendation was that they should be photographed at the same time. That was a good idea, but it had one fatal defect, if deception is regarded as a fatal defect. It was clearly understood that this registration was compulsory. We were told how well it was going on, how successful it was, and it was hoped that we malignants would now be satisfied and keep quiet. The whole thing turned on the point that it was compulsory.

If it had been voluntary, what use would it have been? ... Was it expected that Japanese who had entered the country illegally would come forward and say, "Yes, I came in illegally, take me." Of course they would not. A Jap is not a fool, any more than we are. The guilty ones did not register and the whole thing was a gigantic failure. It could not be otherwise if it were anything but compulsory.

Our main complaint was that many of them had come into the country illegally and this re-registration would have discovered that. Was it expected that those who had come in illegally would disclose that fact? The thing is ridiculous. When the war came on, after Pearl Harbour, it was discovered that it was not compulsory, that it was just a gesture to keep us quiet, just a farce. Then what happened? The war was on and the people know what war means; this government should know what it means. These same people were given two months in which to register; they were given until February 7 to get things fixed up, to get a fake birth certificate or a forged entry card. You can buy them in Vancouver. If they could not get either, they were given two months before they would be subject to the same action as that to which any other enemy alien would be exposed. Why give them two months? We were practically saying to them, "We are at war with you, but we will give you two months in which to get faked papers, or get out of the country." I never heard the like of it before, and I hope I never shall again ...

They were given two months in which to fix things up or get out. If that registration had been compulsory, we would have got the best of these Jap agents and the best of their spies. They have now gone home with their charts and plans and with a local knowledge that could not be bought for any money.

Perhaps we shall see some of these Japs again peering over the side of the bridge of a German gunboat in Vancouver, Nanaimo or Port Alberni, because we now know that many of them were expert naval men ...

Paragraph 6 recommends that the government should seize immediately the Japanese fishing boats. That was done. It was done immediately war was declared, and for that action I have nothing but the utmost praise. It was done promptly and thoroughly ... At any rate it was done, and done well. While this is not part of the report, I may as well finish up that matter by saying that after they had 1,200 Japanese boats in their hands, the question arose, what to do with them? It was desirable to get them back into fishing again, so that white men could catch the fish so badly needed for the British market. Therefore they set up a committee to try to sell these boats ... Like all government offices, it is true that they were rather slow in going about their work, but they got started at last ...

I want to quote recommendation 7 in which was contained the policy of the cabinet. It reads: "For the same period—that is during the war—the sale of gasoline and explosives to persons of Japanese racial origin will be directly controlled under conditions prescribed by the Royal Canadian Mounted Police."

That is a good idea too, a very good idea, but unfortunately I read in the papers—I have to go to the press for information because I cannot get it anywhere else—that these sales are still going on.

Mr. HOMUTH: The sale of powder is still going on?

Mr. NEILL: Explosives. A man wrote to the Vancouver *Province* the other day and suggested that if this order was in effect, why was the Japanese station at the corner still selling gas the same as usual? That has been going on for two and a half months now, and I rather think permission has been extended to the 1st of April. The language is doubtful, but if it can be interpreted to the benefit of the Japanese, be sure it will be so interpreted. You are dealing with clever, subtle, unscrupulous enemies—and they are enemies—and when you say that you are not going to stop the sale for two months, that is just an invitation to them to accumulate as much gas and explosives as they can in the meantime. We say to them: "Remember, on the 7th of February or on the 1st of April we are going to shut down on you." Is that not an invitation to them to get explosives and gasoline against a rainy day? That time limit should never have been put in. The order should have been made applicable at once ...

There are three classes of Japanese we must deal with. There are the Japanese nationals, those born in Japan and never naturalized in Canada; they are Japanese nationals. Then there is the man born in Japan and naturalized in

Canada. He is called a naturalized Japanese or a Canadian. Then there is the Japanese who was born in Canada, who can call himself a Japanese-Canadian if he likes. The government orders with regard to seizing the boats and the sale of gas and explosives applied to all three classes. That was all right.

Now I deal with paragraph 8. It says that Japanese nationals will be forbidden to possess or use short-wave receiving sets or radio transmitters in Canada. A most excellent thing. Hon. members can all understand why it was necessary to do that. That was fine. But it does not come into effect until the 1st of April. Did the Japanese give us four months notice of what they were going to do at Pearl Harbour? Yet we say to them: "Go wandering about with your cameras and take pictures, and use your receiving sets to send word to Japan, and your receivers to get instructions from Japan. You can do this as much as you like until the 1st of April." Even if the order had been withheld, and they had been allowed to continue doing these things without being told of any date when they must stop, it would not have been so bad, because then they would never have known when the order was coming into force. But they were warned—you will not be interfered with until the 1st of April. The order was the equivalent of that. We told them: "Do your dirty work now. Use your radio and your receiving set but, remember, hide or bury them before the 1st of April, and then everything will be lovely." They told the Japanese nationals that they must not use these things in a protected area. But they can use them outside. I have a police order to that effect. It is signed by the police and says:

"No enemy alien shall have in his possession or use while in such protected area any camera, radio transmitter, radio short-wave receiving set, firearm, ammunition or explosive."

... Well, as I said, it is doubtful. There is, however, no question whatever that a man who is not a Japanese national can do these things any time, any place. The order applies only to nationals; that is, to men born in Japan and coming over here, and these are comparatively few in number, something like 1,700 out of 24,000, and only while they are in the area. The remaining 22,000 of naturalized Japanese are free to come and go, as I have said, anywhere. They can photograph what they like, radio what they like. They can do something else which I have not touched upon, and which is—not to make a joke—a burning question in British Columbia. Three, two, one of them can do endless damage in British Columbia with a box of matches. The most deadly enemy of the lumber industry in British Columbia is fire. Lumbermen are so afraid of it, it is so dangerous, that they shut their camps down in the middle of summer, as soon as the humidity reaches a certain point. A man can wander out in that bush, ten, fifty, a hundred miles from anywhere, and do more damage with a box of matches than it would take two armies to put out. The large number of forest rangers whom we have could not touch the fringe of the thing if these aliens were determined to commit sabotage. Some of the biggest lumbermen on the coast are much alarmed at this situation. If the Japanese were out of the area, they could not do this damage, because you can't do a thing if you are not there.

I have spoken of the freedom of Japanese to come and go with cameras, radios and matches. That is not restricted to two months or four months; that is for eternity, if the war lasts that long; it is for the duration of the war that the naturalized or Canadian-born Jap can go out and commit sabotage; he is free to do it the whole time, and he is the most dangerous of the lot. The naturalized Japanese speaks our language fluently, possibly he has been to college. He possesses far greater potentialities of trouble as a spy or an agent than if he had just come from Japan. The fellow dressed up like a white man, speaking our language glibly, is the one who should be interned. It is very hard for me to believe that the government are so remote from what is taking place or may take place as not to understand the situation …

I should now like to make three charges against the government. The first is this, that, with the exception of seizing these boats they have been far too slow in handling the Japanese situation. They have let days go by when it should have been hours, and a month when it should have been days. Look at what was done in Mexico. There the government dealt with the whole lot as soon as war was declared, and ordered into the interior every Jap who was on the coast. They did it; they didn't talk about it. Cuba did the same thing. They arrested, I believe, eighteen Japanese, all but two of whom were naval officers. Nicaragua took the same course, and took it speedily …

I note here that the council of the city of Vancouver has passed a resolution urging the government to get a move on. The report speaks of increasing irritation and criticism at the coast over the apparent failure of the government to implement its announced policy of removing Japanese.

The legislature of British Columbia, before adjourning a few days ago, passed unanimously a resolution urging the dominion government to strengthen Pacific defences. The feeling is very strong at the coast. I wish I could get the government to realize it.

Here is one incident I must quote, reported under a big headline in a leading Vancouver paper, the *Daily Province*:

JAPANESE LIVE UNDISTURBED ON
DIKE ADJOINING AIRPORT.

There are 200 Japanese living a mile west of the airport. They are living on a dike. It would be very easy to blow up or open that dike, and the airport would be rendered useless for a long time to come. Yet they are living undisturbed within a mile of the airport; they are on a dike into which a gap could be blown with a few sticks of powder that would make the airport useless for a long time to come. Why does the government not take some action in this case?

The second charge is that even the small restrictions to which I have referred are applicable only to nationals, and I say it is inexcusable that they are not made applicable to all naturalized Japanese aliens in this country. To whom do you suppose they think they owe loyalty? If they were scattered all over Canada, the case might be different, but think what may happen when they are turned loose in a small area, when 25,000 are concentrated in an area where they could so readily combine to take action against Vancouver, or Victoria, as the case may be. It constitutes an unspeakable menace; I cannot understand why it is allowed to continue.

The third charge is that the government have shown indifference to British Columbia defence, also to air raid precautions work and the like of that. I am not blaming the government for preparations which they might have made six years ago. That is not their fault; I know that. We could not get the appropriation through the house ... But I do blame the government for not having taken the situation in hand since war was declared. They are too slack, they appear to adopt the attitude, "Oh, well, we have to take chances; we are doing the best we can; it will be all right." Well, they told us it would be all right about Hong Kong. But people make mistakes—even military men, even high military men. They told us it would be all right at Singapore. Yet we know that mistakes were made there. Here is the government's paper, the *Vancouver Sun*, expressing this opinion:

> Canada obviously has not made its plan of defence on the assumption of any real attack on the Pacific coast ... That is the plan which must be reconsidered ... we do expect a well-equipped, mobile striking unit which could pounce upon any Japanese landing attempt from Alaska southwards. No such force exists on our coast. No such force exists in Canada.

A.Y. JACKSON (1882–1974)   *The Red Maple* 1914   oil on panel   21.6 x 26.9 cm
Gift of Mr. S. Walter Stewart
McMichael Canadian Art Collection. 1968.8.18
Courtesy of the Estate of Dr. Naomi Jackson Groves.

J.E.H. MACDONALD (1873–1932)   *Oaks, October Morning* 1909   oil on board   17.5 x 12.8 cm
Gift of Mr. R.A. Laidlaw
McMichael Canadian Art Collection. 1966.15.15

FRANKLIN CARMICHAEL (1890–1945) *October Gold* 1922 oil on canvas 119.5 x 98.0 cm
Gift of the Founders, Robert and Signe McMichael
McMichael Canadian Art Collection. 1966.16.1

ARTHUR LISMER (1885–1969) *Forest, Algoma* 1922 oil on canvas 71.0 x 90.8 cm
Gift of the Founders, Robert and Signe McMichael
McMichael Canadian Art Collection. 1966.16.104

FRANK JOHNSTON (1888–1949)   *Moose Pond* 1918   *oil on board*   26.5 x 33.8 cm
Gift of the Founders, Robert and Signe McMichael
McMichael Canadian Art Collection
1972.18.14

LAWREN S. HARRIS (1885–1970)   *Eclipse Sound and Bylot Island* 1930   oil on panel   30.2 x 38.0 cm
Gift of Col. R.S. McLaughlin
McMichael Canadian Art Collection. 1968.7.3
Courtesy of the Family of Lawren S. Harris.

F.H. VARLEY (1881–1969) *Blue Pool* c.1930   oil on 3-ply wood   30.2 x 37.9 cm
Gift of Col. R.S. McLaughlin
McMichael Canadian Art Collection. 1968.7.11
© 2003 Estate of Kathleen G. McKay

A.J. CASSON (1898–1992) *Spring, Lasky* 1932 watercolour on paper 36.0 x 41.3 cm
Gift of Miss Irene Doole
McMichael Canadian Art Collection. 1970.8

I am afraid that is too true. Perhaps in the secret session which is to be held we shall be given more information on this matter. I do not propose to blame the government for things which happened before they had control and knowledge of the situation, or for not having done what at the time was beyond their power. But the government must be ready at that secret session to give us genuine information, not general assurances and smooth-sounding platitudes. There has been too much of this in connection with the management of the war.

There is a certain place—I will not name names, I will call it *Y*. When the government began to think about building aerodromes I thought that *Y* would make a good site for one, and I said so. I put it up to the officials, and they said that they were experts and ought to know better than I did. Well, I accepted that decision—but they are building that aerodrome now with frantic haste. I fear we may have to paraphrase the hymn and say:

Too late, too late will be the cry
"The Japanese gunboats have gone by."

There was another aerodrome at a place we will call *X*. I wrote to the government in connection with this one, informing them that there were two things wrong about it. This was a year or two ago. I pointed out to the officials that there was a Jap village 200 yards from the mouth of it where the Japs could take photographs and keep a record of any aeroplanes leaving, with all the details, so that they could have it all recorded for the benefit of the Japanese: I have in my desk a letter in which some official tried to stall me off. I was told that they would expropriate the Japanese, but that they could not do it because there was some hitch. However, they said they would look into the matter. Imagine looking into the question of expropriating this particular property when other nations, as we know, take first what they require and then talk about expropriation. Again, I pointed out to the officials that there was a Jap who had been seen taking photographs from an aeroplane over the harbour, where the aerodrome was being built. It was a civilian aeroplane. I took this matter up with various bodies—I will not mention any names because I do not wish to give them away —and what was the answer? I was informed that the investigation was closed. They had ascertained the name of the man and had found that he had gone to Japan. I suppose he took photographs with him as a momento of us because he loved us so much. Well, he has gone back to Japan with whatever photographs he took—we do not know how many—and God knows how many more may have gone there. But the officials did not seem to think it was important. I was told that it would be difficult to take photographs through the glass of any aeroplane unless you had a particular sort of apparatus with which to do it. Well, would the Japanese not have that type of apparatus? I submitted all these matters to the department, and I have it all on record. One of the officials said to me, "There is nothing to this anyhow because it is not against the laws of the country to take photographs of an aerodrome."

I took it up with some of the higher officials, and they juggled with it and finally explained that they could get the Japs under the Official Secrets Act. The aerodrome is still there; the Japs are still staying there under their four months' lease of life, and doubtless they are still taking these photographs, which I have no doubt will be sent to the right place.

These men are not all Canadian nationals. Some of them may be the very best class of spies and foreign agents, and I contend that there has been too much sympathy for the Japanese viewpoint and Japanese interests. We must remember that we are at war with these people. Ottawa is 3,000 miles away from us out there …

We who have taken the position that I am now taking have been called all sorts of names. We have been called agitators. It is said that we are willing to exploit the interests of Canada for our own political advantage; that we are rabble-rousers, Jap-baiters, and that we have a very dangerous influence … I have heard that sort of thing, and hints of it even in this house, and certainly in the government press. You can get a man to write any letter you want; you can get a white man to make a tool of himself for a Jap if you pay him enough. There was a man who wrote to the papers saying what fine people the Japs are. I laid a trap for him and I discovered that he was a white man all right, but also a paid agent of a Japanese association, but he did not say that when he signed his name.

Yes, we are all bad because we want a white British Columbia and not a place like Hawaii! Fifty years from now, unless something is done to stop it, all west of the Rockies will be yellow. I submit, Mr. Speaker, that we want but little; we simply want to be left alone, like New Zealand and Australia, all white. I have no ill-will against the Japanese. Perhaps you may think I have been showing ill-will, but I assure you I have none towards the Japs. No Jap ever "did" me—I never gave him the chance. I wish to be fair to the Japanese, and I think that if we expatriated them, as we ought to do, they should be given full justice in regard to their property, because I am strongly in favour of a Japan controlled by the Japanese, just as I am in favour of a Canada controlled by Canadians. Let us continue to trade with them; let us do business with them across the ocean; but do not force into one nation two peoples separated by something that is wider than the ocean, two peoples who are different in race, in religion, in traditions and in their whole philosophy of life. This difference always has prevented assimilation and always will prevent it, between two nations so utterly divergent in every respect. The greatest path towards assimilation is marriage ... the Japs have been here fifty-eight years and there is no record of a single marriage, although there might be one. I asked a Japanese to produce the record of one marriage and he could not do so. We have heard of second generation Japanese born here going to Japanese schools here to learn Japanese, and that has been regarded as a small matter. We went into their textbooks and had them translated and we found that they were very anti-British. Yet there were people who thought that was a small matter—only the sort of thing that irresponsible people like myself would talk about. But when the war came, it was thought wise to shut down the Jap schools. There were fifty-nine in British Columbia, and leaving out small areas where they could not run a school, the great bulk of those children must have attended some Japanese school.

I have one more word ... we should make an arrangement that when peace time comes, we expatriate all the Japanese left in Canada; do it on fair terms, buy them out, pay them liberally ... it is much easier for us to move 25,000, and it is better to move them while their numbers are so small. Let us settle once and for all this canker in the life of Canada which prevents us from being a united white Canada. And that is what British Columbia wants.

3. *This Is My Own: Letters to Wes and Other Writings on Japanese Canadians, 1941–1948.* Muriel Kitagawa.

i. December 21, 1941.

Dear Wes:

... So far as the new war affects us, I really haven't much to say. It is too early to estimate the effects. On the whole we are taking it in our stride. We are so used to wars and alarums, and we have been tempered for the anti-feelings these long years. It has only intensified into overt acts of unthinking hoodlumism like throwing flaming torches into rooming houses and bricks through plate glass ... only in the West End so far. What that goes to prove I don't know. We've had blackouts the first few nights but they have been lifted. Bad for the kids, because it frightens them so. Of course we have to be ready just in case and I sure hope there won't be any emergency ... not with the kids around. All three Japanese papers have been closed down. We never needed so many anyway. It is good for the *New Canadian* though, as it can now go ahead with full responsibility, though at first it is bound to be hard on the inexperienced staff. All Japanese schools have been closed too, and are the kids glad! Of course I have never intended my kids to go anyway so it doesn't affect us in the least. I am glad in a way that they have been closed down. I hope for good. But it is hard on the teachers who depended on them for a living.

There have been the usual anti-letters-to-the-editor in the papers. Some of them are rank nonsense, and some of the writers think like that anyhow, whatever the provocation. The majority of the people are decent and fair-minded and they say so in letters and editorials. The RCMP is our friend too, for they, more than anyone else, know how blameless and helpless we are, and they have already in one instance prevented tragedy when the City Fathers proposed cancelling all business licences, to say that we did not rate such harsh treatment. Now the North Vancouver Board of Trade goes on record to demand that all our autos be confiscated, but I hardly think that could be practical. What then would our doctors and businessmen do? Also, it is hard to take everything away from 22,000 people without the rest of B.C. feeling some of the bad effects. The dog salmon industry is already short-handed because the Japanese cannot fish any more. How they will make up the lack in the next season I don't know, though the 'white' fishermen seem to be confident, if they could use the fishing boats now tied up somewhere in New Westminster.

There was one letter in the *Province* protesting this confiscation of the right to earn a living from 1880 people ... said it wasn't democracy. Yes sir, when a people get panicky, democracy and humanity and Christian principles go by the board. Rather inconsistent, but human nature I guess. Some silly mothers even go so far as to say, what right have the black-haired kids to go to school with their own precious? One schoolteacher had the courage to say to one of the 'white' pupils who wanted all Japs to be kicked out of school—how they reflect their parents' attitude!—that there were no Japs, and in any case they were far better Canadians than the protester. Strange how these protesters are much more vehement against the Canadian-born Japanese than they are against German-born Germans, who might have a real loyalty to *their* land of birth, as we have for Canada. I guess it is just because we look different. Anyway it all boils down to racial antagonism which the democracies are fighting. Who said it was Woman ... or the Moon that was inconstant? Oh well, it is only the occasional one here and there. I personally have had no change in my relationship with my neighbours or my Egg-man, who told me not to worry. Most of the hakujin deplore the war but do not change to their known Japanese friends. It is the small businesses that are most affected ... like the dressmakers, the corner store, etc., because the clientele are rather shy of patronising in public such places, whatever their private thoughts may be. Powell Street is affected too, in that they have a slightly increased volume of sales to people who usually go to Woodwards etc. But so many have been fired from jobs that belts are tightening everywhere. I don't know yet how all this is going to affect Dad. Most of his patients are fishermen or farmers. So far the farmers haven't been touched.

Last Sunday, the national President of the IODE [Imperial Order of the Daughters of the Empire], who must live far from contact from the Nisei because she didn't seem to know the first thing about us, made a deliberate attempt to create fear and ill-will among her dominion-wide members by telling them that we were all spies and saboteurs, and that in 1931 there were 55,000 of us and that that number has doubled in the last ten years. Not only a biological absurdity, but the records of the RCMP give the lie to such round numbers. The trouble is that lots of women would like to believe their president rather than actual figures. Seems to me illogical that women who are the conservers and builders of the human race should be the ones to go all out for savagery and destruction and ill-will among fellow-humans. They are the ones who are expected to keep the peace with their neighbours in their particular block, but when it comes to blackballing some unfortunate people, they are the first to cast the stone. In times like this I always think of that line:

"If there be any among you that is without sin, let him cast the first stone."

Or words to that effect. And certainly we Nisei are neither harlots nor criminals. We're just people.

But more to the point, how are you getting along, there? Is the feeling worse in Toronto where they don't know the Nisei as B.C. does? How does the war affect you personally? Can you get a loan to get through next year and the year after? After all, you are Canadian-born, and the Army needs MD's. How has it affected your living conditions at the Lethbridges? Or your acquaintance with Dent and others? Has it affected the wearing of your uniform? Your standing in class and lab? Have you heard from George Shimo? Please let me know fully. So far Doug hasn't let me know by word or line how he is, but he's never one to write, and he's carefree. I think he is all right. If he doesn't lose his job through this, I'll ask him to send you what he can every month. Dad and Nobi are getting along but I think Nobi's kind of sad that he won't see Mom again, and he does miss a home life. But I can't do a thing to help as Dad rejects every offer. I guess that when gas rationing starts Dad won't be able to use that darned car so often ... He has to report every month to the RCMP, just because when he first came to B.C., which was over forty years ago, and plenty of time to naturalize, he didn't look far enough ahead to know how it would have helped his children. That! for people who live only day to day. Politics never meant a thing to him, and doesn't yet. So long as he can eat and swank in his car he lets important things slide.

We're getting immune to the hitherto unused term 'Japs' on the radio and on the headlines of the papers. So long as they designate the enemy, and not us, it doesn't matter much. The Chinese here were indecently jubilant ... paraded and cheered in their quarters when the war was announced. They are rather childish that way. Of course, now they hope that both the U.S. and Canada will fork over a lot more help than they have so far. I think they are naive. War nowadays is too complicated and can't be compared simply to a street-fight. I am glad however that the Russian army is licking something out of Hitler's troops. The sooner Hitler stops his enslaving of conquered people ... you know, ship-loading them into Poland or into Germany proper to work for nothing in the fields and factories far from home and children; his way of stealing food from the conquered peoples; his system of captive labour; shooting hundreds in reprisal for one ... then the sooner will the little peoples have a chance at life again.

Ugh! I hate wars, and I've had one already, though I wasn't old enough to know anything then. Now I'm going through a worse one. War, active war, is easier to bear with courage than this surging up of mass hatred against us simply because we are of Japanese origin. I hope fervently that it will not affect the lives of Shirley and Meiko and the unborn son [Kitagawa's children], as the doctor believes. After all, my kids, as only proper being my kids, are so thoroughly Canadian they would never understand being persecuted by people they regard as one of themselves. Already Meiko came crying home once because some kid on the block whose father is anti, said something. Yet I try to rationalize things for them, so that they won't be inundated by self-consciousness. Children are so innocent, but they are savages too, and reflect faithfully their parents' attitudes. That was the one thing my doctor was worried about. Otherwise he, with most of the others, tells us not to worry. We're Canadians and can expect decent treatment from decent people ...

ii. January 21, 1942.

Dear Wes:

... Since they are moving the unemployed Nisei first, I don't think Ed [Kitagawa's husband] will be affected. After all, they could hardly expect him to leave a good job for road work when he has a big family to feed. I have my fingers crossed—all ten of them. Of course, since I have been house-bound from October I haven't felt the full force of the changes since Dec. 7th.

[Alderman Halford] Wilson and his bunch are making political hay out of this. He does so with bland half-truths and falsehoods and hypocrisies enough to turn your stomach. So does the *Sun* paper. They are deliberately inflaming the mob instinct and inciting the irresponsible elements to a bloody riot—the kind they had in 1907, the one in which Wilson's father had a dirty hand. Once the flames catch, Powell Street will be in for a bad, bad time, not mentioning the scattered but large number of families in certain suburban districts. How that Wilson can square his conscience, eat three meals in peace, with his brand of patriotism that stinks to hell—I don't know.

The *Province* and *News-Herald* have been editorially condemning Wilson and his bunch and appealing to B.C. at large to give the local Japs a chance. Acts of vandalism make the headlines, and there has been one murder. Yoshiyuki Uno was shot to death by a 17 or 19 yr old bandit.

iii. February 19, 1942.

Dear Wes:

How's things? That was a good letter you wrote to the N.C. [*New Canadian*].

Well, I guess you've read in the papers that there isn't a province in Canada that will take the "Japs," and B.C. just has to have us whether she will or no. Ian Mackenzie has again come out with "Volunteer or else—." Vancouver City Fathers have petitioned Ottawa to put the OK on a ban of trade licences to Japanese here—850 or so. Won't the Relief offices be flooded then! … They don't care anyway—under their hypocritical Christian faces. It beats me how they can mouthe "Down with Hitler," and at the same time advocate a program against "Japs" (4-letter syllable in place of "Jews"). Now that attack on this coast is becoming more of a concrete threat, feeling is running pretty high—tho' the individuals in most cases are pretty decent. The rabble-rousers and the mob— haven't we learned about "mobs" in Roman days and in Shakespeare's works?— they are the ones to cause all the trouble. Even the Youth Congress has come out with a plea to move us all out someplace, anywhere except on the coast.

… Anyway I'm not sure what to believe these days. Dad takes no thought of his eventual transfer to a camp. (They're moving the over-45-year-olds after they get the first batch settled.) In fact, if the war comes any closer we'll all be kicked out.

Gosh, but hasn't 1941 been the awfullest year in our life?

iv. March 2, 1942.

Dear Wes:

What a heavenly relief to get your letter. I was just about getting frantic with worry over you … Oh Wes, the things that have been happening out here are beyond words, and though at times I thank goodness you're out of it, at other times I think we really need people like you around to keep us from getting too wrought up for our own good.

Eiko and Fumi [friends of Kitagawa] were here yesterday, crying, nearly hysterical with hurt and outrage and impotence. All student nurses have been fired from the [Vancouver] General.

They took our beautiful radio … what does it matter that someone bought it off us for a song? … it's the same thing because we had to do that or suffer the ignominy of having it taken forcibly from us by the RCMP. Not a single being of Japanese race in the protected area will escape. Our cameras, even Nobi's toy one, all are confiscated. They can search our homes without warrant.

As if all this trouble wasn't enough, prepare yourself for a shock. We are forced to move out from our homes, Wes, to where we don't know. Eddie was going to join the Civilian Corps but now will not go near it, as it smells of a daemonic, roundabout way of getting rid of us. There is the very suspicious clause 'within and *without*' Canada that has all the fellows leery.

The Bank is awfully worried about me and the twins, and the manager has said he will do what he can for us, but as he has to refer to the main office which in turn has to refer to the Head Office, he can't promise a thing, except a hope that surely the Bank won't let us down after all these years of faithful service. Who knows where we will be now tomorrow next week. It isn't as if we Nisei were aliens, technical or not. It breaks my heart to think of leaving this house and the little things around it that we have gathered through the years, all those numerous gadgets that have no material value but are irreplaceable …

Oh Wes, the Nisei are bitter, too bitter for their own good or for Canada. How can cool heads like Tom's [Tom Shoyama, editor of the *New Canadian*] prevail when the general feeling is to stand up and fight.

Do you know what curfew means in actual practice? B.C. is falling all over itself in the scramble to be the first to kick us out from jobs and homes. So many night-workers have been fired out of hand. Now they sit at home, which is usually just a bed, or some cramped quarters, since they can't go out at night for even a consoling cup of coffee. Mr. Shimizu is working like mad with the Welfare society to look after the women and children that were left when their men were forced to volunteer to go to the work camps. Now those men are only in unheated bunk-cars, no latrines, no water, snow 15' deep, no work to keep warm with, little food if any. They had been shunted off with such inhuman speed that they got there before any facilities were prepared for them. Now men are afraid to go because they think they will be going to certain disaster … anyway, too much uncertainty. After all, they have to think of their families. If snow is 15' deep there is no work, and if there is no work there is no pay, and if there is no pay no one eats. The *Province* reports that work on frames with tent-coverings is progressing to house the 2,000 expected. Tent coverings where the snow is so deep! And this is Democracy! You should see the faces here, all pinched, grey, uncertain. If the Bank fails Eddie, do you know what the kids and I have to live on? $39. For everything … food, clothing, rent, taxes, upkeep, insurance premiums, emergencies. They will allow for only two kids for the Nisei. $6 per., monthly. It has just boiled down to race persecution, and signs have been posted on all highways … JAPS … KEEP OUT. Mind you, you can't compare this sort of thing to anything that happens in Germany. That country is an avowed Jew-baiter, totalitarian. Canada is supposed to be a Democracy out to fight against just the sort of thing she's boosting at home.

And also, I'll get that $39 only if Eddie joins the Chain Gang, you know, *forced to volunteer* to let the authorities wash their hands of any responsibilities. All Nisei are liable to imprisonment I suppose if they refuse to volunteer … that is the likeliest interpretation of Ian MacKenzie's "volunteer or else." Prisoners in war-time get short shrift … and to hell with the wife and kids. Can you wonder that there is a deep bitterness among the Nisei who believe so gullibly in the demo-cratic blah-blah that's been dished out. I am glad Kazuma [Uyeno] is not here.

There are a lot of decent people who feel for us, but they can't do a thing.

And the horrors that some young girls have already faced … outraged by men in uniform … in the hospital … hysterical. Oh we are fair prey for the wolves in democratic clothing. Can you wonder the men are afraid to leave us behind and won't go unless their women go with them? I won't blame you if you can't believe this. It *is* incredible. Wes, you have to be here right in the middle of it to really know.

How can the hakujin face us without a sense of shame for their treachery to the principles they fight for? One man was so damned sorry, he came up to me, hat off, squirming like mad, stuttering how sorry he was. My butcher said he knew he could trust me with a side of meat even if I had no money … Yet there are other people who, while they wouldn't go so far as to persecute us, are so ignorant, so indifferent they believe we are being very well treated for what we are. The irony of it all is enough to choke me. And we are tightening our belts for the starvation to come. The diseases … the crippling … the twisting of our souls … death would be the easiest to bear.

The Chinese are forced to wear huge buttons and plates and even placards to tell the hakujin the difference between one yellow peril and another. Or else they would be beaten up. It's really ridiculous.

And Wes, we are among the fortunate ones, for above that $39 we may be able to fill it out by renting this house. Now I wish I hadn't given my clothes to Kath. We will need them badly. Uncle has been notified to get ready to move. Dad will be soon too.

There's too much to say and not enough time or words.

Can't send you pictures now unless some hakujin takes the snaps … STRENG VERBOTEN [German for "strictly forbidden"] to use even little cameras to snap the twins … STRENG VERBOTEN is the order of the day.

v. April 20, 1942.

Dear Wes:

I went to the Pool yesterday to see Eiko who is working there as steno. I saw Sab too who is working in the baggage … old Horseshow Building. Sab showed me his first paycheque as something he couldn't quite believe … $11.75. He's been there for an awful long time. Eiko sleeps in a partitioned stall, she being on the staff, so to speak. This stall was the former home of a pair of stallions and boy oh boy, did they leave their odour behind. The whole place is impregnated with the smell of ancient manure and maggots. Every other day it is swept with dichloride of lime or something, but you can't disguise horse smell, cow smell, sheeps and pigs and rabbits and goats. And is it dusty! The toilets are just a sheet metal trough, and up till now they did not have partitions or seats. The women kicked so they put up partitions and a terribly makeshift seat. Twelve-year-old boys stay with the women too. The auto show building, where there was also the Indian exhibit, houses the new dining room and kitchens. Seats 3000. Looks awfully permanent. Brick stoves, 8 of them, shining new mugs … very very barrack-y. As for the bunks, they were the most tragic things I saw there. Steel and wooden frames with a thin lumpy straw tick, a bolster, and three army blankets of army quality … no sheets unless you bring your own. These are the 'homes' of the women I saw. They wouldn't let me into the men's building. There are constables at the doors … no propagation of the species … you know … it was in the papers. These bunks were hung with sheets and blankets and clothes of every hue and variety, a regular gipsy tent of colours, age, and cleanliness, all hung with the pathetic attempt at privacy. Here and there I saw a child's doll and teddy bear … I saw babies lying there beside a mother who was too weary to get up … she had just thrown herself across the bed … I felt my throat thicken … an old old lady was crying, saying she would rather have died than have come to such a place … she clung to Eiko and cried and cried. Eiko has taken the woes of the confinees on her thin shoulders and she took so much punishment she went to her former rooms and couldn't stop crying. Fumi was so worried about her. Eiko is really sick. The place has got her down. There are ten showers for 1500 women. Hot and cold water. The men looked so terribly at loose ends, wandering around the grounds, sticking their noses through the fence watching the golfers, lying on the grass. Going through the place I felt so depressed that I wanted to cry. I'm damned well not going there. They are going to move the Vancouver women first now and shove them into the Pool before sending them to the ghost towns.

   … The other day at the Pool, someone dropped his key before a stall in the Livestock Building, and he fished for it with a long wire and brought to light rotted manure and maggots!!! He called the nurse and then they moved all the bunks from the stalls and pried up the wooden floors. It was the most stomach-turning nauseating thing. They got fumigators and tried to wash it all away and got most of it into the drains, but maggots still breed and turn up here and there. One woman with more guts than the others told the nurse (white) about it and protested. She replied: "Well, there's worms in the garden aren't there?" This particular nurse was a Jap-hater of the most virulent sort. She called them "filthy Japs" to their faces and Eiko gave her 'what-for' and Fumi had a terrible scrap with her, both girls saying: "What do you think we are? Are we cattle? Are we pigs you dirty-so-and-so!" You know how Fumi gets. The night the first bunch of Nisei were supposed to go to Schreiber and they wouldn't, the women and children at the Pool milled around in front of their cage, and one very handsome mountie came with his truncheon and started to hit them, yelling at them, "Get the hell back in there." Eiko's blood boiled over. She strode over to him and shouted at him: "You put that stick down! What do you think you're doing! Do you think these women and children are so many cows that you can beat them back into their place?" Eiko was shaking mad and raked him with fighting words. She has taken it on her to fight for the poor people there, and now she is on the black list and reputed to be a trouble-maker. Just like Tommy and Kunio. I wish I too could go in there and fight and slash around. It's people like us who are the most hurt … people like us, who have had faith in Canada, and who have been more politically minded than the others, who have a hearty contempt for the whites ...

By the way, we got a letter from Uncle ... or rather Auntie got it. He's the gardener, and has to grow vegetables and flowers on the side. Takashima is cook and gets $50 clear. Uncle only nets about $10. All cards and letters are censored, even to the Nisei camps. Not a word about sit-downs, gambaru-ing or anything makes the papers. It's been hushed. Good thing for us. I wondered why I didn't read about it. I haven't been to meetings so long now that I don't know what's going on. Uncle's camp is 8 miles from the station up into the hills. Men at the first camps all crowd down to the station every time a train passes with the Nationals and hang onto the windows asking for news from home. Uncle said he wept.

But the men are luckier than the women. They are fed, they work, they have no children to look after. Of course the fathers are awfully worried about their families. But it's the women who are burdened with all the responsibility of keeping what's left of the family together. Frances went to Revelstoke, bag and baggage and baby. When I heard that I felt choked with envy, and felt more trapped than ever. Eiko tells me: "Don't you dare bring the kids into the Pool." And Mr. Maikawa says Greenwood is worse. They are propping up the old shacks near the mine shaft. Sab went through there and says it's awful. The United Church parson there says of the Japs: "Kick them all out." Sab knows his son who had the room next to him at Union College. Vic and George Saito and family went to the beet fields. Sadas are going tonight. They are going to hell on earth, and will be so contracted that they cannot leave the place or move. Whites will not go there.

I pray that Kath and Mom are safe. Mom's got to live through this. Now that Japan proper has been bombed they will come here.

Sab told me his father has applied to get to Winnipeg or to Toronto. Sab is hoping to get to Queens.

Eiko, Fumi and I, and all of us, have gotten to be so profane that Tom and the rest of them have given up being surprised. Eiko starts out with "what the hell" ... and Fumi comes out with worse. It sure relieves our pent-up feelings. Men are lucky they can swear with impunity. (Hell ... I can smell horse all of a sudden ...)

On account of those fool Nisei who have bucked the gov't, everything the JCCL fought for has been lost. Our name is mud. Why they don't arrest Fujikazu I don't know. I kind of feel that the RCMP are just letting us raise such a stink by ourselves ... that is fools like Fujikazu and his ilk ... that the rest of us who are really conscientious and loyal will never have a chance to become integrated with this country. It's damnable. All we have fought for and won inch by inch has gone down the drain. More than the Nationals, our name is mud. There's over 140 Nisei loose, and many Nationals. The Commission thinks the Nationals are cleared but oh boy there are a lot of them who have greased enough palms and are let alone.

By the way if you ever write anything for the NC write it to Tom personally.

How are things there? How are the Pannells and everybody? Three Nisei girls are going to Toronto for housework. Maybe you might get to see them, whoever they are. Aki Hyodo is in Hamilton. If Mrs. Pannell doesn't mind the typewriter, I think I shall write to her.

I'll write again soon.

vi. We'll Fight for Home, 1942.

The tide of panic, starting from irresponsible agitators, threatens to engulf the good sense of the people of British Columbia. The daily press is flooded with "letters to the editor" demanding the indiscriminate internment of all people of Japanese blood, alien or Canadian-born; demanding the immediate confiscation of our right to work as we like, our right to live like decent human beings. One and all, they add the height of sardonic cynicism: if we are as loyal as we say we are, then we ought to understand why we ought to be treated like poison.

If we were less Canadian, less steeped in the tradition of justice and fair play, perhaps we could understand and bow our heads before this strange, undemocratic baiting of thousands of innocent people.

For the very reason that our Grade School teachers, our High School teachers, and our environment have bred in us a love of country, a loyalty to one's native land, faith in the concepts of traditional British fair play, it is difficult to understand this expression of a mean narrow-mindedness, an unreasoning condemnation of a long suffering people. We cannot understand why our loyalty should be questioned.

After all, this is our only home, where by the sweat of our endeavours we have carved a bit of security for ourselves and our children. Would we sabotage our own home? Would we aid anyone who menaces our home, who would destroy the fruits of our labour and our love? People who talk glibly of moving us wholesale "East of the Rockies," who maintain that it is an easy task, overlook with supreme indifference the complex human character.

They do not think what it would mean to be ruthlessly, needlessly uprooted from a familiar homeground, from friends, and sent to a labour camp where most likely the decencies will be of the scantiest in spite of what is promised. They do not think that we are not cattle to be herded wherever it pleases our ill-wishers. They forget, or else it does not occur to them, that we have the same pride and self-respect as other Canadians, who can be hurt beyond repair. In short, they do not consider us as people, but as a nuisance to be rid of at the first opportunity. What excuse they use is immaterial to them. It just happens to be very opportune that Japan is now an active enemy.

We have often been accused of taking the bread out of "white" folks' mouths. Is there anything against the right to enjoy what one has earned? Our little trades and professions ... what golden loot for our would-be despoilers! No wonder they drool to get at them. These hard-earned, well-deserved small successes ... for out of the total of our enterprises, how many are there that can be classed as wealth? So few!

"Man's inhumanity to man makes countless thousands mourn."

Right here in British Columbia is a God-sent opportunity for the government and the people to practise democracy as it is preached. Not in panicky persecutions that do no one any good, but with sensible belief in our very real harmlessness, and consideration for us as a much-maligned people.

Ye gods! Can they not see that we love our home and would fight to protect it from the invader!

vii. On Loyalty, 1942.

The quality of loyalty is difficult to define in exact terms. There is a oneness with one's country, just as there is the blood tie with one's mother. There is the fighting urge to defend that country should it be threatened in any way. There is a passionate, unquestioning, unqualified affinity with the land that excludes the pettiness of a manmade—and therefore imperfect—government. All this and active service for the country is loyalty.

Who can glibly say I am a Japanese National of Japan just because I am of the same race with black hair and yellow skin? Who can rightfully tell me where my heart lies, if I know better myself? Who can assume with omniscience that I am disloyal to Canada because I have not golden hair and blue eyes? What are these surface marks that must determine the quality of my loyalty? Nothing, nothing at all!

Yet because I am Canadian, must hate be a requisite for my patriotism? Must I hate vengefully, spitefully, pettily? Will not hate cloud my good sense, muddy the clean surge of willing sacrifice, the impulse to rally strongly to the flag of this country? Hate never fought as fiercely as love in the fight for one's country. Hate impedes, while love strengthens.

Therefore it is not hate for a country one has never known, but love for this familiar Canadian soil that makes me want to use my bare fists to uphold its honour, its integrity.

Who is there, unless he does not know the quality of loyalty, who will question mine?

viii. Mr. and Mrs. Kitagawa to Custodian of Japanese Properties, Vancouver, B.C., July 1943.

Dear Sir:

This is to register with you our absolute opposition to the proposed liquidation of our house and lot at 2751 Pender Street East, Vancouver, B.C.

This house, bought out of slender earnings, represents our stake in this country of our birth, but sentiment alone is not for withholding our express and voluntary consent to sell.

Our present earnings are even more slender than before. You are doubtless aware, if you have a family of your own, what it costs in dollars and cents to feed, clothe, and house a family of six, excluding the other expenses incidental to schooling, medical services, etc. With four growing children, that $25 a week we receive from the rental of our house is more welcome than you could ever understand. Without that $25, meagre as it is, we could not meet all our monthly obligations. You know, too, that while cost of living rises, salaries do not. But now you [propose] to deprive us of that regular income on which we are desperately dependent. We are not among those who can afford the loss of their dear-bought investment.

Our house, a private residence belonging to a private citizen of this country, is in the capable hands of a trustworthy agent; the tenants are pleasant and punctual. They know they have a bargain, as the house is in good shape, with added improvements to the cost of many hundreds of dollars, boosting the saleable value of the house, too. This piece of real estate is not idle, either, housing as it does the family of a soldier, and also keeping poverty and hardship that much further away from the absent owners.

We cannot understand the official claim that it is necessary to sell over our heads the home from which we were forcibly ejected. We do not quarrel with military measure but this act can scarcely be in accordance with any war measure. Please hasten to assure us that our house is inviolate.

Yours truly,

ix. F.G. Shears, Department of the Secretary of State, Office of the Custodian, Japanese Evacuation Section, Vancouver, B.C., to Mr. and Mrs. Kitagawa, July 2, 1943.

Dear Sir:

I am in receipt of your letter of the 26th instant in which you registered your disapproval of the sale of your property.

The proposed liquidation is of course a general one and not only applies to your particular property. The policy has been decided upon at Ottawa and this Office, acting under advice of an independent Advisory Committee, will endeavour to obtain the best possible results.

You are aware I hope that the proceeds of the liquidation will be available to you from time to time as you have need of same.

At the present moment tenders have not been called on your particular property but I am unable to give you the assurance asked for and it will be disposed of in due course if satisfactory offers are received.

Yours truly,

x. T.M. Kitagawa to Mr. F.G. Shears, July 8, 1943.

Mr. F.G. Shears:

I received your letter of July 2nd, File No. 10004, yesterday and must say was not too greatly surprised. The reason for writing you at all was because the government had vested in you the final authority to sell or not to sell our homes, and perhaps I took a vain-hope gamble.

Would you give up a legitimate fight to defend what is yours though the odds are enough to overwhelm you? Britain didn't, did she? This war, for the common soldier, is a war for Principle: the rights and liberties and the pursuit of happiness for every man; and I'm on the side of the common soldier, giving his heart's blood that the oppressed may be free. Who would have thought that one day I would be unable to stand up for my country's government, out of sheer shame and disillusion, against the slurs of the scornful? The bitterness, the anguish is complete. You, who deal in lifeless figures, files, and statistics could never measure the depth of hurt and outrage dealt out to those of us who love this land. It is because we *are* Canadians, that we protest the violation of our birthright. If we were not we would not care one jot or tittle whatever you did, for then we could veil our eyes in contempt. You … and by "you" I designate all those in authority who have piled indignity upon indignity on us … have sought to sully and strain our loyalty but, I'm telling you, you can't do it. You can't undermine our faith in the principles of equal rights and justice for all, with "malice towards none, and charity for all."

Why can't you differentiate between those owners who don't care one way or the other what happens to their homes, and those who, born in this country, hate to lose their homes? If you are worried for our sakes about the depreciation of property values, then why will you not allow the owners a say in the sale price, the choice of prospective buyers? Can you, with a clear conscience, commit this breach of justice, and face the accusing eyes of all bereft and absent owners? Do you think it is logical, after what happened to the boats, the cars, and radios, that we have any faith in any promise of a fair price, which "proceeds of this liquidation will be available ... from time to time?" What will happen is the gradual dribbling away to nothing of the pitiful price, and then what shall we have left to show for our lifetime of struggling and saving and loving the bit of land we call our own? You may rightly say that wartime sacrifices are inevitable and honourable, but can you say with any truth that this sacrifice forced on us will be sanctified by a spirit of voluntary giving? What are platitudes against this humiliation!

Now you understand a little why I must contest the sale to the last bitter ditch, if we are to hold up our heads. You will concede us that, especially as this is the very principle for which the democracies are fighting.

However, if all fails and you are upheld in your purpose, then kindly send us our "proceeds" in one sum that we may personally reinvest it in something solid ... Victory Bonds, for instance.

There are still a few personal possessions in our home for which I shall send at once. You would not deny us that, I hope.

4. W.L. Mackenzie King, House of Commons, *Debates*, August 4, 1944.

... The government has had certain basic principles before it in formulating the policy which I wish to present to-day. In the first place, it recognizes the concern felt by British Columbia at the possibility of once again having within its borders virtually the entire Japanese population of Canada. In the past that situation has led to acrimony and bitterness. That the feeling is general in British Columbia has been made evident not only by the remarks of hon. members from that province but also through representations received from many west coast organizations and individuals. In view of the concern, it is felt that it must be accepted as a basic factor that it would be unwise and undesirable, not only from the point of view of the people of British Columbia, but also from that of persons of Japanese origin themselves, to allow the Japanese population to be concentrated in that province after the war.

Secondly, account should be taken of the fact that for the most part the people of Japanese race in the country have remained loyal and have refrained from acts of sabotage and obstruction during the war. It is a fact that no person of Japanese race born in Canada has been charged with any act of sabotage or disloyalty during the years of war. For the future protection of those who have remained loyal, as well as to eliminate those who have shown that their true allegiance is not to Canada but to Japan, the government is of the view that persons of Japanese race, whether Japanese nationals or British subjects by nationalization or birth, who have shown disloyalty to Canada during the war, should not have the privilege of remaining in Canada after the struggle is terminated. That is a second principle that is considered to be fundamental.

Thirdly, the government is of the view that, having regard to the strong feeling that has been aroused against the Japanese during the war and to the extreme difficulty of assimilating Japanese persons in Canada, no immigration of Japanese into this country should be allowed after the war. It is realized, of course, that no declaration of this type can or should be attempted which would be binding indefinitely into the future. Nevertheless, as a guiding principle in the years after the war, it is felt that Japanese immigrants should not be admitted.

Finally, the government considers that, while there are disloyal persons to be removed, and while immigration in future is undesirable, and while problems of assimilation undoubtedly do present themselves with respect even to the loyal Japanese in Canada, nevertheless they are persons who have been admitted here to settle and become citizens, or who have been born into this free country of ours, and that we cannot do less than treat such persons fairly and justly. The interests of Canada must be paramount, and its interests will be protected as the first duty of the government. It has not, however, at any stage of the war, been shown that the presence of a few thousand persons of Japanese race who have been guilty of no act of sabotage and who have manifested no disloyalty even during periods of utmost trial, constitutes a menace to a nation of almost twelve million people. Those who are disloyal must be removed. That is clear. Surely, however, it is not to be expected that the government will do other than deal justly with those who are guilty of no crime, or even of any ill intention. For the government to act otherwise would be an acceptance of the standards of our enemies and the negation of the purposes for which we are fighting …

I should add that in handling the Japanese problem we shall attempt, in so far as it seems desirable, to maintain a policy that in a sense can be considered as part of a continental policy. The situation in the United States in a great many essentials, is the same as our own, and to the extent that it seems desirable we shall endeavour to ensure that our policy takes account of the policies which are being applied south of the border. There is no need for an identity of policy, but I believe there is merit in maintaining a substantial consistency of treatment in the two countries.

I might now mention the tentative measures which it is proposed to put into effect in order to carry out a policy based upon the principles I have indicated. The first and, in a sense, the fundamental task is to determine the loyal and the disloyal persons of Japanese race in Canada. The entire policy depends upon this being done. To some extent, of course, the task has been carried out through the examination and internment of suspicious or dangerous persons. It cannot be assumed, however, that all those who have been interned are disloyal. Some may have merely misunderstood their dispossession from their property in the protected zones, and, as peaceful and honest Canadian citizens, may have striven to protect and retain what they considered to be rightfully theirs. Undoubtedly some of these cases exist. Misunderstanding is not the same as traitorous intent, and a stubborn defence of one's own property is not necessarily disloyalty. On the other hand, there may be persons who have committed no act to justify their internment but who are in fact disloyal. What is clearly needed is the establishment of a quasi-judicial commission to examine the background, loyalties and attitudes of all persons of Japanese race in Canada to ascertain those who are not fit persons to be allowed to remain here. The commission I have referred to should, I think, be established in the fairly near future in order that it may begin what will be a large and important task. The result of the work of the commission would be to establish a list of disloyal Japanese persons, some of whom will be Japanese nationals, some British subjects by naturalization, and some British subjects by birth. The government's intention would be to have these disloyal persons deported to Japan as soon as that is physically possible. Prior to deportation, British subjects, falling within this class, would be deprived of their status as such. By the terms of the peace, Japan can be compelled, whether she wishes it or not, to accept these persons. There may also be some persons who will voluntarily indicate a desire to proceed to Japan. For these, no further examination would be necessary. Whatever their national status, they would be allowed and encouraged to go as soon as they can.

Once the examination has been carried out there will be established a list of Japanese persons who are loyal to Canada. These persons, if they have been properly admitted to this country, and wish to remain here, should be allowed to do so. However, as I have said, they should not be allowed once more to concentrate in British Columbia. To prevent such concentration, measures of two types can be taken—a maximum can be set on the number of persons of Japanese race to be allowed to return to British Columbia, and persons of Japanese race can be given encouragement to move and remain elsewhere. It would be most undesirable, I believe, to establish a permanent barrier to the movement within Canada of persons who have been lawfully admitted to Canada or who are nationals of Canada. That would raise the possibility of discrimination and restrictions on movement to and from provinces which might have most unfortunate consequences in the future. Even the establishment of a temporary limitation would be undesirable in principle, but as a practical question of policy it may well be inescapable.

There is little doubt that, with co-operation on the part of the provinces, it can be made possible to settle the Japanese more or less evenly throughout Canada. They will have to settle in such a way that they must be able to pursue the settled lives to which they are entitled, and that they do not present themselves as an unassimilable bloc or colony which might again give rise to distrust, fear and dislike. It is the fact of concentration that has given rise to the problem.

The sound policy and the best policy for the Japanese Canadians themselves is to distribute their numbers as widely as possible throughout the country where they will not create feelings of racial hostility.

… We must not permit in Canada the hateful doctrine of racialism, which is the basis of the Nazi system everywhere. Our aim is to resolve a difficult problem in a manner which will protect the people of British Columbia and the interests of the country as a whole, and at the same time preserve, in whatever we do, principles of fairness and justice.

Readings

Adachi, K. *The Enemy That Never Was: A History of the Japanese Canadians*. Toronto: McClelland and Stewart, 1976.

Broadfoot, B. *Years of Sorrow, Years of Shame: The Story of the Japanese Canadians in World War Two*. Toronto: Doubleday, 1977.

Granatstein, J. *A Man of Influence: Norman A. Robertson and Canadian Statecraft, 1929-68*. Ottawa: Deneau, 1981.

Granatstein, J. "The Enemy Within," *Saturday Night* (November 1986). Reprinted in J. Barman and A. McDonald *Readings in the History of British Columbia*. Richmond: Open University, 1989.

Hillmer, N., B. Kordan and L. Luciuk, eds. *On Guard for Thee: War, Ethnicity and the Canadian State 1939-1945*. Ottawa: Canadian Committee for the History of the Second World War, 1988.

Miki, R., and C. Kobayashi. *Justice in Our Times: The Japanese Canadian Redress Settlement*. Vancouver: Talon, 1991.

Omatsu, M. *Bittersweet Passage: Redress and the Japanese Canadian Experience*. Toronto: Between the Lines, 1992.

Roy, P., M. Iino and H. Takamura. *Mutual Hostages: Canadians and Japanese during the Second World War*. Toronto: University of Toronto Press, 1990.

Sunahara, A. *The Politics of Racism: The Uprooting of the Japanese Canadians during the Second World War*. Toronto: James Lorimer, 1981.

Ward, W. "British Columbia and the Japanese Evacuation," *Canadian Historical Review* 57, 3 (September, 1976).

Ward, W. *White Canada Forever: Popular Attitudes and Public Policy Toward Orientals in British Columbia*. Montreal: McGill-Queen's University Press, 1978.

Chapter Twelve

"Cinderella of the Empire": Newfoundland and Confederation

Newfoundland National Convention Debates, 1946–1948.

1. Joseph Smallwood.
2. Major P.J. Cashin.
3. F. Gordon Bradley.
4. G.F. Higgins.
5. G. Macdonald.
6. H. Harrington.
7. I. Keough.
8. J. Roberts.

Introduction

Federate with Canada or not, that was the question adult Newfoundlanders had to answer when they voted on July 22, 1949. Their answer proved more ambiguous than expected: 52.34% wanted Newfoundland as Canada's tenth province, 47.66% voted against. That, in a democratic system, was sufficient for Newfoundland to take its place in confederation.

This was a runoff referendum: the second on the same issue. The first, held the previous month, offered Newfoundlanders three choices: regain semi-independent responsible government; join Canada as a province; or continue the unhappy Commission of Government then ruling Newfoundland directly from Britain. Voters overwhelmingly rejected the last choice, a mere 23,311 supporting it. Confederationists, however, came out second best with 64,066 votes to 69,400 for responsible government. It looked as though Newfoundland would become an autonomous Dominion in the Gulf of St. Lawrence. In the end, however, most of those who initially voted for the status quo became confederationists on the second ballot.

Newfoundland's reticence to join Canada was hardly surprising considering its unique historical development. Being part of the British Empire and sharing the same continent were arguably the sole things uniting Newfoundlanders to Canada, and if we must join somebody, many islanders proclaimed, let it be the United States with whom we have more in common. From the time they arrived on Newfoundland's craggy coast, most settlers, with their maritime Gaelic and English roots, turned their backs to the North American continent. Instead they faced Europe across the rolling Atlantic, unlike their compatriots on the mainland who looked inward or westward.

The problem, however, was that Newfoundland possessed neither the population nor resource base to prosper independently. Britain provided most of the island's funding, and Newfoundland's standard of living languished as the rest of the continent flourished. England, meanwhile, resented the interminable bills and called for their government to cast "the Rock" adrift. Newfoundlanders saw the writing on the wall well before the Second World War, particularly during the calamitous depression era that cut a bitter swath of social deprivation through the colony. Things had to change. Then, in 1939 and in their moment of despair, Newfoundland miraculously found itself in a strategically critical location, where it served as a vital staging post for Atlantic convoys during the Second World War. The United States leased huge military bases for 99-year terms, and thousands of Canadian soldiers and sailors milled about St. John's, preparing to embark for Europe or patrol duty. The Newfoundland economy reignited, and Newfoundlanders argued that they could indeed support themselves.

Islanders and island administrators had long wrestled with Newfoundland's future and the idea of federation with Canada was not new. While one Maritime Province after the other joined the Canadian federation in the late 1860s and 1870s, Newfoundland hesitated. Newfoundlanders wanted to steer their own course, and Canada's reticence discouraged a confederation courtship. Most Canadians knew little about Newfoundland, and probably cared less. Newfoundland was a foggy rock in the Atlantic inhabited by vaguely odd fishers who spoke peculiar English, drank Screech and served as the butt of jokes. Pragmatic Canadians also feared that Newfoundland's precarious financial situation would make it a financial liability were it to federate. Thus, the average Canadian believed the disadvantages outweighed the advantages of Newfoundland joining Canada.

Newfoundlanders resented Canadian condescension and feared that Canada, patronizing as it was, would absorb Newfoundland and use it as it saw fit with little consideration for islanders' wishes. The very democratic process that finally brought Newfoundland into confederation also posed a significant threat. Newfoundland's population, tiny in relation to the rest of Canada, could easily be outvoted and ignored in future federal elections. Thus islanders feared that their distinct and cherished culture could be legislated out of existence once Newfoundland joined Canada. This suspicion deepened during the negotiation process when Newfoundlanders, with good reason, concluded that a conspiracy existed between Britain and Canada to bring the island into confederation regardless of local opinion.

In 1949 Newfoundlanders voted to join Canada with the slimmest margin after a tumultuous and nasty campaign. No vote was ever taken asking Canadians if they wanted yet another province. Today the Parti Quebecois argues that a simply majority of Quebec voters is sufficient to take their province out of Confederation, while the federal government argues that all Canadians have a right to decide on the disintegration of Canada. Newfoundland's case provides an interesting precedent.

Discussion Points

1. Was it in the interest of Newfoundland's inhabitants to join Canada in 1949?
2. If the benefits to joining Canada were so obvious, why did such a large percentage of Newfoundlanders oppose federation?
3. Who was more nationalistic: Cashin or Smallwood?

Documents

1. Joseph Smallwood.

Our people's struggle to live commenced on the day they first landed here, four centuries and more ago, and has continued to this day. The struggle is more uneven now than it was then, and the people view the future now with more dread than they felt a century ago.

The newer conceptions of what life can be, of what life should be, have widened our horizons and deepened our knowledge of the great gulf which separates what we have and are from what we feel we should have and be. We have been taught by newspapers, magazines, motion pictures, radios, and visitors something of the higher standards of well-being of the mainland of North America; we have become uncomfortably aware of the low standards of our country, and we are driven irresistibly to wonder whether our attempt to persist in isolation is the root-cause of our condition. We have often felt in the past, when we learned something of the higher standards of the mainland, that such things belonged to another world, that they were not for us. But today we are not so sure that two yardsticks were designed by the Almighty to measure the standards of well-being: one yardstick for the mainland of the continent; another for this Island which lies beside it. Today we are not so sure, not so ready to take it for granted, that we Newfoundlanders are destined to accept much lower standards of life than our neighbours of Canada and the United States. Today we are more disposed to feel that our manhood, our very creation by God, entitles us to standards of life no lower than those of our brothers on the mainland.

Our Newfoundland is known to possess natural wealth of considerable value and variety. Without at all exaggerating their extent, we know that our fisheries are in the front rank of the world's marine wealth. We have considerable forest, water power, and mineral resources. Our Newfoundland people are industrious, hard-working, frugal, ingenious, and sober. The combination of such natural resources and such people should spell a prosperous country enjoying high standards, Western World standards, of living. This combination should spell fine, modern, well-equipped homes; lots of health-giving food; ample clothing; the amenities of modern New World civilization; good roads, good schools, good hospitals, high levels of public and private health; it should spell a vital, prosperous, progressive country.

It has not spelt any such things. Compared with the mainland of North America, we are fifty years, in some things a hundred years, behind the times. We live more poorly, more shabbily, more meanly. Our life is more a struggle. Our struggle is tougher, more naked, more hopeless. In the North American family, Newfoundland bears the reputation of having the lowest standards of life, of being the least progressive and advanced, of the whole family.

We all love this land. It has a charm that warms our hearts, go where we will; a charm, a magic, a mystical tug on our emotion that never dies. With all her faults, we love her.

But a metamorphosis steals over us the moment we cross the border that separates us from other lands. As we leave Newfoundland, our minds undergo a transformation: we expect, and we take for granted, a higher, a more modern, way of life such as it would have seemed ridiculous or even avaricious to expect at home. And as we return to Newfoundland, we leave that higher standard behind, and our minds undergo a reverse transformation: we have grown so accustomed to our own lower standards and more antiquated methods and old-fashioned conveniences that we readjust ourselves unconsciously to the meaner standards under which we grew up. We are so used to our railway and our coastal boats that we scarcely see them; so used to our settlements, and roads, and homes, and schools, and hospitals and hotels and everything else that we do not even see their inadequacy, their backwardness, their seaminess.

We have grown up in such an atmosphere of struggle, of adversity, of mean times that we are never surprised, never shocked, when we learn that we have one of the highest rates of tuberculosis in the world; one of highest maternity mortality rates in the world; one of the highest rates of beriberi and rickets in the world. We take these shocking facts for granted. We take for granted our lower standards, our poverty. We are not indignant about them. We save our indignation for those who publish such facts, for with all our complacency, with all our readiness to receive, to take for granted, and even to justify these things amongst ourselves, we are, strange to say, angry and hurt when these shocking facts become known to the outside world.

We are all very proud of our Newfoundland people. We all admire their strength, their skill, their adaptability, their resourcefulness, their industry, their frugality, their sobriety, and their warm-hearted, simple generosity. We are proud of them; but are we indignant, does our blood boil, when we see the lack of common justice with which they are treated? When we see how they live? When we witness the long, grinding struggle they have? When we see the standards of their life? Have we compassion in our hearts for them? Or are we so engrossed, so absorbed, in our own struggle to live in this country that our social conscience has become toughened, even case-hardened? Has our own hard struggle to realize a modest competence so blinded us that we have little or no tenderness of conscience left to spare for the fate of the tens of thousands of our brothers so very much worse off than ourselves?

Mr. Chairman, in the present and prospective world chaos, with all its terrible variety of uncertainty, it would be cruel and futile, now that that the choice is ours, to influence the handful of people who inhabit this small Island to attempt independent national existence. The earnings of our 65,000 families may be enough, in the years ahead, to support them half-decently and at the same time support the public services of a fair-sized municipality. But will those earnings support independent national government on an expanding, or even the present, scale? Except for a few years of this war and a few of the last, our people's earnings never supported them on a scale comparable with North American standards, and never maintained a government even on the pre-war scale of service. Our people never enjoyed a good standard of living, and never were able to yield enough taxes to maintain the government. The difference was made up by borrowing or grants-in-aid.

We can indeed reduce our people's standard of living; we can force them to eat and wear and use and have much less than they have; and we can deliberately lower the level of governmental services. Thus we might manage precariously to maintain independent national status. We can resolutely decide to be poor but proud. But if such a decision is made, it must be made by the 60,000 families who would have to do the sacrificing, not the 5,000 families who are confident of getting along pretty well in any case.

We have, I say, a perfect right to decide that we will turn away from North American standards of public services, and condemn ourselves as a people and government deliberately to long years of struggle to maintain even the little that we have. We may, if we wish, turn our backs upon the North American continent beside which God placed us, and resign ourselves to the meaner outlook and shabbier standards of Europe, 2,000 miles across the ocean. We can do this, or we can face the fact that the very logic of our situation on the surface of the globe impels us to draw close to the progressive outlook and dynamic living standards of this continent.

Our danger, so it seems to me, is that of nursing delusions of grandeur. We remember the stories of small states that valiantly preserved their national independence and developed their own proud cultures, but we tend to overlook the fact that comparison of Newfoundland with them is ludicrous. We are not a nation. We are merely a medium-size municipality, a mere miniature borough of a large city. Dr. Carson, Patrick Morris, and John Kent were sound in the first decades of the nineteenth century when they advocated cutting the apron-strings that bound us to the Government of the United Kingdom; but the same love of Newfoundland, the same Newfoundland patriotism, that inspired their agitation then would now, if they lived, drive them to carry the agitation to its logical conclusion of taking the next step of linking Newfoundland closely to the democratic, developing mainland of the New World. There was indeed a time when tiny states lived gloriously. That time is now ancient European history. We are trying to live in the mid-twentieth-century, post-Hitler New World. We are living in a world in which small countries have less chance than ever before of surviving.

We can, of course, persist in isolation, a dot on the shore of North America, … struggling vainly to support ourselves and our greatly expanded public services. Reminded continually by radio, movie, and visitor of greatly higher standards of living across the Gulf, we can shrug incredulously or dope ourselves into the hopeless belief that such things are not for us. By our isolation from the throbbing vitality and expansion of the continent, we have been left far behind in the march of time, the "sport of historic misfortune" the "Cinderella of the Empire". Our choice now is to continue in blighting isolation or seize the opportunity that may beckon us to the wider horizons and higher standards of unity with the progressive mainland of America.

I am not one of those, if any such there be, who would welcome federal union with Canada at any price. There are prices which I, as a Newfoundlander whose ancestry in this country reaches back for nearly two centuries, am not willing that Newfoundland should pay. I am agreeable to the idea that our country should link itself federally with that great British nation, but I am not agreeable that we should ever be expected to forget that we are Newfoundlanders with a great history and a great tradition of our own. I agree that there may be much to gain from linking our fortunes with that great nation. But I insist that as a self-governing province of the Dominion, we should continue to enjoy the right to our own distinctive culture. I do not deny that once we affiliated with the Canadian federal union, we should in all fairness be expected to extend the scope of our loyalty to embrace the federation as a whole. I do not deny this claim at all, but I insist that as a constituent part of the federation, we should continue to be quite free to hold to our love of our own dear land.

Nor am I one of those, if there be any such, who would welcome union with Canada without regard for the price that the Dominion might be prepared to pay.

I pledge myself to this House and to this country that I will base my ultimate stand in this whole question of Confederation upon the nature of the terms that are laid before the Convention and the country. If the terms are such as clearly to suggest a better Newfoundland for our people, I shall support and maintain them. If they are not of such a nature, I shall oppose them with all the means I can command.

In the price we pay and the price we exact, my only standard of measurement is the welfare of the people. This is my approach to the whole question of federal union with Canada. It is in this spirit that I move this resolution today.

Confederation I will support if it means a lower cost of living for our people. Confederation I will support if it means a higher standard of life for our people. Confederation I will support if it means strength, stability, and security for Newfoundland.

I will support Confederation if it gives us democratic government. I will support Confederation if it rids us of Commission Government. I will support Confederation if it gives us responsible government under conditions that will give responsible government a real chance to succeed. Confederation I will support if it makes us a province enjoying privileges and rights no lower than any other province.

These, then, are the conditions of my support of Confederation: that it must raise our people's standard of living, that it must give Newfoundlanders a better life, that it must give our country stability and security, and that it must give us full, democratic responsible government under circumstances that will ensure its success.

Mr. Chairman, gentlemen, I have given a statement of my faith, but I do not expect members to support this motion for the reasons that impel me to do so.

Members no doubt have a variety of reasons of their own, and their support of this resolution does not at all necessarily imply agreement with mine. There are many cases to be made for submitting and supporting this resolution quite apart from those I have given here today.

In the name of the people of Bonavista Centre and of thousands of other Newfoundlanders throughout this Island, I move this resolution. I believe that this move will lead to a brighter and happier life for our Newfoundland people. If you adopt this resolution, and Canada offers us generous terms, as I believe she will, and Newfoundland decides to shake off her ancient isolation, I believe with all my heart and mind that the people will bless the day this resolution was moved. With God's grace, let us move forward for a brighter and happier Newfoundland."

2. Major P.J. Cashin.

... the total federal debt of Canada amounts to over $18 billion, or a per capita debt on every man, woman and child in Canada of $1,492. From information taken from the Report of the Auditor General of Canada, we find that the total interest charge on Canada's national debt is close to $450 million annually, or at the rate of $35 for every Canadian. But just compare this with our own country's finances. Our national debt is roughly $70 million as against Canada's $18 billion. Our per capita debt is $213 as against Canada's $1,492. Our total interest charge, together with sinking fund payments, is $3,375,000 or slightly over $10 per head, as against Canada's $35 per head. Therefore we find that the difference between the national debt of Canada and that of Newfoundland on a per capita basis is approximately $1,200 in excess of ours, which means that if Newfoundland were to become a Canadian province upon the terms offered us, our country would have to become responsible for this extra debt, which would amount to, in all, nearly $400 million as Newfoundland's proportionate share of the entire debt of the Dominion of Canada. It would mean that every man, woman and child in Newfoundland would pay in annual taxes, directly and indirectly, about $230 instead of $120 which is our present per capita tax annually. In all, the people of Newfoundland would have to pay an additional $38–40 million each year in taxation.

But that is not the worst of it. Canada, we are told, in the event of confederation, will be generous enough to take over our sterling debt, which amounts to approximately $64 million. On the face of it, this would look like Canada was giving us something for nothing, but in actuality it is nothing like that. It means that for this $64 million Canada will buy Newfoundland—our railways, public buildings, wharves, lighthouses, telegraph system, docks, steamers and harbours, everything for a paltry $64 million. Why, Mr. Smallwood himself gives the Canadian government the valuation of our railways and its subsidiaries, just one item, as being $72 million. If ever there was a one-sided bargain, this is it. If ever there was a pig-in-a-bag transaction, this is it. ...

This particular feature of the proposals for the union of Newfoundland with Canada is being stressed with every effort by the advocates of confederation. They feel that it is the one bright spot in their annexation platform. They realise that the other terms of union have no basic or solid foundation, and at every opportunity that is afforded them, they try to drill into the minds of our people that once they become a province of Canada all our difficulties will be ended, and the Newfoundland people will at last have entered into a land of milk and honey. They conveniently forget that the taxpayers of the country will be compelled to find these fictitious monies through either direct or indirect taxation. One would imagine to hear some of these people talk, that money is growing on trees. They deliberately try to avoid discussing the present average tax of Canada as compared with the average tax of Newfoundland, which as I have already said, is favourable to Newfoundland in the amount of $110 per head for every man, woman and child in the country. Let me repeat and further emphasise the fact that union with Canada means extra taxation on our people of an additional $35 million annually.

Now let us make a brief review of the Old Age Pension Act as it exists and functions in Canada. A man or woman, to become eligible for this stipend, must be practically a pauper, and then before he or she receives this $30 per month allowance, he or she must assign to the federal government any property or assets they may have; which in the event of death is taken over by the Canadian government and sold in order to repay the federal treasury the amount so paid.

... The people of Canada are raising Cain over the means test. It is wrong to give a man an old age pension if when he dies the government takes his estate, unless he violates a law and has it made over to his successor some years before. It is an inducement to law-breaking. In our Economic Report we outlined a plan whereby we would be in a position to supplement our present old age pension scheme to bring the stipend up to $25 per month. But never in the history of our country, since the old age pension was first instituted some 40 years ago, has the pensioner been compelled to assign or mortgage his properties or assets to the government in order to become eligible for this pension.

Also, with respect to the unemployment insurance scheme now in force in Canada, it is proper that our people should know that those affected or those eligible for recompense under this particular plan, in the event of union with Canada, would not be our primary producers. It does not affect our fishermen, our loggers, our miners, our farmers, our longshoremen or others of the labouring class, and consequently would be of little help to the employed of Newfoundland ...

During my recent two weeks in Canada I made enquiries about this whole business, and was invariably told by mining men and other business interests that all Canada wants Newfoundland for is for the iron ore of Labrador, as well as the 50 or 60 million cords of timber which is available there for the manufacture of pulp and paper. Canada today, even though she is in serious financial straits, has great national ambitions for the future. Canada is struggling to be one of the future powers of the world. Canada is sparsely populated. Her per capita population per square mile is less than that of our country. Canada carries a huge national debt, far too great for its present population of something over 12 million people. There is only one redemption for this Dominion to the west of us, and that is increased population. In order that Canada may continue to expand, and equitably place the cost, she must increase her population to not less than 20 million. That is necessary if Canada hopes to survive and develop as a nation. By the inclusion of Newfoundland in the Canadian federation, Canada would be in the position of controlling the steel production of the entire North American continent. This would be her salvation from an economic standpoint. I say that our Labrador possession must be guarded for the future generations of Newfoundland. I realise that strong influences are at work, both governmental and financial, to rob from Newfoundland her God-given rights. We, as a people, owe it to the future generations yet unborn, to guard those interests handed to us by a kindly Providence.

This whole Labrador business looks to me something like the deal made between Russia and the United States ... when Russia sold Alaska for about $7 million. Like Labrador, Alaska was considered a barren wasteland, and the Russians thought they were making a good deal; but hardly was the ink dry on the contract when Russia had the bitter experience of seeing their former territory becoming a land worth billions. Will we, by accepting these proposals made to us by the Canadian government, be guilty of a similar folly? Will we grasp at a few dollars and live to see French Canada take to herself the millions which should be coming to us—and which would have made us one of the richest little countries in the world? What a bitter pill that would be for our children to swallow—what a remorse to carry to our graves—to sacrifice hundreds of millions for a baby bonus! ...

In addition to paying an annual federal tax of around $230 per annum, every Newfoundlander, will have to find an additional $30 per year in provincial taxation. In all, therefore, the people of the country would have to find over $80 million each year to pay both federal and provincial taxation. In short, the whole thing means that the people of Newfoundland would be taxed to death—that the dole days would be considered luxurious living and opulence in comparison to the manner in which the people of our country would be forced to live in union with Canada ...

I am not speaking to hear the sound of my own voice. Nor am I trying to warp the judgement of the delegates to this Convention or the people of the country, or influence their minds with any more airy rhetoric or political spell-binding. My purpose has been, at this time particularly, to give hard, cold facts which cannot be denied or talked away. What I have said emanates from my sincere political belief which is based on the solid and eternal doctrine: first, a country belongs to its people; second, it is the solemn duty of the people of that country to shoulder the responsibility of governing it. Any divergence or avoidance of that doctrine, any excuse for acting contrary to that fundamental truth is cowardly, unethical and immoral. The challenge which faces the people of this country today is the patriotic and moral challenge to do their duty and to face their responsibilities like real men and women. It is a clear-cut issue—as clear and unambiguous as the challenge of right and wrong. But again I say, there are those amongst us who have shown that they are unwilling, or have not the capabilities of facing their responsibilities and accepting obligations of democratic decency. They are prepared instead to assume the garb of mendicants and go begging at the back door of some outside country, asking to be taken in out of the rough world which they fear to face. Like Shakespeare's character, they are prepared to crawl under the huge legs of some foreign colossus and find themselves dishonourable graves. But I know that there are many thousands amongst us who are not prepared to form their opinions on mere moral or ethical grounds. They prefer to deal with matters from a more practical standpoint. They ask for facts. Well, I think I have given them the facts.

In my opinion, Canada is today in a position where she finds she has overreached herself. She reminds me of the frog in the fable who wanted to be as big as a bull and who puffed himself up until he burst. Canada is an ambitious country and in the thirties she got the idea that she wanted to become a big nation. She put on long pants before she became of age. She wanted an army, she wanted a navy and all the trimmings. How she might have gotten on if World War II had not come along we do not know. But like other countries, the blast of war hit her, and today she is left in an exhausted position, struggling for her life, and her financial bloodstream is fast running dry. As I said, she is begging Uncle Sam for dollars and her people are on the rocky road of austerity. ...

I have lived in Canada and worked there from coast to coast. I like Canada, it is a great country, but after living and working there, I want to give it as an honest opinion, that if confederation were good for Newfoundland there would not be a stronger supporter of it in Newfoundland today, but I am honest in my opinion when I say that confederation will be the worst thing that ever struck Newfoundland ... Canada is in a worse position financially than Newfoundland ... We are not begging for dollars, all we are trying to do is keep people from plundering our treasury. We can sympathise with Canada in her present plight, just as any other allies made prosperous by the war, but nevertheless we must remember that charity begins at home, and our first duty and our first obligation we owe to ourselves, our families, our children and our children's children ... Canada is well aware, as we are, that if she can take over Newfoundland she can richly benefit by our assets. For instance, if she controlled our rich Labrador possession, it would in a few years place her in a position where she could get all these American dollars which she urgently needs ...

I would ask you to believe me when I say that I have not said these things merely to make a case for responsible government, or because I am against confederation with Canada. I have made my criticisms against these terms as a Newfoundlander rather than a politician—as a Newfoundlander who sees in them a threat to his people and his country, who sees hidden in their beguiling phrases nothing less than an invitation to national disaster. For I say that I was never as certain of anything in my life, as I am of the worthlessness of these so-called Canadian terms ...

To those who, like myself, recognise the fact that the only proper and decent course open to us is to become masters in our own house, no further words of mine are necessary. But to those who may be beguiled to any degree by this confederation mirage, I say do nothing further—make no new steps. Do not consider any negotiations until, as a first step, you have a duly authorised government of your own to consider the whole matter. Any other course is sheer political madness. That is my solemn advice to you. Whether you take it or not rests with yourselves. And if we delegates have failed to carry that one message to the people who sent us here, then I say we have failed dismally in our duty.

In closing I would ask your permission to express a purely personal opinion. I am convinced that although our country and our people are at present enshrouded in a pall of political darkness, they will eventually find their way into the light. This whole matter of bribes and promises will in the end be shown up for what it really is. And I say this not because our people would shrink from the new burden of taxation which confederation with Canada will place on their shoulders, not because of the vision of the thousands of homesteads which may have to be sold to satisfy the Canadian tax gatherers. No. It will not be for these things alone, that our people will spurn this offer for them to sell out the land of their birth. I say our people will win through because of other, greater things. They will triumph, emerge from this ordeal, because there are still in this country such things as pride, courage and faith. Pride in the great traditions which have come down to us through the centuries of independent living. Courage to face up to life and hew out our individual fortunes. And finally faith in our country, and in the great destiny which I am convinced lies ahead of us ...

To trifle with a people and a country, to compromise the lives of future generations, are no small things. Yet that is the very thing that is now being attempted, to the end that we shall cease to exist as an independent country, and that Newfoundlanders shall be no longer Newfoundlanders. ... Does not all this confederation business come down to a matter of a cold, commercial business deal, whereby we were asked to sell out our country and our future to Canada for a certain sum of money? And speaking of this attitude, I confess it seems to me to be a terribly serious thing for any country or any people to place themselves in the balance against the pull of Canadian dollars. What is the price, or shall I say the bribe, they offer us? The prize bait seems to be that a certain number of our people will get this thing called the baby bonus. But do they tell us that this baby bonus is an unsubstantial thing, that it is something that we cannot depend upon? That it may vanish overnight, and that in the event of a depression in Canada it will die a quick death? Indeed, my own personal opinion is that it will not exist longer than two years. Do they tell us that when our babies reach the age of 16 they will spend the rest of their lives paying back to the Canadian government the amount of their bonus? Do they tell us that when our babies reach military age they will almost certainly be conscripted into the Canadian military forces? Do they tell us that in the event of confederation a big percentage of these young people will have to emigrate from this country to seek employment which cannot be found at home? Of course they do not tell us those things, because they know, and know well, that if we saw the truth of these things this baby bonus would be no longer able to bluff and deceive us ...

Soon I trust, Mr. Chairman, our people will be called upon to once again mark their cross upon a national ballot paper ... That "X" will be written by every real Newfoundlander on a day not too far distant. It too will indicate, if correctly placed, our love and our affection for the land of our birth. I ask you gentlemen to ponder and hesitate before you make that little mark by which you, your children, and your children's children can be blessed or blasted. That cross must be the kiss of love given by every loyal citizen to our own mother— Newfoundland. Take care, I say, that it is placed with zeal and loyalty just where it belongs, just where she wishes it, and tremble like Iscariot ere you place it on your own shame and future despair, in the place that means your traitorous denial of your mother country's best interests ... once done it cannot be undone. It is final, irrevocable and unchangeable ...

3. F. Gordon Bradley.

... While the people were expecting what was their undoubted right, a straightforward and impartial and co-operative discussion of what confederation would mean to them, they were treated instead to a senseless barrage of heated misrepresentation and distortion, to pretty prejudice and personal antagonism. The Convention became a veritable battleground. Instead of making an effort to understand the terms and make them plain to our people, some members seemed determined to make it appear that confederation is such a complicated and confused question that nobody in or out of the Convention could possibly understand it ...

Now there is a very urgent need indeed that in the interests of clear thinking a number of misconceptions that have grown up or been thrown up around this whole question should be corrected. Amongst these, sir, is the utterly foolish notion that the very fact that we are discussing confederation at all is the result of a breach of faith by Britain, that if she had carried out her obligation to us no confederation question would have arisen at all. Great currency has been given to this notion. Indeed it has been actively and sedulously circulated. This notion has grown into the more vicious and equally unfounded charge that Britain is false, that Britain is not to be trusted, that Britain is trying to cheat us out of our rights, including the right of responsible government, that Britain is actively plotting to thrust us into confederation whether we want it or not, that Britain is plotting to retain Commission government. In fact about the only political crime that is not charged up to Britain today is that of trying to foist responsible government on us. It is in no way surprising, therefore, to find that almost invariably, if not exclusively, every one of these charges is voiced by a supporter of responsible government.

Now what are the bases of these charges? The argument runs something like this: in 1933–34 the British government promised that when Newfoundland became self-supporting responsible government would be restored if the people wanted it. Newfoundland is now technically self-supporting, and it remains therefore only for Britain to give us back responsible government and clear out. "Give us back what we had, give us back responsible government," that is the cry. What are the real facts? It is quite true that the British government of 1933 did promise to restore responsible government to Newfoundland if and when she became self-supporting, and if the people requested it. Of that there can be no doubt whatever, and it is also true that Newfoundland, at least in the official sense, is self-supporting today—we do not presently require grants from Britain to pay our government bills. But just where and how has that promise of Britain been broken? Is there not to be a national referendum? Are not the people of Newfoundland to vote at that referendum? Will not responsible government be one of the forms for which they may vote on the ballot at that referendum? And if the people of Newfoundland, by a majority, request a return of responsible government does anyone here suggest that Britain will refuse to carry out that wish? Where, I ask you, is the broken promise? What then is it that rouses the ire of these responsible governmentites almost to the pitch of frenzy? I will tell you. It is not that Britain has failed to carry out that promise of 1933, but that she has done more than honour what these people are pleased to term her bond. She has not only undertaken to give us back responsible government if we want it, but also to give us any other form of government (within reason, of course) which we may request.

Let me put the position to you by a very simple illustration. Let us suppose a man takes his young son to a house which he, the father, owns, and says, "Son, when you are 21 years of age I will give you this house if you want it." The boy reaches the age of 21, and the father now says to him, "Son, some years ago I promised you this house if you asked me for it when you became 21. You are now 21, and I intend to keep my promise, but before you ask me for it I want to show you two other houses that I own." Thereupon he shows the young man these two other houses, and says, "Now you can have your choice of the three." Has that man broken his promise to his son? He has not, he has enlarged it, he has extended it. In exactly the same way Britain has fulfilled her so-called bond to the people of Newfoundland. She says to us, in effect, "You Newfoundland people may have a return of responsible government if you want it, or if you prefer you may have Commission government, or confederation; or tell me what you do want and I will give you anything within reason." ...

Sir, I wonder if those who visualise the making of the terms of federal union as something akin to the chattering of a housewife over a basket of vegetables in the marketplace, I wonder if they appreciate the true Canada of today? Do they realise that this Canada is a great and a generous nation, the third largest exporting country in the world, whose generous policy towards the mother country, both during the war and ever since, is eloquent testimony not only to her great wealth, but to her realisation of the high moral obligation which rests upon her as a member of the Commonwealth. While the conflict was in progress she gave and loaned to Britain literally thousands of millions of dollars, and since then she has continued that policy, as well as the policy of supplying that war-torn and impoverished land with millions of tons of food at amazingly low prices. And yet this is the country that the anticonfederates would liken unto a housewife haggling over a basket of potatoes. Don't they realise that confederation is not the making of a merely commercial bargain between a couple of private businessmen? Confederation is a proposal for political union. A partnership between Newfoundland and Canada presupposes that we shall become one more among the provinces that constitute that union.

Far from being a trading corporation, those nine provinces are bound together by a constitution known as the British North America Act. This act, which was passed by the British Parliament 80 years ago, lays down the terms and conditions of that union, and this act must govern the entry of any country into that union, be it Newfoundland or any other. Confederation therefore is not a case of a couple of businessmen driving a bargain; it is not a case of a couple of horsetraders, each trying to outsmart the other; it is not a matter of haggling, or bargaining, or even negotiating, except in the very broadest and loosest sense of that term. It is a case of ascertaining what are the terms of union as laid down by the British North America Act, and by the various regulations and agreements having their roots in that act. Nor can the federal government discriminate against, or unduly favour any province or proposed province. It has a duty not to unduly favour any province at the expense of others. All that any delegation, whether it be from an elected government or from this Convention can do, is to learn the limits of what is possible under Canada's constitution ...

Only once in our history has the question of confederation been submitted to our people. That was in 1869, two years after the then four British colonies on the mainland were united to form Canada. The Canadian union was then in its experimental stage, and there was no certainty that it would succeed or even survive. It lacked financial strength, the prairies were unpopulated, the transcontinental railway not even contemplated, and the country's economy almost entirely agricultural. Here in Newfoundland our people were uneducated. Few ever saw a newspaper. There was no radio. The whole question of confederation was deliberately turned into a political squabble. The anticonfederate party was led by a great merchant who spared no expense to win. An army of party hacks were sent around the Island to poison the people's minds against confederation. These henchmen traded on the people's ignorance and assured them that their property would be taxed—their homes, their furniture, their gardens, boats, flakes, stages, fishing gear, their poultry and animals, the very panes of glass in their homes. A horde of Canadian tax-gatherers would swarm over the land, the anticonfederates declared, and woe betide the unfortunates who didn't have the hard cash to pay up, for the hungry tax collectors would seize their property, put them on the street. Canada would seize their young men to fight her wars, and their bones would be left to bleach on the desert sands of Canada. Their very babies would be used as gun-wads in the Canadian cannon ... There was no secret ballot in those days. There was no manhood suffrage. There was no woman's vote at all. The unfortunate voter had to declare his vote aloud in the presence of the party agent—often the employee of the local merchant, and it was a bold man who would brave the anger of his supplier in those semi-feudal days. As we look back upon that story of 1869, it is difficult to believe that any men voted for confederation; but thousands did, and it is of tremendous significance that out of 30 members elected to the House of Assembly, ten were confederates.

How vastly different is the whole prospect today. Canada is a rich and powerful nation—no longer a strange and foreign land, but a friendly neighbour in which many thousands of our own Newfoundland people are prospering at this very moment. And our Newfoundland people are educated today, they are better informed, they read the newspaper and magazines, they have radios, they have relatives and friends in Canada. No longer are they under the thumb of anyone, merchant or otherwise. They have full manhood suffrage, both men and women. And they have the secret ballot. And, sir, they have something more: they have experience of two forms of government, Commission and responsible.

There is, however, one thing which has not changed. The same policy of twisting and distorting and misrepresenting the facts is again to be seen. The tax scare, which worked so well in 1869, is again put to work.

But these despicable political dodges are a bit stale and ineffectual, and so the anticonfederates have coined a new one, the Labrador scare. "If we become part of Canada, Quebec will chisel us out of Labrador." Sir, these men in their desperation forget that our people know full well that Labrador was awarded to Newfoundland by the Judicial Committee of the Privy Council, and that there is no way whatever to upset that award ...

Notice, please, that it is not a case either of annexation or absorption or taking over. We go in as a partner, retaining our own identity, governing ourselves as to local matters, and sharing in the government of all Canada in matters of national interest. We will retain our own legislature right here in St. John's, with which nobody will interfere. We will also send elected members to represent us in the Canadian House of Commons, just as each province now does. We will not be a dependency without a word in our cheeks, but a partner with a full voice in Canada's councils, and complete control of local Newfoundland affairs.

Eighty years ago it might have been sound to say that to join in the union then would have been risky. The union had no assurance of success or even of continued existence. Today the prospect is far different. Those four weak provinces have grown and expanded into a mighty nation whose institutions have a world reputation for soundness and stability, and whose social, commercial and financial services are in the front rank of sane, modern development, and whose standard of living is far ahead of ours. If you doubt this latter statement, ask the people of the southwest coast, and of Labrador and northern Newfoundland, who are in constant touch with Canada. Truly, Canada has proved that in union there is strength, and it would now appear inevitable that had we joined the union in 1869, the Newfoundland people would be better off today. Of course the standard of living is higher in some parts of Canada than in other parts, just as in Newfoundland the people of the paper towns are better situated than those of the fishing settlements. These variations are inevitable in any country, as they depend on the resources of the particular locality. But there is no province of Canada which cannot show a better standard of living than we have experienced. That is a definite result of union, the system of taxation and distribution of revenue, and the power which the united provinces wield in the world. The individual provinces don't count for very much, but when Canada speaks the nations of the world listen.

Under confederation we would be relieved of the cost of many public services which at present are a terrible load for this little country to carry. We would be relieved of that terrible but necessary burden, the railway. The postal, airport and veterans' services would be taken off our shoulders and improved. In the field of social service we would enjoy the benefits of family allowances, old age pensions, unemployment insurance and sick mariners' and fishermen's hospitalisation.

I have heard some strange pronouncements voiced both in and out of this chamber within the past couple of months, but none more curious than the assertions that Newfoundlanders were lazy and that family allowances were immoral, degrading and would result in people ceasing to earn a living. The first of these statements I pass by as beneath contempt. But the latter cannot be allowed to go unchallenged. Family allowances are paid by the Canadian government to every child in Canada (and that would include Newfoundland if our people chose confederation) from birth to the age of 16 years. The amount varies according to age from $5 to $8 per month for each child, or from $60 to $96 per year per child. The purpose is obvious. It is to ensure that every child in Canada shall have as far as possible appropriate food, sufficient clothing and education, notwithstanding that its parents are not prosperous. And, in order that the stigma of pauperism might not attach to the payments, these allowances are payable to all children, rich and poor alike ...

- Because confederation will reduce the cost of living for our people and raise their standard of living;
- Because confederation will reduce the burden of taxation on our people and apportion the burden more fairly amongst them;
- Because confederation will give our people social services such as no other form of government would give them;
- Because confederation will provide our people with wider opportunities of employment;
- Because confederation will provide our people with greatly improved railway and other transportation services;
- Because confederation will stabilise government revenues by means of definite federal cash grants;
- Because confederation will make Newfoundland one of the family of Canadian provinces and bring her into union with the great, wealthy

and growing Canadian nation, which has flourished under union
while we have marched with snail's pace under isolation;

• Because of these irresistible benefits offered our struggling people, sir,
I am a confederate.

4. G.F. Higgins.

With respect to union with the States. As we are aware, there does exist a very
definite wish amongst a number of our countrymen that the ballot at the referendum should include union with the United States. It is too late now for this
Convention to explore the possibility of union with that great country, and
consequently the Convention will be unable to recommend that this form of
government be placed on the ballot. Whilst it is quite definite that the future
economic security of Newfoundland makes it essential that we have a definite
arrangement with the United States, this now must be left for an elected government to handle. If this country were to federate with Canada, the opportunity to
negotiate with the United States for trade concessions would be impossible, and
any wish to join in union with the United States would be lost forever. Most
thinking people agree that at some time in the future the North American continent will be in union. That is, the United States will assimilate Canada. The
time when such union takes place may be greatly accelerated by world events.
What a position to bargain Newfoundland would be in, if she was independent
when such union takes place!

In mentioning the United States, another most important matter in considering confederation with Canada arises. We have listened for many, many
months to the advantages of joining with this land of heart's desire—Canada.
Would Mr. Smallwood in his reply care to state why so many Canadians are
leaving Canada to reside in the United States? In the 90 years between 1851 and
1941, 6,700,000 people immigrated to Canada. With all the hard work put in
by the Canadian government, and all the money spent in 90 years to encourage
immigration, the net gain was 400,000 people. In the last boom period from
1920 to 1930, Canada lost some 500,000 of her citizens to the United States, an
average of 50,000 a year. Since the end of the war in Europe in 1945, it is stated
that about 40,000 Canadians per year have made applications to emigrate to the
United States. How many Canadians go across the border without being granted
permission is impossible to estimate. It is stated that two-thirds of all those
emigrating to the United States from Canada are under 37 years of age. Due to
United States immigration requirements, those granted permission are usually a

picked group, and the result is Canada is losing her best type of citizens, the thrifty and better-trained people. The chief reason for the immigration appears to be the better wages paid in the United States. The earnings in manufacturing in the United States averaged $1.20 per hour to the Canadian 78 cents per hour. The statement that the increased wages in the United States is equalised by the higher cost of living does not appear to be correct. It would appear that for the same standard of living of a middle-income group, the weekly expenditure for cost of living is $5 higher in the States but wages are $20 higher per week there than in Canada. The reasons given for the difference in the wage scale is that business firms in Canada cannot afford to pay the same wages as paid in the United States. This argument, however, should not apply to the pulp and paper industry in which the Canadians believe they lead the world. In this industry, the average hourly earnings of pulp and paper workers in Canada is 85 cents and in the United States $1.43. The real reason however, for this difference in wages is not in industry, but in the Canadian people themselves, because of what they pay their citizens in Canadian schools, colleges and the civil service ...

5. G. Macdonald.

... but judging wholly by the evidence before us, I have come to the personal conclusion that federal union with Canada is the most acceptable form of government for Newfoundland out of the three choices before us, and the one which will be in the best interests of our country and for the following reasons:

1. We will not forfeit the democratic way of life we talk so much about; no person can reasonably think that the Canadian way of life is not democratic.

2. Federal union with Canada will reduce our cost of living generally. I think that must be admitted.

3. Federal union will do the greatest good for the greatest number; which I am sure is or should be the object of all the members of this Convention. It will place the burden of taxation where it belongs, on the shoulders of those who have the capacity to pay. It will give our people social security in the way of old age pensions to an extent which we have been unable to reach either under our own government or Commission in the past, and I doubt if we could ever hope to reach to that extent in the future under the governments I have mentioned.

Federal union will give us the benefits which family allowances will bring, not only directly to the persons concerned, but indirectly in the way of general business. It is estimated that 120,000 children under the age of 16 would be eligible for the family allowances. At an average of $72 per child per year, this would amount to $8,640,000. It is also estimated that the number of persons over 70 is 10,000. When we allow that 7,000 of these are eligible for pensions at $30 per month, this would amount to another $2.5 million. Making a grand total of over $11 million per year put into circulation in this country each year in these two services alone—and that's no chicken-feed, sir, despite the criticisms levelled against it. It has been stated that we will have to pay for these services. Of course we will have to pay our proportional share as a province, but we will have the help of about 12 million people in doing it. The point is, could we ever hope to accomplish this on our own?

Federal union will also bring us unemployment benefits, ...

Federal union would provide the same facilities to us as enjoyed by Canadian citizens in all nine provinces, viz. that of having free entry to other provinces for our people, particularly our young people who may wish a wider field of endeavour in their chosen professions or trades and not be treated as foreigners and admitted on a quota. It will not be the first time in our history that through depression or other causes, our people have been forced to seek work elsewhere, in times when there were not jobs enough even to go around; from what I can hear there are not enough jobs even now to carry our people over, in spite of an expression made in this Convention in connection with a certain place that there was plenty of work, if the people were not too lazy to look for it.

Mr. Chairman, we have increasing numbers of young people graduating from Memorial University. What have we to offer them in Newfoundland in order that they may carry on their chosen careers? Federal union will give them an opportunity on an equality with the young people of our neighbouring dominion to go forward in their various professions. If we cannot provide sufficient employment for our growing population, let us then in the name of goodness try and clear the way for them to seek it elsewhere ...

6. H. Harrington.

... I have said that confederation would mean a fundamental change in our national life. That need not be a bad thing necessarily. But it can be a bad thing, and will be if the people of this country are stampeded into such a union against what would be, under other circumstances, their better judgement.

What seems to be overlooked in this whole affair is that to be a success and a good thing for Newfoundland, confederation must work, and work a whole lot more smoothly than it does in the Maritime Provinces, for example. For these provinces are part and parcel of confederation, they grew up with it and within it. We have remained aloof until now, and in the meantime we have labouriously built up a country, a culture, traditions, faiths, hopes and, indeed, a certain kind of charity and a hospitableness that is unique. We are as separate a race of people, with ideas and standards of our own, as different from the Canadians as the Canadians are from the Americans. The adjustment of our whole lives, and our outlook on life, government, religion, everything would be a tremendous and shaking process. We might easily never become emotionally, psychologically or mentally adjusted to living under confederation at this stage in our development as a separate people, and might end up as the last and most neurotic and hard-to-live-with member of the confederation family. For a period now of 14 years, over three ordinary parliamentary government administrations, we have been without a vote or a voice in the control of our own affairs. To rush into confederation at this time would be to wake up tomorrow to find we had a vote and a voice—but that the control of our affairs, at a time when that control could be used to immense advantage to ourselves, is gone forever to a capital 2,000 miles away where our faint protests would fail to reach; of if they did, would fall on deaf ears ...

7. I. Keough.

... There is one further matter that should give us cause for concern in considering this whole matter of union, and that is whether union would prejudice the survival of a distinctive national culture and civilisation that we should seek to maintain. There are people in this island to whom the whole confederation issue is like a red rag to a bull, and for about much the same reason they just don't like it no how. Mention confederation, and they'll rant and they'll roar in the approved grand manner about 30 pieces of silver, and niggers in the woodpile, and selling our sacred heritage up the St. Lawrence. Indeed, there has been so much of that sort of thing going on both within and without this Convention that one has to pause to enquire if perhaps there might be a modicum of truth in it all. I must confess that I am not too clear as to just exactly what the poets and the politicians have in mind when they take to being sentimental over our sacred heritage. I remember that I did one time see a fisherman's wife shovel fish guts into a brin bag and spell it on her back to her gardens a mile away. I feel certain that that is not what they have in mind by our sacred heritage. I remember that I did one time spend February in a most picturesque little cottage nailed to a cliff beside the sea. I didn't get warm for a month, and I feel certain that the people living there didn't get warm for the winter. I feel that that is not the sacred heritage over which our poets work themselves up into ecstasies, and over which our politicians work themselves into a lather. Indeed, it must be something altogether different than the most of what one comes across in making the rounds of this country. But if by our sacred heritage the poets and the politicians mean that we know in this island a culture and civilisation so different, and so much more advanced than the culture and civilisation of the North American mainland that they are worth any sacrifice to preserve them, they had better stop wool-gathering on Mount Olympus, and come down and walk among the people and learn how the people live. You know, it could be that the best authority on the desirability of baby bonuses would be the people who have the babies.

I have come to conclude that there would not be involved in confederation any issue of the preservation of a distinct national culture and civilisation. Now that is not to say, mind you, that we have not evolved our own customs, our own institutions, our own peculiar way of life. We have. It so happens that we are the inheritors of what I have sometimes called a fish and brewis culture, ... Of that fish and brewis culture I am as proud as any Newfoundlander. It is true that we are the inheritors of a great national tradition of bravery against the seas, of heroism defying the sea to do its worst—bravery and heroism exemplified for all time on a bleak October day on the bleak Labrador coast when a man named Jackman did 27 times head into the storm and 27 times come ashore with a human life on his back. It is true that in this land we are the inheritors of a great Christian tradition; that at the end of every week, after we have braved the sea and dug the land and cut the pulpwood, we do still after the manner of our fathers land gather in a thousand churches to pray as our fathers prayed ... All these things are true. It is true too that all these things can remain to be so in the event of confederation. The things dearest to our hearts in this land will not in the event of union be at issue. I give it to you as my considered opinion, for what it is worth, that if the confederation alternate shall come to confront us in the referendum, that there shall be involved therein no issue involving our distinct character as Newfoundlanders, no issue involving our national honour, no issue involving our distinct culture and way of life ...

8. J. Roberts.

Mr. Chairman, I wish to state that I will vote for the motion before the Chair. I feel in duty bound to do so, in view of the fact that many thousands of Newfoundlanders wish to vote for confederation. I wish also to state I hold no brief for the people of St. Barbe district, which I represent, as to how they will vote. They will do as they please. I have only one vote, and will do as I please with it. But I would like to tell all anticonfederates that if confederation does not go on the ballot paper, the people of the northwest coast will vote overwhelmingly for Commission of Government. The mention of responsible government stinks with them. After neglect by all responsible governments, and despite all the sentimental poppycock that some of our so-called patriotic Newfoundlanders have been getting off their chests here the past few days, and despite all the taxations they have been hearing about, they know what to expect from responsible government and they are willing to take a chance on confederation. You don't have to take my word for it, let any man who wishes to find out take a trip down that coast and talk about the glories of responsible government; but I warn him to have a plane standing by so as to make a quick getaway, especially if he should tell them they were disloyal or unpatriotic ...

Dozens of my relatives and friends, after vainly trying to make a living, have gathered together a bit of money with the help of their relatives abroad and travelled to Canada. Ask these people if they wish to come back to the living conditions they left, and they would surely think it quite a joke. My own mother, widowed in the early years of her marriage, left with three small children and little means of support, struggled for three or four years to keep her family together and maintain them; she had to give it up, give away her children, and on the advice of a relative in Canada went there and made a comfortable living. So I have a warm spot in my heart for the country which befriended my mother, above all other people on this earth.

We people on the west and northwest coasts have been in close contact with Canadians, both fishermen and financiers, for years and years, and have not found them the big bad wolves that the people in the interior and on the east coast seem to think they are. Surely, so many of our people would not stay in Canada if they were so tax-ridden as some people try to make us believe they are. As I said before, the people of the west coast who have been in close contact with Canadians all their lives, must certainly regard the ravings that have been going on here about all thing Canadian as pure and simple stuff and nonsense.

I wish to touch briefly on two very much ridiculed subjects, namely family allowances and old age pensions. I have in mind a family not far from my home; a man with ten children and a sick wife. You can imagine, or can you, the awful struggle that man is having to make a living. I wonder would he scoff at a family allowance of $60 a month, would he worry about the dozens of taxes on a loaf of bread, if under confederation, he would get his flour for $12 a barrel, when he is paying $22 for it in Bonne Bay today? Would he worry about the hundreds of taxes on a pair of shoes, when under confederation he would be able to buy three pairs in the place of the two pairs he buys today? Boots and bread, sir, take a very large slice out of his budget. His fish he can get a scant half mile from his door, and his vegetables can be grown around his home. If he does pay property taxes, which he knows he is likely to pay, they will be small on his acre of land and his small unfinished, unfurnished home. He is paying plenty now, far more than his pocket can stand. He is not worrying either about the man who can afford to drive a motor car, own a fine house, he figures the man can well afford under confederation to pay his taxes and help pay some for him as well.

Old age pensions. I have in mind an old couple nearly 80 years of age each, living alone, getting very little help from relatives, trying to live on their old age pension. That man still has to go in the fishing boat to try and earn a few dollars to augment his pension. What a help it would be to receive $60 a month instead of the $10 they receive today. His property would not exceed $1,500, and even if it did exceed $2,000 and under Canadian rule the government did take it, would not they be entitled to it after his family had forsaken them and let the government look after them? I think they would have a perfect right to it, and I feel sure the old couple would think so too. The old age pensioners of New-foundland need not worry about the government taking their property. Very few of them whom I have seen in the outports have property over $2,000, and if they have, they would not receive old age pensions. I have made out quite a number of applications the past 20 years. I have a good idea of their property value. I am not going to touch on other taxations, this has been ably and thoroughly gone into by other speakers.

There will, no doubt, be many changes and adjustments in the event of union, especially in the business world. But my thought about all that is, if our business men cannot adjust themselves to competition, they are not the men I take them to be. The proper thing to happen to them is to fold up. But don't worry, Water Street of St. John's, and all the little Water Streets of the outports, will be carrying on under confederation when I am drawing my old age pension.

And please don't let some people make you believe the only reason Canada wants Newfoundland is to make a fortune out of us, and for the inhumane purpose of starving to death our 300,000 people. That has not been the history of the democratic government of Canada. In my opinion Newfoundland has nothing to lose and very much to gain by closer contact with our neighbour, Canada, which fact will strengthen our bargaining power which members like to talk so much about. In union is strength. So let's hope Newfoundlanders will remember that at the referendum. I will, by voting for confederation.

Readings

Blake, R. *Canadians at Last: Canada Integrates Newfoundland as a Province.* Toronto: University of Toronto Press, 1994.

Chadwick, S. *Island into Province.* Cambridge: Cambridge University Press, 1967.

Fitzgerald, J. "The Newfoundland Referenda Campaigns of 1948," *Beaver* (February-March, 1998).

Fitzgerald, J. "Newfoundland Politics and Confederation Revisited," *Newfoundland Studies* 9, 1 (1993).

Gilmore, W. "Law, Constitutional Convention, and the Union of Newfoundland and Canada," *Acadiensis* (Spring, 1989).

Gwyn, R. *Smallwood: The Unlikely Revolutionary.* Revised edition. Toronto: McClelland and Stewart, 1972.

Hiller, J. "Newfoundland Confronts Canada, 1867–1949," in E. Forbes and D. Muise, eds. *The Atlantic Provinces in Confederation.* Toronto: University of Toronto Press, 1993.

Hiller, J., and P. Neary, eds. *Newfoundland in the Nineteenth and Twentieth Centuries: Essays in Interpretation.* Toronto: University of Toronto Press, 1980.

Horwood, H. *Joey: The Life and Political Times of Joey Smallwood.* Toronto: Stoddart, 1969.

Long, G. *Suspended State: Newfoundland Before Confederation.* St. John's: Breakwater Press, 1999.

Mackenzie, D. *Inside the Atlantic Triangle: Canada and the Entrance of Newfoundland into Confederation, 1939–1949.* Toronto: University of Toronto Press, 1986.

MacLeod, M. *Peace of the Continent: The Impact of Second World War Canadian and American Bases in Newfoundland.* St. John's: H. Cuff, 1986.

McCann, P. "Confederation Revisited: New Light on British Policy," *Newfoundland Studies* 14, 2 (1998).

Neary, P. *Newfoundland and the North Atlantic World 1929–1949.* Montreal and Kingston: McGill-Queen's University Press, 1988.

Neary, P. "Newfoundland's Union with Canada: Conspiracy or Choice," *Acadiensis* 12, 2 (Spring, 1983).

Neary, P., ed. *The Political Economy of Newfoundland 1929–1972.* Toronto: Copp Clark, 1973.

Noel, S. *Politics in Newfoundland.* Toronto: University of Toronto Press, 1971.

Walsh, B. *More than a Poor Majority: The Story of Newfoundland's Confederation with Canada.* St. John's: Breakwater, 1985.

Webb, J. "Responsible Government League and the Confederation Campaigns of 1948," *Newfoundland Studies* 5, 2 (1989).

Webb, J. "Confederation, Conspiracy and Choice: A Discussion," *Newfoundland Studies* 14, 2 (1998).

Chapter Thirteen

"A Glow of Fulfilled Femininity": Women in the 1950s and 1960s

1. Beverly Gray, "Housewives Are a Sorry Lot," *Chatelaine*, March 1950.
2. "Housewives Blast Business Girl," *Chatelaine*, June 1950.
3. Doris McCubbin, "How to Live in a Suburb," *Chatelaine*, March 1955.
4. Dr. Marion Hilliard, "Stop Being Just a Housewife," *Chatelaine*, September 1956.
5. Cynthia Steers, "How Much are You Worth to Your Husband?," *Chatelaine*, April 1959.
6. Anna Davies, "I Hate Housekeeping," *Chatelaine*, March 1961.
7. Mollie Gillen, "The Royal Commission on the Status of Women: Will it do any Good?" *Chatelaine*, January 1968.

Introduction

Second wave feminism burst onto the Canadian scene with such unexpected vehemence and vigour that the federal government, in 1967, called a Royal Commission on the Status of Women to examine the issue. Since tectonic shifts of this type do not occur in a vacuum, historians have subsequently wondered why Women's Liberation occurred at that specific point in time and with such force. The 1960s was a time of considerable social upheaval, and some pundits suggested that the new wave of feminism simply rode that tidal wave of discontent. That explanation, however, proved insufficient. The apparent disjunction between the feminist anger of the 1960s and the maternal bliss of the 1950s was particularly puzzling. How, people asked, could the happy cookie-making June Cleaver of the '50s suddenly metamorphose into the raging feminist of the '60s? That question, of course, led historians to reevaluate the 1950s. Research now suggests that, despite the appearances to the contrary, Canadian women actually found considerable fault in both the mythology and reality of that decade, but felt their voices censored until the climate became more conducive to revolt—which it did in the 1960s.

The 1950s were, at least superficially, very good for Canada. The Second World War had partially receded into memory, and Canadian industry worked at full capacity to fill orders from a world rebuilding. Jobs were plentiful and well paid, standards of living rose dramatically, taxes and mortgages remained low, and a pervasive sense of optimism suffused the country. The size of the middle class consequently grew enormously, and hundreds of thousands of formerly marginalized Canadians reached for the Canadian dream. That dream, similar to America's, revolved around owning a detached house, purchasing the plethora of new consumer goods, keeping kids in school past grade eight, annual vacations, and having mom stay at home. A married woman's place, according to the ideal social conventions of the day, was not in the paid workforce, but instead in one of the many new suburbs built for freshly minted middle-class Canadians and their desire for respectable inclusion. There, she was to create her familial nest while dad worked downtown and the kids attended school. This image pervaded the North American psyche, promoted by the popular new mass medium, television. American shows beamed into Canada, like "Leave it to Beaver" and "Father Knows Best," became icons of the decade, their stereotypical descriptions of middle-class suburban life further strengthened by the messages in the frequent commercial breaks.

Despite the seductive promise of suburban coziness, however, there was a dark side to the '50s, one that society subconsciously and consciously hid because it threatened the apple pie image. Life for women in particular, was not all it was cracked up to be. Suburbia, with its much-lauded benefits, suffered a number of very serious and unforeseen shortcomings, the brunt of which women bore. A key issue was the housewife's loneliness. Women now had their own homes and gardens, true, but separate from their neighbours, both emotionally and physically. The kids were in school during the day, and husbands commuted to work. Thus the only daytime company came from radio and television, with its increasingly hollow middle-class boosterism, or from other housewives in the same boat. No one, of course, admitted to being lonely because that suggested a fundamental personal failing.

Canadian women experienced other unexpected problems in the '50s. Modern appliances, for example, turned out to be double-edged swords. They supposedly did away with the drudgery of housework, and indeed helped enormously. Compare an electric wringer-washer, after all, to heating water on the stove and using a washboard. How about a vacuum cleaner to the broom, the electric refrigerator to the icebox, and the electric range to the wood stove? The problem was, however, that the new technology facilitated heretofore impossible standards of cleanliness, and a consequent diminution of what was formerly acceptable. Housewives' work actually increased in some areas as they now strove to match June Cleaver's spotless home, or to conform to standards set by cleaning product advertisements in popular women's magazines. Appliances did indeed liberate time, but not nearly as much as expected, and they created their own relentless tyranny.

Social conformity also became an unexpected problem for the new suburban housewife. Suburbia, with its homogenous physical layout, narrow demographic background, and lack of history, helped generate a sub-current of uniformity that stifled individualism and creativity. The sad irony was that housewives now had the time to nurture their individuality, but found doing so unacceptable.

Other issues plagued Canadian women in the 1950s. The law remained paternalistic, calculated to side with men in cases of divorce, property or custodial rights, rights over children, and employment and pension eligibility. A woman's body remained controlled by a male dominated state that refused her access to abortion and tried to manage birth control as well. Equality in the workforce, either in pay or opportunity, was nonexistent and many institutions, such as the federal government, refused to hire married women.

Enormously popular during this period, the Canadian women's magazine *Chatelaine* was in fact, years ahead of its American counterparts in discussing issues such as suburban boredom, women's sexuality, abortion, birth control, women's legal rights, lesbianism, and issues of gender equality. This was unheard of in a mass circulation magazine, if for no other reason than some of the advice went counter to the message the magazine's advertisers promoted. Nor was it merely middle-class suburban housewives who subscribed. Records show that some 70% of the readership was lower middle class and 30% rural, and that women from all ethnic backgrounds and all regions of the country bought it and made it part of their community. Impassioned letters to the editor plus the significant circulation clearly indicate that *Chatelaine* was an important magazine for a segment of the population. Editor Doris Anderson's feminist campaign did not receive universal support from her readers. What most women appreciated, however, was that Anderson's regular lead editorial columns asked them to think for themselves. Canadian women became used to Anderson's pen, often directed at what she perceived as the complacency of women themselves, and a decade of such thought-provoking material helped build the foundation for Canadian second wave feminism of the 1960s and 1970s.

Discussion Points

1. How significant were the differences between women who stayed at home and those who worked? Would this remain a problem in uniting women into a single, coherent movement?
2. Were the problems of the suburban housewife significant or merely so many tempests in teapots?
3. Who were more likely to become feminists—frustrated housewives or ambitious business women?

Documents

1. Beverly Gray, "Housewives Are a Sorry Lot," *Chatelaine*, March 1950.

Get mad if you like. But somewhere in this article there's a truth for every one of us.

Beverly Gray, a business girl, looks over her married friends, shudders, takes a reef in her girdle and strikes out with these observations:

Marriage brings almost a full stop in mental development.

As soon as the wedding is over a woman drops phoney interests in such things as sports, politics and world events.

Her life channels into a narrow domestic little tunnel.

A girl expects her husband to be a combination of Ronald Colman, Gregory Peck and Humphrey Bogart.

Chat with any housewife and she's sure to bring the conversation round to how terribly frustrated she is.

If the individual housewife is a saddening sight, housewives in the mass are appalling.

YOU CAN'T SAY: "She is a housewife, so she is blond." You can't say: "She is a housewife, so she is fat." You can't even say: "She is a housewife, so she is a good cook." But nine times out of 10 you can say: "She is a housewife, so she is unhappy."

Young or old, fat or thin, pretty or homely, a housewife is not a happy person. She is miserable, frustrated, underprivileged, abused and oppressed. Nobody loves her and she hasn't any money. Chat with any housewife for five minutes, and she will tell you how she suffers.

She has three main complaints: poverty, loneliness and drudgery. Of these, poverty is the most deadly, not because she actually goes around naked and undernourished, but because poverty is a weapon with which she can beat her husband literally into the grave. A housewife, like a baby, is quick to learn: she soon finds that if she talks long enough and loud enough and often enough about what other husbands give their wives, she can goad hers into anything from borrowing money at the bank to embezzling it at the office.

No woman believes for an instant that any other woman is as poor as she is. She is convinced that all husbands but hers ladle out clothes and caviar and cleaning women in a never-ending stream; they give their wives a generous allowance and money besides (as well as paying the rent and the utilities and the grocery bill); they take their wives out to dinner when it's too hot to cook, and on carefully casual occasions they land home with their arms full of roses.

Soap Opera Diet

No wonder she feels badly, this bedraggled drudge, scrubbing the floor on her hands and knees, chained between the kitchen stove and the washing machine, with her current account overdrawn and without a rag to her name. The worst of it is, her poverty is genuine, although she is mistaken in its nature. It's not coin of the realm she lacks, it's currency of the spirit, and a bucketful of ten-dollar bills won't cure it.

Marriage seems to bring about a full stop in mental development. How many wives have any interest outside the home—or inside it? As soon as the wedding ring is safely on her finger, a woman drops the phoney interest in sports, politics, the stock market, or whatever it was that made her seem too remarkable to the bemused bachelor. She lets her mind crystalize into a narrow, dark, domestic little tunnel, with no surprises, no clear, cool streams of thought, and no pleasant sunny places. Almost any married woman can have a baby, but it takes an unusual matron to have a new idea.

Notice what the housewife reads: movie periodicals, love stories, murder mysteries. Or what she listens to on the radio—and don't let her tell you she doesn't. Walk down a middle-class residential street on a hot afternoon when the doors are open, and hear the soap operas.

Other Women Bore Her

As for the housewife's second complaint, her loneliness, since the invention of the telephone there probably isn't an hour in the day when she isn't talking to somebody. The trouble is, it's women she talks to, and women bore her to death. Society has hounded her husband out to provide her with gadgets (and she has nothing to say to him anyway) and she doesn't dare have any men friends. So she is reduced to stultifying, niggling gossip that leaves her unsatisfied and lonely.

Looking at her drudgery from a vantage point behind a hot typewriter, it seems that it must take years of patience and persistence to develop work habits to keep her busy in a modern home from eight in the morning until 10 at night. Even if she has children, in these days of sitters and playsuits (and nursery schools that take babies at three) children shouldn't be too much of a drag on her.

It seems, however, that this idea is wrong, as she will tell you at length. This modern feeling that children are an unmitigated nuisance would have fascinated Freud, with his theories on the scarring of childish minds. "The doctor thinks Mary's little boy is going to be all right. Poor Mary—she's been tied in the house all week."

"Tied" in the house by a sick child.

Obviously, women feel that they are wasting their time looking after a home and family, and that they ought to be out in the world. Yet surely the snappiest adding machine lacks the lure of flesh of your flesh and bone of your bone, all done up in satiny skin and dimples.

Any married man will tell you that a wife is a lovable, warmly affectionate creature—closely resembling a halibut. She is too busy to go to the hockey game, too tired to iron a clean shirt, too bored to be amorous and silly. She is suspicious of every move her husband makes, and automatically jealous of any friend, man or woman—how many masculine friendships ever survive a marriage? A wife's normal attitude seems to be that she doesn't much want her husband herself, but she's going to see to it that nobody else gets him.

As for her suspicions, usually when her husband lies to her, she deserves it. The instinct for self-preservation is strong in husbands, and after one or two unfortunate brushes with the truth, they find it easier to lie. Sooner or later they get caught, and from then on their wives (silently, loudly or tearfully, depending on type) doubt every remark.

Her Wasted Life

This, of course, is the obvious result of expecting too much. When she marries, a girl expects her husband to be a combination of Ronald Colman, Gregory Peck and Humphrey Bogart: a man at once tender, gorgeous and brutal: a man who will praise every shining floor, every fried egg. When he turns out to be a heel who snorts and gurgles in his sleep, who takes all her sacrifices for granted, and who yawns when she tells him about the shooting pains in her heart, she suddenly realizes that she has wasted her life on an insignificant individual who is all running to belly and baldness.

If he's not an outstanding success in business, she never forgets how successful she might have been, if she had not married. There are many, many wives in this world who never forgive their husbands for marrying them, for burying their abilities under a heap of dirty dishes, for cutting short a glamorous career as salesclerk or stenographer. They would be furious if anyone suggested that real talent won't be smothered by circumstances, and that they are merely making marriage a handy excuse for their own shortcomings.

The truth is, most housewives are lazy. They are too lazy to put down their magazine and write the story they think they could; too lazy to walk a block to do their shopping in person; too lazy to learn to sew if they can't afford new underwear. They cover up for their laziness with monologues on their backaches and the cost of meat and how hard it is to get anything for a change when He doesn't like asparagus. As they have nothing to wear, there is no point in combing their hair or mending the lining in their old coat, or in scrounging 40 cents out of the canned goods money to get new heel lifts on their shoes.

And if the individual housewife is saddening, housewives in the mass are appalling.

Look at what comes out from behind the woodwork the morning of a sale, each specimen mistress of some man's castle and queen of his heart. Their transportation manners are atrocious. They elbow their way to the front of a queue waiting for a streetcar, and then make everybody wait while they search for their fare. They forget to ask for transfers as they get on, and then plow their way back through the maimed and dismembered for them later. If they must stand, they look fixedly at a seated man or make pointed remarks to a friend. They discuss personal problems (their own and other people's), complete with names, ages, vices and vital statistics, at the pitch of their voices.

The Militant Matron

Then there is the way they look. One might think, charitably, that they can't possibly be held responsible for that: that God in His infinite wisdom must have created a special type of costume and facial expression for housewives. But when she considers that they must have been, at some time, reasonably attractive, the business girl shudders and takes another reef in her girdle.

The militant matron, shopping bag under her arm and a wild light in her eye, is an object to behold with awe. And where there is one there are usually two or three. Listen to them in restaurants, watch them at bargain counters, hear them on buses and street corners. Discontent rises from them in waves. They have no sense of humor and no sense of honor; they would stone any man who talked about his wife as they talk about their husbands. Ply a housewife with tea and kindness, and she will tell you anything from her husband's weight to what his boss said to him in confidence.

They have one other subject of conversation besides their husbands, and a popular one it is. Any housewife can tell you (and will, unless stopped by force) every lugubrious, gory detail of every childbirth in her acquaintance, even unto the third and fourth generation back. She herself is never without an ailment, whether she is sickening for it, actually in its throes, or convalescing and waiting morbidly for the next.

This illness seems to go with marriage. Perhaps it is because when she is ill a woman can get masculine attention, even if she (or her husband) has to pay for it. All doctors know that half of the illnesses afflicting married women are the result of too much spare time and too little to think about. Judging from the great and growing number of widows, the married state can't be too unhealthy for women, but if you ask any housewife how she feels, any place, any time, in front of any company, she will tell you, ache by ache, retch by retch, flux by flux.

Housewives are a race apart, a separate division of the human species, bearing little relation to ordinary unmarried females. Their complaints fill the air and their horrid plight is obvious. Housewives are a sorry lot.

2. "Housewives Blast Business Girl," *Chatelaine*, June 1950.

"Housewives are a sorry lot," said Beverly Gray in March Chatelaine. "They have three main complaints—their poverty, loneliness and drudgery. Marriage seems to bring about a full stop in mental development. The average woman lets her mind crystalize into a narrow, domestic tunnel."

Developing these ideas, Miss Gray criticized housewives for their appearance and manners.

Over five hundred women protested in letters and articles. Through all of them ran a vein of tolerance and good humor. But the three things which most of them resented were the attacks on their happiness, their mental status, and their laziness.

Since no reply was, in itself, a completely satisfactory answer to Miss Gray, we have selected excerpts—typical of the point of view of Canadian housewives.— The Editors.

MISS GRAY is guilty of the most sweeping generalizations. She has taken a few of the most unattractive human emotions—frustration, envy, suspicion, discontent and laziness, and she has landed them squarely in the housewife's lap. She has allowed for no individual talents or virtues, condemning in one sweep every woman who dares possess husband, hearth and home ... Granted nearly every housewife in her off moments is guilty of one or even all these undesirable traits. She is, however, playing her role, not merely as a housewife but as an individual, or—as any man would maintain—a woman. The editorial comment that there is a truth for every one of us is just. The article mirrors the darker side of all of us, whatever may be our *chosen* profession and should not be directed specifically at the housewife.

IN MY OPINION the term housewife is outmoded. The next time the census man comes to the house and asks, "Occupation?" I am going to reply "Homemaker," or "Nation Builder," or "The most important job in the world," instead of answering meekly, Housewife.

OUR MENTAL development hasn't stopped dead—it's simply changed its direction. From baseball to babies, politics to pastry, stock markets to super-markets. We still have our old interests plus innumerable new ones. And, lady, try just once, baking, marketing or caring for your baby without putting a bit of mental effort into it.

THE BUSINESS GIRL claims that the housewife drops "phony" interests when the wedding ring encircles her third finger, left hand. If these interests were not genuine, but developed merely to please the "bemused bachelor" I'd say it's a good thing matrimony made an honest woman of her.

... You think the "bemused bachelor" who was inveigled into matrimony talked to his girl about politics and stock markets! Well, guess again. And to quote you, "Almost any married woman can have a baby but it takes an unusual matron to have a new idea!" Most married women who get a new idea mention it to their husbands so tactfully that they soon think it was theirs in the first place.

... Any girl who expects that a man is going to marry her because she knows how the Grand Llama of Tibet is elected, or can swim the English Chan-nel in November had better stay with her desk job. Somewhere along the line she has been sadly misinformed. It takes a different kind of brainwork to be a reasonably efficient combination of cleaning woman, dietitian, nurse, teacher, dressmaker, economist, psychologist, sweetheart and mother. While I'm not a grey-haired grandmother, I've been a housewife long enough to see the rewards that come from an established home and family.

B.G. COMPLAINS how voluble a woman is on the subject of her husband's shortcomings. Golly, what a fascinating, tell-all bunch of gals she hobnobs with! I, unfortunately, seem to have gone through life tuned to the wrong wave lengths. I have known women whose husbands were alcoholics, niggardly misers or just plain skunks and I have always believed them to be just too stupid to see the flaws. But obviously they have been deliberately secretive during their visits with me, waiting only until they got into a public restaurant to let down their hair and give with the dirt. Even my best friends have never shown any inclination to let me in on the excitement of their marital tribulations, so you can imagine how furious it makes me to find how unnaturally they have been behaving toward me.

IT REALLY must be terrible for the housewives who are the unfortunate possessors of caddish husbands such as Miss Gray talks of so understandingly. You'd think even smart business girls could recognize the type of character who'd refer to his wife as a "halibut." Of course, such a husband probably has for his motto—"There's lots of good fish in the sea—and if those lucky business girls want to be suckers, that's entirely their business."

WHEN WE'RE poking about the kitchen with runs in our nylons, hair in wisps, we don't look like your Marie Holmes illustrating how to make marmalade (who does?), but give us any day the crowded nursery, the round of ups and downs—of joy and laughter, of heartache and anxiety—for of threads such as these the fabric of life is woven.

You say our lives channel into a "narrow domestic little tunnel." Well, I'll tell you a secret—you don't know it, but you are in a straight and narrow ditch. Same old office hours, same old desk, same old people around you every day, same old letters, same old boss, same old routine, same old restaurant, same old bus—my, but what a variety of exciting things your day contains! Beverly, is that really what you prefer to running a house to suit yourself by day—and having evenings to share with your children and your guy? Reef your girdle and stay at that desk if you will. I'll reef my clothesline and thank my silver polish I'm not there!

... Just now, for us young house wives, life "may channel into a narrow domestic little tunnel," dark in spots, but it's a tunnel with light at the end of it—a family decently reared, our own home and a husband who has helped in the hard work and good planning; and certain sacrifices do come out right at the end of the tunnel. And sister, didn't you hear of "kissing tunnels?" They're fun!

I DENY that as a group housewives are unhappy. We're happy because we know we are loved and appreciated in spite of our curlers and last year's coat. We're happy because we're released from the tension of office competition and the competition for affection and because we can put all our heart into the home and community service.

LAZY? Who are those two million women I meet at the supermarket, those lazy creatures with two armfuls of groceries, pushing a carriage with one or two occupants, holding the harness of a third between their teeth? Housewives trying to fill their empty days?

... If all housewives were as moronic, lazy and lacking in imagination as pictured, how could they raise their daughters to grow into such smart, intelligent and very self-assured young business girls?

NOW WHAT'S all this hullabaloo about us listening to soap operas? Some of us do and some of us don't. So what? They are merely a form of entertainment to occupy part of the mind while, say, washing dishes. Don't tell me we should have a waterproof copy of "The Rise and Fall of the Roman Empire" to reach for instead.

... Suppose we do listen to soap operas—don't we get the news every hour on the hour sandwiched in between? And what husband will take your latest theories on why Russia will wait three years before declaring war, in place of lemon pie for supper?

WE ARE accused of lack of outside interests. How then does B. G. account for the number of women's organizations? In my town every year without exception it has been a married woman who collected for the Community Chest. In our choir are housewives. I see them donating afternoons to all sorts of charitable work. Who bakes the pies and cakes at the fairs, prepares the church suppers? Who makes up the Parent-Teacher groups?

DISCOURTESY is not a disease specifically attributable to the housewife. I have often waited patiently to be served in department stores while giggling clerks stood in a huddle discussing last night's date, until I was finally forced to leave without making a purchase.

UNTIL READING Miss Gray's article, I had always been under the impression that women as such might be grouped en bloc, but that beyond this it became necessary to recognize a vast variation in ability and character. But according to her there are only two classifications—single girls and housewives. Housewives, all having been cut from the same shoddy piece, must be classified under the same generalized accusations. How simple! I should very much like to know whether she keeps her office correspondence in the same type of all-inclusive folders.

This new type of reasoning requires neither consistency nor veracity—how easy it becomes to state a case. For instance, the movie magazines, it seems, are read only by housewives; but it has been my observation that they are to be found in greatest profusion at the beauty parlors where, we are led to infer, no housewife ever sets foot!

SO THE writer thinks housewives are the only females addicted to long telephone calls. I might remark that I know a good dozen firms in one city who have had to deny employees use of the phones for personal use, the reason being that female employees have carried on such interminable gossip sessions with their cronies that incoming business calls were badly delayed.

THE MOVIES have made you "career girls" a very glamorous lot. But from where I stand on my corner waiting for a homeward bus, dinner under my arm, I see a swarm of tired, bedraggled and irritable young business girls who elbow their way just as fast, if not faster, than I to the only available seats.

SO YOU consider our children a nuisance. Well, you're dead right! And who has a better right to say so than we? They haven't invented a toddler yet with a push-button mechanism and if we talk about what we went through producing the little dears, why not? They don't do that with mirrors either. Evidently you have missed the note of living pride usually wrapped up in our complaints about our offspring.

AND WHO ARE "all" the doctors who know that half the illnesses of married women are imaginary? For every wife who fakes illness there are at least 10 who do their day's work, and I mean work with aches and pains that would keep you home from the office for a month, Miss Gray. And since you mentioned widows, statistics prove that married men live longer than bachelors and I'll bet you're just the one who'll come back with "It only seems longer!"

YOU SAY women talk too much about childbirth. One session of pregnancy would put some of the critics out of business completely. Yet the so-called "spineless" housewife, lacking all the determination, strength of character and other virtues of her unmarried sister is supposed to recover and rebound from the ordeal with the elasticity of a rubber band. The amazing thing about her is she does!

BEVERLY, I can't help but wonder who your married friends are. If it is from them you have gleaned your rather wild ideas about us, you had better look up from polishing your nails, open your eyes, and really see. If we had so ghastly an existence—why weren't women frightened away from it generations ago?

WHATEVER IS the matter with you, Beverly Gray—I hope its curable. Stop being a sour-puss and you will find that married women are people too, and very nice. Often they are tense with worries that are not as controllable as a typewriter or adding machine.

In our village the women are clever and kind, some more efficient than others. Our children are healthy and usually very happy. We like our husbands. We give service to our community. We understand municipal affairs and work to improve them. We have political opinions and we don't fight over disagreements. When we are in trouble we help one another. Our women are smart-looking and well-groomed—and I expect they are where you live too.

ONE CAN'T blame these spotless specimens of business girls shuddering at the sight of a housewife going about her business. I shudder myself when I think of it. But that fly-away look in our eyes and hair seems unavoidable when trying to shop in a limited time and keep small fingers from creating too much damage in the store. When those smooth b.gs. approach with their unruffled hair, unblemished make-up and in up-to-the-minute tailoring, my inferior complex reaches a new low. And if the need to speak arises, their cool husky tones are a positive delight—but I've often wondered would their voice pitch rise as high as mine if in an emergency a child tried crossing the street in front of a moving car!

IT SEEMS to me from Beverly Gray's article that her position at the console of her typewriter encompasses a much smaller horizon than the narrow domestic circle in which, according to her, we housewives are groveling. But her ideas will doubtless cause more smiles than scowls—for we realize how very young she must be, at least in experience. Perhaps Chatelaine should sponsor a Womanhood Week—so that one half may learn how the other half lives. But don't let Beverly scare you, girls. Countless thousands of us in Canada are homemaking—and loving it! And it only takes one hug and good-night kiss from sleepy cherubs to bring back all the love and energy which has been given so freely during the day.

WE ARE SORRY to see one member of the female sex allowing her sublime ignorance and noticeably narrow-minded opinions to carry her away. We can only suppose that Miss Gray's vitriolic tongue has reduced her circle of friends to such an extent that she has been forced to retaliate in a verbal barrage against her own kind.

ALL HOUSEWIVES will no doubt agree it's a smart business girl who, knowing her own limitations, decides to sidestep the idea of becoming one of us. But don't think for a moment that we, "a race apart, a separate division of the human species," would change places—oh, no, we're housewives, and darned proud of it!

3. Doris McCubbin, "How to Live in a Suburb," *Chatelaine*, March 1955.

It's 10.24 on a Friday morning. You've just spun two loads of washing through the machine, swished through the breakfast dishes, scooped up a dustpanful of paper cutouts left by your daughter, listened to a lecture by the milkman on the sluggardly rate they are getting around to paving the streets in your six-month-old suburb, and let out the dog for the seventh time.

From the periodic banging as the baby tried to chip his Bugs Bunny off his playpen with the remains of his wooden fire engine, you hopefully calculate that you have about an hour to cut out your new dress before lunch.

You're just about to smooth out the material on the dining-room table when the telephone rings. "Hi!" sings out a voice you recognize as your next-door neighbor. "Coffee time! Bundle up the brat and bring him over. Marg and Dot are coming. Estelle can't. That poor kid of hers has another cold." There is a significant pause.

You make a "m-m-m-m-m" noise at your end of the line, which could or could not be interpreted as your agreement that Estelle doesn't put enough clothes on her only son to keep a polar bear from catching pneumonia. For just a moment you're tempted to say, "Gosh, honey, I'm sorry, but I'm just in the middle of dressmaking. Can't come today."

But at the back of your mind is a nagging question. Why isn't Barbie coming? Has Barbie been marked for a purge—and why? And another thought—suppose you do say you can't come, and suppose they don't ask you the next time? Just for a moment you pause and then you say, "Sure." The dressmaking project is canceled for this morning.

Why, you ask yourself, did I do that? Why do I spend so much time drinking coffee? How is it people who were complete strangers to me six months ago now know more about me than my own mother? Why is it I find myself saying things I don't mean, doing things I don't want to do in an attempt to fit in? Why have I become afraid to speak out on almost any subject from racial intolerance to modern art? How is it that this suburb, where we moved to find freedom to breathe, sometimes seems to be slowly choking us to death?

Your problem is one facing thousands of newcomers to Suburbia all across Canada today. It's an inevitable reaction after the first heady "Hi, neighbor" fever begins to wear off. To seek some solutions to these questions Chatelaine talked to some suburban housewives. The community canvassed most thoroughly was Don Mills, Toronto's new dream suburb, but other districts were also visited. Some Chatelaine staff members are themselves suburban dwellers. Social workers, sociologists and psychologists were interviewed and all the findings were pooled. Out of all this emerged a picture of the pleasures and pitfalls of suburban living.

Suburbia is the friendliest community in North America since the days of stockade life and Indian raids. It provides you with an opportunity to share in building a community. It offers you a chance to give badly needed leadership—a chance you mightn't get in an older, more settled district. Suburbia also supplies a feeling of belonging that is often lost these days when people move about the country more and live outside the larger family circle.

But suburbia can also become a breeding ground of boredom, filled with women isolated by lack of transportation from the rest of the city, who measure out their spare time with cups of coffee and chitchat.

The exhilarating frontier neighborliness starts from the moment the woman moves into her house. Here she is in a brand-new community. Nobody knows anybody else. There are no established customs, no caste system, no elite, no old-timers. Everyone feels they are sharing in an exciting new adventure, all faced with the same problems ...

But long before any borrowing starts she meets her neighbors. While one woman was still unpacking the china and wondering where on earth she put the baby's bottle warmer, coffee-bearing neighbors knocked on her door. They all sat around on packing cases and introduced themselves. Last names were brushed aside like titles in Russia.

Before she was in her house a week she was on the program committee for a three-week-old Home and School Association, a member of a Ping-pong league and vaguely committed to join a drama club. Her husband went off in a car pool every morning as though he had done it all his life. He and a man called Charlie were swapping stories as they built a communal fence.

At this stage she burbled off a letter to mother, "This is a wonderful place. Everyone is so friendly."

Everyone in a new suburb *is* friendly. But one day, about six month after you move in, you'll find yourself wishing the coffee bean had never left Brazil. You'll suddenly discover the pally little puddle has frozen over. Miniature icebergs, no bigger than a woman's hand, appear on the surface with vast potential dangers lurking below. Soon two neighbors, who were swapping chili con carne recipes three days before, pass one another in the supermarket as if each considered the other a display of decaying cabbage.

You'll find yourself forced into joining sides. It takes a strong-minded woman to stand alone, and she's always afraid she might be left there. Your husband will be mystified by all the female fencing. Why Josie is speaking to Gladys one week and not speaking to her the next is just as baffling to him as fashion futures.

You'll be amazed to find that you're growing more like your neighbors by a strange process of homogenization. Wasn't it after one of those coffee sessions that you decided against a Swedish contemporary chair for the living room and got a sectional set like everyone else? Wasn't that big fight you had three months ago with your husband caused by your implication that he was a slothful slob because he wasn't spending every spare minute over a set of power tools in the basement like Marge's husband, Roddy? And since when (you ask yourself) have you hauled down your banner for racial tolerance? Bill Smith tosses around words like mick and dago—words that used to make you buckle on your white armor. Why don't you set the record straight on where you stand? But you don't. Why not?

You may discover that you are unconsciously playing down your education, taste and opinions that might mark you as different. One young suburban housewife told me: "You've got to be mediocre or you become just as big an oddity as the emu. My husband actually had to work up a repertoire of dirty jokes—the barnyard kind—to keep up his end of the conversation with the boys. I buried the fact that I had an M.A. degree in English under the sod of our new front lawn."

Another said, "You find yourself pooh-poohing things you've always been proud of—like good music. We pass off our subscription to the Atlantic as a gift from an eccentric aunt. We hide the fact that we know what people are talking about when they mention French impressionists as though we had a record in dope peddling." ...

But suppose you don't like living a life that has about as much privacy as a newly laid frog's egg. Suppose you want to keep your tastes intact. Suppose you're tired of talking babies and bottle routines or discussing what a mess the woman across the street is making of her child, her marriage and her color scheme. Suppose you don't like parties with the men in one end of the room discussing (a) makes of cars and (b) hockey, and the women in the other end swapping anecdotes about children. Suppose you don't want to start every party with good old Charlie and Margie Brown at the top of the list. Suppose you don't like your next-door neighbor walking in on you at least three times a day with no warning except a hearty "Hi" as she kicks open the door. Suppose you're bored to the breaking point with the meandering kind of conversation that goes with the *Kaffeeklatsch*, in which everyone throws in an anecdote or two and at the end you feel you've swallowed a tubful of pablum?

Well, theoretically you could withdraw from the whole setup, keep to yourself. But you know that would be impossible. Then you would become a curiosity, and an even greater source of interest. Your children would be singled out as the odd offspring of odd parents, and after all you moved out to Suburbia for the children, didn't you?

Besides you can't move anywhere else. You've mortgaged yourself down to your last dollar for this house and the life that goes with it. You can't wipe it off as a mistake and go back to living with in-laws or in a crowded apartment.

Well then, what *can* you do?

In any community since the beginning of time, there is gentle but firm pressure toward conformity, toward the average. The only place where this law doesn't apply is on a desert island inhabited just by you, or smack in the middle of a very big city where your neighbor doesn't care if you're alive—or dead for that matter.

Bedroom Curtains Were Bad

In suburbs as they exist all over Canada the law is exaggerated. The main patterns of conformity were fairly rigidly laid out right from the start. Most of the people in any given suburb fall into the same income group. They often have the same kinds of jobs. They're roughly in the same age group. Old people and teen-agers are rare. There are no Negroes, Chinese. Non-English-speaking families are the exception. There are no slums, no "big" houses, no wrong side of the tracks. Women raise their children by the same baby book, listen to the same radio programs and eat more or less the same kind of food. Everyone is working to improve the property. Slackers who don't cut their grass and keep the place painted become pariahs.

One family who rented their living room to help swing the monthly payments were almost snubbed out of the community, although several people on the same street had tenants in their recreation rooms. "Those bedroom curtains facing out on the street looked bad—pulled down the level of the whole neighborhood," was the reason given.

Much of this pressure toward conformity you approve of—it produces the kind of neighborhood you want for your family. Having sunk your all into one fifty-by-hundred-foot plot you justifiably don't want property values decreased by someone running a boardinghouse. You moved to the suburbs to get the kids away from smoke, dust, traffic, crowded apartments with no place to play, and into an environment where they would be mixing with children like themselves.

"But," protested one mother, "I don't want to turn them into narrow-minded little copies of all the other children on this block. Mary doesn't know what it's like to ride on a streetcar. She can't imagine anyone not owning a car. Young Bill embarrassed me terribly the other day when we were downtown buying shoes and he stared in astonishment at a Negro. In spite of all the things they have—books, radio, TV—they are growing up in a kind of middle-class cocoon. They not only don't know how the other half lives—they don't know how anyone lives outside of Sunnyvale Acres."

In other words, if you are not on guard against the tendency, your suburb can turn into a sort of negative democracy where everyone is as good as everyone else because everyone is *like* everyone else and smugly proud of this white man's white-collar community.

This is where you and your husband begin to show what calibre of parents you are. You can no more raise your children in a small suburban community and expect them to grow up with a broad outlook, with no extra help from you, than you can dump them into our school system and expect them to come out with a first-rate education with no extra help from you. Suburbia will provide them with fresh air, reasonable safety while crossing the street, and a back yard to play in, but you have to face the fact that Suburbia is not an environment rich in experiences to stir a child's imagination.

You're going to have to go to the trouble of taking Mary for a streetcar ride. You're going to have to point out to both Mary and Bill that the rest of the world who don't live in Sunnyvale Acres are not inferior or funny but merely different, and there's nothing terribly wrong with being different. You're going to have to work hard explaining to them about racial intolerance. It's easy to give lip service to this subject but when children hear their parents talking about other people in the same community and criticizing them on such minute details as table manners or how many times a woman washes her bathroom floor, how can they be expected to understand people who talk with a funny accent and have a completely different culture?

But aside from the children, what about you yourself? Will you quietly submerge under a sticky puddle of coffee and gossip?

You don't have to. Many housewives in suburbs have thought and acted their way into a much richer, varied life than they had ever known before. For Suburbia is the best opportunity Canadian women have ever been handed. Its newness is a big plus factor.

There it is—bare as a clean page, with no old established traditions to hamper you, and filled with young people like yourself, loaded with enthusiasm and energy. For most of the day while the men are away at work the women run the community. After the bulldozers have pulled out, the spadework to make a real community out of your particular collection of houses has to be done by you, the homemakers.

You can take part in community life in a big way or in a small way. Get into community life in a big way and you'll find you have earned your right to be different, if you want to be different in smaller and more personal ways.

At this point you may be snorting, "I suppose the answer is clubs! But clubs are even worse gossip dens than coffee parties!" It's true that gossip and backbiting and smallness don't automatically stop when people join clubs. But gossip is the pastime of idle people and in a dynamic group there is too much to do to leave much time for gossip. There is less desire to discuss Mrs. Jones and her strange ways of raising children and keeping house when you both are worrying about how to divide the town's recreation grant to cover all the activities in your program. Besides you'll find if you meet Mrs. Jones on a community rather than a back-fence level, you will view her from a refreshing new angle and find unsuspected talents and qualities which you wouldn't discover in twenty years of peering at her over the rim of a coffee cup.

If you have the courage to stand by your own convictions and tastes you will find that there are probably other people right in your block who are as eager to shrug off lazy conformity as you are. But if you slavishly conform to the general level, you will never find these kindred spirits. If you take an active, positive part in your particular piece of Suburbia, you will discover unsuspected talents and interests yourself—and what is even more surprising, that there are other people with the same desire to find new satisfactions in community projects.

Help in a Crisis

One mother took her little girl over to join a newly formed Brownie company. When she got to the church where the troop was meeting, she found one harassed leader trying to cope with forty little girls. This mother took off her coat and pitched in to help. Now she is the Tawny Owl for the company and in this new role, which she never dreamed of filling six months before, she has found a new interest and is learning a lot about children in the process.

Another woman who had always helped her husband run his ambulance business by taking incoming phone calls, felt lonely when they moved to a suburb. But instead of allowing herself to become unhappy about the situation, she organized a volunteer baby-sitting service. "My telephone rings on an average of every ten minutes," she reports, "and I love it." She has also developed a tremendous respect for her neighbors. "I never realized just how much real kindness people are capable of until I see some woman in a crisis—say a baby arriving six weeks before it's due. The way the neighbors rush in to help renews your faith in humanity."

Another mother reports, "My husband and I moved out to the suburbs because we both had grown up in small towns and we wanted the same kind of community feeling for our children." This couple knew this kind of community spirit doesn't come ready-made like the street plan. They knew they had to work at it. To begin with both of them started organizing a church service to be held every Sunday in one of the schoolrooms. Then the wife and two other women started holding Sunday school in the living room of her home with as many as thirty children attending.

"You can start any kind of a club you want," reports another woman. "It's amazing how many other people you'll find have always wanted to learn Spanish or smocking, or form a Citizen's Club." But one piece of advice everyone stresses, is that you must have a definite program right from the start. There are so many demands on everyone's time that the project has to take off fast or it will be in grave danger of never getting off the drafting board.

To sum it up, Suburbia is as big or as confining as you make it. It can become a tiny, little world as narrow as the view you get from behind your kitchen curtains, or it can become a rich, warm environment in which you, your family and your neighbors can all do a lot of growing.

4. Dr. Marion Hilliard, "Stop Being Just a Housewife," *Chatelaine*, September 1956.

When I was an adolescent in Morrisburg, Ont., I used to sing a song that contained the line, "Men must work but women must weep." The rest of the song is gone from my memory but that one line has been haunting me ever since. I believe that the most important thing I know about women, after twenty-five years as an obstetrician and gynecologist, is that women need not weep, *but they must work*.

I know exactly how most men and a lot of women will feel about my attitude. There is a prevailing image of womanhood, slightly plump in a cotton print dress, surrounded by adoring, golden-haired children as she bends over an oven door to take out a pan of biscuits. In this pink picture, the woman's face is brimming with contentment, tears of tender joy stand in her eyes and she is bathed in a glow of fulfilled femininity. She's wonderful all right, but she's no more real than the fantasy image millions of men have of themselves, exultant and virile, stripped to the waist in the sunshine, splitting rocks with Gargantuan strength.

People in our culture are too complicated to have more than fleeting moments of such acute sensation. Splitting rocks is unprofitable, making it impossible for a man to raise his family in a spacious neighborhood, and it also is incapable of satisfying his intelligence. The desire to be half naked and muscular must give way to the reality of a pallid face and a grey-flannel figure crouched over a desk.

Similarly, women cannot perpetually achieve the ideal state of enriched motherhood. Motherhood, in reality, turns out to be a state with well-spaced-out rewards—the thrill of nursing a baby, the look on a small child's face when he is comforted after a fall, a remark of a school-going child that shows under-

standing and warmth, a shared laugh with an adolescent, a first date, a gradua-
tion, a wedding, a grandchild. In between are periods of monotony and a feeling
of stagnation.

Much of the fault for the current mood of nameless longing that is sweeping modern housewives is to be found in their so-called blessings. Women no
longer weave their own cloth, make their own soap, put down a cellarful of
preserves. Consider the mid-twentieth-century woman: she is alone in her house,
miles from her family and the friends of her childhood; her work has been simplified to the glorious point where she can keep her house glittering in two hours
a day; she stares into her own thoughts while the refrigerator clicks on, the oven
bakes the prepared cake mix and her children play in denims that need no ironing. She has married young, earlier every year in Canada according to the statistics.
She's strong, intelligent and responsible. She sits with a cigarette in her fingers
and feels futile. I say she needs to work.

I'd like to emphasize immediately that I have several convictions about
why women should work, and none of them include money. To take a job merely
for the sake of a pay cheque is a spiritless and degrading business. It's the blight
of our times—men and women working at grey, loathed occupations purely for
the sake of income. It flies in the face of the human necessity to take pride in a
job, and the repetitious agony of an occupation that gives no satisfaction can
lead to mental or physical breakdown. I am shocked by the number of our
adolescents who take light, aimless jobs when they leave school, putting in time
until marriage. College girls wait on tables at summer resorts in order to purchase cashmere sweaters. Young married women stand behind counters in
department stores so they can pay the next installment on the refrigerator—and
when that is paid off they'll make a down payment on a clothes dryer. These
women have settled on a materialistic standard, filling their closets with clothes
and their kitchens with electric appliances. They don't realize that their vitality is
turning to cold ashes and their spirit is impoverished.

Women must work, all women must work. There is no place in our society for an indolent woman. But as a doctor I am certain that it is good health
therapy to work and that women must work for values other than purely economic. Women need to work to gain confidence in themselves. Women need to
work in order to know achievement. Women need to work to escape loneliness.
Women need to work to avoid feeling like demihumans, half woman and half
sloth.

Work, as I mean it, includes any activity that fulfills these needs. It includes hospitality, a complicated and rewarding occupation. It includes active

membership in an organization that is performing a vital function in the community. It includes part-time work in a dress shop, if the woman is stimulated by handling new clothes and meeting a variety of people. It includes full-time work at a job that challenges and delights her, providing she has some enthusiasm and glow left over afterward for her home.

I am not speaking of the unmarried woman, who will work all her adult life. She too needs to choose an occupation in which she can find some expression of her personality, whether it be chatting with people over a bakeshop counter or peering through a microscope in search of a cure for cancer. But she is not fooled, as the married woman is fooled, into believing she can spend her whole life without acquiring a single skill.

This is the deep dark water under the thin ice of a married woman's composure. Frittering away the scant years before she marries, she learns no trade. She comes to marriage with little ability beyond a certain flair for looking attractive in strong sunlight. On this house of cards, she builds her self-assurance. She rises in the morning full of the delight of greeting her young loveliness in a mirror. But time won't hold still and this butterfly reaches her mid-thirties, when her children are almost independent and her one small talent is beginning to weather. The change in her appearance, which had counted for so much, makes her unsure. She is now ready, with her family nearly grown, to take part in the bustle outside her home, but she is newly timid and has no training. Unskilled occupations look wearying, unworthy and dull; so she sits at home and becomes more despondent with each empty, wasted day.

One such woman came to me a few years ago. She was expensively dressed, given to tapping her fingers sharply on the arm of her chair and full of vague symptoms of irritability, sleeplessness and pains that changed location with each medical article she read. Both sons were in high school and her husband was absorbed in a business boom.

"You need to work," I told her.

"My husband is quite successful," she said coldly.

I shifted patiently. "I mean for your own sake," I explained. "What can you do?"

She butted her cigarette viciously. "Dr. Hilliard, I am thirty-six years old. I have two years of university education, sixteen years of marriage and a pretty good IQ. I believe I am qualified to be a baby sitter."

I met an older version of the same woman not long ago. Her husband had died, in his mid-fifties, and she was devastated.

"I know that self-pity isn't helping me," she commented sadly, "but I just sit in our pretty little home and cry."

"You'd better get a job," I said.

"A job!" she exclaimed. "I've never had a job in my life. What could I do?"

"Start down the street of the shopping district nearest you," I advised her, "and go into every store and ask for work until you find a job."

She took my suggestion and landed a job the next day in a dime store. Wrestling with the problems of learning to ring up sales and make change for the purchase of 59-cent wallets, she found new strength to accept her loneliness and an awakened interest in people. She left that job for a better one and I haven't heard from her since. I suspect she is just fine.

It is time women took a good long look at their lives and realized that they will spend most of the years working. Most women realize that they will work before their marriage, but they don't know that this is only the beginning. If their husbands need to finish their educations or become ill for a long period of time, the wives will have to work. If the marriage suffers either separation or divorce, both of which are increasingly common, the women go back to work. When the children are entering their teens, the women can easily fit a job into the home schedule. They'll be grandmothers in their forties, eagerly looking for something to fill their time. Women live longer than men, so it is likely that they'll spend the end of their lives, if they're lucky, working at a job that interests and delights them. In the long view, marriage and childbearing, although a desperate need, may be only an interlude in a woman's life.

Young people today approaching adulthood are betrayed by the ease with which they can make money. They need no skill at all and life is a lark. A teenage girl with indifferent ability to type can make fifty dollars a week in an office and conserve all her animation for the coffee breaks and after-five dates. A boy I know made eighty dollars a week on a road-construction gang, guiding traffic with a red flag. He had the wit to be ashamed of himself, but his savings paid his first-year medical-school fees.

With jobs so easy to come by, many adolescent girls are fooled into believing that only the salary is an important factor in choosing an occupation. The jobs that require training and education, such as nursing and teaching, have little charm. They'll be marrying soon, they figure, so why bother?

Once a generation becomes adjusted to the notion that happiness varies in a direct ratio with dollars, desperate aberrations appear in its behavior. Last winter I had three mothers in three months come to me in their early pregnancies and tell me that they wanted their babies placed for adoption. These mothers were married, giving birth to legitimate babies. "Why give up your baby?" I asked.

"We can't afford to give this new baby the advantages it should have," the first mother told me. "We have two children now and we can't manage another."

"Do you think dancing lessons and brand-new snowsuits are more important to a child than being with his own parents?" I enquired.

The mother was surprised. "Certainly," she answered.

I discovered to my sorrow that the adoption department of at least one children's aid society had to hire a special case worker to deal with the growing number of married couples who place their children for adoption. What has happened to our values if we can give up our babies because they strain the family budget? We pride ourselves on our Western way of life. "What shall it profit a man, if he shall gain the whole world, and lose his own soul?"

This trend is evident in the mothers of teen-age girls who chat with pride about their daughters. "She's so pretty," they tell me gaily. "We belong to the country club because we want her to meet a nice crowd of people and we try to keep her well dressed. She studied at the conservatory for years but now she's more interested in badminton. She's having such a wonderful time!"

I wonder. Does she know what life is about, I think to myself. Does she have a core of serenity, derived from the knowledge that she is a capable, coherent human being? Is she prepared to live a long time and be able to respect herself most of those years? Or will she be bored for twenty or thirty years, turning her bitter venom on her children, her husband, her friendships that show signs of waning? Don't tell me your daughter can figure-skate like Barbara Ann Scott. Tell me instead that she is generous and kind and that she has forethought enough to prepare herself for a creative vocation.

Men preparing themselves for a profession usually continue with their education after marriage, but a woman almost invariably stops her education at the first clang of the wedding bell. She believes, and she is dead wrong, that her training is of no importance. Many women tell themselves that they can always finish the course later, but later never happens. A middle-aged housewife is so rare in a university that she's newspaper copy. No woman should ever be concerned that her training as a teacher, a business-machine operator or a dietician will ever be wasted when she marries. She will be using it, all right, and probably a lot sooner than she expects.

This brings us to the mothers of preschool children. Society agrees that babies and little children need their mother, an absolutely steady and reliable, loving woman. The mother who rushes her children through a dawn breakfast, nags them to hurry with their clothes so she can deposit them somewhere on her way to work and then returns, exhausted, in the early evening to prepare an ugly meal and send her children testily to bed is suffering a defeat on all fronts. She isn't a mother, wife or woman. She's a wage-earner and the $42.97 she gets every week, after deductions, cannot possibly justify what she is doing to herself.

It isn't the time she's away from the children, it's what happens in the hours she has them with her. I have known many mothers of preschool children who stayed home stubbornly to raise their small ones and managed to do as much harm as the working mother I have just described. These are the mothers who can never accept the estrangement of being a housewife. They remember the conviviality of the office they left for motherhood; lunching in laughter-filled restaurants; the lullaby relaxation of routine. They survey their present existence: an adult, spending an entire day in the company of a two-year-old, subject to the whims and demands of the child at erratic intervals, including the middle of the night; a highly skilled office worker, reduced to removing dust from the coffee table. She screams at her child, who is the cause of her plight, and afterward is wracked by guilt. She soaks herself in radio and television to distract her mind, ordering her child to be quiet and go away. When she can't stand it any longer she goes out, leaving the child with some makeshift supervision. She prides herself on being a "good" mother because she isn't working; in her heart she must know she is a terrible mother.

This woman needs to work at something she can be proud of, in order to increase her importance to herself. It doesn't need to be a major occupation, lasting several hours a day, but it must be regular so she can look forward to it and plan the supervision of her child. I know of one woman in a northern Ontario city who discovered there was no kindergarten in the local schools. She campaigned, became a school-board trustee and led a movement to establish kindergartens. Another woman spends an afternoon a week teaching a cerebral-palsy victim of thirty-three how to read. I know another who became an expert gardener, growing hybrid roses, and another who, in a rebellion against depression one grey winter day, started to scrape the finish off the dining-room table and eventually refinished with professional technique all the furniture in her house. All of these fulfill my requirements for working women, since they have the heavy remuneration of self-esteem and worth.

As the children grow older, I believe that they will gain by having a working mother. They can learn responsibility in no better way. There are, of course, two different ways of performing any assigned task. The twelve-year-old who is supposed to do the dinner dishes can feel abused—and be loquacious on the subject—and will try to avoid the chore at every opportunity. But if he understands that this is his contribution to his family and that he is an active participant in the machinery that makes the family work efficiently, there is rarely much difficulty.

Children have a great capacity for responsibility. Without any exception, mothers who have teen-age children and become pregnant tell me that their older children showed a solicitude and thoughtfulness that astounded their parents. "I didn't know they were capable of such understanding," the mother tells me. Those children are capable all right and they and their parents both gain enormously in the discovery.

Although few mothers go back to university to finish courses, a surprising number are taking night-school training in accounting or business machines, or refresher courses in some type of nursing or teaching. A woman social worker I know kept her hand in all through the years her three children were small by intensive reading. She bought a small filing cabinet and kept all useful information in well-organized files. She went back to work, when her youngest child was ten, as knowledgeable as any fresh graduate.

Work is a wonderful antidote to the blues of menopause. This is a period when a woman's sense of uselessness is so acute that she can, literally, be driven to drink, dope or mental illness. Her family is grown, her childbearing years are ending, her husband often could do just as well with a hired housekeeper. If she has some consuming occupation, whether it is a study of fourteenth-century Chinese art or an office to manage, she isn't in much danger of being shattered by what is happening to her physiology.

Work is a great healer, for a woman. A woman who discovered her husband, much adored by their children, was chronically unfaithful, soothed her ravaged emotions by going back to work. Another woman, who was languishing in misery because she was sterile, pulled herself out of her own private pit by spending a morning a week bathing babies at an infants' home. The babies responded instantly to her loving gentleness in the midst of their institutional life; babies and woman helped one another through a bad time.

I'd like to add a special word for a woman trained in some profession such as medicine or law before her marriage. In our busy new country, it is a tragic loss to have such a person disappear into the suburbs, and agonizingly difficult for such a woman to be content with peeling potatoes. Three quarters of the staff of Women's College Hospital where I work are married and many of them have children. Quite a few women dentists and architects continue to work after their marriages. These women cannot possibly be motivated by money, I am delighted to say. The cost of housekeepers, the increased needs of their wardrobes, the whopping income tax they pay, at single-woman rates, all combine to reduce the possibility that a fondness for a bank account is a main factor. I know a woman doctor who last year, after paying her office upkeep, her secretary, her housekeeper and her income tax, made six hundred dollars. She works, as happy, well-adjusted women everywhere work, because it satisfies her need to work, gives her joy in a job she loves.

Every Thursday night for twenty years I have been met by a gentle radiance in my living room. It uplifts my heart and dispels my fatigue. My staunch Scots friend has been there all day "bringing up" the shine, even of the window sills. That room is full of enduring integrity and devotion of one who loves to clean, and loves me too. She did not go to work to meet any deep psychological need, she went to work to feed her children—now they are financially successful but she still works. It is the centre of her life, for we are all dependent on her faithfulness. I pay this special tribute to all those cheerful women who do hard rough work, so that the mother, the business and professional woman can be refreshed and do a better job. I hope they see their reward and we justify their devotion.

Some women have no struggle as to whether they will continue to work outside their home when they marry. No indecision or longing for activity will wrack them. They marry a farmer, a minister or a country doctor and it becomes a two-way partnership. Who will carry the heavier load? Who will sustain and support the community? I'll bet on the wife every time.

Next year I reach retirement age at my hospital. Many friends have asked if this will mean that I will quit work. Quit work! Not until I quit breathing. I'll work wherever I can; somewhere, I'll always work. Work is medicine, good medicine. I wholeheartedly prescribe it for every woman.

5. Cynthia Steers, "How Much are You Worth to Your Husband?," *Chatelaine*, April 1959.

How much is a housewife worth? Even leaving aside the incalculables—for instance, your blue eyes and smiling face, your role as family comforter and psychologist—it's an impressive amount.

Suppose, as we did, that yours is a city family in a middle-income bracket ($5,000 to $8,000), three children, living in a moderate-priced home. Now, you take the month off.

Here's what your husband would have to pay out in cold hard cash—and, if anything, our figures veer to the conservative. The housewives we questioned sometimes also pickled, jammed and canned out of their own gardens, sewed *all* the children's clothes, papered and painted, helped their husbands with office work at home—but the average wife's work added up like this:

HOUSEKEEPER AND CLEANING WOMAN:

For better or worse the wife does all the cleaning, light dusting, heavy scrubbing and floor cleaning. She takes care of the three children all of the time, naturally—a job that lasts usually from at least seven in the morning till eight at night (on a good day).

A paid housekeeper who sleeps in charges $125 to $140 a month, with at least a day off a week. She does the light cleaning but not the heavy work. So a cleaning woman to take care of the onerous duties costs $7 a week plus carfare and lunch—or $30 a month.

LAUNDRESS:

All a part of the day's work, the housewife takes care of the household, children's, her husband's and her own personal laundry, washing, ironing, spot-cleaning, pressing.

A paid housekeeper keeps the children's clothes and household linen in order. She doesn't take care of the husband's attire. Laundry bills for shirts alone total $1.75 to $2 a week for five to six white shirts and a couple of sports shirts—adding up to $8 a month. Turning collars costs 50 cents a shirt, pressing pants, 50 cents, pressing suits, $1.25.

An average $1 a month for valeting would keep the husband fairly neat, making the total for his personal appearance $9 a month.

HOME ECONOMIST AND SHOPPER:

Chicken wings, sausages, beef Strogonoff—the housewife plans economical family meals and shops on her own, usually one big trip a week to the supermarket with a gaggle of children trailing her.

The housekeeper plans the meals but orders supplies from the corner grocery which delivers. This adds dollars to the grocery bill in extra delivery costs and higher charges on most grocery items in the smaller stores which deliver. Add about $5 a month to the food budget.

CHAUFFEUR:

The housewife squires her children about in the family car for visits to the doctor and dentist, for shopping trips for children's shoes and clothes, to parties and extra lessons of one kind or another.

The housekeeper must use a taxi for these expeditions. At three outings a month, taxi fares amount to approximately $5.

BABY SITTER:

Whoever thinks of a mother being a baby sitter? She's baby sitting all the time! However, without her, her husband must still be away from home for business meetings, club meetings, extra working days, on weekends, and days off for golf or skiing. And the paid housekeeper must also have her time off. Thus baby-sitting fees must be added to the account.

The going rate for baby sitters is 60 cents an hour. Since a baby sitter will probably be needed twice a week, for an average four-hour period each time, the minimum total is $20.

HANDYMAN:

Almost without thinking about it, the housewife will pick up a screwdriver or hammer to right some small wrong about the house. Such small extras as the odd painting job (shelves or chairs in the children's rooms), fixing the front-door number plaque that fell off, or putting up the magnetic knife holder, or hammering a few nails into the back steps, or putting a washer into a leaky faucet, are part and parcel of a housewife's day.

Upkeep for a house on this level, considering handyman's charges of $1 an hour, would amount to at least $3 a month.

CLEANER:

Spot-cleaning or cleaning rugs, chesterfields and chairs is another wifely task—especially with grubby small fingers leaving imprints on everything they touch.

Professional cleaners charge $7.50 for a chesterfield and $2.50 for large chairs. Rugs, depending on size, could be cleaned from about $10. Considering once-a-year cleaning, the break-down amounts to about $2 a month, for chesterfield, two chairs, and one rug.

SEAMSTRESS:

Quite aside from the darning, button sewing and sheet mending a wife often acts as professional seamstress—even if only for the children's curtains and bedspreads, or school-play costumes, or cushions for the living room. The cost of making them at home is just half what it costs to have them made outside.

And clothes sewed for the children save fifty percent on their clothing budget. Children's party dresses, velvet or smocked, cost $12 to $15 to buy and can be made at home for $3 to $5. Overalls, smocks, pyjamas can be made for half price. Estimating an average six articles a year for the ordinary, not-mad-about sewing mother, the saving is approximately $5 a month.

GARDENER AND GROUNDSKEEPER:

Into shorts for gardening in summer or on with the toque and mitts in the winter for snow-shoveling duties—it's all part of the working day for a housewife. With gardeners and snow shovelers charging $1 an hour, and working an average hour and a bit a week over the changing seasons, the monthly cost would be around $5.

HOSTESS:

Clean the floor, vacuum, whip up a divine dinner after feeding the children, jump into something glamorous and the housewife is ready to play hostess to her husband's business associates and clients as well as to family friends.

Without his wife, a husband would probably have to entertain (other than personal friends) at a dinner in a restaurant, at a cost of $20 for three, rather than the $5 it might cost at home. And he would probably give one cocktail party a year at home to entertain all his friends. Catering for food for this for thirty people would cost $25 rather than the $10 a wife could manage on. With one dinner a month and a cocktail party a year, entertainment would cost him about $17 a month extra.

TAX DEDUCTION:

And not to be forgotten, the one figure everyone can pinpoint is the $1,000-a-year tax deduction stay-at-home wives are worth to their husbands—which is a pretty $16.65 a month.

Grand total—$257.65 a month at least.

6. Anna Davies, "I Hate Housekeeping," *Chatelaine*, March 1961.

Nothing in my early education prepared me for housekeeping, and I'm not sorry. On the contrary, I'm thankful now for all the hours I spent reading and studying, instead of learning time-honored methods of making short pastry and starching frills.

I was trained for what I fondly hoped would be the life of a modern woman. My educators, assuming this would require an ability to think, taught me to think. And the thinking I have done during fourteen years of marriage, over dishwashing, bedmaking and vacuuming, has led me to the conclusion that our methods of housekeeping in this age of industrial organization and scientific accomplishment are obsolete.

It's time to revolt!

My dissatisfaction, which I share with many others, arises not out of an immature disinclination to do necessary work, but out of the recognition that I spend my days in completely futile and unnecessary toil. And for that reason alone, I hate housekeeping.

Moreover, I am no longer interested in learning how to do housework quickly, painlessly, efficiently or well. I'm only interested in abolishing it. Should this necessitate a social revolution, so much the better. Societies thrive on them.

If a bowling alley can provide mothers with a fully equipped and supervised nursery to care for their children while they bowl, then surely we could make provision for those who want to spend time more constructively—on an afternoon's work which they enjoy and are trained for.

And if an afternoon—why not two or three? Why not a short working week for both men and women? We're always talking about it.

As an enthusiastic proponent of marriage and motherhood, I attack only the outworn image of a backdrop against which the family phase of human existence should be enacted. I'm intolerant of the old routines, increasingly impossible for women to play with conviction.

I realize I was led up the educational garden path, as thousands of girls were and still are, but I do not reproach those responsible, I wish them luck and success with the next generation. As a mother of girls, I'll help from my end.

Some say education is "wasted" on girls who will ultimately be "only housewives." Therefore, we are urged to put the clock back and train them all in the homemaker arts. But the days of the housewife are numbered, and in the meantime we're not wasting education on women, we're wasting educated women!

Women did "men's jobs."

After the Industrial Revolution the home and the women in it lost their former economic and educational function. Until then, the family's livelihood and the children's training largely centred in the home. Now the men went off to factories to earn a living, and much of the training of the children was taken over by schools.

Girls, also integrated into this public-school system, tagged along with a curriculum designed to equip male children to earn a living in industry.

Thus women stumbled upon a means to develop individual talents and achieve economic independence of men. The First World War, by drawing large numbers of them into factories and offices, helped prove they could do "men's jobs" efficiently and well.

The girls born in the years between the two world wars, who are now wives and mothers, were the first to receive, as a matter of public policy, higher educations on a par with their brothers'. They entered business, industry and the professions in the hundreds of thousands, leaving home, mother and domestic service in droves.

So far, so good. That was progress. Now comes the rub.

Although public policy demands equal effort and standards of excellence from all students regardless of sex, the boy who despairs of surpassing the high grades of a female fellow student needn't worry. The competition and challenge she presents in the schoolroom will not be carried into later life. Her abilities will be withdrawn from the world through marriage: her so-called "true" womanly talents better employed within the confines of house and family.

In forty years we have reached a halfway mark. We have created an elaborate, expensive and unnecessary ritual whereby the modern girl prepares to be an old-fashioned wife. Property, dowries, the domestic arts are no longer factors influencing the planning of a marriage. Mutual attraction in looks, common interests, ideas, and other intangibles, are.

Not a word before marriage of cooking, cleaning, washing, polishing, ironing, mothproofing, putting out garbage, cleaning basements, weeding, raking leaves: baby sitters: staying in for cleaner, breadman, deliveryman, picking up clothes, toys, papers, and so on and on. That's conversation for a courting couple? Horrifying thought.

Funny thing though—it's conversational material for many married couples these days. Even we women like to talk about our work occasionally.

With what kind of work do I justify my existence? After the family's clothes have been washed and dried automatically, I am required to fold them and put them away. I see no future in this job, the play-learning potential of which I long ago exhausted. But such jobs are all mine now ...

In other words, while women who would have been domestic workers in the past now go into industry, we try to fill the gap they leave in homes with all our married women—the intelligent, the average and the dumb—regardless of talent, ability or inclination.

No wonder there is frustration and dissatisfaction among women who, brought up in the confident expectation of ultimately achieving satisfaction from the work of their choice, find that merely through marriage they are demoted, left to cope with the disorganized remnants of what was work of purpose and worth—well over a century ago. Even their duties as citizens are subordinated to the traditional housewifely tasks (and as a result, we probably get the world we deserve).

This study was of four countries with older cultures and less initial educational opportunity for girls than we have in North America. The education and training of our girls should lead them to expect more than that "natural order of things"; the tragedy is that it doesn't.

A vote but no real voice

Whatever we women may think about our situation soon goes up in the steam of our electric kettles, down the drain with the water from our washing machines, is lost in the ceaseless daily round from small child to appliance, from telephone to family station wagon. In our secure little nests alone and unaided, we haven't much time for thought about or for contact with the outside world. Regressing willy-nilly to our former childish and dependent state, we leave the affairs of the world to our husbands, to the men of the world everywhere. We have a vote, for what it is worth, but no real voice.

The values of a vote seem remote from daily concern with leaky taps, dribbly noses and meal-planning.

Again Professor Duverger: "Under a democratic system, political activity is essentially adult. It presupposes that anyone engaged in it takes full responsibility for his fate and does not leave it to another to decide for him."

This is interesting, considering that girls, officially encouraged to the dizzy heights of adult freedoms and responsibilities, are as women precipitated back into a world of children, childish tasks and contained horizons. We proclaim the supreme importance of this little world to all women. Then we complain of their inertia and reluctance to take on civic responsibilities.

There is drudgery in every job, in every profession; but in most, early stints of drudgery well done are rewarded by promotion, by more responsibility and less drudgery. Not so for the "career" of homemaker. More responsibility invariably is accompanied by more drudgery. The best, the most interesting part of educating a child is siphoned off by better-organized institutions such as schools and youth groups.

It might be argued that the intelligent woman could find challenge enough in her older children, in guiding and teaching the nascent minds,. But when the baby needs changing, the phone answering ("It's for you, Ma!"), the dinner putting in the oven and tears of a toddler drying, it is useless to discuss political parties or the aims of World Refugee Year with an inquiring nine-year-old—this being the time he is likely to ask for such information. And as the years slip by mother's mental development stagnates for want of exercise.

Husbands are expected to fill this void in their wives' mental requirements and be good fathers, lovers, breadwinners, and do odd jobs around the house besides. Frankly, I think it is too much to expect of any man.

Since we are making no effort to curtail our girls' educational opportunities (on the contrary, the trend being to seek improvements in our co-educational system), the New Class will just keep on growing.

Marriage is *not* a career

More women will embark on careers and professions they enjoy; more mental skills will be developed in the female half of the population; more vocational opportunities will open to them.

Let's face the fact that domestic work is only one job—for someone; not everyone, not every woman. Let's admit that marriage, motherhood and home-making are not careers, but human conditions. With a little reorganization of contemporary society they need not interfere with a woman's chosen work any more than marriage and fatherhood does with a man's.

We can encourage girls to attain and stay in the adult world. Let them have marriage, home and all the babies they want—but not necessarily in our way, on our terms.

Women who go out to work seeking a personal satisfaction missing in the home are reproached by public opinion for neglecting their duties, and so feel guilt. They worry about their children in "empty houses," "running wild in the streets," and so on—all the bogeys conjured up by their critics.

They also worry, with justification, because adequate community care and facilities for children are lamentably lacking.

All we can provide instead of these is one private slave—mother! ...

Our standard of material living may be as high as modern technology permits, but our scale of culture is low because the exploitation of our productive capacity is inefficient. It does not help fulfil the individual's human potential—especially woman's.

The answer lies not in bigger and better and more elaborate mechanical gadgets. It lies in reorganizing our roster of life's priorities; in extending some of our social and commercial services and initiating others.

We need crèches, nursery schools, day nurseries, cafeterias, laundries, home help, more and better public transportation, parks, libraries, and recreation centres. We can do with more and better varieties of precooked, prepackaged family-size meals, with less variety and simpler styles in clothing. There is a limit to the need for Things: in our "affluent society" the need for services is greater.

I am not advocating abolition of the home. I am for abolishing our present understanding of home as a private box; repository of the family's worldly goods. "Home is where the heart is" runs a saying, but for us it seems to be "where the things are kept."

Upkeep of property is deemed more important than development of mind and senses; mom's baking more treasured than her mental health; the monotony of daily life broken only by purchasing yet another luxury.

And every new, private thing requires its routines of care and upkeep.

We haven't begun to use our vast industrial potential and scientific know-how for real, free living. We are still devoted to making, selling and buying merely newer versions of what was made in the past to suit another way of life.

Our industries could provide us with more disposable objects of living than it does. If we can have disposable handkerchiefs and prefabricated kitchens, we can go on up the scale to prefabricated housing assembled and dismantled at will; buildings such as schools that could be added to or subtracted from as the need arises.

Let's throw things away

Plastics haven't begun to come into their own. We make useless toys and copies of conventional articles with a material that, if imaginatively applied, has thousands of original uses. Furniture, utensils, clothes, toys could be cheaply made to last only as long as they are useful, then be discarded without a qualm.

We could have all these things, objects of superb design, utility and variety, but we're so convinced of the enduring values of possessions that when we are told we would not want things any different we believe it.

What is worse, we are never given the opportunity to test our opinions. Extended social services and industry satisfying real consumer needs, instead of catering to obsolescent and artificially stimulated wants, could combine to bring women into the twentieth century before it is over.

Could we not in future divide bread-winning and child care equally between husband and wife? We would then have completed the cycle set in motion by the Industrial Revolution and regained the adult, human partnership which men and women in the home enjoyed before that time.

Nor is my seeking to free women from domestic toil tantamount to advocating the breakup of family life. If we had real faith in ourselves and the future and suffered less nostalgia for a vanished age, we might come up with a fresh and more applicable conception of family life for our day.

Women can be equal

We know we face a challenge from the East, behind and in front of the Iron Curtain. There, people are much less concerned with annihilating us (and themselves in the process) than they are with achieving our standards of education, technology and living—in that order—and eventually surpassing us in all three.

Therefore, if we are truly concerned about the perpetuation of our democratic way of life, we should match their effort with ours. A first step would be to ensure equality of opportunity to be human to our own women, thus doubling the human achievement potential on our side.

If it means that we thereby draw women away from a conventional family-home structure as we long ago drew their husbands out of the home and into the factory, then let's make up for lost time and progress right away. ...

In exercising my critical faculties on hateful housekeeping I am vindicating my early training. I ask others to join me in a battle against futility; in inventing ways to circumvent the accepted and abolish the unnecessary. Let us at last demand unashamedly the means to realize our full potential as women.

A rebellion is justified, for, far from being detractors of our civilization, we are the pioneers of inevitable changes for the better. What was bad for our mothers is no longer good enough for us.

7. Mollie Gillen, "The Royal Commission on the Status of Women: Will it do any Good?" *Chatelaine*, January 1968.

Yes, because there are still plenty of problems in the Canadian woman's Garden of Eden. For example ...

Why are widows taxed unfairly?
Why are deserted wives unprotected?
Why don't equal-pay-for-equal-work laws work?
Why don't women have equal job opportunity?
Why aren't working wives helped more?
Why aren't there enough day nurseries?
Why do divorce laws favor men?
Why can't women decide abortions?

The announcement made on February 3, 1967, that Prime Minister Lester Pearson was setting up a Royal Commission on the Status of Women in Canada was received across the land with a variety of reactions—rejoicing, rejection and outright ribaldry.

Among the rejoicers were women who for many years have seriously studied the position of women in Canada. "It won't be the answer to everything, but I'm delighted to see it," said Laura Sabia, St. Catharines alderman and president of the Canadian Federation of University Women. Margaret Hyndman, QC, former national and international president of the Business and Professional Women's Clubs, called it "a wonderful opportunity to tell the story of Canadian women's potential in relation to all phases of Canadian life." Toronto Controller Margaret Campbell stated flatly that discrimination is still practiced, noting press dismay because *two* of Toronto's four controllers elected in 1966 were women.

The rejecters were led by Ottawa's fiery former mayor and alderman, seventy-one-year-old Charlotte Whitton, "It's the most fantastically inexcusable thing I've ever heard of ... The doors are open now, if women didn't want to be sissy pussies making sandwiches in the ladies' auxiliary." Writer June Callwood called it "a lot of nonsense," and added, "you can't get equality by decree." Toronto alderman Alice Summerville said, "There is no discrimination in Ontario at least ... It sounds to me like just another way to spend money."

Ribaldry—or anyway flippancy—popped up among the columnists, mostly male. Robert Evans of the *Sudbury Star* agreed it's a good thing for women to let off steam to an audience "other than their husbands or friends ... The effect should be therapeutic if nothing else." Toronto columnist Frank Tumpane got old-fashioned cute. "Yes, sir, I'm all in favor of equality for women. Do you know there are people in this country who can actually remember that when a girl married a man she expected him to support her? That was inequality for you ... We've made great strides since then, of course. Nowadays when a girl is married she is expected to get a job and put her husband through university ... Having conceded a great measure of equality, the men want the women to enjoy it, that's all ... Now let's sit back, fellas, and see if they can agree on just what it is they do want."

Perhaps it's inevitable that there should be a great many misconceptions about the meaning of equality for women. Far too many people (including a lot of women) think it means a total reversal of today's sex roles and read the words "domination" or "loss of femininity" for equality. Others insist, like Miss Whitton, that equality already exists, ignoring the dreary and unarguable statistics that still show women's pay at a lower level than men's for the same work in many occupations, laws that take away certain personal legal rights upon marriage, public morality that punishes the prostitute, the unmarried mother, the mistress more severely than her male partner.

A government can legislate married *women* out of jobs (except for wartime, the federal civil service refused to employ married women until 1955) simply by reason of their marital status, though it would never dream of legislation to restrict a man from his right to work for pay. Under Canadian law, a married woman is considered to be her husband's dependent, to be provided for by his earnings and have no need for any of her own. This is often the reason given for higher pay for men, who "have a family to support."

Of course, there are Canadian women teachers, preachers, lawyers, doctors, chemists, engineers, stock-market promoters, architects. But there is still a barrier at the door that limits the number of women who get through, whether it's a quota system, a social attitude, a legal rule. Any rights women have today have been gained drib by drab over the years after tremendous and prolonged pressure. There still remain rights to be gained, trails to be blazed.

As women, we weren't even *persons* according to law, as recently as 1929.

Let's move to specifics and look first at the historical position of women ...

Canadian women were emancipated bit by bit in much the same pattern. Right to custody of children came in provincial statutes from 1914 to 1922, the right to personal property from 1903 to 1923, and Canadian women got the federal vote in 1918.

We have come a long way since those days. But have we come far enough? Our Royal Commission has been set up to try to find answers to just that question.

EDUCATION AND TRAINING

Among the subjects the Commission will be asked to consider will be the education of girls and women. Parents themselves, and social attitudes, have a tendency to regard higher education for daughters as less important than for sons. Today, when every third worker in the labor force is likely to be a woman, the lack of advanced training and skills shows up in their earnings. Although the relative income of working women is probably lowered by the proportion of part-time workers in their ranks, cross-Canada figures for earnings of workers show that the average incomes of men are about double those of women. "The reasons why women generally earn less than men," says the federal Department of Labour's Women At Work In Canada (1964), "are to a considerable extent related to the role of women in society ... The attitude of women toward training for employment tends to be different from that of men ... [they] are less likely than men to take the training necessary to fit them for highly skilled work."

Even where they may have equal training, women tend to earn less than men. "In general, women earn less than men as teachers," comments Women At Work In Canada, "but this is related to the fact that a larger proportion of men teach in secondary schools in urban areas, and have higher certificates. *Apart from qualifications, men probably have more opportunities than women to become principals or assistant principals because of the force of tradition.*" (Our italics.)

Since jobs for women outside the home are an increasing necessity for both the personal and national economy, the Commission will consider the *availability* of proper training for women. It will ponder the reasons for this country's low percentage of women in such professions as law, medicine, architecture, engineering, accountancy, when other countries are using the potential of their female population in vastly higher numbers. Is there an outdated social criticism in Canada that keeps women from entering these fields? A quota system (conscious or unconscious) that limits the entrance of women as undergraduates to these faculties? A failure of business and industry to employ women lawyers, engineers? In percentage comparison with other countries of women students against total number of students in professional university faculties, Canada makes a poor showing:

Country	Law*	Pharmacy*	Medicine*	Science*
Australia (1965)	11	41	17	20
Belgium (1964)	15.8	42.62	14.94	5.2
Canada (1964–65)	4.9	33.3	9.1	16.3

Denmark (1962–63)	26.8	52.5	24.2	22.4
Ireland (N. & S.)	21	40	26	30
Norway (1961)	17	62.5	23	26.65

*Percentages of women students in faculty.

EQUAL PAY

The heavy grouping of women workers in the lower-paid ranks is due not only to lack of proper training. The Commission will be taking a hard look at the implementation of Canada's equal-pay legislation. The federal government and eight of the ten provinces have equal-pay laws, and Quebec has incorporated the principle in its anti-discriminative legislation. But, as suggested by the Canadian Federation of Business and Professional Women's Clubs in their memorandum presented to the Prime Minister in February 1966, we have a long way to go to make this legislation effective. The government's own statistics show that all down the line women come off second best in average income, from the person working 50 to 52 weeks in a year (the figure for men is $5,014, for women $2,634) to the one-to-fourteen weeks' workers (men $839, women $383). Women wage earners in manufacturing earned an average of $49.22 a week in 1963, men $89.96. Women on salary got a weekly $64.17, men $128.50.

For completely identical work, a male assembler of heating and cooking apparatus, for instance, gets $1.89 an hour, his female counterpart $1.71. A male TV-set assembler gets $1.74 an hour, a female $1.48. The male pocketmaker, at $1.93 an hour, earns more than the female by 50 cents. To get redress on unequal pay, the woman worker has to complain and is often afraid to do so; a fairer system would be government enforcement by inspection.

The Commission will also have to consider whether the suggestion by the Business and Professional Women to change the wording of the federal act from "identical or substantially identical work" to "work of comparable character done in the same establishment" would remove the opportunity at present open to an employer to circumvent the law. This can be done, for instance, by what the Bs and Ps call a "weasel" clause, a slight variation in the job description such as adding that a male employee "may" do a certain additional operation though he probably never does, or by defining the selling of women's blouses and sweaters as "different" from selling men's shirts and socks in order to justify a lesser rate for the woman salesclerk.

"It's to men's advantage, too, to have this kind of discrimination abolished," says Ontario Women's Bureau director Lita-Rose Betcherman. "Lower-paid women can undercut higher-paid men for the same jobs." Men who would enjoy nursing, social work, library science and other work now largely dominated by women would be attracted to these fields if the pay were higher. "The best profession for men to get into," said a woman social worker cynically a few years ago, "is one in which there are a lot of women—men will always come to the top as executives."

"The invisible barriers" to the acceptance and promotion of women in every area of business and industry must also be brought into the open by the Commission. The federal government itself has been called to task for failure to open its top positions to women, by no less a voice than that of the Glassco Commission on the civil service. The Business and Professional Women protested the policy in their February 1966 memorandum to the Prime Minister: "The continued dearth of appointments of women by the Government of Canada as deputy ministers and assistant deputy ministers leads this federation to believe that discrimination is being practiced against women because of their sex and for no other reason."

It may be, of course, due less to policy than to a kind of absentmindedness, "The past lays a heavy hand upon the minds of men," says Mirra Komarovsky in *Women In The Modern World.* "It seems so natural that the occupants of certain swivel chairs should be male that the candidacy of a woman may not even enter the mind." Nineteen delegates were sent off to London in 1959 to represent Canada at the Commonwealth Conference on Education, all of them male, though education is a subject acknowledged to be of concern to women as mothers and teachers. The omission was admitted by the then Prime Minister, John Diefenbaker, and a last-minute appointment sent Dr. Mary Quayle Innis, dean of women at University College, Toronto, to join the delegation. The trend continues: The planning committee for the Canadian Conference on Human Rights Year (1968) has no woman member. It remains noticeable how many boards and commissions of vital interest to women consist totally of men, even though there are many qualified women to choose from. Out of the 967 people who were on the 1966–67 governing boards of 44 Canadian universities, for instance, only 33 were women—a sorry showing when almost half the student population was female (179,484 men, 75,217 women).

Business and industry offer many reasons for the failure of women to reach the top in proportionate numbers. Sometimes it's straight prejudice. "I couldn't work with a woman," said a top advertising executive, his only reason for turning down a senior woman writer. Sometimes it's customer acceptance, "I don't think it has been a deliberate policy of the banks to exclude women from the position of bank manager," says Dilys Smith, superintendent in the Canadian Imperial Bank of Commerce's personnel division, "although it is difficult to assess the public's acceptance of women in that post. My personal opinion is that many businessmen feel uncertain of a woman bank manager's abilities. Unfortunately, many women do, too." There are no women in this position at present with the Bank of Commerce, and only three with the Bank of Nova Scotia, the first Canadian bank to appoint a woman bank manager.

"The Bank of Commerce would appoint woman managers, but qualified women whose domestic responsibilities would permit such an appointment are rare," says Dilys Smith. Many women don't want the responsibility, or their energies have to be divided between home and job. As well, there's the problem of domicile. What does such a woman do when her husband is transferred to another city?

THE MARRIED WOMAN

Here the Commission will have to consider the plight of the married woman. Happy wives will rear up at the suggestion that they suffer from discrimination, but marriage does result in legal incompetences for women in certain situations. It's no answer to say that these don't bother most wives. Domicile is only one of the personal rights given up by a married woman in Canada. By law her husband's domicile is hers, too. If he deserts her, or they separate, her legal domicile is considered to be wherever *he* happens to live. Any divorce action she may wish to take must be started in the province of his residence. In other countries— Holland for one—domicile is independent of marital status for a woman as it is for a man. The Commission will be asked to look closely into this restriction operating against women as persons.

Since Canadian law regards wives as their husband's dependents, marriage for the noneworking wife is legally a maintenance institution: There is no monetary value placed on her contribution to the partnership, and she has no right under law to any cash allowance from her husband if he chooses not to give it to her. He is obligated only to provide her with food, shelter, clothing and medical attention, with no minimum set beyond that of "the necessaries of life."

Broken marriages are a tragedy for both parties, if only in terms of broken dreams. Separation, judicial or by private consent, means hardship for both, but often more for the wife. Her "meal ticket" is still, by law her defaulting or absent husband, and the deserted wife, with skills lost and perhaps young children to care for, is in for a long, complicated and humiliating series of forms and formalities before she can receive the small pittance of welfare payments. The law that will garnishee a man's wages for unpaid installments on a color television set won't do so for the subsistence of his deserted wife and children. The economic, legal and social status of the married woman left alone will be intensely studied by the Canadian Federation of University Women and other groups over the coming years, and represents an area of major concern for the Royal Commission.

TAXATION

In 1959, changes in inheritance taxation partially relieved a situation gravely unfair to widows (persistent appeals by women's groups can claim much of the credit for this). The 1959 act granted a basic exemption of $40,000 if the value of the estate exceeds $50,000, but made the exemption $60,000 if there is a widow. In the case of a *house* or other *real property*, but only if it is held in joint tenancy (legal jargon meaning that the surviving wife or husband takes all), a widow is relieved of the obligation to prove that her contribution to the property was her own and not given her by her husband. As well, either spouse may give the other a once-in-a-lifetime interest of $10,000 in their residential property.

Further tax changes have been recommended by the Carter Report (for instance, that no taxes be levied on inheritances between husbands and wives). The Commission on the Status of Women will provide opportunity to interest public opinion in pressing for their implementation.

Tax relief for the working woman will be another important subject of discussion. "The well-heeled businessman who wines and dines his customers can claim the cost as business expenses for tax purposes," wrote the Toronto Star in January 1967. "But the hard-pressed housewife working to help pay off the mortgage, or the divorced or deserted mother, can't deduct the cost of household help." This adds up to more than merely social injustice: It denies the country the skills of many qualified women and often prevents them from taking courses that would upgrade or update those skills.

WORKING MOTHERS

Relief for working mothers is implicit in most of the headings considered so far, in the light of today's reality where married women workers are 52.1 percent of the total female labor force. Among other needs urgently demanding attention are provision of proper day care for young children and maternity leave, in both of which Canada lags far behind European countries.

In Germany, for example, pregnant women get six weeks' leave prior to birth if they want it, plus a mandatory six weeks minimum afterward—with full pay. During pregnancy they must be given easier work if their health requires it;

nursing mothers are granted daily time off. No pregnant woman can be given notice of dismissal until four months after giving birth.

Childbirth leave with full job security is also mandatory in Norway (up to 18 weeks) and France (up to 14 weeks) though not with pay unless the employer grants it. In France, women get half pay from their medical-insurance plan if they stop work for at least six weeks.

More day nurseries for children of working mothers are still needed in Europe's industrialized nations—such as Germany, Scandinavia, France—but they still provide more nurseries than we. As well, both France and Sweden offer limited programs, hiring mothers to go in and look after children in their own homes.

Women trade unionists are particularly concerned with day-care facilities and maternity leave. A June 1967 women's conference sponsored by the Ontario Federation of Labour gave top priority to them.

There will also be vehement and persuasive arguments for (and some against) the abolition of special protective treatment of women—restrictions on night work, provision of transportation after midnight, physical limitations. A job or elective post should be available to and accepted by a man or a woman on its own merits and on the qualifications they bring to it: Adult women, say the unionists, don't have to be babied, and must accept the responsibilities of any job on equal terms with the men. The unionists—and others, too—will be asking why women must retire at the age of sixty while men can keep on working until they're sixty-five, as many companies (a national oil company, for one) insist: and why other companies require, for instance, ten years of service before a woman employee can join a salary-insurance plan open to a man after only one year.

THE WIDER ISSUES

If the Commission does no more than provide an opportunity for bringing to public attention, for thoughtful consideration, the discrepancies, injustices and inequities that still exist, it will have given us our money's worth. For many of the problems are *human* problems, not merely women's alone.

We have reached the point where legislation can be expected before long to amend the relevant section of the Criminal Code, banning the dissemination of information about birth control. The problems of divorce and abortion are also nearer to saner and more sensible treatment than ever before. These are three issues of the utmost importance to all women, and almost all the briefs received by the Commission can be counted on to include sober suggestions and requests for government action.

Issues of supreme importance to women, a uniform minimum age of sixteen for marriage and provision for the child who has been raped, have been the subject of serious study by such organizations as the Voice Of Women and the CFUW. The final report of the Commission will undoubtedly add strength to the tireless pressure on provincial governments for action.

It will, in fact, probably be hard to find any subject—any aspect of life— that is not offered to the Commission from the point of view of women. Jury duty and forensic clinics, part-time work and treatment of sex deviates, penal reform and traffic problems, housing, medical research, you name it—can anyone really believe that these are subjects outside the interest and concern of women?

THE OTHER SIDE

There's a negative side of women's status in Canada that the Royal Commission can't afford to ignore. How far are women themselves to blame for discrimination and prejudices? Are some of the restrictions—limits on insurance levels, exclusion from company pension or other benefit schemes—imposed not by the ill will of employers, but by actuarial difficulties because not enough women are interested in supporting a scheme to make it financially practicable? Have working women absorbed enough of the group philosophy to support a benefit scheme that they don't need personally but that will help their colleagues ("because she's got three kids ... an invalid sister ... a senile father to care for)?" Do men have a sense of brotherhood that women, so far, lack? If this is so, the Royal Commission's educational value will not be its least important one.

NOT THE FINAL ANSWER

Not even the thirty-one women's groups who so ardently urged the establishment of a Commission to examine the status of women in Canada expect miracles from its studies. They do hope that social injustices will be brought into the clearer light of reason, and that women in future will work for and gain the right to be persons in areas where now they are still limited by being female persons.

You can, in spite of writer June Callwood's pessimism, get equality by decree in some cases: A decree could remove tax discrimination, domiciliary inequality, birth-control prohibition. But women can help themselves, too. By taking an interest in civic affairs and qualifying for appointment. By demanding and using the training facilities to upgrade their qualifications. By pressing for reform wherever they see social injustices operating against any section of the community. By fulfilling the obligations of any responsibility they accept.

It's true that women have not yet won all the rights men have, and a Royal Commission can go far to hasten the slow Canadian awareness of its female potential.

Readings

Adamson, N. et al. *Feminist Organizing for Change: The Contemporary Women's Movement in Canada.* Toronto: Oxford University Press, 1988.

Backhouse, C. and Flaherty, D., eds. *Challenging Times: The Women's Movements in Canada and the United States.* Montreal: McGill-Queen's Press, 1992.

Bashevkin, S. *Toeing the Lines: Women and Party Politics in English Canada.* Don Mills: Oxford University Press, 1993.

Bashevkin, S. *Women of the Defensive: Living through Conservative Times.* Toronto: Univesity of Toronto Press, 1998.

Brodie, J. *Politics on the Margins: Restructuring and the Canadian Women's Movement.* Halifax: Fernwood, 1995.

Boyd, M. *Canadian Attitudes Toward Women: Thirty Years of Change.* Ottawa: Government of Canada, 1984.

Gleason, M. "Psychology and the Construction of the 'Normal Family' in Postwar Canada, 1945–1960," *Canadian Historical Review* 78, 3 (1997).

Golz, A. "Family Matters: The Canadian Family and the State in Postwar Canada," *Left History* 1, 2 (1993).

Iacovetta, F. and M. Valverde, eds. *Gender Conflicts: New Essays in Women's History.* Toronto: University of Toronto Press, 1992.

Korinek, V. *Roughing it in the Suburbs: Reading Chatelaine Magazine in the Fifties and Sixties.* Toronto: University of Toronto Press, 2000.

Kostash, M. *Long Way From Home: The Story of the Sixties Generation in Canada.* Toronto: James Lorimer, 1980.

Owram, D. *Born at the Right Time: A History of the Baby Boom Generation.* Toronto: University of Toronto Press, 1996.

Parr, J., ed. *A Diversity of Women.* Toronto: University of Toronto Press, 1995.

Pierson, R. et al., eds. *Canadian Women's Issues: Twenty Five Years of Women's Activism in English Canada.* Toronto: James Lorimer, 1993.

Strong-Boag, V. "Home Dreams: Women and the Suburban Experiment in Canada," *Canadian Historical Review* 72, 4 (1991).

Strong-Boag, V. "Canada's Wage-Earning Wives and the Construction of the Middle Class, 1945–1960," *Journal of Canadian Studies* 29 (Fall 1994).

Vickers, J. et al. *Politics as if Women Mattered: A Political Analysis of the National Action Committee on the Status of Women.* Toronto: University of Toronto Press, 1993.

Wine, J. and J. Ristock, eds. *Women and Social Change: Feminist Activism in Canada.* Toronto: Lorimer, 1991.

Chapter Fourteen

"THE VERY ESSENCE OF CANADIAN IDENTITY": MULTICULTURALISM

1. Government of Canada, Appendix to *Hansard*, October 8, 1971.
2. Neil Bissoondath, *Selling Illusions, the Cult of Multiculturalism*, 1994
3. Dick Field, "Multiculturalism Undermines Values Held by Canadians," *Toronto Star*, December 23, 1994.

Introduction

Canadians often define themselves through comparisons between Canada and the United States. Of these, perhaps the most common is contrasting the Canadian multicultural "mosaic" to the American monocultural "melting pot," lauding the former and condemning the latter. According to this theory, immigrants to Canada maintain and celebrate their heritage, creating a national mosaic of cultures, while newcomers to America must abandon all cultural baggage and melt into homogenous Americans. Fond of this image as Canadians are, it is grossly simplistic. Ask an Uzbek-Canadian how Uzbecky he and his kids can remain while functioning in Canadian society.

Government supported multiculturalism in Canada is, in fact, a recent phenomenon. Until it became official national policy in 1971, many Canadians had an expectation that other cultures, including those already present such as Native and French-Canadian, should assimilate into the dominant Anglo-Protestant society. As a result, the Department of Immigration, usually sought immigrants from the British Isles while discouraging most others. Immigration remained very selective before 1945 and restrictions, such as head taxes and official discouragement (Canada was touted as too cold for people of African origin), kept immigration virtually exclusive of visible minorities. This was particularly true of the 1920 and '30s during which Eastern Europeans and Jews, who earlier came in large numbers, lost access. Canada was, in fact, among the least welcoming democracies to Jews fleeing Nazi persecution. The overriding justification for this precise selectivity was to preserve and promote the "Britishness" of the nation.

Things changed after the war. The Canadian economy leaped from the ashes of war and required significantly more workers than were available—jobs filled by waves of "DPs" (Displaced Persons) escaping the post-war chaos of Europe. Visible minority immigrants from "exotic" homelands also became more common after the war, partly from the (collapsing) British Empire, but also as a result of overtly discriminatory barriers to immigration disappearing from the Immigration Act in 1967, thus encouraging a large influx of immigrants from Africa, South and Central America, the Caribbean, and Asia. The process was accelerated in 1978 with the creation of Canada's refugee program. Consequently, by the end of the twentieth century, 40% of Canada's population was of neither French nor English ancestry. This reality was particularly graphic in Canada's urban environments. Toronto's population, for example, is 38% foreign born (not just of foreign ancestry). Vancouver is similar. In a recent survey of first year students at the University of Toronto, more than half considered themselves non-white and only about 1/3 spoke English as a first language. In contrast, rural regions, particularly in Quebec and in Atlantic Canada, the clear majority remains French, English, or Native.

The huge increase in immigration after the war, both in volume and countries of origin, begged a central question: should Canada expect its newcomers to assimilate into one of the two traditionally dominant cultures? In 1963 the federal government appointed the Royal Commission on Bilingualism and Biculturalism to examine French-English relations, but the Commission's mandate also encompassed recommendations on the new multicultural reality of Canada. The result was a profound shift in cultural policy. The Commission advised that the best solution for Canada, both to heal the rift between French and English, and to acknowledge the multicultural reality of the country, was to promote no single culture—except in the area of language where both French and English would share official status. The Commission argued that ethnicity is the basis of the Canadian identity. Pierre Trudeau accepted the recommendations and made them official on October 8, 1971.

Multiculturalism as a policy came under intense scrutiny. The arguments against it were primarily threefold: that the motivation for multiculturalism was a cynical attempt to grab ethnic votes for the Liberals; that it attempted to diffuse Quebec separatism rather than address the needs of immigrants; and that it was more divisive than constructive. Writers like Neil Bissoondath, for example, argued that it meant little else than encouraging ethnic ghettoization that would perpetuate values from the "Old Country." To him, ethnic parades and festivals also demonstrated superficial patronizing—all at taxpayers expense and rarely translated into anything beyond recreation. If language is the key to cultural retention, some question whether multiculturalism can exist within a bilingual framework. Other critics also maintain that multiculturalism promotes ethnic divisions, therefore reinforcing differences rather than promoting Canadian unity. Some even go so far as to argue that multiculturalism actually encourages racism.

Supporters of multiculturalism state that the policy simply recognizes the Canadian reality and thereby affords protection to those who might be discriminated against by virtue of their ethnicity. They also argue that multiculturalism is anything but divisive: that it generates a sense of harmony by encouraging Canadians to share their heritage, thereby promoting understanding and tolerance. The world is increasingly homogenous, they argue, and official multiculturalism will create significant benefits for the country by creating a vibrant and open cultural climate that invites the best and brightest from across the world. According to its supporters, Canada is simply the vanguard of a general trend, and progressive nations like Australia now borrow from the Canadian legislation. Supporters also point to an increase in mixed marriages since Canada became officially multicultural; suggesting the policy successfully engineered the social fabric in a more inclusive direction. There is also the philosophical question: why should everyone conform to traditional British or French culture when the clear majority of Canadians now no longer traces its heritage to either the British Isles or France? Finally, they claim that racism cannot be eradicated without officially sanctioning cultural background as a badge of honour, not an impediment to inclusion.

Discussion Points

1. In practical terms does multiculturalism exist in Canada?
2. Has multiculturalism gone too far or not far enough?
3. Does multiculturalism produce a sense of national identity and unity?
4. Was Bissoondath right about multiculturalism promoting racism?

Documents

1. Government of Canada, Appendix to *Hansard*, October 8, 1971.

The government accepts and endorses the recommendations and spirit of Book IV of the Royal Commission on Bilingualism and Biculturalism. It believes the time is overdue for the people of Canada to become more aware of the rich tradition of the many cultures we have in Canada. Canada's citizens come from almost every country in the world, and bring with them every major world religion and language. This cultural diversity endows all Canadians with a great variety of human experience. The government regards this as a heritage to treasure and believes that Canada would be the poorer if we adopted assimilation programs forcing our citizens to forsake and forget the cultures they have brought to us.

The federal government hopes that the provinces will also respond positively to those recommendations which the commissioners addressed to them. The Prime Minister has written to each of the provincial premiers outlining the policies and programs which the Federal Government is initiating and asking for their co-operation. Some provinces have already taken the initiative and are responding to the recommendations directed to them.

The government while responding positively to the commission's recommendations, wishes to go beyond them to the spirit of the Book IV to ensure that Canada's cultural diversity continues.

Cultural diversity throughout the world is being eroded by the impact of industrial technology', mass communications and urbanization. Many writers have discussed this as the creation of a mass society—in which mass produced culture and entertainment and large impersonal institutions threaten to denature and depersonalize man. One of man's basic needs is a sense of belonging, and a good deal of contemporary social unrest—in all age groups—exists because this need has not been met. Ethnic groups are certainly not the only way in which this need for belonging can be met, but they have been an important one in Canadian society. Ethnic pluralism can help us overcome or prevent the homogenization and depersonalization of mass society. Vibrant ethnic groups can give Canadians of the second, third, and subsequent generations a feeling that they are connected with tradition and with human experience in various parts of the world and different periods of time.

Two misconceptions often arise when cultural diversity is discussed.

(a) Cultural Identity and National Allegiance.

The sense of identity developed by each citizen as a unique individual is distinct from his national allegiance. There is no reason to suppose that a citizen who identifies himself with pride as a Chinese-Canadian, who is deeply involved in the cultural activities of the Chinese community in Canada, will be less loyal or concerned with Canadian matters than a citizen of Scottish origin who takes part in a bagpipe band or highland dancing group. Cultural identity is not the same thing as allegiance to a country. Each of us is born into a particular family with a distinct heritage: that is, everyone—French, English, Italian and Slav included—has an "ethnic" background. The more secure we feel in one particular social context the more we are free to explore our identity beyond it. Ethnic groups often provide people with a sense of belonging which can make them better able to cope with the rest of society than they would as isolated individuals. Ethnic loyalties need not, and usually do not, detract from wider loyalties to community and country.

Canadian identity will not be undermined by multiculturalism. Indeed, we believe that cultural pluralism is the very essence of Canadian identity. Every ethnic group has the right to preserve and develop its own culture and values within the Canadian context. To say we have two official languages is not to say we have two official cultures, and no particular culture is more "official" than another. A policy of multiculturalism must be a policy for all Canadians.

(b) Language and Culture.

The distinction between language and culture has never been clearly defined. The very name of the royal commission whose recommendations we now seek to implement tends to indicate that bilingualism and biculturalism are indivisible. But, biculturalism does not properly describe our society; multiculturalism is more accurate. The Official Languages Act designated two languages, English and French, as the official languages of Canada for the purposes of all the institutions of the Parliament and government of Canada; no reference was made to cultures, and this act does not impinge urn [upon] the role of all languages as instruments of the various Canadian cultures. Nor, on the other hand, should the recognition of the cultural value of many languages weaken the position of Canada's two official languages. Their use by all of the citizens of Canada will continue to be promoted and encouraged.

The government is concerned with preserving human rights, developing Canadian identity, strengthening citizenship participation, reinforcing Canadian unity and encouraging cultural diversification within a bilingual framework. These objectives can best be served through a policy of multiculturalism composed of four main elements.

1. The government of Canada will support all of Canada's cultures and will seek to assist, resources permitting the development of those cultural groups which have demonstrated a desire and effort to continue to develop, a capacity to grow and contribute to Canada, as well as a clear need for assistance.

The special role of the government will be to support and encourage those cultures and cultural groups which Canadians wish to preserve.

The stronger and more populous cultural groups generally have the resources to be self-supporting and general cultural activities tend to be supportive of them. The two largest cultures, in areas where they exist in a minority situation, are already supported under the aegis of the government's official languages programs. New programs are proposed to give support to minority cultural groups in keeping with their' needs and particular situations.

However, the government cannot and should not take upon itself the responsibility for the continued viability of all ethnic groups. The objective of our policy is the cultural survival and development of ethnic groups to the degree that a given group exhibits a desire for this. Government aid to cultural groups must proceed on the basis of aid to self-effort. And in our concern for the preservation of ethnic group identity, we should not forget that individuals in a democracy may choose not to be concerned about maintaining a strong sense of their ethnic identity.

2. The Government will assist members of all cultural groups to overcome cultural barriers to full participation in Canadian society.

The law can and will protect individuals from overt discrimination but there are more subtle barriers to entry into our society. A sense of not belonging, or a feeling of inferiority, whatever its cause, cannot be legislated out of existence. Programs outlined in this document have been designed to foster confidence in one's individual cultural identity and in one's rightful place in Canadian life. Histories, films and museum exhibits showing the great contributions of Canada's various cultural groups will help achieve this objective. But, we must emphasize that every Canadian must help eliminate discrimination. Every Canadian must help contribute to the sense of national acceptance and belonging.

3. The Government will promote creative encounters and interchange among all Canadian cultural groups in the interest of national unity. As Canadians become more sensitive to their own ethnic identity and to the richness of our country, we will become more involved with one another and develop a greater acceptance of differences and a greater pride in our heritage. Cultural and intellectual creativity in almost all societies has been fostered by the interaction and creative relationship of different ethnic groups within that society. Government

aid to multicultural centres, to specific projects of ethnic groups, and to displays of the performing and visual arts as well as the programs already mentioned, will promote cultural exchange. The Government has made it very clear that it does not plan on aiding individual groups to cut themselves off from the rest of society. The programs are designed to encourage cultural groups to share their heritage with all other Canadians and with other countries, and to make us all aware of our cultural diversity.

4. The Government will continue to assist immigrants to acquire at least one of Canada's official languages in order to become full participants in Canadian society. The federal government, through the Manpower and Immigration Department and the Citizenship Branch of the Department of the Secretary of State, already assists the provinces in language training for adults, but new arrivals in Canada require additional help to adjust to Canadian life, and to participate fully in the economic and social life of Canada.

2. Neil Bissoondath, *Selling Illusions, the Cult of Multiculturalism,* 1994

... Their voices were almost aggressive in dismissing any discomfort that they might have experienced by flaunting the only government policy that seemed to cause no resentment: Canada as a multicultural land. Officially. Legally. Here, they insisted, you did not have to change. Here you could—indeed, it was your obligation to—remain what you were. None of this American melting-pot nonsense, none of this remaking yourself to fit your new circumstances: you did not have to adjust to the society, the society was obliged to accommodate itself to you.

An attractive proposal, then, a policy that excused much and required little effort. It was a picture of immigration at its most comfortable.

And yet I found myself not easily seduced.

The problem was that I had come in search of a new life and a new way of looking at the world. I had no desire simply to transport here life as I had known it: this seemed to me particularly onerous baggage with which to burden one's shoulders. Beyond this, though, the very act of emigration had already changed me. I was no longer the person I had been when I boarded the flight in Trinidad bound for Toronto: I had brought to the aircraft not the attitudes of the tourist but those of someone embarking on an adventure that would forever change his life. This alone was a kind of psychological revolution.

Multiculturalism, as perceived by those at whom it was most explicitly aimed, left me with a certain measure of discomfort ...

Many have long suspected that multiculturalism, proclaimed official policy in 1971, was initially boosted into the limelight not as a progressive social policy but as an opportunistic political one, not so much an answer to necessary social accommodation as a response to pressing political concerns. If the emphasis on federal bilingualism had seemed to favour francophone Quebec at the expense of the rest of the country, enhanced multiculturalism could be served up as a way of equalizing the political balance sheet. As René Lévesque once commented, "Multiculturalism, really, is folklore. It is a 'red herring.' The notion was devised to obscure 'the Quebec business,' to give an impression that we are *all* ethnics and do not have to worry about special status for Quebec."

But even a program born of manipulative cynicism does not necessarily have to be bereft of a certain amount of heart and sincerity. The Act for the Preservation and Enhancement of Multiculturalism in Canada, better known by its short title, the Canadian Multiculturalism Act, offers up—as do all such documents—gentle and well-meaning generalizations.

The act recognizes "the existence of communities whose members share a common origin and their historic contribution to Canadian society" and promises to "enhance their development"; it aims to "promote the understanding and creativity that arise from the interaction between individuals and communities of different origins" and commits the federal government to the promotion of "policies and practices that enhance the understanding of and respect for the diversity of the members of Canadian society." It talks about being "sensitive and responsive to the multicultural reality of Canada."

Recognition, appreciation, understanding; sensitive, responsive, respectful; promote, foster, preserve: these words and others like them occur time and again in the Multiculturalism Act, repeated in the thicket of legalistic phrasing like a mantra of good faith.

Beyond this, the act goes from the general to the concrete by authorizing the minister responsible to "take such measures as the Minister considers appropriate to ... (a) encourage and assist individuals, organizations and institutions to project the multicultural reality of Canada in their activities in Canada and abroad; ... (c) encourage and promote exchanges and cooperation among the diverse communities of Canada; ... (e) encourage the preservation, enhancement, sharing and evolving expression of the multicultural heritage of Canada; ... (h) provide support to individuals, groups or organizations for the purpose of preserving, enhancing and promoting multiculturalism in Canada."

The Multiculturalism Act is in many ways a statement of activism. It is a vision of government, not content to let things be, determined to play a direct role in shaping not only the evolution of Canadian—mainly *English*-Canadian—society but the evolution of individuals within that society. As a political statement it is disarming, as a philosophical statement almost naive with generosity. Attractive sentiments liberally dispensed—but where in the end do they lead?

The act, activist in spirit, magnanimous in accommodation, curiously excludes any ultimate vision of the kind of society that it wishes to create. It never addresses the question of the nature of a multicultural society, what such a society is and what it means. Definitions and implications are conspicuously absent, and this may be indicative of the political sentiments that prompted adoption of the act in the first place. Even years later, the act—a cornerstone of federal social policy—shows signs of a certain haste. In its lack of long-term consideration, in its delineation of action with no discussion of consequence, one can discern the opportunism that underlay it all. One senses the political hand, eager for an instrument to attract ethnic votes, urging along the drafting—and damn the consequences.

In its rush the act appears to indulge in several unexamined assumptions: that people, coming here from elsewhere, wish to remain what they have been; that personalities and ways of doing things, ways of looking at the world, can be frozen in time; that Canadian cultural influences pale before the exoticism of the foreign. It treats newcomers as exotics and pretends that this is both proper and sufficient.

Nor does the act address the question of limits: how far do we go as a country in encouraging and promoting cultural difference? How far is far enough, how far too far? Is there a point at which diversity begins to threaten social cohesion? The document is striking in its lack of any mention of unity or oneness of vision. Its provisions seem aimed instead at encouraging division, at ensuring that the various ethnic groups have no interest in blurring the distinctions among them.

A cynic might be justified in saying that this is nothing more than a cleverly disguised blueprint for a policy of "keep divided and therefore conquered," a policy that seeks merely to keep a diverse populace amenable to political manipulation.

The Canadian Multiculturalism Act is in many senses an ill-considered document, focused so squarely on today that it forgets about tomorrow. And it is this short-sightedness that may account for the consequences that it has brought about for individuals, for communities, for the country and people's loyalty to it.

CONSEQUENCES
The Simplification of Culture

The consequences of multiculturalism policy are many and varied, but none is as ironic—or as unintended—as what I would call the simplification of culture.

The public face of Canadian multiculturalism is flashy and attractive, emerging with verve and gaiety from the bland stereotype of traditional Canada at festivals around the country. At Toronto's "Caravan," for instance, various ethnic groups rent halls in churches or community centres to create "pavilions" to which access is gained through an ersatz passport. Once admitted—passport duly stamped with a "visa"—you consume a plate of Old World food at distinctly New World prices, take a quick tour of the "craft" and "historical" displays, then find a seat for the "cultural" show, traditional songs (often about wheat) and traditional dances (often about harvesting wheat) performed by youths resplendent in their traditional costumes.

After the show, positively glowing with your exposure to yet another slice of our multicultural heritage, you make your way to the next pavilion, to the next line up for food, the next display, the next bout of cultural edification. At the end of the day, you may be forgiven if you feel you have just spent several long hours at a folksy Disneyland with multicultural versions of Mickey, Minnie, and Goofy.

This in fact is all you have really done. Your exposure has been not to culture but to theatre, not to history but to fantasy: enjoyable, no doubt, but of questionable significance. You come away knowing nothing of the language and literature of these places, little of their past and their present—and what you have seen is usually shaped with blatantly political ends in mind. You have acquired no sense of the everyday lives—the culture—of the people in these places, but there is no doubt that they are each and every one open, sincere, and fun-loving.

Such displays are uniquely suited to seeking out the lowest common denominator. Comfortable only with superficialities, they reduce cultures hundreds, sometimes thousands, of years old to easily digested stereotypes. One's sense of Ukrainian culture is restricted to perogies and Cossack dancing: Greeks, we learn, are all jolly Zorbas, and Spaniards dance flamenco between bouts of "Viva España"; Germans gulp beer, sauerkraut, and sausages while belting out Bavarian drinking songs; Italians make good ice-cream, great coffee, and all have connections to shady godfathers. And the Chinese continue to be a people who form conga lines under dragon costumes and serve good, cheap food in slightly dingy restaurants.

Our approach to multiculturalism thus encourages the devaluation of that which it claims to wish to protect and promote. Culture becomes an object for display rather than the heart and soul of the individuals formed by it. Culture, manipulated into social and political usefulness, becomes folklore—as Lévesque said—lightened and simplified, stripped of the weight of the past. None of the cultures that make up our "mosaic" seems to have produced history worthy of exploration or philosophy worthy of consideration.

I am reminded of the man who once said to me that he would never move into an apartment building that housed any East Indian families because the building was sure to be infested with roaches: East Indians, he explained, view cockroaches as creatures of good luck, and they give live ones as gifts to each other. I had known the man for some time, was certain that he was in no way racist—a perception confirmed by the fact that he was admitting this to me, someone clearly of East Indian descent. His hesitation was not racial but cultural. I was not of India: he would not hesitate in having me for a neighbour. So searching for an apartment, he perceived the neighbours not as fellow Canadians old or new but as cockroach-lovers, a "cultural truth" that he had accepted without question. But what would he have done, I wondered later with some discomfort, had he seen me emerging from a building that he was about to visit?

The vision that many of us have of each other is one of division. It is informed by misunderstanding and misconception: what we know of each other is often at best superficial, at worst malicious. And multiculturalism, with all of its festivals and its celebrations, has done nothing to foster a factual and clear-headed vision of the other. Depending on stereotype, ensuring that ethnic groups will preserve their distinctiveness in a gentle form of cultural apartheid, multiculturalism has done little but lead an already divided country down the path to further social divisiveness ...

It has become a commonplace that we who share this land—we who think of Canada as home—suffer an identity crisis stemming from a fragile self-perception.

Certain segments of the population profess a dogged loyalty to the monarchy, a manifestation of mental colonialism hardly in evidence in other parts of the former British empire. Other groups, in contrast, have evolved a sense of self independent of their colonial origins, one that, coalescing around language and distinctive culture, at times hints at a kind of besieged tribalism. There are even some, emerging from both groups, who quietly yearn for a kind of wider continentalism, the self as simply North American: the anglophone who professes to see no difference between Canadians and Americans; the francophone who holds that his rights would be more respected under the American constitutional umbrella.

To such fracturing must now be added a host of new divisions actively encouraged by our multiculturalism policy and aided and abetted by politicians (a cheque here, a cheque there) of every ideological stripe.

When, a few months ago, Yugoslavia was beginning its inexorable slide into horror, a CBC news report stated that an estimated two hundred and fifty sons of Croatian immigrants, young men of able body and (presumably) sound mind, had left this country to take up arms in defence of Croatia. The report prompted a question: how did these young men define themselves? As Canadians of Croatian descent? As Croatian Canadians? Or as Croatians of Canadian birth? And I wondered which country they would choose if one day obliged to: the land of their parents, for which they had chosen to fight, or the land of their birth, from which they had chosen to depart?

It seems an unfair question. Not only does federal law accept the concept of dual citizenship—which implies dual loyalties—but Canadians have a long and honourable history of inserting themselves into foreign wars. Norman Bethune is just one among hundreds of Canadians, for instance, who enlisted in battle on the republican side of the Spanish civil war ...

To leave one's country, to commit oneself to conflict in the land of one's forbears for ideals not intellectual but racial, is at best to reveal loyalties divided between country and ethnicity. The right to decide on the distribution of one's commitments is of course fundamental: freedom of belief, freedom of conviction, freedom of choice. It says much about the new country, however, that its command of its citizens' loyalties is frequently so tenuous.

Divided loyalties reveal a divided psyche, and a divided psyche, a divided country. For these young Canadians of Croatian descent are not alone in their adulterated loyalty to Canada. Others, too, find it impossible to make a whole-hearted commitment to the new land, the new ideals, the new way of looking at life.

Imported Old World feuds—ethnic, religious, and political hatreds—frequently override loyalties to the new country. If the aiming of a gun at one's Old World enemies breaks the laws of Canada, so be it: the laws of Canada mean little against the older hatreds. And multiculturalism, in encouraging the wholesale retention of the past, has done nothing to address what is a serious—and has at times been a violent—problem. In stressing the differences between groups, in failing to emphasize that this is a country with its own ideals and attitudes that demand adherence, the policy has instead aided in a hardening of hatreds. Canada, for groups with resentments, is just another battleground ...

And this insistent vision, passed down to the next generation, has already

led—and will continue to lead—to suspicion, estrangement, vandalism, physical attack, and death threats; it is yet another aspect of the multicultural heritage
that we seek to preserve, promote, and share.

Marginalization

One never really gets used to the conversation. It will typically go something like this:

"What nationality are you?"

"Canadian."

"No, I mean what nationality are you *really*?"

To be simply Canadian untinged by the exoticism of elsewhere seems insufficient, even unacceptable, to many other Canadians. This fact clearly stems,
in part, from the simple human attraction to the exotic. But it seems to me that
it also has much to do with a wider issue: the uncertainty that we feel as a
people.

We reveal this uncertainty by that other quintessential (and quite possibly
eternal) Canadian question: who are we? The frequent answer—Well, we're not
like the Americans ... —is insufficient; a self-perception cast in the negative can
never satisfy. Lacking a full and vigorous response, we search for distinctiveness—exoticism—wherever we can find it. And we find it most readily in our
compatriots more recently arrived.

For professional ethnics—they who enjoy the role of the exotic and who
depend on their exoticism for a sense of self—this is a not unpleasant state of
affairs. For those who would rather be accepted for their individuality, who
resent having their differences continually pointed out, it can prove a matter
of some irritation, even discomfort. The game of exoticism can cut two ways:
it can prevent you from being ordinary, and it can prevent you from being
accepted.

The finest example of this remains the sprinter Ben Johnson. Within a
shattering twenty-four-hour period, Mr. Johnson went in media reports from
being the "Canadian" who had won Olympic gold through effort to the "Jamai-
can immigrant" who had lost it through use of drugs. The only thing swifter
than Johnson's drug-enhanced achievement was his public demotion from "one
of us" to "one of them." The exotic multicultural concept of the ever-lasting
immigrant has come to function as an institutional system for the marginalization
of the individual: Ben Johnson was, in other words, a Canadian when convenient, an immigrant when not. Had he, success or failure, been accepted as
being simply Canadian, it would have been difficult for anyone to distance him
in this way. Thus the weight of the multicultural hyphen, the pressure of the

link to exoticism, can become onerous—and instead of its being an anchoring definition, it can easily become a handy form of estrangement.

There is also evidence of this in the infamous Sikh turban issue that keeps bubbling up on the placid surface of our cultural mosaic. The two well-known controversies—turbans in the RCMP and turbans in Canadian Legion Halls— are in themselves indications of the failure of multiculturalism to go beyond superficiality in explaining us to each other. To view the turban as just another kind of hat, with no significance beyond sheltering the head, is to say that a cross worn on a chain is of no significance beyond a decoration for the neck: it is to reveal a deep ignorance of the ways and religious beliefs of others. To ban either is to revel in that ignorance and to alienate the other by rejecting a funda- mental part of his or her self.

Of greater interest, however, is what these controversies reveal about our idea of ourselves and our traditions. We are not a country of ancient customs, and multiculturalism seems to have taught us that tradition does not admit change: that traditions, in Canada, turn precious and immutable. This helps explain why, although RCMP headgear has changed throughout the years, there are those passionate in their opposition when faced with the possibility of seeing a turban among the stetsons. It also explains, in part, why a Legion Hall's desire to honour Canadian military men by banning headgear cannot make room for turbans. (In Britain, which is often seen as a tradition-bound society, turbans have long been accepted as part of the military and London police uniforms.)

But if, in our cultural insecurity, we have decided that tradition is immu- table, what happens when two contradictory traditions come together? Only conflict can result, the natural outcome of our inflexible view of tradition and multicultural heritage: so that protests with distinctly racist overtones are raised against turbans in the RCMP; so that a Sikh wishing to enter an Alberta Legion Hall is told to use the back door.

A final consequence of the marginalization to which we can so easily sub- ject one another comes frequently in times of economic hardship. The stresses of unemployment—the difficulty of the present and the invisibility of a future— create a need for scapegoats: we need something or someone to blame. We can rail against politicians, taxes, corporations—but these are all distant, untouch- able in their isolation. But no one is more easily blamed for the lack of opportunity than the obvious "foreigner" who is cleaning tables in the local doughnut shop. Maybe he has brown skin, maybe he speaks with an accent: clearly he is out of place here, filling a paid position that should by rights have gone to a "real" Canadian. All differences always so close to the surface, are seized upon; are turned into objects of ridicule and resentment, the psychology of exoticism once more cutting both ways.

Encouraging people to view each other as simply Canadian would not solve this problem—humans, in times of pain and anger, have unique ability for seeking out bull's-eyes in each other—but it may help redirect the resentment, so that in expressing the hurt we do not also alienate our fellow citizens. Differences between people are already obvious enough without their being emphasized through multiculturalism policy.

The Multiculturalism Act suggests no limits to the accommodation offered to different ethnic practices, so that a Muslim group in Toronto recently demanded, in the name of respect for its culture, the right to opt out of the Canadian judicial system in favour of Islamic law, a body of thought fundamental to the life and cultural outlook of its practising members. In the opinion of its spokesmen, this right should be a given in a truly multicultural society.

More recently, the Ontario College of Physicians and Surgeons expressed concern over a rise, unexplained and unexpected, in the number of requests for female circumcision. According to a report in the *Toronto Star* on 6 January 1992, the procedure, long viewed in Western culture as a kind of mutilation, involves "cutting off a young girl's external genital parts, including the clitoris. In some countries, it includes stitching closed the vulva until marriage, leaving a small opening for urination and menstrual flow ... Various health risks have been linked to it, including immediate serious bleeding, recurring infections, pain during intercourse, hemorrhaging during childbirth and infertility ... Charles Kayzze, head of Ottawa's African Resource Centre, believes it is being performed here by members of the community. In some cases, he says, families are sending their children to Africa to have it done."[5] The result is the reduction of the woman to the status of machine, capable of production but mechanically, with no pleasure in the process.

It is curious that such ideas can be brought to this land, survive, and then present a problem to doctors for whom policy guidelines, never before necessary, are now being established. ("The policy," the report states, "is likely to say Ontario doctors should not perform the operation.") Yet one awaits with bated breath calls for public performance of the ancient Hindu rite of suttee in which widows are cremated alive on their husband's funeral pyres.

There is a certain logic to all of this, but a logic that indicates a certain disdain for the legal and ethical values that shape, and are shaped by, Canadian society—and therefore for Canadian society itself.

And why not, given that the picture that the country transmits of itself is one that appears to diminish a unified whole in favour of an ever-fraying mosaic? If Canada, as a historical, social, legal, and cultural concept, does not demand respect, why should respect be expected? ...

Canada has long prided itself on being a tolerant society, but tolerance is clearly insufficient in the building of a cohesive society. A far greater goal to strive for would be an *accepting* society. Multiculturalism seems to offer at best provisional acceptance, and it is with some difficulty that one insists on being a full—and not just an associate—member. Just as the newcomer must decide how best to accommodate himself or herself to the society, so the society must in turn decide how it will accommodate itself to the newcomer. Multiculturalism has served neither interest; it has highlighted our differences rather than diminished them, has heightened division rather than encouraged union. More than anything else, the policy has led to the institutionalization and enhancement of a ghetto mentality. And it is here that lies the multicultural problem as we experience it in Canada: a divisiveness so entrenched that we face a future of multiple solitudes with no central notion to bind us ...

3. Dick Field, "Multiculturalism Undermines Values Held by Canadians," *Toronto Star*, December 23, 1994.

Thirty-five years ago, the majority of Canadians accepted the concept of multiculturalism because we felt that it would help newcomers integrate into Canadian society.

Unfortunately, no sooner had the concept been proclaimed by the federal government than the added concept of a "mosaic of cultures" was pushed on an unsuspecting public. This concept put forth the very damaging idea that newcomers could come to Canada and keep their own culture and that we, the taxpayers, would pay them to do so.

This concept was diametrically opposed to the strongly held Canadian tradition that newcomers should come to Canada, leave their problems and ancient hatreds in the old country, join the majority culture here, and work together to build Canada.

The concept of separate cultures, each of equal value, maintained at the majority taxpayers' expense, has spawned a nightmare of destructive self-interest. Minority spokespeople have built personal political fiefdoms as have an army of bureaucrats, politicians, educators and other people who manipulate the system for their own advantage.

All this at the expense of undermining Canadian values and traditions.

Even worse, at the expense of the good will which the vast majority of Canadians have, in the past, extended to all newcomers.

Canadians are not opposed to having other cultures join us in Canada. We are not opposed to other cultures preserving those parts of their culture that they wish to preserve, provided it is at their own expense and provided those cultural values are not in fundamental conflict with Canadian values and traditions (for example, female circumcision and polygamy).

In a positive sense there is much to learn from all cultures, especially in the area of the arts, foods and perspective.

What we are now experiencing, unfortunately, is a growing sense of being strangers in our own country. Our values and traditions as a free and independent people are under assault.

We do not blame the minorities themselves, when we are thoughtful. We know it is the crassness of our political leaders and the wrongness of the many laws, policies and programs they institute that are causing the upset.

We know it is not the majority within the minorities causing these problems. Unfortunately minorities must bear the brunt of the backlash, when we are pushed beyond thoughtfulness.

There are, however, too many minority members who do not speak out when they know their spokespeople are wrong. There are also too many Canadians willing to accept this chipping away at our values because they fear that if they do speak out they will be labelled as racists or bigots.

The employment equity law of Ontario is but one manifestation of the appeasement policies of insensitive governments reacting to the loud and insistent voices of the taxpayer-funded minorities. This horrendous concept, now law, fractures an unwritten principle of our society, which is that all of us must be equals under and before the law.

This is a law of inequality. This law judges us by skin colour, sex, or whatever other "disadvantaged" designation bureaucrats or politicians may decide is appropriate.

For the last 35 years, Canadian and British history, which embody the fundamental traditions and values of this free society, have been dishonoured. Among other things, they have even been excluded from our school curriculums.

As a consequence, young Canadians of all backgrounds are confused as to their heritage. In an attempt to be fair, the values of all cultures have been taught as being the equivalent of the values of this country.

This is a dangerous and divisive concept, as well as being untrue. Take an honest look at the countries where most recent ethnic and visible minority refugees and immigrants come from. Ask yourselves if those countries operate on the fundamental principles of a free and democratic country such as Canada. That is why it is the duty of all citizens to understand the principles and values underlying our country and to uphold them.

The vast majority of Canadians expect newcomers to do just that. The majority of new immigrants expected to do so when they came here but they are now being taught that Canadians have no values.

We now have many new immigrants who after three years in Canada obtain a piece of paper that says they are citizens, but they have no concept of Canadian values. Such people may be legal Canadians but they are not and never will be Canadians in mind or spirit.

Yes, "official taxpayer-funded" multiculturalism is dead. It is dead because the majority of Canadians no longer accept such a divisive and destructive policy and increasingly, they resent paying for it. All of us must make sure the beast lies down by withdrawing all funding designed to appease the spokespeople of ethnic and racial minority groups.

The answer lies in all of us joining together as Canadians, as unhyphenated human beings, and subscribing to the traditional values of Canada. Until we do, racial and ethnic upset will only get worse.

Readings

Abu-Laban, Y. and D. Stasiulis, "Ethnic Pluralism under Seige: Popular and Partisan Opposition to Multiculturalism," *Canadian Public Policy* 18, 4 (1992).

Angus, I. *A Border Within: National Identity, Cultural Plurality and Wilderness.* Montreal-Kingston: McGill-Queen's University Press, 1997.

Berry, J and J. Laponce, eds. *Ethnicity and Culture in Canada: The Research Landscape.* Toronto: University of Toronto Press, 1994.

Bibby, R. *Mosaic Madness.* Toronto: Stoddart, 1990.

Breton, R. et al. *Ethnic Identity and Equality.* Toronto: University of Toronto Press, 1990.

Cairns, A. and C. Williams, *The Politics of Gender, Ethnicity and Language.* Toronto: University of Toronto Press, 1986.

Cardozo A. and L. Musto, eds., *The Battle over Multiculturalism.* Ottawa: Pearson-Shoyama Institute, 1997.

Dahlie, J. and T. Fernando, eds. *Ethnicity, Power and Politics in Canada.* Toronto: Methuen, 1981.

Dodge, W., ed. *The Boundaries of Identity: A Quebec Reader.* Toronto: Lester, 1992.

Driedger, L., ed. *Ethnic Mosaic: A Quest for Identity.* Toronto: McClelland and Stewart, 1978.

Gairdner, W. *The Trouble with Canada.* Toronto: General, 1991.

Gwyn, R. *Nationalism Without Walls: The Unbearable Lightness of Being Canadian.* Toronto: McClelland and Stewart, 1995.

Hryniuk, S., ed. *20 Years of Multiculturalism: Successes and Failures.* Winnipeg: St. John's College, 1992.

Hutcheon L. and M. Richmond, eds. *Other Solitudes: Canadian Multicultural Fictions.* Toronto: Oxford University Press, 1990.

Kallen, E. "Multiculturalism: Ideology, Policy and Reality," *Journal of Canadian Studies* 17, 1 (1982).

Kaplan, W., ed. *Belonging: The Meaning and Future of Canadian Citizenship.* Montreal-Kingston: McGill-Queen's University Press, 1993.

Kymlicka, W. "The Theory and Practice of Canadian Multiculturalism," *Breakfast on the Hill.* November 23, 1998.

Kymlicka, W. *Multicultural Citizenship.* Oxford: University of Oxford Press, 1995.

McRoberts, K. *Misconceiving Canada: The Struggle for National Unity.* Oxford: Oxford University Press, 1997.

Padolsky, E. "Multiculturalism at the Millennium," *Journal of Canadian Studies* 35, 1 (Spring 2000).

Pal, L. *Interests of State: The Politics of Language, Multiculturalism and Feminism in Canada.* Montreal: McGill-Queen's University Press, 1993.

Palmer, H. *Immigration and the Rise of Multiculturalism.* Toronto: Copp Clark, 1975.

Reitz J. and R. Breton, *The Illusion of Difference.* Toronto: C.D. Howe Institute, 1994.

Roy, P. "The Fifth Force: Multiculturalism and the English Canadian Identity," *Annals of the American Academy of Political and Social Science* 538 (March 1995).

Satzewich, V., ed. *Deconstructing a Nation: Immigration, Multiculturalism and Racism in '90s Canada.* Halifax: Fernwood, 1992.

Taylor, C. *Multiculturalism and the Politics of Recognition.* Princeton: Princeton University Press, 1992.

Chapter Fifteen

"The Whites Were Terrorists": Residential Schools

1. Rev. K. Annett, "Hidden from History: The Canadian Holocaust," *Nexus* (March-April 2002).
2. Government of Canada, "Statement of Reconciliation," January 7, 1998.
3. Ted Byfield, "Weren't We all Physically Abused in Schools? So When do We Get Our Money for Healing," *Alberta Report*, January 19, 1998.
4. P. Donnelly, "Scapegoating the Indian Residential Schools: The Noble Legacy of Hundreds of Christian Missionaries is Sacrificed to Political Correctness," *Alberta Report*, January 26, 1998.
5. David Napier, "Sins of the Fathers: The Legacy of Indian Residential Schools is One of Physical and Emotional Scars, Nasty Lawsuits, A Questionable Medical Study, and Suicide," *Anglican Journal*, May 2000.

Introduction

In January 1998, then Minister of Indian Affairs, Jane Stewart, apologized to Canada's aboriginal community on behalf of the federal government for complicity in the treatment of Natives in government-sponsored residential schools. She said she was "deeply sorry" and established a "healing fund" of $350 million to help aboriginal communities overcome traumas resulting from their residential school experiences. All of this came on the heals of similar confessions of guilt from the Catholic and Anglican churches of Canada.

These apologies came years after former residents of the schools began coming forward en masse with a litany of horrors about life in the schools. Natives are now suing both the federal government and the religious institutions that ran the schools, and prosecutors have successfully convicted a number of former staff members. Some religious organizations presently face potential bankruptcy as a result of court-imposed settlements against them. Native communities, meanwhile, still languish with suicide and substance abuse rates significantly higher than the national average, and the percentage of aboriginals in Canadian jails is out of proportion to their absolute numbers. Indian leaders put much of the blame for this tragedy squarely on the impact of residential schooling.

The most common accusations against the system concern sexual and physical abuse, including neglect, of the children in the institutions' care. There are also more philosophical and ideologically motivated cases. Perhaps the most far reaching and comprehensive of these is the accusation that successive federal governments and their partners perpetrated "cultural genocide" against Canada's aboriginal population by, among other things, forbidding native languages from being spoken in the schools, and forcibly removing Native children from their homes.

Apart from the philosophical and ideological issues of assimilation and "cultural genocide," perhaps the biggest problem, and one never rectified, was chronic underfunding at all levels. This often meant school buildings that were, at best, mediocre, and at worst unfit for habitation. It meant inadequate food and medical care for some children in some areas. Low wages and extreme isolation too often led to unqualified or poor teachers being hired, and to insufficient general staffing levels. Poor funding meant inadequate government supervision of the schools. Abusers and abuses, even when reported—and they rarely were, tended to continue unchecked, sometimes for decades.

The list of complaints against the residential school system is long and the evidence damning, but the story has another side—one far less frequently and stridently voiced. Many native parents supported residential schools and regularly requested more be built. They argued that their children stood a better chance of integrating into mainstream society if they received a European-based education and training, something they could not get from their own people in the traditional villages. This belief became increasingly common as traditional modes of life, such as the buffalo hunt, disappeared or became untenable. Some Natives, such as Reverend Peter Jones, devoted their lives to bringing European education to their people, and there was never a shortage of residential school students who wished to become nuns and priests. Some former residential school residents even reminisce fondly over their years as students, maintaining that the education they received from devoted and friendly staff served them well in later years.

No single date marks the beginning of the residential school system, but one of the most significant early milestones was the 1842 Bagot Commission Report. It advised the government of Upper Canada that Natives should acquire "European industry and knowledge" unattainable, so the report stated, within

the confines of native communities where author Charles Bagot believed "primitive" culture stultified its citizens. Thus his overriding philosophical bent was to
assimilate Native children into mainstream culture by removing them from their
homes and placing them into Eurocentric environments where they would learn
to become "white." His recommendations, by chance, coincided with a period
of intense missionary effort on the part of major Christian denominations seeking to save souls and fill pews throughout the new world. Egerton Ryerson, a
Methodist minister prominent in Canada West's (Ontario) political circles, consolidated the emerging philosophical direction in his 1847 report which
recommended "the education of Indians consist not merely of training of the
mind but of weaning from the habits and feelings of their ancestors and the
acquirements of the language, arts and customs of a civilized life." A symbiotic
partnership between church and state therefore, not surprisingly, emerged whereby
Christian missionaries ran government funded schools for Natives.

Early efforts to create a residential school system remained haphazard, however, until confederation in 1867. At that time the federal government made
Natives wards of the state in a paternalistic move that facilitated further legislation, such as the 1876 Indian Act that consolidated the assimilationist
underpinnings of Native education policy. The 1879 Davin Report did much
the same, recommending the establishment of a comprehensive residential school
system modelled after the ones in the United States. An Order-in-Council in
1892 finally instituted regulations for operating residential schools, and a more
formal contractual agreement between religious groups and the federal government detailed the administrative partnership between church and state.

In 1920 Duncan Campbell Scott, federal Superintendent of Indian Affairs, made school attendance for Natives mandatory for seven to fifteen-year-olds
after discovering how few Indian children attended school. This, of course, required most Native students to board away from their families since facilities
rarely existed in remote villages. Despite subsequent concerted efforts to implement the letter of the law, including accusations of kidnapping, only a small
percentage of Native children ever attended residential schools.

There were, at their maximum extent, some 80 residential schools, with a
total population of approximately 10,000 students, in all provinces and territories except New Brunswick, Prince Edward Island and Newfoundland. Serious
criticism, along several fronts, mounted until bureaucrats in the Department of
Indian Affairs conceded by the end of the Second World War that residential
schools did not, in fact, achieve their goals and also suffered from a number of
grave problems that jeopardized the health and well-being of Native children.

The solution was to phase out the schools and integrate Indian youths into regular provincial schools. It took two more decades, however, for the system to wind down. The federal government took direct control of their management, and subsequently relinquished control of many to Native communities themselves. The last government-run residential school closed in 1983.

Discussion Points

1. Sexual abuse is, by its nature, difficult to prove. Is the evidence and conclusion of sexual and physical abuse from the first document sufficiently convincing? Why or why not?
2. When the anti-Potlatch laws were passed natives protested and found various ways to avoid the law. Why did they keep sending one generation after another of their children to residential schools?
3. Is the residential school experience the primary source of native social problems today or are there other critical factors?
4. Many similarities exist between the abuse natives suffered in residential schools and what occurred in places like Mt. Cashel a Catholic residential school for boys in Newfoundland. Is the basic problem the nature of custodial care, rather than racism?
5. One political scientist argues that the "aboriginal movement depends on the cultivation of grievances," and that the "apology reinforces segregation." Is he right?

Documents

1. Rev. K. Annett, "Hidden from History: The Canadian Holocaust," *Nexus* (March-April 2002).

FOREWORD

Jasper Joseph is a sixty-four-year-old native man from Port Hardy, British Columbia. His eyes still fill with tears when he remembers his cousins who were killed with lethal injections by staff at the Nanaimo Indian Hospital in 1944.

I was just eight, and they'd shipped us down from the Anglican residential school in Alert Bay to the Nanaimo Indian Hospital, the one run by the United Church. They kept me isolated in a tiny room there for more than three years, like I was a lab rat, feeding me these pills, giving me shots that made me sick. Two of my cousins made a big fuss, screaming and fighting back all the time, so the nurses gave them shots, and they both died right away. It was done to silence them. (November 10, 2000)

Unlike post-war Germans, Canadians have yet to acknowledge, let alone repent from, the genocide that we inflicted on millions of conquered people: the aboriginal men, women and children who were deliberately exterminated by our racially supremacist churches and state.

As early as November 1907, the Canadian press was acknowledging that the death rate within Indian residential schools exceeded 50%. And yet the reality of such a massacre has been wiped clean from the public record and consciousness in Canada over the past decades. Small wonder; for that hidden history reveals a system whose aim was to destroy most native people by disease, relocation and outright murder, while "assimilating" a minority of collaborators who were trained to serve the genocidal system.

This history of purposeful genocide implicates every level of government in Canada, the Royal Canadian Mounted Police (RCMP), every mainstream church, large corporations and local police, doctors and judges. The web of complicity in this killing machine was, and remains, so vast that its concealment has required an equally elaborate campaign to cover-up that has been engineered at the highest levels of power in our country; a cover-up that is continuing, especially now that eyewitnesses to murders and atrocities at the church-run native residential "schools" have come forward for the first time.

For it was the residential "schools" that constituted the death camps of the Canadian Holocaust, and within their walls nearly one-half of all aboriginal children sent there by law died, or disappeared, according to the government's own statistics.

These 50,000 victims have vanished, as have their corpses—"like they never existed", according to one survivor. But they did exist. They were innocent children, and they were killed by beatings and torture and after being deliberately exposed to tuberculosis and other diseases by paid employees of the churches and government, according to a "Final Solution" master plan devised by the Department of Indian Affairs and the Catholic and Protestant churches.

With such official consent for manslaughter emanating from Ottawa, the churches responsible for annihilating natives on the ground felt emboldened and protected enough to declare full-scale war on non-Christian native peoples through the 20th century.

The casualties of that war were not only the 50,000 dead children of the residential schools, but the survivors, whose social condition today has been described by United Nations human rights groups as that of "a colonized people barely on the edge of survival, with all the trappings of a third-world society". (November 12, 1999)

The Holocaust is continuing.

This report is the child of a six-year independent investigation into the hidden history of genocide against aboriginal peoples in Canada. It summarises the testimonies, documents and other evidence proving that Canadian churches, corporations and the government are guilty of intentional genocide, in violation of the United Nations Convention on Genocide, which Canada ratified in 1952 and under which it is bound by international law.

The report is a collaborative effort of nearly 30 people. And yet some of its authors must remain anonymous, particularly its aboriginal contributors, whose lives have been threatened and who have been assaulted, denied jobs and evicted from their homes on Indian reserves because of their involvement in this investigation.

As a former minister in one of the guilty institutions named in our inquiry—the United Church of Canada—I have been fired, black-listed, threatened and publicly maligned by its officers for my attempts to uncover the story of the deaths of children at that church's Alberni residential school.

Many people have made sacrifices to produce this report, so that the world can learn of the Canadian Holocaust, and to ensure that those responsible for it are brought to justice before the International Criminal Court.

Beginning among native and low-income activists in Port Alberni, British Columbia, in the fall of 1994, this inquiry into crimes against humanity has continued in the face of death threats, assaults and the resources of church and state in Canada.

It is within the power of the reader to honour our sacrifice by sharing this story with others and refusing to participate in the institutions which deliberately killed many thousands of children.

This history of official endorsement of, and collusion in, a century or more of crimes against Canada's first peoples must not discourage us from uncovering the truth and bringing the perpetrators to justice.

It is for this reason that we invite you to remember not only the 50,000 children who died in the residential school death camps, but the silent victims today who suffer in our midst for bread and justice.

PART ONE: Summary of Evidence of Intentional Genocide in Canadian Residential Schools

Article II: The intent to destroy, in whole or in part, national ethnic, racial or religious group; namely, non-Christian aboriginal peoples in Canada

The foundational purpose behind the more than one hundred Indian residential schools established in Canada by government legislation and administered by Protestant and Catholic churches was the deliberate and persistent eradication of aboriginal people and their culture, and the conversion of any surviving native people to Christianity.

This intent was enunciated in the Gradual Civilization Act of 1857 in Upper Canada, and earlier, church-inspired legislation which defined aboriginal culture as inferior, stripped native people of citizenship and subordinated them in a separate legal category from non-Indians. This Act served as the basis for the federal Indian Act of 1874, which recapitulated the legal and moral inferiority of aboriginals and established the residential school system. The legal definition of an Indian as "an uncivilized person, destitute of the knowledge of God and of any fixed and clear belief in religion" (Revised Statutes of British Columbia, 1960) was established by these Acts and continues to the present day.

Then, as now, aboriginals were considered legal and practical non-entities in their own land and, hence, inherently expendable.

This genocidal intent was restated time and again in government legislation, church statements and the correspondence and records of missionaries, Indian agents and residential school officials (see Documentation section). Indeed, it was the very *raison d'être* of the state-sanctioned Christian invasion of traditional native territories and of the residential school system itself, which was established at the height of European expansionism in the 1880s and persisted until 1984.

By definition, this aim was genocidal, for it planned and carried out the destruction of a religious and ethnic group: all those aboriginal people who would not convert to Christianity and be culturally extinguished. Non-Christian natives were the declared target of the residential schools, which practised wholesale ethnic cleansing under the guise of education.

As well, such "pagans" were the subject of government-funded sterilisation programs administered at church-run hospitals and tuberculosis sanatoriums on Canada's west coast (see Article IId).

According to an eyewitness, Ethel Wilson of Bella Bella, BC, a United Church missionary doctor, George Darby, deliberately sterilised non-Christian Indians between 1928 and 1962 at the R. W. Large Memorial Hospital in Bella Bella. Ms Wilson, who is now deceased, stated in 1998:

Doctor Darby told me in 1952 that Indian Affairs in Ottawa was paying him

for every Indian he sterilised, especially if they weren't church-goers. Hundreds of our women were sterilised by Doctor Darby, just for not going to church. (Testimony of Ethel Wilson to International Human Rights Association of American Minorities [IHRAAM] Tribunal, Vancouver, BC, June 13, 1998)

According to Christy White, a resident of Bella Bella, records of these government-funded sterilisations at the R. W. Large Hospital were deliberately destroyed in 1995, soon after a much-publicised police investigation was to open into residential school atrocities in British Columbia. Ms White stated in 1998:

I worked at the Bella Bella hospital, and I know that Barb Brown, one of the administrators there, dumped sterilisation records at sea on two occasions. Some of the records were found washed up on the beach south of town. That was just after the cops opened their investigation into the schools, in the spring of 1995. They were covering their tracks. We all knew Ottawa was funding sterilisations, but we were told to keep quiet about it. (Testimony of Christy White to Kevin Annett, August 12, 1998)

Legislation permitting the sterilisation of any residential school inmate was passed in BC in 1933 and in Alberta in 1928 (see "Sterilization Victims Urged to Come Forward" by Sabrina Whyatt, *Windspeaker*, August 1998). The Sexual Sterilization Act of BC allowed a school principal to permit the sterilisation of any native person under his charge. As their legal guardian, the principal could thus have any native child sterilised. Frequently, these sterilisations occurred to whole groups of native children when they reached puberty, in institutions like the Provincial Training School in Red Deer, Alberta, and the Ponoka Mental Hospital. (Former nurse Pat Taylor to Kevin Annett, January 13, 2000)

Of equal historical significance is the fact that the Canadian federal government passed legislation in 1920, making it mandatory for all native children in British Columbia—the west coast of which was the least Christianised area among aboriginals in Canada—to attend residential schools, despite the fact that the same government had already acknowledged that the death rate due to communicable diseases was much higher in these schools and that, while there, the native children's "constitution is so weakened that they have no vitality to withstand disease". (A. W. Neill, West Coast Indian Agent, to Secretary of Indian Affairs, April 25, 1910)

That is, the Canadian government legally compelled the attendance of the most "pagan" and least assimilated of the native peoples in residential schools at precisely the time when the death rate in these schools had reached their pinnacle—about 40%, according to Indian Affairs officers like Dr Peter Bryce. This fact alone suggests a genocidal intent towards non-Christian aboriginals.

Article II (a): Killing members of the group intended to be destroyed

That aboriginal people were deliberately killed in the residential schools is confirmed by eyewitness testimonies, government records and statements of Indian agents and tribal elders. It is also strongly suggested by the bare fact that the mortality level in residential schools averaged 40%, with the deaths of more than 50,000 native children across Canada (see Bibliography, inc. the report of Dr Peter Bryce to Department of Indian Affairs Superintendent Duncan Campbell Scott, April 1909).

The fact, as well, that this death rate stayed constant across the years, and within the schools and facilities of every denomination which ran them—Roman Catholic, United, Presbyterian or Anglican—suggests that common conditions and policies were behind these deaths. For every second child to die in the residential school system eliminates the possibility that these deaths were merely accidental or the actions of a few depraved individuals acting alone without protection.

Yet not only was this system inherently murderous, but it operated under the legal and structural conditions which encouraged, aided and abetted murder and which were designed to conceal these crimes.

The residential schools were structured like concentration camps, on a hierarchical military basis under the absolute control of a principal appointed jointly by church and state, and who was usually a clergyman. This principal was even given legal guardianship rights over all students during the early 1930s by the federal government, at least in west coast residential schools. This action by the government was highly unusual, considering that native people were by law the legal wards of the state, and had been so since the commencement of the Indian Act. And yet such absolute power of the school principal over the lives of aboriginal students was a requirement of any system whose killing of aboriginals had to be disguised and later denied.

The residential schools were constructed behind this deception in such a way that the deaths and atrocities that constitute genocide could be hidden and eventually explained. In the Canadian context, this meant a policy of gradual but deliberate extermination under a protective legal umbrella, administered by "legitimate and trusted" institutions: the mainline churches.

It should be clarified from the outset that the decisions concerning the residential schools, including those which caused the deaths of children and resulting cover-ups, were officially sanctioned by every level of the churches that ran them and the government which created them. Only such sanction could have allowed the deaths to continue as they did—and the perpetrators to feel protected enough to operate with impunity for many years within the system, which they universally did.

Exposure to Diseases

In 1909, Dr Peter Bryce of the Ontario Health Department was hired by the Indian Affairs Department in Ottawa to tour the Indian residential schools in western Canada and British Columbia and report on the health conditions there. Bryce's report so scandalised the government and the churches that it was officially buried and only surfaced in 1922 when Bryce—who was forced out of the civil service for the honesty of his report—wrote a book about it, entitled *The Story of a National Crime* (Ottawa, 1922).

In his report, Dr Bryce claimed that Indian children were being systematically and deliberately killed in the residential schools. He cited an average mortality rate of between 35% and 60%, and alleged that staff and church officials were regularly withholding or falsifying records and other evidence of children's deaths.

Further, Dr Bryce claimed that a primary means of killing native children was to deliberately expose them to communicable diseases such as tuberculosis and then deny them any medical care or treatment—a practice actually referred to by top Anglican Church leaders in the *Globe and Mail* on May 29, 1953.

In March 1998, two native eyewitnesses who attended west coast residential schools, William and Mabel Sport of Nanaimo, BC, confirmed Dr Bryce's allegation. Both of them claim to have been deliberately exposed to tuberculosis by staff at both a Catholic and a United Church residential school during the 1940s.

I was forced to sleep in the same bed with kids who were dying of tuberculosis. That was at the Catholic Christie residential school around 1942. They were trying to kill us off, and it nearly worked. They did the same thing at Protestant Indian schools, three kids to a bed, healthy ones with the dying. (Testimony of Mabel Sport to IHRAAM officers, Port Alberni, BC, March 31, 1998)

Reverend Pitts, the Alberni school principal, he forced me and eight other boys to eat this special food out of a different sort of can. It tasted really strange. And then all of us came down with tuberculosis. I was the only one to survive, 'cause my Dad broke into the school one night and got me out of there. All of the rest died from tuberculosis and they were never treated. Just left there to die. And their families were all told they had died of pneumonia. The plan was to kill us off in secret, you know. We all just began dying after eating that food. Two of my best friends were in that group that was poisoned. We were never allowed to speak of it or go into the basement, where other murders happened. It was a death sentence to be sent to the Alberni school. (Testimony of William Sport to IHRAAM officers, Port Alberni, BC, March 31, 1998)

Homicides

More overt killings of children were a common occurrence in residential schools, according to eyewitnesses. The latter have described children being beaten and starved to death, thrown from windows, strangled and being kicked or thrown down stairs to their deaths. Such killings occurred in at least eight residential schools in British Columbia alone, run by all three mainline denominations.

Bill Seward of Nanaimo, BC, age 78, states:

My sister Maggie was thrown from a three-storey window by a nun at the Kuper Island school, and she died. Everything was swept under the rug. No investigation was ever done. We couldn't hire a lawyer at the time, being Indians. So nothing was ever done. (Testimony of Bill Seward, Duncan, BC, August 13, 1998)

Diane Harris, Community Health Worker for the Chemainus Band Council on Vancouver Island, confirms accounts of the murders.

We always hear stories of all the kids who were killed at Kuper Island. A graveyard for the babies of the priests and girls was right south of the school until it was dug up by the priests when the school closed in 1973. The nuns would abort babies and sometimes end up killing the mothers. There were a lot of disappearances. My mother, who is 83 now, saw a priest drag a girl down a flight of stairs by her hair and the girl died as a result. Girls were raped and killed, and buried under the floorboards. We asked the local RCMP to exhume that place and search for remains but they've always refused, as recently as 1996. Corporal Sampson even threatened us. That kind of cover-up is the norm. Children were put together with kids sick with TB in the infirmary. That was standard procedure. We've documented thirty-five outright murders in a seven-year period. (Testimony of Diane Harris to the IHRAAM Tribunal, June 13, 1998)

Evidence exists that active collusion from police, hospital officials, coroners, Indian Agents and even native leaders helped to conceal such murders. Local hospitals, particularly tuberculosis sanatoriums connected to the United and Roman Catholic churches, served as "dumping grounds" for children's bodies and routinely provided false death certificates for murdered students.

In the case of the United Church's Alberni residential school, students who discovered dead bodies of other children faced serious retribution. One such witness, Harry Wilson of Bella Bella, BC, claims that he was expelled from the school, then hospitalised and drugged against his will, after finding the body of a dead girl in May 1967.

Sadly, the two-tiered system of collaborators and victims created among native students at the schools continues to the present, as some of the state-funded band council officials—themselves former collaborators—appear to have an interest in helping to suppress evidence and silence witnesses who would incriminate not only the murderers but themselves as agents of the white administration.

A majority of the witnesses who have shared their story with the authors and at public tribunals on the west coast have described either seeing a murder or discovering a body at the residential school he or she attended. The body count, even according to the government's own figures, was enormously high. Where, then, are all these bodies? The deaths of thousands of students are not recorded in any of the school records, Indian Affairs files or other documentation submitted thus far in court cases or academic publications on the residential schools. Some 50,000 corpses have literally and officially gone missing.

The residential school system had to hide not only the evidence of murder but the bodies as well. The presence of secret gravesites of children killed at Catholic and Protestant schools in Sardis, Port Alberni, Kuper Island and Alert Bay has been attested to by numerous witnesses. These secret burial yards also contained the aborted foetuses and even small babies who were the offspring of priests and staff at the schools, according to the same witnesses. One of them, Ethel Wilson of Bella Bella, claims to have seen "rows and rows of tiny skeletons" in the foundations of the former Anglican residential school of St Michael's in Alert Bay when a new school was built there in the 1960s.

There were several rows of them, all lined up neatly like it was a big cemetery. The skeletons had been found within one of the old walls of St. Mike's school. None of them could have been very old, from their size. Now why would so many kids have been buried like that inside a wall, unless someone was trying to hide something? (Testimony of Ethel Wilson to Kevin Annett, Vancouver, BC, August 8, 1998)

Arnold Sylvester, who, like Dennis Charlie, attended Kuper Island school between 1939 and 1945, corroborates this account.

The priests dug up the secret gravesite in a real hurry around 1972 when the school closed. No one was allowed to watch them dig up those remains. I think it's because that was a specially secret graveyard where the bodies of the pregnant girls were buried. Some of the girls who got pregnant from the priests were actually killed because they threatened to talk. They were sometimes shipped out and sometimes just disappeared. We weren't allowed to talk about this. (Testimony of Arnold Sylvester to Kevin Annett, Duncan, BC, August 13, 1998)

Local hospitals were also used as dumping ground for children's bodies, as in the case of the Edmonds boy and his "processing" at St Paul's Hospital after his murder at the Catholic school in North Vancouver. Certain hospitals, however, seem to have been particularly favourite spots for storing corpses.

The Nanaimo Tuberculosis Hospital (called The Indian Hospital) was one such facility. Under the guise of tuberculosis treatment, generations of native children and adults were subjected to medical experiments and sexual sterilisations at the Nanaimo Hospital, according to women who experienced these tortures (see Article IId). But the facility was also a cold storage area for native corpses.

The West Coast General Hospital in Port Alberni not only stored children's bodies from the local United Church residential school; it was also the place where abortions were performed on native girls who were made pregnant at the school by staff and clergy, and where newborn babies were disposed of and possibly killed, according to witnesses like Amy Tallio, who attended the Alberni school during the early 1950s.

Irene Starr of the Hesquait Nation, who attended the Alberni school between 1952 and 1961, confirms this.

Many girls got pregnant at the Alberni school. The fathers were the staff, teachers, the ones who raped them. We never knew what happened to the babies, but they were always disappearing. The pregnant girls were taken to the Alberni hospital and then came back without their babies. Always. The staff killed those babies to cover their tracks. They were paid by the church and government to be rapists and murderers. (Testimony of Irene Starr to Kevin Annett, Vancouver, BC, August 23, 1998)

Article II (b): Causing serious bodily or mental harm

Early in the residential schools era, the Indian Affairs Superintendent, Duncan Campbell Scott, outlined the purpose of the schools thus: "to kill the Indian within the Indian".

Clearly, the genocidal assault on aboriginals was not only physical but spiritual: European culture wished to own the minds and the souls of the native nations, to turn the Indians it hadn't killed into third-class replicas of white people.

Expressing the "virtues" of genocide, Alfred Caldwell, principal of the United Church school in Ahousat on Vancouver Island's west coast, wrote in 1938:

The problem with the Indians is one of morality and religion. They lack the basic fundamentals of civilised thought and spirit, which explains their child-like nature and behaviour. At our school we strive to turn them into mature Christians who will learn how to behave in the world and surrender their barbaric way of life and their treaty rights which keep them trapped on their land and in a primitive existence. Only then will the Indian problem in our country be solved. (Rev. A. E. Caldwell to Indian Agent P. D. Ashbridge, Ahousat, BC, Nov 12, 1938)

The fact that this same principal is named by eyewitnesses as the murderer of at least two children—one of them in the same month that he wrote this letter—is no accident, for cultural genocide spills effortlessly over into killing, as the Nazis proved so visibly to the world.

Nevertheless, Caldwell's letter illuminates two vital points for the purpose of this discussion of mental and bodily harm inflicted on native students: (a) the residential schools were a vast project in mind control, and (b) the underlying aim of this "re-programming" of native children was to force aboriginals off their ancestral lands in order to allow whites access to them.

To quote Alberni survivor Harriett Nahanee:

They were always pitting us against each other, getting us to fight and molest one another. It was all designed to split us up and brainwash us so that we would forget that we were Keepers of the Land. The Creator gave our people the job of protecting the land, the fish, the forests. That was our purpose for being alive. But the whites wanted it all, and the residential schools were the way they got it. And it worked.

We've forgotten our sacred task, and now the whites have most of the land and have taken all the fish and the trees. Most of us are in poverty, addictions, family violence. And it all started in the schools, where we were brainwashed to hate our own culture and to hate ourselves so that we would lose everything. That's why I say that the genocide is still going on. (Testimony of Harriett Nahanee to Kevin Annett, North Vancouver, BC, December 11, 1995)

It was only after the assumption of guardianship powers by the west coast school principals, between 1933 and 1941, that the first evidence of organised pedophile networks in those residential schools emerges. For such a regime was legally and morally free to do whatever it wanted to its captive native students.

The residential schools became a safe haven—one survivor calls it a "free fire zone"—for pedophiles, murderers and brutal doctors needing live test subjects for drug testing or genetic and cancer research.

Particular schools, such as the Catholic one at Kuper Island and the United Church's Alberni school, became special centres where extermination techniques were practised with impunity on native children from all over the province, alongside the usual routine of beatings, rapes and farming out of children to influential pedophiles.

Much of the overt mental and bodily harm done to native students was designed to break down traditional tribal loyalties along kinship lines by pitting children against each other and cutting them off from their natural bonds. Boys and girls were strictly segregated in separate dormitories and could never meet.

One survivor describes never seeing her little brother for years, even though he was in the same building at the Alert Bay Anglican school. And when children at the schools broke into each other's dormitories and older boys and girls were caught exchanging intimacies, the most severe punishments were universally applied. According to a female survivor who attended the Alberni school in 1959:

They used the gauntlet on a boy and girl who were caught together kissing. The two of them had to crawl naked down a line of other students, and we beat them with sticks and whips provided by the principal. The girl was beaten so badly she died from kidney failure. That gave us all a good lesson: if you tried having normal feelings for someone, you'd get killed for it. So we quickly learned never to love or trust anyone, just do what we were told to do. (Testimony of anonymous woman from the Pacheedat Nation, Port Renfrew, BC, October 12, 1996)

According to Harriett Nahanee:

The residential schools created two kinds of Indians: slaves and sell-outs. And the sellouts are still in charge. The rest of us do what we're told. The band council chiefs have been telling everyone on our reserve not to talk to the Tribunal and have been threatening to cut our benefits if we do. (Harriett Nahanee to Kevin Annett, June 12, 1998)

The nature of that system of torture was not haphazard. For example, the regular use of electric shocks on children who spoke their language or were "disobedient" was a widespread phenomenon in residential schools of every denomination across Canada. This was not a random but an institutionalised device.

Specially constructed torture chambers with permanent electric chairs, often operated by medical personnel, existed at the Alberni and Kuper Island schools in British Columbia, at the Spanish Catholic school in Ontario, and in isolated hospital facilities run by the churches and Department of Indian Affairs in northern Quebec, Vancouver Island and rural Alberta, according to eyewitnesses.

Mary Anne Nakogee-Davis of Thunder Bay, Ontario, was tortured in an electric chair by nuns at the Catholic Spanish residential school in 1963 when she was eight years old. She states:

The nuns used it as a weapon. It was done on me on more than one occasion. They would strap your arms to the metal arm rests, and it would jolt you and go through your system. I don't know what I did that was bad enough to have that done to me. (From *The London Free Press*, London, Ontario, October 22, 1996)

Such torture also occurred at facilities operated by the churches with

Department of Indian Affairs money, similar to the sterilisation programs identified at the W. R. Large Memorial Hospital in Bella Bella and the Nanaimo Indian Hospital.

Frank Martin, a Carrier native from northern BC, describes his forcible confinement and use in experiments at the Brannen Lake Reform School near Nanaimo in 1963 and 1964:

I was kidnapped from my village when I was nine and sent off to the Brannen Lake school in Nanaimo. A local doctor gave me a shot and I woke up in a small cell, maybe ten feet by twelve. I was kept in there like an animal for fourteen months. They brought me out every morning and gave me electric shocks to my head until I passed out. Then in the afternoon I'd go for these X-rays and they'd expose me to them for minutes on end. They never told me why they were doing it. But I got lung cancer when I was eighteen and I've never smoked. (Videotaped testimony of Frank Martin to Eva Lyman and Kevin Annett, Vancouver, July 16, 1998)

Such quack experimentation combined with brutal sadism characterised these publicly funded facilities, especially the notorious Nanaimo Indian Hospital. David Martin of Powell River, BC, was taken to this hospital in 1958 at the age of five and used in experiments attested to by Joan Morris, Harry Wilson and other witnesses quoted in this report. According to David:

I was told I had tuberculosis, but I was completely healthy; no symptoms of TB at all. So they sent me to Nanaimo Indian Hospital and strapped me down in a bed there for more than six months. The doctors gave me shots every day that made me feel really sick, and made my skin all red and itchy. I heard the screams of other Indian kids who were locked away in isolation rooms. We were never allowed in there to see them. Nobody ever told me what they were doing to all of us in there. (David Martin to Kevin Annett Vancouver, November 12, 2000)

A recurring and regular torture at the residential schools themselves was operating on children's teeth without using any form of anaesthesia or painkiller. Two separate victims of this torture at the Alberni school describe being subjected to it by different dentists, decades apart. Harriett Nahanee was brutalised in that manner in 1946, while Dennis Tallio was "worked on by a sick old guy who never gave me painkillers" at the same school in 1965.

Dr Josef Mengele is reputed by survivors of his experiments to have worked out of Cornell University in New York, Bristol Labs in Syracuse, New York, and Upjohn Corporation and Bayer laboratories in Ontario. Mengele and his Canadian researchers, like the notorious Montreal psychiatrist Ewen Cameron, used prisoners, mental patients and native children from reserves and residential schools in their efforts to erase and reshape human memory and personality, using drugs, electric shocks and trauma-inducing methods identical to those employed for years in the residential schools.

Former employees of the federal government have confirmed that the use of "inmates" of residential schools was authorised for government-run medical experiments through a joint agreement with the churches which ran the schools.

According to a former Indian Affairs official:

A sort of gentlemen's agreement was in place for many years: the church provided the kids from their residential schools to us, and we got the Mounties to deliver them to whoever needed a fresh batch of test subjects: usually doctors, sometimes Department of Defense people. The Catholics did it big time in Quebec when they transferred kids wholesale from orphanages into mental asylums. It was for the same purpose: experimentation. There was lots of grant money in those days to be had from the military and intelligence sectors: all you had to do was provide the bodies.

The church officials were more than happy to comply. It wasn't just the residential school principals who were getting kickbacks from this: everyone was profiting. That's why it's gone on for so long. It implicates a hell of a lot of top people. (From the Closed Files of the IHRAAM Tribunal, containing the statements of confidential sources, June 12–14, 1998)

Such experiments and the sheer brutality of the harm regularly inflicted on children in the schools attest to the institutional view of aboriginals as "expendable" and "diseased" beings. Scores of survivors of 10 different residential schools in BC and Ontario have described under oath the following tortures inflicted on them and other children as young as five years old between the years 1922 and 1984:

- -tightening fish twine and wire around boys' penises;
- -sticking needles into their hands, cheeks, tongues, ears and penises;
- -holding them over open graves and threatening to bury them alive;
- -forcing them to eat maggot-filled and regurgitated food;
- -telling them their parents were dead and that they were about to be killed;
- -stripping them naked in front of the assembled school and verbally and sexually degrading them;
- -forcing them to stand upright for more than 12 hours at a time until they collapsed;
- -immersing them in ice water;
- -forcing them to sleep outside in winter;
- -ripping the hair from their heads;
- -repeatedly smashing their heads against concrete or wooden surfaces;

-daily beating without warning, using whips, sticks, horse harnesses,
    studded metal straps, pool cues and iron pipes;
-extracting gold teeth from their mouths without painkillers;
-confining them in unventilated closets without food or water for days;
-regularly applying electric shocks to their heads, genitals and limbs.

Perhaps the clearest summary of the nature and purpose of such sadism are the words of Bill Seward of Nanaimo, a survivor of the Kuper Island school:

The church people were worshipping the devil, not us. They wanted the gold, the coal, the land we occupied. So they terrorised us into giving it to them. How does a man who was raped every day when he was seven make anything out of his life? The residential schools were set up to destroy our lives, and they succeeded. The whites were terrorists, pure and simple. (Testimony of Bill Seward to Kevin Annett and IHRAAM observers, Duncan, BC, August 13, 1998)

2. Government of Canada, "Statement of Reconciliation" January 7, 1998.

Learning from the Past

As Aboriginal and non-Aboriginal Canadians seek to move forward together in a process of renewal, it is essential that we deal with the legacies of the past affecting the Aboriginal peoples of Canada, including the First Nations, Inuit and Métis. Our purpose is not to rewrite history but, rather, to learn from our past and to find ways to deal with the negative impacts that certain historical decisions continue to have in our society today.

The ancestors of First Nations, Inuit and Métis peoples lived on this continent long before explorers from other continents first came to North America. For thousands of years before this country was founded, they enjoyed their own forms of government. Diverse, vibrant Aboriginal nations had ways of life rooted in fundamental values concerning their relationships to the Creator, the environment, and each other, in the role of Elders as the living memory of their ancestors, and in their responsibilities as custodians of the lands, waters and resources of their homelands.

The assistance and spiritual values of the Aboriginal peoples who welcomed the newcomers to this continent too often have been forgotten. The contributions made by all Aboriginal peoples to Canada's development, and the contributions that they continue to make to our society today, have not been properly acknowledged. The Government of Canada today, on behalf of all Canadians, acknowledges those contributions.

Sadly, our history with respect to the treatment of Aboriginal people is not something in which we can take pride. Attitudes of racial and cultural superiority led to a suppression of Aboriginal culture and values. As a country, we are burdened by past actions that resulted in weakening the identity of Aboriginal peoples, suppressing their languages and cultures, and outlawing spiritual practices. We must recognize the impact of these actions on the once self-sustaining nations that were disaggregated, disrupted, limited or even destroyed by the dispossession of traditional territory, by the relocation of Aboriginal people, and by some provisions of the Indian Act. We must acknowledge that the result of these actions was the erosion of the political, economic and social systems of Aboriginal people and nations.

Against the backdrop of these historical legacies, it is a remarkable tribute to the strength and endurance of Aboriginal people that they have maintained their historic diversity and identity. The Government of Canada today formally expresses to all Aboriginal people in Canada our profound regret for past actions of the federal government which have contributed to these difficult pages in the history of our relationship together.

One aspect of our relationship with Aboriginal people over this period that requires particular attention is the Residential School system. This system separated many children from their families and communities and prevented them from speaking their own languages and from learning about their heritage and cultures. In the worst cases, it left legacies of personal pain and distress that continue to reverberate in Aboriginal communities to this day. Tragically, some children were the victims of physical and sexual abuse.

The Government of Canada acknowledges the role it played in the development and administration of these schools. Particularly to those individuals who experienced the tragedy of sexual and physical abuse at residential schools, and who have carried this burden believing that in some way they must be responsible, we wish to emphasize that what you experienced was not your fault and should never have happened. To those of you who suffered this tragedy at residential schools, we are deeply sorry.

In dealing with the legacies of the Residential School system, the Government of Canada proposes to work with First Nations, Inuit and Métis people, the Churches and other interested parties to resolve the longstanding issues that must be addressed. We need to work together on a healing strategy to assist individuals and communities in dealing with the consequences of this sad era of our history.

No attempt at reconciliation with Aboriginal people can be complete without reference to the sad events culminating in the death of Métis leader Louis

Riel. These events cannot be undone; however, we can and will continue to look for ways of affirming the contributions of Métis people in Canada and of reflecting Louis Riel's proper place in Canada's history.

Reconciliation is an ongoing process. In renewing our partnership, we must ensure that the mistakes which marked our past relationship are not repeated. The Government of Canada recognizes that policies that sought to assimilate Aboriginal people, women and men, were not the way to build a strong country. We must instead continue to find ways in which Aboriginal people can participate fully in the economic, political, cultural and social life of Canada in a manner which preserves and enhances the collective identities of Aboriginal communities, and allows them to evolve and flourish in the future. Working together to achieve our shared goals will benefit all Canadians, Aboriginal and non-Aboriginal alike.

3. Ted Byfield, "Weren't We all Physically Abused in Schools? So When do We Get Our Money for Healing," *Alberta Report*, January 19, 1998.

That the government of Canada should apologize and compensate for any sexual abuse of native children at government-supervised residential schools between the 1930s and 1980s seems altogether appropriate. What we consider sexual abuse of children has not changed at all from the 1930s until today, although we are under increasing pressure to do so.

But the government apology and compensation for physical abuse of children raises a fundamental question. What's considered physical abuse has changed radically since the 1950s. So the question is: Did the commission whose report led to this apology and accompanying half-billion-dollar compensation package judge those schools by today's standards or by yesterday's? The former, one suspects—in which case Ottawa, to be consistent, had better apologize to several million other Canadians as well.

Suppose, that is, that some investigator, thoroughly imbued with the current theories of raising children, was asked to peer into the typical urban elementary school back in the '30s, '40s or even '50s. At the public school I attended in suburban Toronto between about 1936 and 1940 here is what she would have seen:

When the school bell rang, children from kindergarten to Grade 8 marched in to martial music played on a gramophone, while the principal kept time like a drum major. Standing rigidly by their desks, they sang "God Save the King" and recited the Lord's Prayer. In the younger grades, they chorused to the teacher,

"Good morning, Miss Smith" before seating themselves. To ask a question, you raised your hand, rising when acknowledged. Teachers were addressed as "Mr. Jones," "Miss Smith" (or "Sir" or "Ma'am").

Discipline came in three levels—a sharp verbal reprimand, a detention to stay after class, or "the strap." The latter was a flat, stiff 14-inch leather instrument, administered sharply across the outstretched palm, anywhere from three to maybe eight strokes per occasion. How often this happened depended on the teacher: in some classes almost daily, in others perhaps once a month. The recipient was almost invariably male—I can't actually remember a girl ever "getting it." From what I've heard, country schools were much the same, perhaps even more prone to corporal punishment.

Such was emphatically the case at a private boys' residential school I attended for two years at great expense to my parents and grandparents. Known as Lakefield, near Peterborough, Ont., it is still very much operative today. Here the instrument was not a strap but a stick about two feet long, often a hockey stick handle, administered across the hind end while the accused bent over. Three to maybe 10 swats was the usual quota, which could be delivered not only by teachers (whom we called "masters") but also by "prefects," senior students who shared in the school's administration. These "beatings" occurred routinely in classes, dormitories, wherever and whenever misconduct occurred, which was everywhere and often.

Now the point, of course, is this: Any educator or social worker schooled since the '60s would regard these institutions as houses of horror. She would see rigid "authoritarianism" in their methodology, individual spontaneity being endlessly stifled, and repugnant brutality in their methods of discipline. Her report would denounce and deplore them, and if compensation for the "victims" of such appalling institutions were available, she would surely recommend it.

Without doubt, the inquiry into native residential schools found instances of physical injury that exceeded what I've described here. But I'm equally sure that an exhaustive examination of public schools of that era would have produced much the same. I heard of a teacher once breaking a youngster's arm, for example, and another in high school who punched a kid in the face. My Grade 1 teacher at a Toronto school suffered a nervous breakdown and was eventually carted off the premises after doing heaven knows what. (I alone cannot claim credit for this, but I likely contributed.) With such incidents incorporated in the investigator's report the case for compensation would grow accordingly.

So one suspects that by the reasoning of the native residential school inquiry, most Canadian-born citizens over the age of, say, 55 were "abused" in like manner. Are we all to receive an apology from the government? What will be our compensation? Will there be a provision for counselling us? How much will we get for "healing initiatives"?

Two points need to be added to my portrayal of education in the '30s and '40s. In the elementary school I have described, Courcellette Road in Toronto, I received a grounding in English language and grammar out of which I have made a living all my life. However "authoritarian," the teachers were competent, dedicated, in no rational sense whatever "abusive," and probably ill-paid. As for Lakefield, the two years I spent there were among the happiest in my life, and I became acquainted for the first time with two realities. One was history and the other was God. And while I can easily believe some of the native residential schools were far from idyllic, I have read a woman's published memory of one of them that is both fond and thankful, and categorically denies that either sexual or physical abuse occurred in it.

All this casts real doubt on what the government is now doing, but it accords with everything else we see in Ottawa's approach to the aboriginal peoples. What Ottawa does today at great expense it will no doubt be apologizing for tomorrow at even greater expense. You can look back at an unbroken record of muddle-headedness.

Consider this, for instance. We have enshrined in our Charter of Rights and Freedoms an absolute prohibition against racism, which is regarded as anathema—something to be abhorred and outlawed. Yet at the same time we are zealously establishing and segregating with the full thrust of the law an entire category of citizenship, founded rigorously and exclusively on racism. The definitions of who is, and who is not, a native read like Hitler's racial purity laws. The government has abandoned its past policies of "assimilation," says a news story, explaining the official "apology." It is now intent on preserving the cultural and communal identity of the native peoples, and this "reconciliation statement" is "the centrepiece" of the new policy.

How will they square this bold new venture into legislated racism, you wonder, with the charter's condemnation of it? How is Canada to ride two horses at the same time when they're galloping in opposite directions? Nobody in the Ottawa hierarchy ever seems to raise this question, let alone answer it.

You get the impression that our native policy is directed, not by moral principle nor even by common sense, but by whatever is currently fashionable. That's how we got the residential schools, and that's why we're now apologizing for them. Soon no doubt some other liberal fad will take hold and Ottawa will be apologizing for the apology. How luckless for the natives that they were left under federal jurisdiction.

4. **P. Donnelly, "Scapegoating the Indian Residential Schools: The Noble Legacy of Hundreds of Christian Missionaries is Sacrificed to Political Correctness," *Alberta Report*, January 26, 1998.**

In the week following the Chretien government's apology to natives for residential schools, news media characterized the historic institutions as "brutal," "miserable," "genocidal" and "horrendous." They were repeating vaguely recounted and unchallenged testimony to a royal commission which concluded that the poorly funded and allegedly abusive schools bear large responsibility for the woeful present plight of many Indians. In none of the media coverage was the possibility raised that the schools were on the whole beneficial and widely supported by the Indians who attended them and voluntarily sent their children to them. Nor was the possibility admitted that the Indian leaders who now revile the schools might be motivated by the prospect of federal compensation.

On January 7 the Chretien government said it was "deeply sorry" for the treatment of natives in residential schools. The apology, part of the government's official response to recommendations of a Royal Commission on Aboriginal Peoples, carried with it a "healing" fund of $350 million, or $500,000 on average per reserve.

Initiated in 1991 by then-prime minister Brian Mulroney, the commission's mandate was to examine all aspects of the federal government's relationship with aboriginal people. There were seven commissioners, four native and three white, balanced also for gender and region. By the time they had wrapped up their cross-country hearings in 1996, the aboriginal commission had become the most expensive in Canada's history, with a final cost of$58 million and 445 recommendations, the cost of which were estimated in total at $20 billion. While it dealt with a broad range of issues including treaty rights, self-government, social programs, education and land-claims, the commission's most damning indictment was reserved for residential schools.

Travelling in threes, the commissioners held meetings in communities all across Canada, from cities to Inuit villages and Indian reserves. At the height of its undertaking, the commission employed over 100 staff in Ottawa and countless others in local communities who encouraged people to come forward and make submissions. Paul Chartrand, a Metis commissioner from Manitoba, explains that witness testimonies were not tested for accuracy or truthfulness. "We were a body of inquiry and were not there to cross-examine people appearing before us. We were not a judicial process. We listened to submissions, applied our understanding of the issues, and came up with policy recommendations."

Mr. Chartrand concedes that not all the testimony was critical of residential schools. "The report acknowledges that attendance for many people was not an unhappy experience," he says carefully. "[And] the report doesn't contain a blanket condemnation of the schools."

Fellow commissioner Mary Sillett, an Inuit from Ottawa representing Labrador, agrees that there were positive stories. However, she believes that the negative testimony far outweighed the positive. "Residential schools hurt a lot of people very deeply. Little kids were forcibly removed from their homes, beaten, and taught to despise their families. The stories were absolutely horrifying. How can you ever apologize adequately for the abuse those children suffered?" she says. "However, it's significant that the decision-makers have shown the courage to recognize the hurt and damage that was caused by residential schools."

The commission concluded, "Tragically, the future that was created [by the schools] is now a lamentable heritage for those children and generations who came after ... The school system's concerted campaign to obliterate Aboriginal languages, traditions, and beliefs was compounded by mismanagement and the woeful mistreatment, neglect, and abuse of many children ... The memory has persisted, festered and become a sorrowful monument, still casting a deep shadow over the lives of many Aboriginal people and over the possibility of a new relationship between Aboriginal and non-Aboriginal Canadians."

Since the commission's report was published in November 1996, the federal government has been preparing its response. Amid sweetgrass smoke and the beating of drums, on January 7 Indian Affairs Minister Jane Stewart expressed "profound regret" for the residential schools. The apology was hailed by aboriginal leaders as a first step in recognizing the suffering of the aboriginal people over the 300 years of Canada's history. Phil Fontaine, grand chief of the Assembly of First Nations, told the *Calgary Herald*, "Let this moment mark the end of paternalism in our relations and the beginning of the empowerment of First Nations, the end of the official victimization of First Nations." Chief Fontaine, from Pine Falls, Man., has said in the past he was sexually molested at one of the schools, but was travelling last week and could not be reached for an interview.

However, it remains a question, in many Indian minds as well as white, whether the general legacy of the Indian schools may actually have been quite good. While there have been some documented cases of sexual abuse over the 120-year history of the schools, a handful of which still operate, the available evidence is vague and almost entirely anecdotal.

Far-removed from Ottawa's corridors of power, many native people say they are bewildered by the vilification of residential schools. For example, Dora and Donald Cardinal of Onion Lake, Sask. near Lloydminster attended St. Anthony's Residential School on the reserve in the 1950s.

"It was a great, big white-frame building," recalls Mrs. Cardinal of the structure which was demolished in 1972. "I was sad to see it go; I have a lot of fond memories from that school, I really liked it there." One of her most vivid memories is of the kitchen, with big wood-burning stoves all along one wall. "There was a lot of food, we were practically forced to eat," she recalls wistfully. "Every day there was delicious fresh bread, porridge, peanut butter and lots of stew. I was a picky eater back then, and the food was always very good." Mrs. Cardinal explains that children from the reserve attended one of several area boarding schools, depending on their religious affiliation. As Roman Catholics, she and her older brother and sister were sent to St. Anthony's, operated by the Oblates of Mary Immaculate and the Grey Nuns.

Donald Cardinal adds that although speaking their native Cree was against the rules, he can not remember ever being punished for it. "It was the boys' job to look after the garden," he explains. "We chopped wood, worked on the farm, and looked after the cows while the girls learned to sew, mend, crochet." Dora Cardinal recounts that the Onion Lake reserve was very poor, and so was her family with six children. "We lived in a cabin, my dad did a little trapping; we had to survive somehow. I remember nights at home that were so cold, and we never had enough blankets. Sometimes my mother's bread wouldn't rise because it was so cold. I also remember that if we got some second-hand, old clothes, mother would cut off the sleeves and we used them for socks. Many parents at the time thought the school was a blessing."

The Blood Reserve near Lethbridge had two residential schools; Catholic St. Mary's and the Anglican St. Paul's Residential School. Rufus Goodstriker, a retired pro rodeo rider and boxer, and now a rancher and herbalist, attended St. Paul's for eight years in the 1940s. A three-storey, steam-heated brick building, St. Paul's at one time had over 500 students. "We were supposed to speak English, but I spoke Blackfoot all the time anyway," Mr. Goodstriker remembers. "It was good teaching for survival in society. We learned reading, writing, history, science, as well as how to operate machinery and farm chores. I really appreciated being able to learn all that. I'm a rancher now, and I use a lot of what I learned at the school."

A typical day began at 6:45, with breakfast and chapel before morning classes. After a half-day in the classroom, boys worked on the farm or in the shop. The children often went on hikes and camping trips through the surrounding countryside, and the older students were allowed to visit nearby Cardston on Saturdays. Each Friday night there was a co-education social event, usually a dance.

Although the children often visited their parents on weekends, school was a lonely experience at first. Mr. Goodstriker recalls that once his older brother ran away. "But my father immediately loaded him up in the wagon and brought him right back and said 'you don't run away from school' although, looking back, it probably would have been better to keep the children with their parents."

For Mr. Goodstriker, the sports program was the real highlight of school. Although St. Paul's lacked an indoor gym, the students were coached in soccer and softball. In the winter they flooded a rink for hockey, and numerous social events were organized by staff and students. Notwithstanding all these pleasant recollections, indeed almost as an afterthought, Mr. Goodstriker remarks that the schools were practising "cultural genocide." Asked to elaborate, he declines.

Another former resident at St. Paul's remembers that each week began with a chore work-list, which the students worked through in groups. "We worked together on everything; repairing equipment, cleaning washrooms, sweeping dormitories. I really enjoyed my time at the school; not only did I learn to work with other people, I also learned to respect them and respect myself."

The informant, who did not wish his name to be used because he says it could cause trouble, attended the school for eight years in the late 1940s. "I was never lonely there," he says. "When I went home on holidays, I was always lonesome for the school. The staff was very supportive of the students, and there were always lots of activities organized. Besides sports there was choir, piano, even a first-aid course. I even remember the staff reading stories to the younger children."

In the 1940s, the schools were already two generations old. Following the decimation of the buffalo and the movement of the nomadic plains Indians to reserves, the first residential schools in the West were started in 1884 by Catholic Father Albert Lacombe and Bishop Vital Grandin. With the plains steadily filling up with settlers, and game scarce, the schools were envisioned as a means of endowing native children with the skills necessary to survive in their changed world.

Initially termed "industrial schools," the facilities were established by the churches and staffed by religious workers, in an era when few white people had much sympathy for Indians. Besides core academics, various schools taught blacksmithing, woodworking, carpentry, cobbling, tailoring and farming. By the 1890s the federal government had established control over the schools, and provided enrolment grants while the churches continued running them. The number of schools peaked in 1946 when there were 76 scattered across Canada, most of them in the West.

Of those schools, 45 were affiliated with the Roman Catholic Church, 19 with the Anglican Church, 10 with the Presbyterians and two with the United Church. By most estimates, over 150,000 native children were educated in residential schools between 1867 and the late 1960s.

Some schools, located on reserves, operated as day schools and the students went home to their parents at night. Others had day populations and boarders from farther afield. Some served very scattered populations and were entirely residential; prohibitions against speaking Indian were more common at these, especially where the students came from different tribes historically at war with each other. Some of the early industrial schools, for example the Dunbow School near Calgary, were established in white communities so that the students could apprentice with local tradesmen.

According to Gerry Kelly, coordinator for the National Catholic Working Group on Native Residential Schools, the Indian people themselves recognized the need for education. "In several cases, Indian bands asked the government to establish schools," he explains. "In the 1930s, the Sechelt band near Vancouver lobbied the Oblates for such a school; some aboriginal communities wanted the schools so badly that they built them themselves. It's disrespectful to the natives' history to suggest that they played no part in the system, that they were herded mindlessly along by the government. Natives exercised some authority."

Mr. Kelly points out that, often, problems resulted after the native students left the industrial schools and attempted to find work in white communities. "For instance, a boy would train as a blacksmith, but then no one would hire him, however good he was at blacksmithing." Mr. Kelly is disappointed that the residential schools have been made scapegoats for all the suffering of the Indian people. "In some cases," he argues, "the very existence of these schools saved communities, for example in the North. In times of epidemics, the institutions were there to care for people. Also, the irony is that the only [white] people who were concerned about the Indians worked in the schools."

Mr. Kelly explains that, after the Second World War, there was a growing movement to shut down the residential schools and transfer the responsibility of educating native children first to the provinces, and then to the natives themselves. "The viability of the provincial systems was growing, and there was a growing movement to integrate native children with non-native." In 1946 a joint committee of the House of Commons and Senate recommended that Indian children be schooled with non-native children wherever possible. According to the compilation of essays entitled Indian Education in Canada, by 1960 nearly 25% of Indian children in Canada were being schooled in provincial institutions.

However, there was also a growing desire among Indian people to control their children's education directly. In 1971, the federal government handed control of the Blue Quills Residential School near St. Paul, Alta., to local bands, making it the first federal Indian school to be run by natives. The process of turning over the schools, both residential and day facilities, to local bands accelerated during the 1970s and 1980s. By 1993, there were only seven residential schools left in Canada and these were administered solely by native bands.

By the late 1980s many natives, especially politicians, were pointing accusing fingers at the residential schools. Highly-publicized incidents of sexual abuse, coupled with white liberal guilt about cultural assimilation, transformed the old residential schools into symbols of "degradation" and "cultural genocide" where the native children were systematically stripped of their culture, forced to adopt non-native ways, and undergo physical torture and sexual abuse by the school staff.

Chief Greg Smith of the Peigan reserve told the *Calgary Herald* that the legacy of the residential schools was terrible. "It was appalling, I see the effects of those schools everywhere. For me to lose my language, being part of the residential school system hurt me later on. I've had to go back and learn my language because it was taken away by someone else." However, he conceded that he suffered no abuse worse than having his hair cut. Warner Scout attended St. Paul's on the Blood Reserve after his mother froze to death while drinking and his alcoholic father was unable to care for him. He also told the *Herald*, "A lot of us graduated from there to jails. We knew nothing else to do except get drunk."

Flora Northwest of Hobbema, Alta., attended the Ermineskin Residential School in the 1950s. She told the *Edmonton Journal* that the loneliness at the school was terrible. "Because of what happened, I became the alcoholic that I never wanted to be," she said. "I became a woman with no values."

Though it is true that many Indians feel this way, many others are appalled at the demonization of residential schools. Rod Lorenz, a Metis Catholic lay missionary at Lloydminster, is sceptical of the government's apology for imposing residential schools on the native people. "If you look at it historically, the priests were very well-travelled and intelligent. They realized that the natives' food supply was diminishing, and they realized that the schools were one way the natives would learn the new tools they needed to survive—and a lot of those kids did learn.

"My own mother attended the residential school in Lebret from 1909 to 1916 in Saskatchewan and she loved it. The nuns taught her everything; how to sew, cook, read and write. How would she have learned otherwise? Certainly, the European style of discipline was different than native culture, but what could you do? If you let the children leave, a lot of them would have starved. You needed discipline." Mr. Lorenz points out that, in some cases, the separation of children from their parents was difficult. "Sure, mistakes were made but there are two sides to this story and you have to look at the positive side."

Rev. Stanley Cuthand, a Cree Indian and retired Anglican priest, grew up on Saskatchewan's Little Pine Reserve, boarded at the La Ronge Residential School in 1944, and was chaplain of Saskatchewan's La Ronge and Gordon Residential Schools, and of St. Paul's School at the Blood Reserve in the 1960s. "The schools weren't terrible places at all," he recalls. "They were certainly not prisons, although the principals were a little strict."

Rev. Mr. Cuthand recalls only one incident of sexual abuse of a student, at the Gordon Reserve, where one of the staff members was later convicted and sent to prison for several years. "Most of the kids had no complaints about sexual abuse; if they did, they would have told me. However, they did get homesick and some tried to run away. There was also plenty of food; raisins, fish, potatoes, bread with lard, stew. In those days everyone lived on fish."

As for the oft-alleged conscription of unwilling students, Rev. Mr. Cuthand recalls that the only children who were "forced" to attend a residential school were orphans or children from destitute families. "The idea that all children were forced into the schools is an exaggeration," he explains. "The idea of the separation of students [from parents] came from England. Practically all the [upper class] English were brought up in residential schools. In Canada, the main idea at the time was to civilize and educate the children; and that couldn't be done if the kids were at home on the trapline."

Mr. Cuthand also scoffs at the accusation that Indians had no influence in their children's education. "The Little Pine reserve wanted its own day school, and in 1910 after petitioning Ottawa, we got our own day school. Our parents had never had schools before, but they wanted us to learn English. When the school was built, there was so much cooperation between everyone that everyone on the reserve sent their kids there." He explains that the reason the children were forbidden to speak their language was because they used to swear in Cree, and had nicknames for their supervisors. "Of course they would be punished for swearing," he says. "The kids were not saints. But generally, language was not an issue. The La Ronge school also allowed fiddle dances every Saturday night; that was the students' culture. By then, most of them had already forgotten the traditional Cree dances."

Rev. Mr. Cuthand enjoyed his time on the Blood Reserve in southwest Alberta. "It was an exciting place to live," he recalls. "The Bloods were rich and very traditional. The school was a fine place with some very good teachers." The parents were involved in the school, with some parents living there as staff members. "[Blood] Senator Gladstone sent his kids there, and many of the students from St. Paul's went on to university." Mr. Cuthand remembers that his school was particularly committed to recognizing the native culture. "One principal had tepees set up on the front lawn," he remembers with a laugh.

That principal, Archdeacon Samuel H. Middleton, with the support of the tribal leadership, was a resourceful school promoter starting in the 1920s. "He started the honorary Kainai chieftainships," explains Mr. Cuthand, whereby prominent people were named as honorary chiefs to support the school. It was an exclusive club: the Prince of Wales, later King Edward VIII, and John Diefenbaker, to name only two. It also came to include three former principals and three former superintendents. Mr. Cuthand remembers the archdeacon, who spoke Blackfoot, changing the Sunday School curriculum to make it more relevant to native culture. "The school was well respected by the Bloods," Mr. Cuthand says. "We used to take students climbing up Chief Mountain because the Indians there believed it was a sacred place." Though not universal, respect for native culture was fostered elsewhere: for example, at the Blue Quills Residential School near St. Paul, religion classes were often conducted in Cree and Chipewyan.

Father Antonio Duhaime of the Oblates was principal at the Duck Lake Residential School from 1962 to 1968, and then principal at St. Mary's Residential School on the Blood reserve from 1968 to 1980. Given the name Black Eagle, Fr. Duhaime speaks some Blackfoot and in 1988 was made an honourary chief of the Blood. "The parents brought us their kids in September, and said 'Father, I want my children to learn English' and now they're accusing us of forbidding them to speak their native languages," he says, shaking his head. "If some of the natives are successful today, they can thank the residential schools. No one else was interested in the Indian people back then."

Fr. Duhaime remembers the schools as a defence against assimilation, not a promoter of it. "At the time, there was a low budget for each school. The federal government was insisting on assimilating the natives, and they were pressuring the children to attend non-native schools off the reserve." However, the sports program at St. Mary's remained an attraction. "We had two provincial highschool basketball championships," he says proudly. "Our teams travelled all over the world; Ireland, Mexico City, Europe. The kids loved to play because on the basketball courts, they were equal or superior to whites."

Dora Cardinal can recall only one instance of physical punishment at St. Anthony's School at Onion Lake. "One time one of the older girls was strapped because she had run away. But the nuns were generally very caring, and a lot of fun," she says. "My Grade 1 teacher in particular was always trying to cheer me up, and she never yelled at us. The way I see it, kids were better off then than today," she says firmly. "Kids today get away with everything; they have no respect for anyone. When I was at the school, I learned a lot about patience and self-discipline, and I learned to persevere."

That Indian reserves today are riven with social problems is everywhere admitted. According to Statistics Canada, the suicide rate among natives is five to eight times the national average, infant mortality is almost double the Canadian average, poverty is three to five times more common, and 60% of reserve residents depend on welfare. In Saskatchewan, the mortality rate on Indian reserves is an annual 5.0 per 1,000, compared to a provincial rate of 3.5. In 1995–96, 22% of all inmates sentenced to prison in Canada were aboriginal, about five times their share of the Canadian population.

But can the residential schools be blamed for this horrific misery? Rita Galloway grew up on the Pelican Lake Cree reserve in Saskatchewan. Today she is a teacher and president of the Saskatchewan-based First Nations Accountability Coalition. "I had many friends and relatives who attended residential schools," she comments. "Of course there were good and bad elements, but overall their experiences were positive. Today those people are now productive citizens; professionals, consultants, and business people. They learned the ethic of hard work."

Mrs. Galloway believes that it is unfair to blame residential schools for the conditions found on many reserves. "The suicide rates are very high, there is a lot of sexual abuse on the reserve; some of my siblings were sexually abused by band members. But my parents never attended a residential school, and they still had problems; my father lost his logging business because of drinking. A lot of these problems were present before the schools. When you put a group of people together in a small area like a reserve there will be problems. But it's always easier to blame others."

"The real problem is lack of financial accountability," insists Mrs. Galloway. "Each year, Indian Affairs doles out $13 billion to 680 reserves across Canada; and we don't know where a lot of it goes. And now, with this apology, the government is handing out another $350 million. When that money is gone, we'll be having the same discussion in 10 years, and there will be the same excuses for more money. But more money doesn't solve anything. Someone has to have the guts to say we need accountability; only then will you see real changes and growth."

Mrs. Galloway taught at the Prince Albert Indian Residential School from 1988 to 1990, when the school was operated by the Prince Albert tribal office. "Within the last five years, there was a police investigation for sexual abuse," she reports. "They didn't run a clean school themselves, and they're pointing the finger at others. As aboriginal people we have to be aware that other aboriginal people are abusers, and it's an oversimplification to blame the residential schools."

Mrs. Galloway also believes that residential schools still have a vital role to play. "Nowadays, there's lots of children who don't even attend school," she points out. "There is a very high drop-out rate among native children who attend school off-reserve. It's attributed to racism, but the deeper problem is that these kids don't get the support at home that they need. There are too many distractions, and many reserve homes are overcrowded. The morning after welfare day, children come to school tired because their parents were partying all night. We have to give these children some normalcy in their lives. When I taught at the Prince Albert school, I was able to give the students the academics they needed, and they were able to focus on their studies."

One of two residential schools still operating in Saskatchewan is the Whitecalf Collegiate in Lebret. Formerly the Oblate-run Qu'Appelle Industrial School, in a 1983 land claims deal the school and 55 acres of surrounding land were ceded to the nearby Star Blanket Cree Reserve. Verne Bellegarde, today executive director of the collegiate, attended the school for Grades 1 to 12, from 1947 to 1959. Mr. Bellegarde says that the band now operates the school with a great deal of success. "For only 200 positions, we have over 500 applicants from Indian reserves all across western Canada." The school's attraction, he believes, is its solid academic record plus its strong emphasis on sports. "Nearly 90% of our graduates go on to some form of post secondary education; with 50% of our grads attending university."

Mr. Bellegarde believes that most parents feel their children would be better-educated at the collegiate than in reserve-based schools. "I would definitely say that we don't have an absentee list," he points out, "and we can isolate them from home to some extent." Mr. Bellegarde points out that, while he was a victim of sexual abuse himself, he doesn't believe that such abuse was widespread through the residential school system. "You can't dwell on that," he reflects. "I've put it behind me, because I can forgive." He prefers to remember his positive experiences. "I learned discipline, and the 3 Rs. Through my experience that I could compete against non-Indians. Through my experience with sports I realized that I could compete against non-Indians."

Rod Lorenz agrees. "There can be a lot of distractions on the reserve," he says. "I think boarding school can be a great way to study and apply yourself. My own son is attending a residential school; but it's a Ukrainian residential school in Manitoba. Residential schools—or boarding schools—have a lot of resources and can be a real advantage to young people. They're a good idea for the advanced grades, but not the younger children. They need mom and dad."

Mr. Lorenz believes that it is convenient for the native political leadership to overlook the positive side of residential schools. "Victimhood gets money," he says simply, "and there are certain vested political interests who have no reason to say anything good about residential schools. If you're trying to get money, balance is not what you want." Mr. Lorenz also believes that adherents to native religions like to discredit Christianity by smearing the residential schools. "There are definitely some people who see Christianity as a rival religion. Those who spearhead the native spirituality revival are very hostile. If they can use the schools as a stick to beat the Catholics, they're going to use it. If someone says that the schools weren't so bad, they become pariahs; they sold out to the whites."

The churches have been brow-beaten into line. In 1992, the Oblate order issued an apology for "certain aspects of their ministry" including "recent criticisms of Indian residential schools." The wordy document, delivered by Father Doug Crosby, then president of the Oblate Conference of Canada and now Bishop of Labrador, apologized for imposing "cultural, linguistic and religious imperialism over the native people."

Retired Oblate priest Duhaime believes that the smear of residential schools cheapens the sacrifices of many lay workers and missionary priests over the years who gave their lives in the service of Indian children. "It's very disappointing," he remarks. "All the years we worked in these schools, trying to make a difference, and all you hear today is negative. It's very hard to take."

5. **David Napier, "Sins of the Fathers: The Legacy of Indian Residential Schools is One of Physical and Emotional Scars, Nasty Lawsuits, A Questionable Medical Study, and Suicide,"** *Anglican Journal,* **May 2000.**

... Must current generations of non-Natives take responsibility for backward-thinking government officials and zealous church leaders of the past, who wanted to permanently erase Native culture and tradition? Few Canadians alive today have any direct ties to the federal government's original policy of assimilation, which required Indian children to attend residential schools, and condemned Native culture by outlawing such gatherings as potlatches and sweat lodges.

But many non-Natives are members of one of the four churches—Anglican, Roman Catholic, Presbyterian, and Methodist (now represented by the United Church)—that ran approximately 130 Indian residential schools that dotted the national map from Alert Bay on Vancouver Island to Shubenacadie, N.S., which some 105,000 children attended. Anglicans were involved in 28 schools—26 through the church's missionary society, two run by the independent New England Company based in London, England. The first Anglican school opened in 1820. The last one closed in 1971. In all, about 35,000 students are thought to have attended Anglican schools; and some of the individuals who stand accused of physically and emotionally abusing Native children are still alive, and named in the growing number of lawsuits.

For the last few years, former attendees of residential schools have been coming forward in droves, claiming they were physically, sexually and mentally abused while students at these mostly remote schools that operated in Canada for more than a century. Thousands have retained lawyers and turned Canada's justice system into the backdrop for the ultimate national story of crime and punishment. Their financial claims total billions of dollars, and may reach tens of billions.

As of mid-April 2000, the Government of Canada was being sued by an estimated 7,000 survivors of residential schools, with the Anglican Church named as a co-defendant in 359 cases involving about 1,600 plaintiffs. Various dioceses within the Anglican Church of Canada, and possibly the national General Synod itself, could go bankrupt as a result of the lawsuits. The General Synod, the national church body that created and is responsible for the missionary society, is already facing claims of more than $2 billion, but has assets of only about $10 million.

Several dioceses, the regional divisions of the church, face similar problems.

"If just 20 of the cases the church faces go the way the first one did, we will be bankrupt, there's no doubt about it," says Bishop Duncan Wallace of Saskatchewan's Diocese of Qu'Appelle, that encompasses Regina and the Gordon Reserve. Wallace is referring to a 1999 Supreme Court of British Columbia decision in which a judge found the Anglican Church and the federal government liable (60 and 40 per cent, respectively) for the abuse that dormitory supervisor Derek Clarke inflicted on Floyd Mowatt in the early 1970s, while Mowatt was a student at St. George's Indian Residential School near Lytton, B.C. The amount was settled before the judge's final decision. Although the amount is confidential, no one has challenged the Journal's reported figure of about $200,000.

The collective dollar amounts from such cases are huge, but the hurt is even greater. This piece of Canada's past has scarred not only former students, but also former staff, many of whom feel their reputations have been damaged, even though they personally did not abuse students. And it has pitted Native Anglicans, the Anglican Church of Canada and the federal government against one another in a series of legal battles that are proving costly, and even deadly; some former students are resolved to suffer the consequences of going public, but others who have not launched lawsuits, but were abused, have been so shocked to learn that their secrets will be revealed in a public forum that they have taken their own lives rather than face the scrutiny and shame of appearing as witnesses at trials.

This painful reality was underscored for me again and again during the eight months I spent crisscrossing Canada by airplane and telephone, en route to being humbled, threatened, hugged and hung-up on. Along the way I met Ben Pratt and dozens of other men and women who attended residential schools, as well as those who staffed and administered these religious/educational outposts (two convicted abusers would not agree to be interviewed). All the former residential school students with whom I spoke physically changed as they told their stories, sinking like loose change into the cushions of their chairs and sofas as they detailed the abuse. Some were fondled in their beds, others were sexually assaulted in washrooms. "I learned that it was safer to pee sitting down," said one man who attended St. George's. These reminiscences were usually accompanied by tears and stories of nasty divorces, alcohol and drug use and attempted suicides. Invariably, these people have the bitter, ironic impression that they are treated like second-class citizens in a country that espouses multiculturalism and equality. Nothing underscores this second-class status more dramatically than documents found at the National Archives in Ottawa, which, quite apart from the issue of individual incidents of abuse, raise real concerns about widespread malnutrition among students at residential schools.

The original mission of the 19th- and early-20th-century Church and State, in their design of residential schools for Native children, was assimilation. "Church and government leaders had come to the conclusion that the problem (as they saw it) of Aboriginal independence and 'savagery' could be solved by taking children from their families at an early age and instilling the ways of the dominant society during eight or nine years of residential schooling far from home," reads the 1996 Royal Commission on Aboriginal Peoples. "Attendance was compulsory. Aboriginal languages, customs and habits of mind were suppressed. The bonds between many hundreds of Aboriginal children and their families and nations were bent and broken, with disastrous results." Today, Native people have the highest suicide rate of any demographic group in Canada, with young Natives eight times more likely to kill themselves than non-Natives. Economic hardship is endemic, especially on reserves. While seven in 10 adult Natives generally are either working or looking for work, less than half those on reserves are working or looking for work—most of the rest being on welfare according to 1990 figures.

And of those Natives that had jobs in 1990, they earned 30 per cent less than the average Canadian wage of $27,880.

The real cost to the country? It has been estimated that if these disparities did not exist, Aboriginal people would have added $5.8 billion in goods and services to the Canadian economy in 1996. The Royal Commission reported the economic toll appears much bleaker when we realize that in 1992–93, the latest year for which information on all governments is available, Ottawa and the provinces each spent about $6 billion on Aboriginal people, mostly on programs for registered Indians and Inuit—a total of $11.6 billion. Government spend money on all citizens, mostly for health care and education, to stimulate the economy, and facilitate transportation. But the amount spent on general programs per person for Aboriginal people is 57 per cent higher than for Canadians generally.

These national statistics are symptoms of what Natives say is a greater ill— the attempted theft of the "vehicle that drives Native culture"—namely, languages, and the oral traditions that get passed along in Cree, Ojibway and various other Native communities. Without oral histories to build upon, many Native Canadians have struggled for any sense of self-identification and roots. It began at many residential schools where children were banned from speaking their mother tongues, and often beaten when they tried. "As a passive people, we put up with this for a long time," says Christine (Willie) Hodgson of the Plains Cree Nation, a teacher who chaired the Qu'Appelle Diocesan Advisory Council of Indigenous Peoples. "It's like Alabama for Indians up here," says Hodgson of life in Saskatchewan. "There's going to be civil strife." Clashes between Native and non-Native cultures do occur, in volatile situations such as the standoff at Oka, Que., the shooting of J.J. Harper in Manitoba, and the recent accusations of police abuse of Natives in and around Saskatoon.

Conflicts like these have their roots in a lack of understanding and appreciation sparked in large part by residential schooling, and fuelled by the government policy that once established an educational system that has been called "a national crime." It has left a legacy on reserves, street corners and prisons crowded with Native people so far down-and-out they cannot dream of being up-and-in. It makes it very difficult for many young Native people to walk in what their elders refer to as "both worlds." And today, churches, governments—sons of a flawed system—and individual abusers, are being held accountable.

Not all students, not all teachers.

But if all perspectives of Indian residential schools are to be taken into account, it must be understood that these schools were not all bad places run by bad people. "I don't like to be thought of as a villain. I don't think I was ... I think I was a fairly decent person and still am," says Berit Rasmussen, an 83-year-old Norwegian woman who came to Canada as a missionary in 1949, spent decades at residential schools in Ontario, Saskatchewan and British Columbia, and now lives in Lytton. Sitting in her living room knitting a large blanket, Rasmussen fields questions about the schools at Gordon's Reserve, Pelican Falls and St. George's where she worked. One of the highlights of her time at these schools came when she tucked an eight-year-old gift named Lilly into bed one night. "She pulled my face to hers and whispered, 'When I came to school last year I thought you were a white woman.'" The girl was so comfortable with Rasmussen that she gladly mistook her for a Native mother or aunt.

"My experience does not reflect what some Native activists and much of the media are saying," says Eric Carlson, a status Indian who attended St. Anthony's Indian Residential School at Onion Lake, Sask., for 12 years. "I don't recall ever going hungry and the nuns did their best to clothe us and keep us in good health. The academic instruction was such that I had no difficulty keeping up when I moved on to St. Thomas College," adds Carlson, who eventually went on to teach at a residential school ...

As with the abusive act itself, there is a certain degree of shame attached to cash settlements awarded in such cases. "Around here it's called 'arse money.' It's supposed to be dirty," says Pratt, who believes that such taunts often come from people who have suffered abuse themselves and are simply hiding behind catcalls rather than face their own demons. "I laughed and made fun of others, until it got to my door," admits the man whose residential-school experience came back to haunt him not as a nocturnal image that startled him from his sleep, but in the form of people on the reserve going door-to-door asking who had been abused at Gordon's. When faced with the question, Pratt made the toughest decision of his life, and told his well-kept secret. By his own estimation, he is feeling more empowered and in control—even if his emotions still run high on occasion.

But for every Ben Pratt, there is a man or woman who will not, or cannot, step forward and revisit the horror they endured as children. Some simply choose to remain silent, while others put guns to their heads or ropes around their necks. Nothing illustrates the despair some former residential-school students feel like the phone call Pratt received awhile back. It was a Tuesday night, and his cousin, a grown man and fellow resident of Gordon's, was on the other end of the line, crying. Between sobs, he told of his abusive past and the taunts and criticism from those who claimed to be friends, but who now simply made fun of him. It was all too much to bear, he said. Pratt tried to reassure him that things would get better. You must be strong and not walk away from this fight, Pratt said. His cousin said he would try, then hung up. But he couldn't do what Pratt begged of him. Instead, he walked down to a nearby set of train tracks. Just before a locomotive whipped by, he stepped on to the tracks—to his death, his Creator, and the possibility of peace.

When Pratt finishes telling this story his eyes overflow with tears, and his ballcap is a crinkled mass of black cotton. "I wish I could write," he says, wiping his eyes. I attempt to be encouraging and supportive, assuring him that he can write down his story if he simply takes the time to do so. Pratt looks at me. "I am illiterate," says the graduate of Grade 6 at residential school. Pratt doesn't give me a chance to apologize before he continues. "If I could write, I would tell everyone what happened to me. I have even come up with a name for my story. I'd call it Number 38 Speaking Out."

Not everyone is so willing to talk. "If you come onto my reserve, I'll get you." These are some of the last words I hear before Chief Janet Webster of the Lytton Indian Band slams down the phone, bringing our brief conversation to an abrupt end. I had called Webster because I wanted to let her know I would be visiting British Columbia and was hoping to speak with residential-school survivors, some of whom are members of her band. Webster was not happy to hear from me, because other reporters had visited the reserve and left behind a powerful emotional fallout that has, she says, resulted in suicide ...

Readings

Assembly of the First Nations. *Breaking the Silence: An Interpretive Study of Residential School Impact and Healing as Illustrated by the Stories of First Nations Individuals.* Ottawa: Assembly of First Nations, 1994.

Barman, J. et al., eds. *Indian Education in Canada.* Vancouver: University of British Columbia Press, 1986.

Bull, L. "Indian Residential Schooling: The Native Perspective," *Canadian Journal of Native Education* 18 (1991).

Canada, *Looking Forward, Looking Back: Report of the Royal Commission on Aboriginal People.* Ottawa: Canada Communication Group, 1996.

Chrisjohn, R. and S. Young, *The Circle Game: Shadows and Substance in the Indian Residential School Experience in Canada.* Penticton: Theytus Books, 1997.

Coates, K. "'Betwixt and Between': The Anglican Church and the Children of Carcross (Chooutla) Residential School," *B.C. Studies* 64 (Winter 1984–85).

Deiter, C. *From our Mothers' Arms: The Intergenerational Impact of Residential Schools in Saskatchewan.* Etobicoke: United Church, 1999.

Dyck, N. *Differing Visions: Administering Indian Residential Schooling in Prince Albert 1867–1995.* Halifax: Fernwood, 1997.

Fiske, J. "Gender and the Paradox of Residential Education in Carrier Society," in J. Gaskell and A. McLaren eds. *Women and Education: A Canadian Perspective.* Second edition, Edmonton: Detsileg Enterprises, 1991.

Fournier, S. and E. Crey. *Stolen From our Embrace: The Abduction of First Nations Children and the Restoration of Aboriginal Communities.* Vancouver: Douglas and McIntyre, 1997.

Furniss, E. *Victims of Benevolence: Discipline and Death at Williams Lake Indian Residential School, 1891–1920.* Williams Lake: Cariboo Tribal Council, 1992.

Graham, E. *The Mush Hole: Life in Two Residential Schools.* Waterloo: Heffle Publications, 1997.

Grant, A. *No End of Grief: Indian Residential Schools in Canada.* Winnipeg: Pemmican Publications, 1996.

Grant, W. *Residential Schools: An Historical Overview.* Ottawa: Assembly of First Nations, 1993.

Haig-Brown, C. *Resistance and Renewal: Surviving the Indian Residential School.* Vancouver: Tillacum Library, 1988.

Ing, R. "The Effects of Residential Schooling on Native Child-Rearing Practices," *Canadian Journal of Native Education* 18 (1991).

Jack, A. *Behind Closed Doors: Stories from the Kamloops Indian Residential School.* Penticton: Secwepemc Cultural Education Society, 2001.

Jaine, L., ed. *Residential School: The Stolen Years.* Saskatoon: University of Saskatchewan, 1993.

Knockwood, I. *Out of the Depths: The Experiences of Mi'kmaw Children at the Indian Residential School at Shubenacadie, Nova Scotia.* Lockeport: Roseway Publishing, 1992.

Miller, J. *Shingwauk's Vision: A History of Native Residential Schools.* Toronto: University of Toronto Press, 1996.

Miller, J. "The Irony of Residential Schooling," *Canadian Journal of Native Education* 14 (1987).

Miller, J. "Owen Glendower Hotspur, and Canadian Indian Policy," *Ethnohistory* 37, (1990).

Milloy, J. *National Crime: The Canadian Government and the Residential School System, 1879 to 1986.* Winnipeg: University of Manitoba Press, 1999.

Nuu-chah-nulth Tribal Council. *Indian Residential Schools: The Nuu-chah-nulth Experience.* Port Alberni: 1996.

Raibmon, P. "A New Understanding of Things Indian: George H.Raley's Negotiation of the Residential School Experience," *B.C. Studies* 110 (Summer 1996).

Titley, B. "Red Deer Indian Industrial School: A Case Study in the History of Native Education," in N. Kach and K. Mazurek, eds. *Exploring our Educational Past: Schooling in the Northwest Territories and Alberta.* Calgary: Detselig Enterprises, 1992.

Titley, B. *A Narrow Vision: Duncan Campbell Scott and the Administration of Indian Affairs in Canada.* Vancouver: University of British Columbia, 1986.

Urion, C. "Introduction: The Experience of Indian Residential Schooling," *Canadian Journal of Native Education* 18 (1991).

Chapter Sixteen

"Winter in Our Souls": Quebec and Independence

1. Marcel Chaput, *Why I am a Separatist*, 1961.
2. Front de Libération du Québec, "A Message to the Nation," 1963.
3. J. Leger, "Sovereignty the Condition of Salvation," 1967.
4. René Lévesque, "Quebec Independence," 1978.
5. Gilles Vigneault and Marie Laberge, "Preamble, Sovereignty Declaration," September 6, 1995.

Introduction

Some Quebecois have always sought to leave this country and form an independent nation. This became more obvious with the formation of the Parti Quebecois. Since its inception in 1968, this provincial political party dedicated to separatism, has remained at the forefront of Quebec and national politics. It was, however, only the latest and most successful manifestation in a long tradition of separatist thought and organizations emanating from *La Belle Province*.

French Canada had, by 1763 when Britain officially conquered it, developed a unique and distinct culture—one its people cherished and wished to preserve. This, of course, was awkward with Quebec under British tutelage and an official policy of Anglo-assimilation. Though assimilationist efforts largely failed and led to some acceptance of French Canada's uniqueness within British North America, as enshrined in the 1774 Quebec Act, the latent expectation of assimilation remained. Thus many French Canadian nationalists concluded that the only way to preserve and nurture Quebec's culture was to create an independent nation beyond England's grasp. That was what the rebels of 1837 sought, and what nationalists like the conservative Abbé Lionel Groulx promoted in the 1920s and '30s. It was not before the late 1950s, however, that French Canadian separatism emerged in its modern version and became a formidable and popular force.

Economic conditions in Quebec not only played a major part in fomenting modern separatism, they still contribute to the waxing and waning of separatist support. French Canadians discovered by the late 1950s that most things worth owning in their province, be it the wood, minerals, electrical generation potential, commerce, banking—belonged to *les etrangers* "foreigners," most either Montreal Anglophones or American corporations. Meanwhile, disproportionately high unemployment and narrow job prospects haunted the French Canadian majority.

If, argued separatists in the 1950s and '60s, the Quebecois wished to change their lot, then it must happen by leaving Canada to create a new and independent nation in which French Canadians could truly rule their own house. Conversely, they argued, tinkering with the federal system, no mater how noble the intentions, must leave Quebec unable to manage its own affairs because it would remain "colonized" by the federal government. There was no shortage of enthusiasm for independence in the heady social flux of the 1960s, especially on Quebec's campuses; the question was how to achieve it. Some argued that the Anglo "bosses" would never voluntarily relinquish control because it suited their ends. This group of Marxists contended that independence could logically only come through revolution—and the militant underground organization, the *Front de Libération du Quebec* (FLQ) was born. Though the FLQ's campaign of bombing and kidnapping symbols of Anglo-domination through the 1960s cost it mass support, the organization's eloquent fury and ultimate goals struck a responsive chord within Quebec. But most Quebecois separatists preferred to follow legal channels, however, and here a number of political organizations dedicated to separatism emerged; the major one being the *Rassemblement pour L'indépendance Nationale* (RIN). When René Lévesque quit the provincial Liberal party in 1967, he brought much of the RIN on side, fused it with his own converts to independence, and created the dynamic *Parti Quebecois* (PQ) in 1968.

Pundits across Canada who gleefully prophesized René Lévesque's political suicide soon had to eat their words. Separatism gained popularity among many progressive Quebec urbanites, and the party's support rose to the point where it won a quarter of the popular vote in the 1970 provincial election. This astonishing victory, however, translated into only 7 seats in the National Assembly—which separatists held up as proof that the system was stacked against French Canadians and their aspirations. The 1973 provincial election increased the PQ's popular vote to almost one third—and they still lost a seat. The tide turned in the 1976 provincial election, and René Lévesque's party swept to power with three quarters of the seats—and 41% of the popular vote, largely on the promise to hold a referendum on the right to begin negotiating separation with the federal government within its first term in office.

Terry Mosher, drawing as cartoonist "Aislin," captured Canada's mood the day after the PQ gained power. His predictably scabrous editorial cartoon depicted a dishevelled Lévesque, ubiquitous cigarette in hand, against a black background. The caption: "Okay, everybody take a Valium." Canada awakened from its post-war complacent slumber to discover that one of the country's provincial governments and some 30% of the nation's population apparently wished to leave what was supposedly the finest country on earth.

The PQ kept its promise to hold a referendum on the right to negotiate sovereignty association, doing so in 1980 after postponing it for as long as politically feasible. Polls taken early in the Parti's mandate proved that separatist support was, in fact, dangerously soft. The PQ knew, however, that a large percentage of Quebecois were unhappy with the federal-provincial status quo. Thus Lévesque and his team spent four years carefully cultivating the idea of separatism, casting it as a logical, safe, and advantageous route for the province—or at least as implied leverage in federal-provincial negotiations. Gentle persuasion was the order of the day. Lévesque de-emphasized the PQ's avowed independence agenda in favour of simple good government, thereby hoping to gain credibility and support among "soft separatists" and undecided voters. Claude Morin, one of the separatist referendum architects, logically pointed out that "you don't make a flower grow by pulling at it."

Prime Minister Pierre Trudeau responded to the PQ's 1976 electoral victory and to the 1980 referendum by promising to address Quebec's concerns and to work toward creating a sense of inclusion for the Quebecois within Canada. A made-in-Canada constitution, he argued, would begin the process by removing the symbolic thorn of English domination. Vote "no," he promised, and Canada will ensure that Quebec gains its deserved sense of equality.

The 1980 referendum results became official on May 20th. The vote in favour of a mandate to negotiate sovereignty-association was 40.4%; opposed, 59.6%. While separatists wept over their seemingly catastrophic defeat, federalists collectively sighed with relief. Closer examination of the referendum results, however, allowed sovereignists to dry their tears and draw comfort from a result that was far more ambiguous than simple numbers initially suggested. Federalists certainly had no cause for smugness. The sizable non-Francophone community in Quebec, for example, predictably voted overwhelming *non* to sovereignty-association. Francophones, however, voted almost 50-50 *oui*, and young secular urbanites, the next generation of Quebec leaders, supported independence by a reasonably wide margin. The 1981 provincial election saw the Parti Quebecois, still dedicated to a sovereign Quebec, swept back into power, winning 80 out of the 122 seats—a two-thirds majority, and this despite losing the referendum. The dream of an independent Quebec certainly did not die in 1980.

Trudeau was as good as his word and set to creating a new constitution immediately after the referendum. Reaching consensus with the other provinces, however, proved all but impossible. At the end of the day, the new Canada Act of 1982 became law without Quebec's support, and with grudging acceptance from the rest. Quebec separatists saw this development as just the latest incarnation of colonialism: a constitution that Quebec did not support but must obey, this time imposed by Ottawa rather than London. Subsequent federal governments, particularly Brian Mulroney's Progressive Conservatives, sought to placate Quebec and gain that tenth signature on the Canada Act. Negotiations such as the Meech Lake and Charlottetown Accords offered glimmers of hope of achieving this by calling for a significantly decentralized federation and special status for Quebec within Canada. The rest of Canada, however, found this unacceptable and all negotiations ultimately failed—just as the separatists predicted.

As promised, the PQ held a second referendum on separatism in 1995. This time the *non* side won by less than one percent after a calamitous campaign that saw thousands of Canadians from across the country reach out to Quebec. PQ Premier Jacques Parizeau blamed Quebec's ethnic minorities for the referendum's failure. The PQ vowed to hold yet another when conditions appear ripe for victory—which had not occurred by the turn of the new millennium. Other issues pushed separatism to the back burner at the beginning of the twenty-first century, but the stove remains lit and there is no reason why the pot may not boil again. The political journalist who dubbed the process the "neverendum" was probably correct.

Discussion Points

1. Do the aims, ambitions and grievances of the separatists justify the creation of an independent state?
2. Is Sovereignty Association a contradiction in terms? Utopian? Realistic? Does it fit into the movement towards larger units of economic and political co-operation such as the EEU and NAFTA, or not?
3. Is the Quebec situation simply the most severe version of regional forces that threaten to de-confederate Canada? Do any other regions of Canada have a similar basis for claiming a separate identity?

4. Should Canadians recognize Quebec's claim to distinct status?
5. Would Canada be better off without Quebec?
6. During his tenure as premier of Quebec, Lucien Bouchard stated that Canada is not a country. Was he right?

Documents

1. Marcel Chaput, *Why I am a Separatist,* 1961.

PREFACE

The world is made up of Separatists. The man who is master of his home is a Separatist. Each of the hundred nations striving to maintain its national identity is Separatist. France and England are mutually Separatist, even in relation to the Common Market. And you who long for a real Canadian Constitution, you are a Separatist. The only difference between you and me is that you want Canada to be free in relation to England and the United States, and I want Quebec to be free in relation to Canada. In mathematical terms, Quebec's independence is to Canada as Canada's independence is to the United States and England. But Quebec is far more justified than English Canada in asserting its individuality, since of the four territories, Quebec alone has a distinct culture, whereas English Canada, the United States and England tend to be very similar.

In spite of this, Separatism has always received a poor press in Quebec. The very term Separatism is certainly responsible in part. It is negative and doesn't seem to encourage a constructive approach.

And yet, for anyone who pauses to reflect on it, Separatism leads on to great things: to Independence, Liberty, Fulfilment of the Nation, French Dignity in the New World.

It has become fashionable in some quarters to treat Separatists as dreamers. Thank heaven that there are still men and women in French Canada capable of dreaming! But to grasp the distinction between a practical dream and a utopia, you must at least be able to put aside the sort of subjective dogmatism which immediately rejects the idea of independence for Quebec without a thought.

It is true that independence is a matter of character rather than of logic. Everyone is not capable of being independent. A feeling of pride is even more essential than having a reasonable claim.

If you possess this pride of which free men are made, if you can shake off all preconceived notions about the subject and bring a sincere, discerning attitude to the discussion, then, and only then, should we sit down and talk. ...

Most of all, you would be wrong to think that I consider independence the solution to all of Quebec's problems; on the contrary, I believe that it would create many more new ones.

Why independence then?

Because it is highly desirable that a normal man or nation be free.

I just don't believe, as do certain M.P.'s, that the bilingualism of French-Canadians is an indication of their superiority, but rather a proof of their enslavement. I cannot stand by silently, as others seemingly can, and watch the day-by-day extermination of my people, even if by our own foolishness we are more to blame than the "damned English."

The six million French-Canadians are no longer obliged to accept this minority position, which makes of us a people without a future, shut up in the vicious circle of destructive bilingualism.

Since I naturally owe my first allegiance to French Canada, before the Dominion, I must ask myself the question: which of two choices will permit French-Canadians to attain the fullest development—Confederation, in which they will forever be a shrinking minority, doomed to subjection?—or the independence of Quebec, their true native land, which will make them masters of their own destiny?

But judging by the reaction of some of my compatriots to this basic question, its seems to me that truly free French-Canadians are even harder to find than you would think, which is after all normal for a people in bondage.

Faced with Separatism, some smile ironically, others hide their eyes, the established well-to-do have proved to themselves that independence isn't necessary to the Good Life, the bourgeois have other things on their minds, and the petty workers are afraid of losing their jobs.

And then, after all, we aren't so badly off. Actually, we are quite well off. Who do these Separatist people think they are, coming along to disturb our serenity? Do they want to shut themselves up in the "Quebec reservation"?

And so on through the whole list of current objections.

But let's not get ahead of ourselves. Let us start at the beginning. ...

The Historical Dimension

A world-wide trend to independence

We of the mid-twentieth century are living historic years. Since the Second World War more than thirty former colonies have liberated themselves from foreign domination to attain national and international sovereignty. In 1960 alone, seventeen African colonies, fourteen of them French-speaking, have obtained their independence. And now it is the turn of the French-Canadian people to arise and claim their rightful place among free nations.

Why independence? We are free

Why independence? you may ask. What is this Separatism that is making so much fuss? We French-Canadians are free. We are free to speak our language, to practise our religion. We have the right to vote, even the right to be elected. Is not the very presence of a French-Canadian as Governor-General an outright refutation of Separatist claims? And what of the two French-Canadian Prime Ministers? And the head of the Supreme Court? And the generals? Are the Separatists trying to compare the French-Canadians to the African tribes who have recently won their independence? These Negroes, often illiterate, sometimes deprived of the most basic rights, exploited, living in under-developed countries, had a right to claim the independence they lacked. But as for us French-Canadians, the situation is quite different.

Similarity and difference

It is true that our situation in French Canada is not identical with that of the African Negroes. It is true that we have enjoyed rights for a long time which these people have only recently acquired. But we are not assured of total independence by the mere fact that we have certain rights which give us a partial control of our national affairs, even if this control be much greater in practice than that held by the newly decolonized countries. You may be closer to your goal than a neighbour is, without having reached the goal.

In the rise of people toward independence, no two cases are identical. But French Canada *is* like all these new sovereign nations in that she too has been taken by force, occupied, dominated, exploited, and in that even today, here destiny rests to a great extent in the hands of a nation which is foreign to her ...

Confederation: the lesser of two evils

To affirm, as some do, that Confederation was freely accepted by the French-Canadians of the time, is to play with words, to distort the meaning of liberty. First of all, the B.N.A. Act was never put to the vote. It was imposed by a decree of parliament at Westminster, and by a majority vote of twenty-six to twenty-two among the Canadian representatives.

For Confederation to have been labelled the free choice of the French-Canadians, it would have been necessary to have given them the freedom of choice between Confederation or total sovereignty. And this freedom was not granted, either by the London parliament or by the English-speaking colonies of America.

In 1867, French Canada, Lower Canada, old Canada in short, was a British colony, and the alternatives offered her did not include independence. She was a colony and was to remain so, inside or outside Confederation. If there was any freedom of choice, it was that of the convicted man who is allowed to choose between a fine and prison. Just as the prisoner chooses the fine, if he can afford it, French Canada entered Confederation. It was, in her opinion, the lesser of two evils ...

What about the Canadian nation?

There is no Canadian nation. We cannot have a Canadian nation and a French-Canadian nation at the same time. There is a Canadian State.

Certain groups, invariably English, would like to see a genuine Canadian nation. But this would involve the negation of the French-Canadian group as such.

The Canadian State is a purely political and artificial entity formed originally by armed force and maintained by a submission of the French-Canadians to the federal government.

On the contrary, the French-Canadian nation is a natural entity whose bonds are those of culture, flesh and blood.

If the American army were to invade Mexico and force its amalgamation with the United States, there would still be a Mexican nation. In the same way there is still a French-Canadian nation.

The confrontation of two nationalisms

The Separatists also urge French-Canadians to make their presence felt everywhere in Canada, in America, in the world. But we feel just as strongly that French-Canadians must be *in control* somewhere, in a country of their own, specifically in Quebec.

That is why modern Separatism constitutes an irreconcilable opposition to traditional nationalism. Whereas the latter is employed to uphold rights in a vast Canada in which French-Canada is a minority group, Separatists, the Freedom Fighters of Quebec, are aspiring to set up the French-Canadians as masters of their own destiny.

It has nothing whatsoever to do with Anglophobia, chronic discontent, or vengefulness. The removal of each individual injustice suffered by the French-Canadians will not cause the idea of an independent Quebec to disappear.

We want independence for a totally different reason. It is because dignity requires it. It is because of the idea that minorities, like absentees, are always wrong ...

A pact between two great races

French Canada is unfortunately populated with people who, for want of reality, like to tell themselves stories. One of the dangerous ones is that Confederation is a sacred pact between two great races, French and English. It is a poetic idea. It inspires you. But the fact remains that it is an illusion. For you can search in vain, in the texts and especially in the facts, without finding a single word or action to justify it.

All political decisions of importance in Canada are made by the Parliament or the Cabinet, where the French-Canadians are in a minority. Proof? Newfoundland's entrance to Confederation, Canada's membership in the UN, in NATO or in NORAD, had no need of French-Canada's approval. Even if we had been consulted, we couldn't have done anything because of our minority position.

You may retort that French is still an official language, but you would be wrong—or at least you would be only partly right. French is, along with English, official in Quebec—this makes us the *only* bilingual province in our dealings with the Ottawa Parliament and the Federal Courts of Justice. This limitation puts French on an unequal footing with the English from the outset.

In Parliament, nine per cent of the speeches have been given in French since the installation of simultaneous interpretation. Are the members from Quebec less talkative than their English colleagues? Or perhaps they simply want to show off their "bilingual superiority"? Nonsense! It is nothing but a minority reflex, conditioned by two hundred years of subjection.

The final result is that, internally, Canada is a predominantly English country and, from the outside, Canada is also an English country, a country in which, they say, English and French live in perfect harmony for the edification of humanity.

The Economic Dimension
After all, we're not so badly off

For many people, not only French-Canadians, the economic aspect of a problem is always the most important. Faced with the prospect of Quebec's independence, they invariably say that they will support the idea as soon as they see proof that Quebec would gain economically.

This subsection was not written to prove that an independent Quebec would be an economically sound proposition. We shall discuss this later. My only purpose for the moment is to remind you that the French-Canadians have gained nothing from Confederation; on the contrary, they are losing continuously.

Perhaps the relative comfort you enjoy makes you fear a lowering of your standard of living, a serious change in your habits, a prolonged economic recession. After all, the French-Canadians aren't so badly off, no matter what they say.

Let me hasten to remind you that individual liberty is not under discussion here. Certainly there are rich men, even millionaires, among the French-Canadians, which seems to show that a French-Canadian can make a lot of money, even under Confederation. But we are discussing French-Canadians as a people, as a nation, in their province of Quebec. The French-Canadian nation is economically weak and economically under-developed, living in economic bondage ...

A people in bondage

There is no need to be an economist, statistician or informed industrialist to realize that the French-Canadians are not the masters, are not the proprietors of their own province or cities. You have only to take a stroll through any city in Quebec with your eyes open, to seize at a glance our economic insignificance. Our contribution is limited to furnishing cheap raw materials, cheap manpower and five million docile consumers. All this for the sake of a few crumbs.

We French-Canadians made up twenty-nine per cent of Canada's population in 1951, but our participation in the economy was limited to five or ten per cent, closer to five than to ten. In Quebec we are eighty-three per cent of the population, but less than twenty per cent of the economy is in our hands. At the Montreal Stock Exchange (you rarely hear it called *la Bourse de Montréal*), it is said that one per cent of the business is based on French-Canadian capital—in a city containing at least a million French-Canadians! Scarcely a month goes by that you don't learn in the papers or by word of mouth that another French-Canadian enterprise has sold out to a big American or Anglo-Canadian firm. It is a well-known fact, appearing in the papers every year, that Quebec has the greatest number of bankruptcies in Canada. The corner grocery, which used to be our own, has been supplanted, or rather, strangled, by the supermarkets, all of which are under foreign control. And the small grocer who has managed to survive has done so only by joining some *chain*, and the main link of this chain is invariably in the hands of foreign control as well.

The labour market

On the labour market, the French-Canadians are at the bottom of the ladder. You may insist that it is their own fault, that all they have to do is get more education to prepare themselves for better positions. But I insist that I am not attempting an assessment of commendation and rebuke—I am establishing facts.

For equal labour, workers in Quebec are paid less than in Ontario. If there is an economic recession or unemployment, Quebec always has the longest list of unemployed. If anyone receives a good salary, he is almost certain to be in the employ of a foreign company. But at the higher levels of these foreign companies, at directorship-level, French-Canadians are no longer found. Even in the Federal corporations our compatriots are significantly rare. Out of the seventeen directors of the Bank of Canada, one is a French-Canadian; out of the seventeen vice-presidents of the C.N.R., none is French-Canadian. Out of the seven top officials in the new Federal ministry of forests, none is French-Canadian, although Quebec has twenty-five per cent of Canada's commercial forest area. In public office, the higher you go, the fewer French-Canadians you meet. The situation is the same in the armed forces. We are good enough when it comes to paying taxes, or playing the role of consumer and soldier, but we are not good enough to take our rightful place on the well-paid levels of Canadian life.

Quebec—Ottawa's private treasure chest

If only Quebec got back in service what it gave to Ottawa. But far from it—it pays to have itself Anglicized and to maintain its state of bondage.

Quebec pays two billion dollars a year to Ottawa in taxes. It gets back only five hundred million dollars per year, twenty-five per cent of its contribution ...

English, language of labour and thought

Any country in the world must have its bilinguals. Interpreters and translators are required in diplomatic service, transport, communications, hotels, the army, even in the civil service. But in what proportion? That is the problem. Let us be generous and say five per cent. But in French-Canada, at least half the workers must know English to earn their living. Of these, at least half must, like me, throw off their native language with their overcoats at the office or factory entrance each morning—their native language, French, an international language, used by one hundred and fifty million people.

For the majority of French-Canadian workers, even in Quebec, English is the language of labour and thought. French? It is used in translations, in the family, in folk-lore. In his own language, the French-Canadian leads a fairy-tale existence. Active life, the life of earning enough to keep bread on the table, the life of entertainment, the life of the mind, is carried on in English as often as not ...

You think you are going to a French show—if you can find one at all. Two times out of three you will see the French version of a Hollywood hit. You open your French newspaper and read the French translation of an English translation of a speech given in French by General de Gaulle. The Canadian Press (there is no such thing as *la Presse Canadienne*) has not even passed on the original, and this in a country where they say French is an official language. You subscribe to a Canadian magazine of genuinely French content, only to find that it has recently been bought out by Anglo-American capital. You pass by a large building, even in Montreal—you will find three words of French on a bronze plaque and a bilingual elevator-boy. Seek no further. That is the extent of the French. "Patrons are requested to leave their tongue in the umbrella rack."

What about the schools?

Why should our schools teach French, real French, if the language is of so little use here? It is English that we need, and more and more of it. Really, can you imagine a more absurd situation than the one in which you and I have found ourselves? Six, eight, ten, twelve years of French studies, when this language, which is supposedly so beautiful, is of no use in earning your daily bread. So many long years spent learning a language when English is what you really need when you leave school. As a result, parents demand more English, and those parents are right. Far be it from me to criticize them, for their logic is impeccable. Parents see things in their true light, and children too. They realize quite well that without English you might not be able to earn your keep in Canada, that without English you run the risk of swelling the ranks of Quebec's unemployed.

But what is the result of these repeated demands, which are heard today more than yesterday, and tomorrow more than today? The more bilingual our children become, the more they will use English; the more they use English, the less use they will get from French; and the less use they get from French, the more they will use English. *It is a paradox of French-Canadian life: the more bilingual we become, the less need there is to be bilingual.* This is a path which can lead us only to Anglification. Moreover, we have already come such a long way in this direction that we would be better off to know only English—so let's get on with the process and speak no more about it ...

Bilingualism—a sign of bondage or superiority?

It may seem strange to some people that a French-Canadian like me, who earns his living in English, should not appreciate the benefits of bilingualism.

Well, I do; I am very happy that I know English, and if I didn't know it yet, I would learn it. I derive satisfaction from knowing English, just as I should like to do with several more languages, English even more than other languages because it is the most widespread in North America. But it is not a question of deciding whether it is useful or not for French-Canadians to know English, but of discovering what this knowledge and its constant use is costing them.

They learn English to the detriment of their native language which is deteriorating, their French culture which is wilting away, their dignity which is being insulted.

I didn't learn English out of intellectual curiosity. I learned it because it was the language of the stronger side, because I needed it to earn my living. Perhaps a man who knows two languages is worth two men, but a man who is forced to speak the Other Fellow's language in order to eat is worth only half a man. The misfortune of the French-Canadian people is to mistake the fetters of its bilingualism for a sign of superiority. Just as a little boy afraid of the dark will whistle to bolster his courage, the brow-beaten French-Canadian prides himself on his bilingualism to hide his inferiority complex ...

The Social Dimension

We are inferior to ourselves

As in other spheres, or perhaps even more here than elsewhere, French-Canadians are inferior to themselves. You often hear it said: What have we to complain about? We have accomplished a great deal. Haven't we produced two prime ministers, a governor-general, a chief justice? Don't we have our artists, our scientists, our writers?

It is true that, in spite of serious difficulties, French-Canadians have nevertheless produced a lot. But, for nations, just as for men, it isn't enough to know whether they have produced; we must ask whether they have produced enough— whether they have produced as much as their capabilities permit. This is the parable of the talents.

Far be it from me to excuse my compatriots by blaming the "damned English" for our inferiority. But all the same we must recognize the fact that the French-Canadians have not had the same history as the English-speaking Canadians during the past two hundred years, not even in the ninety-four years of Confederation. Armed with abundant capital, political authority and numerical superiority, the English Canadians had an easier time of it than we. We had the talents—and we still have—but we lacked the financial boost and political favour, so that, socially, we are second-rate citizens.

In the workaday world

In the workaday world of industry and commerce, we are on the bottom rung of the ladder. Quebec is the place to go for cheap labour; in times of crisis or economic recession, Quebec always has the greatest number of unemployed. This was obvious in the winter of 1960–1961. Across the country, eleven per cent of the working force was idle in March, according to the papers; in Quebec, the figure was fourteen per cent. Do you remember Elliot Lake, the mining town in Ontario which was one day declared a ghost town? Out of all the miners thrown into the streets, seventy-five per cent were French-Canadians from Quebec.

All you have to do is open your eyes: all the large industries in Quebec make excessive use of the English to the detriment of the French. In so doing, they are merely following the example of those around them, but this marked predominance of English places the French-Canadian worker in an inferior position from the start. That is obvious. There is a dividing line between the management and the labour force. The first is English, the second French. ...

But in the face of the imminent dangers confronting the French-Canadian nation, I fear that the outgrown methods of this noble society are no longer sufficient. Confederation, pan-Canadianism, bilingualism and the whole Canadian way of life have depersonalized the French-Canadian, have even robbed him, over the years, of his capacity for indignation. At his most brash, he is no more than a beggar. The schools have forgotten about nationalist education, and life in Quebec doesn't even teach us our language. Something better than the repetition of the same old reports must be found if we are going to change things ...

Independence of Quebec

The rejection of liberty

You have just read, a few pages back, that a minority which wishes to live cannot hand over the control of its affairs to a foreign majority. That is the simple reason why the Separatists want Quebec to be independent. As long as the French-Canadians form a linguistic and cultural minority, they will be doomed to subjection and mediocrity. It is not because of hostility or a desire for revenge against the English; it is not a way of finding an alibi for all our stupidities and cowardly acts; it is not a way of excusing men by blaming the institutions. On the contrary, it is based on a purely mathematical truth of democracy—the majority prevails over the minority. Either we must bow to the decisions of the majority and stop complaining, or withdraw from Confederation. The desire to stick with Confederation at all costs is a search for excuses to justify the rejection of liberty.

Commonwealth and Crown

Why should we kid ourselves any longer? For two hundred years the French-Canadians have been trying to free themselves from the British Crown, the symbol of foreign domination. All the French-Canadian nationalist movements of the past have embodied this subconscious or avowed refusal to submit. It is high time that English Canada realized the fact that, outside of a few rare politicians, the French-Canadians have *never* accepted subjection to British Royalty. They simply endured it. We had to submit to it under force of arms; you can't reproach us all the same if we want to free ourselves from it now.

The formation of a new confederation with English Canada can only mean continued domination for the French. It is normal that English Canada should be attached to the British Crown and all its symbols—the Union Jack, the Red Ensign, protocol, etc., and they cannot be reproached for it, but nothing holds the French Canadians to these things.

In the year 1961, the British Crown can mean only one thing: the free, voluntary and intentional acceptance of a tie, on the part of a people which has the right to turn down this tie. If the British Crown is imposed where it is not wanted, then it becomes imperialistic ...

Well, we French-Canadians *do* form a nation, simply by possessing all necessary attributes. We are certainly large enough—five or six million is more than necessary for the foundation of an independent nation. Half of the members of the U.N. are smaller.

But the population figure alone does not make us a nation. We have numerous institutions—we have a territory which we have occupied for almost four centuries, Quebec, which belongs to us by virtue of Article 109 of the B.N.A. Act, we speak the same language, French; above all, we have maintained a collective will to live unbroken even by the events of the past two centuries.

A nation we certainly are, all the more since our ties are those of flesh and blood and spirit, whereas our membership in what some people call the Canadian nation is a merely political one imposed by circumstances ...

In practice, this situation is at our throats every day. Every day we have to choose between being French-Canadian or Canadian because there is no longer any equivalence or conciliation possible between the two. Nowadays, if you want to be *Canadian*, you must be English ...

Nevertheless, the theory of Quebec's independence has other claims to desirability than that of being normal. As surely as Confederation has kept us in an unfavourable position by making us into a minority group, Quebec's independence will ensure our advancement by handing over to us the control of our own destiny.

Quebec's independence is therefore desirable for the same reasons that Confederation, in which we are the minority, is not.

Historically, Quebec's independence would allow the French-Canadians to enjoy liberty. History intended that there should be a free French people on American soil. By claiming independence for Quebec, we are merely leading our people back to its historic destiny. After being conquered by armed might, dominated by a foreign nation, after having fought the hard battle for survival, French Canada, by leaving Confederation, will be doing nothing more than leaving behind it one further stage in its long march toward full sovereignty.

Politically, Quebec's independence is desirable because it would take the French-Canadians out of their position of numerical helplessness. In politics as in everything else, for the French-Canadians as for all people, numerical balance is essential to the smooth running of affairs. Starting with our Independence Day, Quebec will negotiate on equal terms with other countries, including the rest of Canada. Once it has become the recognized master of its destiny, a sovereign Quebec can then approve any unions, sign any treaties, practise any amount of friendly relations, set up any plans for helping under-developed countries or Canadian provinces, that are dictated by its own responsibilities and interests.

Independence is politically desirable because it is always good for people to be free, and because no nation has ever become great by leaving the political control of its destiny in the hands of another.

Economically, political independence is desirable for Quebec because, without control over political power, economic independence remains a sweet day-dream ...

There will always be some who assert that the economy has nothing to do with nationalistic spirit, but this is only true for the man without a country. It is also true, however, that nationalistic spirit is not something you can acquire at will. It is something permanent which penetrates into all realms of activity and which springs from a deeper feeling—that of a nation that is well-defined, and quite capable of conducting its own affairs.

Culturally, independence would be the nation's salvation. Do you realize what life would be like in a unilingual country? Morning to night you would hear the same language, the national language.

It would mean the end of the absurd and deadly situation, economically and culturally, for the majority of French-Canadians, the situation of working in English after having gone to French schools.

It would mean the end of this noxious co-existence of two languages and two systems of thought which makes French-Canadian bilingualism into the *doubtful art of speaking two languages at once.*

Do not misunderstand me; I consider English to be a beautiful language, when spoken properly. It is the mutual penetration of two languages, of two thought-patterns, which is harmful. And Quebec's independence would separate them—not by raising a cultural wall around Quebec, which would be impossible and undesirable. Since it is geographically part of America, a totally French Quebec will obviously have to open its doors to Anglo-American culture.

But as in everything, it is a question of balance. A French Quebec can make no cultural progress unless it feeds principally on French cultural traditions, in lesser proportions on traditions from English Canada, America and elsewhere.

At present, under Confederation, Anglo-American language and culture are weighing down too heavily on the French consciousness ...

Basing our case on the United Nations Charter which stipulates—Article 1, paragraph 2—that all peoples have the right of self-determination, we will then begin negotiations with Ottawa. And Ottawa, which has also signed this Charter, cannot do other than agree.

2. Front de Libération du Québec, "A Message to the Nation," 1963.

Patriots,

Ever since the second world war, the various enslaved peoples of the world have been shattering their bonds to acquire the freedom which is theirs by right. Most of these peoples have overcome their oppressors, and can today live in freedom.

Like so many others before us, the people of Quebec have reached the end of their patience with the arrogant domination of Anglo-Saxon colonialism.

In Quebec, as in all colonized countries, the oppressor fiercely denies his imperialism and has the support of the so-called national élite which is more interested in protecting its own entrenched economic interests than in serving the vital interests of its nation. This servile group persistently denies obvious facts and raises up endless problems, aimed at distracting the hard-pressed population's attention away from the only vital problem: INDEPENDENCE.

Despite all this, the workers' eyes are daily becoming more attuned to reality: Quebec is a colony!

We are a colonized people, politically, socially, and economically. Politically, because we do not have any hold on the political instruments necessary for our survival. Ottawa's colonial government has full powers in the following fields: economic policy, foreign trade, defence, bank credit, immigration, the criminal courts, etc. Moreover, any provincial legislation may be repealed by Ottawa if it so decides.

The federal government undividedly stands behind the interests of the Anglo-Saxon imperialists who both constitutionally and in practice play an overwhelming part in ruling the country. The government therefore serves to maintain and indeed to intensify the inferior position of Quebeckers. Whenever a conflict arises between Anglo-Saxon and Quebec interests, it is Quebec's interests that must yield. In the military field, we had conscription; demographically, the pressure has always been towards anglicization; internationally, priority has in all our diplomatic dealings invariably been given to the English-speaking. Hence, the Ottawa government has always, without exception, favoured Anglo-Saxon interests to the detriment of Quebec. At times, even force was used. Quebec blood then flowed for the greater glory and profit of colonial financiers. Quebec is thus certainly a colony in the political sense.

It is also economically a colony. A single statement will serve to prove it: over 80 per cent of our economy is controlled by foreign interests. We provide the labour, they bank the profits.

Socially, too, Quebec is a colony. We represent 80 per cent of the population, and yet the English language prevails in many fields. French is gradually relegated to the realm of folklore, while English becomes the people's working language. The Anglo-Saxons' contempt for our people is as high as ever. Expressions such as 'Speak White!', 'Stupid French Canadians', and others of the same ilk are common. In Quebec itself, thousands of people who can speak nothing but English are unashamed to exhibit this in public. The colonizers see us as inferior beings, and have no compunction about letting us know that they do.

Here is the historical background of the problem: On 8 September 1760 Monsieur de Vaudreuil, Governor of New France, signed Montreal's capitulation, thereby sealing its fate. Shortly thereafter England was to take official possession of the French colony and of the 60,000 French Canadians living in it. This was the beginning of a long story of Anglo-Saxon domination over Quebec. Ours was a rich country, and London's capitalists were already counting future gains. In order to establish undisputed Anglo-Saxon supremacy over Quebec, the 60,000 French settlers had at all costs to be anglicized, by one means or another. It seemed easy enough at the time, for what did this handful of men represent beside the crushing power that was then England? But, suddenly, the American Revolution broke out. For a time it became important to go easy on the French Canadians. Yet the efforts at anglicization were not thereby set aside. One day, the English Canadians went too far; and the 1837 rebellion flared up. It was drowned in blood. Then came the Durham report. Since it was proving impossible, said Lord Durham, to absorb the French Canadians by force, let us go about it in other ways: slow assimilation takes longer, but is just as effective. Union having proved a failure, Confederation was devised—assimilation's perfect tool—its very name embodying a falsehood. Since then, all of Quebec's efforts to get recognition for its people's basic rights have been thwarted by colonialism.

What if today, in 1963, there are over five million of us? Assimilation continues to make its insidious inroads. While in 1940 our numerical strength came close to 40 per cent of the Canadian population, today we only represent 28 per cent of the total. This, we are told, is the only thing that counts. Time plays into their hands, and well do they know it.

The colonizers have, however, overlooked one factor, an important one. Its force is now becoming evident. Patriots' eyes have opened to the fact that they are being colonized, exploited, dominated. They have also become aware that only immediate and total action can break their chains. They know this has to be action in which there is no room for petty personal gain, for the corrupt outlook which seeks utopian compromises at any cost, or for national inferiority complexes. Such weaknesses have to be thrown overboard.

Quebec patriots have, over the centuries, had their fill of fighting for trifles, of squandering their vital energies upon the winning of illusory gains that forever need to be reconquered.

Only think of our jobless people by the hundred thousands; of the grinding poverty of our Gaspé fishermen; of the many farmers all across Quebec whose annual income barely reaches $1,000; of the young people in thousands who are too poor to continue their studies; of the thousands who cannot afford the simplest medical care; of the misery of our miners; of the widespread insecurity of job-holders! This is what colonialism has brought us.

Quebec is also suffering from the unjust and paradoxical situation which can best be illustrated by a look at two neighbouring communities: Saint-Henri and Westmount. Here, we find the typical poverty and overcrowding of a French district; there, we see an English minority living in shameful luxury. Our progressive economic enslavement, and an ever-fuller foreign control, will not be arrested by provisional, short-sighted solutions. Patriots say NO to COLONIALISM, NO to EXPLOITATION.

However, a situation cannot merely be rejected; it also needs to be corrected. Our situation amounts to a national emergency. It is now that the search for alternatives must begin.

Let us acquire the essential political instruments, let us take over control over our economy, let us get a radically reformed social leadership! Wrench off the colonial yoke, get rid of the imperialists who live off the toil of our Quebec workers. Quebec's tremendous natural resources must belong to Quebeckers!

There is only one way to bring this about: a national revolution in a framework of INDEPENDENCE. Otherwise, the Quebec population cannot hope to live in freedom.

But it is no longer enough to want independence, to work within the existing political separatist parties. The colonizers will not so easily yield up their tempting loot. The separatist political parties will never gain sufficient power to overcome the colonizers' political and economic hold. Moreover, independence alone will not resolve anything. It must, at all costs, be accompanied by a social revolution.

Quebec's patriots are not fighting over a name, but over a situation. A revolution is not a parlour game, played for fun. Only a full-fledged revolution can build up the necessary power to achieve the vital changes that will be needed in an independent Quebec. A national revolution cannot, of its very nature, tolerate any compromise. There is only one way of overcoming colonialism: to be stronger than it is! Only the most far-fetched idealism may mislead one into thinking otherwise. Our period of slavery has ended.

QUEBEC PATRIOTS, TO ARMS! THE HOUR OF NATIONAL REVOLUTION HAS STRUCK!

INDEPENDENCE OR DEATH!

3. J. Leger, "Sovereignty the Condition of Salvation," 1967.

... True Life or Slow Death

For Quebec today the choice is not between two systems more or less favourable to its overall progress. The choice is simply one between a good life and a slow death. And we cannot play hide-and-seek with history by saying, "We aren't ready yet ... but we will be in fifteen, twenty or twenty-five years." There is very little chance that in a quarter of a century we will still be free to choose. The factors that supposedly conspire today against independence will be ten or twenty times more powerful then, and today's impetus toward independence will be measurably weakened. For Canada is devouring Quebec: demographically, economically, constitutionally, culturally. There will come a time when the gravity of the problems and the deterioration of the situation will be such that radical action must be taken; but when we finally do realize this we no longer will have the moral or physical strength for the necessary effort.

The Last Chance

The truth is that we are a people in danger of death, and we now have, doubtless for the last time in our history, the opportunity for a genuine choice on the most essential point. It is childish to think that we can plan our collective future in the way one plans the various stages of building some industrial complex: that we might first try out the "special-status" solution for ten years or so, after which we could go on to the system of associate states for another decade and finally, if circumstances seemed favourable, proclaim our independence. It certainly would take less than ten years before French Canada would have to choose between life and death, between having a fatherland and consenting to a slow submersion in the Anglo-Saxon sea.

A Life of Dignity and Co-operation for Quebec and Canada

Far from being the daydream or the mad adventure that some would call it, independence is at the same time the only logical result of our situation and the absolute pre-condition for a natural life. Without its inspiration the struggle for survival would be only a rear-guard action, an odious deception. If we can control our irrational reflexes of conservatism and false sentiment, we will recognize that the independence of Quebec and Canada represent (in a world of diversity and interdependence) a formula of dignity and reason and our great chance for organic co-operation. Tomorrow English Canada would be grateful to Quebec for bringing it about.

For Quebec, in fact, independence is a vital necessity; for Canada, Quebec's independence is the prerequisite to a fuller development. For the two states this would provide a new and fruitful start. For we are a dead weight on English Canada, and we ourselves lead a mutilated existence. Canada in its present form is condemned to mediocrity. In a permanent atmosphere of mistrust, bad-humour, and general dissatisfaction, what do we find? An endless series of delicate and crippled compromises, negotiations forever underway on age-old problems and new situations, a shocking waste of time, money, and talent in attempts to hold the pieces together and, above all, to preserve the illusion in the weaker of the two partners that he is "just as equal as the other." Does anyone believe that a country can survive and progress in the atmosphere that has prevailed for the last few years? And things are not about to improve, for the requirements of our time and the natural inclinations of the Anglo-Saxons will lead to increased centralization. And at every stage this will be less favourable for Quebec, until the day when its very name no longer expresses a distinct entity, for the Franco-Quebec nation will have become a minority in its own home.

Fifteen years of difficult discussions between ministers of justice and heads of governments were needed to reach a difficult agreement on the simple matter of amending the constitution—an agreement which Quebec was finally to discard. At the most optimistic estimate, Quebec would need twenty-five years of negotiations to obtain an *ersatz* special status (and by that time, in the year 2000, the probable English-speaking majority in Quebec, made up of Britons and anglicized New-Quebeckers, would not even want such a special status). Quebec and English Canada will expand great amounts of energy in this melancholy and disappointing struggle, while the great tasks of development and social and cultural progress stand crying for action, in a merciless world where, once we have fallen behind, it is more and more difficult to catch up. This federation has the cross of death on its forehead, and we share this doubtful decoration. To be sure, it can survive a few more decades if the two nations are willing to go on with their sterile game of squaring the circle, and if the French-Canadian nation agrees to its own slow disappearance and gives up any idea of acquiring the tools to create its own future.

If the people of Quebec, adopting the terms of the preamble to the American Declaration of Independence, should be asked to "declare the causes which persuade it to independence," it would be obliged to add to the "free right of peoples to self-determination" another reason: the slow suicide that membership in this federation means to us. Under siege for so long, our nation now is under attack: its economic position is continually worsening, not only in Canada as a whole but in Quebec itself. The masses of immigrants arriving in its territory add the weight of their numbers to the English-speaking minority (who would, without them, amount to eight or nine per cent rather than twenty or twenty-one per cent). The use of the French language, and its usefulness, recede continually, especially in Montreal. We are on the way to losing Montreal, if we have not already done so, and the rot in the metropolis, the cancer of French Canada, is an indication of what will happen tomorrow in all Quebec.

Only a sovereign state can exercise absolute control over immigration policy or make French into the necessary language—*i.e.*, the only language—officially and in practice. Only a sovereign state can institute the psychological climate and set up the structures indispensable to economic emancipation and development-planning in the interests of the *Québécois*. Only a sovereign state can integrate broadcasting with a national educational and cultural policy that is determined and progressive. And, finally, only a sovereign state can carry out a policy of foreign relations as a function of the cultural and material interest of Quebec society allowing the latter to participate as an adult nation in the great movement of international co-operation. These tools for action—to name only these—are all equally indispensable: if only one is lacking, the whole edifice is endangered.

When a nation sees ninety per cent of its immigrants join the ranks of the minority and adopt the latter's language and go to its schools, when a nation must resign itself to the fact that the majority of its sons work in a foreign language in their own country, when a nation does not even control twenty per cent of the economic activity in its own territory, it is not only gravely ill, it is threatened with extinction. If it does not quickly change the conditions that have given rise to such a state of affairs, it will be able to do [not] more than fill the breaches, which will continue to gape wider and wider, trying to stem the forward march of an inexorable process. But the tools of our collective salvation are incompatible with any diminished status whatsoever, with any "special" status whatsoever—(the latter being, moreover, illusory and at the same time incompatible with federalism): the tools of salvation can be found only in national independence ...

But it is not only a question of satisfying a normal aspiration, nor of avoiding the destiny of being reduced to the level of a group quaintly interesting for its folklore values but destined to assimilation. It is also, and perhaps primarily, a question of founding in America a modern and progressive society that is distinct from the modern Minotaur, the U.S.A. This society's first concern would have to be the human progress of the masses of Quebec, which today are in complete disarray. By the healthy shock it will create, and the new psychological climate it will establish, independence will be the first step in an authentic "quiet revolution," for that revolution is not worth undertaking if it consists merely of sticking new labels on social and cultural facts and attitudes which remain unchanged. A sovereign Quebec first and foremost must represent an act of liberation and progress for the masses, who must be given back a consciousness of their dignity and culture. It is the promotion of these in every sphere that must be the primary objective of independence.

Independence: A Point of Departure

For independence is not a final achievement but merely a point of departure. Its actual embodiment will come about through the building of a new society, and through a concern for the human values which today, like democracy and liberty, tend to take refuge in small nations. In short, national sovereignty will be springtime for Quebec, after the exhausting and monotonous winter of a grey and mediocre era of bare survival.

In this world of innovation and change which has, in the last few decades, undergone immense and often unforeseen political and social upheavals, where an effort is being made to reconcile the need for human dignity with that of efficiency (*i.e.*, national liberty with international co-operation), why should Quebec's independence—and Quebec's alone—be something abnormal or shocking or dangerous, almost monstrous? It would be harmful perhaps to certain interests and to the traditional "establishment," but it would not be a true threat to anyone. It would be good for both Quebec and Canada. The former needs it simply to live, the latter in order to live better.

Of all the rights that are recognized—or at least proclaimed—by twentieth-century man, is there a more fundamental one than the right to a genuine homeland, the right to live (and hence to work) in one's own language, the right to have a daily environment in harmony with one's culture and mentality, the right to take part in the concert of nations freely and directly? This is known as freely choosing and creating one's destiny: it is known as independence. Dignity and reason urge us to take this path, all the more forcefully because by taking it we preserve for ourselves and for "the others" those things which are today the most essential: liberty, expansion, and co-operation. For Quebec and for Canada this is an historic opportunity to be seized together in the common interest. On the other hand, if Canada is to be progressively absorbed by its great neighbour, is it not important for that part of Canada with the greatest chance of resisting (and the greatest significance) to detach itself while there is still time, to preserve at least one independent voice in North America and to ensure that this voice is not just the echo *de jure* or *de facto*, of the U.S.A.?

Dignity and liberty are not things for which one begs: one deserves them and fights for them, or rather one deserves them through fighting for them. Quebec will never survive or develop if its survival and development are left to the goodwill, the benevolence or the sympathy of the Anglo-Saxon world, however real and widespread these might be. It will exist and grow only by its own actions and—most important—by its own choice. The coming time is one for courage, and also one for lucidity and fervour.

A state which is economically free, socially just, culturally progressive, and politically sovereign: this is what Quebec should be, and its citizens should be assured of the benefits of such a state. This can come about only through full independence, along with many varieties of organic co-operation with its neighbours. The objective can still be decided and attained. If Quebec denies itself this, let's at least find some good arguments to justify such "living" on borrowed time.

4. René Lévesque, "Quebec Independence," 1978.

After the Seven Years' War and the conquest of New France, Old England was particularly strapped for money and went after it with a vengeance in the colonies. The Boston Massacre followed in 1770, and then, even more decisive, the Boston Tea Party, which opened the door in 1773 to the ultimate demand of independence ... it was recognized by all in 1783.

Thus, the collective liberty of a small nation of three million people ... was imposed on the greatest power of all. And it showed the way to others ...

So the American example, begun in Boston, inspired many people on their own path to national emancipation. And it still does, remaining one of the greatest proofs of the validity of national existence for the progress of nations and the evolution of mankind.

I am confident, therefore, that here in Boston, here at Harvard, there will be, if not necessarily agreement, a basic understanding of our aspirations. And here, too, I know that among many there is a solid knowledge of Quebec, just a few hundred miles away, and of its Canadian environment; of the uncertain perspectives arising out of very rapid change over the last generation or so, particularly in our Quebec society, and the way the fallout affects the whole of Canada.

Some Vital Statistics

I was warned, before my visit, that some Americans may suffer slightly from that minor visual defect bred by proximity, a sort of farsightedness that makes a situation blurred, even uninteresting, when it is too close. China is more exotic, or Africa, than good gray Canada (as it is usually called), even when it works itself into a small turmoil. So let me offer a few vital statistics about Quebec.

First: with 636,000 square miles (most of it a northern vision, but nevertheless there), Quebec is the equivalent of about 18% of the United States land mass. Physically, it is rather visible. Quebec's population of 6 1/4 million people, however, is only about 3% of that of the United States. Still, we are in a world where 78 of the now 155 recognized sovereign states have less than 5 million people. Quebec counts among the top 77 in population. That is the second important statistic.

Third: our Gross Provincial Product for 1977, for the first time, crossed the 50 billion dollar mark. And the year before, 1976, per capita production was over $7,400 (U.S.), putting Quebec's production ahead of all but a handful of the most economically advanced national societies in the world. Quebec is highly industrialized and solidly based on hydroelectric power, on forest and mineral resources, and even more so on the human society. Our society for a long time was considered, justifiably, to be behind the times. It has mostly caught up, is as competent, well trained, and educated as other industrialized societies.

The Roots of Quebec's Discontent

The picture of our society is not one of misery or persecution comparable to many parts of the world. But everyone is familiar with the perception of unfairness, or inequality, or injustice, which is tied to one's environment. You compare yourself with others, with people in your neighbourhood, and with your peers. That is where the feeling grows.

The results of over 110 years of Canadian federal institutions, with their consistent preferences in economic and development policies, have led Quebec to build a strong feeling of being too often overlooked and neglected and even the object of discrimination. The feeling is essentially one of a colonial people (although no doubt a well-fed colonial people). As in other countries where an important segment, though smaller than the majority, feels more or less cooped up, depending on circumstances, in institutions that are controlled outside themselves, we in Quebec are an inner colony. The feeling of being cooped up inside the Canadian structure, inhibited, basically dependent, has been growing in Quebec over many years, and it is based primarily on the following statistic.

More than 80% of Quebec's people are French, and that is not folklore or museum French. It is a language with its own accent, its own quirks, its North American flavor (we are old North Americans). It is not only a living language; it is also vibrantly alive because it is the essential tool of communication, of cultural expression. It is the tool of everything: work, play, love, for practically each and every one of five million people.

The central fact of language makes Quebec the one Canadian province out of ten which is radically (in the root sense of the word) different from the rest of Canada. It makes Quebec the home base, the homeland, of a compact, very deeply rooted, and rapidly evolving cultural group; a cultural group—there should be no mistake—which sees itself as a national group. Democratic control of provincial institutions in Quebec supplies the Quebec people with a powerful springboard for self-affirmation and self-determination. And self-determination is rooted in the tradition of democracy, in bills of rights internationally recognized, in the rights of different peoples to choose their own institutions.

Since the French people in Quebec are surrounded by a continental ocean of English-speaking people both in Canada and in the United States, the question is often asked: "Why don't you just give up the ghost? What is the use of holding on and going on, more and more insistently in recent years, having all that noise and that confrontation and tension about your century-old and eminently respectable political structure? After all, all of us in North America—the United States, Canada, even Mexico—we are all under federal systems, federal institutions and structures. Nobody has been complaining all that much until now; why not go on? If it has been good for the United States, and not so bad for Canada, apparently, why are you guys in Quebec raising such a ruckus, such a lot of sound and fury about the whole thing—even talking about opting out of such a good deal?"

These questions make it look as if we came from the same mold, but words can be misleading. The vocabulary is basically the same, but I want to emphasize how false is the impression. The federal system, modern style, was invented by Americans; it was a free people, recently emancipated, that invented its own set of institutions. In our case, the story was not exactly the same. In Canada, one hundred years later, there was not much debate, nor much consultation. There was certainly no great interest except among Canadian Pacific lawyers and other railroad builders. It started with four colonies, which were still colonies, and which were resigned to remaining colonies for some time to come.

Those four colonies, Quebec included, were the starting point of federal Canada. They were still tied closely to the imperial parliament in London and all of them worried about American expansionism. America was talking about manifest destiny and flexing its muscles all over the place. To try to hold on to the bits north of the United States that were left to British realm and to cement them together, a colonial adaptation of the federal system was devised. It was established by a decree of a European parliament.

There is an even more basic contrast. Two hundred years ago, the unity of the United States was firmly established on a uniform basis of language and culture; English was the one and only vehicle for a tradition built from the Pilgrim Fathers to the Puritan tradition. That was strong enough to sustain the melting pot, integrating immigrants from all over into an organized and essentially united nation.

In Canada, when our federal system developed, some 40% of the population was French. More than 25% still is, with a language, tradition, cultural outlook, and aspirations different from those of the English-speaking majority. I believe that the most essential ingredient determining whether a political structure works, whether it has staying power, does not depend on it being federal or unitary. It depends, rather, on cultural and national homogeneity.

And that is the story of Quebec. Not only are we a different cultural body, a different society in many ways, but among all European settlers we were the first on this continent (excluding Mexico). We were the first discoverers, the first pioneers, the first settlers, and now our roots go back a bit further than those of Boston, 370 years. We have worked the same land. We were born on it in the Valley of the St. Lawrence; all our forefathers are buried there. The tradition is tied also to a language which made us different; it is not our fault, but we keep going on. It is tied to the fact that there is this will, with the ups and downs we shared throughout the generations, of staying together. And now it is also tied to something which ties up with the central misunderstanding of our federal institutions.

A nation is made in 370 years. Nationalism often has a bad connotation, but it can be either positive or negative. Quebec nationalism, the tie to home, and the driving aspirations, the urge for development, is not anti-anyone; it is pro-us. I think it is positive, a national feeling of a national group deeply rooted, durable for the future. There lies the central misunderstanding of the whole Canadian structure.

Two Solitudes

From the very start, Canadian federalism has been a dialogue of the deaf. To the English majority in Canada, we are nothing. The feeling has not been hidden very well through history. We are little more than a conquered and dependent minority. The English hoped this relatively small group would dwindle and eventually fade away like old soldiers.

When Canada was devised structurally, the main effort on the English-Canadian side was to develop federal institutions as central and powerful as possible. The French view was exactly the opposite. The federal system was looked upon as decentralization, enhancing, in American parlance, a state power, state rights, and a better chance for the future. And the French dreamt a normal dream for any cultural, national group—that somewhere, sometime, the nation would achieve self-government.

This competing vision of the founding explains, in a nutshell, the century of two solitudes. More recently, since World War II and especially since the "Quiet Revolution" of the 60s, Quebec at a dizzying speed has come of age; what used to be called "cheap-labor Quebec," "priest-ridden," a folkloric society, is growing by leaps and bounds.

We are entitled, like all societies, to this growth, but the structures have become a constraint on our development. Quebec and Ottawa have been at loggerheads practically on a permanent basis for the last 35 years. Quebec citizens have been caught up in a schizophrenic tug-of-war between the two levels of government for which they pay, with an incredible waste of energy, of time, of resources and, more worrisome, with an evergrowing danger of bad blood between the two communities.

The Growth of the Parti Québécois

It is in the context of two solitudes and federal-provincial discord that the *Parti Québécois* (PQ) grew from a few hundred members in 1967 to 23% of the voters in the first election three years later, in 1970. We polled 31% in 1973 and we emerged as the official opposition. In 1976 we became the government with a 41% plurality.

The *Parti Québécois* is the first political party in the Western world, as far as I know, to rise from nothing to become the government while refusing, year after year, any money from any group—either corporate on the right or union on the left—because groups do not vote. We made it a basic principle to keep them at arm's length. No slush funds. With thousands of canvassers all over the place, door to door, we solicited citizens' money, which is not supposed to be, of course, a serious factor in politics. It was serious enough to build a party into the government of a society of six million people. And our government has passed Bill No. 2, the legislation of which I am proudest, requiring all parties to open their books.

When people start, subtly or otherwise, to give us lessons in basic democracy, they should come to see how democracy now works in Quebec. We are in a very imperfect world where democracy has never quite been a reality, but we are the most staunchly dedicated to democracy of all parties anywhere in the Western world. We were elected promising good government, and over the last 16 months we have tried to do the job. We intend to keep government clean.

Sovereignty-Association and the Referendum

We were elected for good government. We were also elected on a platform of sovereignty with association. Those are two key words, "sovereignty" and "association," and we are committed to a democratic referendum about them before the next election. The enabling legislation is passing laboriously, for the wheels of parliament turn slowly, but the referendum will be held as promised.

Many people say the referendum creates uncertainty in Canada and in Quebec. In fact, uncertainty has been with us because of the many misconceptions and misunderstandings, grown in like barnacles, around our federal structures. Uncertainty has been with us for 35 years. It has shaken Canada's structures and the relationship between Quebec and Canada. For the first time, we are offering a chance to get rid of uncertainty, to get rid of it democratically, when people have had a chance to make up their minds, to be consulted, to get information. It is up to Quebecers to decide what they want. It will be the first chance ever for our people to decide for themselves about their institutions and about the whole future of their community.

If Quebecers vote as we hope, then soon afterwards we will acquire sovereignty, self-government. To use a good phrase of basic democracy, there would be no more representation of Quebec in Ottawa because no more taxation would go to Ottawa from Quebec.

The trend is universal. There were 50 recognized sovereign countries when World War II ended. Now there are 155, and many are comparable to Quebec. Denmark and Norway each has 4 million people; there are 6 million in Switzerland and 8 million in Sweden. These countries are leaders, not just in standard of living, but also in many other accomplishments. No fraternal counsels, no propaganda, will convince us that 6 million should give up the ghost and not pursue democratically normal accomplishments. It is the trend of the last half century.

In addition to sovereignty, we have been proposing from the beginning what we call "association." It is inspired by another universal trend; it is not contradictory. We are convinced that it is just as inevitable as sovereignty. Whatever its eventual shape—whether as a customs union or a common market—it will require still further research and study. The most open-minded people in the rest of Canada, however, are now giving it serious consideration, even though the present climate is hostile. Those courageous enough to look are becoming convinced that some form of association is common sense, responding to the real, hard facts of the situation.

Consequences of Sovereignty-Association

Politically, Canada without Quebec, a lot of people say, would disintegrate. It is the old domino theory, and after all the pieces go, the huge maw next door (that's you) will just gobble it up. I think Canada has a lot of staying power. I know Canada well, both because I have lived there and because I am a former newspaperman. Without the foreign body, which more and more we are, Canada would have more coherence and a chance to reorganize according to its own views and its own preferences. Quebec is a roadblock now because Canadians fear that any change must pose the question, "What the hell is going to happen to Quebec?"

We propose association, first, in order not to "pakistanize" Canada between the Maritimes to the east of Quebec and Ontario and the rest to the west. It is not to build walls of hostility that would take years to break down again. We care about Canada. We do not care about the structures, but we care about the people. We care about the common things we have, many of them, with the Maritimes, with practically as long a tradition as ours and the same kind of outlook in many ways. We care for the fruitful relationships, very mutually profitable, between Quebec and Ontario mostly, and growing with the rest of Canada. But we also care about our own identity. There is no reason why there should be any contradiction, except for people who think that institutions become sacred because they are old. You do not change them like you change your shirt, but not because they are old do you hang on to them when they have passed their day and become obsolete, when they have become like straitjackets.

For political reasons, then, we have proposed a new association, if and when Quebec democratically decides to opt out. There is no reason why it should not be arranged on a free-flow basis. When Alaska became a state of the Union, with some 1100–1200 miles between the state of Alaska and the continental United States, I did not hear any voices of doom. Two civilized countries made arrangements about the free flow of communications and goods. In our case, it would be good for Canada, and so we should do it.

There are also economic reasons for association, recently spelled out by one of those serious minds in English Canada, in Toronto itself, a well-known and reputed economist, Abraham Rotstein, not a party member of ours. He demonstrated that 105,000 jobs next door in Ontario are tied directly to the Quebec market, and there is more or less the equivalent in Quebec facing Ontario. Western beef, with some protection, finds its major market in Quebec. The existence of the Maritimes is tied to a new rapport with Quebec. Newfoundland needs Quebec as a buyer or transmitter of its enormous undeveloped energy resources. We are initiating negotiations with Newfoundland on that subject. Prince Edward Island needs to sell potatoes to the voracious Montreal market.

The Western European Union is our inspiration. It finally gave the French and the Germans the first chance, for centuries, to bridge a chasm of blood and of world war. Adapted to our own needs, sovereignty-association will give our two societies what we think is terribly needed leeway—breathing space—to protect us from the dangerous risk of growing too far apart.

The Challenge of Major Change

Almost everybody, even staunch federalists, even Mr. Trudeau, are at long last admitting publicly the need for a rethinking and a revamping of our political and constitutional arrangements. The temptation is always present, and I can see it in Mr. Trudeau's eyes when we meet occasionally, for the true believers of the *status quo*, for the hangers-on and the careerists, to try to sell or con people into accepting superficial arrangements, mere plastic surgery. But we are convinced that it would not work. There are too many generations of more solitudes facing each other. There is a danger of bad blood. And all the cosmetic constitutional operations over the last 25 or 50 years have failed to give Canada a truly new face.

The only true solution, from our point of view, for our two peoples, has to lie somewhere in the direction we are indicating. And there, also, lies the first chance for real understanding, the only base for mutual respect and equality and cooperation. Maybe, at long last, there is a promise of real friendship between our peoples which up until now we have not really found ...

5. Gilles Vigneault and Marie Laberge, "Preamble, Sovereignty Declaration," September 6, 1995.

The time has come to reap the fields of history. The time has come at last to harvest what has been sown for us by four hundred years of men and women and courage, rooted in the soil and now returned to it. The time has come for us, tomorrow's ancestors, to make ready for our descendants harvests that are worthy of the labours of the past. May our toil be worthy of them, may they gather us together at last.

At the dawn of the 17th century, the pioneers of what would become a nation and then a people rooted themselves in the soil of Québec. Having come from a great civilization, they were enriched by that of the First Nations, they forged new alliances, and maintained the heritage of France.

The conquest of 1760 did not break the determination of their descendants to remain faithful to a destiny unique in North America. Already in 1774, through the Quebec Act, the conqueror recognized the distinct nature of their institutions. Neither attempts at assimilation nor the Act of Union of 1840 could break their endurance.

The English community that grew up at their side, the immigrants who have joined them, all have contributed to forming this people which became in 1867 one of the two founders of the Canadian federation.

We, the men and women of this place,

Because we inhabit the territories delimited by our ancestors, from Abitibi to the Îles-de-la-Madeleine, from Ungava to the American border, because for four hundred years we have cleared, ploughed, paced, surveyed, dug, fished, built, started anew, discussed, protected, and loved this land that is cut across and watered by the St. Lawrence River;

Because the heart of this land beats in French and because that heartbeat is as meaningful as the seasons that hold sway over it, as the winds that bend it, as the men and women who shape it;

Because we have created here a way of being, of believing, of working that is unique;

Because as long ago as 1791 we established here one of the first parliamentary democracies in the world, one we have never ceased to improve;

Because the legacy of the struggles and courage of the past compels us irrevocably to take charge of our own destiny;

Because it is this land alone that represents our pride and the source of our strength, our sole opportunity to express ourselves in the entirety of our individual natures and of our collective heart;

Because this land will be all those men and women who inhabit it, who defend it and define it, and because we are all those people;

We, the people of Québec, declare that we are free to choose our future.

We know the winter in our souls. We know its blustery days, its solitude, its false eternity and its apparent deaths. We know what it is to be bitten by the winter cold.

We entered the federation on the faith of a promise of equality in a shared undertaking and of respect for our authority in certain matters that to us are vital.

But what was to follow did not live up to those early hopes. The Canadian State contravened the federative pact, by invading in a thousand ways areas in which we are autonomous, and by serving notice that our secular belief in the equality of the partners was an illusion.

We were hoodwinked in 1982 when the governments of Canada and the English-speaking provinces made changes to the Constitution, in depth and to our detriment, in defiance of the categorical opposition of our National Assembly.

Twice since then attempts were made to right that wrong. The failure of the Meech Lake Accord in 1990 confirmed a refusal to recognize even our distinct character. And in 1992 the rejection of the Charlottetown Accord by both Canadians and Quebecers confirmed the conclusion that no redress was possible.

Because we have persisted despite the haggling of which we have been the object;

Because Canada, far from taking pride in and proclaiming to the world the alliance between its two founding peoples, has instead consistently trivialized it and decreed the spurious principle of equality between the provinces;

Because starting with the Quiet Revolution we reached a decision never again to restrict ourselves to mere survival but from this time on to build upon our difference;

Because we have the deep-seated conviction that continuing within Canada would be tantamount to condemning ourselves to languish and to debasing our very identity;

Because the respect we owe ourselves must guide our deeds;

We, the people of Québec, declare it is our will to be in full possession of all the powers of a State: to vote all our laws, to levy all our taxes, to sign all our treaties and to exercise the highest power of all, conceiving, and controlling, by ourselves, our fundamental law.

For the men and women of this country who are the warp and weft of it and its erosion, for those of tomorrow whose growth we are now witnessing, to be comes before to have. And this principle lies at the very heart of our endeavour.

Our language celebrates our love, our beliefs and our dreams for this land and for this country. In order that the profound sense of belonging to a distinct people be now and for all time the very bastion of our identity, we proclaim our will to live in a French-language society.

Our culture relates our identity, it writes of us, it sings us to the world. And through varied and new contributions, our culture takes on fresh colour and amplitude. It is essential that we welcome them in such a way that never will these differences be seen as threats or as reasons for intolerance.

Together we shall celebrate the joys, together we shall suffer the sorrows that life will set upon our road. Above all we shall assume not only our successes but our failures too, for in abundance as in adversity the choices we make will have been our own.

We know what determination has gone into achieving the successes of this land. Those men and women who have forged the dynamism of Québec are eager to pass down their efforts to the determined men and women of tomorrow. Our capacity for mutual support and our appetite for new undertakings are among our greatest strengths. We commit ourselves to recognize and encourage the urge to put our hearts into our work that makes us builders.

Along with other countries of like size, we share the virtue of adapting quickly and well to the shifting challenges of work and trade. Our capacity for consensus and our spirit of invention will enable us to take a good and rightful place at the table of nations.

We intend to uphold the imaginative powers and the abilities of local and regional communities in their activities of economic, social and cultural development.

As guardians of the land, the air, the water, we shall act in such a way as to be respectful of the world to come. We, the men and women of this new country, acknowledge our moral duties of respect, of tolerance, of solidarity towards one another.

Averse to authoritarianism and violence, honouring the will of the people, we commit ourselves to guarantee democracy and the rule of law.

Respect for the dignity of women, men, and children and the recognition of their rights and freedoms constitute the very foundation of our society. We commit ourselves to guarantee the civil and political rights of individuals, notably the right to justice, the right to equality, and the right to freedom.

To battle against misery and poverty, to support the young and the elderly, are essential features of the society we would build. The destitute among us can count upon our compassion and our sense of responsibility. With the equitable sharing of wealth as our objective, we commit ourselves to promote full employment and to guarantee social and economic rights, notably the right to education and the right to health care and other social services.

Our shared future is in the hands of all those for whom Québec is a homeland. Because we take to heart the need to reinforce established alliances and friendships, we shall safeguard the rights of the First Nations and we intend to define with them a new alliance. Likewise, the English-speaking community historically established in Québec enjoys rights that will be maintained. Independent and hence fully present in the world, we intend to work for cooperation, humanitarian action, tolerance and peace. We shall subscribe to the Universal Declaration of Human Rights and to other international instruments for the protection of rights.

While never repudiating our values, we shall devote ourselves to forging, through treaties and agreements, mutually beneficial links with the peoples of the earth. In particular, we wish to formulate along with the people of Canada, our historic partner, new relations that will allow us to maintain our economic ties and to redefine our political exchanges. And we shall marshal a particular effort to strengthen our ties with the peoples of the United States and France and with those of other countries both in the Americas and in the Francophonie.

To accomplish this design, to maintain the fervor that fills us and impels us, for the time has now come to set in motion this country's vast endeavour;

We, the people of Québec, through our National Assembly, proclaim:

Québec is a sovereign country.

Readings

Behiels, M., ed. *Quebec Since 1945: Selected Readings.* Toronto: Copp Clark Pitman, 1987.

Bercuson, D., and B. Copper. *Deconfederation: Canada without Quebec.* Toronto: Key Porter, 1991.

Bothwell, R. *Canada and Quebec: One Country, Two Histories.* Vancouver: University of British Columbia Press, 1995.

Bourgault, P. *Now or Never: Manifesto for an Independent Quebec.* Toronto: Key Porter, 1991.

Brym, R. "Some Advantages of Canadian Disunity: How Quebec Sovereignty Might Aid Economic Development in English-Speaking Canada," *Canadian Review of Sociology and Anthropology* 29, 2 (May 1992).

Carens, J, ed. *Is Quebec Nationalism Just?: Perspectives from Anglophone Canada.* Montreal: McGill-Queen's University Press, 1995.

Clift, D. *The Decline of Nationalism in Quebec*. Montreal: McGill-Queen's University Press, 1982.

Coleman, W. *The Independence Movement in Quebec, 1945–1980*. Toronto: University of Toronto Press, 1984.

Covell, M. *Thinking About the Rest of Canada: Options for Canada Without Quebec*. North York: York University Centre for Public Law and Public Policy, 1992.

Dion, S. *Straight Talk: On Canadian Unity*. Montreal: McGill-Queen's University Press, 1999.

Fournier, L. *F.L.Q. The Anatomy of an Underground Movement*. Toronto: NC Press, 1984.

Fraser, G. *The PQ: Rene Levesque and the Parti Quebecois in Power*. Toronto: Macmillan, 1984.

Gairdner, W. *Constitutional Crack-Up: Canada and the Coming Showdown with Quebec*. Toronto: Stoddart, 1994.

Griffen, A. *Quebec: The Challenge of Independence*. Rutherford: Fairleigh Dickinson University Press, 1984.

Guindon, H. *Quebec Society: Tradition, Modernity and Nationhood*. Toronto: University of Toronto Press, 1988.

Jacobs, J. *The Question of Separatism: Quebec and the Struggle over Sovereignty*. New York: Random House, 1980.

Jones, R. *Community in Crisis: French Canadian Nationalism in Perspective*. Toronto: McClelland and Stewart, 1972.

Lemco, J. *The Quebec Sovereignty Movement and Its Implications for Canada and the United States*. Toronto: University of Toronto Press, 1994.

McRoberts, K. *Quebec: Social Change and Political Crisis*. Third edition. Toronto: McClelland and Stewart, 1988.

Moniere, D. *L'Independence: Essai*. Montreal: Quebec/Amerique, 1992.

Saywell, J. *The Rise of the Parti Quebecois*. Toronto: University of Toronto Press, 1977.

Weaver, R., ed. *The Collapse of Canada*. Washington: Brookings, 1992.

Young, R. *The Secession of Quebec and the Future of Canada*. Kingston: McGill-Queen's University Press, 1995.

Chapter Seventeen

"THE SLIPPERY SLOPE": FREE TRADE AND CANADIAN CULTURE

1. James Laxer, *Leap of Faith*, 1986.
2. Ted Byfield, "Keeping things cozy for Canadianism," *Alberta Report*, March 31 and April 14, 1986.
3. Susan Crean, "Reading Between the Lies: Culture and the Free-Trade Agreement," *This Magazine* 22, 2 (May 1988).
4. Anthony DePalma, "Tough Rules Stand Guard Over Canadian Culture," *New York Times,* July 14, 1999.
5. Henry N.R. Jackman, "Canada's Culture," Speech to the Canadian Club (November 1999).
6. Peter Herndorf, "Massey Commission at 50: The State of the Arts," *Canadian Speeches: Issues of the Day* 15, 6 (January-February 2002).

Introduction

During free trade negotiations between Canada and the United States in the 1980s, the influential and unerringly perceptive British weekly, "The Economist," declared that Canadians would now unfortunately become Americans. Implicit in that declaration, was a recognition that American and Canadian culture are not the same. But what is the difference? Is Canadian culture, the performances of the Winnipeg Ballet, the writings of Margaret Atwood, the music of the Bare Naked Ladies or simply hockey, Canadian beer and toques? Though the answer is subjective, Canada has a long history of fighting to preserve its alleged distinctiveness against the American cultural juggernaut. This was somewhat awkward since both share the world's longest undefended border and 85% of Canadians live within one hundred kilometres of it. Most Canadians speak English, as do Americans, so transmitting culture northward requires no translation. If, however, nationalist George Grant was correct, the major reason Canadian culture will die is because Canadians don't care.

A minority of Canadians believe that there is a distinct Canadian culture; that it must be preserved, and that American cultural encroachment poses the most significant threat to its existence. It is this group that traditionally pushed hardest to preserve Canadian culture, doing so through protectionism, arguing that arts and communications create and preserve the essence of Canada. Without support, they claim, Canadian arts and media would drown in a sea of Americana.

The idea of the government supporting Canadian media to protect culture goes back to 1903 when Ottawa offered an annual grant of $60,000 to Canadian Associated Press to collect information rather than relying so much upon copying reports of American foreign correspondents. When commercial radio began broadcasting in 1922, a number of thorny questions arose due to its huge potential as a cultural disseminator and because controlling the airwaves was awkward. The United States promptly appropriated every clear channel on the band, including those used by Canadians, to the point where the four leading Toronto stations had to jostle for one spot on the dial. There was also a real fear that Canadian stations might simply rebroadcast Americana because it was cheaper than producing local shows. The result was the Aird Commission hearings which advocated government control of broadcasting free from foreign interference, similar to the system in England. Lack of funds stalled the idea until 1932 when Prime Minister R.B. Bennett introduced the Canadian Radio Broadcasting Act. The Act not only authorized state-regulated airwaves, it also created the precursor to the Canadian Broadcasting Corporation, itself born in 1936 with the clear mandate to unify Canadians by creating and transmitting stories about Canada and Canadians. Despite the best intentions, however, most programming on Canadian radio remained American. Music stations, for example, limited their play lists to American popular songs and excluded Canadian artists. This eventually led to the Broadcasting Act of 1968 that, among other things, required private and public radio and television stations to "safeguard, enrich and strengthen the cultural, political, social and economic framework of Canada." The new Act confirmed that the airwaves were public, that they should serve the national interest, and that stations would be strictly regulated by a new watchdog: the Canadian Radio-television and Telecommunications Commission. It also reiterated the importance of a publicly funded broadcaster, the CBC. In 1971 the head of the CRTC, Pierre Juneau, required all Canadian stations to play at least 30% Canadian material. This was very unpopular with private broadcasters who complained about having "to reach into the Beaver Bin for some droppings," but the result was a music revolution. "Can-con," as its Canadian content regulations became to be known, ably illustrated the potential impact of cultural protectionism.

The Canadian film industry died in the early 1920s, victim of Hollywood competition and an American cartel that quickly owned and controlled film distribution in Canada. Once again the federal government interceded to promote what it saw as an important cultural medium. It created the National Film Board in 1939 with the mandate to "interpret Canada to Canadians and other nations." Though the Board became internationally famous, it never overcame the vexing problem of distributing its films to Canadian viewers. By creating the Canadian Film Development Corporation (now Telefilm) in 1968 the government sought to encourage Canadian film making by allowing tax write-offs for investors, but the result was a string of cinematic abominations (the "Porky's" films, for example) that still faced the old distribution problem. By the end of the twentieth century, only 3-5% of screenings in Canadian cinemas were of Canadian films, and 95% of the profits from films shown went south. Canadian cultural nationalists argued that such gluttony of cinematic Americana, with its different worldview, was eroding Canadian cultural distinctiveness.

Magazines are also important cultural transmitters. Here too, Canadian publications struggled to swim against the surge of American publications pouring across the border. In 1925, for example, four American magazines had greater circulation in Canada than the leading Canadian publication. R.B. Bennett responded in 1930 by introducing a major tariff on magazine imports, and by the mid-thirties Canadian magazine circulation rose by 65% while US publications fell the equivalent. But Canada remained the single biggest American magazine export market. One explanation for the proliferation of American magazines in Canada was the right of Canadian advertisers to deduct the cost of their advertising in them. Prior to 1976, for example, more than half of all Canadian magazine advertising went to Canadian editions of *Time* and *Reader's Digest* alone. Bill C-58 of 1976 eliminated the tax exemption, much to the chagrin of advertisers and American publishers, and *Maclean's* became Canada's largest circulation magazine. C-58 also applied to radio and television too, and also provoked considerable wrath from Canadian and American entrepreneurs who hated the state interference in free enterprise. The Americans were particularly incensed and successfully lobbied Ottawa to modify the Act.

Television remains the most potent acculturator because of its ubiquitousness and the fact that Canadians, in 1999, watched an average of 21.6 hours per week. Three quarters of TV programming in Canada is American, which will grow with the proliferation of technology that accesses ever more channels. Why is Canadian programming largely nonexistent? Chiefly because it costs ten times as much to produce a Canadian show as it does to buy the rights to rebroadcast an American one. Again, many fear that the American programs, with their different worldview, will doom Canadian culture and distinctiveness. Bill C-58 supposedly addressed this by increasing Canadian programming quotas for TV too, but private broadcasters simply fulfilled their requirements with no frills game shows. The American response to Canadian concerns over cultural invasion on TV was to point out that Canadians simply choose to watch Americana, which they should be able to do in a free society.

Protectionism, however, is not ubiquitously popular in Canada, and many, particularly entrepreneurs, resented subsidizing culture through tax dollars, retorting that it should sink or swim just like any other industry. The dispute, both internally and with the US, peaked during the Free Trade Debate in the 1980s. To Americans, culture is a commodity, which could be bought and sold like everything else. Canadians rejected this view and Canada's cultural industry quickly became the debate's lightning rod. Filmmakers, publishers, broadcasters, musicians, and others worried that an open border would sweep them away in a wave of American culture. That, after all, was the idea of free trade: governments would stop supporting industry through tariffs, subsidies, quotas, or anything else that impeded free enterprise. This was serious since the Canadian federal government spent more on culture than its American counterpart, despite representing a population one tenth as large. Estimates varied, but total annual expenditures on the arts by all governments in Canada amounted to some $2.9 billion—which did not include the many policies and regulations that really amounted to subsidies too. All that would presumably disappear. Under the FTA there would be no Canadian music quotas, no low postage rates for Canadian magazines, no tax breaks for Canadian films, American cultural products like CDs would hit the Canadian market without tariffs. The reverse, of course, was also true, with Canadian cultural industries gaining equal access to America. This, however, was cold comfort since Americans statistically do not buy foreign culture, as indicated by the $1.5 billion annual balance of trade surplus in cultural commodities in America's favour over Canada. Under the FTA, said cultural activists, Canadian culture and Canada would disappear.

Prime Minister Mulroney's Conservatives were unconcerned about Canada's cultural industries under the FTA, and the depth of Canadian anxiety caught them off guard. In advance of the talks, for example, bureaucrats were to create 84 profiles of Canadian industries that needed addressing during the negotiations, not one of which dealt with culture. The Americans, ironically, studied the impact of free trade on Canada's cultural scene, commissioning a report from Statistics Canada through the American embassy in Ottawa. The controversy about culture and free trade, however, finally forced the Canadian government to reassess culture, and to assert that it was off the negotiation table. The Americans, not surprisingly, pointed out the logical absurdity of Canada wanting free trade, but not total free trade, and US trade negotiator Carla Hill promised the American Congress that "we'll negotiate, but if that doesn't work, we'll use a crowbar." In the end, the "compromise" was two points in Article 2005 of the Agreement. The first declared that Canadian cultural sovereignty legislation is exempt from the Agreement, but the second permitted the US to retaliate against this in any sector it wishes. If nothing else, this implied that the Canadian government conceded that culture was, in fact, a commodity like any other. Brian Mulroney and President Ronald Reagan signed The Free Trade Agreement in January 1988, which subsequently expanded into NAFTA in 1994 with the inclusion of Mexico. Since then, Canadian governments have significantly cut cultural industry funding, but insist this was for budgetary, not free trade reasons.

Discussion Points

1. Was Byfield right that Canadian culture does not exist?
2. To what extent can or should culture be regulated and nurtured through government intervention?
3. With its distinct language, how would Quebec fit into this debate?
4. Will new technologies like e-mail and the internet help to support Canadian culture or further threaten it?
5. Could the Free Trade Agreement and NAFTA eventually lead to Canada's total demise?

Documents

1. James Laxer, *Leap of Faith*, 1986.

Canadians have often been told that the stakes in the debate about free trade with the United States are purely economic, that the issue is whether a sound business deal can be had. There is evidence, however, that what will be on the table in the trade negotiations is no less than a series of key decisions about our way of life, the values of our society, the character of our communities. What is involved is "culture," not in the narrow sense of specific institutions and their products, but in the broad sense of the world view of our society.

For some people, concern about the impact of a trade deal on culture is a red herring, used to lure Canadians off the path of making a sound economic decision. One of the people who feels this way is Simon Reisman, Canada's chief trade negotiator. In the spring of 1985, before the Prime Minister picked him to head the Canadian negotiating team, Reisman said in a speech to the Ontario Economic Council that he could not understand why some people made so much fuss about the protection of Canadian culture.

He confessed himself unable "to find convincing evidence" that any threat to Canadian culture could be a by-product of full free trade with the United States.

Another supporter of free trade who dismisses the concern about culture in a particularly frank way is Anthony Westell, Associate Dean of Arts at Carleton University. He believes, quite simply, that there is no problem because there is no Canadian way of life. In December 1984, in a lengthy article in the journal *Perspectives*, Mr. Westell contended that it "is misleading in modern circum-stances to think of national cultures."

"To be a Canadian," he contended, "does not signify a way of life, or a set of values beyond attachment to the community and loyalty to the national state. So the fear that closer association with the United States will erode a Canadian identity in the making or abort a Canadian culture about to be born is unfounded."

Are there values, ways of living, that divide Canadians from Americans, and if so, will those values be on the table in the trade talks? To make sense of this, we have to get past the obvious impact of American popular culture on societies all over the world. Huge portraits of American movie idols in Paris, and giant renderings of the Flintstones on the walls of buildings in Tokyo were two examples of that influence that struck me during my travels in recent months. But, beneath this surface sameness, are there enduring and important differ-ences between societies that matter to their inhabitants?

I believe there are such differences between Canada and the United States, and that they are tangible, important to the way Canadians live, and that they are at stake in the trade talks.

Four areas come to mind:

Violence in the two countries

The tone and design of Canadian and American cities

Attitudes to social programs

The importance of the military in the two countries

Violence is important to the way a society lives, because it places limits on the sense of safety citizens have in going about their everyday activities. It is all well and good to talk about the common culture of North America, but if it turns out that one country is immensely more violent than the other, then perhaps it is the similarities that are superficial and the differences that are profound. American sociologist Seymour M. Lipset, a long-time observer of the two countries, has made the point that there is a sharply lower level of violence in Canada compared to the United States.

The United States is wracked with violence on a scale unique in the developed world. In the spring of 1985, a report by twelve prominent university experts for the Eisenhower Foundation concluded that the "level of crime in the United States remains astronomical when compared with that of other industrialized democracies."

In Atlanta, Georgia, where medical epidemics have long been studied, the Violence Epidemiology Branch now analyzes the American problem with violence. There are nearly twenty thousand murders a year in the United States, compared with about six hundred per year in Canada. On a per capita basis, while there are about 2.5 murders per hundred thousand people per year in Canada, in the United States the rate runs at 8.3 per hundred thousand.

In many large American cities, the murder rate is much higher. In New York, it runs at 23 per hundred thousand, in Philadelphia at 18—and in Detroit at an astronomical 49, twenty times the Canadian rate. To put Detroit's murders in perspective, at that rate Metropolitan Toronto would have over 1000 murders a year, instead of the 57 it actually had in 1985.

Of course, all industrial societies have their violence and their mass murderers, including British Columbia's Clifford Olson. The difference is one of scale. In the United States the problem of violence is epidemic in comparison to other industrial countries. In the past year I felt quite comfortable exploring Tokyo, Paris, and Stockholm at night, but not New York, Washington, and Chicago, although presumably as a Canadian I have much more in common with people in the American cities.

Feeling more at home in Canadian, Japanese, and European cities than in American cities has to do not only with the fear of violence but with the design and shape of American cities in comparison to those in other industrial nations. The design of American cities reflects much wider values that get at the very core of the American "way of life."

The typical American city is, as Toronto historian William Kilbourn describes it, "a doughnut"—it is made up of rings of affluence around a ruined, often empty, shell at the centre. Detroit, Philadelphia, Chicago, and countless smaller American cities share this pattern of wealthy suburbs surrounding frightening, desolate city centres. Even New York, often cited as a major exception, is much more like this than are the great cities of Europe, Japan—and Canada. Metropolitan Toronto, a city of three million, works—much to the astonishment of many Americans— because it has not died at the centre.

The reasons American cities have taken the shape of the doughnut are not hard to find. In the American quest for individual freedom, the flight to the suburbs, away from the need to pay taxes to keep up the core of a city, has reawakened the ancient spirit of the frontier in Americans. The result is decaying city centres inhabited by those whom the larger white, middle-class society has rejected.

If the American emphasis on individual mobility has had its impact on the shape of U.S. cities, it has also had its effect on social programs across the border. The idea of providing a government-operated safety net on behalf of the sick, the old, the disadvantaged, and the unemployed is a much more controversial one in the United States than in Canada. While in Canada state-supported universal medicare is something that no political party dares to attack, in the United States, universal medicare does not exist and it is routine for the White House to propose cuts to the meagre government spending for medical services for the poor now in place (as it did in preparing its 1987 budget proposals).

While government payments for social programs are widely supported in Canada, they are increasingly under attack in the United States. While in Ottawa, the government retreated from plans to de-index old-age pensions, in Washington conservative authors like Charles Murray, who want to scrap all federal involvement in social programs, are very popular with the White House. In his book, *Losing Ground*, economist Charles Murray, Senior Research Fellow at the Manhattan Institute for Policy Research, warned against the rise of a culture of dependency due to welfare spending by the U.S. government. He linked welfare payments to the prodigious rise in illegitimate births in the United States and advocated the complete elimination of all federal government programs directed at the poor.

One of the reasons that social programs receive wider support in Canada than in the United States is that Canada has a less extreme disparity of income distribution that has its neighbour. While south of the border, the bottom fifth of the population makes only 4.7 per cent of national income, in Canada the figure is 6.3 per cent. In the United States the top fifth of the population enjoys 42.7 per cent of national income, while in Canada it gets 38.9 per cent. As Richard Gwyn wrote in *The 49th Paradox*: "Canada is a middle-class nation, by no means as equalitarian as the Scandinavian ones, but far more so than the U.S."

If Canadian society places much higher value on the public funding of social programs, it accords military spending a much lower priority than does the United States. Among the seven major non-communist industrial countries, Canada spends the second lowest proportion, 2.2 per cent, of its gross national product (GNP) on defence, while the United States spends the highest proportion, 6.4 per cent.

If it is fair to conclude that Canadian society differs significantly from American society, is there any reason to believe that the Canadian way of life is threatened by a full free trade deal with the United States?

If the trade talks turned on the removal of tariff barriers to trade alone, there would be no such threat. However, the most significant aspect of the talks deal not with tariffs, but with the countless other ways that governments operate in society that can have an impact on exports and imports. It happens that the list of areas in which government has an impact is very long indeed.

As we have seen, U.S. negotiators have made it clear that what the Americans want in a trade deal is the achievement of what they call a "level playing field," that is, an economic environment in which the market is allowed to operate on its own. The problem is that the existence of Canada as a separate society in North America has always depended on large-scale government intervention in the economy. Without such intervention, we would not have built our railways, our telecommunications links, or the Trans-Canada Highway; we would not have established cultural institutions, such as the CBC and the National Film Board, to interpret our society to itself and the world.

If there is one thing that distinguishes the American way of life from all others, it is a singular belief in the ability of the market-place to set priorities for society. The United States has been the world's most perfect example of a society based on individualism. That has given the United States its great energy and its strong conviction that it has much to teach the rest of the world. All other developed western countries, including Canada, have believed in government intervention in the economy and the development of the welfare state to a much greater extent than has the United States. For Canada to go over to the concept of an economy with much more limited government intervention—in other words, "the level playing field"—is precisely to adopt that which is most central to the American way of life, and to give up that which has been central to our way of life.

Concretely, how could that affect us?

The many programs employed by government in Canada to bolster the economies of disadvantaged regions could be eliminated as a series of export-support measures. The payment of unemployment insurance to Canadian workers on a seasonal basis could be barred as an export-support measure.

In addition, the deal will mean that Canadian governments cannot use any direct means to Canadianize the ownership of industries or to attract or keep industry in this country as opposed to the United States. That would mean that our industries would operate in a completely American environment, in an economy fully integrated with that of the United States. And, in that context, the Canadian way of life has no chance. This country's more expensive social programs could wither, under the ceaseless pressure to keep our economy competitive with regions to the south where such programs are not in place. Employers who do not want to contribute to such programs directly, or indirectly through taxation, could move their operations south to jurisdictions with less expensive programs. And our governments would have bargained away the right to stop them.

A way of life does not exist in a vacuum. It is the product both of the ideas and traditions of people and the institutional arrangements they make for themselves in their society. If we decide to adopt American institutional arrangements, let us not imagine that this will not affect our way of life.

We are already familiar with the American insistence that in trade talks between Canada and the United States "everything must be on the table." Clayton Yeutter, the U.S. Trade Representative, insists that "everything" includes cultural industries.

The American insistence on including cultural issues makes it clear that in the upcoming trade negotiations public policies to support Canadian culture could be attacked as barriers against the free importation of American culture— or, to use the jargon, as non-tariff barriers. Once on the table, such cultural supports could be eliminated or used as bargaining counters to help make a deal possible. In the fall of 1985, a secret memorandum, prepared by the External Affairs Department at the senior-deputy-minister level, proposed the possible use of Canadian cultural programs as "trade-offs" in the negotiations.

The seriousness of the cultural side of the talks became evident with the revelation in a leaked document authored by Allan Gotlieb, Canada's ambassador to Washington, that the giant U.S. firm Gulf + Western threatened a "scorched earth" policy if its takeover of the publishing company, Prentice-Hall in Canada, was blocked. Gotlieb advised his government to take the side of Gulf + Western or face serious rancour south of the border. In the days after the Gulf + Western affair, a large number of American congresspersons indicated they were prepared to go to bat to clear away Canadian restrictions on imported American culture. Eventually, as we have seen, the Gulf + Western takeover went ahead.

The Prentice-Hall issue was, of course, only the tip of the iceberg. The basic American concern had to do with the policy of the Canadian government, enunciated by Communications Minister Marcel Masse, that when foreign-based publishers decided to sell their Canadian subsidiaries, they should be required to sell them to Canadians. The purpose of the policy was to expand the 20 per cent share of the publishing market in Canada now held by Canadian-owned companies. It was also to expand the opportunities for Canadian authors, over 75 per cent of whose works are published by Canadian companies, despite their small share of the national market.

Moreover, beyond book publishing, there is the issue of film distribution in Canada, which is overwhelmingly controlled south of the border. For years it has been evident that Canadian film-making is seriously limited by the absence of major domestically owned film-distribution companies. Far more important to Gulf + Western than Prentice-Hall is its ownership of Famous Players in Canada.

Determined to scotch any renewed drive toward Canadianization of cultural industries, the United States deployed Secretary of State George Shultz, who lobbied External Affairs Minister Joe Clark on behalf of Gulf + Western when the two men met in Calgary in the fall of 1985.

Embarrassed by the leaked documents and by continuing American insensitivity on the issue, Canadian cabinet ministers, including the Prime Minister, have tried to make the cultural issue go away by proclaiming that Canadian cultural sovereignty will not be undermined in the talks. Such reassurances, however, have repeatedly been followed by U.S. statements that the cultural industries must be on the table.

Aside from the book publishing controversy, other cultural issues that could be at stake in the trade talks are:

The controversial practice of inserting Canadian advertising into the cable signal from border U.S. television stations, protecting the territorial copyright the Canadian broadcaster has bought.

The advertising tax write-off provision which promotes Canadian ownership of periodicals and which drove Time Canada out of business and allowed *Maclean's* to operate as a weekly newsmagazine.

Postal rate advantages for Canadian magazines.

Tax support for films made in Canada.

The large-scale operation of the public sector in the cultural field in Canada, and restrictions on the operations of foreign-owned companies in the cultural field are viewed by Americans as limitations on the free operations of the market system in Canada. It is that issue—"the freedom of the market-place"—that is the real bottom line in Canadian-American trade negotiations. The U.S. insistence on the removal of any interference with the market is for Americans not only an economic issue, but a matter of culture and ideology as well.

When Allan Gotlieb warned his government about the Gulf + Western issue, it was clear that much more was at stake than simply the fate of one book publishing company. The real issue was the way the U.S. administration and Congress would see Canada and Canadians. Gotlieb warned Ottawa in his confidential memo that if it pushed its publishing policy, the U.S. media could "infect the general perception of Canada as a destination for the U.S. investment dollar."

Since coming to office, the Mulroney government has gone to great lengths to make American law-makers see Canada as a country that respects the American way of doing things. The elimination of the National Energy Program, and particularly the replacement of the Foreign Investment Review Agency (FIRA) with Investment Canada have been aimed at changing the way Americans view Canada. Although during its years of operation FIRA blocked few foreign take-over bids, its very existence was seen as an offence to Americans. It was removed for symbolic reasons, for cultural reasons.

But in dealing with Americans, symbolism is of great importance. That is because of the special character of the United States as a country that takes ideology very seriously. For Canadians who have spent a great deal of time considering their own national identity, it is useful to consider how the American identity matters when it comes to negotiating a trading relationship.

The United States has a special history which separates it from the rest of the industrialized world, including Canada. American identity is rooted in the great revolutionary tradition of the eighteenth century, and the unparalleled American faith in individual freedom and the market-place.

At the core of the American reality is the fact that the United States is the product of the first modern revolution—a revolution, which like its Soviet counterpart, produced a messianic society, convinced that its ideas and institutions were founded on universal values that could liberate all mankind.

To a very considerable extent, the United States is a country with a "one myth" culture. The "one myth" that is central to everything in American life is the idea of individual freedom. American law is founded on the freedom of the individual, as is the American economic system. To Americans, the truths that are enshrined in their Constitution and Declaration of Independence are the central tenets in a national religion. To feel differently about such matters is to be un-American. Moreover, as the American sociologist Louis Hartz concluded, U.S. society has a paradoxical nature—it is the most liberal of societies, and yet it has a compulsive intolerance of ideological differences. While the British, the French, the Swedes, and the Canadians can have legitimate differences of opinion about the proper balance between the individual and society, between the market-place and government, for Americans these questions have a quasi-religious character that is born of revolution.

That the revolutionary tradition is very much alive today is seen clearly, and ironically, in the ideas of today's American neo-conservatives.

Irving Kristol, the godfather of American neo-conservatism, recently wrote in a new journal, *The National Interest*, about the conflict between American and Soviet messianism:

In our own era, the distinction between religious ideas and political ideas is blurred ... We live in an era of 'ideologies'—of political ideas that breathe quasi-religious aspirations and involve quasi-religious commitments ... The basic conflict of our times—that between the USSR and the United States—is ideological.

Kristol here is speaking approvingly, urging his fellow Americans to join the religious war against the Soviet Union—on behalf of American messianism. Messianism, of course, does not operate only against foes. It directs its compulsive message, on behalf of a way of life, especially effectively toward the citizens of friendly and smaller countries.

And so it is in the attitude of the U.S. government to trade negotiations with Canada. To Americans it is natural to demand that everything be put on the table in trade talks. After all, how else can one achieve the desired end—the dismantling of government intervention in the economy and society—so that free enterprise (the American way) can have unimpeded sway.

The Americans insist on discussing culture when they discuss trade, because for them there is a natural ideological dimension to the talks. The idea that a smaller country needs special measures to protect its identity does not resonate south of the border. Such an idea smacks of state intervention. It is an affront to the free working of the market system, and therefore to the American way of life.

It will be difficult for the Mulroney government, in the trade talks, to meet the clear Canadian desire for cultural sovereignty, if it wants to convince the Americans that we are prepared to do things their way.

2. Ted Byfield, "Keeping things cozy for Canadianism," *Alberta Report*, March 31 and April 14, 1986.

Public support for the Mulroney government's free trade movement has dropped from 78 per cent two years ago to 54 per cent in January 1986, according to the polls, while opposition to it has more than doubled from 17 per cent to 35 per cent. We need scarcely wonder why. Free trade with the U.S. would sacrifice the immediate interests of Ontario to the long-term interests of the West. Since the ordained economic purpose of the West, from the dawn of its settlement onward, has been to serve the manufacturing industry of Ontario, then obviously free trade would reverse the master-servant relationship. Ontario would be serving us, a decidedly un-Canadian arrangement, at odds with our whole historical tradition. It is not, however, the resistance of the manufacturing industry that is undermining the free trade cause. The business that sees itself most imperilled is what could be called the "Canadianism industry," the people who have assigned themselves the onerous task of manufacturing, distributing and marketing Canadianism for the rest of us to consume. They are headquartered, naturally, in Toronto with a show branch office in Edmonton. Free trade, they have decided, would be very bad for Canadianism.

If the majors of this industry require identification, it isn't difficult because the list is short. The big player is, of course, the Canadian Broadcasting Corporation which, from the vantage point of Jarvis Street, defines Canadianism something like 18 hours a day. In Ottawa the National Film Board makes a more academic definition, detailing in its widely acclaimed productions the non-beliefs of Canadians: we do not believe in militarism; we do not believe in atomic war; we do not believe in moral absolutism; we do not believe in "violence." We may believe in God so long as we do not insist that our beliefs are true (i.e., that what conflicts with them must be false), and we may believe in free enterprise provided (a) that the participants restrict themselves to things like the hand-turning of pottery in Peggy's Cove, Nova Scotia, and (b) that they make no money at it. Central to our beliefs, however, is the cardinal quality of Canadianism, preferably recited by school children each day. "What is a Canadian?" the teacher ritually asks. Answer: "A Canadian is not an American." The central fraud of the canadianist is this: the Canada he purports to show us is not the Canada that exists today. Nor did it ever exist. Nor, one hopes to heaven, will it exist in the future.

For what, when you get right down to it, is the national heritage? How did we get here? Are we not a people who crossed the seas, pushed back the forests, charted the rivers and lakes, rammed the railways through the mountains, broke the prairies, and tamed the barrens of the Arctic? Are we not a people who found gold in the Pre-Cambrian, oil in the Beaufort, and grew food for the world where men could hitherto scarcely find food enough for themselves?

Are we French? Are we English? We are both, and German, Polish, Ukrainian, Dutch, Chinese and who knows what else. Why did we come here? For most, there was a single answer: land. For land, the Carignan-Solières Regiment established the first substantial settlement in Quebec. For land, the Loyalists came. For land, the eastern Europeans peopled the western prairie. For land, the Chinese built with their blood the railways, the Japanese opened the fishery, and the Jews of Russia created Winnipeg's north end and the thousand cultural endeavours that have flowed from it. What all these people wanted, in other words, was private property, safe from expropriation, safe from tax collectors, safe from thief and marauder. Property, that is, meant freedom, and freedom was worth life itself.

What did we believe? We believed in God. Religion was either the chief motive for, or indispensable companion of, almost every settlement. It was both puritanical and authoritarian, be it the authority of the Bible or the authority of the church. It was narrow, intolerant of non-conformity, and quick to condemn what it viewed as corruptive. But it was not anti-intellectual. Religion, in fact, established our school system. And a tough system it was, sparing neither rod nor child. It knew its goals, and against them it examined pupil and teacher remorselessly, overworking both. Indeed, work was a thing it revelled in, lots of it, with back and brain, dawn till long past darkness, men, women and children included. If a man would work, he should live. If he would not work, he should starve. If he could not work, it was up to the community to care for him, generously and positively with the hope that he would one day care for himself.

With the faith came the family. In families we arrived. In families we divided the land. In families we saw our children grow and prosper. In families we found companionship, purpose, comfort, warmth, guidance and an occasional clout on the ear. Was the mother of this family exploited and oppressed? She certainly was. Being exploited and oppressed was at once her burden, her privilege and her delight. That's what motherhood was about. In fact, in a sense, that's what the whole family was about. Either you believed in it, or you didn't.

We believed in it so much we quite readily fought for it, whether in the schoolyard or in the trenches. For we are indeed a fighting nation. Scarcely had the first shots been fired when we plunged into two world wars, years before the Americans, and those years we spent berating them for their backsliding cowardice. We left our blood and bones on the slopes of Vimy Ridge until we had hacked our way to the top of it, something the army of no other nation had been able to do. We were tied to posts and bayoneted at Hong Kong. We tore through the skies in the Battle of Britain, and we littered Germany with the corpses of our bomber crews. But these were wars of justice and we won them. We do not apologize for this.

Who would have us do so? The canadianists, that's who. For the clear goal of the Toronto media propagandist is to reshape what we are, into something we are not. Every one of the values out of which the country has emerged he repudiates. He debunks our religion and he undermines our families. He tells our women that raising children is contemptible, and aborting them an act of heroism. He plumps and pleads every cause from state day care to pansy parsons. He lets the killer stalk the streets while jailing parents who spank their children, and he has helped create governments so bloated and beyond control that more than 50 cents of every dollar we earn is required to feed and pamper them.

If sufficiently subsidized he will package and peddle our history. Mostly, however, he's ashamed of it. Our forefathers did not overcome the natural barriers of a continent, they "despoiled" them. They did not break the prairie. They seized it from its rightful owners. They were duped into fighting their wars, and most of their heroes were fakes. Our responsibility as a nation is to abandon the Americans, leave ourselves at the mercy of the Russians (who really aren't that bad, after all), let the trained professionals of government raise our children, and provide bigger and better budgets for the CBC and the National Film Board so they can continue to tell us all these wonderful things.

If we are going to have a Canada, surely the first thing we should do is dump the canadianists. The second is to realize whence we came, who we are, and what we believe.

Neither do the giants of the industry require identification. All are widely know to us because all are professional Canadians: Pierre Berton, Margaret Atwood, Knowlton Nash, June Callwood. All have done their part in exposing free trade for the menace that it represents, though most of this work has been left to their Edmonton branch manager, Mr. Mel Hurtig, publisher of *The Canadian Encyclopedia*.

Publishing is, alas, one of the industries lost to Canadianism over the last two decades, a scandalous loss, caused solely by negligent governments that denied the subsidies without which Canadianism cannot exist. Thus the industry has slid into American ownership, its demise, curiously enough, precisely paralleling its adoption of the Canadianist philosophy. That is, the more it espoused the social cause and became sensitive to the "true role" of Canadianism, as defined by the Canadianism industry, the less money it made. For the disconcerting truth is that there is almost no market for Canadian authors outside Canada. The world does not seem to appreciate them. They are simply not able to compete. Their stuff won't sell. It therefore becomes the soulbound duty of Canadians to keep them alive here. And that, they are telling us, is why we cannot possibly allow free trade.

It behoves us in the West, however, to assess the price to be paid for preserving this Canadianism industry. For it is we—not Ontario—who are going to pay most of that price. We in the West live on the basis of four key industries: grain production, oil and gas, mining, and forestry. Such manufacturing industries as we possess—not all, but nearly all—are related directly to these four. If they failed, most of our manufacturing enterprise would fail with them. The health, in fact the survival, of all four depends solely upon their ability to gain access to markets beyond the country, many of them in the United States. Hence, trade barriers of any kind work directly against the West, just as freedom of trade works for us.

We would be brainless indeed, therefore, if we did not hear the warnings that are being shouted at us by people of considerably more economic authority than Toronto's self-serving media community and its branch office management in Edmonton. I mean, that is, by people like the C.D. Howe Institute, the senior banks, the premiers of the three western-most provinces, and the leaders of all four key industries. That message is utterly consistent and alarmingly relevant to our economic survival, and it is this:

That the United States for four decades since the end of the Second World War has worked hard and expensively to develop the production potential of its former enemies and of the Third World. It has succeeded so well that its creatures, with Frankensteinian menace, have now threatened its own industry. The demand grows feverishly for high tariffs in the United States against foreign competition. This will logically include competition from Canada unless arrangements are made to bring us within the American wall. If we are left outside that wall the economic catastrophe to the West will be unparalleled in our history. We will suffer as we have never suffered before.

Now what Mr. Hurtig and his Toronto friends are telling us is that this suffering is well worth it, that Canadianism requires sacrifice, and that we should be prepared to make it. Whether they're right, surely, depends on what Canadianism actually is. If it is merely anti-Americanism, then that is strange reason to undertake such a sacrifice, for the vast majority of us are not anti-American. And if it is simply socialism, then that is stranger still, since over two-thirds of us aren't socialists either. And if it is goodness-knows-what then that is strangest of all because it means we have no reason whatever for rejecting free trade. So why reject it?

3. Susan Crean, "Reading Between the Lies: Culture and the Free-Trade Agreement," *This Magazine* 22, 2 (May 1988).

For something that was not supposed to be part of the free-trade deal at all, culture has a large and pervasive presence in the text of the final agreement between Canada and the United States. It has been given special treatment and is mentioned mainly by way of exceptions to the new rules, but it most assuredly has not been left out. This is not surprising. Anyone who has been following the trade talks attentively, or is aware of the history of Canada-U.S. cultural relations, knows that the Americans are intensely interested in culture—always have been—and will not be persuaded to set it aside. Moreover, they have a number of scores to settle with Canada, and so far as their negotiators were concerned, these were always on the agenda and part of the talks. Only the Canadian representatives were willing to pretend otherwise.

The Deal

From the outset of the free-trade talks, the concern about the effects of the deal on the cultural sector, and its impact on our freedom to make cultural policy for ourselves, has been answered by the Mulroney government in two ways: with protestations that Canadian cultural sovereignty will remain inviolate, and, when that failed to convince the cultural community, with an undertaking to keep the cultural industries off the bargaining table. Had either promise been kept there would presumably be nothing to say on the matter, and no interpretation necessary. This chapter could begin and end with a recitation of Article 2005 which reads:

1. Cultural industries are exempt from the provisions of this Agreement except as specifically provided in Article 401 (Tariff Elimination), paragraph 4 of Article 1607 (divestiture of an indirect acquisition) and Articles 2006 and 2007 of this chapter.

2. Notwithstanding any other provision of the Agreement, a Party may take measure of equivalent commercial effect in response to action that would have been inconsistent with this Agreement but for paragraph 1.

Leaving aside, for the moment, the question of how exempt the exemption is, we can begin with the exceptions, which are fourfold. First, the cultural industries—defined as book, magazine and newspaper publishing, film and video, audio and video recording, music publication and radio and television broad-casting—will be subject in the same way as other industries to tariff elimination. This means that the last remaining duties on recordings and printed matter imported into Canada will be removed. Second, in the event that a cultural enterprise located in Canada is acquired indirectly by American interests, and following a review under the Investment Canada Act a divestiture is requested by the Canadian government, the agreement states that Canada must offer to purchase the company from its American owners "at a fair, open market value, as determined by an independent, impartial assessment." Third, Canada has agreed to recognize copyright in the retransmission of television programming by cable, something the Americans have been agitating for since amending their Copyright Act in 1978. Whether the original transmission was intended for free, over-the-air reception by the general public or not (as in the case of pay television and other specialty service channels), permission must be sought and payment made to the copyright holders. Canada has undertaken to make the necessary legislative amendments and to have a repayment scheme in place by 1990. Fourth, the Print-in-Canada requirement of the Income Tax Act will be repealed so it will no longer be necessary for publications to be printed in this country in order for advertisers to claim legitimately the cost of advertising space as a deduction against income.

These exemptions are significant and revealing. By the first, the tariff pro-tection—which along with the 30 per cent Canadian content ruling for AM radio allowed the Canadian recording industry to take root in a hostile environ-ment—will be abolished seven years ahead of the gradual phasing-out that is already underway. In addition to the immediate effect the loss of the 11.8 per cent tariff will have on jobs and original production in this sector, there is the principle to consider. Although few tariffs now remain in the cultural area they are nevertheless a standard means for a country to ensure indigenous production (especially critical when the "products" are works of the collective imagination). Without a backward glance—and with no forward thinking about what our culture, including the cultural industries, may need in the future—we have re-nounced tariffs as an instrument of public policy.

This makes the next exception all the more curious, for it suggests that the Canadian government is preparing to move in a completely new direction, breaking ground in policy terms and, for that matter, apparently breaking its own commitment to privatization by introducing public ownership in the mass media. Outside of the CBC and National Film Board (and more recently, pro-vincial educational broadcasting), public ownership has not been pursued in this country as a means of Canadianizing the media. Public subsidy and regulation have been the options preferred, partly because they maintain a hands-off relationship between the state and culture. It is hard to believe that the Mulroney government is serious here, and we will have to wait for the other Gucci loafer to drop to discover what it intends to do with the cultural firms acquired in this manner, if indeed it envisages making such acquisitions at all, for it is entirely possible that divestiture will never be requested—as it was not in the case of the much publicized Prentice-Hall takeover in 1985. Pretexts can be found again, and this provision could be a powerful incentive to hunt for them diligently.

The retransmission right, while costly to Canada, is legitimate and desirable, and is supported by the cultural community as a matter of principle. Moreover, one of that community's long-standing criticisms of Canadian television has been that broadcasters and cable companies have never had to pay the full price for the American programming that fills their schedules to the marginalization of Canadian content. Abundantly available, cheap American shows have historically stifled original Canadian production. But if there is a good side to this article, there is also a hidden razor-blade—an agreement to establish a joint advisory committee "comprised of government and private sector experts to review outstanding issues related to retransmission rights in both countries and to make recommendations to the Parties within twelve months." In other words, the tough issues which would not submit to resolution in the talks are being referred to a new round of negotiations, and both countries have bound themselves to a time limit. Furthermore, underneath the term "retransmission right" lie most of our broadcasting, informatics (information technology) and telecommunications activity, and it would appear that the U.S. has just acquired the right to oversee the formulation of Canadian broadcasting policy.

The fourth exemption, like the third, only tells part of the story. The Print-in-Canada requirements are contained in Section 19 of the Income Tax Act which defines a Canadian magazine using quite stringent criteria of ownership, residency, editorial content as well as typesetting and printing. These provisions were introduced by Bill C-58, the famous *Time-Reader's Digest* bill. Since the late 1950s, it had been apparent that, so long as these two American magazines were allowed to soak up 50–60 per cent of advertising revenues in Canada, a viable Canadian magazine industry could not develop. In the early 1960s, the Canadian government got as far as drafting legislation to correct the situation. It was envisaged that only advertising placed in *Canadian* magazines would qualify as a tax-deductible business expense, thus making American magazines with Canadian editions a less attractive vehicle for advertisers. But the Auto Pact was then under discussion, and the White House had only to make a few veiled threats to get the Diefenbaker cabinet to recant. *Time* and *Reader's Digest* were made honorary Canadian citizens and the Auto Pact became reality. Thirteen years later the Liberals took another swing at the problem, and amid howls of protest from across the border Bill C-58—which had the same provisions as the earlier legislation—was passed into law in 1976. In the intervening decade, a domestic magazine industry has, indeed, been built on that legislative foundation; the predictions for C-58 were proven accurate. However, the U.S. has never accepted our law as the final word. American magazine publishers, printers as well as broadcasters (U.S. border television stations were also affected by the law), have been lobbying Congress without rest for a decade; the issue has remained near the top of the American list of "irritants." So it was obvious from the outset of the talks that the Americans would insist that C-58 be on the table. Only innocents or charlatans could deny this history, maintaining that C-58 would be kept out of play.

And C-58 is not alone. The American negotiators are also after the postal subsidy programme which is a vital element of support for Canadian magazines, and the draft agreement actually included a commitment to equalize postal rates for some publications. To the surprise of many, this was dropped from the final text, apparently because the two sides were so far apart on the issue (Canada was talking about letting *Time* and *Newsweek* in; the U.S. was talking about all publications with a circulation over one thousand). According to the Canadian Periodical Publishers Association (CPPA), the Americans have simply decided to change tactics, figuring they will have better success taking their complaint to the General Agreement on Tariffs and Trade (GATT). Moreover, they have a longer-term goal, which is to clear the way for American printers to expand their business into Canada.

Since eliminating the manufacturing clause in American copyright law, thereby dropping the requirement that foreign publications be printed in the U.S. if more than 1,500 copies are to be distributed, American printers have been lobbying for access to the Canadian market. The agreement gives them two important concessions. Besides the removal of the Print-in-Canada part of C-58, printing and typesetting have been omitted from the definition of the cultural industries and are therefore ... not exempt from the agreement. This leaves just two regulations in their path. First, item 99221–1 of Schedule C of the Customs Tariff, which prevents the importation of magazines in which more than 5 per cent of the advertising is directed to Canadians (this would mean that if Canadian magazines were printed in the U.S. they could not re-enter Canada). Second, there are the postal regulations which stipulate that periodicals qualifying as Second Class mail must be printed in Canada. The CPPA does not believe repealing the Print-in-Canada requirement will by itself be harmful, for the remaining definition is still very strict. But read in the long-term context, these two concessions are less innocuous than they seem. Canadian magazine publishers regard them as the thin end of a wedge which will guarantee the intensification of pressure for the removal of other programmes designed to assist the industry. And, when all the ramifications of the agreement are played out, our magazine industry could be severely damaged.

Although there are many intangibles in Clause 1 of the agreement's Article 2005, it is actually crystal clear when compared to the second clause. This so-called "Notwithstanding clause" is the conundrum, though on the surface it too seems straightforward. Both countries, it says, can go right ahead promoting their cultural industries, but both risk retaliatory action from the other in response to anything which would be inconsistent with the agreement but for the exemption. Translation: the cultural industries are not part of the agreement unless they involve actions which are not otherwise permitted.

There is, of course, good reason why double negatives are considered bad grammar; being indirect statements, they inject imprecision into the discussion and open the door to multiple meanings. This clause will probably keep several dozen lawyers warm through many winters trying to divine its meaning and it will be years more before any definitive interpretation is possible. For, by its vagueness, the clause raises a host of questions and none of these can be answered by the government with any degree of assurance. For example, though tariffs are now being eliminated in the cultural industries, can they be reintroduced as a "measure of equivalent commercial effect"? What limitations, if any, are there on the scope of retaliatory action? Since the article as a whole ostensibly removes the cultural industries from the body of the agreement, does this preclude recourse to the disputes-settlement mechanism? If one side takes retaliatory action to recoup the commercial effects of cultural policy, and the other side considers this illegitimate or excessive, what recourse is there? Who decides what a "measurable commercial effect" is and how that effect is to be calculated? If the compensatory commercial action taken by one country falls within the definition of dumping or countervailing duties, is there an argument to be made that would give the other country access to the disputes-settlement mechanism? Or, as the prevailing legal opinion has it at the moment, does the Notwithstanding clause amount to prior agreement giving the United States a free shot at any part of the Canadian economy?

Despite its murky legal implications, the main thrust of Article 2005 is perfectly clear. The first clause obviously came from the Canadian side and represents an attempt to live up to the government's promise to protect Canadian cultural sovereignty. The second constitutes the price exacted by the Americans. Canada can make whatever cultural policies it wants, but if in doing so the commercial status quo of American interests is affected, the U.S. has the right to extract its pound of flesh. That much at least is clear: the deal gives the U.S. the right, (leave in advance, as it were), to retaliate. Such a concession, it can be argued, actually leaves the cultural industries with less protection than the other sectors of the economy included in the deal. Certainly it is the kind of special treatment that makes you pine for ordinary dispensation.

Cultural Surrender

The most disturbing and probably the most far-reaching aspect of the Notwithstanding clause is the precedent it sets by accepting the American definition of culture. Early on in the trade talks External Affairs Minister Joe Clark was heard ruminating on the differences between Canadian and American approaches to book publishing. He said: "To us it's culture; to them it's business." Clark was right, there is a difference. And true, in the United States, culture does mean business—the biggest, in fact, if you include the entire information sector. He also correctly acknowledged that, in Canada, we have historically reserved economic judgment on culture, recognizing that there are justifications, besides monetary gain, for making our own films, writing our own books and gathering our own news. But it would be most accurate to say that culture and business are inextricably intertwined and interdependent. As innumerable commentators around the world have noted, American entertainment functions as publicity for the products and services of American industry. Just as the function of the programmes on American commercial television is to supply advertisers with an audience (appropriately skewed as to age, income, sex etc.), so the American media can be viewed as delivering consumers and devotees to the American way of life. To imagine that these activities can be separated, that culture and economics can be carved into discrete compartments where they will not impinge on other aspects of life in the body politic, is one of the reigning conceits of our time. The idea that the economy operates entire of itself, that it is even possible to make a "purely economic" decision, is an idea which is loaded with cultural values.

In the past two decades, Canadian society has experienced a cultural expansion of epic proportions which has repeatedly found access to the mass media barred from without. Driven by the determination of a generation of creators who decided to flaunt convention and work in Canada for Canadian audiences, the movement has succeeded in establishing a Canadian presence and voice in the media and the arts where one did not really exist before. This has been achieved by prodigious personal effort, but without access to the Canadian marketplace through the national systems of communication, the Canadian voice has mostly been heard in local and regional registers. It is still not easy to address a national audience.

The essential dilemma which cultural policy has been grappling with since it was invented in the early 1970s is how to break into the mainstream of popular culture which, in this country, is mostly American. Governments have introduced all sorts of programmes to subsidize the development of the cultural industries over the years, but these have been directed almost exclusively to production. Time and again, secretaries of state and ministers of communications, revved up by the demands of the cultural community and convinced by their own industry studies, have gone to Cabinet to get a policy that would do something about distribution. Time and again, as one wag put it, the minister went in with a tiger of a policy and came out with kitty litter, as Cabinet shied away from action and buckled under pressure from the Americans. As a result, the structural changes which are absolutely necessary if Canadian culture is ever to have a national presence in this country, have never materialized.

The figures tell the tale: 3–5 per cent of the screen time in Canadian movies houses is devoted to Canadian films; 2–4 per cent of videocasettes sold are Canadian; 20 per cent of books sold are published by Canadian-owned firms which publish 80 per cent of the Canadian-authored titles; 97 per cent of film revenues leave the country, 95 per cent headed for the U.S.; 85 per cent of records and tapes sold in Canada are non-Canadian; 77 per cent of the magazines sold are foreign; 95 per cent of the drama aired on television is non-Canadian.

So American culture remains the one cultural common denominator for all Canadians. And the cultural industries, far from being made an exception to prove the rule, ought to be read as an object lesson. There are no barriers now preventing Canadian producers from selling in the United States—except American attitudes. Though Canadian policy-makers rarely stop to notice the fact, Americans are loath to purchase culture from abroad. They import almost no television programming (except for PBS), very few books, fewer feature films, and only a smattering of music since most foreign artists are either produced on American labels or distributed by them. It is highly unlikely that this will be changed by a free-trade deal with Canada, even though we are their biggest cultural customer. The one-way flow across the forty-ninth parallel will not be reversed or modified by the agreement; there will not be new revenues for original Canadian film production, and in the cultural sector as a whole the most we can hope for is 20 per cent of our own market. With no plans, real or rhetorical, for adjusting this picture, we have to conclude that as little as 3 per cent of the domestic market is just fine for the Tories, and to them an acceptable definition of cultural sovereignty. Perversely, then, C-58—the one and only stake the Liberals ever made on the marketplace on behalf of Canadian culture—was one of the first offerings made by Ottawa to lure the slyly diffident Americans to the bargaining table.

By the terms of the free-trade agreement it will now become harder to do anything about American domination of our mass media. Whatever we do try will elicit immediate retaliation, which means that whatever is accomplished will have to be paid for twice—over and above the cost of the programme itself, we will have to pay off the Americans. The agreement therefore dramatically raises the political odds against any affirmative action for Canadian culture, for now we will not just have to convince the politicians about the rightness of such action, we will have to convince them it will be worth it even if other Canadians in other sectors will be penalized. This pits Canadian workers and artists against each other and forces us all into a situation of having to "choose" between bread and books. Very adroitly, the American negotiators set the cat among the Canadian chickens and have settled back to watch us self-destruct.

Notwithstanding the exemption, this agreement will irrevocably change Canadian cultural policy. Contrary to the government's claim, the agreement does not retain our full capacity to support the cultural industries. It commits us to pursuing culture as a business, the American way. And it signifies a renunciation of Canadian efforts to modify American presence in our media. Not bad for one sentence and thirty-two words.

Loopholes

Culture adds up to more than the cultural industries. Likewise, the cultural industries are greater than the definitions given them in an agreement which leaves out a great deal—all the creative professions which are the well-spring of any cultural industry, for example, as well as printing and typesetting and bookselling. The arts are not mentioned either, presumably because they are non-profit and non-profitable. Yet there are pockets of profitability in the arts (commercial theatre, for instance) and all sorts of arts-related professions and services which support Canadian art by providing artists with freelance incomes. There is nothing in the agreement to suggest that the arts will be protected from the indirect effects of the deal as it applies to these subsections of the economy.

By the same token, artists will have no recourse to the Notwithstanding provision of Article 2005 should their commercial position be adversely affected by
American actions. Artists who make a living typesetting (and I do know several
who do just that), who fall victim to American competition and have to close
down their studios and go out of business, are out of luck. There is no way for
Canada to extract repayment for that kind of loss.

Just formulating that observation, however, lights up other quirks in the
thinking behind the agreement. The wording of Article 2005 indicates that the
trigger for retaliatory measures is government action, as is the case under GATT
agreements. Damage caused by private enterprise in the marketplace, which is,
after all, the kind of damage Canadian cultural industries are most likely to face,
is untouchable and designated fair game. Yet, so far, no one in authority seems
to have wondered whether the Notwithstanding clause works in reverse or even
if it is meant to. When, and under what sort of circumstances, would Canada be
in a position to extract a little "equivalent commercial" compensation of our
own? The fact is that it has been designed for American retaliation, not Canadian, as the American summary of the text makes explicit: "Canada faces no
constraints on its ability to promote the development of Canadian culture through
economic measures. The United States can take measures of equivalent economic effect to respond to actions taken by Canada in the cultural area. The
U.S. recognizes the importance to Canada of maintaining its cultural identity.
At the same time, however, the U.S. wants to ensure that Canadian cultural
policies do not constitute an unnecessary barrier to U.S. trade."

In sum, then, Article 2005 adds up to this: some cultural industries have
been exempted, but on the understanding that we will not do anything about
the status quo of American media in our marketplace; the U.S. is guaranteed
continued access to the billions of dollars its cultural industries extract annually
from the Canadian economy; and Canada has acceded to conditions which will
make it impossible for us to fashion policies that will shape the content of our
own mass media.

Realizing that the bulk of Canadian cultural activity is not exempted or
dealt with comprehensively inevitably sends us off on a fishing trip through the
text, searching for places where culture may be implicated. The service sector is
an obvious place to look as many cultural activities fall into this category. There
is nothing in Chapter 14 which would prevent the growth of U.S.-based design, publicity and management services in the cultural sector—cultural
industries included. Indeed, private American firms have already been contracted to run some university bookstores, though publishers and booksellers

vociferously protested the move and in one case forced a retreat. Under the free-trade agreement, however, this will be allowed to continue and expand. It is not impossible to imagine such private sector services, including exhibition, design and management, being brought into public museums and art galleries. But the exact status of sectors not specifically named will only be determined by invoking the disputes-settlement mechanism.

There are two places where the arts are specifically mentioned in Chapter 14 of the agreement, although the first one is stated in code, (literally, it is identified only by a Standard Industrial Classification number), and thus in such a way that most people (maybe even our negotiators) missed it. Among non-university, post-secondary educational institutions included in the deal are schools of art and the performing arts which will be open to the private sector and American competition in management and all commercial services. And in Annex 1404, architecture is singled out for special treatment and Canada has therein agreed to the development of mutually acceptable professional standards and criteria regarding education, examination, experience, conduct and ethics, and professional development, and has undertaken to harmonize provincial licencing practices so that the profession will operate on a smooth and level continental playing field.

And then there is the tricky little question of subsidy, left to further negotiations to be worked out. How will the subsidy to the cultural industries be regarded—particularly the support provided to those sections not exempted or otherwise covered in the agreement? What will prevent American cultural firms operating in Canada from demanding equal treatment and access to Canada Council support for, say, writers and book promotion tours? And in the investment section, there are, likewise, implications for culture which are difficult to forecast. There, neither the cultural industries nor the arts are exempted from direct investment; whatever money wants in, is apparently welcome. Databanks, information processing and the software side of informatics governed by copyright law are all open to foreign involvement and exploitation. Although these represent the growth industries of the future, they have been renounced as instruments of cultural development, or as strategic sites for Canadian job creation and Canadian content. (And has anyone thought through the legal implications for the privacy of Canadian citizens now that our data can be processed in a foreign country under foreign law?)

The only concession to Canadian cultural tradition—and in reality more a concession to the political sensitivity of the moment—is the special rule regarding indirect takeovers. As previously noted, this is an extraordinary rule. Not only does the government seem to be agreeing in advance to purchase cultural firms affected by a takeover at a price to be determined by independent assessment, it is conceding to the rule of North American rather than Canadian market forces. It also appears to be agreeing to public ownership in the cultural sector, or at least to public participation in the purchase of certain American branch-plants which, most likely, would not remain in government hands but be turned over to private owners for a subsidized price.

Down the Road

It is not easy to predict what the ultimate effect of the free-trade agreement will be on the cultural life of the country, or even the cultural industries. Change there will be, without doubt, even if it will occur only slowly and subtly. However, for the sake of trying to understand the phenomenon, to at least give it a face and some dimensions, let's try to imagine.

Take the business of book publishing. Of all the mass media in Canada, book publishing has arguably developed the most distinctively Canadian voice. Canadians know and read Canadian writers, (and so do a growing number of people in other countries), and the majority of them are published by Canadian-owned firms. Some Canadian writers have even acquired celebrity status; so have a few publishers—Jack McClelland, Mel Hurtig, Anna Porter and Adrienne Clarkson among them. Moreover, these people are not just famous for being famous. They have had a lot to say over the years about the political issues of our time and are quite likely to turn up on "The Journal," or at public hearings to deliver their considered opinions about free trade, the Meech Lake Accord or pornography legislation. In short, it is possible to talk about a Canadian book publishing culture, and one of its most remarkable qualities is its regional character. However inept book distribution and publishing policy may have been, they have been premised on the idea that literature is regionally bound and that regional presses ought to feed into a nation-wide system. Regional, in Canadian English, refers to cultural as well as geographic location.

By comparison, American book publishing, which also has a regional side to it, is organized more in the direction of specialization, and the division of intellectual labour is done according to categories and markets. The definition, therefore, is primarily economic. The clue is in the way the printing industry is structured. According to Willy Cooper, president of the Canadian Printing Industries Association, the difference can be described as follows: "Large American undertakings tend to have fewer manufacturing locations than do Canadian companies. Typically, in the United States, such facilities are dedicated to the production of huge quantities of a limited number of product lines. The Canadian situation, reflecting the linguistic and geographic reality of this nation, is altogether different. Canadian printing firms often have a large number of plants located across the country, producing a wider variety of products for local or regional distribution."

Life after free trade will immerse Canadian book publishing in a business milieu ever more powerfully driven by the beat of American enterprise. This suggests that the single most important change will be the sea-change of attitudes and habits which will engulf the business community at large as it reorients itself to regional and cross-border markets. The full force of American commercialism will thereby be unleashed and it will feel like a steroid injection. In such an environment, some Canadian publishers may actually do very well, and all sorts of new players will appear with new ideas and wheels to deal. The literary presses will likely survive, with public funding, but only for show; the concept of their participating in a genuine national market probably will not. McClelland & Stewart will not disappear overnight; yet when next its bottom line crashes, the cultural imperative *cum* political will to bail it out with public money may just not be there. In short, the transformation of Canadian book publishing will not be a case of the immediate demise of the Canadian-owned sector but the reorientation of the industry as a whole so that it ceases to have much meaning or weight in the culture that surrounds it. As it is by-passed it will become marginalized.

The Canadian negotiators, however, have not understood this; they seem to be able to contemplate the complete transformation of economic and trading relations between our two countries, and among the regions of our two countries, and still imagine that culture is off the table. And by inaccurately gauging the American agenda, they have failed to achieve what they set out to achieve in the cultural sector and do not even recognize their own error. The text may say that the cultural industries are exempted—but that is not what it means. Culture is about values, and cultural policy is about ensuring that our values have a voice in the commercial hubbub that explicitly celebrates American values. With the free-trade agreement, the Mulroney government has completely abandoned the project of a national market for Canadian culture. All of our cultural industries will, by coercion or force of commercial circumstance, eventually rationalize and reorganize themselves to harmonize with the patterns of American enterprise. They may survive, but only as specialty producers.

In this sense, the agreement is a monumental statement of failure and surrender. The failure of the central government and central Canada to live up to its rhetoric of nation-building and cultural and regional development. Ontarians cannot blame Westerners or Maritimers or Northerners for opting to do business for a time with their neighbours to the south. It cannot be any worse than trying to extract a decent arrangement out of Ontario, and they will not be made to feel inferior to Seattle or Dallas or Baltimore, as they are now to Toronto. (The irony of ironies is that Toronto is likely to become an important North American city, but it will have decreasing importance, in every way that matters, to other Canadians.) The free-trade advocates may then be, pathetically, looking at the wrong thing. The issue is not who is braver or stronger or more confident about taking on the Americans and winning; the issue is who are we cosying up to, and how far we want to let the vast pulsing dynamo of American consumerism rule our lives. The issue is not access to the American market for Canadian culture, but access to our own.

To say that cultural sovereignty has been protected because the cultural industries (or parts of them) have been exempted (sort of) from certain aspects of the agreement is sheer duplicity. In thirty-two words the Mulroney government has committed us forever to asking, first, what the Americans will let us have, and, second, what we want and need as Canadians. If that is not a violation of cultural sovereignty, what is?

4. Anthony DePalma, "Tough Rules Stand Guard Over Canadian Culture," *New York Times,* July 14, 1999.

Lenny Kravitz's raunchy remake of the '70s classic "American Woman" had been thoroughly dissected, and the music director of Toronto's CHUM-FM radio station was satisfied that it was, indeed, Canadian. Surprising, since neither the singer nor the subject of the song has a direct connection to the Great White North. But the music and anti-American lyrics—reflecting common Canadian views—were written by members of the Guess Who, a popular Canadian band of the 1970s. That gives "American Woman" the two points it needs under Canada's intricate system of rankings to help meet CHUM-FM's government-imposed requirement that 35 percent of its daytime playlist be devoted to Canadian content.

Determining what to do with "Baby Feel My ..." by Patria, a young Filipino artist, was not so easy. "She came to Canada at age 2, but I think she's a landed immigrant now," said Barry Stewart, CHUM-FM's music director, as the weekly music meeting dragged on. "That makes her Canadian, right?"

Welcome to the bizarre world of Canadian cultural regulation, a sometimes arbitrary, often contradictory system of rules and measures cobbled together over several decades to protect Canadian culture—not just music but film, television, magazines and literature—from what some Canadians consider the menace of American cultural imperialism. Canada is not alone in trying to draw a Maginot line against Mickey, Rambo and Homer Simpson. France required theaters to reserve 20 weeks of screen time a year for French feature films. Australia demands that 55 percent of a television broadcaster's schedule be filled with domestic programs. And while Mexico allows foreign films to be shown, with subtitles in Spanish, it does not allow them to be dubbed because that would increase the mass appeal of new Hollywood films in a country where literacy rates are low.

By most counts Canada is the Death Star of cultural fortifications, bristling with regulatory armaments to preserve what little is left of its own cultural territory. But at a glance it might appear the battle is already lost. Eighty percent of what Canadians watch on television, outside of news, comes from the United States. So do up to 80 percent of English-language magazines on Canadian newsstands; 65 percent of the songs heard on the radio, 60 percent of English books and 95 percent of feature films. No other country is so vulnerable to invasion by the American colossus. Except for the French-speaking province of Quebec, Canada shares the same language with the United States and is separated from its loud neighbor to the south by a peaceful, 3,000-mile border that is largely invisible. Where cultural differences exist, they tend to be subtle.

At the same time, few people in the world match Canadians' appetite for American cultural goods, everything from Walt Disney to "Fresh Prince of Bel Air." And Canadians enjoy being a part of a cultural scene much larger than their own population of 30 million people, spread over a vast and wild continent, could ever support. Thus, as barriers are thrown up to keep Hollywood from dominating the Canadian scene, both Vancouver and Toronto welcome film production crews with incentives and a cheap Canadian dollar to dress up Canadian streets to look like New York and Chicago. The efforts have been so successful that the Screen Actors Guild in the United States estimates that Canada lured away the equivalent of almost 19,000 full-time film production jobs last year. It has vowed to get them back.

Critics say the maze of cultural restrictions really is intended to protect the 700,000 Canadians who depend on culture for their jobs. But those like Norman Jewison, the director of "Moonstruck" and "Fiddler on the Roof," argue that much more is at stake. "This isn't just cars or refrigerators for sale; this is ideas," Jewison said. "And when you start exporting ideas, philosophies, behavior, products, ways of living, it becomes an assault on the culture. Americans have to understand that."

It isn't always clear that Americans do, especially since entertainment is now one of the most important United States exports. For Washington, every question involving culture and trade has assumed enormous importance because of the impact it might have on business. For example, the office of the U.S. trade representative threatened to start a trade war over a proposed Canadian law intended to protect Canadian magazines. The law would have made it a criminal offense for Canadian companies to take out advertisements in the Canadian editions of American magazines like Sports Illustrated.

Canada's position is that domestic magazines are important conveyors of Canadian voices and will be undercut if Americans can simply place a maple leaf on a magazine cover, call it a Canadian edition and sell cut-rate advertising that would otherwise go to Canadian magazines. The Americans respond that if magazines are so important, Canada can subsidize outright; otherwise, free trade laws mean that the market is open to all comers. After months of argument, Canada's cultural minister, Sheila Copps, agreed to allow Canadians to provide up to 18 percent of the advertising in an American magazine. The percentage could increase only if more than half the content of the magazine is Canadian.

Ms. Copps was pilloried from coast to coast for selling out Canadian culture, although the compromise represented a crack in Washington's defense against cultural restrictions. "This decision gives France and other countries the opportunity to argue that the precedent of taking cultural considerations into account has already been set," said William S. Merkin, a former U.S. deputy chief trade negotiator.

In defending itself against brashly aggressive American culture, Canada sometimes seems like a fastidious gardener who fumes and fusses over the riot of dandelions on his neighbor's lawn while realizing that ultimately there is little he can do to keep them from encroaching on his property. But that doesn't keep him from trying. Elaborate systems have developed to preserve a portion of the culture market for Canadian products, and they are largely considered here to have been successful in helping the nation break out of its colonial independence—first on Britain, then on the United States—and develop its own creative universe.

Celine Dion, Shania Twain, Alanis Morissette, Sarah McLachlan, Bryan Adams, the Tragically Hip and the Barenaked Ladies are all Canadian stars in the music field. In film, Mike Myers, Jim Carrey, David Cronenberg, Atom Egoyan, James Cameron and Norman Jewison share Canadian roots. Television programs like "The Outer Limits" and, until recently, "The X-Files," have been filmed in Canada. In literature, Margaret Atwood and Alice Munro have been joined by a stable of accomplished writers including Michael Ondaatje, Rohinton Mistry and Guy Vanderhaeghe. What is less clear is the degree to which the system of percentages and regulation is responsible for such cultural blossoming. Many Canadian pop stars signed contracts with major labels after leaving Canada, suggesting that the Canadian content regulations cannot be credited with their success.

In fact, stars like Ms. Dion are penalized by the regulations. The point system for determining Canadian content goes by the acronym MAPL—music, artist, production, lyrics—and assigns one point for each category where a Canadian is predominantly involved. At least two points are required for a record to be treated as Canadian. So while Rod Stewart's "Rhythm of My Heart" is accorded the two points because the music and lyrics were written by Mark Jordan, a Canadian, Celine Dion's hit "My Heart Will go On" from the movie "Titanic" cannot be counted in a radio station's quota for Canadian content because it gets only one point, for the artist.

The Canadian content rule also creates a kind of musical ghetto in which songs that are not popular enough to make it on their own are replayed endlessly just to meet requirements. Stewart, the CHUM-FM music director, said that because there are not enough hits meeting the criteria that identifies them as Canadian, a song by an artist like Shania Twain has be kept on a playlist for more than five months—an eternity in radio. Listeners tire of it, he said, and are tempted to tune in to radio stations from the United States that can play whatever they wish.

The radio regulation is intended to support up-and-coming Canadian artists. But some argue that it can foster mediocrity or generate an artificial popularity that comes back to haunt Canadian groups. "If an artist has success in Canada, international markets often see that as 'rigged' because they believe that artist 'has to be played by law,'" Steven Page, lead singer for the Barenaked Ladies, said in an e-mail interview conducted while he was backstage at a concert in England.

At times, Page said, Canadian artists don't know where to turn. The impression that Canadian songs are played only because they must be played "can make taking your success elsewhere a more difficult endeavor," he said. And the government's protectionist attitude sometimes trickles down to fans who "turn their backs on artists they feel are not Canadian enough," he said. With its overwhelming impact, television is the fiercest battleground for Canada's protectionist policies—and the most controversial, because broadcasters often find themselves opposing government regulations.

Canadians watch Canadian television channels, but they see very little that is produced in Canada by Canadians. Regulations allow commercial stations to broadcast popular American programs at the same time they are broadcast on American channels—which most Canadians can receive. But the law allows Canadian broadcasters to substitute their own commercials. So while Canadians saw the Super Bowl at the same time as Americans did, they were treated to dated Canadian beer ads instead of flashy new American commercials.

Regulations now require 60 percent of a television station's schedule to be Canadian. But with unceasing opposition from broadcasters, regulators are constantly redefining what Canadian content is, and even what prime time is. "Top Cops," a CBS program that tells American police stories, fulfills Canadian content regulations because it is produced in Canada. But the Disney company's "Never Cry Wolf," a 1983 film version of the Canadian author Farley Mowat's book about the Arctic, is not Canadian enough because it was produced in the United States. Broadcast executives like Ivan Fecan, president of CTV, one of Canada's largest commercial television networks, argue that while Canada's cultural regulations may be necessary, their effect is limited because they can never overcome a fundamental promise: popular culture must be popular.

"You can't force people to read Canadian magazines or watch Canadian dramas, but you should provide them with the choice," he said. "I don't think anyone would confuse this with being anti-American. It's not. Canada is not another state, and we don't want to be one."

5. Henry N.R. Jackman, "Canada's Culture," Speech to the Canadian Club (November 1999).

Madam Chairman, it is indeed an honour to be invited to be a speaker at one of your meetings celebrating the millennium, although I must say I was very nervous when you suggested that I should talk about culture, particularly that rather elusive entity, Canadian Culture.

I looked up three dictionaries to find a definition for culture—one Canadian, one American and one English. The dictionaries, of course, all gave many definitions, but it was interesting to see which definition each dictionary listed first.

The first definition in the English dictionary said that culture was "a refined understanding of the arts and other human intellectual achievement."

The American Webster Dictionary called culture "a set of shared attitudes, values, goals and practices that characterize a company or a corporation, or traits of a racial or religious group." Note the difference.

The Canadian dictionary stated as its first definition "the cultivation of plants, the rearing of bees, silkworms, etc.," or "a quantity of bacteria grown for study."

I am being, of course, somewhat facetious here as all the dictionaries gave alternative definitions and came around to approximately the same position.

But of the definitions cited I personally prefer the first definition in the Oxford English Dictionary, "a refined understanding of the arts and other intellectual achievement," which implies a knowledge and understanding of the arts acquired through intellectual and aesthetic training. Culture so defined transcends national boundaries. It represents the highest quality of the human spirit. It rejects a narrow "jingoistic" definition. Appreciation of fine art, music and literature is a personal attribute attained through study, rather than a national characteristic. Encouragement of art and cultural expression of all kinds, not just Canadian, is a legitimate avenue for government support as the greater appreciation of art and culture enriches our lives.

I suspect, however, for the purposes of your Canadian Club Millennium series, we are attempting to define the word culture in the American Webster Dictionary sense as being "a set of shared attitudes and values" which might characterize us as a nation. This is a much broader definition and could include social attitudes, consumer preferences, the sports we enjoy, attitudes towards government, etc., all of which might define us, but are hardly examples of artistic expression. In this sense the word "culture" is synonymous with "identity" and is far broader than simply appreciation of the arts.

The problem in Canada, particularly when it comes to government policy, is that we tend to confuse the two definitions. Policies that encourage an exploration and appreciation of arts and the humanities should and do receive government support in most civilized societies. Government policies on the other hand that deal with *"identity"* are much more of a problem. Much of Canada believes that the state should have no role in promoting a specific identity. The problem is compounded by the fact that there seems to be no consensus in this country as to what our identity truly is.

Can we define Canadianness with a country spread out over thousands of miles with differences which in the past 100 years have grown greater rather than lessened? The twin forces of globalization on one hand and the growth of regionalism are much stronger now than they were 100 years ago. Does this make the search for our Canadian identity or culture even more elusive?...

That the government is concerned about the lack of a Canadian identity goes without saying, as witnessed by the myriad of programs and dollars that are lavished on our so-called cultural industries in an attempt to define "identity" with questionable relevance to artistic merit. Developing cultural police is not an easy task, particularly in the absence of any consensus as to what culture it is we are trying to protect.

And yet, in spite of this cultural ambiguity, artistic expression in Canada seems to be in pretty good shape.

At the moment our so-called "cultural industries" are enjoying remarkable growth. Canada is becoming a cultural powerhouse. Canada's artists and cultural entrepreneurs have made Canada one of the top exporting nations against countries two or three times its size. Books by Canadian authors in terms of both titles and sales have trebled in the past decade and foreign-rights sales are booming. In the 1960s only 5% of books sold in Canadian bookstores were by Canadian authors. Now the figure is over 30%.

Much of this growth is fuelled by the 1988 Free Trade Agreement and the cheaper Canadian dollar. Canadian film and TV production, according to a recent Price Waterhouse survey, now totals $3 billion, double the figure seven years ago. Between them Alanis Morissette, Shania Twain and Celine Dion have sold 155 million albums, of which 95% are sold outside of Canada. Private TV networks are voluntarily increasing Canadian content, a development that would have been unheard of only a few years ago.

Yet in spite of all this, many Canadians suggest that much of this may be simply a symptom of further Americanization of our society.

One of the chief problems with our quest to find our identity is that we keep making comparisons to the United States. In fact, we are in danger of developing a mega-sized inferiority complex which seems to tell us that if only the United States were not here we could develop on our own and that the huge U.S. engine south of the border is somehow destroying our separate and distinct culture. We label American culture as self-assertive, expansive, vigorous and robust. In spite of the tremendous growth in Canadian film, theatre, music, and books we still continue to say that our culture is fragile and undernourished. Our federal arts bureaucrats, concerned with their own budgets and those dependent on government handouts, encourage this perception.

Since Americans are characterized as being brash or harsh, we take refuge in calling ourselves "a kinder and gentler people," an assertion that may have little ground for legitimacy. In other words, our obsession with the United States means that discussion of culture in this country, which should be a celebration of the remarkable achievements Canadians have made in the "arts," tends to be a hand-writing wake where we wallow in our own supposed cultural deficiencies and ask for more government funding.

This has led ot a huge cultural establishment at the federal level which supports organizations like the CBC and the National Film Board, and the Museum of Civilization which gobble up the lion's share of the Department of Heritage budget. The question of what it is we are trying to protect, however, never seems to be answered.

A Canadian magazine may get a different tax treatment from an American magazine. What is the difference between an American and a Canadian magazine? Answer: the Canadian magazine gets a different tax treatment. Does this mean that it is only the extent of government support that defines its Canadianness?

What is a Canadian book? I just finished reading a biography of the late John Marshall, former chief justice of the United States during the early 19th century. A friend of mine asked me why did I not read a comparable book about our Canadian judicial system? The book I read was certainly published by an American publisher, but when I read the flyleaf the author was a professor at the University of Toronto who wrote the book in Canada. Is this book Canadian? A biography of Laurier published by the Oxford University Press—written by an Oxford professor who did his graduate work in Canada—is this a Canadian book? Probably not by our government definition.

Some years ago I was walking to my home and my way was blocked by a film crew who were shooting a movie. I asked someone who appeared to be in charge whether this was a Canadian movie. The person I questioned turned out to be the Executive Producer, who said, "Hell, no, this is definitely not a Canadian movie." I asked him "Why not?" It was my understanding there were a lot of grants given to Canadian productions. He said, "If this were a Canadian movie the distributors would not touch us." Admittedly this was some years ago, but it was obvious that Canadian government funding was the last resort of bad movies. Good movies, or at least commercially successful movies, could and did receive money from the private sector.

Canada as a movie capital at the moment is booming. Twenty-five per cent of Hollywood's movies are now made outside of the United States, most of them in Canada. Are these Canadian movies? According to our cultural bureaucrats most of them are not. By definition Canadianness of a film can only be defined, like publishing or magazines, by reason that they receive government subsidies. If you do not get a Canadian government grant you are not a Canadian movie and presumably are not contributing to our cultural fabric. Yet until you see the credits at the end of the film it is often very difficult, if not impossible, to determine the film's nationality.

The biggest threat to Canadian culture, in my opinion, is the faulty logic coming from Ottawa which defines our identity in terms of government support. The CBC, which soaks up over a billion dollars of our taxpayers' money, presumes to give Canadians a common sense of identity even though its television audience is only a small fraction of what it once was a few years ago. Any discussions of the CBC, including the present press surrounding the hiring of the new president, makes it very clear that the CBC itself has no clear idea as to what its mandate should be. Yet this lack of purpose does not prevent the CBC from asking for more money. CBC supporters will say the very existence of the CBC is a reflection of our identity. What it may or may not broadcast therefore becomes secondary. In other words, according to Ottawa and our cultural mandarins, Canadian identity is defined by government policy and largesse. In the absence of any clear ability fo define who we are, perhaps they may be right. Government handouts have certainly become part of our culture.

Although we do not have an authoritarian regime in this country, cultural policy still remains subject to political pressure and the dictates of what might be called the politically correct. The CBC a few years ago came up with a documentary entitled *The Valour and the Horror* which, according to some, denigrated the service of the Canadian armed forces during the Second World War. The issue here was not an artistic question but their interpretation of history which was vigorously criticized by veterans groups. The CBC apologized.

There is a lesson to be drawn here. Surely an artist may write or publish or produce anything he or she wishes, but should they do so if it is produced and funded by governments? Contrast this with the tremendous number of anti-Vietnam War feature-length films that have come from Hollywood. These movies, I am sure, were to some Americans as equally offensive as *The Valour and the Horror.* Yet there was no public outcry. Why? The difference was that they were not funded by governments. In a country that believes in free expression no one really has the right to complain. But if it is the government or the CBC that funds one point of view to the exclusion of other viewpoints you can see the problem.

The Canada Council, which again prides itself as an agent for allowing the "avant garde" to express itself, came out with a program to celebrate the millennium. What were these avant garde themes the Canada Council wished to promote? Well, there was giving our Native peoples a voice which had so long been denied them; expressions of celebrating our multiracial, multicultural diversity; recognizing the place of women in our history and our society; and recognizing the duality of French and English languages across Canada.

Now these sentiments, however laudable, are hardly "avant garde." "Avant garde" is meant to shock and to raise questions and challenge established tastes and values. The Canada Council here is simply reconfirming what our government feels is politically correct.

Similarly, government funding, as practised by the Canada Council, simply because it is *one* Council, inevitably leads to a uniformity of cultural choices which everyone must agree is detrimental to the creative process. It is far better to have a multiplicity of funding sources. Patron "A" may be eccentric in his choice of art but his or her eccentricities are cancelled out by the eccentricities of hundreds of other patrons. It is only from this variety of tastes that true art or culture can emerge. There are still many in the federal government who feel that private sector funding is somehow corrupting and that government should be the exclusive funder of the arts. The truth of the matter is that private sector donors are far less subject fo political pressures than governments.

What, therefore, is the answer? I have said earlier that our preoccupation with our identity, particularly our insecurity relative to the United States, is self-defeating, perhaps even soul destroying. It prevents a healthy, robust culture from ever developing at all. I believe that we should not try to define ourselves; we should simply let it happen. We are very different people living in this country. The fact that we are different does not make any of us less Canadian. It is not the government or the CBC that gives us our identity. The government should be a reflection of what we are, not someone who tells us who we should be.

What then do we have in common? For 200 years now the northern half of this continent has decided to live separately from our neighbour to the south. Why did we do it? Our history tells us why, which leads me to ask, why in the interests of political correctness have we stopped teaching our history in Canadian schools? But that is another story. Our history would show that Canada is not the product of a revolution against authority as was the United States, but is the product of the counter-revolution. We are the product, not of a proclamation of a set of principles or a way of life, but are the product of a pragmatic, evolutionary process which perhaps resists ringing declarations such as an "American" or a "Canadian" way of life. Perhaps because of the evolutionary nature of our development, our culture or identity is therefore incapable of being defined. Nor should it be defined. For in spite of our differences we have created a nation on the north half of this continent, sprung from ancient traditions, nourished and enriched by the countless millions who came to these shores to join their destiny with ours.

We do not need the government to tell us who we are or what we should be. Culture and artistic expression, however you define it, must come from within; it cannot be imposed.

Government funding of the arts should be limited to art in its truest sense. I again quote the Oxford Dictionary, "a refined understanding of the arts and other human intellectual achievement." We do this through the support of our schools, universities and other cultural institutions.

I said earlier that we have been told that we are a kinder and more generous people, particularly when compared with the United States. That statement only rings true if we talk about government programs. If we measure the words "kind" and "generous" in terms of volunteerism or charitable giving, the facts show otherwise. Volunteerism as measured by the number of volunteers relative to population is three times greater in the United States than in Canada. Charitable giving, according to the house of Commons Finance Committee, is also three times as great in the U.S. relative to personal incomes.

Why then do we seem to be less generous? It is not because on a personal level we care less, but simply because in Canada our government leaders have told us they would do more and therefore as individuals we need to do less. We therefore have a system of medicare, hospital and unemployment insurance, government grants to arts, culture and public broadcasting which are much greater here than in the United States. Whether these should be carried out by the government or whether the private sector should play an increased role can be a matter of debate. However, there is no question that there is a correlation between government support and lack of private sector support ...

6. Peter Herndorf, "Massey Commission at 50: The State of the Arts," *Canadian Speeches: Issues of the Day* 15, 6 (January-February 2002).

... Instead, on this 50th anniversary year of the Massey-Levesque Report—a report that's often been described as the Magna Carta of Canadian cultural life— I want to talk about the remarkable impact that Canadian artists are having on the world around them.

Let me start by telling you a little about the Massey-Levesque Report— and the Canadian cultural revolution that it spawned.

The Massey-Levesque Report was a Royal Commission initiated by Prime Minister Louis St. Laurent in 1949, and the members of the Royal Commission— led by Vincent Massey—conducted the broadest investigation of the state of the arts, letters and sciences in Canada ever done. They held 114 public meetings throughout Canada, and more than 1,200 witnesses appeared.

Their report was published in 1951, and the reverberations are still being felt. The report described a litany of problems facing the arts in Canada in the post war period—artists couldn't earn a decent living in Canada, they argued. The country relied almost entirely on touring foreign companies for performing arts productions. And few books were being published in Canada.

They challenged conventional wisdom even more fundamentally when at the beginning of the "cold war," they questioned the purpose of elaborate national defence strategies—if, as a nation, we weren't clear about the values that we were defending.

Their prescription was also far reaching. They argued that Canadian culture played a critically important role in our nation building, and that the federal government had a clear obligation to nourish Canada's intellectual and cultural life. Let me quote a paragraph from the report that is typical in its directness:

"The second essential is money. If we in Canada are to have a more plentiful and better cultural fare, we must pay for it. Good-will alone can do little for a starving plant; if the cultural life of Canada is anemic, it must be nourished, and this will cost money."

Most of that money, they suggested, should come from the three levels of government.

The report went on to make a powerful and persuasive case for the creation of a national "arms length" funding agency for the arts, a recommendation which led almost immediately to the establishment of the Canada Council. The report argued for the creation of a National Library; it supported the launch of CBC Television—which occurred the following year; and without question, Vincent Massey and his colleagues provided the cultural framework that led to the emergence of several generations of gifted, innovative and fiercely independent Canadian artists.

Today—50 years later—we're in an enviable position. There's more artistic talent—and more creativity—in this country than at any time in our history.

Our artists have the skill, the imagination and the commitment to create powerful and original work, and they have the drive and energy to compete with the very best in the world.

Our artists are arguably Canada's most important "export" product—and they symbolize Canada for much of the world.

When you go on your next international trip, ask the people you meet what they know about Canada. People in Europe, in Asia or in South America will probably tell you that they've never heard of most of our politicians, our business leaders, or even our hockey players. But I suspect that they'll tell you that the individuals who really define Canada for them are almost always our artists—artists from a wide range of disciplines.

Take literature for example. For years, Alistair MacLeod's stunning short stories have been Canada's best kept secret. But since his first novel "No Great Mischief" won the International Impac Dublin Literary Award—the world's richest literary prize—he's a huge star. He joins such other internationally acclaimed Canadian writers as Margaret Atwood, who won last year's Booker Prize for "The Blind Assassin;" Michael Ondaatje, who became a literary cult figure after "The English Patient;" and Carol Shields, who continues to delight readers around the globe.

And just last Wednesday, the *New York Times* devoted a significant part of its arts section to exploring the narrative landscape of three wonderful Canadian writers—Richard Wright, Dennis Bock and Jane Urquhart. It was a clear sign of how much "can lit" has become an international household word.

What about theatre? Director Robert Lepage regularly stages new productions around the globe. Stratford and Shaw continue to set the standard for the classics in North America. And Cirque du Soleil has created a new theatrical art form, by completely reworking our ideas about circus. They started out performing acrobatics in communities across Quebec and Ontario. Now you can take in their multi media shows when you go to Las Vegas, Disney World, or the Far East.

Last week, the NAC's Denis Marleau opened his new play in Paris to rave reviews in Le Figaro, and Louise Pitre is generating the same kind of notices in the smash Broadway hit Mamma Mia.

And in Music? Well Diana Krall is the best known jazz singer in the world. Shania Twain and Terry Clark have cornered the market in country music. Sara McLachlan and Alanis Morissette have done the same in alternative rock.

And in most parts of the world, people line up for blocks to see a Robert Carsen opera, to attend a Ben Heppner performance, or to hear a Céline Dion, Leonard Cohen or Oscar Peterson concert. And Americans are just beginning to discover the blandishments of The Barenaked Ladies.

Take our filmmakers. For years, we've been making a splash at the Cannes Film Festival for our creativity and innovation. David Cronenberg did it with his unique brand of the cerebral and the quirky—in movies like "Crash" and "The Fly." Atom Egoyan was the next to make an impact at Cannes with his evocative and idiosyncratic films like the "Sweet Hereafter" and "Felicia's Journey." And this year, Inuit filmmaker, Zacharias Kunuk, won the best first film award at Cannes for "The Fast Runner," shot with a cast of Inuit people on Baffin Island.

What about comedy? I only have to mention one name to get a debate going between the generations—Tom Green. Love him or hate him, but you have to admit that his madcap energy and creativity is having an impact on the world of comedy. How about some of the others—Jim Carey, Martin Short, Dan Ackroyd—Lorne Michaels and his wonderful group of Canadian writers from Saturday Night Live. The cast of Twenty-two Minutes and the Royal Canadian Air Farce. And of course, Mike Myers. We can only guess at how many people around the world continue to regale their friends with their best Austin Powers imitations.

If we had a little more time, I'd love to talk about some of our other arts disciplines. We have great dance companies like the National Ballet and Marie Chouinard in Montreal—and despite their current financial difficulties, we have superb orchestras and composers. We're fortunate to have both the Canadian Opera Company and Tapestry in this city, each of them bringing originality and great professionalism to the stage. We have exceptional visual artists, and a number of internationally acclaimed galleries and museums across the country.

We've also produced some of the great cultural impresarios in North America: Moses Znaimer, who's completely redefined the concept of local television over the past 20 years; Mark Starowicz of the CBC, who instinctively understood that millions of Canadians would watch hours of television about Canadian history; Garth Drabinsky, who's brought such passion and showmanship to the theatre; Robert Lantos, who makes films that matter—and make money; and David Mirvish, who proves year in, year out that Canadian commercial theatre can be both successful and adventurous.

My point in all of this is that we live in an amazing time for creativity in Canada, and all of us should be very proud of that.

The artists, and the arts organizations that I've mentioned all have several important characteristics in common. They had the audacity to dream big dreams. They've had the courage to pursue those dreams. And they've had the tenacity to keep going until those dreams came true.

I should really end my remarks on that note of triumph. A kind of David and Goliath story, with Canada winning in the end.

But it's not an accurate picture, and I have to conclude with one significant caveat. The arts in Canada may have been a great success story over the past 50 years, but in the difficult and uncertain days ahead, we need your help more than ever.

We need a clear signal from all levels of government across the country that, even in tough times, they recognize the importance of the arts, and the benefits of a strong and vibrant Canadian culture.

Even in tough times, we need ongoing government support for our key arts organizations, and for our most promising young artists.

And even if the TSE isn't performing very well these days, we need increased levels of philanthropic support for the arts from the individuals and corporations that flourished in Canada over the past decade. We need, as well, a willingness on the part of federal tax officials to make increased charitable contributions more attractive to the donor or, at the very least, as attractive as it is in the United States.

Despite the concerns about the economic downturn, we need your support as patrons in concert halls, theatres, galleries, museums and bookstores. The arts community, in turn, will promise to "make it worth your while."

And most of all, we need you to take a real sense of pride in the extraordinary achievements of our artists. They symbolize, in many ways, the changing character of this country—more dynamic, more adventurous, and more of a player on the international stage.

They deserve your admiration—and they deserve your enthusiastic support.

Readings

Atwood, M. "Blind Faith and Free Trade," in R. Nader, ed. *The Case Against Free Trade: GATT, NAFTA and the Globalization of Corporate Power.* San Francisco: Earth Island Press, 1993.

Audley, P. "Cultural Industries Policy: Objectives, Formulation and Evaluation," *Canadian Journal of Communication* 19 (1994).

Ayers, J. "From National to Popular Soverignty? The Evolving Globalization of Protest Activity in Canada," *International Journal of Canadian Studies* 16 (Fall 1997).

Barlow, M. *Parcel of Rogues: How Free Trade is Killing Canada.* Toronto: Key Porter, 1990.

Barry, D., ed. *Toward a North American Community: Canada, the United States and Mexico.* Boulder: Westview, 1995.

Bowker, M. *On Guard for Thee.* Ottawa: Voyageur, 1988.

Bradfield, M. *The Free Trade Claims: Smoke and Mirrors.* Ottawa: Canadian Centre for Policy Alternatives, 1988.

Campbell, K. "Why We Must Protect Canadian Culture from the US Juggernaut," *Canadian Speeches: Issues of the Day* (March 1997).

Carr, G. *Trade Liberalization and the Political Economy of Culture: An International Perspective on FTA.* Orono: University of Maine, 1991.

Clarke, M. *Restoring the Balance: Why Canada should reject the North American Free Trade Agreement.* Ottawa: Council of Canadians, 1993.

Clarkson, S. *Canada and the Regan Challenge: Crisis and Adjustment.* Toronto: J. Lorimer, 1985.

Clarkson, S. *Uncle Sam and Us: Globalization, Neoconservatism and the Canadian State.* Toronto: University of Toronto Press, 2002.

Cohen, M. *Free Trade and the Future of Women's Work: Manufacturing and Service Industries.* Toronto: Garamond, 1987.

Crean, S. *Who's Afraid of Canadian Culture?* Don Mills: General, 1976.

Crispo, J., ed. *Free Trade: The Real Story.* Toronto: Gage, 1988.

Doern, B. and B. Tomlin. *Faith and Fear: The Free Trade Story.* Toronto: Stoddart, 1991.

Doran, C. and A. Drishler eds. *A New North America: Cooperation and Enhanced Interdependence.* Westport: Praeger, 1996.

Eggleton, A. "Our Culture Too Must Compete in the Global Marketplace," *Canadian Speeches: Issues of the Day* (March 1997).

Flaherty, D., ed. *Southern Exposure: Canadian Perspectives on the United States.* Toronto: McGraw-Hill Ryerson, 1986.

Flaherty, G. and F. Manning, eds. *The Beaver Bites Back: American Popular Culture in Canada.* Kingston and Montreal: McGill-Queen's University Press, 1993.

Fox, A. *Settling U.S.-Canada Disputes: Lessons for NAFTA.* Orono: University of Maine, 1992.

Gold, M. and D. Leyton-Brown, eds. *Trade-Offs on Free Trade: The Canada-United States Free Trade Agreement.* Toronto: Carswell, 1988.

Granatstein, J. *Yankee Go Home: Canadians and Anti-Americanism.* New York: Harper Collins, 1996.

Hart, M. et al. *Decision at Midnight: Inside the Canada-US Free Trade Negotiations.* Vancouver: University of British Columbia Press, 1994.

Hurtig, M. *The Betrayal of Canada.* Toronto: Stoddart, 1991.

Hutcheson, J. "Culture and Free Trade," in M. Hendersen ed. *The Future on the Table: Canada and the Free Trade Issue.* Toronto: Masterpress, 1987.

Lapierre, L., ed. *If You Love This Country.* Toronto: McClelland and Stewart, 1987.

Lipsey, R. *The Free Trade Deal: Shall we forsake the bird in the hand?* Toronto: C.D. Howe Institute, 1988.

Litt, P. "The Massey Commission, Americanization and Canadian Cultural Nationalism," *Queen's Quarterly* 98, 2 (1992).

Litvak, I. and C. Maule. *Cultural Sovereignty: The 'Time' and 'Reader's Digest' Case in Canada.* New York: Praeger, 1974.

Mahant, E. *Free Trade in American-Canadian Relations.* Melbourne: Krieger, 1993.

Mahant, E. and G. Mount. *Invisible and Inaudible in Washington: American Policies Toward Canada.* Vancouver: University of British Columbia Press, 1999.

McArthur, J. *The Selling of 'Free Trade': NAFTA, Washington and the Subversion of American Democracy.* New York: Hill and Wang, 2000.

Merrett, C. *Free Trade: Neither Free nor About Trade.* Montreal: Black Rose, 1996.

Mulcahy, K. "Cultural Imperialism and Cultural Sovereignty: US-Canadian Cultural Relations," *American Review of Canadian Studies* 30, 2 (Summer 2000).

Murray, J., ed. *Canadian Cultural Nationalism.* New York: Council of Foreign Relations, 1977.

Radebaugh, L. and E. Fry, eds. *Canada/US Free Trade Agreement.* Provo: Brigham Young University, 1986.

Randall, S. and H. Konrad, eds. *NAFTA in Transition.* Calgary: University of Calgary Press, 1995.

Schwartz, M. "NAFTA and the Fragmentation of Canada," *The American Review of Canadian Studies* (Spring and Summer 1998).

Smith, A. "Canadian Culture, the Canadian State and the Management of the New Continentalism," *Canadian-American Public Policy* 3 (October 1990).

Smith, G. and F. Stone, eds. *Assessing the Canada-US Free Trade Agreement.* Halifax: Institute for Research on Public Policy, 1987.

Spry, I. "Canadian Culture: Past and Future," in Ian Parker and P. Craley, eds. *The Strategy of Canadian Culture in the 21st Century.* Toronto: TopCat Communications, 1988.

Thompson, J. "Canada's Quest of 'Cultural Sovereignty': Protection, Promotion and Popular Culture," in H. Holmes and D. Taras, eds. *Seeing Ourselves: Media Power and Policy in Canada.* Toronto: Harcourt Brace, 1992.

Watson, W. *Globalization and the Meaning of Canadian Life.* Toronto: University of Toronto Press, 1998.

Chapter Eighteen

"A Cherished Reputation":
Peacekeeping

1. Barbara McDougall, "Peacekeeping, Peacemaking and Peacebuilding": Statement to the House of Commons Standing Committee on External Affairs and International Trade, Ottawa, February 17, 1993.
2. Unnamed Canadian soldier, "To Jane Snailham," Sirac Croatia, April 29, 1992.
3. Unnamed Canadian soldier, "To Jane Snailham," Daruvar Croatia, July 28, 1993.
4. Unnamed Canadian Lieutenant Colonel commanding the 12 RBC assigned to the Canadian contingent of UNPROFOR, "To Jane Snailham," Visoko, Bosnia-Herzegovina, February 12, 1994.
5. Unnamed Canadian Warrant Officer serving with Canadian contingent to UNAMIR, "To Jane Snailham," somewhere in Rwanda, December 21, 1995.
6. Richard Sanders, "Canada's Peacekeeping Myth," The Canadian Centres for Teaching Peace, 1998.
7. Peter Topolewski, "Canadian Soldiers Die For the UN," *Laissez Faire City Times*, 3, 33, August 23, 1999.

Introduction

Few images warm the collective Canadian heart more than the blue-helmeted soldiers with Canadian flags on their sleeves leaping into the world's hotspots, politely separating the warriors and shepherding the women and children to safety. Though much divides the country, Canada-as-peacekeeper rallies Canadians in a bond of justified pride that statistically transcends political, regional or ethnic affiliation. The idea makes us feel important: we may be unable to fix our own internal problems, but we can solve the world's. The 100,000 Canadian men and women soldiers who have served in virtually every United Nations peacekeeping operation since 1949, some 30 in total and more than any other nation, have brought comfort to thousands. Though some operations failed in their objectives, and though over one hundred Canadian peacekeepers have died for their efforts (not counting the 516 Canadians who died in the Korean War, which some refer to as a "police action"), polls consistently show popular support for peacekeeping. It has gained a mythology that may transcend reality—and may mask less noble aspects of Canada's international military role.

Peacekeeping did not officially emerge until the creation of the United Nations, in which Canada played a significant role. Canada's first peacekeeping role was neither well planned nor well executed. Mediating the rift over Kashmir between India and Pakistan in 1949 a handful of Canadian soldiers, under UN auspices, acted as observers. It was, however, Suez in 1956 that inextricably linked Canada to peacekeeping, both to its own eyes and to those of the world. The Suez operation also began inauspiciously when Minister of External Affairs Lester "Mike" Pearson proposed that British and French troops, who had just invaded Egypt, be converted into international policemen. Egypt's president Nasser naturally refused. From that emerged Pearson's alternative plan—for which he later won the Nobel Peace Prize—for creating an international United Nations force that would wedge itself between the combatants, while politicians brokered a resolution. Nasser agreed, but without Canadian troops, their "neutrality" compromised by the Union Jack on Canada's flag and its British uniforms. Nasser eventually, and grudgingly, acceded to Canada playing a minor communications role in the operation.

Despite initial internal reservations, something about the role fired the public imagination, and just three years later, when Prime Minister John Diefenbaker refused to send Canadian peacekeepers to the Congo, public outrage forced him to reconsider. Next it was off to Cyprus in 1964, a mission that lasted thirty years. The federal government elevated peacekeeping to top priority for the Department of Defence in 1964. But the scope of peacekeeping was not particularly ambitious in its first three decades. There was little talk of humanitarianism, international justice, or even of maintaining peace after violence ceased. Instead, Canada and other peacekeepers simply encouraged the pre-conflict *status quo*. Disputes such as civil wars were also initially off limits to peacekeepers because the United Nations mandate did not allow meddling in a nation's internal affairs. Thus two key reasons for the relative success of the earlier missions were the limited mandates of the peacekeeping forces, and the fact that most conflicts erupted along clearly delineated borders between sovereign nations. This kept missions straightforward and mandates unambiguous.

Peacekeeping also created a strong sense of national unity and identity in Canada itself. Canadians found comfort in their heroic peacekeepers when domestically they struggled with mundane problems like inflation, unemployment, and national discord. A high peacekeeping profile also let Canada believe that it upheld its international obligations, despite simultaneously cutting defence spending and reneging on obligations to organizations like the North Atlantic Treaty Organization. Furthermore, peacekeeping generated enormous international prestige, partly because the operations occurred under United Nations mandate, thereby creating distance between Canada and the United States— which suited the Canadian public especially during the Vietnam War. Finally, peacekeeping diverted attention from the fact that Canada was, and remains, one of the world's leading producers and exporters of military equipment.

Canadian peacekeeping efforts changed in the late 1980s. Reasonably clear-cut UN missions suddenly became murky and deadly in Yugoslavia, Somalia, Rwanda, and parts of the Middle East and Southeast Asia. To make matters worse, the new flashpoints ignored recognized national borders, often involved far more than two combatants, and erupted with unimaginable violence. Civilians, too, became more involved, often with unprecedented levels of barbarism. Finally, the combatants frequently no longer wanted or respected the peacekeepers' presence—or worse, used them as leverage for their own ends. All this, of course, made peacekeeping very difficult and dangerous.

Canada's position on peacekeeping had to change. In 1991 Minister of External Affairs, Barbara McDougall, stated "the concept of sovereignty must respect higher principles, including the need to preserve human life from wanton destruction." This called for a dramatic shift from traditionally passive peacekeeping to aggressive peacemaking—and it could involve interfering in the internal affairs of a sovereign state. Canada suggested a peacekeeping force for Yugoslavia, the first nation to do so, fully aware that Canadian forces would have to create peace against the will of zealous and nihilistic combatants. Some 1,200 Canadians arrived in the former Yugoslavia in March 1992, their mandate to make peace as members of the UN force (UNPROFOR). The mission indeed proved as deadly as feared, and a number of international peacekeepers lost their lives. There were other problems, the major one being the lack of a clear mandate in a fluid war zone where rules of engagement and conduct simply ceased to exist. Despite enormous adversity, peril, frustration, and some tragic failures—particularly in Bosnia, UN peacekeepers undoubtedly saved countless lives, but at a cost.

The Canadian public initially reacted positively to this new shift. Strange bedfellows like the NDP and Reform (now the Alliance) parties abandoned their traditional reticence and, if anything, called for greater peacekeeping action with even stronger force. Then when Canadians perceived how aggressive and dangerous peacekeeping really was, they became very skittish. The United Nations, after all, created 14 new peacekeeping missions between 1988 and 1993, as many as over the previous four decades, and Canada participated in them all. Not only that, Canadian peacekeepers now died, or were injured, or captured and abused. And peacekeeping was very expensive at a time when the Canadian government teetered on insolvency.

Jean Chretien's Minister of Finance, Paul Martin, gutted defence spending from $12.83 billion in 1992 to $10.5 billion by 1995—while the government simultaneously increased the country's peacekeeping obligations from $12 million in 1992 to $130 by 1994. Canadian forces became so stretched by cutbacks and mounting international obligations that some doubted their ability to contend with potential domestic problems.

Two further events forced Canada to rethink its international role. On March 16, 1993 a group of Canadian Airborne soldiers, sent to Somalia, caught and tortured to death Somali Shidane Arone. At least a dozen other Canadian soldiers witnessed the event and did nothing as the teenaged thief died repeating the only English words he knew: "Canada," "Canada," "Canada." The trophy-photograph of grinning trooper Kyle Brown holding Arone's bloody body rocked the country and burst the myth of the noble Canadian peacekeeper. Some mused on the apparent contradiction of sending trained killers, which soldiers are, to make peace.

Then came Rwanda where the international community's selective impotence in the face of savagery became crystal clear. Canadian Major-General Romeo Dallaire arrived early in the conflict with his peacekeepers, but quickly realized that he could not fulfil his mandate with the very limited resources the UN sent him. Meanwhile, the situation in the tiny African country worsened. Ten Belgian UN peacekeepers were killed and the UN, rather than reinforce its forces, panicked and evacuated 2,050 of Dallaire's 2,500 soldiers. Dallaire, in fury, warned the UN and Canada in January 1994 that he needed at least 5,000 peacekeepers to avert genocide. His bosses demurred and Dallaire witnessed approximately 800,000 men, women and children butchered, mostly by Hutu tribesmen. A humiliated world looked away and muttered about the impossibility of peacekeeping in the new reality.

The cumulative effect of increasingly difficult peacekeeping missions, economic constraints in Canada, tarnished peacekeepers, and a realization that Canada's forces were stretched beyond endurance led to profound soul searching by Canadians on the nature of peacekeeping and Canada's role in it.

Discussion Points

1. Does Canada deserve the title "international boy scout"?
2. Have we followed a consistent international policy with respect to international conflicts?
3. American military commanders have rejected using regular soldiers as peacekeepers. Should Canada continue with peacekeeping operations or do these assignments actually work to weaken the military?
4. Explain the difference between peacekeeping and peacemaking.
5. In an era of fiscal restraint when we can't defend our own soil or even air-lift our heavy military equipment, should we continue to act as peacekeepers elsewhere? Is peacekeeping still something "we can't afford not to become involved with"?

Documents

1. Barbara McDougall, "Peacekeeping, Peacemaking and Peacebuilding": Statement to the House of Commons Standing Committee on External Affairs and International Trade, Ottawa, February 17, 1993.

Canadians are the most experienced peacekeepers in the world. Since the first United Nations peacekeeping forces were sent out 45 years ago, our forces have always been in demand. Ten percent of all peacekeepers now on duty in the world are Canadian. Canadians have always seen peacekeeping as a reflection of Canadian values, as a way of promoting our international objectives—peace and security, respect for human rights and democratic freedoms, and a say in decisions that shape the world.

The specific challenges that face us, however, have changed dramatically in the last five years. The end of the global Cold War has been followed by outbreaks of conflicts in many parts of the world. These conflicts are very different one from the other—just compare the situations in Somalia and the former Yugoslavia, for example—and the range of diplomatic and military tools needed to deal with them has correspondingly expanded.

At the same time, the sheer volume of demand for international crisis management is now overwhelming. More such UN operations have been authorized in the last five years than in the previous forty. Partially as a way of sharing the burden, more and more regional organizations have also become involved such as the Organization of American States (OAS) in Haiti, the Commonwealth in South Africa, or the Conference on Security and Cooperation in Europe (CSCE), the European Community (EC), and the North Atlantic Treaty Organization (NATO) in former Yugoslavia. There are many situations where traditional peacekeeping, based on the consent of all parties, will not lead to a resolution of the conflict. We are faced with situations where the consent of all parties cannot be obtained, or where effective authority does not in fact exist. The use of force has had to be considered more often, as other measures have failed.

If you work closely with the UN, you cannot fail to observe the extreme pressure on the crisis management system, which has built up since its creation.

This system threatens to become seriously overloaded, not just in terms of the management of all these crises, but also in terms of the personnel and financial resources needed to deal with them on the ground. The UN budget for peacekeeping operations jumped from $700 million in 1991 to $2.8 billion in 1992. Associated financial and personnel costs have begun to stretch the resources of even major powers.

It is against this background that I would like to focus on six instruments for crisis management. These derive from the Agenda for Peace issued last summer by UN Secretary General Boutros-Ghali. Taken together, they reflect a spectrum of ways to handle potential or actual conflict situations.

At one end of the spectrum, we find preventive diplomacy: the attempt to head off the outbreak of hostilities by dealing with the underlying problems. It includes such measures as early-warning mechanisms to ensure that potential conflicts can be anticipated, perhaps in time to head them off; fact-finding missions and monitoring; confidence-building measures, such as mutual military inspections; warnings to potential combatants; sponsorship of consultations; and offers to mediate.

Canada is already active in this area. In the former Yugoslavia, Canadians have taken part in a wide range of initiatives, including the EC-led CSCE monitoring mission, the Canadian-led CSCE fact-finding mission last June on the military situation in Kosovo and subsequent CSCE conflict-prevention missions in other parts of the former Yugoslavia. Canada also provided logistical and expert support to the fact-finding mission of the CSCE chairman-in-office to Nagorno-Karabakh, and will shortly be participating in the CSCE mission to Estonia. This is intended to stabilize relations between the Estonian majority and the large Russian minority in Estonia.

A related option in the crisis management spectrum is preventive deployment or preventive peacekeeping. This involves the deployment of peacekeeping forces before hostilities break out for purposes such as the separation of forces, the observation of frontiers and the creation of demilitarized zones.

A recent example is the UN decision to send such a force to the former Yugoslav republic of Macedonia. Canadians in the UN Protection Force II (UNPROFOR) were asked to establish this operation pending the arrival of a Scandinavian force.

Next is peacemaking following the outbreak of conflict. This can include, for example, large-scale international peace negotiations like the ones in Cambodia, which resulted in the Paris accords of 1991. In this process, Canada chaired the key First Committee on Peacekeeping. Another example would be the International Conference on Former Yugoslavia, co-chaired by the UN and the EC, in which Canada participated.

Also included under peacemaking are indirect means of exerting pressure on recalcitrant parties, without actually engaging in military action. One well-known method is, of course, sanctions and embargoes. Canada has participated in the naval embargo on Iraq and supplied a ship last year to the Adriatic sanctions monitoring fleet organized by NATO. A Revenue Canada customs officer leads the mission in the former Yugoslav republic of Macedonia, which is helping to implement sanctions on Serbia. Let me draw your attention to another such form of pressure: the establishment of an international court or tribunal for the consideration of criminal charges under international humanitarian law. Canada urged that this be set up to hear charges arising out of the situation in the former Yugoslavia. A team of war crimes investigators and a leading legal expert have been provided to the UN Commission of Experts that is compiling and analysing the evidence of atrocities.

Peacekeeping, as generally understood, occurs in an environment where the parties to a dispute agree to a cessation of hostilities. This has been the case in Cyprus, the Golan Heights, and the first UNPROFOR operation in Croatia. Peacekeeping has evolved to incorporate objectives over and above supervising a cease-fire. In the case of Somalia, for instance, the initial goal was the protection of humanitarian assistance under conditions of on-going conflict. In El Salvador, in Central America, the peacekeeping mission was essentially political and human-rights related. There were at times more civilians and police officers in place than military. In Namibia, from 1989 to 1990, operations involved overseeing the creation of a new state and, in Cambodia, essentially managing the country while competing factions shift from military to political competition.

We currently have 4,700 men and women with UN operations, plus RCMP and civilian personnel.

Should peacemaking or peacekeeping fail, the fifth option is peace enforcement. Enforcement has been sanctioned by the UN under Chapter VII of the Charter only as a last resort—Korea, the Congo, the Gulf War, and Somalia being the main examples so far. Canada has taken part in these UN enforcement actions; our largest current contingent is in Somalia, where we have 1,300 military personnel. The main emphasis in Somalia, as in many enforcement actions, has been to establish a secure environment in which civil peace can be restored and humanitarian relief operations carried out. Enforcement has also been discussed in the case of former Yugoslavia. However, the situation there is radically different from that in Somalia and it is widely recognized (most recently by the new U.S. Administration) that imposing a political settlement by military force is unlikely to achieve a viable long-term solution.

Finally, the UN Agenda for Peace raises the concept of peacebuilding. It is not always enough simply to end a conflict, whether by peacemaking, peacekeeping, or peace enforcement. The society in question must often be assisted to heal itself and rebuild, whether in political, social, or economic terms. Some aspects are military, such as helping local armed forces to reshape for democratic conditions or clearing mines, which Canada is doing in Cambodia and the Iraq-Kuwait border area.

More dramatic examples of peacebuilding involve long-term nation building as envisaged by the UN in Namibia and Cambodia, or in its original plan for Somalia. I am speaking here of measures that run the gamut from refugee relief to resettlement operations and from free elections to restoration of civil administration. Peace does not automatically continue once the troops leave, but it can be maintained if there is an opportunity for a better life. The idea that international security has roots in development and democracy has, of course, long been part of Canadian policy.

Each of these options involves a different basic approach, different strengths and constraints, and different types and levels of resource commitment. Clarity of objective is fundamental. When we are contemplating action to handle a current or potential conflict, it is important to know whether we are sending troops for preventive deployment, peacekeeping, or peace enforcement. Each involves different risks and costs, training, equipment, and rules of engagement.

This being said, real life is not political science. Realities on the ground rarely lend themselves to definitions as clear as the six foregoing options. Conditions in Bosnia, for example, have never been those of a classic peacekeeping operation and yet Canada is participating because the reality of human suffering is so compelling. As well, situations evolve. Somalia (like the Congo) began as a peacekeeping operation and moved to enforcement when that was judged necessary by the UN Security Council.

Experience has made it clear that one kind of action used in isolation may well lead to partial, short-term, or ineffective conclusions. Canada has been peacekeeping in Cyprus for almost 30 years, without a political solution coming noticeably closer: peacekeeping has become a permanent fixture there rather than the means to an end. This is one reason for Canada's announcement that it would no longer contribute forces to this operation. Peacekeeping is not an end in itself.

The international community is seeking new approaches to crisis management. We have at our disposal a full range of potential actions, but we need to apply them more coherently. Better early-warning mechanisms, triggering earlier international responses, should be a priority. In this context, we are addressing how Canada can best support and contribute to international efforts to prevent or resolve conflicts. For example: Are there ways in which we can help the international community to improve its early-warning capabilities? What are the most effective Canadian contributions? Should we be concentrating, for example, on military tasks or on civilian activities? Can we better assist the UN in efforts to strengthen its own crisis management capabilities?

These are not theoretical questions. Our answers will affect the futures of men, women, and children around the world. Also, we must ensure that Canada's limited resources—political, diplomatic, civilian, and military—are used in the most effective way possible.

2. Unnamed Canadian soldier, "To Jane Snailham," Sirac Croatia, April 29, 1992.

Dear Jane,

First of all, thank you very much for sending the card and letter of support, you have no idea what it means to a soldier whose mind is being tested every moment. I guess it is only polite to tell you who I am and a little of my background. I was born in a small town in Nova Scotia and finished high school with no future to look forward to. I spent six years in the Militia [in the infantry] then joined the regular force in 1985. My first posting was Winnipeg for three years, then off to Germany in 1988 for a five-year tour. I have obtained the rank of master-corporal and have been on many courses dealing with the infantry. I have seen every province in Canada and been in many countries around the world. And I can assure you that Canada comes out on top. I am married to a wife who goes through everything I do and supports me in whatever I do. I also have been blessed with two boys who were born in Germany [and] who I would die for at the blink of an eye.

As I write, the sun is going down in Croatia and I have no idea of what tomorrow brings. I have never in my life seen or witnessed the death and destruction as I have in this past month. Our company is positioned in a small town [called] Sirac, which is 10 kilometres southeast from Daruvar, which is 20 kilometres south from Zagreb. If you have a good enough map you can probably locate it. The fighting continues seven kilometres from our position. Every night the silence is broken with gunfire and artillery which lights up the sky. The people here are very grateful for the UN being here, but are sometimes confused with our purpose. Everyone from the age of 16 and up carries a gun and whatever else he or she likes to carry.

Our first night here, 232 soldiers from my company were welcomed with 14 rounds of artillery from Serbia into our position. I still have no idea how or why no one was killed. It was the first time since Korea that Canadian soldiers were shelled.

My job consists of policing the area. I have an armoured personnel carrier with one driver and radioman. Every day we go out and patrol the front lines to observe what is going on. At the present time all the UN soldiers in our area have not arrived, only the Canadians, until the remaining soldiers arrive we cannot start working towards peace. I have no idea what the news programmes are saying as I have not heard or saw any news since I left Germany. But I believe in about four months, this is only my opinion, that [the] fighting will stop in Croatia. For the rest of the remaining country, your guess is as good as mine. The men I work with are pretty well much like my brothers. The morale is very high among the soldiers and we enjoy and believe in what we are doing. My stay will only be six months but long enough to miss out on my children's progress.

We are being looked after very well, being fed and equipped with the proper weapons and protective clothing. I find it very difficult to write as I hope you understand. The land here is much like Nova Scotia with mountains only slightly higher. Every town has been destroyed and burnt. Dead animals and the remaining livestock roam the streets; the old money is blowing in the wind. It is really hard to enter a house to check for life when everything is destroyed, usually the family picture is hanging on the wall and it's hard to understand how something like this can happen. Please be very thankful that you live in a safe place. I know [Canada] is being harassed by the language issue and unemployment, but this does not even compare to a lot of places here ...

3. Unnamed Canadian soldier, "To Jane Snailham," Daruvar Croatia, July 28, 1993.

Our situation here is deteriorating, that's why most of our battalion has deployed south. Sometimes we have Croatians that do get restless and tend to get a little violent by throwing grenades at the camp or fire their weapons and there have been gang beatings when entering the town. Most of this violence comes from the young Croatians probably with nothing else to do. They no doubt see us UN soldiers as a threat. I just assume leave this country and let the Croatians and Serbs continue with what they want most and get it over with, genocide. After all, it seems that they have their heart set on it. We're just in their way. Sorry for being so negative, but I think you'd understand if you've had to live around these people. These people just don't comprehend that their little war has taken me away from my family and home.

I don't mean to be so pessimistic, but this place is starting to get to me. Not much longer before I head home so I keep reminding myself.

My UN tour here is a little hectic. Twice a week, I have a duty called a roving patrol. At all hours of night, two of us on duty have to patrol Camp Polom's three gates and also the interior of the camp. This certain duty was started due to threats and gun and mortar fire around the camp.

I live in a small trailer with another girl, and our shower and bathroom facilities are across the camp. There are approximately 30 military girls and over 1,000 guys camped here with me. Mind you, the guys are spread out around the camp in different areas. Some of the trades that the girls are in are, medical assistants, pay clerks, administrative clerks (like myself), vehicle mechanic, truck drivers, military police and cooks. There are still a lot of men here that don't believe that women should be allowed in a combat zone or wear a uniform, but if women can do the job just as good as the men, why not. The camp's kitchen and drinking mess are located in tents, like a MASH [mobile army surgical hospital] unit, and my office is in a building riddled with bullet holes. The Croatian army had control of this camp before the Canadian UN troops moved in, so most of the buildings have either been blown up or shot up. Our construction engineers teams are still making repairs around the camp. The odd time our vehicles hit anti-tank mines that have been planted in the road, there were no serious injuries ...

4. Unnamed Canadian Lieutenant Colonel commanding the 12 RBC assigned to the Canadian contingent of UNPROFOR, "To Jane Snailham," Visoko, Bosnia-Herzegovina, February 12, 1994.

... The beginning of February heralded the halfway point of our duty in Bosnia. As you can well understand, all the "horses" can now smell the barn; however, I've had to tighten the disciplinary reins in order to ensure that no one forgets where they are and the danger that lurks beyond the defensive perimeter. To this point in time, I'm satisfied that we've done everything we can to reduce the levels of misery and hardship experienced by the people. So far, we've escorted 80 humanitarian aid convoys, delivering approximately 5,050 tonnes of food and over 100,000 litres of fuel. To do this, we've had to skirt running battles between the warring factions. Unfortunately, we've had two men killed, four wounded and two trucks have been badly damaged by machine gun and artillery fire.

I very recently returned from a visit to Muslim enclave of Srebrenica in Northeast Bosnia. Notwithstanding, the marvellous job done by the 160 women and me I have stationed in that particular area, there is only so much that we can do. The living conditions of the 44,000 people trapped in the pocket are atrocious. The hills surrounding the town are a moonscape, having been totally denuded of all foliage, which is being burned to produce heat. Piles of rotting garbage picked clean by the inhabitants, are infested with rats and other vermin. There are thousands of streetwise, orphaned children, their parents having been killed in the fighting. Srebrenica has been machine gunned, bombarded and mortared back to the last century.

The last 30 kilometres of the road we use to reach Srebrenica bears witness to the full fury of the wave of hatred and ethnic cleansing which washed over the area last spring and summer. All of the 15 or so villages and hamlets which lie astride the east-west road have been totally destroyed. There are no people, no animals, no stray dogs or cats, even the birds have gone. In the fields, are low piles of dirt. One can only imagine what lies buried beneath them. These images will forever remain indelibly etched in my mind and those of my women and men ...

5. Unnamed Canadian Warrant Officer serving with Canadian contingent to UNAMIR, "To Jane Snailham," somewhere in Rwanda, December 21, 1995.

Dear Jane,

Letters and cards from all across Canada, addressed to Canadian peace-keepers in Rwanda have been flooding into our contingent mail room for the past couple of weeks. When we can find the time, soldiers have been happily responding to any which included a return address. Since I am from the Halifax area, I would like to say hello from Rwanda and take this opportunity to tell you about some of the things we do here.

I am a warrant officer and I have been in Rwanda since July. It is a very small country, being only half the size of Nova Scotia. There are a little more than 100CE personnel serving with the UN in Rwanda. UNAMIR was established in October 1993 to police a cease-fire between the Hutu and Tutsi tribes who were fighting for control of the country. UNAMIR is helping the Rwandan people rebuild their nation by assisting in national reconciliation and providing for the voluntary and safe return of refugees to their homes. The job of Canadian peacekeepers is firstly, to provide logistical support to UNAMIR, and secondly, to support humanitarian activities throughout the country, in general. ...

Last year, fighting erupted once again. This time it was genocidal in nature, and hundreds of thousands of people died over a period of a few months. It has to rank among the most socially destructive and tragic events of this generation. Men, women and children killed and were killed. Even now, a year later, the evidence of this horrific event still lingers. From the despair of genocide, UNAMIR has assisted the Rwandan people in many ways to alleviate their grim predicament. We have rebuilt and supported schools and orphanages for tens of thousands of children, helping them to deal with the trauma of war. UNAMIR has contributed to the building of extensions to prisons to ease the appallingly overcrowded conditions for those incarcerated. In Rwanda today, over 55,000 prisoners are housed in facilities designed for a maximum of 13,000. Other assistance includes training of police, provision of more advanced medical care and the restoration of national medical services, repairing of roads and bridges, restoration of telephone services and the building of refugee transit camps. These contributions have helped bring back some normalcy to a country severely disrupted by war. Not that long ago, the capital city of Kigali was dead in every sense of the word. Bodies still lay in the street, packs of dogs fattened from the corpses ruled the city, houses were destroyed and there was no electricity, water, nothing. All that seemed to remain was the stench of genocide and children abandoned by war, pathetically wandering the streets, traumatized by the death and destruction they had witnessed. Today, with UNAMIR's assistance, Kigali is essentially, a fully-functioning city. You won't see any dogs, though, since many had to be shot to prevent the spread of disease.

There are over 12,000 orphans in Rwanda. The Canadian Contingent sponsors a number of orphanages and visits them regularly, providing medical care, water supplies, repairs to electrical and plumbing problems, building playgrounds and donating medical supplies, blankets and shoes. It is important to let these children know that someone cares about them and that they have a reason to hope and believe in the future. I helped deliver some food to an orphanage, recently. The children seemed rather amused at my white skin, but were very happy to see us. Before we left, they gathered outside the orphanage and sang and danced for us. On a separate occasion, I viewed some drawings made by children from another orphanage. Sadly, many of the drawings depicted the terrible experiences endured by the littlest victims.

As we carry out our duties, we travel all around the country. There are only a few good roads, and it can take a long time to travel a short distance. When it rains, the dirt roads become very muddy and slippery, as if covered with a layer of snow and ice. There are few trees, because they have been cut down to clear land for farming and for heating. In many areas, there are buried mines, so we are careful to exercise mine awareness, wherever we go. Everybody has so far stayed safe, but some of us have been very, very lucky. Unfortunately, many Rwandans are still being hurt by these mines. These weapons do not discriminate. Men, women and children are being killed or maimed almost everyday. There is still an ongoing low-level insurgency war which can make traveling through some parts of the country somewhat entertaining on occasion. Certainly, we try to avoid moving by night wherever we are and have adopted measures to enhance our security when we do ...

Outside of Rwanda and adjacent to its borders, there are still close to two million Rwandan refugees. The vast majority refuse to accept assurances from the international community and the Rwandan government that it is safe for them to return. They continue to fear being arrested as suspected genocidaries and thrown into one of Rwanda's notoriously appalling prisons, where they could languish for months until their case is brought to trial. Another reason many will not return, is that they enjoy a better quality of life in the refugee camps than do their counterparts living in Rwanda. However, the presence of these refugees, concentrated as they are into camps close to the country's border, is causing significant environmental damage.

The UN is not well liked by some Rwandans. It is important for us to remember though, that the UN was slow to intervene when so many people were being killed here last year. Rwandans are still distrustful of us, and only grudgingly accept our presence. However, despite the frustrations and the dangers, we must now allow ourselves to turn away from the challenges we face. I become concerned when I hear some Canadians complaining about our participating in UN missions because it is too expensive, too risky, or because they don't understand why we should care about problems in Rwanda or other places like Haiti and the former Yugoslavia. I can only respond that based on my personal experiences in Rwanda and other UN missions, we can't afford not to become involved. The Blue Beret with UN badge, and the distinctive red and white Canadian flag we wear on our shoulders, symbolizes Canada's long-standing and consistently demonstrative commitment to promoting peace and stability in the world's trouble spots and to safeguarding human rights. It is what we are known for the world over, and it is what helps to define us as Canadians. Peacekeeping is among the noblest of any nation's undertakings. I hope it is something that we will never allow ourselves to forget, nor cease to find reasons to keep doing.

I would like to think that we can stop the fighting here or anyplace where the UN has its troops, but conflict can only really end when the warring sides agree to resolve their problems, peacefully. Meanwhile, we try to deter the use of deadly force by any of the sides, and work to encourage a dialogue between them that will foster peace and stability. Sometimes it can be very exasperating work. The importance of any success is often measured against the efforts applied to achieve it. Consequently, in peacekeeping, even a little progress can be perceived as monumental and tantamount to having scaled Mount Everest to reach it.

We were able to follow the great referendum debate, but our circumstances here lead many of us to wonder why we can't accommodate each other in a country as rich in resources and stable as Canada is. We are a mixed group here: men, women, French and English speaking. We work with a unity of spirit and purpose. We have to. Because failure to do so would undermine the job that we have been sent here to do, and could jeopardize the safety and well being of each other. We recently had an occasion to sing Canada's national anthem as a group. It was spontaneous, and we sang it in French (those of us who didn't know all the words just hummed along). When we finished, there were not afterthoughts, save one. Whatever language we sang in, it was no less the national anthem of our country. I'm not sure what one can infer from this, but from my perspective in this reality, our Canadian-made problems at home quickly lose that precipitous aspect that we tend to award them, especially when one starts to make the inevitable comparisons ...

6. Richard Sanders, "Canada's Peacekeeping Myth," The Canadian Centres for Teaching Peace, 1998.

The belief that Canada is a major force for global peace forms the basis of a powerful myth that is integral to our culture. This myth shapes the image that we have constructed of ourselves and moulds the way that others see us. Like all myths, it has very little basis in reality.

The symbolic gestures and diplomatic postures that our government parades in public, compose a carefully calculated mask to hide their behind-the-scenes actions. Our government makes proud statements about its restrictive arms trade guidelines while encouraging and assisting military producers to make deals that undermine international peace and security. During this, the UN Year for a Culture of Peace, Canadian peace activists will continue to challenge our national "peacemaker" myth by helping people face the truth about this country's real role as a "war maker." To do this, it is important to expose Canada's active participation in:

- the international arms trade,
- undeclared wars against Iraq, Somalia and Yugoslavia, in the 1990s,
- the provision of weapons testing ranges (air, land and sea) for use by foreign militaries,
- a military alliance that threatens to use nuclear weapons, i.e., NATO,
- the proliferation of uranium and nuclear power plants.
- International Arms Trade

Canada was the world's ninth largest arms exporter in 1997. We ranked even higher, however, in terms of our military exports to the "Third World." In that category, we ranked seventh. Data on Canada's military exports are contained in reports published by the Department of Foreign Affairs and International Trade (DFAIT), called Export of Military Goods from Canada. These reports are significantly flawed. They omit all data on military exports to the U.S., which is by far, our largest buyer. The magnitude of this flaw is evidenced by DFAIT's estimate that 80% of Canadian military exports in 1997 went to the U.S.

Toothless Guidelines

As anyone who has written to protest Canada's military exports will know, DFAIT is proud of its 'guidelines' governing military exports. These guidelines state, in part, that: "Canada closely controls the export of military goods and technology to countries that are involved in or under imminent threat of hostilities ... and whose governments have a persistent record of serious violations of the human rights of their citizens, unless it can be demonstrated that there is no reasonable risk that the goods might be used against the civilian population."

These guidelines are worse than toothless, they are essentially meaningless. They do not state that Canadian companies cannot sell military equipment to governments engaged in war, or that might be used against civilians. They merely state that such sales will be "closely controlled." In the bureaucratic, through-the-looking-glass world of government bureaucracies, "closely controlled" can actually refer to concerted efforts to assist corporations in their relentless drive to increase military exports (as long as that increase is "closely controlled"). DFAIT's most recently published policy document on aerospace and defence sector exports, states that: "China, Japan, India, South Korea, Taiwan and the Philippines offer potential for Canadian defence products ... Australia offers important opportunities for defence ... in addition to good prospects for the development of strategic alliances aimed at penetrating markets in Southeast Asia ... Countries such as Chile, Argentina, Mexico and Peru represent emerging markets that require strategic positioning by Canada and Canadian A&D [i.e., "aerospace and defence" (sic)] firms, especially in terms of follow-up to the success of Canadian participation at FIDAE '96 [Latin America's largest arms bazaar!]. The Middle East remains an important market, particularly for defence-security firms ... The region accounts for more than 40% of all defence-product transfers and is expected to absorb over $150 billion by the year 2000. Saudi Arabia is expected to purchase $32 billion worth of military equipment and other targets include the United Arab Emirates and Kuwait."

Aiding and Abetting Wars

During the 1990s, Canada exported military equipment to several governments engaged in war. Chief among these was, of course, the U.S. that has always been Canada's largest purchaser of military equipment. Even during the worst excesses of the 1960s—during the Vietnam War, when three million people were killed in Southeast Asia—Canadian industries were assisted by our government in ensuring a steady supply of military hardware to fuel the U.S. war machine.

The fact that the U.S. has engaged in more interventions and invasions than any other country this century has never stopped the Canadian government from actively promoting military exports to our friendly neighbour to the south. Neither have Canada's military exports been stopped because the U.S. has armed, financed, trained and equipped dozens of covert wars, organized death squads, backed military coups against elected governments, undermined and rigged elections, assassinated foreign leaders and propped up ruthless dictators who offer bargain basement, union-free factories and all-round cheap access to natural resources.

In 1991, the U.S. led the devastating war against Iraq, and with the support of Canada and the UN, has lead the economic blockade which has killed almost two million people! Canada also supplied military hardware to many of the other "coalition forces" which participated in that war. In 1998, the U.S. overtly bombed Afghanistan, Iraq and Sudan.

One might reasonably expect that the U.S. government's standing as the world's rogue superpower and its unbridled thirst for starting wars and backing military dictatorships, should mean that it would be subject to more arms export restrictions than other, less violent governments. Unfortunately, as usual, the opposite is true. Our government has never placed any restrictions on military exports to the U.S. In fact, there is only one country for which Canadian companies have never been required to obtain military export permits from our government. That country is, of course, the U.S.

In the 1990s, DFAIT permitted military exports to at least 17 governments that engaged in wars during the late 1990s. These mostly internal wars, which SIPRI and the Center for Defense Information called "major armed conflicts," were in: Algeria, Bangladesh, Cambodia, Ethiopia, India, Indonesia, Israel, Kenya, Pakistan, Peru, Philippines, Russia, Sri Lanka, Turkey, the United Kingdom, Yugoslavia and Zaire. Canada's declared military exports to these warring nations, during the 1990s, totalled just over $300 million.

Supporting Repression

One need only examine the evidence amassed here to see that Canadian corporations and the government are still very much complicit in crimes against peace, crimes against humanity and war crimes. Some of the governments purchasing Canadian military hardware are notorious for violating human rights. Many so-called "security" forces armed by Canada are well known to routinely engage in torture and extrajudicial executions. In 1998, the following countries purchased Canadian military hardware, even though torture by their military and/or police was reported that year by Amnesty International to be "widespread," "endemic," "systematic," "officially sanctioned," "frequent" or "commonplace": Argentina, Brazil, China, Egypt, Israel, Mexico, Peru, Philippines, Turkey and Venezuela. Between 1990 and 1998, the Canadian government permitted the military exports to numerous undemocratic and repressive regimes. For instance, Canada has sold arms to:

- Brunei, Qatar, Saudi Arabia and Oman: Countries which have never had any elections;
- Bahrain: Its only legislature has been dissolved by decree since 1975;
- Kuwait: Women still do not have the right to vote or stand for election;
- Algeria, Egypt, Jordan, Kenya, Mauritania, Morocco, Lebanon, Pakistan, Singapore, St. Vincent, Togo and Turkey: Women held less than 5% of the seats in parliament in 1999;
- Bahrain, China, Oman, Qatar, Saudi Arabia and the UAE: Unions, strikes and collective bargaining are strictly outlawed; and
- India, Kuwait, Lebanon, Mozambique, Oman, Pakistan, Russia, Saudi Arabia, Singapore, Sri Lanka, Tanzania and UAE: Central governments spent more on their militaries than on health and education combined.

Canada is selling military hardware to foreign police and military institutions that are well known to be regularly and systematically abusing human rights. The regimes that our government continues to prop up are guilty of the most extreme forms of civil rights violations: secret arrests, unfair trials, cruel treatment of prisoners, torture, disappearances and extrajudicial executions. Economic and social rights to education, health, housing and employment are ignored or undermined by many recipients of Canadian military exports. Canada is selling tools of war and repression to many regimes spending vast amounts on security structures to quell demonstrations and strikes by those striving for a better life. For several years, the UN has declared Canada to be the best place in the world to live. Does this privileged rank depend upon exploiting our position in an unjust global economic order? When purchasing inexpensive products from farms, mines and factories around the world, we might ask ourselves: Why are these products so cheap? Do the workers receive fair wages? Are their living and working conditions safe and healthy? Dismantling the myth of "Canada the Peacemaker," is one step toward building a culture of peace in which citizens refuse to support corporations and governments that are profiting from war and repression.

7. **Peter Topolewski, "Canadian Soldiers Die For the UN,"** *Laissez Faire City Times*, **3, 33, August 23, 1999.**

Lethal contaminants. Shredded files. Unwitting victims. Mysterious illnesses. Is it beginning to smell like a Clinton scandal around here or are these the ingredients for the latest episode of the X-Files?

Neither. These are keys in another case of the hierarchy in the Canadian Armed Forces abandoning its soldiers. And in the recent history of giving short shrift to the men and women who volunteer their lives to the whim of the Prime Minister and the minister of defense, this shrift is the shortest of them all. The lack of respect for human life that has become institutionalized in the military has evolved from years of neglect—neglect that has let the condition of the military sink to new depths ...

While the quality of Canadian troops has never slipped, and the military to this day meets Canada's NATO and UN obligations shiningly, Canada's forces offer little protection from an attack against the home turf. Canadians and interested observers openly acknowledge that the military is wholly inadequate to protect the country's people and land. It is reasonable to argue that no army in the world could capably protect Canada's huge landmass, nor any navy properly patrol the largest coastline in the world; nevertheless, since the end of the Second World War, Canada has come to maintain a force of about 60,000 regulars with less than 200 CF-18s. Upgrading a thirty-year old fleet of rescue helicopters has become a shameful embarrassment to the government—bickering over dollar signs has sent several crewmen to their deaths in antique aircraft and rendered the rescue forces virtually useless.

The penny pinching has understandably hurt morale. No wonder. Perennially low wages trap many soldiers below poverty level. In the last year national television newscasts have run stories on soldiers who are forced to visit food banks to feed their families. Two soldiers in Winnipeg, Manitoba garnered some much needed media attention for their food-drive—they promised to camp out atop a few stories high scaffold for food donations for their base. Well-wishers and supporters stopped at the foot of the scaffold and gave what they could.

That the Canadian military could come to this is hard to conceive. Yet the wonder grows greater when we see the politicians so willing to send this military on UN missions. In the early 90s Canada shipped troops to Somalia, a hell on earth so volatile and confused that a Somali prisoner sadly, but not surprisingly, was beaten and killed while held in custody by Canadian soldiers. To the hate war in Bosnia, Canadians went as unarmed gatekeepers and to stuff body bags.

Their role was much the same in Croatia, enforcing peace in a place where nothing was what it seemed—even the dirt.

The UN, Dealer of Death

Six years after Canadian troops went to work in Croatia on behalf of the UN, they are learning that they made their bunkers out of earth contaminated with PCBs and bauxite. These days scores of those who served in Croatia are sick. Some are going blind, others deteriorating at the joints. Who has stepped forward to treat them, to provide them with a pension? Not the organization (the UN) that sent them to Croatia. Actually, since the story has hit the media, the military is grudgingly offering some assistance, but this story gets much worse. In 1993 a doctor had a memo placed in the files of all soldiers who served in Croatia that year, stating that they might have been exposed to harmful substances and faced a risk of illness. Those memos were systematically removed and shredded.

With overwhelming predictability, the Ministry of Defense has convened an inquiry to determine the source and nature of possible illnesses caused by materials or events in Croatia. A separate criminal investigation into the memo shredding has also commenced. Meanwhile, Matt Stopford, a former Canadian soldier who served in Croatia, is leading the charge for compensation. Already blind in one eye and swallowing handfuls of medication a day, he's lived through six years of zero progress with his onetime employer. He claims that he's been contacted by more than 30 people just like him, and 70 others have spoken with veterans groups and another soldier who is compiling a list of sick former servicemen. Not surprisingly, Stopford says that none of the affected are contacting the military, not only because the Forces are downplaying complaints, but the soldiers don't trust the military leadership.

Maintaining the armed forces is one of the few duties the federal government should consider an obligation. Somehow the best fighting force Canada can produce in the 1990s is a bunch of soldiers who do not believe their leaders will look out for them. A defense budget that has armed soldiers with outdated equipment and left them in the poorhouse might reflect the priorities of peace-loving Canadians. Other ventures and adventures and programs are more important to the voters, you can almost hear the politicians saying. And so the obligation to maintain a national defense has instead become very much more like a luxury.

This might be how it is, but it is totally wrong. The "luxury" spending on the military comes at cost to the men and women who volunteer to offer their lives for Canada's protection. If the government cannot properly pay and supply its soldiers it cannot justify sending them on peacekeeping missions. In these circumstances the Canadian contributions to UN and NATO missions look more and more like efforts to maintain a cherished reputation in the international community. I find it hard to believe that any human could send others into such danger easily, or without the decision weighing heavy in the heart. And yet the evidence shows, at the home base and the on the peacekeeping mission, that the Canadian leadership treats Canadian soldiers as if their lives have no value. This cannot be tolerated. They must have proper supplies, whether that means more money or fewer soldiers.

Though treated like it, these soldiers are not toys.

Readings

Arbuckle, J. *The Level Killing Fields of Yugoslavia: An Observer Returns.* Clementsport: Canadian Peacekeeping Press, 1998.

Bercuson, D. *Significant Incident: Canadian Army, the Airborne and the Murder in Somalia.* Toronto: McClelland and Stewart, 1996.

Bercuson, D. and J. Granatstein. *War and Peacekeeping: From South Africa to the Gulf-Canada's Limited Wars.* Toronto: Key Porter, 1991.

Brodeur, J-P. *Violence and Racial Prejudice in the Context of Peacekeeping.* Ottawa: Queen's Printer, 1997.

Canada, *The Dilemmas of a Committed Peacekeeper: Canada and the Renewal of Peacekeeping.* Ottawa: Queen's Printer, 1993.

Cohen, L. and A. Moens. "Learning the Lessons of UNPROFOR: Canadian Peacekeeping in the former Yugoslavia," *Canadian Foreign Policy* 6, 2 (1999).

Commission of Inquiry into the Deployment of Canadian Forces to Somalia, *Dishonoured Legacy: The Lessons of the Somalia Affair.* Ottawa: Queen's Printer, 1997.

Cox, D. "Canada and the United Nations: Pursuing Common Security," *Canadian Foreign Policy* 2, 1 (Spring 1994).

English, J. and N. Hillmer, eds. *Making a Difference: Canada's Foreign Policy in a Changing World.* Toronto: Lester, 1992.

Gaffen, F. *In the Eye of the Storm: A History of Canadian Peacekeeping.* Toronto: Deneau and Wayne, 1987.

Gammer, N. *From Peacekeeping to Peacemaking: Canada's Response to the Yugoslav Crisis.* Montreal: McGill-Queen's University Press, 2001.

Gizewski, P. *The Burgeoning Cost of UN Peace-keeping: Who Pays and Who Benefits?* Ottawa: Canadian Center for Global Security, 1993.

Granatstein, J. "Canada and Peacekeeping: Image and Reality," *Canadian Forum* 54 (August 1974).

Granatstein, J. *Shadows of War, Faces of Peace: Canada's Peacekeepers.* Toronto: Key Porter, 1992.

Granatstein, J. "Peacekeeping: did Canada make a difference? And what difference did peacekeeping make to Canada?" in J. English and N. Hillmer, eds. *Making a Difference: Canada's Foreign Policy in a Changing World*. Toronto: Lester, 1992.

Grant, T. "The History of Training for Peacekeeping in the Canadian Forces, 1956–1998," in Y. Tremblay, ed. *Canadian Military History Since the 17th Century*. Ottawa: Department of National Defence, 2001.

Hewitt, D. *From Ottawa to Sarajevo: Canadian Peacekeepers in the Balkans*. Kingston: Center for International Relations, 1998.

Jockel, J. *Canada and International Peacekeeping*. Toronto: Canadian Institute of Strategic Studies, 1994.

LeBeuf, M-E. *Participation of Members of the Royal Canadian Mounted Police as Civilian Police Monitors in United Nations Peace-keeping Missions: Assessment and Perspectives*. Ottawa: RCMP, 1994.

Legault, A. *Canada and Peacekeeping: Three Major Debates*. Clementsport: Canadian Peacekeeping Press, 1999.

Loomis, D. *The Somalia Affair: Reflections of Peacemaking and Peacekeeping*. Ottawa: DGL, 1997.

Mackenzie, L. *Peacekeeper: The Road to Sarajevo*. Vancouver: Douglas and McIntyre, 1993.

Martin, P. and M. Fortmann. "Canada Public Opinion and Peacekeeping in a Turbulent World," *International Journal* 50, 2 (Spring 1995).

Morrison, A. "Canada and Peacekeeping: A Time for Reanalysis?" in D. Dewitt and D. Leyton-Brown, *Canada's International Security Policy*. Toronto: Prentice Hall, 1994.

Morrison, A., ed. *The Changing Face of Peacekeeping*. Toronto: Canadian Institute of Strategic Studies, 1993.

Morrison, A., ed. *Peacekeeping and International Relations*. Clementsport: Canadian Peacekeeping Press, 1991.

Ross, D. *In the Interests of Peace: Canada and Vietnam 1954–73*. Toronto: University of Toronto Press, 1984.

Savard, C. *Journal Intime d'un Beret Bleu Canadien en ex-Yugoslavie*. Outremont: Quebecor, 1994.

Sens, A. *Somalia and the Changing Nature of Peacekeeping: The Implications for Canada*. Ottawa: Queen's Printer, 1997.

Sigler, J., ed. *International Peacekeeping in the Eighties: Global Outlook and Canadian Priorities*. Ottawa: Carleton University Press, 1982.

Sokolsky, J. *The Americanization of Peacekeeping: Implications for Canada*. Kingston: Center for International Relations, 1997.

Taylor, A. et al. *Peacekeeping: International Challenge and Canadian Response*. Toronto: Canadian Institute of International Affairs, 1968.

Taylor, S. and B. Nolan. *Tested Mettle: Canadian Peacekeepers at War*. Ottawa: Esprit de Corps, 1998.

Worthington, P. and K. Brown. *Scapegoat: How the Army Betrayed Kyle Brown*. Toronto: Seal, 1977.

Wirick, G. and R. Miller. *Canada and Missions for Peace: Lessons from Nicaragua, Cambodia and Somalia*. Ottawa: International Development Research Centre, 1998.

Chapter Nineteen

"OUR PASSION FOR SURVIVAL": THE BIRTH OF ENVIRONMENTALISM

1. Grey Owl, *The Men of the Last Frontier*, 1931.
2. Haig-Brown, *Measure of the Year*, 1950.
3. R. Hunter and R. Weyler, *To Save a Whale: The Voyages of Greenpeace*, 1978.
4. Farley Mowat, *Sea of Slaughter*, 1984.
5. David Suzuki, *Time to Change: Essays*, 1994.
6. Tzeporah Berman, *Clayoquot and Dissent*, 1994.

Introduction

Consideration for the Canadian environment is no longer the parvenu of yogurt-eating hippies, as it was in the 1960s. It has become part of mainstream culture. Nobody at the beginning of this new millennium bats an eye at a "blue box" and we all agree we should ride the bus—though we don't. This may offer a cushion of comfort: a feeling that Canadians have seen the error of our ways and now strive for a healthy national ecosystem. While there is room for such optimism we do, however, remain deeply mired in the problem. The federal government estimates that 5,500 Canadians die of smog-related causes per year. Canadians are the per capita world's highest energy consumers—SUVs, for example, remain wildly popular despite their antisocial gas guzzling. Corpses of beluga whales turning up in the St. Lawrence are sufficiently full of chemicals to be declared toxic waste. Meanwhile, only 8% of the world's population lives in North America but we produce 50% of the world's garbage and, despite a successful recycling program that lowered by 60% the amount of paper reaching Canadian landfills, Toronto alone produces enough garbage to fill Sky Dome every four months. The amount of Canadian garbage washing up on Scottish beaches increased by 1,000% since 1988. If that is not enough, flying over British Columbia, in particular, reveals a cancerous carpet of devastation from clear-cut logging. The list goes on. If it isn't Atlantic cod, then it is the grizzly, and if not them, any one of the myriad of plants and animals teetering on extinction from human activity. This sorry situation, of course, begs two central questions: how did Canada find itself in this state; and what wrought the change that now offers cause for cautious optimism?

That the Canadian landscape appeared as an inexhaustible storehouse of natural resources ripe for the picking, forms a major explanation for the ongoing environmental predation that began off the coast of Newfoundland in the 16th century. Explorers, trappers, settlers, administrators, all were mere specks on the vast Canadian landscape. Surely, they believed, no amount of beaver hunting, whaling, tree cutting, fishing, mining, or other extraction could possibly empty the larder, and any civilizing of the landscape that might occur was, of course, a good thing.

Capitalism also contributed to Canada's present sorry environmental state. It is, after all, an economic system that puts private shareholder profits above public social needs, particularly if the latter costs money or impedes development—as it often does.

Finally, a number of women activists, ecofeminists, charge that environmental degradation results from men dominating world political and economic systems. Men, they assert, are biologically aggressive and predatory conquerors who cannot naturally nurture—as women can. Put women in positions of economic and political power, they say, and the environment has a chance.

Regardless of the cause, the result conjures up false images of Canadian men engaged in an unrelenting orgy of environmental rape until the 1960s when Greenpeace saved the day. Environmentalists, in fact, championed their cause throughout the twentieth century, and we have certainly not fixed the environmental ills that plague us.

The kernels of an attitudinal sea change toward the environment emerged in industrialized nations around the beginning the twentieth century. Progressive social theorists concluded that rubbing shoulders with nature was highly beneficial for humankind, as was a more symbiotic relationship between our environment and us. This new mindset, for example, led to the creation of inner city parks where fresh air and greenery supposedly cured working people's social and physical ills. It also facilitated the first five national parks in Canada between 1885-97, and to the federal government enacting the world's first dedicated parks service in 1911. The idea was to protect and preserve specific chunks of national splendour for future generations of Canadian tourists. Thus parks did not emerge from any recognition that we should be less polluting, less consuming, and more nurturing to the environment. The plunder of the rest of Canada, after all, continued unabated and with ever increasing ferocity as technology streamlined the process. Technological innovation, the chainsaw for example, allowed relatively few individuals to harvest hitherto unimaginable quantities throughout the extraction industries.

There were, however, voices in the wilderness warning of unconscionable and irreparable damage to the Canadian ecosystem without major attitudinal modifications toward the environment. Lone souls like the popular Grey Owl worked, wrote, and lectured tirelessly on environmental issues in the 1930s, and were largely responsible for Canadians reconsidering, or at least considering, their relationship to nature. Though the alleged half-Apache Grey Owl turned out to actually be an Englishman named Archie Belaney, nobody discovered that until after his death, and his eloquent pleas and personal example did much to encourage the nascent environmental movement. Men like Roderick Haig-Brown took up the cause in the post-Second World War era, and helped set the foundation for the Canadian environmental movement that burst on the scene in the 1960s.

Environmental degradation was worse in the United States, largely because of greater population pressures and very aggressive industrialization. There, in the 1950s and '60s, seminal books like *Silent Spring* and *River of Grass* led directly to creating populist movements that saved areas like the Florida everglades from the ravages of civilization. The American socio-political situation was also far more tense than the Canadian. Vietnam and civil rights, in particular, focused popular protest and inspired activism among the normally disengaged. Impending environmental calamity, not surprisingly, became one of the key issues of the day—a motherhood concern anyone could support. Similar to most protest of the era, the environmental movement claimed the moral high ground by employing Gandhian non-violent and consciously public tactics.

The threat of nuclear catastrophe, whether by war, testing, or accident, fused peace movements with environmentalism and internationalized both. Nuclear fallout, after all, respects no borders. American and French nuclear testing, for example, contributed to the creation of Greenpeace in Vancouver. Greenpeace's success, from day one, derived partly from empowering ordinary citizens—initially by attempting to sail an old halibut boat into a nuclear blast zone and daring the Americans to risk the fallout from frying the Canadian crew. From protesting nuclear testing in Amchitka and French Polynesia, Greenpeace activists set their sights on the whaling industry, this time putting themselves between the whales and the harpoons on the high seas—and on camera. This very dramatic television footage brought a formerly invisible carnage to the world and led to international outrage and condemnation. The impact on whaling was swift and stark. Next Greenpeace tackled the sealing industry, cruise missile testing, pollution, and other environmental threats, both at home and abroad. In the 1980s, clear-cut logging in British Columbia, particularly on Vancouver Island, became one of the critical battlegrounds between the now sophisticated environmental movement and a forest industry increasingly on the defensive. Environmental activists were by then very successful at shutting down markets for environmentally dubious practices. Convincing European women that sealskin coats were morally reprehensible, for example, essentially killed the Canadian sealing industry and saved the Harp seal. Convincing Home Depot in the United States not to sell lumber from old growth forests meant that Canadian lumber producers could not simply carry on as before and dismiss environmental activists as dope smoking tree huggers and social misfits.

The 1980s saw two shifts in the Canadian environmental movement, one small and possibly short lived, one major. A number of activists abandoned pacifism for direct action, arguing that peaceful protests took too long—so long that success might come too late. Greenpeace veterans like Paul Watson became unrepentant "ecoterrorists," in his case outfitting a ship to hunt, ram and sink rogue whalers, which he did with great effect. Others spray painted fur coats, smashed logging equipment, spiked trees, or engaged in other forms of illegal, and sometimes very dangerous, activity. Ecoterrorism, however, remains marginal to an overall movement that perceives non-violence and legal protest as a key philosophical tenant.

The second shift will, in the long run, be much more significant. Women now lead much of the environmental movement, both in Canada and internationally. Seeking inspiration from the peace camps in England, such as the one outside the airbase at Greenham Common, Canadian women joined forces, found strength in their community, and became a formidable force throughout the environmental movement. Thus two thirds of the 856 people arrested at Clayoquot Sound on Vancouver Island in 1993, were this new breed of ecofeminists. By the beginning of the new millennium, Canadian women played key roles in Greenpeace, the Sierra Club, the Green Party, and most other environmental groups.

All told, the Canadian environmental movement has enjoyed considerable success; both in elevating environmental issues into the mainstream national debate, and also in achieving significant environmental protection. However, environmental degradation continues in Canada, and Canadians still live with the legacy of four centuries of environmental damage.

Discussion Points

1. Internationally Canada's reputation for strip mining, clearcut-ting, seal bludgeoning, acid rain, over-fishing and reluctance to sign the Kyoto Accord has overshadowed local environmen-tal movements. Greenpeace has moved its international headquarters to Amsterdam and Canada's Green Parties lack significant popularity. Why haven't we been able to advance the environmentalist cause further?
2. Are environmentalists chiefly urban dwellers with romantic no-tions of nature, unfamiliar with the reality of wilderness life? In other words is it easy to talk about saving nature when you actually don't live and work in rural areas?
3. What explains the fact that most of these documents were generated by people living in British Columbia? Does envi-ronmentalism have a peculiar regional focus in Canada?
4. Is ecoterrorism justified?
5. Early environmentalist leaders tended to be men. Now they are women. Why?

Documents

1. Grey Owl, *The Men of the Last Frontier*, 1931.

... Yet the scene around me had its influence, and a guilty feeling possessed me as I realized that of all present in that place of peace and clean content, I was the only profane thing, an ogre lurking to destroy. The half-grown ferns and ever-green sedge grasses through which the early breeze whispered, would, if I had my way, soon be smeared with the blood of some animal, who was viewing, perhaps with feelings akin to my own, the dawning of another day; to be his last. Strange thoughts, maybe, coming from a trapper, one whose trade it is to kill; but be it known to you that he who lives much alone within the portals of the temple of Nature learns to think, and deeply, of things which seldom come within the scope of ordinary life. Much killing brings in time, no longer tri-umph, but a revulsion of feeling.

I have seen old hunters, with their hair silvered by the passage of many winters, who, on killing a deer would stroke the dead muzzle with every appear-ance of regret. Indians frequently address an animal they are about to kill in terms of apology for the act. However, be that as it may, with the passing of the mist from the face of the mountains, I saw a large beaver swimming a short distance away. This was my game; gone were my scruples, and my humane ideas fled like leaves before the wind. Giving the searching call of these animals, I cocked my rifle and waited.

At the call he stopped, raising himself in the water to sniff; and on the summons being repeated he swam directly towards me, into the very jaws of destruction. At about fifteen feet I had a good view of him as he slowed down, trying to catch some indication of a possible companion, and the beautiful dark fur apprised me of a hide that would well repay my early morning sortie. The beaver regarded me steadily, again raising himself to catch an expected scent, and not getting it he turned lazily to swim away. He was at my mercy, and I had his head snugly set between the forks of my rear sight, when my heart contracted at the thought of taking life on such a morning. The creature was happy, glad to be in God's good sunlight, free after a winter of darkness to breathe the pure air of the dawn. He had the right to live here, even as I had, yea, even a greater claim, for he was there before me.

I conquered my momentary weakness; for, after all, a light pressure on the trigger, a crashing impact, would save him many days of useless labour. Yet I hesitated, and as I finally laid my rifle down, he sank without a ripple, out of sight. And I became suddenly conscious of the paeans of praise and triumph of the feathered choir about me, temporarily unheard in my lust to kill; and it seemed as though all Nature sang in benediction of an act which had kept inviolate a sanctuary, and saved a perfect hour from desecration.

I went home to my cabin and ate my breakfast with greater satisfaction than the most expertly accomplished kill had ever given me; and, call it what you will, weakness, vacillation, or the first glimmerings of conscience in a life hitherto devoted to the shedding of blood, since the later experiences I have had with these animals I look back on the incident with no regret ...

Misinformed and apparently not greatly interested provincial governments aided and abetted this destructive and unwarranted encroachment on the rights of their native populations who were dependent entirely on the proceeds of the chase, by gathering a rich if temporary harvest in licences, royalties, etc. A few futile laws were passed, of which the main incentive of enforcement often seemed to be the collection of fines rather than prevention. Money alone can never adequately pay the people of Canada for the loss of their wild life, from either the commercial, or recreational, or the sentimental point of view ...

Although in the north they are now reduced to a few individuals and small families scattered thinly in certain inaccessible districts, there has been established for many years, a game reserve of about three thousand square miles, where these and all other animals indigenous to the region are as numerous as they were fifty years ago. I refer to the Algonquin Provincial Park in Ontario. This game sanctuary is guarded in the strictest manner by a very competent staff of Rangers, and it is a saying in the region that it would be easier to get away with murder than to escape the consequences of killing a beaver in their patrol area ...

With her timber gone, the potential wealth of the Dominion would be halved, and her industries cut down by one-third; yet the forest is being daily offered up for a burnt sacrifice to the false gods of greed and waste, and the birthright of future generations is being squandered by its trustees. Not only is the interest, the merchantable timber arriving at maturity, being used up faster than it accumulates, but the capital, the main body of the forest, is fast disappearing. Year by year for three-quarters of a century, this useless and costly destruction has been going on for five months out of every year ...

The fire-fighting machinery is now one of the most efficient and highly organized branches of the government service. Only men of known ability are employed. Districts where much travelling is done are patrolled by airplanes, which are also used for transporting fire-fighting apparatus to places to which it would be otherwise impossible to move it. Steel towers, hauled in sections by dog-teams during the winter, are erected on commanding situations and connected by telephone, and in them sentinels are posted every day of summer. Portages are kept in first-class condition, and short-cuts established, so that gangs of men and equipment may be rushed to the scene of a fire in the shortest possible time. Professional woodsmen and Indians are kept on the pay-roll for the express purpose of discovering blocks of valuable timber, and opening up routes to them ...

Most of the companies are honest in their dealings with timber on Crown lands, but unfortunately some of these concerns have passed out of the hands of the big-hearted lumber kings, and under a new regime fail to keep up the traditions. There are a number of them now being operated by foreign amalgamations with huge sums of money behind them, and having no special interest in the country, their only concern being to get what can be got whilst the getting is good. They employ labour certainly, as long as it lasts, even as the beaver supported a large population for a time and are gone now. The two cases are parallel.

The white pine, king of all the Forest, at one time the mainstay of the lumber industry, is now only existent in a few remote districts, or in reserves set aside by a wise government. But the pine is hard to save. Politics have still a little to say, for it is a profitable tree, and many are the hungry eyes turned on the rolling dark green forest of the reserved lands. Certain unscrupulous lumber companies, of foreign origin, have been the cause of fires designed to scorch large areas of timber on Crown lands. Burnt timber must be immediately sold or it will become a total loss. The burning of an old lumber camp, and the sacrifice of some logging gear in the fire establishes innocence on the part of the company, and they come into possession of a nice, juicy cut of timber which rightly belongs to the public. The money is paid over but the pine is none the less gone.

Too many regard the wilderness as only a place of wild animals and wilder men, and cluttered with a growth that must somehow be got rid of. Yet it is, to those who know its ways, a living, breathing reality, and has a soul that may be understood, and it may yet occur to some, that part of the duty of those who destroy it for the general good is to preserve at least a memory of it and its inhabitants, and what they stood for.

The question of re-forestation immediately crops up.

I feel that the planting of a few acres of seedlings to compensate for the destruction of thousands of square miles of virgin timber, whilst a worthy thought, and one that should be extensively carried out, seems much like placing two cents in the bank after having squandered a million. Let us keep on with the good work by all means, but why not at the same time devise means to save a little of what we have?

This re-forestation may salve the consciences of those who would ruthlessly sell or cut the last pine tree, but by the time the seedlings arrive at maturity, a matter of a hundred and fifty years or more, the rabble of all nations will occupy so much territory that the trees will have no room to grow.

No one seems to have thought of ascertaining just how long a soil impoverished by being systematically denuded of its natural fertilizer, by the removal of all mature timber, will reproduce a forest worthy of the name. In these domestic woodlands there will fall no logs to rot and nourish the trees growing to take their places, especially in the unproductive barrens to which the interests of practical forestry have been relegated by the somewhat over-zealous land-hunters.

We have already to-day examples of this depreciation in "land-power" in some of the great wheat-growing areas of the West. The ruinous "scratch-the-land-and-reap-a-fortune" policy of the propagandists of settlement schemes in the past has been followed only too closely; and, insufficiently fertilized, the soil, having given all it had, is beginning to run out.

There are to-day in Canada large concerns that in the guise of a benevolent

interest in Wild Life, and under cover of a wordy forest preservation campaign
(of which re-forestation, *not* conservation, is the keynote), are amalgamating in
order to gain possession of practically all of Canada's remaining forests.

And, let us be warned, they are succeeding handsomely.

Enormous areas are already beyond the jurisdiction of the people. As a sop
to public opinion the benefits of re-forestation are dwelt on, not as a contributing factor in silviculture (and a very necessary one it is), but as a substitute for
the timber they wish to remove. According to those interested the forests will
burn, fall down, decay, or rot on the stump if they are not cut immediately, and
in return they will plant comparatively infinitesimal areas with tiny trees, to
replace the fast disappearing forests on which they are fattening.

So we have the highly-diverting spectacle of one man, standing in the
midst of ten million acres of stumps and arid desolation, planting with a shovel
a little tree ten inches high, to be the cornerstone of a new and synthetic forest,
urged on to the deed by a deputation of smug and smiling profiteers, who do not
really care if the tree matures or not—unless their descendants are to be engaged
in the lumbering business.

How have the mighty fallen, and will continue to fall!

Even the policy of girdling the hardwood species where they are not useful
as firebreaks, woods whose beautiful fall colouring and grateful shade are a tradition in Canada, has been advocated to allow the growth of more easily
merchantable species in their place at some future date. The virtual drying-up of
springs, lakes, creeks and even fair-sized rivers consequent on this wholesale
removal of forest growth, we hear nothing about.

Even an Act of Parliament to preserve a few hundred square miles of Canada's
natural scenery intact for the benefit of the people, has to be fought through a
number of sessions before it can wrest from destruction beauty spots of inesti-
mable value to the nation, the benefits of which will accrue to the greater number
and for all time, not only temporarily to an individual or a company.

And until the politics in which the issue is obscured are kept out of the
matter and replaced by public-spirited altruism and a genuine forest conservation
policy, the will of the people will be over-ridden, and the forest will continue to fall
before the hosts of the God of Mammon, until the last tree is laid in the dust ...

Beauty spots such as this little Lake of Calling Waters, groves redolent with
the clean smell of the leaves, carpeted in Spring with a myriad flowers, must
soon be laid waste and trampled underfoot by the unsavoury hordes of Southern
Europe, and their silence broken by a babel of uncouth tongues.

A frenzied and misdirected immigration policy, *encouraged by the demands of a wage-cutting type of employer by no means rare, and promoted by shipping and transportation companies whose only interest is to collect fares,* is fast filling up Canada with a polyglot jamboree of languages, among which English is by no means the predominating feature. The unskilled labour market in Canada is glutted. Every city has its unemployment problem. Prosperity there is, but not enough to provide a livelihood for the adult male population of all Europe ...

The South-eastern European will work for less wages than the "white" races, and has therefore to a very large extent supplanted the old-time, happy-go-lucky lumberjack of song and story. This is to say nothing of other occupations he has seized on and monopolized, for no one will work with him.

He lowers the standard of living by existing under conditions that the English-speaking and French-Canadian nationalities would not tolerate, and in order to live the cheaper, in places where he boards himself, will kill every living creature from a whiskey-jack up, to eke out his niggardly diet.

The "Bohunk" or "Bolshie" is seldom seen without a home-made cigarette, hanging from his lower lip, which he will carelessly spit out into the inflammable forest litter. For days perhaps the dry muck will smoulder along, until a breeze springs up and fans the "smudge" into a blaze which leaps quickly from one resinous tree to another, till the whole forest is in flames.

This type herds together in communities where the whole output of his labour is just sufficient to support life, and generally in sections where the timber he cuts and destroys is worth infinitely more than his contribution to the wealth of the country ...

The forest-fire menace in Canada is very real, yet the continued carelessness of unintelligent vandals, who get into the country simply because they have so much money, can't speak English, and do not happen to have consumption or a wooden leg, is destroying as much, if not more, valuable timber than is cut for useful purposes. Hundreds of square miles of the finest forests now remaining on the American Continent, trees that were old when Wolfe stormed the citadel at Quebec, will be carelessly burnt every summer to provide a Roman holiday for an alien race. It would not be fair to blame the "Hunky" for all the fires, but with less of him the fire risk would be much reduced.

FOR A WOODSMAN TO REVISIT A COUNTRY THAT HE ONCE knew as virgin and find it has been destroyed by fire is like coming home and finding the house burnt. Trappers and Indians rarely set fire; if they did their occupation would be soon gone. No man will burn his own property, and the proprietary feeling of these people towards their stamping grounds is very real. Most of them are the best unofficial Fire Rangers we have ...

2. Haig-Brown, *Measure of the Year*, 1950.

LET THEM EAT SAWDUST

I HAVE BEEN, ALL MY LIFE, WHAT is known as a conservationist. I am not at all sure that this has done myself or anyone else any good, but I am quite sure that no intelligent man, least of all a countryman, has any alternative. It seems clear beyond possibility of argument that any given generation of men can have only a lease, not ownership, of the earth; and one essential term of the lease is that the earth be handed on to the next generation with unimpaired potentialities. This is the conservationist's concern.

It is in the history of civilizations that conservationists are always defeated, boomers always win, and the civilizations always die. I think there has never been, in any state, a conservationist government, because there has never yet been a people with sufficient humility to take conservation seriously. This is natural enough. No man is intimately concerned with more than his lifetime, comparatively few men concern themselves seriously with more than a fraction of that time; in the last analysis all governments reflect the concerns of the people they govern, and most modern democratic governments are more deeply concerned with some brief, set term of office than with anything else. Conservation means fair and honest dealing with the future, usually at some cost to the immediate present. It is a simple morality, with little to offset the glamor and quick material rewards of the North American deity, "Progress."

Living near a settlement like Elkhorn one sees both sides of the argument lived out, and inevitably takes part. Elkhorn is entirely dependent on natural resources in their first state. Almost the whole of Vancouver Island is, or was, timber; possibly the finest softwood saw-log timber in the world. Next in importance to timber are the recreational assets—game, game fish, and scenery; after these, commercial fishing, coal mining, agriculture, and water power. Elkhorn is touched by all of them, but timber is overwhelmingly the most important factor in its existence; the whole forty-year life of the village has been built on service to the logging camps and loggers of the surrounding country. And during those years the importance of a tourist trade based mainly on sport fishing has steadily increased.

It would be logical to suppose that everyone in Elkhorn would be interested in forestry and forest conservation, but almost no one is. Vancouver Island's forests were at first considered "inexhaustible"; then, as it became clear that they were being rapidly exhausted, the forests became an expendable asset, to be used in "opening up the country" so that some unspecified phenomenon, probably "industry," could come in and take over. In spite of some very halfhearted at-tempts at a sounder forest policy by the government, that is where things rest at present. Elkhorn and other little towns like it watch the big logging camps draw farther and farther away as the more accessible timber is cleared off; they know vaguely that the end of saw-log timber is in sight, that millions of deforested acres are reproducing only slowly if at all; yet they retain a mystic faith in the future, a belief that "progress" in the shape of roads and wharves and airplanes and hydroelectric power will somehow lead them on to a continuously more abundant life. Perhaps they will. But even that could not excuse or justify the fire-destroyed acres, the incredible waste of timber in logging, the long barren years through which magnificent forest land has grown little or nothing.

Elkhorn is in no way unique. This frantic dream of progress and develop-ment has cursed nearly every hamlet and village in North America at some time or another, bringing with it premature sidewalks and false-front stores, fantastic real-estate projects, fierce neon signs and an orgy of public services planned with a solidity that might better have gone into the jerry-built houses. Usually it is a recurrent frenzy, starting with each sizable economic boom, dying back between whiles to surge up again on some new promise of oil or minerals or large con-struction, any high and easy road to sudden wealth. And it is not wholly bad. It has built a continent's material civilization, blatantly, wastefully, with an enor-mous cruelty in the shattering of men's hopes and dreams, and frequent distortions of true values; but it has built it, and perhaps it was necessary to build so fast and so extravagantly.

But now that the continent is crossed and secured the method seems stu-pid, the haste merely destructive. The sanctity of "progress" with its tricky little catch phrase, "We can't stand in the way of progress," seems suddenly false and treacherous. It is a good time to ask, "Why can't we?", to pull progress apart and take a new look at it, to examine everything called "development" in terms of values that already exist, in its relationship to the economy of the whole nation and the whole continent; above all, in its relationship to human happiness.

Progress seems to mean, all too often, the projection of slums into the wilderness. Incredibly, for all its village size, Elkhorn achieved slums for itself on land that had been bush only a year previously. This came about in a sudden flux of temporary jobs on a major construction project; people poured in, found high wages, then paid higher rents for tar-paper shacks set in mud, where each family shared a single room and a dozen families shared a hand pump for water, and an outside toilet. The project was finished, many of the families moved out and the village had time to wonder what had happened to it. Meanwhile the timber has drawn back two or three years farther into the mountains. But more people than ever before are dependent on it.

So the more abundant life has arrived briefly and departed, much of it spent in failure and waste. High wages have little meaning if they will buy only tar-paper shacks as transient homes for growing children. Boom and progress and development add up to high real-estate prices, houses scattered among vacant lots that no one can afford to buy, a few short lengths of sidewalk, some no-parking signs, and a multiplicity of stores with little reason to be doing business. And the village settles back to consolidate. Strangely, there is something to consolidate. More people are living in the community, even though there is apparently less reason for them to be doing so. There is a framework of community organization, something beyond the simple mutual help of the older days. There are many improved services, such strange exotic things as street lights and an up-to-date water system and an extremely modern school. Some of these things may prove difficult to maintain and pay for; but they exist and merely by doing so they make a village out of what had been only a settlement. Somehow timber and tourists will support them until another boom comes and a few more of the vacant lots between the houses are filled and a small town begins to grow out of the village. But the solidity, the real existence of the town, as of the village, will be built only slowly, between the booms.

It is difficult to know how much or how little human happiness grows out of such a boom, but the total seems less than before. There are more worried and anxious and uncertain people than there were before. Even small businessmen who have done well are strained by their expansion, working harder, worrying more, remembering the quieter, more logical times with regret. Even the most ambitious of them speak regretfully of simplicities they loved in the earlier Elkhorn, which now seem lost in the surge of progress they called for. Yet they must seem to call for more progress because the deity is sacrosanct; no North American businessman can deny her lip service, no matter what may be in his heart.

A conservationist fights many battles, varying in scale all the way from the attempted protection of some individual species of wildlife to the supreme issue of proper use of soil, air, and water; and every fight is complicated, if not forced, by the false urgency and outdated sanctity of progress. The speed of modern development is such that the conservationist is always under attack, rarely has time himself to attack. He needs only breathing space, a little time for thought to creep in and temper progress with wisdom. Development is rarely a matter of urgency. Timber, soil, fisheries, oil and minerals, even water power, become more, not less, valuable with delay. The problem is to use the self-reproducing resources within their safe yield and to develop the wasting resources without injury to others already producing.

Elkhorn, when a government was damming its river, had to fight and fight hard to save the salmon run on which its tourist trade is built. She had to fight again, still harder, to win clearing of the land that would be flooded by the dam. She expects, and needs, a pulp mill; probably it will come one day and if it does she will have to fight again, harder than ever before, to save her waters from pollution.

Such conflicts as these go on throughout the continent, and none of them is necessary. Hydroelectric developments, pulp mills, and other such manifestations of progress are not dreamed up overnight. There is always ample time for mature and careful consideration of every issue involved. But early planning is always left to the single-track minds of the developers, often buried in deepest secrecy for purely commercial reasons, and the conservationist is left with a last-ditch battle. In this way the burden of proof is always forced upon him. He is standing in the way of progress—reactionary, narrow, without real vision.

It seems clear to me that all destruction it causes should be reckoned in the direct cost of any project, and that no preventable destruction should ever be permitted. Obviously flooded land is no longer land in any useful sense; but it should be cleared of timber and debris before flooding so that a lake with good bottom and clean shores will take its place. If the cost of this is too great for the project to bear, then the project is uneconomic. Runs of game and commercial fish can be destroyed by poorly planned dams; but sound planning can always find some way to compensate and may even save the whole resource. The onus here is just as clear, if not clearer, since a run of fish properly looked after will maintain itself indefinitely into the future, while a hydroelectric development may be outdated within twenty years, almost certainly will be within fifty years. Pollution of air and water by industrial plants is the simplest issue of all. There are adequate means of preventing all such pollutions. Admittedly they are sometimes costly, but if the industry cannot support the cost it is economically unsound. No nation can afford polluted air or polluted waterways.

These are sweeping statements, and I mean them to be. A civilization built on foul air and polluted water, on destroyed timber lands, overgrazed ranges, exhausted farm lands, on water sucked from one river system to make cheap electricity on another, is too costly and too insecurely based to last. I saw recently a newspaper editorial happily forecasting that before very long the world's timber supplies will be too valuable for any such simple use as building houses or making paper; they will all be needed for human food—processed, no doubt, into pulpy palatability, but still essentially sawdust. Any civilization that can cheerfully contemplate such a morbid future for its multiplied grandchildren needs a new philosophy.

Industrial development has produced such an enormous material prosperity, so widely spread, that its sanctity is easy to understand. But in North America it has done so largely by using capital assets as income. That is why conservation is now far more important than further development. It seems to me that the people of the continent, both Canadians and Americans, have everything to gain, nothing to lose, by stopping to take stock and understand what they have got and how it can soundly be used. Exhausting a continent and overpopulating it to the point at which its inhabitants must start eating trees seems a strange way to a more abundant life.

It is difficult to believe the theorists who say that a nation to be sound must have an increasing population. Thousands of years ago the human race had to breed tolerably fast to survive. After that nations had to grow large populations in fear of wars. And there was always the idea that man must multiply until he had overrun the earth. He seems to have achieved this and surely he can be allowed to pause to recognize that there is no virtue in population for the sake of population; if there were, India, China, even Russia would be more prosperous nations than they are. It is difficult to believe that there is any true morality in producing children, or any essential immorality in not producing them. Certainly there is little to be said for raising men to be slaves to "progress" and cities, to industry and all the machines of a civilization frantically producing substitutes for the natural things it has destroyed.

Conservation is wise use of natural resources, which ultimately are the whole life of any country, even one that imports most of its natural resources. And it is axiomatic that no special interest, whether it is industrial or governmental, can be trusted to use raw materials wisely. All resources are interdependent; soil, for instance, cannot be separated from water tables, nor water tables from forests; and all life that moves on the land, in the water, or in the air is affected by every use of these resources. Government departments work independently and with blind irresponsibility to achieve specialized departmental ends; British Columbia has an Electric Power Act that restricts the function of a powerful commission to the production of cheap electricity; it has a Water Act that recognizes fourteen uses for water, but does not include its use by fish, though the commercial salmon fishery is one of the three or four main resources of the province. The logging industry has to pay only slight attention to forest regeneration, none at all to economical use of timber stands, preservation of soil or water resources. So it is through the whole picture. The conservationist's hope—perhaps dream is the better word—is to change all this, to establish a coordination of effort that will make sure that every factor is properly weighed and every resource fully protected against exploitation or wanton destruction. There are a few slow signs that we are beginning to think on these lines; the existence of a minor government department called the Land Utilization Branch is one of them, and an annual conference of experts on natural resources initiated by this branch is another. But this is a feeble result for the last west, with a whole continent's lessons of waste and destruction to draw on. Perhaps I take too much pleasure in prophesying doom, perhaps I am too much countryman and woodsman to understand the dream of progress through cities and machines, to feel the romance of the bulldozer and the earth mover, the concrete mixer and the four-lane highway. But I think we are on our way through the whole tragic story, that we shall live well on it. Our children and grandchildren and great-grandchildren will have to solve the slow, difficult problem of restoration as best they can. Perhaps atomic power will help them. It seems to be our only legacy.

3. R. Hunter and R. Weyler, *To Save a Whale: The Voyages of Greenpeace*, 1978.

... It was early October in 1971. We were en route, we thought, to the remote Aleutian Island of Amchitka, where the U.S. Atomic Energy Commission was planning to trigger an underground nuclear blast. Our plan was to park our chartered vessel—an ancient eighty-foot halibut seiner—within three miles of Ground Zero, thus making the test all but impossible without the risk of us being blown out of the water or sprayed with vented radiation.

It was a good plan. Ours was a Canadian vessel. The Americans could not seize it in international waters without committing an act of piracy. But we were already in trouble. The test had been delayed a month, forcing us to put into Akutan, the easternmost major island in the chain extending almost to Russia. Within a week, although we had not yet guessed it, we would be arrested by the U.S. Coast Guard and sent packing back to Canada. We would never get to Amchitka.

Instead, we were to encounter something that was to move us even more deeply than our dread of nuclear Armageddon. Unknowingly, we had anchored next to an abandoned whaling station, one of the hundreds which dot the shores of the Aleutians, Alaska, and British Columbia.

Crossing the Gulf of Alaska westward on a great circle route from far down

Prince Rupert to Akutan Pass, we had not seen a single whale. Our captain, John Cormack, a veteran fisherman who had traveled these waters for over forty years, had remarked, "Used to be, when you came out here on the Gulf, you could see them whales from horizon to horizon. They'd come up to the boat like big puppies. 'Course you don't see them any longer. They're *extinct*."

It had been gray and lonely and oppressive out on the Gulf. The captain's words rang in our ears. They gave a new dimension of despair to our action. We had been filled for years with the fear that the human race might wipe itself out through nuclear weaponry. Our efforts to try to save ourselves and to spare our children had seemed such an urgent matter. Now it seemed that saving human lives was somehow not quite enough. There was a sense that some major point had been missed, that incalculable damage had already been done, and that we were, in some fundamental way, too late ...

The whaling station might have been in operation as little as thirty years earlier, perhaps right up to the onset of the Second World War ...

The wind tugged at our scarves and jackets. No one tried to speak. We separated, each to wander alone. Somehow the ruins seemed to have more to do with our own future than with the long-dead whales. Perhaps we were thinking of the thermo-nuclear bomb being fashioned only a few hundred miles away ...

Bones. They were like dry pulp, their surfaces pitted with tiny holes. Ribs stuck up like parts of an old picket fence. Vertebrae the size of toilet bowls lay half-buried, barely visible through clumps of horsetail rush. Part of a jawbone jabbed out of the ground like a gray sheet of plywood ...

Out in the bay, our battered old seiner looked like nothing much more than a toy itself. It had taken so much effort just to get this far, and while we had not yet reached the gateway to the bomb, it seemed we had come to some other, unexpected, gateway. The silence spoke as clearly as the roar we had been bracing ourselves to hear. The holocaust that was coming seemed, for the moment, to hold no more horror than the holocaust that had already come.

New Directions

The sail on our boat was dark green. On it, painted in a yellow that had already been blackened by soot from the stack, was the word we had chosen to express our goal: *Greenpeace*.

We began as the Don't Make A Wave Committee, a coalition of West Coast environmentalists and antiwar protesters. The name *Greenpeace* was chosen temporarily for the vessel that would sail to Amchitka simply because the word nicely expressed the spirit of both the ecology and the peace movements. It was not until the boat was almost back home in Vancouver that the decision was made to rename the organization and start preparing for another attempt in the following year to sail into the Amchitka bomb test zone. Thus, a new name: The Greenpeace Foundation.

Before the new group could even begin to form its plan for a second assault on Amchitka, the U.S. government announced that no further tests would be carried out there. The island was to be turned into a game sanctuary. The Greenpeace voyage, as well as other forms of protest, had generated enough political pressure that the Pentagon decided that Amchitka was too vulnerable a test site and closed down the operation.

The Greenpeace Foundation immediately turned its attention to French nuclear tests in the South Pacific. In the spring of 1972 a group sailed a small ketch into the test zone at Mururoa Atoll, where it was rammed by a French navy mine-sweeper and towed away. The vessel returned to the site in 1973. Its owner was beaten with rubber truncheons, suffering permanent damage to his right eye. But the action succeeded in triggering a storm of international protests. By the spring of 1975, the French government had halted its atmospheric tests at Mururoa, just as the Americans had closed their underground facilities at Amchitka three years earlier. In both cases, Greenpeace ships had provided a spearhead of opposition.

As soon as the news came through that France had abandoned its atmospheric nuclear program, Greenpeace began to develop the idea that had been slumbering in the backs of our minds ever since that October day in the Aleutian Islands amid the ruins of the whaling station. We had often sent boats into atomic test areas for the sake of human life. Now, with Amchitka left in peace and the nuclear monster driven down into the darkness beneath the coral at Mururoa, we might send a boat out to defend the sacredness of another awesome kind of life.

With the announcement in January, 1975, that the Greenpeace Foundation would attempt to go to the rescue of the world's last remaining great whales, a frightening energy became available to us. Earlier, pitting ourselves against the bomb, we had acted in the defense of our own homes, our own land, our own people. There was nothing really new about it. The bomb itself might provoke terror, and even a sense of awe, but it was finally nothing more than another human invention. There had been great energy spent to protest the atomic testing, but that was merely war; now our campaign for the whales became religion.

Compared to a great whale, even a nuclear bomb is just a gadget. In announcing that we would put ourselves between the harpoon and the whale—that we were willing to die to save the whales—we committed ourselves to something greater than anything we had undertaken before. We had committed ourselves finally to something that was greater than the human race itself. It was as though a moment had come for us to crawl up out of some dark sea and perceive a whole new world on the horizon. Suddenly it seemed so simple. If there was to be any salvation on this planet, it was not enough to shield human beings from their own folly. We would have to shield the non-humans too, for without them there would be a weakening and deterioration of the great system of order underlying the whole flow of life on the planet.

At first, the idea of sending a Greenpeace boat out to try to intercept the whaling fleets was greeted by scepticism and scorn. It caused a major rift among Greenpeace veterans themselves, many of whom thought the whaling issue to be frivolous in comparison to the problem of nuclear weapons. Some others in the group rejected the idea on the grounds that finding the whaling fleets in the vastness of the ocean would be utterly impossible for it was no longer a matter of setting a course for an island or atoll, however remote. This time we would be seeking a moving target. One Greenpeace advisor, a former U.S. Navy captain, said flatly: "It's too big an ocean and those guys can move at twenty knots. You haven't got a chance."

Indeed, at the early stages of organization, it was difficult to avoid the feeling that we had passed into some crazy New Age fantasy world. On previous expeditions there had been a hard core of veteran seamen, former military men, and toughened antiwar protesters. Most of them withdrew, not wanting to be associated with what they thought of as a "hippie thing."

At the time we announced our plan, we did not, in fact, have a clue as to where the fleets might be found. We thought vaguely that they might be operating near the Sea of Okhotsk northeast of Japan. Or perhaps they were somewhere off the west coast of Canada. It was not a strong basis on which to launch any kind of an expedition and if were going to carry on in the face of such odds, it could only be as an act of faith. From a purely rational point of view, the whole exercise was hopeless.

During this initial stage of doubt and misgiving, it was due to the conviction of one man that we were able to carry on. That man was Dr. Paul Spong, an expatriate New Zealand physiological psychologist, who had spent a year studying a captive whale named Skana at the Vancouver Public Aquarium. Paul's studies, like those of John Lilly, led him to the conclusion that the whales possessed a high order of awareness, comparable to, if not superior to, humanity's. It was Paul Spong, more than any other person, who put us on the track of saving the whales and kept us on the track. It was Paul who convinced the doubters among us, who shored up the faith that repeatedly crumbled. He never wavered: "You can count on help from the whales."

This belief was to be our secret ace in the hole, our only ace, for we knew that the chances of finding the whale fleets were just about zero. We knew that, even if we found them, they would be able to move so much more swiftly than we could that the chances of successful interference amounted to yet another zero. We knew that on all counts the undertaking was irrational and futile, unless ... unless Paul Spong was right.

And so, from the beginning, we were embarked on a quest no less mystical than the search for the Holy Grail. It would take the equivalent of a twelfth-century miracle for it to work. Yet, when we accepted the fact that we were looking for a miracle, and nothing less, it brought people to us in droves. And not just in random droves—if we needed an electronics expert, one would appear. If we needed a shipwright, a shipwright would show up at the next meeting. If we decided we needed a musician, or a photographer or an engineer, they, too, would appear as though on cue. It was either a grand illusion or else some kind of psychic tom-tom was at work in the jungle of the collective unconscious. It was impossible to avoid the feeling that we were in harmony with a force so much greater than ourselves that no one dared to talk about it. We simply lived it.

There is a centuries-old Cree Indian prophecy that says a time will come at last when the birds are dropping from the sky, the rivers poisoned, and the deer dying in the forests, when the white man's greed and technology have all but destroyed Mother Earth. At that time, the Indian people will find their lost spirit and communicate it to the other races. Together, as warriors of the Rainbow, these people will go forth to restore the sense of the sacred. A great part of our inspiration, from the beginning, came from this Indian prophecy.

It was therefore, not surprising to find, in short order, that we had been joined by numerous nature mystics, shamans, Indian revolutionaries, Buddhist monks and even a renegade Brahman from India. From the Kwakiutl Indians of British Columbia's west coast we borrowed an image of the whale which became our symbol and our banner. By "coincidence" the head of the oldest school of Tibetan Buddhism, Gyalwa Karmapa XIV, a man believed by his followers to be the personification of the Divine Compassion, showed up in Vancouver, and, told of our plans, announced that such effort "is in accord with the will of the Buddha." He gave us his personal blessing. A white-haired mystic, who lived in an old wooden shack in east Vancouver, emerged from his retreat to donate five acres of land which we were allowed to raffle off to raise money. He promised as well to control the weather for us so that we could not be stopped.

All this was a bit too bizarre for the existing conservation organizations, so we soon found ourselves operating on the outer edge of the environmental movement. It did not seem to matter that we had at least four Ph.D.'s working closely with us. Nor did it seem to make much difference that our crew was going to include people from Japan, France, England, Australia, New Zealand, Czechoslovakia, the United States and Canada. Or that we had electronics experts, navigators, oceanographers, divers, doctors, and lawyers involved as well. We were definitely on the fringes of respectability.

It was a fine, if unconventional, blend of human talents and skills. There were, as well, dozens of people who regularly consulted the *I Ching*, astrology charts, and ancient Aztec tables. Yet for every mystic there was at least one mechanic, and salty old west coast experts on diesel engines and boat hulls showed up at the early meetings to sit next to young vegetarian women. Hippies and psychologists mixed freely with animal lovers, poets, musicians, marine surveyors, housewives, ballet dancers, computer programmers, biologists, and photographers.

We set up a trust fund, organized several benefit concerts, a raffle, and started selling buttons, T-shirts, posters and bumper stickers, using volunteers ranging in age from six to seventy years. By April of 1975 we had worked out an arrangement with John C. Cormack, the tough old captain who had taken us up to the Aleutian Islands in 1971, to make use of his eighty-foot halibut seiner, *Phyllis Cormack*, again. A second skipper, a silver-haired former law professor and Second World War pilot named Jacques Longini, had volunteered the use of his own sailing vessel, *Vega*, which meant that we could theoretically cover twice the area of ocean which we could otherwise patrol.

The fact remained, however, that our lead vessel could make only a maximum of ten knots, and the sailing vessel only seven with a good stiff wind behind it. Our total range was obviously less than a tiny portion of the North Pacific. And so while we had succeeded in raising money and attracting the attention of the media, the essential ingredient was very much still lacking. How were we ever to find the fleets?

Most of the people closely involved in the process of creating a reality out of our fantasy—to actually find a way to get our bodies out onto the ocean and save some whales—were firmly of two minds as to what was happening. With one mind it was easy to see that we were involved in the flowering of an inevitable miracle. The weather itself seemed to be on our side. The things that were needed, appeared. When a certain kind of talent became essential, some individual or another materialized on our doorstep. We seemed definitely blessed. Certainly we *felt* blessed.

But with the other mind, we could see clearly that what faced us was simply an enormous amount of work: hours and hours and hours of hassles to find parts for an engine, paint for a deck, guarantors to sign for a loan, all of that and more. (Yes, we raised most of the money by borrowing from a bank. Protest now, pay later.) At that level, the first five months of 1975 were a burn-out. No fewer than three hundred people showed up at one time or another to volunteer their services. We went through them, exhausting their energies, in weeks. Only a hard core of about one dozen people held the project together, and the toll, psychologically, was dreadful. Seven of our brothers became so mentally and emotionally drained that they ended under sedation in hospitals or else behind bars. It was a disorganized attack, deeply inspired and trembling with high levels of energy, but incredibly wasteful.

By April 27, we came to the end of what seemed to have been a very long and frantic journey—the point where the first antiwhaling expedition was about to be launched. There had been a tremendous storm the night before. It left broken telephone poles and ships smashed against their docks. Rooftops had been shredded. Yet on the morning of the day Greenpeace was to set sail the light came clear for the first time in months. Rainbows appeared over the bay. With twenty thousand people cheering us as we set out from the beach to our ships in a recycled Army landing craft, there was nothing that we could feel except that we were on our way to an ecological crusade ...

We sense that we are near the end of the era in which human beings unwittingly slaughter the whales to the brink of extinction. In Japan hundreds of workers are laid off each year as the industry winds down. The Russians have indicated officially that they are soon to stop whaling. At this writing the International Whaling Commission has been forced to lower the quotas in light of the unexpectedly low catch figures. But what a grand day it would be in the evolution of human consciousness if we could collectively decide to stop killing the whales now, not for economic or political reasons, but because we were finally able to see through the barrier of specism that has separated us from all the other sentient beings with whom we share this planet.

Many people have already made that breakthrough. They are the whale people, and the motifs of their stories indicate some mysteriously shared shift of consciousness, brought on by their encounters with the whales. Suddenly we see ourselves face to face with an alien intelligence right here on planet earth. And perhaps we have heard the signals that mark the end of the childhood of the human race. Perhaps we have begun to break the bonds of our humanness, and to accept ourselves, not separate from, but as a part of wild nature ...

4. Farley Mowat, *Sea of Slaughter*, 1984.

... Goaded by this alien presence on their traditional sealing grounds, and with their cupidity belatedly aroused by the increasing value of seal fat, Newfoundlanders now returned to the ice. By 1947, they were again manning a small handful of sealing ships. However, theirs was a nondescript fleet consisting mostly of small motor vessels normally employed in the cod fishery or the coastal trade. These were hopelessly outclassed by fourteen brand-new Norwegian sealers, which by 1950 were ravaging the Front while the Karlsen fleet did the same in the Gulf. Amongst them, the Norwegians landed better than 200,000 sculps that year. A year later they brought back twice as many—a slaughter the like of which had not been attained since 1881. The fire had flared up anew.

Not content with killing pups and adult females on the whelping ice and adults of both sexes at the moulting patches, the Norwegian offshore fleet took to pursuing the migrating herds northward, even as far as west Greenland waters, killing all the way. The seals they killed would normally have returned south to pup the following spring. Most were not given the chance. In a single year, the new Vikings landed 60,000 sculps out of probably 300,000 adults shot in water and on ice.

This was bloodletting on such a scale as to quickly wipe out whatever gains the harp and hood nations had made since 1919. By 1961, according to Dr. David Sergeant, the western harp nation had declined to an estimated 1,750,000 individuals, or about half of what it was thought to have numbered ten years earlier ...

During the late 1950s, Norwegian chemists had finally discovered a way of treating whitecoat pelts so that the soft and silky hair would remain fast to the skin. The resultant fur delighted the fashion market in affluent Western countries. Although in 1952 a whitecoat sculp unloaded at the docks had only been worth about a dollar, and this mostly for the fat, by 1961 it was worth $5, four of which were for the fur alone. Since a single sealer loose in a whelping patch could kill and sculp as many as 100 whitecoats a day, truly enormous profits could now be made. In1962 the price for whitecoats rose to $7.50 as a mindless passion for seal fur swept fashion salons and fired the acquisitive desires of civilized women in Europe and America. The result was a frantic rush to the ice that spring, one that turned the harp and hood nurseries of eastern Canada into bloody abbatoirs as sealers sculped 330,000 hoods and harps, of which more than 200,000 were whitecoats.

In the light of what followed it is only fair to emphasize that, up to this point, Canadians had played a relatively small, and usually menial, part in the post-war history of the sealing industry. For the most part they served as low-paid butchers and draft animals, assisting a foreign nation to destroy a Canadian resource. Not that there was anything new about this. Canada has always been content to divest herself of natural resources in exchange for jobs for her citizenry as haulers of water and hewers of wood.

Canadian governments, federal and provincial, did everything in their power to assist the Norwegians. Aerial ice reconnaissance was provided to the sealing fleet. Canadian Coast Guard icebreakers were made available to assist the sealers. Most helpful of all perhaps was the refusal of the federal government to implement conservation legislation that would have interfered with the uninhibited pursuit of profit at the ice.

In the 1960s, the so-called seal "hunt" became a veritable orgy of destruction as get-rich-quick entrepreneurs congregated like vultures over the ice floes. Nor is this simile far-fetched. In the spring of 1962 some ships began using helicopters to transport sealers to distant pans and to ferry sculps back to the vessels. The following year, with whitecoat pelts fetching $10 each, an airborne assault was launched against the Gulf seals by dozens of light planes equipped with skis or balloon tires so they could operate on ice.

These planes were mostly owned by the pilots who flew them: aerial gypsies who knew little or nothing about sealing, but who were hot on the scent of a literal quick killing. The pilot-owners hired local men from the Magdalens or Prince Edward Island, flew them out to the whelping patches at dawn, then spent the rest of the day ferrying sculps to makeshift landing strips ashore.

The rivalry that developed amongst these airborne raiders, landsmen sealers, and the sealing fleet brought anarchy to the ice. Whatever rules of sense or sensibility might previously have been observed were now abandoned. Air sealers even hijacked panned sculps left on the ice by sealing ships, and not a few aircraft arrived back at their shore bases with bullet holes in their wings and fuselages. The whelping nurseries of the harp seal nation became a grisly shambles ...

Most of the pilots did go back, however, and were joined by many more, since the rewards for two weeks of hard living and considerable risk-taking could exceed $10,000. In 1964, whitecoat sculps went up to $12.50 each, fuelling a carnage that was becoming wanton beyond belief. At least sixty-five light aircraft, together with several helicopters, "worked" the Gulf seals that spring, along with hundreds of landsmen and the sealing fleet. The competition was ruthless, and the sealers pitiless. Even the best of them became driven machines, wasting or abandoning many pups in their frenzied haste to forestall competitors.

Eighty-one thousand whitecoats were removed from the Gulf ice that spring.

Although the actual number killed will never be known, there is agreement amongst those who were there that the year's "crop" was effectively wiped out. At the Front, where light aircraft could not operate, things were almost as grim. An estimated 85 per cent of the pups born were killed by the Norwegian fleet. The saving grace, if it could be called such, was that at the Front the butchers were at least professionals and there was comparatively little waste.

Meanwhile, seal products continued to diversify. Aprés-ski slippers for women and boots and sports jackets for men made of the silvery skins of adult seals led to a renewed slaughter of mature animals after the annual whitecoat and blueback massacre ended. Even the net fishery flourished anew, particularly along the south Labrador coast. Fishermen who had never previously bothered with seals began catching adults and bedlamers on huge, baited hooks. Worse still, crowds of men and youths started gunning for bedlamers and beaters from every sort of boat, using lightweight .22 calibre rifles. Only a lucky hit in the brain with a .22 was likely to kill even a beater. The accountant of a fish plant in northern Newfoundland who got seal fever and went swatching told me he estimated the ratio of hits to kills at about ten to one.

Not since the mid-nineteenth century had the ice seals endured such merciless persecution. In 1963, reported landings from the northwestern Atlantic totalled 352,000—"reported" because the Norwegians were believed to always land many more than were admitted. Assuming a most conservative loss ratio, the kill that year must have been close to 500,000. The following spring the death toll was almost as huge.

By the summer of 1964 it had become brutally obvious to everyone involved in the business that the ice seals were destined to commercial, if not actual, extinction. From as many as 10 million (the estimates vary) in its aboriginal state, the western herd of the harp nation had been reduced to little more than a million. As for those at the West Ice, not more than 200,000 survived. The Soviets had also joined in the outbreak of uncontrolled avarice by grossly over-killing whitecoats in the White Sea in order to profit from the Western world's mania for sealskin artifacts.

Those departments of the Norwegian, Canadian, and Soviet governments entrusted with the regulation and protection of fisheries were fully aware of what was happening. They had been briefed by their own scientists, most of whom, it must be said in all fairness, were predicting a devastating collapse of harp and hood populations unless the mayhem on the ice was quickly halted.

Norway and Canada ignored the warnings. However, in the autumn of 1964 the Soviet government prohibited further ship-borne sealing in the White

Sea. When challenged to follow suit, a spokesman for Canada's Department of Fisheries asserted that, far from declining, harp seals were actually increasing in numbers. Furthermore, there could be no thought of interfering with the rights of free enterprise to continue making a legitimate profit from this "rational harvesting of a natural resource which was of great importance to the Canadian economy."

The Norwegian response was to point out that, since the Front and West Ice seals lived in international waters, it was nobody's business what their sealers did. Norway would accept no restraint on her freedom to "fish" on the high seas.

Up until this time, the world at large had remained in ignorance of what was happening. This condition might well have continued until the western Atlantic harp and hood nations had been totally destroyed had it not been for a singularly ironic twist of fate. In 1964 a small, Montreal-based company called Artek won a contract from Quebec's tourism department to make some television films extolling the attractions of La Belle Province. Having filmed the usual subjects, it occurred to the producer that something special would add spice to the series. One of his staff, a Magdalen Islander, mentioned a seal hunt that took place there every spring, and this sounded like the very thing. So, in March of 1964, the Artek crew went to the archipelago and filmed what was intended to show an archaic but exciting struggle between man and nature on the harsh world of the ice fields—a glimpse, as it were, of Old Quebec in pioneering days.

The resulting film was exciting enough—but excruciatingly gory. Not only did it show the stark vista of crimson slush on white ice, which is the hallmark of the seal hunt, it captured harrowing scenes of sealers with steel-hooked staves gaffing what may well be the most appealing young creature in the animal kingdom, together with stunning close-ups of one of these attractive little animals—being skinned alive.

When the French television network of the Canadian Broadcasting Corporation screened this film, the audience response was so overwhelming that the corporation decided to broadcast it on the national network, with English subtitles. The subtitles were hardly needed. The images were so devastatingly revolting that words were superfluous.

The reaction of many viewers, including a number of Americans who tune in to CBC, was a massive outpouring of revulsion and outrage. Local branches of the Humane Society and the Society for the Prevention of Cruelty to Animals obtained copies of the film and showed them across the country in church basements, community halls, and schools. Members of Parliament and the federal

Department of Fisheries were inundated by a wave of indignation as thousands of ordinary people registered their protests and demanded that the massacre of baby seals be stopped forthwith. An appalled Quebec Bureau of Tourism did its best to squelch the film. It was far too late for that.

Copies had already gone overseas, there to be further copied and distributed. In West Germany, Dr. Bernard Grzimek of the Frankfurt Zoo not only showed it on television, Europe-wide, but launched a popular crusade to force the Canadian government to "halt this murderous atrocity." Bewildered Canadian embassy staffs soon found themselves beleaguered by picketers and showered with hate mail. As one unhappy spokesman for the sealing industry put it, with surely unconscious humour, "The fat was in the fire."

Indeed it was. Although the Canadian and Norwegian governments, supporting and supported by the sealing industry, did everything in their power to smother the uproar, they only succeeded in intensifying it. In the words of a federal employee, "The combination of that lovable little seal-pup image and the visible result, when what was really just a sack of blood and guts was spilled onto the ice, couldn't be handled rationally ... facts and figures can't counter stuff like that. If we'd been killing baby squids we could've held our own maybe, but baby seals?"

Goaded and prodded into angry reactions, Canadian authorities counterattacked by stigmatizing those who complained about the seal slaughter as deluded dupes, bleeding hearts, or self-serving publicists. The Department of Fisheries rallied its experts and set them to disseminate the "true facts." Having vehemently denied that any cruelty was involved in commercial sealing—"such accusations amount to an unwarranted slur on honest, working fishermen"—departmental spokesmen insisted that the sealing industry was a vital and sustaining element in the Canadian economy and was being rationally and humanely managed.

"The seal fishery is properly regulated," said the Honourable H.R. Robichaud, the federal Minister of Fisheries, as he hurriedly introduced the first regulations ever to be imposed on the sealers. As of the spring of 1965, he announced, access to the seal fishery would be reduced by the introduction of a licensing system requiring the owner of each ship or aircraft to pay a fee of $25 for the right to "harvest" harp or hood seals. Furthermore, in order to protect the stock, a quota of 50,000 seals would be imposed on the Gulf sealers and Fisheries officers would be assigned to supervise the operation and ensure adherence to the laws. Finally, in order to give the lie to accusations of cruelty, representatives of animal welfare groups would be escorted to the Gulf ice fields so they could satisfy themselves, and the world, that the seals were being killed with all due consideration.

Licensing ships and aircraft was a mockery. Even had the fee imposed been realistic, it would have had little or no effect unless the *number* of licences issued was limited, and it was not. Supervision of the slaughter in 1965 by Fisheries officers consisted of counting the sculps delivered by planes and ships—a rather rough count, too, since the quota was exceeded by some 4,000 whitecoats. The visit of the observers to the ice that season was thoughtfully scheduled for the *second* week of the "harvest" and therefore did not take place, because the quota, quite predictably, had been filled in the first four days by ten big ships and sixty or more aircraft that ravaged the Gulf whelping patches.

Finally, the quota of 50,000 whitecoats applied *only* to the Gulf, and *only* to big ships and aircraft. Landsmen, small vessel operators, gunners, and netters everywhere remained free to take all the seals, young or old, that they could kill. As for the slaughter at the Front, by mutual agreement between Canada and Norway, it continued without any supervision or restrictions, pretended or real ...

Such was the beginning of a singularly unedifying battle between various humane and animal welfare agencies, with some vehemently supporting the official contention that the baby seals perished, if not happily, at least painlessly, while others insisted that many whitecoats died agonizing deaths ...

When our forebears commenced their exploitation of this continent they believed the animate resources of the New World were infinite and inexhaustible. The vulnerability of that living fabric—the intricacy and fragility of its all-too-finite parts—was beyond their comprehension. It can at least be said in their defence that they were mostly ignorant of the inevitable consequences of their dreadful depredations.

We who are alive today can claim no such exculpation for our biocidal actions and their dire consequences. Modern man has increasing opportunity to be aware of the complexity and inter-relationship of the living world. If ignorance is to serve now as an excuse then it can only be wilful, murderous ignorance.

Five centuries of death-dealing on this continent is not to be gainsaid; but there are at least some indications that we may finally be developing the will and the conscience to look beyond the gratification of our own immediate needs and desires. Belatedly we seem to be trying to rejoin the community of living beings from which we have, for so long, alienated ourselves—and of which we have, for so long, been the mortal enemy.

Evidence of such a return to sanity is not yet to be looked for in the attitudes and actions of the monolithic organizations that dominate the human world. Rather, the emerging signs of sanity are seen in individuals who, revolted by the frightful excesses to which we have subjected animate creation, are beginning to revolt against the killer beast man has become.

Banding together in groups of ever-increasing potency, they are challenging the licence of vested interests to continue savaging the living world for policy, profit, or pleasure. That they are having an effect is attested to by what they have already accomplished in just the past few years. A prime example is their achievement on behalf of the ice seals. Although they are being furiously opposed by the old orders, it would appear that they are slowly gaining ground.

It is to this new resolution to reassert our indivisibility with life, to recognize the obligations incumbent on us as the most powerful and deadly single species ever to exist, and to begin making amends for the havoc we have wrought, that my own hopes for a revival and continuance of life on earth now turn. If we persevere in this new way, we may succeed in making man humane ... at last.

And then the Sea of Slaughter may once again become a sea of life.

5. David Suzuki, *Time to Change: Essays*, 1994.

The Northern Cod

For Canadians, fish on our three long coasts have been a vital part of our culture. The lives of many aboriginal people were built around fish. When John Cabot encountered the vast shoals of northern cod, he set off 500 years of European exploitation of the eastern coastal waters. That five-century-long history of seemingly limitless abundance came crashing to an end with frightening speed. The fate of the northern cod and the plight of Newfoundlanders who depend on them are an allegory for what we have been doing to the planet.

In a Newfoundland outport, the environment is an intimate part of daily life. Here the word *fish* means cod, the focus of life in most villages. On a visit in 1991, it was sad to watch boats dock while men kept up a veneer of bravado and good humour to mask the pitiful catches.

The fishermen knew the fish were disappearing. They depend on them to survive. I spoke to an elder in the village of Salvage who began fishing as an 11-year-old in 1926. He went to sea for five to six months at a stretch, sailed along the Labrador coast at 15 and earned $90 a season. "We're fishing too hard," he said bluntly. "It's not just the foreign boats. Our gear is too efficient and the fishing season too long. We should stop all fishing to let the stocks come back, but they will never return to what they were."

I met an elderly woman who still goes fishing with her disabled husband just for the joy of being at sea. As she cut cod tongues (a delicacy) from discarded heads, she told me with eloquent simplicity, "I watch all of those 'britches' [codfish ovaries] being thrown out. I see the lumpfish eggs [for caviar] taken in such quantities that those fish will disappear. Eggs are future fish. If they're not being laid, there's no fish."

The fabled abundance of codfish off the Grand Banks has long been exploited by many countries. But now the pressure is too great. Far offshore, huge factory ships take massive numbers of fish with deadly efficiency. Closer to land, fishermen take more in large traps where the cod gather.

The Newfoundland fishery is a symbol of a sustainable resource that is being pushed to extinction. But it's not just overfishing that is to blame. Our failure to control human depradation of fish habitat and interconnected food chains has also taken a toll.

Smeltlike fish called capelin abound in these waters and are the base of the vertebrate food chain for cod as well as seabirds, seals, and whales. The vast numbers of capelin seem to act like a buffer against overharvesting. But Newfoundland, like British Columbia, has found a hungry market in Japan for fish roe, and the eggs are taken from "ripe" females while the rest—whole males, female carcasses, whole immature females—are simply discarded.

Apparently still looming ahead is the huge Hibernia offshore oil development with promises of infusion of jobs and money into a troubled economy. But in "Iceberg Alley" it will add another inevitable stress to the marine ecosystem.

There are troubling hints of worse to come. During my visit in 1991, the capelin failed to appear on time. Some predicted an unprecedentedly late July arrival. Capelin spawn within a narrow window set by water temperature, and that year an abnormal number of icebergs and chunks of pack ice kept the waters around Newfoundland cool. Increased calving of Arctic ice could reflect a decade of record-high world temperatures. In nature, exquisitely choreographed cycles like the capelin-cod connections will be highly sensitive to such environmental change.

There are too many unknowns. What are the effects on cod of pollution, overfishing, decrease in capelin, habitat destruction, and global warming? Do such factors interact synergistically? What are the interconnections in the web of marine ecosystems? In truth, we have no idea.

Meanwhile, the future of cod populations hinges on political decisions, not ecological principles. The "cod problem" is a biological matter that extends far beyond the jurisdiction of the Department of Fisheries and Oceans. Fish are affected by energy policies, by pollution from industries and municipalities, by agriculture and forestry practices, and by transportation, whereas catch levels are arrived at after being filtered through government bureaucracies and political priorities.

The people of Newfoundland's outports know the cod have to be relieved from fishing pressure and their habitat given time to recover, and they are prepared to make more sacrifices to save a future. But faced with the realities of dwindling stocks and reduced income and jobs, the fisher folk don't have the options to escape the political and economic imperatives.

The cod crisis illustrates our failure to balance immediate job and profit needs with long-term protection of the fish. So now 35,000 jobs, to say nothing of a way of life, are on the line. Development of the Hibernia offshore oil field will only provide a temporary infusion of jobs and cash that, once exhausted, will leave people all the more helpless and dependent. And the risk of oil spills puts the fishery at even greater risk.

It didn't have to be this way. The fish population could have been sustained indefinitely even with human predation. But it would have required a radical shift in perspective and priorities. It would mean adapting our lives and economy around the health and survival of the fish. Thus, for example, an inland fishery relying primarily on hand-line fishing from small boats could have employed far more people with far less impact on the fish. But an exploding global market, the availability of a deadly technology for finding and "harvesting" cod, and the lure of big bucks may have depleted them below a critical threshold.

There are plenty of scapegoats—pollution, seals, parasites, whales, foreign fleets, bad weather, cold waters, incompetent bureaucrats, and scientists. But the simple fact is the cod have been overfished and we have no idea how to manage them in a sustainable way.

In 1991, only 127,000 tonnes of the allotted Canadian cod quota of 185,000 tonnes were actually caught. The fish weren't there! The government's decision in February 1992 to "cut" the quota by 35 percent to 120,000 tonnes was just a token gesture that put off the inevitable decision to shut down the cod fishery completely for a few years and pray the fish would come back.

Newfoundland fisher folk are paying the terrible price for society's short-sightedness, and their experience offers a priceless lesson to all sectors of society. We cannot expect nature to increase its productivity to fulfill our economic and political needs. Since the cod do not remain within human boundaries, ecological distribution, not politics or economics, must determine our quotas.

To preserve "stocks," we always have to restrict ourselves very conservatively, since our knowledge is so limited. Small-scale, long-term jobs that are rooted in the culture of local communities make far more sense than short-lived megaprojects like Hibernia. During this unavoidable transition to a sustainable way of life, Newfoundlanders must be helped with real jobs that make sense, like enforcing of the fishing moratorium and Canadian sovereignty on the oceans, rehabilitating habitat, doing more marine research, promoting energy conservation, and adopting a lifestyle that takes into account the natural factors that are so vital a part of Newfoundland life.

The cut in quotas on northern cod announced in early 1992 was followed by a complete moratorium. It was a tragedy for all Canadians. The reverberations went far beyond the catastrophic consequences for the people immediately put out of work and their families. They were also felt by the many more whose services were indirectly affected by the layoff and by all Canadians who treasure the rich cultural diversity of the Canadian mosaic.

But it will be a greater tragedy if we fail to recognize the painful lessons that must be applied to many other sectors of society, such as the forest industry, hydroelectric megaprojects, mining operations, aluminum, pulp and nuclear industries, coal-burning plants, and so on. These are some of the expensive lessons we've gained:

Since our ignorance about the natural world that sustains us is vast, everything we do ought to be done cautiously and conservatively. The two-year moratorium on cod fishing is based on sheer guesswork. The fact is, we simply don't know enough about the biology of the northern cod to "rehabilitate" the species or to predict what will happen when the fishing pressure is off. All we can do is back off and hope nature can do it for us.

Everything is interconnected. We cannot even pretend to "manage" a wild species. Inshore and offshore fishing, bottom dragging, seine nets and longlines, Canadian and foreign fleets, capelin, seals, whales, industrial pollution, soil erosion, and oil spills all impact on cod. We have no mechanisms to deal with cod as a biological entity in an all-encompassing way.

In attempting to mitigate human suffering, we must keep the long-term fate of northern cod as the highest priority. The cod must not be held hostage to human economic, political, and social needs, such as the threats by fishers to continue fishing to get more money. Nature cannot be shoehorned to conform to our priorities, demands, and jurisdiction. The natural regenerative capacity of the cod "stocks," not jobs or economic pressures, must determine the fishing seasons and catch limits to which we must then adapt.

Management of resources must be *ecologically* based. Fish do not recognize borders that delineate our provincial or international territory; they are distributed according to their biological needs. Everything under the ocean surface is not homogeneous and infinitely self-regenerating. Massive drift nets and heavy dragnets pulled along the ocean floor disrupt whole communities of organisms and their habitats and ought to be stopped.

Technology, even in resource extraction sectors like fishing and logging, has become too large and powerful for natural systems to absorb its impact and replenish themselves. We must learn to curtail the use of such technologies to protect the integrity of ecosystems and "harvest" fish at levels that are readily replenished.

Conventional economics cannot be allowed to dictate our policies; its emphasis on growth and maximal short-term profit is inevitably destructive. If we liken fish to basic capital on which wealth is built, then annual yields will represent far lower returns than can be obtained from the stock market. But unlike the financial world, the returns on the fish can be maintained in perpetuity.

Politicians respond primarily to voters who form a rather limited constituency. Immediately after the moratorium on cod, Newfoundland Premier Clyde Wells explained his province's helplessness: "We have seven votes out of 300 in the House of Commons." But how representative is government? Excess representation of business and law skew government preoccupation toward economic or jurisdictional matters.

Furthermore, if politicians respond to an electorate, who speaks on behalf of those who can't vote? At the Earth Summit in Rio, Holland was the only country to name children as official delegates. Holland must be congratulated, but why didn't all countries have child and youth delegates? Our generation is a mere moment within a historical continuum linking all of our ancestors with all generations to come. Who weighs our current actions against the past and all the still-to-be-born of the future? And who speaks on behalf of the northern cod, whales, seals, and capelin that are so interrelated? Who represents the trees, air, water, or soil?

Newfoundlanders are becoming environmental refugees, displaced by ecological disturbances, and are a warning to us that something is wrong. If we don't learn from our mistakes and tragedies, then we are truly doomed to repeat them. Today, as the planet's biosphere careens into the future, we can't afford to ignore the costly lessons.

6. Tzeporah Berman, *Clayoquot and Dissent*, 1994.

Takin' it Back

The protests in Clayoquot Sound represent one of the largest civil disobedience actions in Canada's history. In the summer of 1993 over 800 people were arrested for standing on a logging road in one of the largest areas of temperate rainforest left in the world. Many were there for less than ten minutes. Hundreds have gone to jail. The people who protested in Clayoquot Sound have been referred to as "spoilt children," "welfare bums," "hippies" and most recently by Patrick Moore of the industry-funded "B.C. Forest Alliance" as "wacked out nature worshippers who pray to the moon." They have also been called heroes. In reality they were courageous grandmothers, children, students, seniors and others from all walks of life who found freedom in incarceration and strength in the ability to stand together and make change.

In 1969 the Canadian Council of Christians and Jews wrote that, "Law and order, though vital for society, can often be used to cover injustice. It is no longer sufficient merely to advocate obedience to law. The attainment of justice is first; without it, law is merely a facade."[1] Law is the product of an evolving process and as such it should reflect issues important to society. As values and perceptions change, the law must be recast to reflect new realities.[2] Throughout history, social conflict has proven necessary to attain dramatic social change. At one time blacks were treated as slaves and women were considered their husband's property. For many people who stood on the road in Clayoquot Sound, viewing "nature" as a commodity which humans have the right to exploit seems equally as absurd. Before thousands of black people were given their freedom or women were given the right to vote, there were the lunch counters and buses in the South and thousands of women jailed for picketing polling stations and chaining themselves to legislatures. Any attempt to reevaluate our basic perceptions of worth and value will not be easy and will not come without a dramatic struggle. For many, the catalyst necessary to begin to see the forests for the trees and to reevaluate our relationship with "nature" was the summer of 1993 in Clayoquot Sound.

Located on the west coast of Vancouver Island, Clayoquot (pronounced Klak'wat) Sound is one of very few areas of coastal lowland temperate rainforest left on the planet. It is a unique and beautiful region of white sand beaches, deep green valleys with rich salmon spawning streams, fjords, fresh water lakes, and snow-capped alpine mountains. Clayoquot Sound is home to ancient western red cedars over a thousand years old and Douglas firs that tower 250 feet above the ground. Because of its diverse geography, the area provides habitat for the black bear, cougar, wolves, bald eagles, the elusive marbled murrelet, orca and grey whales and some of the rarest sharks in the world.

Given its intense beauty and high "resource" value, it is not surprising that Clayoquot Sound has become the scene of a showdown of epic proportions. The protests in Clayoquot Sound began over a decade ago on Meares Island. After a two-year planning process, timber giant MacMillan Bloedel pulled out and refused all three options presented by the negotiators. When the logging boats headed out to the island, they were met with a blockade of Nuu-chah-nulth First Nations people and local environmentalists. Eventually the Nuu-chah-nulth obtained an injunction to prevent the company from logging the island, but the issue is still before the courts and has already cost the native community over a million dollars in legal fees.

The first protests were the beginning of a growing relationship between First Nations and the environmental community, a relationship that has matured considerably over the last year. Non-native environmentalists are gradually coming to realize what had been obvious from the First Nations' perspective all along: people don't live in parks and an ancient burial ground is not a recreational site. While the environmental community has still much to learn, Clayoquot Sound has sparked a deeper understanding of the links between social and environmental issues. We are at a point of consensus between the environmental and native communities—that clearcutting irreparably damages our ecological, social and cultural landscapes.

The committees, government processes and subsequent blockades and protests continued intermittently over the years, but didn't reach a fever pitch until 1993, after the provincial government's announcement of the Clayoquot Land Use Decision. After much time and fanfare, Premier Harcourt announced that 62% of Clayoquot Sound would be open to clearcut logging; 33% of Clayoquot Sound would be "protected." What the Premier didn't say is that almost half of the protected area was previously protected and the 62% of Clayoquot Sound open to clearcut logging translates into 74% of the rainforest. Adding insult to injury, the government designated some areas of forests as "scenic corridors" and others as "special management zones." In reality, scenic corridors have proven to be thin strips of trees left along the water while the mountains above are stripped clean. For all intensive purposes "special management zones" appear to be another term for what was previously "modified landscape"—clearcuts.

Almost 70% of Vancouver Island's ancient forests have been clearcut. Where there were once 170 intact watersheds on the island, now there are only eleven.

Five are in Clayoquot Sound. Under the new decision, two intact watersheds would be protected. The decision was touted far and wide as a "responsible compromise." Before the decision, the industry was clearcutting 540,000 cubic metres of rainforest a year in Clayoquot Sound; after the decision they were allowed to log 600,000 cubic metres.

The Clayoquot Land Use Decision sparked cries of protest around the province which quickly spread around the globe. On July 1, the Clayoquot Sound Peace Camp opened and protests were held at Canadian consulates in Austria, Germany, England, Australia and the United States.

The Peace Camp was set up by the Friends of Clayoquot Sound to provide a meaningful forum for grassroots protests. It was a ramshackle village of tents and trailers symbolically situated in an old clearcut known as "the Black Hole." In the four months that it was operating, over 12,000 people visited the camp and joined the protests. In the Peace Camp we created a fluctuating, chaotic and warm community that functioned somewhat as a large extended family, through intense stress and upheaval. In this community, business people rolled up their sleeves beside students, musicians and doctors to wash dishes, help with twenty-four-hour security, or plan the protests to come. Functioning solely on donations, the camp managed to feed at least 200 people a day with healthy vegetarian meals.

In many respects the Peace Camp was a vehicle for and an embodiment of social change. Everyone who entered the camp agreed to abide by a basic set of principles that formed the foundations upon which the community functioned and the context within which we protested. The Peaceful Direct Action Code, as it was called, was developed through an analysis of the philosophies of nonviolent civil disobedience. It was built upon Gandhian principles and the lessons learned from civil rights and environmental protests around the globe. It is as follows:

Peaceful Direct Action Code

1. Our attitude is one of openness, friendliness and respect toward all beings we encounter.
2. We will not use violence either verbal or physical towards any being.
3. We will not damage any property and we will discourage others from doing so.
4. We will strive for an atmosphere of calm and dignity.
5. We will carry no weapons.
6. We will not bring or use alcohol or drugs.

Each day at the Camp, workshops were held which explored the philosophy of nonviolence and civil disobedience, consensus decision-making and legal issues, as well as the history and ecology of Clayoquot Sound. The workshops and "Peaceful Direct Action Code" helped to ensure that the massive protests and the camp community remained peaceful at all times. People learned how to work together, diffuse anger, to refocus fear and anxiety constructively, and most of all, to listen to and respect one another. The philosophy of nonviolence has a great deal to do with abolishing power as we know it and redefining it as something common to all. *Power over* is to be replaced by *shared power*, by the power to do things, by the discovery of our own strength as opposed to a passive receiving of power exercised by others, often in our name. Individuals feel, and in many ways are, powerless against the state, but when we are more than individuals we can find strength, confidence and real power in working together. The success of the Peace Camp was not only in the peaceful daily blockades at the Kennedy River Bridge but the skills, knowledge and experience that thousands of individuals took back to their communities. What grew out of the "Black Hole" was a common understanding that we have a right, indeed a responsibility, to stand up for what we believe in—and together we have the ability to do it effectively.

The government and industry have responded to the protests with fear and aggression. They have called environmentalists "hysterical," and worse. We've heard this before. The took a similar line up to the day the Atlantic cod stocks collapsed. For years Dupont called environmentalists "hysterical" for claiming that CFC's eat away at the ozone layer. Our challenge is to reverse the burden of proof. It is the corporations and governments who now must prove that their practices are ecologically and culturally responsible.

Government and industry have characterized the present debate as a choice between liking trees or liking workers. But the thousands of people who came to Clayoquot realized that we simply cannot negate our dependence on natural systems; scientists call it biodiversity. "Biodiversity is no frill. It is life and all that sustains life." Biodiversity resembles a hammock: as destructive industrial practices like clearcutting dramatically alter existing ecosystems, species go extinct, the hammock unravels. Eventually the hammock can no longer hold anything. We need to begin to understand our dependence on natural systems and to develop mechanisms to have this understanding translate into socio-economic and political realities.

Ultimately, the struggle for Clayoquot Sound is not only a struggle for "wilderness" or sound forest practices but fundamentally a struggle with how we interact with the natural world; and whether we have a right to irreversibly change, and in some cases irreversibly damage the environment. It is a struggle to value the future over monetary gain and, in so doing, to recognize that short-term economic gain will not benefit human or non-human communities. It is a struggle for justice. And may be no more complicated than simply recognizing that we all need to breathe air and drink water ...

The message rings clear: When we stand, we stand for our lives.

Readings

Benedickson, J. *Idleness, Water and a Canoe: Reflections on Paddling for Pleasure.* Toronto: University of Toronto Press, 1997.

Berger, C. *Science, God and Nature in Victorian Canada.* Toronto: University of Toronto Press, 1982.

Bohlen, J. *Making Waves: The Origin and Future of Greenpeace.* Montreal: Black Rose, 2001.

Burns, B. and M. Schintz. *Guardians of the Wild: A History or the Warden Service of Canada's National Parks.* Calgary: University of Calgary Press, 2000.

Carroll, J. *Acid Rain: An Issue in Canadian-American Relations.* Toronto: C.D. Howe Institute, 1982.

Flader, S., ed. *The Great Lakes Forest: An Environmental and Social History.* Minneapolis: University of Minnesota Press, 1983.

Foster, J. *Working for Wildlife: The Beginnings of Preservation in Canada.* Toronto: University of Toronto Press, 1978.

Gaffield, C. and P. Gaffield. *Consuming Canada: Readings in Environmental History.* Toronto: Copp Clark, 1995.

Gillis, P. and T. Roach. *Lost Initiatives: Canada's Forest Industries, Forest Policy and Forest Conservation.* Westport: Greenwood, 1986.

Hood, G. *Against the Flow: Rafferty-Almeda and the Politics of the Environment.* Calgary: Fifth House, 1994.

Hunter, R. *Warriors of the Rainbow: A Chronicle of the Greenpeace Movement.* New York: Holt, Rinehart and Winston, 1979.

Judd, R. "Policy and Ecology in Forest History," *Acadiensis* 23, 1 (Autumn 1993).

Killan, G. *Protected Places: A History of Ontario's Provincial Parks System.* Toronto: Dundurn, 1993.

Kline, M. *Beyond the Land Itself: Views of Nature in Canada and the United States.* Cambridge: Harvard University Press, 1970.

Lambert, R. *Renewing Nature's Wealth: A Centennial History of Public Management of Lands, Forests and Wildlife in Ontario, 1763–1967.* Toronto: Ontario Department of Lands and Forests, 1967.

Lorimer, R. et al., eds. *To See Ourselves/ To Save Ourselves: Ecology and Culture in Canada.* Montreal: Association of Canadian Studies, 1991.

Mies, M and V. Shiva. *Ecofeminism.* Halifax: Fernwood, 1993.

Nelles, H. *The Politics of Development: Forests, Mines and Hydro-Electric Development in Ontario, 1849–1941.* Toronto: University of Toronto Press, 1974.

Nelson, J., ed. *Canadian Parks in Perspective.* Montreal: Harvest House, 1970.

Ommer, R. "One Hundred Years of Fishery Crisis in Newfoundland," *Acadiensis* 26, 2 (Spring 1994).

Rogers, R. *Solving History: The Challenge of Environmental Activism.* Montreal: Black Rose, 1998.

Sandberg, L., ed. *Trouble in the Woods: Forest Policy and Social Conflict in Nova Scotia and New Brunswick.* Fredericton: Acadiensis Press, 1992.

Smith, C. and D. Witty. "Conservation, Resources and Environment: An Explanation and Critical Examination of the Commission of Conservation," *Plan Canada* 11, 1 (1970).

Warecki, G. *Protecting Ontario's Wilderness: A History of Changing Ideas and Preservation Politics, 1927–1973.* New York: Peter Lang, 2000.

Wilson, J. *Talk and Log: Wilderness Politics in British Columbia.* Vancouver: University of British Columbia Press, 1998.

Sources

1 **"Our Rightful Place": Continentalism, Imperialism, or Nationalism**
William Norris, "Canadian Nationality: A Present-day Plea," *The Canadian Monthly and National Review*, February 1880; Hon. Mr. Longley, *Speech, Debates and Proceedings of the House of Assembly of the Province of Nova Scotia* Nova Scotia, May 8, 1886; George M. Grant, *Imperial Federation* Winnipeg: Manitoba Free Press, 1890; Goldwin Smith, *Canada and the Canadian Question* Toronto: Hunter Rose, 1891; Jules-Paul Tardivel, La Vééritéé, March 18, 1893 reprinted in K. McKirdy, J. Moir and Y. Zoltvany eds. *Changing Perspectives in Canadian History* Don Mills: J.M. Dent and Sons, 1971; Henri Bourassa, "The French Canadian in the British Empire," *The Monthly Review*, October 1902.

2 **"The Insane Exuberance of Generosity": Anti-Potlatch Legislation**
All of these documents were reprinted in Charles Hou (comp), *To Potlatch or Not to Potlatch: An In-depth Study of Culture-Conflict between the B.C. Coastal Indian and the White Men.* Vancouver: British Columbia Teachers' Federation, 1973.

3 **"Two Distinct Personalities": The Question of Riel's Sanity**
Documents A through E can be found in D. Morton ed. *The Queen v Louis Riel.* Toronto: University of Toronto Press, 1974; a copy of Valade's document is included in T. Flanagan, "The Riel 'Lunacy Commission': The Report of Dr. Valade," *Revue de l'Université d'Ottawa* 46 (1976); Lavell's report is included in H. Bowsfield ed. *Louis Riel: Selected Readings.* Toronto: Copp Clark Pitman, 1988; Alexander Campbell, Minister of Justice, "Memorandum Respecting the Case of the Queen v. Riel," November 25, 1885 *Canada Sessional Papers* 1886, vol 19, No. 43a; Dr. Daniel Clark, "A Psycho-Medical History of Louis Riel," *Journal of Insanity,* July, 1887.

4 **"Unceasing Conflict and Unrelenting Determination": Unions and Industrialization**
Goldwin Smith, "The Labour Movement," *Canadian Monthly,* December, 1872; "The Nine Hour Movement," *Globe* March 23, 1872; *Royal Commission on the Relations of Labor and Capital in Canada* 1889; Jean Scott, *The Conditions of*

Female Labour in Ontario. Toronto: Warwick, 1889; "There is a Reason for it," *Industrial Banner*, February 1897; *La Presse*, December 6, 1902 reprinted in *L'Action Politique des Ouvriers Quebecois* Montreal: Université de Quebec Presses, 1976; A. Siegfried, *The Race Question in Canada.* London: E. Nash, 1907; "The Glace Bay Strike," *Canadian Mining Journal*, August 1,1909; E. Bradwin, *The Bunkhouse Man: A Study of Work and Play in the Camps of Canada 1903-1914.* New York: Columbia University Press, 1928, reprinted with permission from University of Toronto Press; "The Winnipeg Strike," *The Gazette*, May 22, 1919; *Western Labour News*, May 28, 1919.

5   "The Unfriendly Reception": Immigration

"Chinamen," *Saturday Night,* September 1906 and "Western Blacks," *Saturday Night,* April 1911 reproduced in M. Wolfe ed. *Saturday Night Scrapbook.* Toronto: New Press, 1973; W. Scott, "The Immigration by Races," in A. Short and A. Doughty eds. *Canada and Its Provinces* vol 7. Toronto: Glascow, 1914; W. A. Cum Yow, *Evidence before the Royal Commission on Chinese and Japanese Immigration*, Canada Sessional Papers No. 54, 1903; Dr. Sundar Singh in *Empire Club of Canada, Addresses Delivered to the Members during the Session of 1911-12.* Toronto, 1913; Maria Adamowska "Beginnings in Canada" reprinted in H. Piniuta ed. and trans., *Land of Pain, Land of Promise.* Saskatoon: Western Prairie Books, 1978.

6   "The Smell of the Good Green Earth": Rural vs. Urban Life

E. B. Mitchell, *In Western Canada Before the War.* London: John Murray, 1915, reprinted with permission; Nellie McClung, *In Times Like These.* Toronto, McLeod and Allen, 1915; Rupert Brooke, *Letters from America.* London: Sidgwick and Jackson, 1916; Mary Joplin Clarke, "Report of the Standing Committee on Neighbourhood Work," *Canadian Conference of Charities and Correction September 23-5 1917*, Ottawa: King's Printer,1917, reprinted with permission; William Irvine, *Farmers in Politics.* Toronto: McClelland and Stewart, 1920; Maude Newcombe, "The Farm Woman's Lot," *Grain Growers' Guide*, April 15, 1925, reprinted from *Country Guide*, Winnipeg, MB; Mrs. R.C. Phillips, "A Farm Woman's Reply", *Grain Growers' Guide*, May 27, 1925, reprinted from *Country Guide*, Winnipeg, MB. The last two articles were reproduced in B. Kelcey and A. Davis eds. *A Great Movement Underway: Women and the GrainGrowers' Guide, 1908-1928.* Winnipeg: Manitoba Record Society, 1997.

7   "Perfect Justice and Harmony": Votes for Women

Document 2 was reproduced in R. Cook and W. Mitchenson eds. *The Proper Sphere: Women's Place in Canadian Society.* Toronto: 1976; Hon. John Dryden, Minister of Agriculture, *Womanhood Suffrage.* Toronto: Warwick, 1893; the Bate article was reproduced in B. Kelcey and A. Davis eds. *A Great Movement Underway: Women and the Grain Growers' Guide,1908-1928.* Winnipeg: Manitoba Record Society, 1997; Henri Bourassa, "Le Suffragisme Féminin, Son Efficacité, Sa Légitimité," *Le Devoir*, April 24, 1913; Nellie McClung, *In Times Like These.* Toronto: McLeod and Allen,1915; Stephen Leacock, "The Woman Question" in *Essays and Literary Studies*. New York: John Lane, 1916; H.D.P., "The Failure of the Suffrage Movement to Bring Freedom to Women," *Woman Worker*, December 1928 recently reproduced in J. Sangster and M. Hobbs ed. *The Woman Worker, 1926-1929*. St. John's: Canadian Committee on Labour History, 1999.

8   "What is Our Duty?": Military Service in World War I
B. Wilson ed. *Ontario and the First World War 1914-1918*. Toronto: University of Toronto Press, 1977 contains copies of documents A, B, and F, reprinted with permission of the Champlain Society; *Saturday Night,* August, 1915 excerpt in M. Wolfe ed. *Saturday Night Scrapbook*. Toronto: New Press, 1973; Talbot M. Papineau, "An Open Letter from Capt Talbot Papineau to Mr. Henri Bourassa," March 21, 1916 *in Canadian Nationalism and the War*. Montreal: 1916; Henri Bourassa, "Mr. Bourassa's Reply to Capt. Talbot Papineau's Letter," August 2, 1916. same source; Robert Borden's speech on conscription is found in R. Borden ed. *Robert Laird Borden: His Memoirs vol 2*. Toronto, Macmillan 1938 and Hansard, 1917; Francis Marion Beynon, "Women's View of Conscription," *The Grain Growers' Guide,* May 30, 1917, reprinted with permission; Joseph Ainey, "Canadian Labour and Conscription," *Le Devoir* July 5, 1917; Rev. S.D. Chown, "An Open Letter on the Duty of the Hour," *Christian Guardian*, Dec 12, 1917.

9   "National Art": The Group of Seven
Percy Moore Turner, "Painting in Canada", *Canadian Forum*, December1922; "Canadian Art," *Saturday Night*, May 1924; "Canada and her Paint Slingers," *Saturday Night,* November 8, 1924; "Freak Pictures at Wembley," *Saturday Night*, December 13, 1924; Hector Charlesworth, "The Group System in Art," *Saturday Night*, June 24 1925; "The Group of Seven," *Canadian Forum*, February 1927; "The Group of Seven," *Canadian Forum*, June 1930.

10 "This is My Last Chance": Depression and Despair
With the exception of the last document, "Experiences of a Depression Hobo," *Saskatchewan History* 22 (Spring, 1969); all other materials were reproduced in L.Grayson and M. Bliss eds. *The Wretched of Canada: Letters to R. B. Bennett, 1930-1935*. Toronto: University of Toronto Press, 1971, reprinted with permission.

11 "The Question of Loyalty": Japanese Canadians and World War II
Report and Recommendations of the Special Committee on Orientals in British Columbia, December 1940; A. Neill, House of Commons, *Debates*, February 19, 1942; Muriel Kitagawa's material was reprinted with permission from *This is My Own: Letters to Wes and Other Writings on Japanese Canadians 1941-1948,* edited by Roy Miki, © 1985, Talon Books Ltd., Vancouver, BC; Prime Minister W. L. Mackenzie King, House of Commons, *Debates* August 4, 1941.

12 "Cinderella of the Empire": Newfoundland and Confederation
Smallwood's speech is found in *I Chose Canada*. Toronto: Macmillan,1973 and reproduced with permission from the Smallwood family; all other speeches are

found reproduced in *The Newfoundland National Convention 1946-1948* edited by J. Hiller and M. Harrington, Montreal-Kingston: McGill-Queen's University Press, 1995, reprinted with permission.

13 "A Glow of Fulfilled Femininity": Women in the 1950s and 1960s

Beverly Gray, "Housewives are a Sorry Lot," *Chatelaine*, March 1950; "Housewives Blast Business Girl," *Chatelaine*, June 1950; Doris McCubbin, "How to Live in a Suburb," Chatelaine, March 1955, reprinted by permission of Doris Anderson; Dr. Marion Hilliard, "Stop Being Just a Housewife," *Chatelaine*, September 1956, reprinted by permission of June Callwood; Cynthia Steers, "How Much are You Worth to Your Husband?," *Chatelaine*, April 1959; Anna Davies, "I Hate Housekeeping," *Chatelaine*, March 1961; Mollie Gillen, "The Royal Commission on the Status of Women: Will it do any Good?" *Chatelaine*, January 1968, reprinted by permission of Mollie Gillen.

14 "The Very Essence of Canadian Identity": Multiculturalism

Government of Canada, Appendix to *Hansard*, October 8, 1971, reprinted with permission; the second document comes from *Selling Illusions, the Cult of Multiculturalism* © Neil Bissoondath, 1994. Reprinted by permission of Penguin Books Canada Limited and Neil Bissoondath; Dick Field, 'Multiculturalism Undermines Values Held by Canadians', *Toronto Star*, December 23, 1994, reprinted by permission of Dick Field.

15 "The Whites were Terrorists": Residential Schools

Author's note: "Hidden from History: The Canadian Holocaust," *Nexus* (March-April) 2002 was written and edited by Reverend Kevin Annett, a former United Church minister who was fired without cause and expelled from that church in 1997 after he unearthed evidence that native children were allegedly killed by staff at the United Church Residential School in Port Alberni, B.C. Reverend Annett organized the first independent Tribunal into Canadian Residential Schools in June, 1998 in Vancouver, under the auspices of the United Nations affiliate IHRAAM. The full report contained in "Hidden from History" can be found at this website **http://canadiangenocide.nativeweb.org**; Government of Canada, Indian and Northern Affairs, "Statement of Reconciliation" January 7, 1998, reprinted with permission; Ted Byfield, "Weren't We all Physically Abused in Schools? So When do We Get Our Money for Healing," *Alberta Report*, January 19, 1998, reprinted by permission of Ted Byfield; P. Donnelly, "Scapegoating the Indian Residential Schools: The Noble Legacy of Hundreds of Christian Missionaries is Sacrificed to Political Correctness," *Alberta Report*, January 26, 1998; David Napier, "Sins of the Fathers: The Legacy of Indian Residential Schools is One of Physical and Emotional Scars, Nasty Lawsuits, A Questionable Medical Study, and Suicide," *Anglican Journal*, May 2000, reprinted with permission.

16 "Winter in Our Souls": Quebec and Independence

M. Chaput, *Why I Am A Separatist*. Toronto: Ryerson, 1961, with permission of

McGraw-Hill Ryerson Ltd.; the FLQ 1963 statement was reproduced in C. Savoie *La Veritable Histoire du FLQ*. Montreal: Editions du jour, 1963; Leger's document is found as an appendix to *Option for Quebec* by R. Levesque, Montreal: © Editions Typo et succession Rene Levesque,1997, reprinted with permission; Levesque's Harvard speech is reprinted with permission from *Authority and Influence: Institutions, Issues and Concepts in Canadian Politics*, edited by Carla Cassidy, Phylis Clarke and Wayne Petrozzi, Mosaic Press, Oakville, 1986, and Harvard Centre for International Affairs; G. Vigneault and M. Laberge's preamble was reprinted by the Council for Canadian Unity.

17 "The Slippery Slope": Free Trade and Canadian Culture

James Laxer, *Leap of Faith*. Edmonton: Hurtig, 1986, reprinted by permission of James Laxer; Ted Byfield, "Keeping things cozy for Canadianism," March 31 and April 14, 1986 *Alberta Report*, reprinted by permission of Ted Byfield; Susan Crean, "Reading Between the Lies: Culture and the Free-Trade Agreement," *This Magazine* 22, 2 (May, 1988) in D. Cameron ed. *The Free Trade Deal*. Toronto: Lorimer, 1988, by permission, first published in *This Magazine* May 1988; Anthony DePalma, "Tough rules stand guard over Canadian culture," *New York Times*, July 14, 1999, with permission; Hon. Henry N.R. Jackman, "Canada's Culture," An Address to the Canadian Club Millennium Series, November 1999, with permission; Peter Herndorf, "Massey Commission at 50: the State of the Arts", *Canadian Speeches*: *Issues of the Day* 15, 6 (January-February, 2002) by permission of Peter Herndorf.

18 "A Cherished Reputation": Peacekeeping

Barbara McDougall, "Peacekeeping, Peacemaking and Peacebuilding: Statement to the House of Commons Standing Committee on External Affairs and International Trade, Ottawa February 17, 1993, reproduced in *Canadian Foreign Policy, 1977-1992* by A.E. Blanchette, Ottawa: Carleton University Press, 1994, reprinted with permission; documents 2, 3, 4 and 5 were reprinted with permission from *Eyewitness to Peace: Letters from Canadian Peacekeepers* by Jane Snailhan and published by the Canadian Peacekeeping Centre © 1998 by the Canadian Peacekeeping Press; Richard Sanders, "Canada's Peacekeeping Myth," The Canadian Centres for Teaching Peace, 1998, with permission from Richard Sanders Coordinator, Coalition to Oppose the Arms Trade, Editor, Press for Conversion; Peter Topolewski, "Canadian Soldiers Die For the UN," *LaissezFaire City Times*, Vol. 3, no. 33, August 23, 1999.

19 "Our Passion for Survival": The Birth of Environmentalism

Grey Owl, *The Men of the Last Frontier* Toronto: Macmillan, 1931; Haig-Brown, *Measure of the Year*. Toronto: Collins, 1950, © Roderick HaigBrown 1950, reprinted by permission of Valerie Haig-Brown; excerpt from *To Save a Whale: The Voyages of Greenpeace* by R. Hunter and R. Weyler, © 1978, text Robert L. Hunter, Photographs: Rex Weyler, published by Douglas and McIntyre Ltd. reprinted by permission of the publisher; Farley Mowat, *Sea of Slaughter* Toronto: McClelland

and Stewart, 1984, reprinted by permission of Farley Mowat Limited; David Suzuki, *Time to Change: Essays*. Toronto: Stoddart, 1994, reprinted by permission of David Suzuki; Tzeporah Berman, *Clayoquot and Dissent*. Vancouver: Ronsdale, 1994, reprinted with permission.

Every attempt has been made to acquire permission to reprint articles in this book. We would be grateful for information that would allow us to correct any errors or omissions in a subsequent edition of the work.